The ENTREPRENEUR'S Guide to BUSINESS LAW

2nd Edition

Constance E. Bagley
Harvard Business School

Craig E. Dauchy
Cooley Godward LLP

THOMSON
SOUTH-WESTERN
WEST

Australia · Canada · Mexico · Singapore · Spain · United Kingdom · United States

THOMSON
SOUTH-WESTERN
WEST

The Entrepreneur's Guide to Business Law, 2nd Edition
Constance E. Bagley and Craig E. Dauchy

Editor-in-Chief:
Jack W. Calhoun

Vice President/Team Director:
Michael P. Roche

Senior Acquisitions Editor:
Rob Dewey

Senior Developmental Editor:
Jan Lamar

Marketing Manager:
Nicole C. Moore

Production Editor:
Emily S. Gross

Manufacturing Coordinator:
Rhonda Utley

Design Project Manager:
Michelle Kunkler

Internal Designer:
Lisa Albonetti

Cover Designer:
Lisa Albonetti

Compositor:
Carlisle Publishers Services

Printer:
Webcom Ltd.
Toronto, Ontario

Printed in Canada
2 3 4 5 06 05 04 03

For more information contact
West Legal Studies in Business,
5191 Natorp Boulevard,
Mason, Ohio 45040.
Or you can visit our Internet site at:
http://www.wesbuslaw.com

Library of Congress
Cataloging-in-Publication Data
Bagley, Constance E.
The entrepreneur's guide to business law / Constance E. Bagley,
Craig E. Dauchy.—2nd ed.
p. cm.
Includes bibliographical references and index.
ISBN 0-324-04291-4
I. Business law—United States.
2. Business enterprises—Law and legislation—United States—Popular works. I. Dauchy, Craig E.,
II. Title.
KF390.B84 B34 2003
346.7307—dc21

2002067215

Brief Contents

CONTENTS

Preface

PREFACE

Individuals starting a new business or expanding an existing one face a sometimes daunting set of legal hurdles. The purpose of this book is to identify the legal challenges inherent in entrepreneurial activities and to suggest strategies for meeting those challenges while achieving the core business objectives.

Apart from sharing a name based on the French word *entreprendre* (to undertake), entrepreneurs may at first appear to have nothing in common. Entrepreneurial ventures range from the small start-up firm operating on a shoestring budget to a fully developed enterprise ready to take advantage of the public equity markets. Yet, most entrepreneurs face common issues, ranging from "Should I incorporate?" "Where can I raise money?" and "How can I protect my intellectual property?" to "Should I sell my company or try to take it public?" Even after the burst of the dot-com bubble in 2000, new ventures continue to be an engine for economic growth in the United States and the rest of the world.

INTENDED AUDIENCE

This book is intended not only for entrepreneurs but also for investors, attorneys, consultants, advisers, and board members who work with growing companies. This book will enable CEOs, managers, and other businesspersons to spot legal issues before they become legal problems and to use the law and the legal system to maximize value, marshal resources, and manage risk.

What Distinguishes This Book from Others

Numerous other self-help and reference books for entrepreneurs cover a host of legal issues, and many are quite good. Often, however, the available literature is too general or too technical, impractical, or incomplete. Frequently the authors are not acknowledged experts in their fields and may have unproven track records. This book satisfies the need for a single definitive source that covers the main legal aspects of starting and growing a business, written in a manner that allows the reader to learn about the relevant law and at the same time benefit from practical tips based on experience. We offer the reader a comprehensive book that presents the substantive and practical legal guidance necessary to excel in business.

In particular, our book distinguishes itself from the current literature in the following ways:

- **Integration of Law** Much of the relevant literature sees the legal aspects of business as distinct from such aspects as sources of capital or marketing. Because we see the law as integral to these other important aspects, we have interwoven the law and its business applications by including real-life business examples that illustrate how in practice the law directly affects business success.
- **From the Trenches** Throughout this book, a number of examples appear in a boxed feature called "From the Trenches." When the example is based on a reported court case, we have provided the citation to the legal reporter in which the case can be found. However, many examples are drawn from our own practice representing entrepreneurs and venture capitalists. Sensitivity to confidentiality often required us to use fictitious names, but rest assured that the entrepreneurs and companies involved are real and that everything described in the "From the Trenches" examples actually occurred. Our hope is that our readers will avoid traps others failed to recognize.
- **Examples That Challenge the Nuances of the Law** We use examples from the high-tech arena that push the edge of the envelope as the law is applied to new products and services.

- **Running Hypothetical** A hypothetical that runs throughout the book follows the progress of Kendra Commodore as she leaves her former place of employment, starts a database management software company, raises money from venture capitalists, and ultimately takes the company public in an initial public offering. Much of working effectively with the law entails knowing the appropriate questions and when to ask them. This hypothetical, which is presented at the end of each chapter under the heading "Putting it into Practice," highlights the key concerns entrepreneurs need to contemplate as the business progresses. By following the thought processes and progress of this hypothetical entrepreneur, the reader learns how to spot the issues and put them in a factual context.
- **Getting It In Writing** Samples of certain key legal documents appear in a feature called "Getting It In Writing." They include a venture capital term sheet and an independent contractor services agreement.
- **Crucial Information in One Readable Source** Current literature with more detailed information exists, but often the entrepreneur has to search through many books to find it. We believe that it is important to have the key information available in one book. We have worked hard to achieve this balance—providing a practical source of information without overloading the reader.

PURPOSE

The purpose of this book is twofold. The first is to provide guidance regarding the legal issues that entrepreneurs should consider when launching a new enterprise. The second is to serve as a reference book and resource for those who are already active in the entrepreneurial world.

This book is intended to encompass all phases of the entrepreneurial journey. It is not intended to take the place of an attorney but to help the entrepreneur select one with whom he or she can work in an intelligent, informed, efficient, and economical manner.

CONTENTS

The book contains seventeen chapters that follow the progression of a start-up and anticipate its legal concerns from inception to an initial public offering. Each chapter is self-contained and may be read on its own.

The book begins with a brief description of the rewards and risks of entrepreneurship and introduces the hypothetical that will be discussed throughout the book under the heading "Putting it into Practice." Chapter 2 explores the steps that an entrepreneur who is contemplating leaving an employer can take to make the departure amicable, and it offers guidance regarding the significance of documents (such as a noncompete clause or an assignment of inventions) that the entrepreneur may have signed. The chapter also offers insights into intellectual property issues involved in leaving a company to form a new venture and how the entrepreneur might safely (i.e., legally) go about recruiting colleagues.

Chapter 3 focuses on the role of an attorney and provides practical tips for selecting and working effectively with counsel. The next two chapters detail the considerations entailed in choosing an appropriate legal form for the business and offer suggestions on how to structure the ownership of the business among the founders and the investors. Chapter 6 deals with the proper governance structure for the entrepreneurial venture and examines the role of the board of directors. Chapter 7 discusses sources of funds, and the pros and cons of different ways of raising money, including complying with the federal and state securities laws.

Chapter 8, on contracts and leases, explains what is necessary for a legally binding agreement and highlights contractual issues often faced by entrepreneurs. Chapter 9 highlights special issues associated with electronic commerce and the sale of goods and services. Chapter 10 considers the legal issues faced by a growing company when dealing with employees and independent contractors, including sexual harassment and monitoring of employee e-mail. Chapter 11 discusses a variety of business torts and regulatory issues that an entrepreneur may face and suggests ways (including insurance) to manage risk. Chapter 12 deals with creditors' rights and gives an overview of bankruptcy. Chapter 13 explores venture capital in depth and highlights the aspects of the term sheet and other venture capital documents of greatest importance to the entrepreneur. Chapter 14 takes an in-depth look at intellectual property, the lifeblood of many entrepreneurial ventures.

Chapter 15, new to this edition, discusses factors to consider when expanding internationally, including tax considerations and employment issues. Chapter 16, also new to this edition, explores the processes of buying and selling a business. Sale of a company is a frequent exit strategy for growing companies, and acquisitions are often a way to accelerate growth and increase market share. Chapter 17 concludes the book with insights on another exit strategy, an initial public offering.

New to This Edition

The second edition contains two new chapters—Chapter 15 "Going Global" and Chapter 16 "Buying and Selling a Business." Electronic commerce is discussed extensively in an expanded chapter on e-commerce and sales of goods and services and elsewhere as appropriate. Cyberlaw, including such cutting-edge developments as the Digital Millennium Copyright Act, the enforceability of "click-wrap" agreements, and the patenting of business processes, is given an expanded treatment in a redesigned chapter entitled "Intellectual Property and Cyberlaw." Several existing chapters have been reorganized and reordered to better reflect the sequence in which entrepreneurs are likely to confront certain issues. The running hypothetical "Putting it into Practice" is new, as are many of the "From the Trenches." Finally, the second edition includes an extensive list of Internet sources.

Acknowledgments

The authors gratefully acknowledge the guidance, comments, and helpful suggestions provided by a number of professors who reviewed the manuscript and the first edition.

Reviewers for this edition include:

Joan T.A. Gabel, Georgia State University
James L. Hunt, Mercer University
Michael J. O'Hara, University of Nebraska at Omaha
Frances E. Zollers, Syracuse University

Reviewers for the first edition include:
Robert J. Borghese, University of Pennsylvania
Frank Cross, University of Texas at Austin
Kiren Dosanjh, National University
Richard P. Mandel, Babson College
Sandra J. Perry, Bradley University

Constance Bagley acknowledges with thanks the assistance of Harvard Law School students Michael K. Shah and Matt Zisow. Craig Dauchy gratefully acknowledges the contributions of the following Cooley Godward LLP attorneys who helped in writing the first and second editions of this book: Bill Morrow (Chapter 4); Dan Frank and Deborah Marshall (Chapter 5); Frederick Baron, Dan Westman, Laura Owen, and Erica Rottenberg (Chapter 10); Bob Eisenbach (Chapter 12); Deborah Marshall and Jeff Zimman (Chapter 13); Janet Cullum, Andy Basile, Dan Mummery, and Diane Savage (Chapter 14); Julie Wicklund (Chapter 15); Suzanne Sawochka Hooper (Chapter 16); Christopher Kearns and Deborah Marshall (Chapter 17); and, in addition, Cooley Godward attorneys Luke Bergstrom, John Cummerford, Bill Freeman, Greg Lanier, Mark Pitchford, Frank Rahmani, Tom Reicher, Mike Stern, Lois Benes, and Cooley Godward paralegal Maura Coffin.

The authors are pleased to acknowledge the able assistance of Mark Lamoureux and Joyce Warren in the preparation of the manuscript of the second edition and the generous support of the Harvard Business School Division of Research.

The authors would like to thank Rob Dewey, acquisitions editor; Jan Lamar, senior developmental editor; and Emily Gross, production editor. As always, working with the pros at West was a pleasure.

Conclusion

This area of the law is exciting and challenging. We have done our best to bring to life the power of the law and the strategies necessary to make the law work for the entrepreneur. We had a lot of fun writing this book, and we hope the reader will have just as much fun using the book as a guide when embarking on the exciting but sometimes perilous journey of entrepreneurship.

About the Authors

Constance E. Bagley is Associate Professor of Business Administration at the Harvard Business School, where she teaches legal aspects of entrepreneurship. Before joining the Harvard Business School faculty in 2000, she taught for more than ten years at the Stanford University Graduate School of Business, where she received Honorable Mention (first runner-up) for the Distinguished Teaching Award. Before teaching at Stanford, she was a corporate securities partner at McCutchen, Doyle, Brown & Enersen, a 250-lawyer firm based in San Francisco. She was also a member of the faculty of the Young Presidents' Organization (YPO) International University for Presidents in Hong Kong. Professor Bagley is the author of one of the leading business law textbooks, *Managers and the Legal Environment: Strategies for the 21st Century* (4th ed. 2002). She is also on the Editorial Board of the *Journal of Internet Law,* a staff editor of the *American Business Law Journal,* and a member of the Advisory Board for the Bureau of National Affairs Corporate Practice Series. Professor Bagley received her J.D., *magna cum laude,* from the Harvard Law School and was invited to join the *Harvard Law Review.* She received her A.B., with Honors and Distinction, from Stanford University, where she was elected to Phi Beta Kappa her junior year. She is a member of the State Bar of California and the State Bar of New York.

Craig E. Dauchy is the managing partner of Cooley Godward LLP's Menlo Park office, located in the heart of Silicon Valley, and is in charge of Cooley Godward's venture capital practice firmwide. With more than 600 lawyers and additional offices in Palo Alto, San Francisco, and San Diego, California; Broomfield, Colorado; Kirkland, Washington; and Reston, Virginia, Cooley Godward is one of the nation's leading law firms providing counsel to entrepreneurs and venture capitalists. The firm has represented both issuers and underwriters in nearly 400 public offerings in recent years and consistently ranks among the Top 10 law firms handling venture-backed initial public offerings for companies in the United States. In just the past five years, the firm has represented companies or underwriters in more than 200 public offerings, including more than 100 IPOs. Mr. Dauchy has represented entrepreneurs, emerging companies, and venture capitalists in diverse industries, including medical devices, software, health care, electronics, and consumer products, for more than twenty-five years. He is a frequent lecturer on matters relating to securities law and public offerings, mergers and acquisitions, and venture capital. He also serves on a number of advisory boards and boards of directors. Mr. Dauchy has a J.D. and an M.B.A. from Stanford University and graduated *magna cum laude* with a B.A. in history from Yale University. He is a member of the State Bar of California.

Dedication

DEDICATION

To Bucky
Angels' wings and light perpetual.
C.E.B.

To my wife, Sue Crawford, and to my mother and father,
Philippa and Walter Dauchy.
C.E.D.

Chapter 1

TAKING THE PLUNGE

Individuals start businesses for any number and combination of reasons: to be their own boss, to pursue a passion, to achieve financial rewards, to establish a new livelihood after corporate downsizing, to fill an unmet need with an innovative product or service, or to create something enduring. Despite the vast variety of entrepreneurs and their companies, once individuals decide to become entrepreneurs, they will encounter many of the same issues. These issues will include whether to work alone or with one or more partners, what products or services to provide, and where to obtain the necessary capital.

One recent example of a highly successful entrepreneur is Bob Davis, the founder and chief executive officer (CEO) of Lycos, the first truly global Internet media company. Davis began his entrepreneurial career at age twelve when he mailed in an advertisement from the back of *Boy's Life* that promised "Big Cash." After earning about $30 from selling magazine subscriptions and flower seeds door-to-door, in front of supermarkets, and outside church, Davis felt that he "had struck it rich."[1]

After both his parents died before he reached the age of twenty-one, Davis was left with a total inheritance of $3,500 and the resolve to "take care of myself."[2] To pay his way through college, he worked a series of odd jobs ranging from driving a grocery delivery truck to being a lifeguard. After an internship with IBM and a brief stint with General Electric, Davis began an eleven-year career at Wang Laboratories, then a leader in the burgeoning world of office automation. While at Wang, Davis met Dan Nova, who had left a sales job at Wang to attend Harvard Business School and then joined CMGI, a small venture capital firm that was investing solely in the then emerging Internet. While at CMGI, Nova negotiated the rights to the Lycos Internet search engine, the brainchild of a Carnegie Mellon computer scientist nicknamed Fuzzy. After writing a business plan for a company based on the Lycos technology and a series of interviews with people at CMGI and Carnegie Mellon, Davis was named CEO of Lycos in June 1995. Seven months later, Lycos completed the fastest initial public offering in Nasdaq history. In 2001, Lycos was sold to Spanish phone giant Telefonica for more than $5.4 billion, which represented a 269,900 percent return on the initial $2 million in venture funding provided by CMGI just five years earlier.[3] Davis remained as vice-chair of the combined company Terra Lycos and rejoined Dan Nova as a partner in the venture capital firm Highland Capital Partners.

Before taking the plunge, the would-be entrepreneur must consider the sacrifices, both professional and personal, that will be required. These sacrifices may include accepting several years of low pay and long hours in exchange for a large potential payoff later. Successful entrepreneurship also requires a willingness to take risks. As Sandra Kurtzig, founder of Ask Computer Systems (a company she grew to $400 million in sales), points out, the act of quitting one's job and starting a new business is only the beginning.[4] An entrepreneur must continually take risks and be prepared to make the bet-the-company decisions that will determine the venture's ultimate success or failure.[5]

FROM THE TRENCHES

In the early 1980s, Ron Kipp left a $100,000-a-year job at IBM to acquire a nearly moribund scuba diving shop on Grand Cayman Island. He initially paid himself $12,000 a year and lived in a converted warehouse with no bathtub or stove. Although Kipp spent long hours filling tanks, leading tours, and sweeping floors, they were his floors. Twenty years later, Kipp was a millionaire and the owner of the largest dive shop on Grand Cayman, with seven boats, five locations, and forty-five employees. When asked when he planned to retire, Kipp responded, "Never. . . . How could I? Ninety-nine percent of the poor slobs in the world wish they could do this."

Source: Mark Henricks, Soulful Proprietors, Am. Way, Jan. 15, 2002, at 63.

Regardless of how carefully one deliberates before making decisions, an entrepreneur will make mistakes. As Kurtzig puts it, "Screwing up is part of the process."[6] One key to being successful is to make fewer mistakes than the competition.

Most entrepreneurs and their backers are not risk *seekers;* rather they are risk *takers* who attempt to manage the risks inherent in pursuing new opportunities by making staged commitments and conducting a series of experiments.[7] In selecting an opportunity to pursue, savvy entrepreneurs look for an attractive risk/reward ratio, that is, the set of possible negative and positive cash flows and the likelihood of each possible outcome.[8]

When harnessed correctly, the law and the legal system can be a positive force that can help entrepreneurs to increase predictability, maximize realizable value, marshal the human and capital resources needed to pursue opportunities, and manage risk. Failure to comply with the law can result in crippling lawsuits, devastating fines, and, in egregious cases, imprisonment for the individuals involved. Because legal risks are among the most important of the many risks faced by a young company, an entrepreneur can increase the likelihood of success by understanding and minimizing legal risk, that is, by spotting legal issues before they become legal problems.

PUTTING IT INTO PRACTICE

Kendra Commodore (our fictitious entrepreneur) has been an employee of Creative Software Solutions, Inc. (CSS), a corporation headquartered in Massachusetts, for the past ten years. CSS is a successful software company that develops and markets a broad range of software products aimed at two primary areas: (1) database management software (DBMS) and related development tools that allow for creation, retrieval, and modification of various types of computer-stored data; and (2) a suite of Internet business application software and service solutions that allow customers, partners, and employees to access and automate various business processes over a collaborative Internet environment. It had revenues of more than $4 billion in 2001.

Kendra began as a software development programmer and now heads CSS's Enterprise Consulting Group and directs all of CSS's DBMS consulting practice aimed at *Fortune* 1000 customers. She spends most of her time developing custom solutions that increase the performance and capability of CSS's DBMS products for her clients and building interfaces and software tools that leverage the Internet and corporate intranets. During her time at CSS, Kendra has made full use of the company's tuition reimbursement program and recently earned a Master of Science degree in computer science.

Eighteen months ago, while on a company-sponsored outing, Kendra began chatting with Winston North, a colleague from the Financial Services Group. North told Kendra that many companies, such as financial institutions, brokerage houses, and insurance companies, that utilize and depend on large and complex databases for services to their customers and end-users were interested in a database search engine "booster" that could improve the response times for queries on complex databases. Ideally, the booster would have two characteristics: (1) to preserve the companies' existing investment in DBMS, they should be able to add the booster to their existing DBMS without a costly overhaul or modification of the system; and (2) the user should be able to turn the booster on or off depending on the complexity and time-sensitive nature of the query. Finally, it was critical that the booster not in any way jeopardize the integrity of the database itself.

Shortly after that discussion, Kendra decided that the problem would make a challenging thesis project, and she began working on it at home

continued...

continued...

during her spare time. She devised a revolutionary data extraction algorithm, based on a unique mathematical theory, which was embodied in a software program that could be either integrated into the existing DBMS utilized by the customer or simply added on to reside on top of the existing DBMS.

Based on preliminary benchmark comparisons that Kendra ran on a set of queries, her software program yielded search results ten to twelve times faster than three of the top-selling DBMS programs on the market. Her software program could also be utilized as an Internet search engine booster; preliminary benchmark testing showed significantly improved response times over existing search engines. Additionally, both sets of search results were found to be comparable in accuracy and exhaustiveness to most of the existing DBMS and Internet search engines.

To develop her software, Kendra worked alone outside regular work hours until six months ago, when Philip Colgate (a CSS Internet Applications Group programmer) and his wife, Kristine (a Harvard MBA), began working with her. The three signed a brief, handwritten agreement to form a partnership to develop what Kendra dubbed the Saturn Data Booster (SDB). The agreement stated that they would "divide any profits fairly." Kendra was careful not to discuss her outside project with coworkers but occasionally borrowed technical manuals from work and attended CSS in-house presentations on related topics.

Kendra has just returned from a six-week leave of absence, during which she prepared a presentation for potential investors and completed plans for commercializing the technology. Kendra envisions creating a company that would exploit her breakthrough technology to develop and sell specialized applets. She estimates that she will need $2 million to purchase the necessary development tools and to hire programmers to create a beta-test version of the SDB with a higher result accuracy and an improved range of scalability over medium to large databases. In addition, she believes that the SDB will need to include a functionality for creating a unique parallel database, which could be updated and searched in real time while the original database was being updated. Having this parallel database would also prevent the SDB from jeopardizing the integrity of the original database.

Kendra believed that it was important to get her new venture under way as soon as possible, and she realized that, to do so, she and Philip would have

continued...

continued...

to leave CSS. For geographic and family reasons, Kendra, Philip, and Kristine decided to set up their new business in California.

In preparation for her departure, Kendra asked to review her personnel file to determine what agreements she had signed when she joined CSS. Kendra vaguely remembered being given a stack of papers to sign and return on her first day. In her file, she found forms for health insurance and tax withholdings, along with a long nondisclosure agreement that she had signed without reading. After reviewing the agreement, she realized that it contained provisions assigning her inventions to CSS, a nondisclosure provision, a one-year covenant not to compete, and a no-raid provision, which prohibited her from actively hiring the company's employees. (For a further discussion of these provisions, see Chapter 2.)

Before taking any action, Kendra knew that she needed to investigate a number of crucial issues. Below are some of the questions Kendra pondered in the initial and later stages of forming her business and the corresponding chapters of this book in which her questions are addressed.

1. Who owns the Saturn Data Booster? What rights, if any, can CSS claim to it? (Chapter 2: Leaving Your Employer)
2. What can Kendra do to make her departure from CSS amicable? Should she have left sooner? What ongoing obligations does she have to CSS? (Chapter 2: Leaving Your Employer)
3. Can Kendra ask some of her colleagues at CSS to join her new enterprise? (Chapter 2: Leaving Your Employer)
4. Should Kendra hire an attorney? How does she select the right one? (Chapter 3: Selecting and Working with an Attorney)
5. Given her limited budget, can Kendra afford an attorney? Can she afford not to have one? (Chapter 3: Selecting and Working with an Attorney)
6. What would be an appropriate legal form for the business from a liability and tax standpoint? (Chapter 4: Deciding Whether to Incorporate)
7. How should Kendra approach the issue of splitting the equity in her new venture among the three founders? (Chapter 5: Structuring the Ownership)

continued...

continued...

8. How will the three manage the venture? What happens if one of the founders leaves? (Chapter 5: Structuring the Ownership)

9. What are the advantages and disadvantages of having an active board of directors? Who should sit on the board, and what should Kendra expect the directors to do? (Chapter 6: Forming and Working with the Board)

10. What are Kendra's options for financing the new venture? (Chapter 7: Raising Money and Securities Regulation)

11. How can Kendra ensure that her customers pay her on time and that her suppliers ship goods in the quantity and of the quality she needs for her business? What should she consider before signing a standard-form lease for office space? (Chapter 8: Contracts and Leases)

12. What warranties are implied when the company sells a product? Can the company disclaim all warranties and limit its liability to replacement of the product or refund of the purchase price? Can the company in its advertising speed up a videotape of the product in operation so that the product appears to execute queries faster than it actually does? (Chapter 9: E-Commerce and the Sales of Goods and Services)

13. Does the company have to pay software engineers the minimum wage and overtime? When is the company required to withhold taxes from a worker's check and pay Social Security taxes? What accommodations must the company make for workers with physical or mental disabilities? How should the company resolve a claim by a forty-one-year-old Asian woman that she was laid off because of her age, race, national origin, and gender, and how can the company protect itself against such claims in the future? How should the company resolve a sexual-harassment claim brought by a male employee against a female supervisor? (Chapter 10: Marshaling Human Resources)

14. Does the company need to be concerned that the property it is considering leasing was previously used by an automotive store that sold oil and other lubricants? How should the company resolve a claim for assault, battery, and false imprisonment arising out of an altercation with one of the company's employees, and how can the company protect

continued...

continued...

itself against such claims in the future? (Chapter 11: Operational Liabilities and Insurance)

15. What happens if the company runs out of cash and cannot pay its debts? (Chapter 12: Creditors' Rights and Bankruptcy)

16. If Kendra seeks venture capital financing, how should she approach the venture community? What business and legal provisions in the term sheet and other financing documents should concern her? What is negotiable? Is any of the terms a deal breaker? (Chapter 13: Venture Capital)

17. How can the company protect its proprietary technology? Does the company need to worry about violating other companies' patents or copyrights? (Chapter 14: Intellectual Property and Cyberlaw)

18. Should the company expand beyond the United States? What are the advantages and disadvantages of going global? (Chapter 15: Going Global)

19. What risks are involved in growing the business by acquisition? Is it better to grow the business internally? When should the entrepreneur consider selling the business to a larger competitor? (Chapter 16: Buying and Selling a Business)

20. When is an initial public offering an appropriate exit strategy? What is involved in going public? What does it mean to be a public company? (Chapter 17: Going Public)

NOTES

1. BOB DAVIS, SPEED IS LIFE 5 (2001).
2. *Id.* at 7–8.
3. *Id.* at 189.
4. SANDRA L. KURTZIG, CEO: BUILDING A $400 MILLION COMPANY FROM THE GROUND UP 2 (1994).
5. *Id.* at 2–3.
6. Kurtzig, *supra* note 4.
7. *See* Howard Stevenson, *The Heart of Entrepreneurship,* HARV. BUS. REV. 85–94 (Mar.–Apr. 1985).
8. William A. Sahlman, *Some Thoughts on Business Plans, in* THE ENTREPRENEURIAL VENTURE (Sahlman et al. ed. 2d ed. 1999).

Chapter 2

LEAVING YOUR EMPLOYER

Sometimes an entrepreneur will start a new business right out of school or while between jobs. More often, a person decides to start his or her own company while still employed by a more established company. The idea for a new business may come from a project the person was working on for the current employer. Depending on the agreements the entrepreneur has with the current employer, the entrepreneur's position, and the nature of the proposed new business, the entrepreneur may not be free to work on the venture while still employed or for some time thereafter.

For example, the employee may have signed an agreement containing a *no-moonlighting clause,* which prohibits the employee from engaging in any business activities (even after-hours activities) unrelated to the employee's job with the employer. A signed nondisclosure agreement (discussed later) prohibits the entrepreneur from using or disclosing any of the employer's trade secrets (such as a customer list) unless the employer authorizes it. The prohibition continues even after the entrepreneur quits. In some cases, the entrepreneur may have signed an agreement in which he or she agreed not to compete with the former employer for some period of time after leaving the employer (a *covenant not to compete*). The entrepreneur's ability to recruit former coworkers to join the new enterprise may also be restricted.

Awareness of these restrictions is crucial. A lawsuit arising out of the entrepreneur's duties to a former employer can be so expensive and occupy so much management time that it sinks the venture. At a minimum, the new company would be greatly impeded by the threat of a lawsuit by the former employer.

This chapter discusses both restrictions that are applicable while a person is still employed by another and postemployment restrictions, including a covenant not to compete. It then presents strategies for leaving on good terms.

Restrictions While Still Employed

The employer-employee relationship is based on confidence and trust, which give rise to certain legal duties. For example, the employer has a duty to maintain a good working environment and to compensate employees for their efforts. In return, the employees have a duty to use their best efforts on behalf of the employer and not to act in any way that is adverse to the employer's interests. The extent of an employee's duties to a former employer depends on the position held at the company and whether the new venture will compete with the employer. In addition, the employee needs to consider the issue of solicitation of coworkers.

Position with the Company

Absent a covenant not to compete and a no-moonlighting clause, the employee's position will largely determine what he or she can legally do while contemplating starting a new business. In large part, employees' rights and duties depend on whether they are classified as key employees, skilled employees, or unskilled employees.

Key employees (such as officers, directors, or managers) and *skilled employees* (such as software engineers, marketing specialists, or sales representatives) owe a duty of loyalty to the company. This duty, which exists regardless of whether there is an employment contract, prohibits an employee from doing anything that would harm the employer while he or she is still employed. This includes operating a business that competes with the employer or that usurps any business opportunities that the employer might be interested in exploring. A key or skilled employee may make plans to compete with an employer but may neither actually compete nor solicit employees to work for the new business during the period of employment.

The duties of *unskilled employees* (and other employees not in positions of trust) are generally confined to the period of time during which they are actually working. Their off-hour activities are not restricted unless these activities are detrimental to the employer's interests. However, even unskilled employees can be restricted from competing with the company during their nonworking hours by a covenant not to compete or a no-moonlighting clause in an employment agreement.

Type of New Venture

The activities in which an employee can engage to further a new venture while still employed also depend on whether the venture will compete with the current employer. If the new enterprise is a noncompeting business, the employee (whether a key employee, skilled employee, or unskilled employee) is essentially free to establish and operate the new venture as long as it does not interfere with current job performance or violate any provisions (such as a no-moonlighting clause) in any employment agreement. An employee may make telephone calls, rent an office, hire employees (but not coworkers, except as explained below), and retain attorneys and accountants provided that two conditions are met. First, the employee may not use any of the employer's resources (e.g., telephone, fax machine, printer, copying machine, laptop or home computer supplied by the employer, or conference room). Second, all activities must be conducted after hours.

FROM THE TRENCHES

When cofounder Steve Jobs left Apple Computer, Inc. in 1985, he outraged Apple's board by persuading five top Apple managers to join in starting NeXT, Inc. Jobs had been chairman and CEO but was stripped of the CEO position and control over day-to-day operations in May 1985. Thereafter, he began planning his new company. Five days before resigning as chairman, Jobs gave then Apple CEO John Scully a list of the five employees who would be joining him at NeXT. Jobs also inquired about the possibility of licensing Apple technology for his new venture. Apple responded by suing Jobs for breach of his fiduciary responsibilities as chairman and for misappropriation of confidential and proprietary information. Four months later, Apple agreed to settle the suit in return for Jobs's promise that NeXT would not hire any additional Apple employees for a six-month period and would not solicit Apple employees for a year. NeXT also granted Apple the right to inspect NeXT's products before they were marketed.

What constitutes *after hours* is not always clear. For an employee with specified work hours, defining what is after hours may be easy. It becomes more difficult when the entrepreneur is a key employee whose working hours are not strictly defined and who has a duty to use best efforts to further the interests of the employer. For example, software engineers are famous for doing their best work between midnight and dawn. For them, there may be no clear after hours during the workweek. Instead, vacations may provide the only truly free time to develop an outside venture.

If the new venture will compete directly with the current employer, the entrepreneur's actions are significantly more restricted. Key employees and skilled employees may not prepare for and plan the new venture if doing so would interfere with their job responsibilities. Under no circumstances may they be involved in the actual operation of a competing venture while still employed by the employer.

Once plans for the competing business are in place, it is almost always advisable to terminate the employment relationship. Although it may be tempting to continue working, the potential liability and the time required to straighten out any legal or business conflicts that may arise will probably outweigh the benefit of the extra income.

The rules are summarized in Exhibit 2.1.

FROM THE TRENCHES

A consultant wanting to open a new restaurant went to his employer and worked out explicit arrangements for his new venture. He told the consulting firm that he was starting a new, noncompeting business and that, if it did well, there was a possibility that he would work on it full-time. The parties agreed that he would be responsible for fulfilling his duties as a consultant while working on his culinary interest after hours.

EXHIBIT 2.1

SUMMARY OF PERMISSIBLE ACTIVITIES WHILE STILL EMPLOYED BY ANOTHER

	Type of Venture	
Type of Employee	**Noncompeting Venture**	**Competing Venture**
Key employee Skilled employee	Can prepare for and operate the venture so long as it does not interfere with responsibilities and fiduciary duty. If subject to a no-moonlighting clause, the employee cannot operate it.	Can prepare for the venture so long as it does not interfere with responsibilities and fiduciary duty. Cannot operate it.
Unskilled employee	Can prepare for and operate the venture so long as it does not interfere with responsibilities. If subject to a no-moonlighting clause, the employee cannot operate it.	Can prepare for the venture so long as it does not interfere with responsibilities. If under a covenant not to compete or a no-moonlighting clause, the employee cannot operate it.

Solicitation of Coworkers

Solicitation of coworkers to leave their employment and come to work for the new company can be a sensitive issue. If the coworker has an employment contract for a definite term (e.g., two years), the entrepreneur seeking to lure the coworker away may be liable for damages for intentionally and improperly encouraging the coworker to break that contract and to leave the employer before the specified term is over. The employer could sue for intentional interference with contract, a tort discussed further in Chapter 11.

Even if the coworkers do not have a written employment contract and their employment is terminable *at-will* (i.e., at any time, by either party, for any reason), an entrepreneur can still be held liable if his or her conduct leads coworkers to violate any applicable restrictive covenants. For example, an entrepreneur may want to hire away a coworker who has access to the company's confidential information and who has developed special expertise that could be of great value to the new business. Doing so, however, may result in the violation of the coworker's nondisclosure agreement or of a covenant not to compete. (As discussed below, even in the absence of a nondisclosure agreement, the entrepreneur and the coworker may be opening themselves up to liability for misappropriation of trade secrets.)

Key employees are even more restricted in how they may approach coworkers. Generally, if a key employee induces another employee to move to a competitor, and the inducement is willfully kept from the employer, the conduct is a breach of fiduciary duty. Everyone who has participated in or benefited from that breach may be held liable. In one case, several key management employees induced several coworkers to leave their employer and enter into employment with their newly formed competing air-freight forwarding company. The management employees were held liable to the former employer for breach of fiduciary duty, fraud, and interference with contractual relations. The fact that none of the employees had employment contracts was irrelevant.

A distinction is generally drawn between soliciting coworkers and telling them about future plans. Although pretermination solicitation may be problematic, some courts would not prevent an entrepreneur from discussing future plans with coworkers. If coworkers are interested, they can contact the entrepreneur later and discuss any potential job opportunities.

Often employees are asked to sign an agreement expressly prohibiting them from soliciting coworkers, inducing coworkers to leave, or hiring them for some stated period of time after leaving the former employer. Such a provision is referred to as an *antipiracy* or *no-raid clause*. If the entrepreneur has signed such an agreement and solicits or hires in violation of it, the former employer could successfully sue for breach of contract and perhaps even obtain an injunction or court order preventing the former coworkers from working for the entrepreneur.

Postemployment Restrictions and the Covenant Not to Compete

Once an entrepreneur leaves the former place of employment, he or she may still be restricted by an antipiracy clause (discussed above) or by a covenant not to compete (also known as a *noncompete covenant*). A *covenant not to compete* is an agreement between an employer and an employee that is designed to protect the employer from potentially unfair competition from a former employee. Prohibited competition usually includes dealing with or soliciting business from the former employer's customers, or using the former employer's confidential business information for the benefit of the new employer.

To be binding and legally enforceable, the covenant not to compete must meet certain requirements. It must be ancillary to some other agreement; designed to protect a legitimate interest of the employer; reasonably limited in scope, geography, and duration; and not contrary to the interests of the public. In addition, it must be supported by adequate consideration; that is, the person agreeing to the covenant must receive something of value from the other party. If a court finds that a legally valid covenant has been breached, the court may issue an injunction ordering the entrepreneur to stop the offending activities and/or award damages.

Ancillary to Another Agreement

For a noncompete covenant to be valid, it must be subordinate to some lawful contract that describes the relationship between the parties, such as a formal employment agreement, a sale-of-business contract, or an agreement dissolving a partnership. A stand-alone covenant not to compete is a naked restraint on trade, which, in many states, is *per se,* or by itself, invalid. For example, the Texas Supreme Court refused to enforce a noncompete covenant executed during an employment-at-will relationship (which is characterized by the absence of an employment contract) because the covenant was not ancillary to an otherwise enforceable agreement.[1]

Legitimate Interests

A noncompete covenant may legally protect only legitimate interests of the employer. A general interest in restricting competition is insufficient. For the employer to enforce a restrictive covenant, the employee must present a substantial risk either to the employer's customer base or to confidential business information. Employer interests that have been found to be legitimate include protection of trade secrets and other confidential information, long-term customer relationships, and customer lists and other confidential customer information, as well as protection of the goodwill, business reputation, and unique skills associated with the company.

FROM THE TRENCHES

Jeffrey Hirshberg was employed in the Buffalo, New York office of BDO Seidman, a national accounting firm. As a condition of receiving a promotion to the position of manager, Hirshberg was required to sign a "Manager's Agreement," which provided that if, within eighteen months following the termination of his employment, Hirshberg served any former client of BDO Seidman's Buffalo office, he would be required to compensate BDO Seidman "for the loss and damages suffered" in an amount equal to one-and-a-half times the fees BDO Seidman had charged that client over the last fiscal year of the client's patronage. After Hirshberg resigned from BDO Seidman, the accounting firm claimed that it lost 100 former clients to Hirshberg who were billed a total of $138,000 in the year he left the firm.

The New York Court of Appeals found that the agreement was reasonable and enforceable except to the extent that it required Hirshberg to compensate BDO Seidman for fees paid by: (1) his personal clients whom he had brought to the firm through his own contacts or (2) clients with whom he had never acquired a relationship through his employment at BDO Seidman.

Source: BDO Seidman v. Hirshberg, 712 N.E.2d 1220 (N.Y. 1999).

Limited in Scope

The restrictions imposed by the noncompete covenant must be reasonably related to the interests protected. To be valid, these restrictions must be limited in time, geographic area, and scope of activities affected. In a dispute, the court will closely scrutinize the imposed restrictions to determine how they relate to the employer's business. If the court finds the restrictions overly broad, it will typically either modify some terms of the covenant to make them reasonable (e.g., shorten the duration) or declare the whole covenant invalid. A well-drafted covenant will contain a provision that invites the court to enforce the covenant to the greatest extent possible under applicable law and to modify the covenant as needed to make it enforceable. This is called a *blue-lining clause.*

The determination of the validity of restrictions varies greatly from case to case and is very fact specific. For example, one court upheld a two-year covenant not to compete that prohibited a dermatologist from practicing dermatology within a thirty-mile radius of the offices of the doctor for whom he had worked. Two years was considered reasonable to erase from the public's mind any identification of the dermatologist with his former employer's practice and to allow the former employer to reestablish his relationship with patients who had been referred to the dermatologist. The

FROM THE TRENCHES

Even in states permitting noncompete agreements, courts will enforce only reasonable restrictions on competition. Unreasonableness can be found on many grounds, including duration of limitation, geographic scope, scope of activities prohibited, and the employer's relation to the interests being protected. For example, the Nevada Supreme Court invalidated a noncompete agreement restricting a lighting-retrofitting employee from competing with his former employer within a 100-mile radius of the former employer's site for five years. The duration placed a great hardship on the employee and was not necessary to protect the former employer's interests.

thirty-mile radius covered the territory from which the dermatologist's former employer drew most of his patients.[2]

With respect to the time restriction, courts have generally found one year or less to be a reasonable limitation; a court probably would never enforce a covenant for a period of more than five years, except perhaps in connection with the sale of a business. Some courts will not enforce a covenant extending beyond the geographic area where the employer currently does business. One court refused to enforce a covenant prohibiting an employee who was fired for poor performance from competing with his former employer for two years in a 300-mile area. The court held that it was unreasonable "to permit the employer to retain unfettered control over that which it has effectively discarded as worthless to its legitimate business interests."[3]

Interests of the Public

In determining the validity of a noncompete covenant, the court will also look at the interests of the public affected by the covenant. Noncompete covenants can prevent the uninhibited flow of labor necessary for a competitive market. The public policy of preserving free labor markets disfavors any such restraints on trade and puts limits on the use of restrictive covenants. In addition, there is a basic belief that a person must be able to ply his or her trade to earn a living. But covenants not to compete also help deter unethical business practices, such as stealing trade secrets. If companies cannot adequately protect legitimate interests, entrepreneurs may be less likely to start new businesses and spend time and money developing and marketing better and cheaper products that increase consumer wealth. The balance struck between these competing public policies varies from state to state and is reflected in each state's legislation and judicially created law (called *common law*).

STATE LEGISLATION A number of states have enacted legislation restricting the enforceability of noncompete covenants. Such legislation generally falls into three categories. Some states, such as California, have statutes that broadly prohibit covenants restraining anyone from engaging in a lawful profession, trade, or business. Some credit this California law with providing part of the impetus for the growth of Silicon Valley, as many companies were founded by former employees of existing companies. Other states, such as Oregon, have statutes that regulate some aspects of noncompete covenants without broadly prohibiting them. Texas and a number of other states have taken yet another approach, adopting statutory reasonableness standards that must be satisfied for the covenants to be enforced. Some states prohibit enforcement of noncompete covenants in their state constitutions. States that do not have special legislation or a constitutional provision governing the use of covenants not to compete usually have common-law rules of reason for determining the validity and enforceability of such covenants.

Exceptions to Legislation Many states that have broad prohibitions against covenants not to compete have exceptions permitting such covenants in certain limited circumstances. For example, California has statutory exceptions permitting reasonable restrictions, not to exceed five years in duration, when the covenantor sells all of his or her shares in a corporation in a transaction in which the company is sold as a going concern. The covenantor is typically the owner selling the business and, upon the sale, may be restricted from starting a similar business in a certain location. Restrictions are also permissible in the case of a partnership dissolution or the sale of a limited liability company. California's statutory exceptions have been further narrowed by judicial rulings that limit restraints against the pursuit of an entire or substantial part of a profession, trade, or business and allow restrictions only if the effect is not significant.

CHOICE OF LAW With the high degree of employee mobility in the information economy, it is common for employees to move from state to state for a transfer or a new job. Such moves may affect the enforceability of noncompetition agreements. In particular, some provisions may be enforceable in the state where the employee began working but not in the state to which the employee moves. It may be difficult for any company with employees in many different states to use a single noncompetition agreement that will be enforceable in every state where employees are located.

Companies can use forum selection clauses and consents to personal jurisdiction—agreements to litigate any dispute in a specifically named jurisdiction—to achieve more predictability about the enforceability of their noncompetition agreements, but these clauses will not always be honored. In particular, even when an employment agreement specifies that the law of the employer's principal place of business should govern disputes, a state may refuse to enforce a covenant not to compete against an employee living in that state if the covenant is not consistent with the state's own law. For example, a California court would probably not enforce a covenant not to compete against a California resident even though the employer's principal place of business was in Massachusetts (which does honor reasonable postemployment covenants) and the employment agreement provided that Massachusetts law would apply.[4] On the other hand, if the employer secured a money judgment against an employee who had consented to jurisdiction in the employer's principal place of business, then the employer might be able to invoke the Full Faith and Credit Clause of the U.S. Constitution to require that the employee's home state court enforce the judgment.

The U.S. Court of Appeals for the Ninth Circuit upheld provisions in a noncompete agreement requiring Dr. Bajorek, an executive to whom IBM had granted stock options worth more than $500,000, to return any profits he obtained from the options if he worked for a competitor within six months after exercising the options.[5] Although the stock option agreement stated that New York law should apply to any disputes, Bajorek sued IBM in federal district court in California and argued that California law should apply. The district court agreed, after finding that applying New York law would violate California public policy against both recoupment of wages paid to employees and employee noncompetition agreements. The appeals court reversed on the grounds that these California policies were inapplicable. In addition to finding that stock options were not wages, the appeals court ruled that California restricts only agreements that completely restrain an individual from pursuing his or her profession. The court commented:

> *It is one thing to tell a man that if he wants his pension, he cannot ever work in his trade again . . . and quite another to tell him that if he wants a million dollars from his stock options, he has to refrain from going to work for a competitor for six months.*[6]

FROM THE TRENCHES

Stultz worked for Medtronic in Minnesota and signed a noncompetition agreement governed by, and enforceable under, Minnesota law. Stultz was hired by Advanced Bionics, a California company and a competitor of Medtronic. Advanced Bionics relocated Stultz to California. Advanced Bionics and Stultz brought a lawsuit in California to invalidate Stultz's noncompetition agreement with Medtronic, which was not enforceable according to California law. The day after the filing of the lawsuit in California, Medtronic removed the California lawsuit to federal court, which temporarily put a hold on the California lawsuit. That same day, Medtronic filed a lawsuit in Minnesota to enforce Stultz's noncompetition agreement. The Minnesota court issued an order preventing Stultz from working at Advanced Bionics. The California court issued orders to the effect that the Minnesota court order need not be followed by Stultz and Advanced Bionics.

Comments: As this case illustrates, noncompetition issues often involve a "race to the courthouse," in which the person who files a lawsuit first in a jurisdiction with favorable law may prevail in the dispute.

Source: Advanced Bionics Corp. v. Medtronic, Inc., 105 Cal. Rptr. 2d 265 (Cal. Ct. App. 2001), rev. granted, 25 P.3d 1078 (Cal. 2001).

DISMISSAL FOR REFUSAL TO SIGN AN UNENFORCEABLE COVENANT NOT TO COMPETE The California Court of Appeal held that Playhut, Inc. could not legally discharge an at-will employee for refusing to sign a confidentiality agreement that contained an unenforceable covenant not to compete.[7] Other jurisdictions have reached the opposite result, arguing that the employee should sign the covenant, then assert its invalidity if later sued by the company for violating it.

Breach of a Noncompete Clause

If a court finds that an employee breached a valid noncompete covenant, it will impose liability on the offender. The most common form of relief for an employee's breach of a noncompete covenant is an injunction that requires the employee to stop competing against the former employer. In some cases, actual damages may be assessed against an employee in an amount calculated to put the employer in the same position that it would have been in had there been no breach.

TRADE SECRETS

Most states expressly prohibit the misappropriation of trade secrets as a matter of law, regardless of whether the employee signed an agreement prohibiting use or disclosure. Unauthorized use or disclosure of the employer's trade secrets is generally prohibited both during and after employment. Even if a particular state will not enforce a covenant not to compete, all courts will generally enforce an agreement by an employee not to disclose or use trade secrets belonging to the former employer.

What Is a Trade Secret?

A *trade secret* is information used in one's business that is neither generally known nor readily ascertainable in the industry and that provides the business owner a competitive advantage over competitors who do not have access to this information. (Trade secrets and programs for their protection are discussed further in Chapter 14.) A trade secret can be a formula, pattern, program, device, method, technique, process, or customer list. What constitutes a trade secret is not always evident. The two critical factors in determining whether a trade secret exists are (1) the value of the information to the business owner and competitors and (2) the amount of effort made to maintain the secrecy of the information. These two factors are closely related: the more valuable a certain piece of information is to a business owner, the more likely he or she will make efforts to keep it secret.

Misappropriation of Trade Secrets

A prohibition on the use or disclosure of trade secrets and confidential information is usually included in a specialized agreement called a *nondisclosure agreement* (*NDA*). (Nondisclosure agreements are discussed in detail in Chapter 14.) The purpose of an NDA is to put employees on no-

FROM THE TRENCHES

Peak Computer maintained computer systems, including MAI Systems Corporation computers, for its clients. Peak's maintenance of MAI computers accounted for between 50 and 70 percent of Peak's business. MAI also maintained MAI computers for its customers. MAI's customer service manager and three other employees left to join Peak. Thereafter, MAI began to lose maintenance business to Peak. MAI sued Peak and its former employees for, among other things, copyright infringement, misappropriation of trade secrets, trademark infringement, and unfair competition.

MAI sought and received a temporary restraining order and preliminary injunction. The preliminary injunction was ultimately converted to a permanent injunction. The permanent injunction enjoined Peak from infringing on MAI copyrights, misappropriating MAI trade secrets, maintaining MAI computers, soliciting MAI customers, and maintaining certain MAI customer contacts.

The court determined that MAI's customer database was a protectable trade secret that had potential economic value because it allowed a competitor such as Peak to direct its sales efforts to those potential customers that were already using MAI's computer system. The court was not swayed by Peak's contention that the former customer service manager did not take MAI's customer database or put such information into the Peak database.

Source: MAI Sys. Corp. v. Peak Computer, Inc., 991 F.2d 511 (9th Cir. 1993).

tice that they are exposed to trade secret information in their work, to inform employees about their duties with regard to such information, and to create a covenant restricting their disclosure or use of trade secrets or other confidential information after the termination of their employment. The validity of an NDA is conditioned on the existence of the trade secrets it is designed to protect. If trade secrets do exist, then a reasonable NDA will be upheld even in states (such as California) that will not enforce postemployment covenants not to compete.

Under the *inevitable disclosure doctrine,* some courts will enjoin a former employee from working for a competitor firm for a limited period of time if the former employer is able to prove that the employee's new employment will inevitably lead him or her to rely on the former employer's trade secrets. The leading case involved a former PepsiCo employee who was privy to sensitive, confidential, strategic plans for the marketing, distribution, and pricing of PepsiCo's sports drink All Sport and its ready-to-drink tea products and fruit drinks. The employee left PepsiCo to work for Quaker Oats, seller of market leaders Gatorade and Snapple. The court concluded that the former employee would necessarily rely on his knowledge of PepsiCo's trade secrets when making decisions at Quaker Oats about Gatorade and Snapple. This put PepsiCo "in the position of a coach, one of whose players has left, playbook in hand, to join the opposing team before the big game."[8] The court prohibited him from working at Quaker Oats for a period of six months.

Criminal Liability

People who steal trade secrets not only risk civil liability but also may face criminal penalties. For example, Guillermo "Bill" Gaede, a former Intel Corp. software engineer, pled guilty in March 1996 to mail fraud and interstate transportation of stolen property for stealing copies of Intel's designs for its 486 and Pentium microprocessors and sending them to Advanced Micro Devices, Inc. (AMD), a rival microprocessor company.

FROM THE TRENCHES

General Motors Corp. (GM) became involved in a heated dispute with Volkswagen AG (VW) over the defection of GM's former purchasing chief to the German carmaker. GM filed suit in March 1996 against VW, Jose Ignacio Lopez de Arriortua, and ten former GM managers, alleging that Lopez and the other former employees took numerous boxes of secret GM documents when they quit GM to join VW. The documents in question allegedly contained confidential GM information about prices for parts, new models, and marketing strategies. The parties settled in early 1997, with VW agreeing to pay GM $100 million and to buy at least $1 billion worth of GM parts over seven years. Lopez resigned from VW and was criminally indicted by German authorities.

Source: Gabriella Stern & Brandon Mitchener, GM Agreed to VW Pact to Avoid Further Costs, Risks, WALL ST. J., Jan. 13, 1997, at B4.

AMD returned the plans to Intel and contacted the Federal Bureau of Investigation. The engineer faced a maximum penalty of fifteen years in prison and $500,000 in fines and restitution. Theft of trade secrets may be prosecuted as a federal crime under the Economic Espionage Act.

Even if there is no nondisclosure agreement, most states have passed statutes, such as the Uniform Trade Secrets Act (UTSA), that prohibit an employee from disclosing or using trade secrets belonging to the former employer. In those states that have not adopted the UTSA or comparable legislation, judges have developed common-law rules that prohibit misappropriation of trade secrets.

Invention Assignment Agreement and Works Made for Hire

An *invention assignment agreement* is another type of agreement an employee often is asked to sign. This document requires the employee to assign to the employer all inventions conceived, developed, or reduced to practice by the employee while employed by the company. Some states restrict the scope of such agreements. California, for example, prohibits the application of such agreements to inventions that the employee developed entirely on his or her own time without using the employer's equipment, supplies, facilities, or trade secret information, except when such inventions relate to the employer's business or to current or demonstrably anticipated research and development, or result from any work performed by the employee for the employer. Thus, if, for example, an employee of a software development company involved in developing database management software creates, on her own time and using her own home computer, a new and improved way to input files, that new program will belong to her employer because it is related to her employer's business.

Invention assignment agreements may provide for the assignment of inventions not only during the period of employment but also within a certain time, typically one year, after the termination of employment. Such agreements are not *per se* invalid. One court found, for example, that an agreement was valid and enforceable as it related to ideas and concepts based on secrets or confidential information of the employer even if conceived within one year after the termination of employment.

It is important that any restriction on an employee's further inventive activities be limited in time. Thus, although some agreements providing for assignment of inventions made within one year of employment termination have been found valid, other agreements requiring assignments for longer periods have not been enforced. One court, for example, found a contract provision requiring an employee to assign ideas and improvements conceived by him for five years after termination of employment to be unreasonable and void as against public policy.

As explained further in Chapter 14, even if there is no assignment-of-inventions agreement, by law the patent to any invention by a person expressly "hired to invent" belongs to the employer. The courts construe this narrowly, holding, for example, that a person "hired to improve" is not subject to this rule. Similarly, as a matter of copyright law, the copyright to any work created by an employee acting within the scope of employment belongs to the employer, even if the employee has not signed an assignment-of-inventions agreement.

Strategies for Leaving on Good Terms

To the extent possible, an employee should try to leave the current employer on good terms. To do this, the employee must be honest with the employer about the real reasons for leaving. The employer is likely to think the worst of former employees who say they are going to set up a noncompeting business but then in fact start a competing company. Such behavior will spark fears of stolen trade secrets and other misdeeds.

FROM THE TRENCHES

Two employees of a software company told their employer that they were leaving to start a restaurant. In fact, they founded a competing software company. Their former employer was furious—in part because he had been lied to and in part because he suspected misappropriation of trade secrets—and was successful in getting a court to issue an injunction that prevented the closing of the start-up's financing arrangement.

When the employee tells the employer of his or her future plans, it may be appropriate to offer the employer an opportunity to invest in the new venture. The employer will be most likely to invest if the entrepreneur's prospective business will make products that are complementary to the employer's products. Complementary products can increase a product's market and help establish it as an industry standard. For example, one reason Autodesk's AutoCAD (Computer Aided Design) program has been so successful is that it contains "hooks" that allow other software companies to design applications for AutoCAD. The availability of these additional applications has helped make AutoCAD an industry standard.

Having the employer invest in the new business offers several benefits. First, it may provide an easy source of funding for the entrepreneur. In addition to money, the employer may contribute technology, commercial expertise, and industry contacts. Second, it generates goodwill between the parties by aligning the interests of the employer with those of the entrepreneur. This alignment is important because the employer may be a valuable customer or supplier of the entrepreneur's business. Additionally, with an equity interest in the new enterprise, the employer may be more willing to allow the entrepreneur to hire other current employees. The entrepreneur should be careful, however, about how much of an ownership stake and control is given to the former employer. Allowing the former employer

FROM THE TRENCHES

When Chiron Corp., a leading biotechnology company, bought Cetus Corp., a neighboring biotechnology firm, for $300 million in 1992, it did so based largely on the strength of Cetus's cancer research. Shortly after the acquisition, Frank McCormick, the head of cancer research, and his staff decided to leave Chiron to start a new cancer research company financed with venture capital. When Chiron learned of the pending defection, it persuaded McCormick and the venture backers to restructure the deal to give Chiron a noncontrolling 42.8 percent stake in the new company, named Onyx Pharmaceutical. In return for the equity stake and first rights to diagnostics and vaccines developed by Onyx, Chiron contributed $4 million and technology to the new venture.

to be more than a passive investor may create the same situation that the employee left in the first place—namely, that the entrepreneur will again be working for someone else.

The entrepreneur should avoid soliciting coworkers while still employed. Active solicitation of employees by a skilled or key employee during employment constitutes a breach of the entrepreneur's duty of loyalty and could lead to an injunction preventing the entrepreneur from hiring anyone from the prior employer. A good strategy is for the entrepreneur to tell people that he is leaving. If people ask about his future plans, he is permitted to tell them he plans to start a new business and to give them a phone number where he can be reached. In this way, employees of the entrepreneur's former employer will contact the entrepreneur directly, thereby shielding him from allegations of solicitation.

Putting it into Practice

Kendra decided that the time had come to inform her boss at CSS of her future plans. Before discussing her departure, she contacted Ginny Washington, a college roommate who had graduated from Stanford Law School, for advice on the enforceability of the agreement that she had signed. Ginny told her that the agreement specified that Massachusetts law governed its interpretation and enforcement. However, Ginny believed that a California court would not enforce a posttermination noncompete covenant against a California resident, even though the contract stated that Massachusetts law governed the employment relationship.

Ginny told Kendra that she was bound by the provisions covering the assignment of inventions, however, and by the no-moonlighting, nondisclosure, and no-raid clauses. Of the four provisions, the one covering assignment of inventions was potentially the most problematic. Even though Kendra had developed the SDB technology on her own time, CSS probably owned the technology, because the invention related to CSS's business and she had used some of CSS's resources (her CSS computer and CSS training sessions).

Ginny explained that the no-moonlighting clause prohibited Kendra from starting her business while employed at CSS. Kendra breached this agreement when she and the Colgates signed a partnership agreement to develop the SDB technology. Although it would have been all right for Kendra to make plans for her new venture before quitting, she should not have begun operating until she left. The nondisclosure provision prohibited Kendra from using or disclosing any confidential information that she learned while working for CSS. The no-raid clause prohibited Kendra from soliciting employees from CSS. She was permitted, however, to hire employees if they contacted her about a potential job. Kendra and the Colgates did not plan to hire any other employees in the initial phases, so this was not an issue.

Armed with this advice, Kendra went to see her supervisor. After she informed him of her plans, the supervisor told her that she would need to speak to the director of research regarding the rights to the SDB technology. A few days later Kendra and Ginny met with the director of research and CSS's corporate counsel. After some negotiating, both parties agreed that

continued...

continued...

CSS would transfer all of its rights to the SDB technology to Kendra's new company and release all claims against Kendra and her co-founder Philip Colgate in exchange for 15 percent of the equity.

Satisfied with the agreement she had reached, Kendra gave official notice of her resignation. If people asked about her plans, she informed them that she was leaving to start a new business and gave them a phone number where she could be reached.

Kendra realized that if she took any CSS documents or disks, she could be accused of stealing trade secrets. She returned all non-SDB-related documents and disks to her supervisor, deleted all non-SDB-related information on the hard drives of her office and home computers, and walked out of CSS carrying only her personal effects.

Although Ginny had been helpful in advising Kendra about issues related to leaving CSS (and seemed willing to do so for little or no fee), she was not experienced in representing start-ups. Kendra next turned her attention to selecting a lawyer for her new venture.

NOTES

1. Travel Masters, Inc. v. Star Tours, Inc., 827 S.W.2d 830 (Tex. 1991).
2. Weber v. Tillman, 913 P.2d 84 (Kan. 1996).
3. Insulation Corp. of America v. Brobston, 667 A.2d 729 (Pa. Super. Ct. 1995).
4. *See, e.g.*, Hollingsworth Solderness Terminal Co. v. Turley, 622 F.2d 1324 (9th Cir. 1980).
5. International Bus. Mach. Corp. v. Bajorek, 191 F.3d 1033 (9th Cir. 1999).
6. *Id.* at 1041.
7. D'Sa v. Playhut, Inc., No. B139673 (Cal. Ct. App. Dec. 21, 2000).
8. PepsiCo, Inc. v. Redmond, 54 F.3d 1262 (7th Cir. 1995).

Chapter 3

Selecting and Working with an Attorney

Early in the development of the business, the entrepreneur should consider the need for an attorney. Depending on what the entrepreneur is looking for and the ability of the attorney, a corporate attorney can play a variety of roles. In some cases, the corporate attorney is called on only periodically to address a potential legal issue; at the other extreme, the attorney may provide invaluable assistance by acting as a sounding board for both business and legal issues. In the long run, a good attorney can enhance the bottom line of the enterprise by providing sound advice and preventing unforeseen liabilities. Yet, no matter what role the attorney plays, the costs associated with retaining legal counsel can be substantial. Most attorneys charge hundreds of dollars per hour for legal guidance.

This chapter explains the need for an attorney and suggests how to choose the right one. It addresses the challenge of deciding when and to what extent to work with an attorney, given the financial constraints of the new enterprise. It summarizes typical billing options and provides suggestions for keeping fees under control. The chapter concludes with a brief description of the attorney-client privilege, which is key to keeping communications with an attorney confidential.

The Need for an Attorney

Although there is no scarcity of published legal guides and prefabricated forms on the market, it is highly advisable that the entrepreneur not rely on these materials to the exclusion of expert legal guidance. The law can

FROM THE TRENCHES

One entrepreneur knew the time was ripe for getting an attorney on board when he attempted to put together a financing package and structure a founders' agreement. The entrepreneur wanted an agreement that would recognize the complexity of the founders' situations. When the business was initially starting, the four founders put in different amounts of time because of their diverse strengths. The cofounders wanted to capture the value that each was adding to the business during its different stages of risk.

be quite complicated, and mistakes are costly. Although an entrepreneur may feel that he or she can turn to published sources for specific answers, often the most valuable service a corporate attorney can perform is pointing out potential problems that the entrepreneur never thought about.

Furthermore, at a certain stage, most start-ups need attorneys. Certain matters require the legal experience and skills that only an attorney can provide. In addition, as the business grows, issues related to real estate, employment, intellectual property, securities, tax, and other areas of specialty may arise. They can be quite complicated and are best delegated to an outside expert so that the entrepreneur can focus on the day-to-day running of the business.

In assessing when to start looking for an attorney, an entrepreneur must weigh the financial costs and administrative hassle of finding an attorney against the potential benefits in terms of business and legal advice and document production. Although certain law firms may offer reduced rates and deferred-payment plans until the entrepreneur gets started, typically the costs are significant.

Choosing an Attorney

As is the case with finding an appropriate doctor, finding an appropriate attorney is not as easy as looking in the yellow pages of the local telephone book. Although any attorney licensed to practice in the state can theoretically fulfill many of the legal requirements of the entrepreneur, only a small percentage of the attorneys will have the experience and expertise necessary to provide adequate legal guidance.

An efficient search requires diligence on the part of the entrepreneur. First, the entrepreneur should consider whether he or she wants to work with a large or a small firm and then identify through referrals several attorneys to investigate. Next, the entrepreneur should interview as many of them as possible to ensure a good fit.

Large Firm or Small Firm

A large firm and a small firm will differ mainly in two ways: one will offer specialists, and the other, generalists; their costs and billing procedures will also differ.

Large firms typically have many groups of attorneys who specialize in discrete areas of law. Smaller firms, on the other hand, typically have practitioners who have a greater breadth of knowledge. Small boutique firms usually specialize in a specific area, such as patents. Thus, the trade-off may be seen as depth versus breadth.

In a large firm, however, each attorney has access to many specialists, so the entrepreneur will have access to a vast amount of internal knowledge. Also, some large firms have attorneys who specialize in representing

FROM THE TRENCHES

A small entertainment company that wanted to incorporate and have ownership agreements drafted went to a major San Francisco Bay area firm. The founders were directed to a second-year associate who was assigned the work. After a few weeks, it was apparent that the associate was listening to one founder and not the other. When the entrepreneurs complained to a partner, they were told that the firm usually did not handle clients as small as their company. The partner also said, however, that the firm was not used to people being dissatisfied with its work and so would not charge the entrepreneurs. The entrepreneurs went to a solo practitioner who was able to meet their needs. They continue to use the solo practitioner.

entrepreneurs and thus have the breadth of knowledge found in smaller firms. For the young start-up with general and common business issues, the difference may be inconsequential. Initially, an entrepreneur may want to focus on finding an attorney who has experience in meeting the entrepreneur's immediate concerns in an efficient and timely manner.

The cost and billing structure of large and small firms may differ greatly. Larger firms tend to charge more per hour but may be better able to accommodate a deferred-payment structure and may be more efficient (thereby spending fewer billable hours) because of their expertise. In addition, attorneys from larger firms have lower-paid assistants helping them, which, again, brings down the cost of services. On the flip side, although an entrepreneur may benefit from this cheaper-by-the-hour help, the inefficiencies of involving more persons who are also less experienced may outweigh the benefits.

Referrals

Although it may seem that the numerous lawyer referral services or law directories could help the entrepreneur make a good decision, these sources are usually insufficient. Choosing an attorney is a very personal decision, and these sources are impersonal and often untested. The choice of the best attorney depends on the entrepreneur's type of business and his or her own business expertise, personality, and skills. One of the best ways to find a good lead is to ask friends, colleagues, and other entrepreneurs in the geographic area who have used a particular law firm and attorney for similar purposes. Venture capitalists can also be a good source of referrals. For example, an entrepreneur starting a high-tech company should find an attorney with prior experience in this realm. Find out what others like or do not like about their attorneys and what they consider the most important factors in an effective working relationship. Also ask whether they have had any bad experiences.

Local community groups or universities may be able to provide good leads. Attorneys who specialize in working with start-ups often frequent local entrepreneur conventions or meetings. Consider attending these and meeting with these attorneys. Classes on entrepreneurship at local colleges often feature attorneys as guest speakers.

The director of the state bar's continuing legal education (CLE) program, the local chamber of commerce, accountants, or the local bar committee for business lawyers may also provide some good leads. In addition, entrepreneurs should keep an eye on the trade journals or newspapers for articles written about or by attorneys who have the experience they seek.

Shopping Around

It is important to sit down with various attorneys to determine which one best meets the entrepreneur's needs for a provider of legal work and legal (and perhaps business) advice, as well as a potential information broker. Personality and a compatible working relationship are among the most important factors entrepreneurs should look for when choosing an attorney. If a person has not worked with an attorney before, it makes sense to bring along someone who has. When first exploring a relationship with an attorney, the entrepreneur should take advantage of an opportunity to have lunch with members of the law firm to become better acquainted with the attorney(s) and to obtain some free legal advice.

Factors many entrepreneurs consider important in deciding which attorney to retain include:

- ***Personality.*** Most entrepreneurs look for an attorney who is a good listener, can communicate, understands what the entrepreneur wants from the relationship, and is trustworthy.
- ***A Compatible Working Relationship.*** It is important to determine whether the attorney uses assistants and if so, how. If assistants are used extensively, the entrepreneur should ask to meet with them also. An effective working relationship between the entrepreneur and the law firm may involve a legal team consisting of an experienced partner and a more junior associate who would do most of the actual drafting. In this case, the entrepreneur should focus on whether there is a good personality fit with the associate. Some tasks, such as registration of a trademark, state securities filings, and drafting of minutes, are best done by a legal assistant or paralegal.
- ***Use of Technology.*** The level of technology at a law firm can make a significant difference in the choice of an attorney. Having up-to-date

computer systems and software allows attorneys to rapidly retrieve and modify documents and easily customize standard agreements and forms, thereby creating significant cost savings for the entrepreneur. For companies that have divisions in different time zones, or are international or contemplating international expansion, it scarcely matters where the attorney is located. The entrepreneur should confirm that the firm uses e-mail with appropriate security safeguards to ensure confidentiality. Entrepreneurs who use e-mail find it very efficient, as it is often difficult to reach attorneys over the telephone, and leaving a long voice message can be awkward. Correspondence via e-mail is less interruptive, responses typically come within the day, and the entrepreneur (and the attorney) have written documentation for reference. Using e-mail may also reduce legal fees, as many attorneys do not bill the time they spend reading e-mail but start the meter running as soon as they pick up the phone.

- *Timeliness in Returning Telephone Calls.* Often an entrepreneur needs to resolve a legal question or issue quickly. A timely response from an attorney, ideally within a day, is critical. To some clients, a prompt reply reflects the importance of the entrepreneur to the attorney. If the attorney does not return phone calls promptly, the entrepreneur may conclude that his or her business is not a high priority for the attorney.
- *General Business Acumen and Understanding of Industry.* Some entrepreneurs view their attorneys solely as legal consultants, whereas others view them as an important source of business acumen and, in some cases, as coaches or partners. For some entrepreneurs, especially those who do not have a business partner, it is important to have an attorney with whom they can discuss ideas and go over the business plan. For example, one entrepreneur in the restaurant business finally chose an attorney because of the attorney's prior experience with clients in a retail business similar to that of the entrepreneur. For entrepreneurs involved in very technical ventures, it is important to have an attorney who understands the technology and the industry involved. Such an understanding typically implies that the attorney has contacts in the industry. In addition, it shows that the attorney knows how to view the

business and which contingencies to consider. On a more practical level, familiarity with the industry jargon helps minimize the legal costs.

- ***Information Brokerage and Network with Potential Investors and Venture Capitalists.*** Attorneys can serve an important information brokerage function and provide a path to potential investors and venture capital funds. They have the personal and business connections in the industry that an entrepreneur may need to tap into later to finance the business. For the entrepreneur considering venture capital, it is advantageous to work with a firm that has good relations with the venture capital community and can provide introductions. Attorneys who have done prior work with entrepreneurs may also be able to provide other good networking leads such as commercial bankers, accountants, business partners, and investment bankers.
- ***Cost Sensitivity.*** It is important to have an attorney who understands the business in terms of budgetary constraints. Having an attorney who watches costs carefully and has a good sense of the appropriate amount of time to spend on a matter is important.
- ***Cost.*** Attorneys charge different rates per hour and per task. These rates can appear to differ vastly. Sometimes, however, an attorney who charges significantly less by the hour may take significantly longer to accomplish the task because he or she is moving up the learning curve on the start-up's dime. In that event, the "cheaper" lawyer ends up costing more than the "expensive" but experienced lawyer. An appropriate way to assess this component is to comparison shop and ask each candidate how much the firm typically charges to do certain basic legal work such as drafting incorporation documents and shareholder agreements. The entrepreneur should also ask the candidate about his or her recent experience in drafting such documents.

Working Cost-Efficiently with an Attorney

Most start-ups monitor their spending carefully, so it can be daunting for the entrepreneur to be faced with thousands of dollars in legal fees. Although many law firms will negotiate a fee arrangement with an entrepreneur, the legal fees can still be a significant component of the start-up's operating expenses. Nevertheless, an entrepreneur can take several steps to prevent unpleasant surprises and to keep the fees at a manageable level.

The cost of an attorney can be broken into time- and nontime-related costs. Although nontime-related costs can be substantial, the bulk of the costs come from being billed for someone's time.

The Structure of Billing Time Costs

A client is typically charged for the time spent by attorneys and legal assistants on the client's affairs. Generally, fees fall into one of four categories: hourly fees, flat fees, contingent and deferred fees, and retainers. Firms differ in how they structure fees, and entrepreneurs should insist on a written employment letter that spells out the billing arrangements.

Law firms generally charge by the hour, and depending on the firm and the seniority of the attorneys working with the entrepreneur, prices can range from $150 to $600 per hour. It is important for the entrepreneur to inquire about what services are considered billable because billing practices can vary significantly from firm to firm. For example, some firms will agree that a partner will attend one board meeting a month at no charge. Unless the engagement letter specifies otherwise, any time that an attorney or other staff member spends on the entrepreneur's affairs may be consid-

FROM THE TRENCHES

In April 1980, three venture capitalists and a UCLA scientist met at the law firm Cooley Godward for the purpose of starting a biotechnology company to be called Amgen. Cooley Godward's partners aided Amgen in recruiting a Scientific Advisory Board for the company and Dr. George B. Rathmann as CEO. In January 1981, Cooley helped Amgen obtain $18.9 million in its only round of venture capital financing. The firm designed Amgen's equity program, dealt with several critical personnel matters, and assisted in preparing Amgen to go public in 1983, which resulted in $39 million in capital being raised. In ten years, Amgen became the nation's leading independent biopharmaceutical company.

ered billable time. Thus, for example, the clock may be running for the time spent in meetings or on the telephone, researching a topic or writing a memo or e-mail message, traveling, and discussing matters with other attorneys or legal assistants in the firm.

Flat fees often can be arranged for discrete tasks such as drafting a specific contract or registering a trademark. In this case, the attorney will charge a fixed rate, barring unforeseen circumstances, no matter how much time is spent on the matter.

For noncriminal cases, an attorney may be willing to arrange a contingent fee structure, whereby the attorney receives a fixed payment or a certain percentage of some potential cash flow when a certain event occurs. A contingent payment structure is not uncommon in a trial setting (such as a personal injury case), where, for example, an attorney may receive 40 percent of the settlement. An entrepreneur may wish to structure the fee so that the attorney can continue to bill at the normal high hourly rates but will not expect payment for the bulk of the fee until (and perhaps unless) venture capital or other investor funding is provided. This type of fee structure may be ideal for the entrepreneur who is still testing the feasibility of the venture.

An attorney may agree to defer billing but not make payment contingent on financing. For example, one large Silicon Valley firm gave a start-up client a break on the up-front time charged and agreed that the entrepreneur could defer all payments without interest for up to nine months. Sometimes a firm will ask for stock in the enterprise in exchange for deferring its billing. This can create a conflict of interest, however, as the law firm itself becomes an investor, so the entrepreneur should proceed cautiously.[1] Equity is often a start-up's most precious asset. If the entrepreneur is willing to offer the law firm stock, it is usually preferable to give the firm the right to invest in the first round of financing on the same terms and conditions as the outside investors rather than giving the firm stock for free or at the founders' price.

Some attorneys will request an up-front payment, called a *retainer,* to ensure that they get paid. Because cash is tight in start-ups, the entrepreneur should resist this arrangement and agree to advance only out-of-pocket costs (such as filing fees) as incurred.

The entrepreneur can use the attorney more economically and minimize the time the attorney spends on the work by being organized, preparing an outline for a term sheet, doing a rough draft of some documents, and otherwise remaining proactive in all legal affairs. As mentioned earlier, sometimes an attorney will agree to attend one board meeting a month at no charge. This keeps the attorney abreast of business developments and available for a certain amount of free legal advice without bankrupting the start-up.

NONTIME-RELATED COSTS Besides charging for the time spent directly on the legal matter, law firms typically will bill for other costs that the entrepreneur may not expect to pay for separately. Nontime-related costs may include charges for photocopying, word processing, online research, faxing, long-distance telephone calls, messenger service, and travel, as well as filing fees. Firms usually bill these costs directly to each client rather than absorbing them and raising rates for all clients to cover the added expense. The entrepreneur should determine the protocol of the firm and negotiate how he or she will be billed for these incidental costs. The entrepreneur can try to negotiate better rates or terms—to pay only for faxing and not photocopying, for example—or propose paying a fixed monthly fee or a fee based on a percentage of the professional fees incurred that month.

HIDDEN HEAD COUNTS Even though the entrepreneur may have spoken initially only to a particular attorney, it is likely that some of the work will be farmed out to others in the firm. This delegation has positive and negative aspects. More senior attorneys are typically more adept at looking at the big picture and setting up business structures, whereas mid-level associates are typically more efficient at preparing documentation. The junior associates gain experience by working on assignments under the supervision of more experienced attorneys. Although this process is beneficial to junior associates, the cash-poor entrepreneur needs to be careful that he or she is not financing this training. The entrepreneur may find junior associates sitting in at meetings and on conference calls. In that case, the entrepreneur should find out whether anyone is unnecessarily involved, and if so, whether the entrepreneur is being charged for that person's presence. The entrepreneur may wish to establish a policy that no new person may be brought in without the entrepreneur's approval. The entrepreneur should not hesitate to say that he or she thinks a certain person should not be on the clock.

In most law firms, each attorney is responsible for billing a certain number of hours per month and per year. Attorneys record how they spend their time, often in six-minute increments, and then the firm bills the individual clients for the attorneys' time. Junior attorneys bill out at lower rates than the more senior attorneys. Many entrepreneurs prefer working with partners because of the prestige and because they believe they are in more knowledgeable hands. However, seniority does not necessarily ensure that the best or ideal person is handling a certain transaction. Use of junior associates, who are cheaper per hour and often have more free time to focus on the entrepreneur's concerns and to return phone calls, is often appropriate.

Sometimes, however, the cheaper per-hour rate is not worth the extra time that a less experienced person may take. Usually, first-year associates are not cost-efficient unless the billing partner is willing to write off substantial blocks of time as training. Once associates have two or three years' training, they usually will have a level of competency that, coupled with the lower rate, makes them a good choice for drafting and negotiating documents.

Drafting

Accurately drafting a document that includes all the necessary nuances and covers all possible contingencies can be difficult and time-consuming. Typically, the entrepreneur knows the company's business issues, and the lawyer knows the legal issues. A thorough understanding of both is critical to drafting certain documents, such as shareholder agreements. No document is so completely standardized that a form can just be churned out. Depending on the potential risks, some customization must always be done. Even if no extensive customization is needed, the entrepreneur should understand the significance of the terms and their application to his or her business because ultimately the contract will become legally binding. Thus, by the time the document is finalized and the signatures obtained, the entrepreneur could end up spending a significant amount of money for what may seem at first to be a simple document.

Although lawyers can be instrumental in drafting documents, the impecunious entrepreneur may want to handle the bulk of the drafting. Depending on the type of document being produced, the entrepreneur could write the first draft, using the most appropriate and detailed sample forms from the attorney, preferably on a disk, as a model. By working with the most detailed forms, the entrepreneur will gain a better understanding of all the issues to consider. Although the sample forms may include many terms that are not relevant to the entrepreneur, it is much more efficient to cross out unnecessary terms than to risk forgetting to include a salient feature. Before attempting to customize the forms for his or her business, the entrepreneur might want to ask the attorney to quickly summarize the main features of the document. The attorney should also review the draft to ensure legal compliance and to consider whether any legal or business issues are not adequately covered. It should be noted that if a firm has standardized documents, such as a certificate of incorporation and bylaws, it may be far more expensive to have the attorney review the entrepreneur's draft than to just plug the company information into the firm's standard form.

Furthermore, the entrepreneur, when negotiating a term sheet with another business party, should draft the most detailed term sheet possible before passing it off to the attorney. It is much more expedient if the entrepreneur puts in the terms, as opposed to saying nothing about a certain issue and then having the lawyer negotiate something without knowing what the entrepreneur would have wanted.

Finalizing standard employment forms is one area where the entrepreneur can save money. The entrepreneur should ask the attorney whether employees will need to sign a standard agreement. If so, the entrepreneur should obtain the standard forms on disk and then insert the employee's name. This method may be appropriate for certain assignment-of-invention agreements, nondisclosure agreements, and letters offering employment.

Often drafting can also be left to the entrepreneur when letters that are legally significant but also contain substantial business content are needed. Certain letters of intent, strongly worded demand letters, or contract proposals can be substantially prepared by the entrepreneur before any legal review.

Organization

Because lawyers often keep track of their time in six-minute increments, it is prudent to be as organized as possible to avoid wasting time. The entrepreneur will be billed for the time spent describing an issue. Thus, before calling the attorney, the entrepreneur should prepare by making sure that the necessary documents are on hand and that he or she can explain the situation clearly and concisely. By keeping chronological notes on what has been covered with the attorney, the entrepreneur can help ensure that no important details are omitted. The entrepreneur should also consider minimizing the frequency of interactions by maintaining a running list of questions and being prepared to discuss various issues during one meeting or conversation.

Being Proactive

The entrepreneur's working relationship with the attorney is often enhanced if the interaction does not always involve a specific legal issue. Although it is important to try to educate one's self before seeing an attorney and avoid asking unnecessary questions, the client should not err on the side of being too independent. It is a good idea to keep the attorney informed of important business issues even when they seemingly have insignificant legal implications. Not only may the entrepreneur have failed to recognize the legal implications, but more important, keeping the attorney informed keeps him or her excited about the client and keeps the entrepreneur's business in the forefront of the attorney's mind should any pertinent legal issues arise or new legal developments occur.

An entrepreneur can be proactive in keeping the attorney current on the relevant law. In scouting industry-specific trade journals, an entrepreneur may run across legal issues or precedents. Legal research time can be reduced if the entrepreneur makes it a habit to send relevant clippings to the attorney and asks the attorney to do the same.

The Billing Process

Attorneys and the legal realm can be overwhelming and intimidating. Nevertheless, the entrepreneur should remember that he or she is paying the attorney for a service, and, as when visiting a doctor, it is advisable to speak up about any concerns.

Especially when first starting to work with a law firm, the client should ask for a price estimate or upper price limit on a certain assignment. Although the attorney can never be sure how much time a certain task will take, barring unexpected contingencies, he or she should be able to provide a reasonable cost estimate. Asking for an estimate is important for several reasons. First, as when purchasing anything, it is always a good idea to get a sense of how much something costs. Second, it forces the attorney to anchor around a reasonable price. For competitive reasons, a law firm will not quote a ridiculous price for a certain transaction. Third, if the task takes longer than anticipated, the law firm may absorb the extra costs rather than charge a higher price than originally quoted.

When first negotiating the fee structure for the business, the entrepreneur should ask to see a sample bill. Ideally, the bill should be detailed enough that the client knows exactly why he or she is being charged. The descriptions of work performed should not be vague, such as "produced documents," but should contain specifics about the agreements being drafted. Some firms have a policy of establishing minimum billable hours, whereby they charge a minimum for a certain task, and more if the assignment takes more time. If this method seems inappropriate, the entrepreneur should voice concern. The entrepreneur may desire to pay only for the time actually spent and may ask that work be billed in tenth-of-an-hour increments, as is done in many firms. Some entrepreneurs go to the extent of writing out how they are to be billed. They might specify that all clerical activities performed by an attorney are to be billed out at a paralegal's hourly rate, telephone calls fewer than a certain number of minutes are not billable, express-mail or air-courier costs will be paid only if such services were requested by the client, and any charge over a certain number of minutes must be broken out separately and described.

The entrepreneur should examine each invoice closely. If the amount of time billed for a particular task seems out of line, challenge it. Firms will often write down (or adjust) bills to keep the client happy. Of course, if the partner on the account is asked to spend an inordinate amount of time delving into billing minutiae, it may be harmful to the relationship.

Given that many start-ups live month to month, the entrepreneur should demand monthly billing. Although the entrepreneur should keep a written log of incurred legal expenses, if the bill comes too long after the service, he or she may not be able to recall the work the bill covers.

Attorney-Client Privilege

When retaining an attorney, it is important to be clear about who the client is. Communications with a lawyer are not protected by the *attorney-client privilege* unless they are between a lawyer and a client seeking confidential legal advice. If the client is a corporation, the privilege protects the communications or discussions of any company employee with counsel as long as the subject matter of the communication relates to that employee's duties and the communication is made at the direction of a corporate superior. For example, if a corporation hires a lawyer to do an internal investigation of possible misconduct, and an officer instructs an employee to cooperate in the investigation, a third party (such as the government or a competitor) cannot compel the disclosure of the communication between the employee and the lawyer. The privilege belongs to the corporation as client, however, so the corporation may require the disclosure of the communication between the employee and the lawyer in a case brought by the corporation or the government against the employee. For example, if the CEO of a corporation tells company counsel that the corporation has been booking earnings on sales not yet consummated, then company counsel will be free, if so requested by the board of directors, to report that disclosure to the authorities for criminal prosecution of the CEO.

An attorney retained to incorporate a company will normally view the company as the client, at least once it is organized. This relationship should be clearly spelled out in an engagement letter with the attorney.

Although the founders may initially be the sole representatives of the company, they are usually not considered to be the client. This means that if a dispute occurs down the road and the board of directors votes to fire a founder, the attorney cannot ethically represent both the founder and the company. In addition, any conversations between the attorney and the founders will not be privileged.

Attorneys often recommend that each founder retain separate counsel from the outset, especially when structuring the ownership and negotiating buy-sell agreements. In practice, this rarely happens because it is too

FROM THE TRENCHES

Company X and Company Y were the majority and minority shareholders, respectively, of Company Z. Under the terms of a contract between companies X and Y, Company X had the right to appoint a majority of Company Z's board of directors. Company X determined that an initial public offering (IPO) of stock would be in the best interest of Company Z. Company X retained counsel to advise it on its rights under certain contracts between companies X and Y and, under Company Z's articles of incorporation, to cause Company Z to initiate the IPO process. In the course of the discussion, Company X realized that it would be prudent to invite Company Z's management into certain of the discussions so that Company Z's management could be part of the IPO planning process.

A dispute arose between Company X and Company Y. Company Y made a motion to require Company X's directors to answer questions about the discussions with counsel and to produce their notes of those discussions. Company X asserted attorney-client privilege.

The court held that the attorney-client privilege, which would otherwise have protected Company X's communications with its counsel, was waived as to those conversations in which Company Z's personnel participated. Although Company X was entitled to receive confidential advice from its own counsel concerning its rights and obligations, Company Z's personnel were not strictly necessary to the accomplishment of this end, and their presence destroyed the privilege. As a result, Company X's directors were required to give deposition testimony concerning the conversations with their attorneys in which Company Z's representatives participated and to turn over their notes of those conversations.

expensive. A founder should, and usually will, retain separate counsel if there is a dispute or threatened dispute with the company or its board of directors.

The attorney-client privilege applies only to legal advice, not business advice. It does not protect client communications that are made to further a crime or illegal act. For example, if an entrepreneur asks the attorney the best way to steal a competitor's trade secrets, that conversation is not privileged. In addition, the attorney-client privilege is lost if the client shares the attorney's advice with outsiders or permits outsiders to listen in on a discussion between the client and the attorney.

Putting it into Practice

Because Kendra thought that an attorney would be useful in the initial structuring of the company and issuance of equity, she decided to find an attorney before officially launching her business. Although her college roommate Ginny had been helpful in sorting out her obligations to CSS, Kendra and Ginny agreed that she needed someone experienced in representing software start-ups as counsel for the company.

Kendra believed that it would be helpful to develop a relationship with an attorney sooner rather than later. In addition, another entrepreneur had told her that even though you think you do not need an attorney until you are raising money, an attorney can handle many matters in the beginning, from making sure that stock is issued properly to reviewing a lease for office space.

To find a suitable attorney, Kendra asked friends and business associates for recommendations, then pruned her options down to two: a solo practitioner and a partner in a large regional firm. Kendra made an appointment to talk with both attorneys, who each agreed to meet with her free of charge.

At her meeting with Janet Winslow, the solo practitioner, Kendra learned that she had a generalized legal practice. Janet said that she would do all the legal work herself at a rate of $315 per hour. She warned Kendra that her practice was quite busy, so her turnaround time on documents would vary depending on other client demands. Janet explained that she had done a number of jobs for start-up companies and that, in most cases, she would be able to modify existing documents to meet Kendra's needs. However, Janet would have to draft certain documents from scratch. Janet had contracted with a local patent firm that would handle any patent applications that Kendra needed filed. Janet promised that regardless of how busy she was, she would always return Kendra's phone calls the same day.

Although Janet used e-mail, she had not yet invested in security software. As for a payment plan, Janet said she could be flexible for a couple of months but ultimately would have to be paid.

Kendra's second meeting was with Michael Cruz, a highly regarded corporate partner in a large regional firm. Michael explained that although he would ultimately be responsible for Kendra's company's legal work, a third-year associate, Sanjay Datar, would actually draft the documents, which Michael would then review. Michael said that his billing rate was $495 per

continued...

continued...

hour and that Sanjay billed at $295. Michael told Kendra that the firm's resources would allow it to turn around documents as quickly as Kendra needed them. His firm had several patent counsel, and the firm was capable of handling all patent work that Kendra would need.

Michael also explained that the firm had invested heavily in technology and had a computer program that allowed an associate to enter certain information about a company and its needs, after which the program automatically generated customized documents. The firm also had e-mail and a Web site and used encryption and other security measures to safeguard both the firm's intranet and sensitive e-mail communications. Michael said that because his schedule entailed significant travel, he might take a day or two to return phone calls. Sanjay, however, would be able to respond to calls immediately and would have access to Michael for advice. In addition, Michael offered his and Sanjay's home phone numbers to Kendra and said that if time-sensitive issues arose, she should not hesitate to call them at home.

Michael said that his firm would agree to postpone billing Kendra until her company received venture capital or other financing. If the company did not receive financing, the company would still technically be responsible for the legal fees, but Michael assured Kendra that his firm would not expect the company or the entrepreneur to pay the full amount of the fees.

Michael then introduced Kendra to Sanjay. Kendra was impressed by his enthusiasm and intelligence.

After the two meetings, Kendra decided to hire Michael. She was particularly impressed by the firm's commitment to technology and felt that the improved efficiency would offset the higher billing rates. She also felt that because most work would be done by the associate, she would save money. Although Michael might not be accessible at all times, she felt comfortable knowing she would be able to reach the associate whenever she had a legal question or concern. Finally, she thought the firm would have the flexibility and sophistication to accommodate the company's growing legal needs. Kendra discussed her thoughts with the Colgates, and they agreed with her decision.

Content with her choice, Kendra called Michael, told him of her decision, and set up an appointment to discuss what form of legal entity would be best for the new business.

NOTE

1. For a discussion of ways to mitigate the possible conflict of interest, see American Bar Association Formal Opinion 00-418 (July 7, 2000).

Chapter 4

DECIDING WHETHER TO INCORPORATE

By carefully considering the forms of business entity that are available and then intelligently choosing the most appropriate one, entrepreneurs can reduce exposure to liabilities, minimize taxes, and ensure that the business is capable of being financed and conducted efficiently. In addition, formalizing the business helps prevent misunderstandings among the participants by defining their ownership stakes, roles, and duties in the business.

The primary considerations in the choice of business entity will be the degree to which the entrepreneur's personal assets are protected from liabilities of the business; the availability of favorable tax strategies such as maximizing the tax benefits of start-up losses, avoiding double (or even triple) layers of taxation, and converting ordinary income into long-term capital gain, which is taxed at lower rates; attractiveness to potential investors and lenders; availability of attractive equity incentives for employees and other service providers; and costs (start-up and ongoing).

This chapter first describes each of the principal business forms and then explores the considerations and strategies involved in making an appropriate selection. A brief discussion of name selection follows.

THE FORMS OF BUSINESS ENTITY

A business may be conducted as a corporation (including the S corporation, which has special flow-through tax attributes); a general, limited, or limited liability partnership; a limited liability company (LLC); or a sole proprietorship. Each state has its own laws under which businesses may organize and operate.

A corporation is a distinct legal entity owned by its shareholders and managed by a board of directors. A partnership is a separate entity for some purposes and a group of individual partners for other purposes. It does not pay taxes on its activities; instead, its partners pay taxes on its activities based on their respective interests in its profits. The LLC, a relatively new form of business organization, attempts to combine the best attributes of the corporation and the partnership. An LLC is generally taxed the same as a partnership unless it elects to be taxed as a corporation.

A *sole proprietorship* is a business owned by one person. It has little legal significance separate from its owner and usually requires no governmental filing except a fictitious-business-name statement, which discloses the name under which the business will be conducted and the owner's name and address. The owner reports the income and expenses of the business on a schedule (usually Schedule C) to his or her own personal income tax return. Although the sole proprietorship is probably the most prevalent form of small business in the United States, it is often a poor choice because the owner has unlimited liability for the losses of the business, thereby putting all of the owner's personal assets at risk.

Most large business organizations operate as corporations despite the tax incentives to use the partnership or LLC form of doing business. The corporation is the most familiar business entity and is governed by the most highly developed laws. A principal advantage of the corporate form is the limited liability it provides to its shareholders: Creditors are limited to the assets of the corporation for payment and may not collect directly from shareholders if corporate assets are insufficient to pay all debts and liabilities. Other advantages of the corporate form include its familiarity and well-understood governance laws, its permanence, and the ability to transfer corporate stock more easily than partnership or LLC interests (particularly in the public securities markets). In addition, many venture capital and other investment funds are unable to invest in partnerships and LLCs because their major investors are pension and profit-sharing trusts and other tax-exempt entities that are subject to certain tax restrictions. Despite these advantages of the corporate form, partnerships, proprietorships, and, increasingly, LLCs are also widely used for smaller businesses and when tax and other considerations warrant.

Corporations

A *corporation* is a distinct legal entity owned by its shareholders. Unlike a partnership, a corporation may be owned by a single person who can be the corporation's sole director and serve as any required officer (e.g., president, treasurer, and secretary). The shareholders elect the corporation's board of directors but are not otherwise active in the management of the corporation. The board of directors is responsible for major corporate decisions. Day-to-day management is carried out by the corporation's officers, who are appointed by, and serve at the pleasure of, the board of directors. A corporation has an unlimited life, so it is not terminated or changed on the death of a shareholder or other changes in its ownership. Instead, shares are transferred upon a shareholder's death to the shareholder's heirs.

Unless a corporation elects to be taxed as an S corporation, it is taxed as a separate legal entity. (A corporation that does not elect S corporation treatment is sometimes referred to as a *C corporation* because it is taxed under Subchapter C of the Internal Revenue Code.) Under current federal income tax law, a corporation is taxed on its net income (gross income less allowable deductions) at rates ranging from 15 to 35 percent (the rate is 34 percent on income over $75,000 up to $10 million). Property, other than money, contributed to a corporation will be subject to tax unless the person, or group of persons, contributing the property owns at least 80 percent of the corporation. Money or other property distributed by a corporation to its shareholders is subject to tax again when distributed in the form of dividends; shareholders pay that tax.

Preserving Limited Liability: Piercing the Corporate Veil

The proper operation of a corporation limits the liability of the shareholders because the creditors of the corporation usually cannot reach the shareholders to satisfy the corporation's obligations. Under the *alter ego doctrine,* however, a court may disregard the corporate entity and hold the shareholders personally liable for the corporation's obligations if the shareholders used the corporation to perpetrate a fraud or promote injustice. In determining whether to *pierce the corporate veil,* that is, whether to disregard the corporate form and make the shareholders directly liable for the corporation's obligations, a court will examine many factors, such as:

1. Was the corporation undercapitalized, given the risks inherent in its business?
2. Were corporate assets used for personal reasons?
3. Were corporate assets commingled with personal assets?
4. Were the corporate and personal books kept separately?
5. Were corporate actions properly authorized by the board of directors or the shareholders?

To preserve limited liability for its shareholders, the corporation should observe at least the following procedures:

1. Obtain and record shareholder and board authorization for corporate actions. An annual shareholders' meeting and regular board meetings should be conducted, and accurate minutes should be prepared and kept as part of the corporate records.
2. Keep corporate funds separate from personal funds.
3. Maintain complete and proper records for the corporation separate from personal records.
4. Make clear in all contracts with others that they are dealing with the corporation, and sign all contracts as shown:

   [CORPORATE NAME]

   By: ___________________________

   [Name and Title of Person Signing]

5. Maintain an arm's-length relationship between the corporation and any principal shareholder. Transactions with any of the directors or principal shareholders (or entities in which they have an interest) should be subject to approval by the disinterested members of the

board, if any, without the vote of the interested directors, after all the facts material to the transaction are fully disclosed.

6. Start the business with sufficient equity and liability insurance in light of the future capital needs of the business and its inherent risks.

S Corporations

The Internal Revenue Code permits certain shareholders to operate as a corporation while taxing them as individuals. Such corporations, known as *S corporations,* generally do not pay federal income tax but pass the tax liability for their profits through to their shareholders. Consequently, profits earned by an S corporation will be taxed only once. Similarly, an S corporation's losses flow through to the shareholders and may be deducted by the shareholders on their individual tax returns (subject to certain significant limitations). Profits and losses must be allocated based on share ownership for taxation purposes. The shareholders include as individual income all of the profits earned by the S corporation regardless of whether any cash amounts were distributed to shareholders.

A distribution of earnings by an S corporation to its shareholders is generally not taxed a second time. In contrast, a similar distribution by a corporation other than an S corporation will be taxed twice: The C corporation must pay federal corporate income tax on profits when earned, and shareholders must treat distributions as dividends subject to tax. An S corporation is the same as any other corporation except for the way it is taxed.

Shareholders generally elect S corporation status when the corporation is profitable and distributes substantially all of its profits to the shareholders, or when the corporation incurs losses and the shareholders wish to use the loss deductions on their personal income tax returns. The case for S corporation status is weaker when the corporation is owned solely by insiders who work for the company and receive their share of the profits in the form of salary and bonuses, which are deductible as expenses by the corporation. The presence of outsiders, who do not receive their share of profits in the form of deductible salary and bonuses, makes the technique of extracting profits by paying salaries and bonuses unavailable and the argument for an S corporation more compelling.

There are substantial limitations on the availability of the S corporation election and the allocation and deduction of S corporation losses by the shareholders. To qualify for S corporation status, a corporation must satisfy the following requirements:

1. The corporation must have no more than seventy-five shareholders, all of whom are individuals, certain tax-exempt organizations, qualifying trusts, or estates, and none of whom are nonresident aliens.
2. The corporation must have only one class of stock (although options and differences in voting rights are generally permitted).
3. The corporation may generally not own 80 percent or more of any other corporation unless special requirements are satisfied.

The requirement that an S corporation essentially have no shareholders other than individuals will prevent any business that intends to raise equity capital from venture capital funds, corporations, or other institutional investors from qualifying as an S corporation. In addition, because an S corporation can have only one class of stock, it cannot issue inexpensively priced founders' stock to key employees. Founders' stock is discussed in Chapter 5.

As discussed further in Chapters 7 and 13, most corporations that raise money from outside investors issue two classes of stock: convertible preferred stock to the investors and common stock to employees. The common stock is typically issued at a small fraction of the price of the preferred stock because it lacks the liquidation, dividend, voting, and other preferences that the preferred stock possesses. Because an S corporation can issue only common stock, it must issue the stock to employees at the same price paid by the investors (unless sold to the founders well in advance of the sale to the investors) if the employees are to avoid being taxed on receipt of their shares. Accordingly, the S corporation is most commonly used for family or other closely owned businesses that obtain capital from their individual shareholders and/or debt from outside sources and do not provide equity incentives to their employees on any significant scale.

A qualified corporation may elect to be taxed as an S corporation by filing Form 2553 with the Internal Revenue Service, together with the written consent of all the shareholders. This election must be filed on or before the fifteenth day of the third month of the taxable year of the corporation for which S corporation status is to be effective. If a corporation does not meet all of the S corporation requirements during the entire year, the election will not be effective until the following year.

PARTNERSHIPS

A partnership is a business carried on by at least two persons. A partnership is generally treated as a distinct legal entity separate from its partners. A partnership can sue and be sued, for example, and can own property in its own name. A creditor of a partner must proceed against that partner's interest in the partnership, rather than directly against the assets of the partnership. Similarly, a creditor of the partnership must first proceed against the assets of the partnership before going after any of the partners individually. For some purposes, however, a partnership is treated as an aggregate of its individual partners. For example, a partnership will dissolve on the death of any partner unless the remaining partners elect to continue the partnership. As discussed below, however, even if a partnership dissolves, the partnership business need not terminate.

A partnership may be a general partnership, a limited partnership, or a limited liability partnership. In a *general partnership*, each partner is a general partner, each has unlimited liability for the debts of the partnership, and each has the power to incur obligations on behalf of the partnership within the scope of the partnership's business. Some liability concerns, such as potential claims for personal injuries or those resulting from errors or omissions, can be alleviated through insurance. Each general partner acts as an agent for the partnership. As a result of this agency relationship, great care must be exercised in the selection of general partners.

A *limited partnership* has one or more general partners (each of whom has the same liability and power as a general partner in a general partnership) and one or more limited partners. The limited partners' liability is limited to the amount of their capital commitment. Generally, limited partners may not participate in the control of the partnership, or they will be treated as general partners for liability purposes.

A limited liability partnership is a hybrid used by certain professional partnerships (such as law and accounting firms) that are restricted by state law from organizing as limited partnerships. In a *limited liability partnership,* each partner can participate actively in the business and has unlimited personal liability for his or her own actions (such as medical malpractice) but is liable for the misdeeds of other partners only to the extent of the partnership's assets.

Partnership Agreements and Mechanics

Although most states have a general partnership and limited partnership act, as well as provisions governing limited liability partnerships (many of which are patterned on uniform acts), the partners may generally establish their own business arrangements among themselves by entering into a written partnership agreement. The partners may thereby override most provisions in the partnership acts both in terms of how a partnership is managed and how profits and losses are allocated and distributed. In the absence of an agreement to the contrary, profits and losses are split evenly among the partners.

Unlike a corporation, a partnership will dissolve (cease to be) on the death or withdrawal of a general partner unless the remaining partners elect to continue the partnership. However, a partnership agreement can, and should, provide for alternatives to liquidation after dissolution. For example, the partnership agreement can provide for the buyout of a deceased or withdrawn partner, the election of a new general partner, and the continuation of the business of the partnership by the remaining partners. In a limited partnership, the death of a limited partner typically does not result in the liquidation of the partnership; the limited partnership interest can be passed on to the deceased limited partner's heirs.

Partnerships require few legal formalities. A general partnership does not even require a written agreement; it can be formed with nothing more than a handshake and a general understanding between the partners. For example, students agree to work together on a business plan; a baker and a chef agree to open a restaurant together; two software programmers agree to collaborate on writing a program. In each case, a partnership of sorts is formed. However, the intention of one party alone cannot create a partnership. There must be a meeting of the minds: Each party must intend to establish a business relationship with the other. A limited partnership must have a written partnership agreement and file a certificate with the applicable secretary of state.

For the protection of the parties, a detailed written partnership agreement is strongly suggested for both general and limited partnerships. In the absence of a written agreement, state partnership laws will govern the partnership. Some provisions of the laws may lead to unfavorable results. For example, state laws may require partners to share the profits and losses equally regardless of their original capital contributions. A written partnership agreement can prevent future misunderstandings by including the term of the partnership's existence, the division of profits and losses between partners, the allocation of responsibility for any needed capital contributions, the payment of partnership salaries or withdrawals of capital, the duties of the partners, and the consequences to the partnership if a partner decides to sell his or her interest, becomes incapacitated, or dies. The agreement can also provide for a dispute resolution mechanism. As a practical matter, because a partnership is largely governed by the partnership agreement, which will vary significantly with each partnership, more expense is involved in forming a partnership than a corporation because a corporation's governance is largely controlled by statute. Standard or *boilerplate* forms should be avoided.

Tax Treatment

A key attraction of a partnership is that it pays no income tax. Income or losses flow through to each partner and are reported on the partner's individual tax return. Unlike an S corporation, which must allocate income or loss based on stock ownership, a partnership can allocate income and loss flexibly. For example, income can be allocated differently from losses. In a partnership in which one partner contributes services and another contributes money, the tax losses generated from the expenditure of funds contributed by the cash partner can all be allocated to that partner. In addition, allocations can provide for preferred returns to a certain partner or class of partners and can change over time or as higher profit levels are achieved.

Even though partnership losses flow through to the partners based on the loss-sharing arrangements in the partnership agreement, a number of limitations restrict the partners' ability to deduct these losses on their personal tax returns. For example, the tax code restricts the ability of partners (or shareholders in an S corporation) to deduct passive losses against most income. A partner's losses from a partnership are passive losses unless the partner materially participates in the partnership's business. A limited partner will rarely be able to treat partnership losses as other than passive. Other tax limitations prevent a partner from deducting losses that exceed his or her tax basis (the amount paid for the partner's partnership interest plus his or her share of partnership liabilities, as adjusted over time). In certain circumstances, a limited partner may not deduct losses attributable to nonrecourse debt (debt for which the debtor is not personally liable).

Property can generally be contributed to and distributed from a partnership without being subject to tax. Section 351 of the Internal Revenue Code permits a partnership to convert to a corporation without tax if the incorporation is properly structured. Once a partnership converts to a corporation, however, any distribution from the corporation will generally be subject to two levels of tax: a corporate tax and a shareholder tax.

Limited sources of operating capital are available to a partnership. It is generally restricted to capital contributed by partners and funds loaned by partners and outsiders. It is uncommon for a partnership to raise capital in a public offering, in part because publicly traded partnerships are taxed as corporations. Most venture capital funds have tax-exempt investors who would receive disadvantaged tax treatment if the fund invested in a partnership. Therefore, a business that expects to attract capital from a venture capital fund generally should not organize as a partnership.

Foreigners (that is, persons who are not citizens or permanent residents of the United States) are generally disinclined to invest in a partnership that is carrying on an active business because participating as a partner would cause them to be treated as being engaged in a U.S. trade or business. In that case, the United States would tax any of their U.S. income that is connected with the trade or business. Foreigners generally do not pay tax on income from U.S. corporations in which they invest.

Traditionally, limited partnerships were the entity of choice for activities such as investing in real estate or securities where flow-through tax treatment is desired. In addition to permitting profits and losses to flow through directly to the owners of the business, partnerships can distribute property in kind without incurring tax on the partnership or the partner. Many investment funds distribute highly appreciated securities to their partners after a liquidity event (e.g., an initial public offering or acquisition by a public company in a tax-free reorganization), thereby allowing each partner to make an individual decision as to when to sell the securities received. The advent of the LLC, discussed below, has resulted in many businesses organizing as LLCs instead of as limited partnerships to achieve limited liability for all members, even those who actively participate in the business.

Limited Liability Companies

The limited liability company (LLC) is a form of business organization that has rapidly gained popularity in the United States. All states now have laws that permit a business to organize and operate as an LLC. A properly structured LLC combines the pass-through federal tax treatment of a partnership with the liability protections of a corporation. Thus, an organization that would otherwise organize as a general or limited partnership, or as an S corporation if it met the requirements, will generally derive the most benefit from organizing as an LLC, because it will have limited liability protection while retaining favorable partnership tax treatment.

The owners (referred to as *members*) of an LLC have no personal liability for the obligations of the LLC (but, as is also true for corporate directors

FROM THE TRENCHES

Donald Lanham and Larry Clark were managers and also members of Preferred Income Investors, L.L.C. (P.I.I.), a limited liability company organized under the Colorado Limited Liability Company Act. Clark contacted Water, Waste & Land, Inc. (Westec) about the possibility of hiring Westec to perform engineering work in connection with the construction of a Taco Cabana fast-food restaurant. In the course of their preliminary discussions, Clark gave representatives of Westec a business card bearing Lanham's address, which was the same address listed as P.I.I.'s principal office and place of business in its articles of organization filed with the secretary of state. Although the name Preferred Income Investors, L.L.C. was not on the business card, the letters "P.I.I." appeared above the address on the card. There was, however, no indication as to what the acronym meant or that P.I.I. was a limited liability company. Although Westec never received a signed contract from Lanham, Clark gave verbal authorization to begin work. When P.I.I. failed to pay for the work, Westec sued P.I.I. as well as Clark and Lanham individually.

Even though P.I.I. had been properly formed, Westec argued that the members had failed to make it clear that they were acting on behalf of an LLC. The Colorado Supreme Court agreed, reasoning that the members were agents acting on behalf of a partially disclosed principal. Under traditional agency principles, agents are personally liable unless they fully identify the person on whose behalf they are acting.

Thus, as with corporations, it is critical for persons acting on behalf of an LLC to make clear the capacity in which they are acting. For example, all stationery and business cards used by managers and members of an LLC should include the name of the LLC and its status as a limited liability company if that is not clear from the name itself. In addition, as with officers of corporations, a member or manager of an LLC should execute contracts as follows:

[NAME OF LIMITED LIABILITY COMPANY]
By: ______________________________
[Name and Title of Person Signing]

Source: Water, Waste & Land, Inc. v. Lanham, 955 P.2d 997 (Colo. 1998) (en banc).

and officers, members still have personal liability for their individual acts and omissions in connection with the LLC's business). For all practical purposes, an LLC operates as a limited partnership without the legal requirement of having a general partner who bears ultimate liability for the obligations of the partnership. As discussed above, an S corporation also has both the limited liability and most of the federal tax pass-through features found in the LLC, but ownership is limited to seventy-five shareholders, all of whom must be individuals, certain tax-exempt organizations, qualifying trusts, or estates, and none of whom may be foreigners; in addition, the S corporation can have only one class of stock. An LLC has none of these restrictions.

An LLC has two principal charter documents. The first is a short (one to two pages) document filed with the secretary of state, which sets forth the name of the LLC, its address, its agent for service of process, the term (which may be perpetual), and whether the LLC will be governed by the members or by managers appointed by the members. This document is generally called the *certificate of formation* (Delaware) or *articles of organization* (California).

The second charter document for an LLC is its *operating agreement,* which is analogous to, and closely resembles, a partnership agreement. The operating agreement specifies how the LLC will be governed; the financial obligations of the members (e.g., additional capital calls could be forbidden, voluntary, or mandatory); and how profits, losses, and distributions will be shared. As with a partnership agreement, the operating agreement for an LLC will be tailored to suit the needs of each individual LLC, with the attendant expense of a specialized legal agreement. Again, boilerplate documents should be avoided. The so-called check-the-box regulations promulgated by the Internal Revenue Service generally allow LLCs and partnerships that are not publicly traded to be taxed as flow-through entities unless they elect to be taxed as corporations.

An LLC is not suitable for businesses financed by venture capital funds because of tax restrictions on the funds' tax-exempt partners. But an LLC can be very attractive for businesses financed by corporate investors and, to a lesser extent (because of the passive-loss limitations), wealthy individuals.

An LLC is the entity of choice for a start-up entity seeking to flow through losses to its investors because (1) it offers the same complete liability protection to all its members as does a corporation; (2) it can have corporations and partnerships as members (unlike an S corporation) and is not subject to any of the other limitations that apply to S corporations; and (3) losses can be specially allocated entirely to the cash investors (in an S corporation, losses are allocated to all the owners based on share ownership). In addition, the LLC can be incorporated tax-free at any time. For example, after the initial start-up losses have been allocated to the early-round investors, the LLC could be incorporated to accommodate investment from a venture capital fund in a conventional preferred-stock financing. Alternatively, incorporation could be deferred until a public offering.

Selecting a C Corporation, S Corporation, Partnership, or Limited Liability Company

Three issues are critical in selecting the form of business entity: (1) Who will be the owners of the business? (2) How will the earnings of the business be returned to its owners? and (3) Is the business expected initially to generate profits or losses?

Who Will Be the Owners?

If a business is owned by a few individuals, any of the above entities may be an appropriate business form, and factors other than the type of owner will be determinative. If the business will be widely held, the C corporation is usually the entity of choice for a variety of reasons. A corporation has unlimited life and free transferability of ownership. The corporation's existence is not affected by changes in its ownership resulting from transfers of stock (by a living shareholder or upon a shareholder's death) or the issuance of new shares (i.e., additional shares issued directly by the corporation). Free transferability of interests and unlimited life are more difficult to achieve in a partnership and, to a lesser extent, an LLC. An S corporation is not suitable for a widely held corporation because it cannot have more than seventy-five shareholders (all of whom must generally be U.S. citizens or resident aliens or eligible trusts or estates).

If the business is so widely held that its ownership interests will become publicly traded, the corporation is the entity of choice. Investors are more receptive to offerings of corporate stock than partnership or LLC interests because they are easier to understand. In addition, publicly traded partnerships and LLCs lose their tax advantages and are taxed as corporations (i.e., no flow-through tax treatment).

If ownership interests in the business will be provided to employees, the C corporation will generally be the preferred entity for several reasons. First, stock ownership is easier to explain to employees than equity interests in partnerships and LLCs. Second, creating favorably priced equity incentives is easiest to accomplish in a C corporation because ownership can be held through various classes of stock. It is quite common for a corporation to issue preferred stock to investors and common stock to management and other employees. If properly structured, the common stock can be sold at a substantial discount from the preferred stock because of the special rights and preferences of the preferred stock. For example, preferred stock will usually have a liquidation preference equal to the price paid for the preferred stock. If the corporation is sold or liquidated, this liquidation preference must be paid to preferred-stock shareholders before any funds can be paid to common-stock holders. Preferred stock is usually convertible into common stock at the option of the holder and would ordinarily be converted in an upside situation in which the company is successful and goes public or is sold.

Finally, the tax law gives favorable tax treatment to incentive stock options (ISOs) granted by a corporation. The holder of an ISO generally incurs no tax until the shares purchased through an option exercise are sold. The recognized gain is taxed at the more favorable long-term capital gains rate, rather than as ordinary income. Incentive stock options are available only for corporations, not partnerships or LLCs. When options do not qualify as ISOs, the option holder recognizes ordinary income when the option is exercised and must pay tax on the difference between the exercise price of the option and the fair market value of the underlying stock at the time the option is exercised.

A business that expects to raise capital from a venture capital fund will usually be formed as a C corporation because most venture capital funds raise money from tax-exempt entities such as pension and profit-sharing trusts, universities, and other charitable organizations. These nonprofit entities would incur unrelated business taxable income on which the nonprofit must pay tax if the venture capital fund invested in a flow-through entity such as a partnership or LLC.

How Does the Business Expect to Return Its Profits to Its Owners?

A business can either distribute earnings currently to its owners or accumulate and reinvest the earnings with the goal of growing the business so that it can either be taken public or sold to another business for cash or marketable stock of the acquiring business. Current earnings are taxed as ordinary income, whereas the gain on the sale of stock held for at least one year is taxed at the more favorable long-term capital gain rate.

If a business intends to distribute earnings currently, a tax flow-through entity such as a partnership, LLC, or S corporation is the entity of choice because the earnings can be distributed without incurring a second level of tax. If a C corporation is used, earnings can be paid out without being taxed at the corporate level only if they are paid as salary or other reasonable compensation to shareholders who work for the business. (Such compensation is deductible by the corporation against its taxable income.) Distributions of earnings by a corporation to its shareholders, other than as compensation for services, will not be deductible by the corporation and will be taxed as ordinary dividend income to its shareholders. Most small businesses that distribute the business's earnings currently and do not have owners who work for the business have a strong incentive to use a tax flow-through entity such as an S corporation, partnership, or LLC.

The income tax law provides an additional incentive for businesses that seek to build long-term value, rather than the current distribution of earnings, to organize as C corporations. With a C corporation (but not any other business entity) that qualifies as a small business corporation (SBC), stock issued after August 1993 that is held for at least five years is generally eligible under Section 1202 of the Internal Revenue Code for a 50 percent deduction in capital gains tax, reducing the effective tax rate to approximately 14 percent. High-income-tax payers subject to the alternative minimum tax may incur a higher rate.

Is the Business Expected Initially to Generate Profits or Losses?

If the business is expected initially to generate losses, then a tax flow-through entity such as a partnership, LLC, or S corporation is the entity of choice because it allows the owners to deduct the losses from their taxable income. For example, biotechnology companies frequently operate at a loss because of the extraordinary costs of developing products, conducting clinical trials, and obtaining the approval of the Food and Drug Administration. Even in the best-case scenario, a biotechnology company will typically experience several years of multimillion-dollar losses before reaching profitability. Depending on the sources of start-up funding, use of a flow-through entity may be attractive, as it allows the investors to deduct the start-up losses against taxable income. Otherwise it may be years before the business earns a profit and can use tax loss carryforwards.

Exhibit 4.1 sets forth the relative advantages and disadvantages of the various forms of business organization.

FROM THE TRENCHES

Adobe Systems, Inc., the leading desktop publishing software company, was founded as a partnership in 1982. It was initially organized as a partnership so that its investors, Hambrecht & Quist Investors, and its founders, John Warnock and Charles Geschke, could deduct the losses against their individual taxes. It operated as a partnership until December 1983, when its partners traded their interests for stock in the newly formed corporation. Adobe went public in 1986.

EXHIBIT 4.1

CHOICE OF BUSINESS ENTITY: PROS AND CONS

The following chart lists the principal considerations in selecting the form of business entity and applies them to the sole proprietorship, C corporation, S corporation, general partnership, limited partnership, and limited liability company. The considerations are listed in no particular order, in part because their importance will vary depending on the nature of the business, sources of financing, and the plan for providing financial returns to the owners (e.g., distributions of operating income, a public offering, or a sale of the business). Other factors that are not listed will also influence the choice of entity. In addition, the "yes or no" format oversimplifies the applicability of certain attributes.

	Sole Proprietorship	C Corp	S Corp	General Partnership	Limited Partnership	Limited Liability Company
Limited liability	No	Yes	Yes	No	Yes[a]	Yes[a]
Flow-through taxation	Yes	No	Yes	Yes	Yes	Yes
Simplicity/low cost	Yes	Yes	Yes	No	No	No
Limitations on eligibility	Yes	No	Yes	No	No	No
Limitations on capital structure	Yes	No	Yes	No	No	No
Ability to take public	No	Yes	Yes[b]	No[c]	No[c]	No[c]
Flexible charter documents	Yes	No	No	Yes	Yes	Yes
Ability to change structure without tax	Yes	No	No	Yes	Yes	Yes

continued...

EXHIBIT 4.1 (CONTINUED)

CHOICE OF BUSINESS ENTITY: PROS AND CONS

	Sole Proprietorship	C Corp	S Corp	General Partnership	Limited Partnership	Limited Liability Company
Favorable employee incentives (including incentive stock options)	No	Yes	Yes/No[d]	No[e]	No[e]	No[e]
Qualified small business stock exclusion for gains	No	Yes[f]	No	No	No	No
Special allocations	No	No	No	Yes	Yes	Yes
Tax-free in-kind distributions	Yes	No	No	Yes	Yes	Yes

a. Limited liability for limited partners only; a limited partnership must have at least one general partner with unlimited liability.
b. An S corporation would convert to a C corporation upon a public offering because of the restrictions on the permissible number of S corporation shareholders.
c. Although the public markets are generally not available for partnership or LLC offerings, a partnership or LLC can be incorporated without tax and then taken public.
d. Although an S corporation can issue ISOs, the inability to have two classes of stock limits favorable pricing of the common stock offered to employees.
e. Although partnership and LLC interests can be provided to employees, they are poorly understood by most employees. Moreover, ISOs are not available.
f. Special low capital gains rate for stock of U.S. C corporations with not more than $50 million in gross assets at the time stock is issued if the corporation is engaged in an active business and the taxpayer holds his or her stock for at least five years.

Conducting Business in Other States, Local Licenses, and Insurance

Before commencing operations in other states, the business should determine whether such operations will require it to register as a foreign corporation, partnership, or LLC in those states. Some states have significant penalties for failure to register properly. Even if it need not register as a foreign business entity, the company may be required to pay income and other taxes (including sales and use taxes) in the states where it operates. If the business has employees in other states, it may be subject to withholding from employees' wages, workers' compensation insurance, and other regulatory requirements in those states. If the business owns real or personal property in other states, it may be required to pay property taxes in those states.

State licensing is required for a wide variety of businesses and professions. Cities, counties, and other municipal agencies require local licenses. Because licensing requirements vary greatly among cities and counties, a business may wish to consider local licensing requirements and taxes before choosing a location for doing business.

As discussed further in Chapter 11, new businesses should obtain insurance coverage for all anticipated contingencies, not only to protect the individual participants from personal liability but also to protect the assets and future retained earnings of the business. The coverage may include general liability insurance (including product liability), errors and omissions insurance for directors and officers, fire and casualty insurance, business interruption insurance, key-personnel life and disability insurance, insurance to fund share purchases in the event of the death or disability of a shareholder, and workers' compensation insurance.

Choosing and Protecting a Name for a Business

Proposed names for new corporations, LLCs, and limited partnerships should be precleared through the name-availability section of the secretary of state's office before filing documents. Unless the name is precleared or reserved, the business's filing documents may be rejected by the secretary of state because of a name conflict.

Most secretaries of state maintain a consolidated list of the following: (1) the names of all corporations, LLCs, and limited partnerships organized under the laws of that state in good standing; (2) the names of all foreign corporations, LLCs, and limited partnerships qualified to transact intrastate business in the state and in good standing; and (3) the names reserved for future issuance. Charter documents will not be accepted for filing if the stated name is the same as, resembles closely, or is confusingly similar to any name on the consolidated list.

An organization should also determine whether its preferred name is available for use in other states where it will be conducting business. State laws generally provide for the use of an assumed name in a foreign state when an organization's true name is not available in that state. If a corporate, limited partnership, or LLC name is not available because that name or a similar one is in use, it may still be possible to use that name by obtaining the consent of the entity using the name.

It is important to understand the difference between the actions of a secretary of state in allowing the use of a name and the issues involved in the use of a name or trademark for purposes of identifying a good or service. Approval of a name by the secretary of state merely means that the entity has complied with the state law prohibiting a business from using a name that closely resembles the name of another business organized or qualified to do business in that state. Therefore, the fact that the secretary of state does not object to the use of a particular name as the name of a business does not necessarily mean that other people or entities are not already using the proposed name in connection with similar goods or services. If they are, the law of trademarks (discussed in Chapter 14) will prohibit the new company from using the name. A promising start-up business may find its business plan abruptly derailed when it receives a demand to change its name or faces an injunction and penalties for trademark infringement. To prevent this, the entrepreneur should conduct a search of the existing names in the proposed area of activity to determine, prior to its adoption, how protectable a particular name or trademark will be and whether it will infringe the rights of others.

Because many companies will want to use their corporate name as their domain name on the Internet and World Wide Web (such as Ford.com), entrepreneurs should check with the applicable domain name registry to see what domain names are available before selecting a corporate name. Domain names are granted on a first-come, first-served basis and, as with trademarks, approval of a name by the secretary of state has no bearing on whether a particular domain name is available.

PUTTING IT INTO PRACTICE

Michael Cruz outlined the forms of business organization available and their pros and cons. He told Kendra and Philip and Kristine Colgate that they had probably already formed a general partnership by signing the brief handwritten agreement and carrying on joint business activities. No special form of agreement or governmental filing is required to establish a general partnership. They did, however, need to quickly reorganize their business as an LLC or a corporation to protect themselves from the liabilities of the business because in a general partnership each partner has unlimited liability for the obligations of the business and the obligations incurred by the other partners in conducting the partnership business. In addition, reorganizing as an LLC or a corporation would formalize their ownership interests by specifying how they would share profits, losses, and distributions and what their respective roles, powers, and obligations would be in the business. (These topics are discussed in more detail in Chapter 5.)

The choice between an LLC and a corporation depended primarily on the expected source of the anticipated $2 million start-up funding required. If the financing is to come from venture capital funds, the business should be organized as a C corporation because most venture capital funds cannot invest in businesses that are taxed as flow-through entities such as partnerships and LLCs. If the financing is to come from other sources, such as corporate investors, wealthy individuals, debt, or some combination of these, an LLC would be attractive from a number of perspectives.

An LLC offers the same liability protection as a corporation. An LLC would likely be organized with Kendra and the Colgates as the managers and with the investors as passive members (the voting and other participation rights of the investors would, of course, be the subject of negotiation). As an LLC is a flow-through entity for tax purposes, the LLC operating agreement would allocate start-up losses to the LLC members who provided the financing. A corporate investor would generally be able to deduct start-up losses allocated to it against its other income, but because of the limitations on losses from passive activities, individual investors would generally have to carry their shares of start-up losses forward to use against future income from the

continued...

continued...

LLC. Individuals who had qualifying passive income from other investments could use such losses sooner, however.

An LLC would be the appropriate entity if Kendra and the Colgates expected to license the Saturn Data Booster (SDB) technology to another business solely for royalties and would not create specialized applets for sale. In a royalty-only situation, earnings would be distributed to the owners, rather than retained to grow the business with the view toward selling it or taking it public.

Because an LLC is not a separate taxpayer, the royalty income would be taxed only once (although at ordinary income rates). In a C corporation, the royalties would be taxed first at the corporate level, and the shareholders would be taxed again (at ordinary income rates) on all dividends they received.

Because Kendra and the Colgates intend to grow the business with a view toward taking it public, they plan to reinvest their earnings in the company and thereby shelter substantial amounts of the business's income. Upon sale of the business or an initial public offering of its stock, the gains of Kendra and the Colgates would be taxed at the long-term capital gains rate, which is lower than the ordinary income rate.

An LLC might have an additional attraction to Kendra. Because she is the one contributing the SDB technology to the business for all or part of her equity, she might want to keep a "string" on it so that the SDB technology would revert to her if the participants elected to dissolve the business. Using an LLC would permit the business to be dissolved and its assets divided among the owners without any tax (either to the entity or to the members). In contrast, if the business were a corporation, Kendra and the Colgates would be taxed twice if they parted ways and dissolved the business. Michael pointed out, however, that institutional investors such as venture capital funds would be highly unlikely to permit Kendra to retain any reversionary interest in the SDB technology. With internal financing, such an arrangement would not be unusual.

The founders planned to seek venture capital financing within twelve months.That financing would not be available if they organized as a partnership or LLC. Organizing as an S corporation was not an option because DataAccelleation would have a corporate shareholder, CSS. In addition, Kendra and the Colgates wanted to issue founders' shares at a fraction of the price to be paid by investors and to be able to issue easily understood and tax-favored employee stock options.

continued...

continued...

Kendra and the Colgates decided to organize their business as a C corporation. After checking name availability with the secretaries of state in the states where the company expected to do business, doing a trademark search, and acquiring the DataAccelleation.com domain name, they selected the name DataAccelleation, Inc.

Having decided to use a C corporation, the founders now turned to understanding the issues involved in incorporating the business and in dividing up the equity.

Chapter 5

Structuring the Ownership

After selecting the form of organization best suited to the new business, the entrepreneur's next important step is structuring the initial ownership and the relationship among the founders. If done correctly, the resulting structure will protect the rights of each founder, provide incentives for hard work, and divide the rewards fairly. In addition to formalizing the relationship among the existing founders, the process should be forward-looking and include other considerations, such as whether additional founders or new employees will be added in the near future and whether the company will seek venture capital financing. The structure ultimately put in place should anticipate these events and provide the flexibility to deal with them.

The process of structuring the initial, formal relationship is often the first time the founders are forced to sit down and discuss the details of their deal. In the early stages, when the founders often have little more than an idea, their relationship tends to be vague and informal. If the topic is not discussed formally, each participant probably expects to be treated equally and to receive a pro rata share of the equity and control. Even when the relationship is discussed, the result may be nothing more than an oral agreement to "divide any profits fairly." The problem, of course, is that fairness is in the eye of the beholder.

When the time comes to formalize the relationship, hard questions must be addressed to minimize future disputes. These questions include:

- Who will own what percentage of the business?
- Who will be in the position of control?

- What property and how much cash will be contributed to the business?
- How much time will the participants be required to devote to the business?
- What incentives will there be to remain with the company?
- What happens if a founder quits?
- What protections will a founder have against being forced to leave the company?
- Is there a *wayward* or *forgotten founder,* someone who was involved with starting the venture and may have put work into the project, but is no longer actively involved?

In some ways, the mechanics of implementing these decisions may appear trivial to entrepreneurs who simply want to get on with the important tasks of developing and marketing a product or service. Nevertheless, thoughtful consideration at this stage will minimize serious problems in the future, problems that can threaten the very survival of the business. An added benefit of carefully planning the initial structure can come when venture financing is sought. A well-planned structure can anticipate the concerns of the venture capitalist, make for smoother venture financings, and provide evidence that the founders "have their act together" and can work through difficult issues as a team.

This chapter describes the basic documents that need to be prepared and the decisions that must be made to get the new business launched, including where to incorporate, how to allocate the equity among the founders, which vesting arrangements to impose, and what restrictions to impose on stock transfers.

INCORPORATION

Most entrepreneurs view the formal paperwork of starting a new business as a necessary evil best left to lawyers. After all, the entrepreneur has more important things to do than review documents. Although much of the incorporation paperwork may be boilerplate, entrepreneurs should recognize that careful attention to initial structuring details can help avoid future misunderstandings. On a very basic level, founders should understand the critical terms of the business's charter documents (the certificate of incorporation and bylaws, discussed below). Although a thorough understanding of all of the details probably is not necessary, a general understanding of the controlling documents is important.

The formal documents required to form a new company will, of course, depend on the type of entity that will be used. Chapter 4 described the various forms of entities available and the pros and cons of each. This section provides a brief description of the documents necessary to legally establish a corporation and set the ground rules by which the owners will deal with each other. It assumes that the founders have decided to form a corporation, rather than a partnership, a limited liability company, or some other entity. Even if a noncorporate entity is used, however, most of the issues discussed must still be addressed.

Where to Incorporate

As a preliminary matter, the state of formation must be chosen. Generally, it is best to form the entity either in the state where its principal business will be located or in another state with a well-developed body of corporate law, such as Delaware.

Delaware is chosen by many larger companies that are not based in that state because of its favorable and well-developed corporate law, which can, in certain instances, increase the power of management and give the majority shareholders more flexibility in dealing with the minority. Delaware allows a corporation to have only one director whereas California, for example, requires at least three directors unless there are fewer than three shareholders. Delaware can also be advantageous from an administrative perspective. Delaware was among the first states to permit electronic proxy voting and to authorize shareholder meetings in cyberspace via the Internet. Amendments to the certificate of incorporation can be quickly filed in Delaware by facsimile. In contrast, California has a prefiling review process that can take several days or more to complete. In addition, Delaware has a specialized and very experienced court (the Court of Chancery) dedicated to the swift resolution of corporate law disputes. In the event of a hostile takeover or other time-critical development, an appeal from a Court of Chancery decision can be heard by the Delaware Supreme Court in a matter of days. Other areas where state laws differ include the type of consideration that can be used to purchase stock, the enforceability of voting agreements among shareholders, the ability of less than all of the shareholders to act by written consent, the ability to elect directors for multiple-year terms (and thereby *stagger* the election of directors), the availability of arrangements regarding indemnification of directors and officers, the ability to have certain kinds of *poison pills* (antitakeover defenses), and the ability of shareholders to demand appraisal rights upon certain events.

Incorporating in a state other than the state of the principal place of business usually results in somewhat higher taxes and other costs because of the need to comply with certain tax and regulatory requirements in both states. Finally, if a corporation operates in a state other than the one in which it is incorporated, it will still need to qualify as a foreign corporation and pay a filing fee in each state in which it does business. The founders should review their choice of state of incorporation with counsel.

The California corporations law has several restrictions worth noting. A California corporation may buy back shares or pay dividends only to the extent that it meets certain asset coverage or retained earnings tests. Companies that have negative retained earnings are prohibited from paying dividends, repurchasing shares, or making other distributions to shareholders. The penalties for violating this provision are stiff, and directors are personally liable for any violations of this law. Privately held California corporations must give shareholders the right to vote cumulatively, which may give minority shareholders the opportunity to elect one or more directors. Under cumulative voting, each shareholder can cast a total number of votes equal to the number of shares owned multiplied by the number of directors to be elected; the shareholder can allocate those votes to such nominees as he or she sees fit. (Cumulative voting is discussed more fully below.) All directors must be elected yearly so there can be no staggered (*classified*) board.

One of the most significant differences between California and Delaware law is the right of common shareholders in a California corporation to vote as a separate class in the event of a proposed merger of the corporation. A similar right does not exist in Delaware, where a merger must be approved by a majority of all classes of stock, voting together. Although it is customary for the preferred shareholders to negotiate a right to vote as a separate class on significant matters (such as a merger), the right of the common shareholders to approve a merger under California law can give meaningful leverage to the common shareholders.

A corporation is usually subject to the corporate governance laws of only the state where it was incorporated, even if it is not headquartered there. California is perhaps unique in applying its generally pro-shareholder corporate governance laws to corporations that are incorporated elsewhere but are closely linked with California (so-called *quasi foreign corporations*). In particular, a privately held corporation is subject to California corporate governance laws, regardless of where it incorporates, if more than 50 percent of its shares are owned by California residents and more than 50 percent of its business is conducted in California. For this reason, a corporation that will be owned primarily by California residents and will have most of its property, employees, and sales in California may decide to incorporate initially in California and then reincorporate in Delaware in the event of a public offering.

Certificate of Incorporation

The legal steps needed to form a corporation are surprisingly simple. Once the state of incorporation is chosen, most state statutes simply require that a very short *certificate of incorporation* (sometimes called *articles of incorporation*) be filed with the secretary of state in the state of incorporation, together with payment of a filing fee. Although laws differ from state to state, the certificate of incorporation normally sets forth the following.

First, the certificate must state the name of the corporation, which typically must include the word "Corporation," "Company," or "Incorporated" (or an abbreviation thereof) and usually cannot contain certain words such as "insurance" or "bank" unless the corporation satisfies certain other criteria. In some states, a person's name may not be used as the corporate name without adding a corporate ending, such as "Inc.," or some other word or words that show that the name is not that of the individual alone. The corporate name also must not be so similar to an existing name as to cause confusion and must not infringe anyone's trademarks. (The desirability of doing a name search is discussed in Chapter 4.)

Second, the business purpose of the corporation must be described. In most states, including California and Delaware, the purpose can be as broad as "engaging in any lawful activity for which corporations can be organized in this state."

Third, the certificate must state the authorized capital of the corporation, including the aggregate number of shares that can be issued, the par value of the shares (if any), and the classes of shares if the shares are divided into classes. If the company expects to seek venture financing, the founders can avoid the need to amend the certificate by providing for preferred stock in the certificate at the outset even though only common stock will be issued to the founders. Because the terms of any preferred stock issued in a venture financing will be negotiated, it is best, if the law of the state of incorporation allows, to authorize so-called blank-check preferred stock to facilitate the first round of preferred-stock financing. *Blank-check preferred stock* is authorized by providing in the certificate that classes of preferred stock are authorized and will have such rights, preferences, and privileges as the board of directors sets in board resolutions; no further action by the shareholders is required.

Fourth, the certificate must list the name and address of an agent resident in the state for purposes of service of legal process (such as delivery of a summons). Although it is tempting to use an individual who is otherwise involved with the company, this would require amending the company's certificate of incorporation promptly if the individual moves or is no longer in a position to accept service of process on behalf of the company. Otherwise, a court could enter default judgments against the corporation on behalf of plaintiffs who were unable to serve process on the company. As a result, it is advisable to use one of the many professional service corporations that perform this service for a small fee rather than naming an individual.

Fifth, the certificate should set forth provisions providing indemnification for directors, officers, employees, and other agents and limiting the monetary liability of directors with respect to certain breaches of the duty of care. *Indemnification* means that the company will reimburse the parties indemnified for certain damages and expenses (including attorneys' fees) resulting from their activities on behalf of the corporation.

Certain statutory provisions can be varied only if express language is included in the certificate of incorporation. For example, to impose *supermajority voting requirements* (which require more than a simple majority vote) for shareholder or director actions in California, a provision requiring a supermajority vote must be included in the corporation's articles of incorporation. In Delaware, cumulative voting of shares is permitted only if expressly provided for in the certificate of incorporation.

Some states give all shareholders preemptive rights unless the certificate of incorporation provides otherwise. *Preemptive rights* give each shareholder the right to participate in future rounds of financing and to buy whatever number of shares is needed to maintain the shareholder's percentage ownership interest. This can wreak havoc when the entrepreneur goes out to raise more money in future financings.

The certificate of incorporation may be signed by anyone. The person signing is called the *incorporator.*

Bylaws

Although the certificate of incorporation establishes the legal existence of the corporation, it provides little guidance for determining how the shareholders, officers, and directors deal with each other and with third parties. The operating rules of the company generally are set forth in a document called the *bylaws.* However, certain operating rules established by the applicable corporation statute cannot be varied or will apply by default if the bylaws do not provide otherwise. In most cases, the standard bylaws prepared by legal counsel working with the company will both comply with the applicable statute and sufficiently address most issues of concern to the start-up company. As corporation statutes impose very few restrictions on what the bylaws can contain, the founders should not hesitate to propose specific provisions needed to effectuate their business deal. The founders should carefully review the bylaws before they are adopted to confirm that they accurately reflect the founders' intent.

The founders should focus on a variety of subjects governed by the bylaws, including provisions relating to the number of directors, calling board meetings, directors' voting rights, the process for filling board vacancies and removing directors, the term for which directors are elected, and whether there will be different classes of directors. Most states permit the bylaws to specify a fixed number of directors or a range (e.g., not less than three and not more than five).

The board of directors normally controls all but the most crucial decisions for the company; these decisions, such as a sale of substantially all of the corporation's assets, are left to a vote of the shareholders. Thus, even if a founder owns a significant amount of stock, that ownership alone may not guarantee a real influence on many decisions. Instead, each founder should carefully consider whether he or she should sit on the board and, if so, how to guard against removal or replacement if there are disagreements. The minimum number of directors that must be present at a board meeting to legally transact business (known as a *quorum*) and provisions for supermajority votes should also be considered.

The founders should review the shareholder voting provisions to make sure that they understand how directors will be elected, which matters will require a vote of the shareholders, whether there will be separate class voting on certain matters, how a quorum will be determined, and what degree of shareholder approval will be needed for each action. If a founder believes that, by reason of his or her stock ownership, he or she is ensured a seat on the board or will be able to elect more than one director, special attention should be given to how the shareholder votes are counted in the election of directors.

If cumulative voting is either allowed or required, the ability of a relatively small shareholder to elect a director might be surprising. For example, under cumulative voting, if five board seats are being voted on, a shareholder owning as little as 17 percent of the stock will be able to elect a director. The percentage of stock ownership required to elect one director under cumulative voting can be calculated by taking the number 1 and dividing it by the sum of the number of directors being elected plus one. The formula to determine the percentage interest necessary to elect one director (x) is:

$$x = \frac{1}{\text{number of directors being elected} + 1}$$

Accordingly, if six directors are being elected, a shareholder holding 14.3 percent of the stock [1 ÷ (6 + 1)] could elect one director; a shareholder would need to hold at least 28.6 percent of the stock (14.3 percent × 2) to elect two directors. Given the importance of this issue, it is often best to have a separate voting agreement among the shareholders to ensure that the board's composition will be as expected.

While forming the company, the founders typically will have expectations as to who will fill various officer positions (although these appointments are technically made by the board of directors). The bylaws will specify the principal duties and responsibilities of the officers, and the founders should confirm that particular provisions accurately describe the functions that each officer will perform.

Bylaws often contain restrictions on the transferability of shares and may grant a right of first refusal to the company or its assignees to pur-

FROM THE TRENCHES

A disaffected founder of a California computer peripheral start-up company proposed to transfer a large block of stock to a third party. The company was unable to exercise its right of first refusal because it had negative retained earnings. Under California law, a repurchase would have been an illegal distribution, subjecting the company's directors to possible personal liability to creditors. The bylaw right of first refusal was assignable, however, so the company was able to transfer its repurchase right to a major shareholder, who exercised the right and purchased the founder's shares. Later, when the company could legally make the purchase, the major shareholder sold the stock back to the company at cost. The company then used the stock as an incentive for new employees.

chase shares at the time of a proposed transfer to a third party. Such provisions can be especially important in a new company when it is vital that stock be owned by those individuals and entities that are directly involved in the success of the business. This right should be assignable by the company in case the company itself is not able to exercise the right due to capital constraints or corporate law restrictions on the repurchase of shares.

Bylaws generally provide for the broadest indemnification of directors, officers, and agents allowed by the controlling state statute. The founders should consider whether such indemnification should be mandatory or permissive and whether it should extend to employees and agents of the company. They should also consider whether the company should be required to advance attorneys' fees if a director, officer, or agent is sued. The founders should also consider entering into an indemnification agreement with the company that reflects the indemnification provisions in the certificate of incorporation and bylaws and gives those entitled to indemnity a contractual right to an advance of attorneys' fees and the maximum indemnification permitted by applicable law.

Each founder should fully understand the mechanics of amending the bylaws. Including an important provision in the initial bylaws provides little comfort if the provision can easily be deleted or amended later.

Mechanics of Incorporation

In a document generally called the *action by incorporator,* which can be executed as soon as the certificate of incorporation has been filed with the secretary of state of the state of incorporation, the incorporator named in the certificate of incorporation adopts the bylaws, appoints the first directors, and then resigns. The board of directors then usually elects officers, authorizes the issuance of stock to the founders, establishes a bank account, and authorizes the payment of incorporation expenses. In addition, at the first meeting the board may adopt a standard form of proprietary information and inventions agreement for use by employees and consultants; a form of restricted stock purchase agreement, which typically imposes vesting and rights of first refusal on employee stock; and an employee stock purchase and/or stock option plan. The board may also select the fiscal year of the corporation and determine whether to elect to be taxed as an S corporation. The board generally takes these actions at a meeting called and noticed in accordance with the new bylaws. Written minutes of the meeting should be approved by the board at its next meeting. However, many states permit the board to take actions without a

FROM THE TRENCHES

In the early 1990s, four individuals—A, B, C, and D—decided to build a cogeneration power plant to take advantage of available tax subsidies. A and B hired a lawyer to prepare incorporation documents. The lawyer prepared the documents, which listed his secretary as the incorporator. She signed the articles of incorporation and filed them with the Illinois Secretary of State.

A and B then ended their involvement with the project. The two remaining individuals, C and D, then signed a document they called "Action by Incorporator," in which they purported to adopt bylaws and elect themselves as directors. In their capacity as directors, they issued themselves stock and elected officers. The corporation subsequently entered into a joint venture with a large Canadian electric company to build the plant.

The construction was financed with a permanent loan from a bank. When interest rates fell and retail power prices also declined, the company needed to renegotiate the loan to make the plant economically viable. The lender requested an opinion from counsel for the joint venture that the cogeneration plant was owned by the joint venture. After reviewing the corporation's organizational documents, counsel for the joint venture discovered that the person who had signed the articles of incorporation was different from the persons who had signed the action by incorporator appointing the directors. This error created doubt about the legal status of the corporation's directors and the officers they had appointed, and thus their ability to enter into the joint venture.

A and B, the original two parties who had dropped out of the project, learned of the mistake and claimed that they owned 50 percent of the corporation. The joint venture could not get the refinancing closed without resolving A and B's claim, and the joint venture ended up settling with them for a substantial sum.

Comment: Although having the wrong person sign the action by incorporator designating the directors is a seemingly simple mistake, it created a massive problem, generating very high legal bills. This costly mistake could have been avoided by following the correct legal formalities.

meeting if all directors sign a document approving the action, called an *action by unanimous written consent.*

A privately held corporation's organizational documents (i.e., the certificate of incorporation, bylaws, and organizational minutes) are largely boilerplate, and canned organizational documents are readily available for entrepreneurs who desire to incorporate without hiring a lawyer. Because this documentation is usually straightforward, however, experienced counsel can prepare it inexpensively. Experienced counsel's real value is less in preparing the basic documentation than in providing expert advice on choosing an appropriate capital structure, allocating ownership among the founders, transferring assets to the corporation in the most tax-efficient manner, adopting appropriate equity incentive programs, and generally avoiding pitfalls.

Splitting the Pie

Perhaps the most difficult decision in structuring the new business is how to divide the equity ownership, which will determine who participates in the financial success of the business and at what level. The participants often avoid this topic initially due to its sensitivity. Delay in working out these details can be disastrous, however. When the time comes to formally structure the ownership of the business, the founders must be forthright in their discussions.

The founders should take into account almost any contribution to the business that they believe should be recognized. Factors commonly considered include the following:

- What cash and property will be contributed at the outset?
- If property is contributed, what is its value, and how was it acquired or developed?
- What are the founders expected to contribute to the business in the future, whether in terms of cash, property, sweat equity (time and effort), technical or business expertise, or any other valuable addition?
- What opportunity costs will the founders incur by joining the business?

FROM THE TRENCHES

Two young entrepreneurs received $50,000 from a wealthy individual (an angel investor) to finance the test marketing of a new handheld device containing updatable financial information. It was the understanding of the parties that the cash would purchase equity in a new entity if the device proved promising but that the money would not have to be repaid if the venture did not proceed. The equity split was not discussed. The test marketing was successful, and the two entrepreneurs incorporated the company. They issued 45 percent of the company's stock to each of them and proposed issuing the angel investor the remaining 10 percent of the stock in exchange for his $50,000. They reasoned that because they conceived of the product concept and would be the driving force behind the company, 10 percent for the angel investor was fair.

However, the angel investor believed that advancing the initial risk capital for the enterprise entitled him to be an equal partner. He sued the founders and the company. The entrepreneurs offered to pay back the $50,000. The angel would not settle and insisted that he was entitled to one third of the equity of this now-promising enterprise. Protracted litigation ensued.

Comment: This situation could have been avoided if the parties had either incorporated and issued shares earlier or set forth their deal in writing at the time the $50,000 was advanced.

In the end, the objective should be to treat each founder as fairly as possible. It is not necessarily in the best interest of an individual to negotiate the best deal possible for himself or herself. Success of the company will depend on the hard work of each member of the team over a long period of time. If the business is to grow and be successful, each founder will need to be satisfied that the equity allocation was fair. If members feel slighted, they may be tempted to look for opportunities elsewhere or may not be as dedicated to the business as the other founders.

In addition to considering ownership among the initial founders, the founders need to determine how they will "split the pie" with future employees. If the management team is incomplete and one or more high-level participants will be recruited, the dilutive effect of issuing additional stock and the impact of its issuance on voting control should not be overlooked. For example, if the initial team consists solely of technical people, a chief executive officer (CEO), a financial officer (chief financial officer, controller, or vice president of finance), and a vice president of sales/marketing will be needed. Depending on the caliber of the people recruited, the company may have to issue 5 to 10 percent of the equity to the CEO and another 7 to 10 percent to other senior management. Similarly, venture capitalists who invest in the first round of financing could acquire up to 40 to 60 percent of the company and may require that 10 to 20 percent of the equity be reserved for employee stock options for key hires as well as rank and file employees. The dilutive effect of these potential events should be considered when allocating equity among the founders.

Finally, the expectations of persons who may have contributed to the enterprise during its preincorporation phase, but who are no longer part of the founders' group, must be considered. It can be very harmful to the company if a so-called wayward or forgotten founder suddenly appears at the time of a venture financing or, worse, at the time of the company's initial public offering and asserts an ownership right. The claim could be based on oral promises by the other founders or, more commonly, on early

FROM THE TRENCHES

While attending State University, engineering students A, B, C, and D conceived of an innovative design for a hospital management software system but did not actually write the code. There was some talk of starting a business after graduation, but there was no formal agreement. After graduation, D went to work in a distant city. After four months, A, B, and C formed a company to develop the system. They initially took the position that D was not entitled to share in the new enterprise because of the enormous amount of work that would be required to develop the code and to make it commercially viable. After consulting with a lawyer, however, they reached an agreement with D, whereby D was given 5 percent of the new company in exchange for any rights he might have in the technology. Without such an agreement, D might later have been able to claim a one-fourth interest in the company.

contributions to, and therefore partial ownership of, the company's underlying technology or other intellectual property. If such persons exist, it is best to settle their claims at the incorporation stage rather than having to deal with them at a time when the company has increased in value or when their claims could destroy a pending transaction.

Issuing Equity, Consideration, and Vesting

Once a decision has been made as to how the ownership of the new business will be divided, it is time to formally issue the stock.

Types of Stock

Stock initially issued to founders upon formation of a new company is almost always common stock, while stock issued to venture capital investors is usually preferred stock. There are two primary reasons for this structure.

First, the venture investors can reduce their risk by purchasing preferred stock that includes a liquidation preference over the common stock. A *liquidation preference* gives the preferred shareholders first claim on the company's assets in the event that the company is dissolved. Thus, if the business does not succeed but retains some valuable assets (e.g., patents or other intellectual property), the preferred shareholders may be able to recoup some or all of their investment.

Second, by issuing venture investors stock that has preferential rights over the common stock, the common stock can be valued at a discount to the price paid by these venture investors. As a result, even if the preferred stock is issued at a premium over what the founders paid for their common stock, the founders can still maintain that they paid fair market value and thereby avoid any tax in connection with their acquisition of the common stock.

The benefit of valuing common stock at a discount to the preferred stock continues as the company expands and begins to grant stock options. As additional employees are hired, it is often desirable to switch from issuing common stock for cash or promissory notes to granting stock options. For either tax or securities law reasons, the exercise price of these stock options usually must be at or near fair market value at the time they are granted. Once again, by issuing preferred stock in venture financing rounds, the company can keep the common stock's value relatively low, resulting in a lower option exercise price for employees.

Consideration for Stock

The applicable state statute under which the corporation was formed will contain certain restrictions on the type of consideration that can be used to pay for stock. Cash is always acceptable, as are most types of property. Past services may be acceptable. Under both Delaware and California law, future services are not valid consideration, and promissory notes are acceptable only in certain cases. Given these restrictions, care must be taken to ensure that each founder provides adequate consideration to purchase his or her allocable portion of the company's stock.

CONTRIBUTIONS OF PROPERTY If property is to be contributed to the company, the founders should understand the tax considerations. An exchange of property for stock in a newly formed corporation will be tax-free if it qualifies under Section 351 of the Internal Revenue Code, which imposes two requirements. First, the property must be transferred solely in exchange for stock (or securities) of the company. If the transferor receives any cash or other non-stock consideration (*boot*) in exchange for the property, then the exchange may still qualify under Section 351, but the transferor will be required to pay capital gains taxes on the lesser of the value of the boot and the gain (that is, the fair market value of all stock and non-stock consideration received, minus the transferor's tax basis for the property given up in the exchange). Second, immediately after the transfer, the transferor(s), including those contributing cash but not those contributing only services, must own (1) stock possessing at least 80 percent of the combined voting power of all classes of stock entitled to vote and (2) at least 80 percent of the total number of shares of each nonvoting class.

When there is more than one transferor, the contributions of property do not have to be simultaneous. When the contributions are not simultaneous, however, the rights of the parties must have been previously defined, and the execution of the documents necessary to effect the transfer must proceed at a speed consistent with orderly procedure. As a result of these rules, if property is contributed by a founder who alone will not meet the 80 percent tests, then sufficient other contributions should be made at or around the same time by others so that the contributing group satisfies the 80 percent tests.

Additionally, the founders should confirm that the person contributing property has the right to do so and that the transfer is complete and binding. If technology or other intellectual property is being contributed and will be improved upon, the founders should be absolutely certain that the company has obtained adequate ownership of the property so that the company can both use the property in its development efforts and retain and exploit any advances or improvements that it makes.

Sometimes founders who are contributing intellectual property are reluctant to make the transfer until funding has been assured, or they may wish to license the technology or other intellectual property to the company with a right to terminate the license if funding does not occur or the company fails. Once property has been contributed to the corporation, all shareholders have a pro rata interest in that property. If the corporation is later dissolved, the corporate property will be distributed among the shareholders in accord with their stock ownership interests. At the same time, venture capitalists generally expect the founders to transfer all of their rights to the technology or other intellectual property, not just a

FROM THE TRENCHES

A young entrepreneur made an informal deal with a retired engineer to exploit proprietary technology owned by the engineer. The entrepreneur formed a company and spent more than $100,000 to develop and market a product. When the entrepreneur went back to the engineer to negotiate a formal transfer of the technology to the company, the engineer not only refused to complete the transfer but threatened to sue the company and the entrepreneur for misappropriation of the intellectual property. As a result, the company was never launched, and the entrepreneur lost $100,000.

license. The founders should work closely with counsel to establish the optimum timing for their transfers.

Tax Treatment of Founders' Stock and Employee Stock Options

CHOOSING BETWEEN STOCK AND OPTIONS At the formation stage of the business and for some time thereafter, it is usually best to issue stock outright rather than to use stock options. Stock can be issued for little cost and thereby provide the founders certain benefits of direct stock ownership and avoid some of the drawbacks of stock options. As the company matures and the value of the stock increases, stock options are used extensively to allow employees and others the opportunity to participate in the growth of the business without putting up cash or otherwise having their capital at risk.

TAX TREATMENT OF STOCK If stock is issued to an individual providing services to the company, the recipient must either pay the fair value of the stock or recognize ordinary taxable income to the extent that the value of the stock exceeds the amount paid. If the stock has more than a nominal value, the purchase price or the amount recognized as income can be quite high. Consequently, companies whose stock has more than a nominal value normally elect to use options as a way to allow employees to participate in the growth of the business.

For a newly formed company, the value of the underlying stock normally is not an issue. Upon formation, the company's assets usually consist of a limited amount of cash and property. The prospects of the new business are still in doubt. As a result, the value of the company's stock often is low enough that early participants can afford either to pay for the stock or to recognize taxable income on receipt of the stock.

The value of the stock will continue to be low until some event indicates that it should be higher. Although the valuation event may be as undefined as advances in product development, increased sales, and the like, it can be more concrete, such as a round of venture capital financing in which third parties put a higher value on the business. To take full advantage of this ability to issue *cheap stock* or *founders' stock,* entrepreneurs should attempt to incorporate the business and issue the initial equity as early as possible. The greater the time that separates the founders' stock acquisition from a subsequent event that establishes a higher value, the lower the risk that the founders will be treated as purchasing their stock at a discount with resulting taxable income.

Until the value of the stock is high enough to cause the purchase price or tax consequences to be prohibitive, direct stock ownership offers a number of advantages over stock options. When stock is received, whether for cash or in exchange for property or services, the stock becomes a capital asset in the hands of the recipient (assuming that the stock is vested or a Section 83(b) election is made, as described below). As a result, any subsequent increase in the value of the stock will be treated as a capital gain when the stock is sold. If the stock is held for more than one year, the gain will be a long-term capital gain, which is taxed at a lower rate than ordinary income.

Additionally, stock in a start-up company can often be classified as *qualified small business stock* under Internal Revenue Code Section 1202. Subject to certain limitations, one-half of the gain from the sale of qualified small business stock that has been held for at least five years is excluded from taxation. By owning stock rather than receiving a stock option, a founder can start the holding period both for this exclusion and for purposes of various securities laws, thereby making it easier to sell the stock later.

TAX TREATMENT OF INCENTIVE AND NONSTATUTORY STOCK OPTIONS The receipt of an option by a service provider normally is not a taxable event, and the option itself is not a capital asset. Generally, to realize the value of the option, the holder must first exercise the option and then sell the underlying stock. The tax consequences of exercising an option and selling the underlying stock depend on whether the option is an incentive stock option or a nonstatutory stock option.

To qualify as an *incentive stock option* (*ISO*), the option must be granted to an employee (not a nonemployee director or consultant, who can receive only nonstatutory options), and the exercise price must be at least 100 percent of the fair market value of the underlying stock at the date of grant (110 percent if the grantee is a greater-than-10 percent owner of the company). Any options that do not meet these requirements are called *nonstatutory* or *nonqualified stock options* (NSOs). An incentive stock option generally receives more favorable tax treatment than a nonstatutory stock option.

Upon exercise of a nonstatutory stock option, the optionee normally recognizes ordinary taxable income, which, if the optionee is an employee, is subject to income and employment tax withholding. The optionee must pay tax on the difference between the fair market value of the stock purchased on the date the option is exercised and the amount paid to exercise the option (the *spread*). Any additional gain on the sale of the stock, or any loss, is a capital gain or loss that is long term or short term depending on whether the stock was held for more than one year from the date of exercise. As a result, appreciation in the value of the stock from the option's grant date through the exercise date is taxed as ordinary income. This results in a lower after-tax return than would be achieved if stock had been issued directly at the outset.

Incentive stock options allow the optionee to avoid ordinary income recognition at the time the option is exercised (although if the spread is substantial, alternative minimum tax may be due). Income is not recognized, and thus generally no tax is due, until the underlying shares are sold (although, beginning in 2003, Social Security and other employment tax withholding will be required at the time of exercise). The optionee then pays income tax on the difference between the fair market value of the underlying shares on the date they are sold and the exercise price (the *gain*). To achieve capital gains treatment on the spread existing at the time an ISO is exercised, the optionee must have held the stock for more than one year from the date of exercise and more than two years from the date the option was granted. Otherwise, the spread on exercise will be taxed as ordinary income at the time of sale.

Vesting

When individuals form a new business based on their own ideas, assets, and labor, many founders at first believe that the stock they acquire should be theirs no matter what happens in the future. After all, the business would not exist but for their initial efforts, so why should their ownership be subject to forfeiture? On the other hand, most founders would also agree that a cofounder who leaves the business shortly after it begins should not continue to own a large part, or perhaps any part, of a business that will require substantial future efforts to grow and be successful. Consequently, a mechanism is needed that recognizes that forming the business is only the beginning of the enterprise and that to earn the right to participate in the future rewards the recipients of stock, including the founders, should have to continue working for some period of time.

If the founders expect to seek venture capital financing in the future, they should also recognize that the venture investors will have similar concerns. Venture capitalists invest in people as much as in ideas and technologies. The typical venture capitalist will spend as much time evaluating the team as the product and, before investing, will want to make sure that incentives are in place to keep the team intact. If the founders do not impose restrictions on the stock owned by themselves or other important team members, they can be sure that the venture capitalist will raise this issue before investing. Except in the most unusual situations, a vesting requirement must be imposed before venture capitalists will invest.

It can be a good strategy for founders to self-impose a reasonable vesting schedule up front as a preemptive measure before negotiating with venture capitalists and as a way to prevent any one founder from slow-

FROM THE TRENCHES

Three founders formed a new company to develop adapter cards for connecting high-performance workstations and personal computers over local area networks. Their initial contributions carried the business for eighteen months. When venture financing was sought, the potential investors insisted that stock owned by the founders be subject to vesting over a four-year period. One founder refused, arguing that he had already devoted two years to the business, counting time before the company was formed, and that that should be enough for full vesting. After long negotiations, it was agreed that four-year vesting would be imposed but that one year's credit would be given for past services.

ing down the financing. In addition, there are tax advantages to the founders if they impose vesting at the time the stock is initially issued rather than waiting until later. Often venture capitalists will agree that some portion of the founder's stock (for example, 25 to 33 percent) should be fully vested at the time of the financing, with the balance subject to monthly vesting.

Consequently, although there are exceptions, stock issued in a start-up company is usually subject to some type of vesting. In its most common form, vesting occurs if the individual holding the stock continues to be employed by or otherwise performs services for the company over a specified period. In these cases, vesting usually occurs gradually. A common vesting schedule is for the stock to be completely unvested at the time of issuance, with one-fourth of the stock vesting after one year (so-called *cliff vesting*) and the remaining stock vesting monthly over the next thirty-six months.

If an employee leaves before becoming fully vested, the company will have the right to repurchase the unvested stock at the lower of the stock's market value or the cost of the stock to the employee. The purchase price may be paid in cash, or in some cases, the company may be allowed to repurchase the stock with a promissory note. The use of the promissory note alternative is especially important if the purchase price is high and the company is cash poor. Often, if the company itself is unable to purchase the stock due to a cash shortage or legal restrictions, the company will be allowed or required to assign its repurchase right to the shareholders.

Tax Treatment of Unvested Stock and Section 83(b) Elections

As stated earlier, an individual who receives stock in connection with the performance of services is normally taxed at ordinary income tax rates to the extent that the value of the stock when received exceeds the amount paid for the stock. If the stock is subject to a substantial risk of forfeiture, however, the taxable event (including the measurement of taxable income) is normally delayed until the risk of forfeiture lapses. This is true even if the recipient pays full value at the time the stock is received. In general, a *substantial risk of forfeiture* exists if the recipient's right to full enjoyment of the stock is conditioned upon the future performance of substantial services. Therefore, if stock issued to founders or others is subject to repurchase by the company at less than fair market value upon the termination of employment (i.e., the stock is subject to vesting), the stock will be treated as subject to a substantial risk of forfeiture.

Under these rules, if a founder is issued stock that will vest over a period of time, he or she will recognize taxable income on each vesting date equal to the difference (if any) between the fair market value of the stock on the date it becomes vested and the purchase price paid. For example, assume that the founder pays $25,000 for 500,000 shares of common stock ($0.05 per share) and that one-fourth of this stock will vest after one year with the balance vesting on a monthly basis for the next three years. Assume that $0.05 per share was the value of the stock on the date the stock was issued, and that at the end of the first year the value of the stock has increased to $1.00 per share. Unless the founder has filed a timely Section 83(b) election (discussed below), he or she will recognize ordinary taxable income at the end of year one in an amount equal to $118,750 (the value of one-fourth of the stock [$125,000] minus one-fourth of the exercise price [$6,250]). This income will be recognized and tax will be due even though the stock is still held by the founder and is usually totally illiquid. Similarly, on each monthly vesting date occurring thereafter, the founder will recognize additional ordinary taxable income measured by the then current value of the shares that become vested minus the amount paid for those shares. This income will be treated as if it were wages paid by the company in cash, and (assuming that the founder is an employee) it will be subject to income and employment tax withholding from the employee's cash salary.

As an alternative to recognizing taxable income upon each vesting date, the founder should always consider filing an election under Section 83(b) of the Internal Revenue Code. An 83(b) election must be filed with the Internal Revenue Service within thirty days of the initial purchase of the shares. If an employee exercises an option to acquire unvested stock, then the election must be filed within thirty days of exercising the option.

By filing a timely *Section 83(b) election,* the founder is electing to pay tax at the time the stock is purchased in an amount equal to what would be due if the stock were not subject to vesting. If the founder pays full market value at the time of the purchase, no tax will be due because the value of the stock on that date will not exceed the purchase price. Once this election is made, subsequent vesting of the stock will not be taxable.

FROM THE TRENCHES

A number of employees of a software company received stock subject to vesting. By making a Section 83(b) election, they were able to value the shares at the time purchased at a fraction of the value established when the company went public eighteen months later. Those who did not make a Section 83(b) election had their shares valued at the public trading price on the date the shares became vested. Because they had paid a fraction of that price for the shares, these employees realized very substantial amounts of ordinary income as the shares became vested. This tax expense could have been avoided with careful tax planning.

The founder will be required to pay tax only when the stock is ultimately sold, and any gain recognized on the sale will be a capital gain. Thus, the filing of a Section 83(b) election both allows a deferral of tax beyond the vesting dates and enables all appreciation in the stock's value to qualify for capital gains tax treatment.

Filing the election is not always advantageous, however. If the stock subject to vesting is sold at a discount from its fair market value at the time of sale, then an employee electing to file a Section 83(b) election will recognize as ordinary income in the year in which the stock is issued the spread between the fair market value at the time of issuance and the price paid. For example, assume that an employee pays $10,000 for 200,000 shares of common stock ($0.05 per share) and that one-fourth of this stock will vest after one year with the balance vesting on a monthly basis over the next thirty-six months. Assume that the value of the stock on the date the stock was issued was $0.20 per share, and that at the end of the first year the value of the stock has increased to $1.00 per share. If the employee makes an 83(b) election, then the employee will recognize ordinary income in year one equal to the $30,000 differential between the fair market value of the stock when issued ($40,000) and the price paid ($10,000) and will be required to pay income tax on that amount. If the employee is terminated before the end of the first year, thereby forfeiting all of his or her stock, then the employee will have paid tax at ordinary income rates on a paper gain of $30,000 that evaporated when all of the shares were forfeited. Furthermore, this loss cannot be recognized for tax purposes.

Consequently, the employee will be out of pocket the taxes paid by reason of the Section 83(b) election. In contrast, if the unvested stock's fair market value when issued is the same as the purchase price, then there usually is no real cost to filing the election. As a result, it is almost always advantageous to file an election when the differential is zero or very small; the decision becomes more difficult only when the differential is substantial.

Summary of Tax Consequences of Various Forms of Equity Compensation

Exhibit 5.1 summarizes the federal tax consequences of various forms of executive compensation under the Internal Revenue Code in effect as of January 1, 2002. State taxation may differ. When choosing a tax-favored business strategy, managers should take into account the non-tax features and consequences of various tax-planning alternatives. In addition, the tax

EXHIBIT 5.1

TAX TREATMENT OF RESTRICTED STOCK AWARDS, NONQUALIFIED STOCK OPTIONS, AND INCENTIVE STOCK OPTIONS[a]

EVENT	EMPLOYEE TAX CONSEQUENCES	EMPLOYER TAX CONSEQUENCES
Issuance of Stock Subject to Vesting (Restricted Stock)	None until shares vest unless file an 83(b) election. If file 83(b) election, ordinary income equal to fair market value of shares at time of issuance minus price paid by employee (the *spread*).	None, unless an 83(b) election was made, in which case compensation deduction equal to spread.
Restricted Stock Vests	Ordinary income equal to fair market value of the shares on date shares vest minus price paid by employee, unless an 83(b) election was made, in which case no tax is due upon vesting.	Compensation deduction equal to spread, unless an 83 (b) election was made.

continued...

EXHIBIT 5.1 (CONTINUED)

TAX TREATMENT OF RESTRICTED STOCK AWARDS, NONQUALIFIED STOCK OPTIONS, AND INCENTIVE STOCK OPTIONS[a]

Event	Employee Tax Consequences	Employer Tax Consequences
Property (including Under Certain Circumstances Intellectual Property) Is Contributed to Newly Formed Corporation in Exchange for Stock	Under Section 351, as long as the investors (1) contribute property, not services; (2) receive stock in the corporation; and (3) collectively control 80% or more of the corporation after the transaction, the investors pay no tax on the *gain* (i.e., the fair market value of the stock and other property received minus the cost basis of the property contributed), unless they receive cash or other non-stock property (*boot*). Investors receiving boot are taxed on the lesser of their realized gain and the amount of boot.	None.
Founder Contributes Services in Exchange for Stock Issued Upon Incorporation	Ordinary income equal to the fair market value of the stock received.	Compensation deduction equal to fair market value of stock.
Grant of Nonqualified Stock Options (NQOs)	None.	None.
Grant of Incentive Stock Option (ISO)	None.	None.
Exercise of NQO	Ordinary income equal to fair market value of stock on date of exercise minus option exercise price (the *spread*).	Compensation deduction equal to the spread.

continued...

EXHIBIT 5.1 (CONTINUED)

TAX TREATMENT OF RESTRICTED STOCK AWARDS, NONQUALIFIED STOCK OPTIONS, AND INCENTIVE STOCK OPTIONS[a]

Event	Employee Tax Consequences	Employer Tax Consequences
Exercise of ISO	None, except that the spread will be included as a preference item in calculating the individual's alternative minimum tax (AMT), which could trigger AMT for the year in which ISO is exercised. The employee will receive a tax credit for any AMT paid that can be applied against taxes due in future years. Effective 2003, Social Security and other employment tax withholding will be required at the time of exercise.	None.
Sale of Stock Acquired Upon Exercise of NQO	Capital gains equal to sale price minus fair market value on date of exercise.	None.
Sale of Stock Acquired Upon Exercise of ISO	Capital gains equal to sale price minus exercise price provided that the stock is not disposed of within two years of the grant date or within 12 months after exercise (a *disqualifying disposition*). In the event of a disqualifying disposition, the gain (i.e., the sale price minus the exercise price) is taxed as follows: any gain up to the amount of the spread on date of exercise will be ordinary income and the balance of the gain will be capital gains.	None, unless a disqualifying disposition. If disqualifying disposition, compensation deduction equal to ordinary in come recognized by the employee.

a. Many thanks to Professor Henry B. Reiling of the Harvard Business School for his contributions to this exhibit.

preferences of all parties to the transaction should be taken into account. In the context of executive compensation, this means the tax consequences for both the employer and the employee.

Agreements Relating to the Transfer of Shares

Unvested stock normally is not transferable due to restrictions contained in the purchase agreement for the stock. In addition, it is quite common for other restrictions on transfer to continue even after the stock has become vested. The primary reasons for these restrictions are to keep the ownership of the company with those individuals and entities that are directly involved in the success of the business, to provide liquidity to shareholders in certain situations, to allow other shareholders to participate in transfers of a controlling interest in the company, and to maintain the balance of power among the shareholders. Although a separate document might be prepared for each of these restrictions and provisions, they also can be reflected in a single agreement among shareholders. Common agreements include a right of first refusal, buy-sell agreements, and co-sale agreements.

Right of First Refusal

The most common form of transfer restriction imposed on shareholders of a newly formed company is a right of first refusal. Under a *right of first refusal,* if a shareholder wishes to transfer his or her stock in the company, either the company, its assignees, or the other shareholders (depending on the agreement) must first be given the opportunity to buy the stock pursuant to the terms being offered by the third-party purchaser. Typically, the party or parties with the right have thirty to sixty days to purchase the stock after receiving notice of the pending sale. If they fail to purchase the stock, the selling shareholder is free to sell to the identified third party on the terms presented to the company and the other shareholders within a designated period of time. If the sale to the third party is not consummated within the designated period of time, any subsequent sale may again be made only after application of the right of first refusal. This type of restriction is so common that in many cases it is contained within the bylaws of the company. Sometimes a more elaborate right of first refusal is contained in a separate agreement among shareholders.

The primary benefit of a right of first refusal is that it allows the company and other shareholders to prevent transfers to outsiders who might be uninterested in, or disruptive to, the business. On its face, a right of first refusal appears to allow an existing shareholder to sell his or her stock at its fair value. As a practical matter, however, the effect of a right of first refusal is to severely limit the transferability of stock. A potential third-party buyer will often be disinclined to negotiate a potential purchase because he or she knows that the negotiated terms will then have to be offered first to the company and/or the other shareholders. Even if the right of first refusal is not exercised, the delays caused by the procedures are often enough to dissuade a potential purchaser.

Buy-Sell Agreements

Buy-sell agreements are another device used to provide some liquidity to shareholders while limiting stock ownership to a small group. Buy-sell agreements typically contain three operative provisions. First, the signing shareholder is prevented from transferring his or her shares except as permitted by the agreement. Second, transfers are permitted to certain parties (e.g., family members or controlled entities) or upon certain events (e.g., death), subject in most cases to the transferee's agreeing to be bound by the buy-sell agreement. Third, the company or the other parties to the agreement are either granted an option, or are obligated, to purchase at fair value another party's stock and that other party is obligated to sell the stock upon certain events (e.g., termination of employment).

Often the most difficult aspect of a buy-sell agreement is determining the price to be paid for stock purchased under the agreement. Because the event giving rise to the purchase and sale does not involve a third-party offer, as with a right of first refusal, there usually is no arm's-length evidence as to the stock's value. Alternatives for determining value include valuation formulas based on a multiple of earnings, revenues, and the like; the use of outside appraisers; a good-faith determination by the board of directors; and a price to be agreed on. In some agreements, the method for determining or paying the purchase price will vary depending on the event giving rise to the sale. For example, selling stock as a result of voluntarily leaving employment might result in a lower price than selling stock as a result of extenuating circumstances (e.g., death). Due to their complexity, buy-sell agreements are less common in venture-backed companies than in family and other closely held businesses.

Co-Sale Agreements

Co-sale agreements are commonly used by venture capital investors to allow them to participate in sales by other shareholders. These agreements are especially common when one or more of the founders owns a controlling interest in the company. Such a controlling interest could, absent transfer restrictions, be sold to a third party, thereby leaving the venture investors in a minority position in a business that has lost at least one of its founders. Conversely, a founder concerned that the venture capitalists might sell out to a third party and leave the founder as a minority shareholder could propose a co-sale agreement covering the venture capitalist's shares; however, many venture capitalists are unwilling to agree to such a provision. Co-sale agreements in venture capital deals are discussed further in Chapter 13.

Shareholder Voting Agreements

Although effective control of a business is often tied to the level of equity ownership, this is not always the case, particularly if the company has obtained venture financing and has granted one or more of the investors the right to designate directors through voting agreements. Even before the first venture financing, it may be appropriate to implement a voting agreement to ensure that the composition of the board is defined. Normally, all or a controlling group of the shareholders enter into such an agreement. Under the agreement, the parties pledge to vote their shares for designated individuals as directors. The individuals can be named in the agreement, or the agreement can allow one or more of the shareholders to nominate the director at the time of each election. Although shareholders can agree to elect certain named persons as directors, a shareholder agreement purporting to name the officers would be invalid. Only the directors have the legal authority to name and remove the officers.

When the company is being structured initially, the number of shareholders may be small enough that a voting agreement appears to be unnecessary. For instance, if there are three equal shareholders and three board seats, then, if there is cumulative voting, each shareholder will be able to elect himself or herself to the board. Even in these simple cases, however, a voting agreement could be useful. If, for example, two of the three shareholders are related and are expected to vote together at the board and shareholder levels, the third shareholder might demand that a fourth board seat be established and that, pursuant to a voting agreement, the third shareholder be entitled to designate two of the board members.

In general, larger venture investors will expect the right to designate one director, and founders should expect that their own board representation will be reduced to one, or even to just the CEO, over time. When negotiating voting agreements, the parties should consider a "sunset" clause on board representation if an investor does not continue to invest in the company and is significantly diluted in subsequent rounds of financing.

FROM THE TRENCHES

Two "seed fund" investors led a Series A preferred-stock round of financing to a start-up. As part of the financing, they required that the Series A shareholders be given the right to elect two directors and that the other shareholders agree to vote their shares for nominees of the two original Series A investors. Over time, the company required significant additional capital. Although the initial investors did not continue to invest, they refused to relinquish their board seats, which greatly hindered the company's financing efforts.

Proprietary Information and Inventions, Employment, and Noncompete Agreements

In structuring and forming a new business, the founders should not only focus on equity ownership and control issues but should also consider the appropriateness of individual agreements between the company and the founders and other employees. At the very least, a proprietary information and inventions agreement should be required from all employees, including the founders. The proprietary information (or nondisclosure) provisions will require the employee to keep the company's proprietary information confidential and to use such information only as authorized by the company. Provisions dealing with inventions will effectively assign to the company any inventions that (1) result from work performed for the company; (2) are discovered during company time; or (3) arise from the use of company materials, equipment, or trade secrets. Proprietary information and inventions agreements, as well as other techniques for protecting trade secrets and other types of intellectual property, are discussed further in Chapter 14.

At the very early stages of the company, employment agreements are uncommon, but in the right circumstances, they can be useful. Under the law of most states, employment is considered to be at-will unless there is an express or implied agreement to the contrary. *At-will employment* means that the company can terminate the relationship at any time, with or without cause. As a result, the company may have little incentive to implement an employment agreement if it has otherwise obtained a proprietary information and inventions agreement and, if allowed under state law, a noncompete agreement. However, a founder who feels vulnerable to the whims of his or her cofounders may find some comfort in such an agreement, which can provide for cash severance payments, additional stock vesting, or both if the employee is terminated without good cause. Care should be taken, though, to ensure that any employment agreement is not so airtight that the employee, including a founder, cannot be terminated even for good reason. If the contract effectively guarantees employment, or imposes substantial costs on the company for terminating employment, venture investors could be concerned. These investors must believe that as the business grows, the company will be able to make necessary personnel changes without having to pay too high a price. (Employment agreements are discussed further in Chapter 10.)

In states where an agreement not to compete with a previous employer is enforceable, the founders should consider whether such an agreement between themselves and the company is appropriate. Sentiment will probably be against noncompete agreements at this stage of the company's development because the founders all should believe that they will be with the company for a long time. In addition, each founder may want to ensure that he or she is able to establish a competing venture in the event of being forced out. Nevertheless, founders should not be surprised if venture investors in the first financing round seek to impose these agreements as yet another way of protecting their investment. (Covenants not to compete are discussed in Chapter 2.)

Putting It into Practice

As a first step in structuring their new enterprise, Kendra, Philip, and Kristine met to discuss their expectations for the business. Their simple agreement to "divide any profits fairly" might have given them some comfort on an informal basis, but they recognized that it was now time for them to be clear and forthright about their expectations as to equity ownership and control. Given that Kendra had devised the initial software application for the Saturn Data Booster (SDB) and had been working on the project longer than Philip and Kristine, she indicated that she expected a disproportionate piece of the equity. The group concluded that Kendra should be given 43 percent of the equity, Philip, 20 percent, and Kristine, 20 percent. Kendra had already agreed to give CSS a 15 percent stake in return for licensing the SDB technology. They decided that Winston North, the CSS engineer who gave Kendra the idea for the SDB, should be offered 2 percent of the equity in exchange for his release of any claims to the SDB or against DataAccelleation.

After working out the business deal among themselves, Kendra, Philip, and Kristine met with their legal counsel, Michael Cruz, and his associate, Sanjay Datar, to discuss incorporating the enterprise. Michael asked them to describe the agreements they had reached and their expectations as to foreseeable events (e.g., whether they would seek venture capital financing and, if so, when). Kendra said that DataAccelleation intended to seek venture capital financing in about six months. Philip indicated that until the company received venture financing, it would be financed by family loans and a modest equity investment by a wealthy family friend. The founders asked Michael and Sanjay what legal documentation was needed to ensure the equity ownership and board structure they had agreed upon. Because stock was being issued with the expectation of continued employment, they inquired about mechanisms to keep the stock with the company if one of them were to leave. Finally, Kendra said that she wanted to talk about an employment agreement for herself.

Michael began by outlining the pros and cons of incorporating in Delaware or in California, and suggested that they choose California. He pointed out that for at least the next few years, significant aspects of California corporate law likely would apply to the company no matter where it

continued...

continued...

was incorporated because the company would be based in California and most of its stock would be held by California residents.

The situation with Winston was briefly discussed. Michael expressed the view that 2 percent of the initial common stock was quite generous, given Winston's limited contribution, but said that obtaining his release was certainly a good idea, particularly if it could be accomplished quickly. At Michael's suggestion, Kendra agreed to contact Winston immediately to discuss the founders' plans and to seek his release of any claims to the SDB technology in exchange for common stock.

To reflect the agreement regarding equity, Michael proposed that the company's articles of incorporation authorize 10 million shares of common stock and that 1 million shares of common stock be issued at a price of $.01 per share, with 430,000 to Kendra, 200,000 to Philip, 200,000 to Kristine, 150,000 to CSS, and 20,000 to Winston (assuming he agreed to sign a release). He also suggested the authorization of 1.5 million shares of blank-check preferred stock, based on his assumption that the initial venture investors would seek 40 to 60 percent of the equity. Michael explained that to sell 60 percent of the company's equity to the venture investors, the company would issue 1.5 million shares of preferred stock convertible one-for-one into shares of common stock; thus, after the closing, the 1 million shares held by the founders would represent 40 percent of the 2.5 million shares outstanding. This capital structure would enable the board of directors to issue convertible preferred stock to venture investors without the need for a shareholder vote and would leave a cushion of shares of common stock available to issue to venture investors upon conversion of their convertible preferred stock and to new employees directly or through options.

Michael next discussed the board arrangements, pointing out that cumulative voting would apply as this was a privately held California corporation. Kendra, Philip, and Kristine reported their conclusion that a four-person board would make the most sense, with Kendra having the right to elect two directors and with Philip and Kristine together having the right to elect two directors. Under this arrangement, neither group could control the board if disputes arose. Sanjay told the founders that with a four-person board, Kendra automatically would be able to elect two directors because she held at least 40 percent of the stock, and that Philip and Kristine each

continued...

continued...

would be able to elect one of the four directors because they each owned at least 20 percent of the stock. He also advised that it was unlikely that a venture capital investor would agree to a board composition that included three founders or allowed the founders as a group to elect four directors. In all likelihood, after a venture financing, only Kendra as CEO and perhaps one other founder would remain on the board.

Nevertheless, Michael advised the parties to sign a voting agreement to reflect their decision on board representation because the ownership percentages would change as additional shares were issued to employees, consultants, or investors. Philip asked Kendra if he could have a veto over Kendra's choice of a fourth director. Kendra agreed, subject to her right to veto any director nominated by Philip or Kristine if Philip and Kristine did not nominate themselves.

Sanjay said that he could include all of these provisions in the proposed voting agreement. He suggested that the agreement expire at the time of the company's initial public offering because the company's investment bankers would insist on this. He also advised that the even number of directors could result in a deadlocked board that would be unable to take any action. Kendra said that she would rather have a situation where the directors were forced to agree to an action than one where one side could dictate a decision or where an outside director would have the swing vote on any important issue. Michael said that he was not particularly troubled by the deadlock possibility because these voting arrangements would most certainly change once the company received venture capital financing.

Sanjay then discussed vesting on the common stock to be issued to the founding group. He started to say that the venture investors would insist on vesting, but Philip interrupted to state that the founders did not need to be persuaded to install vesting now. Sanjay did note that if additional restrictions were imposed on the founders' shares later, after the fair market value of the common stock had increased, then the founders would have to consider filing new Section 83(b) elections and possibly would have to recognize some income on the spread. The founders decided that, for Philip and Kristine, monthly vesting over four years would be fair and would set an example for future employees, but that vesting for Kendra should be shorter because she had been the driving force behind the project and had been

continued...

continued...

involved for a longer time. The parties agreed to vest one-fourth of Kendra's shares immediately, with the balance to vest monthly over the next three years. Sanjay asked whether any credit toward vesting should be given in the event of death, but the founders decided against it because of the need to use unvested shares to attract replacements for key personnel who left the business regardless of the reason. Michael advised Kendra, Philip, and Kristine to file Section 83(b) elections within thirty days after the date their stock was issued.

Next, Michael raised the need for controls on the shares to be issued to the founders and future shareholders. He pointed out that because the founders' shares were not registered with the Securities and Exchange Commission but were issued pursuant to certain exemptions from registration (namely, Section 4(2) of the Securities Act of 1933 and Regulation D adopted thereunder), the shares would be subject to restrictions on transfer. A legend on their stock certificates would provide that the shares could not be sold unless registered under the Securities Act of 1933 or sold in an exempt transaction. In general, for a sale to be exempt from registration under Rule 144, the founders would have to hold their stock for at least one year before sale. Even after one year, they would be unable to sell it publicly unless the company was regularly filing periodic reports with the Securities and Exchange Commission, which normally is not done until the company goes public. In addition to these restrictions, all agreed that it made sense to prevent transfers of shares outside the existing shareholder group. Michael suggested an assignable right of first refusal in favor of the company, with exceptions for estate planning transfers, gifts, and transfers to existing shareholders. Kendra thought that there should be no exceptions to the right, even for gifts to family members. The others agreed, as long as the board could waive the right of first refusal in particular cases. Sanjay said that he would include the right of first refusal, and the ability of the board to waive it, in the company's bylaws. Michael pointed out that venture investors might not agree to a right of first refusal on their convertible preferred stock, but he suggested that for now the right should apply to all stock of the company.

Finally, Kendra asked about an employment agreement for herself. She was concerned that the venture investors might insist on board control and then use their poser to terminate her without compensation. Michael indicated

continued...

continued...

that employment agreements for executives were uncommon in Silicon Valley start-ups and that such an agreement would probably have to be eliminated before a venture capitalist would invest. Kendra replied that she would rather face that issue at the time of financing than have nothing in place, and Philip and Kristine reluctantly agreed. Sanjay was instructed to prepare a three-year agreement providing for basic compensation of $100,000 per year with a year's severance pay plus an additional twelve months of vesting on her stock (that is, vesting the number of shares that would have vested had she remained employed for another twelve months) in the event the company terminated her without good cause. Kristine asked Kendra if the commencement of salary payments could be postponed until the company was able to raise capital, and Kendra agreed.

The final step was for Kendra, Philip, and Kristine to review the draft legal documents prepared by Sanjay as a result of their meeting. The founders believed that they had communicated their deal clearly to counsel and asserted that they did not feel a need to review the resulting documents in any detail. Sanjay explained that it was much better to discover any differences between what was intended and what the documents said at this early stage rather than in the future, when it might be more difficult to reach an agreement.

Kendra, Philip, and Kristine then carefully reviewed the drafts and asked questions about several of the more technical drafting points. With one minor modification, they agreed that the drafts reflected their intentions and then signed the final documents. Having successfully incorporated the venture, divided the ownership, and issued stock to the founders, Kendra, Philip, and Kristine turned their attention to selecting their board of directors.

Chapter 6

FORMING AND WORKING WITH THE BOARD

A corporation is legally required to have a board of directors to protect the interests of the corporation and its equity holders. But there are other reasons to have an active board. A board of directors that brings together people with a variety of strengths and skills can be a valuable asset to a young company and contribute to its success by functioning as a strategic sounding board. The most effective boards give independent, informed advice to management and challenge the CEO, rather than acting as a rubber stamp.

When asked to identify the most difficult aspect of starting a business, many entrepreneurs respond that they never realized how many details they would need to be mindful of and how difficult it would be to do so many things simultaneously. Keeping an eye on the big picture while being continually concerned with day-to-day operational issues can be challenging. As they try to solve countless problems, entrepreneurs often turn to the directors for answers and advice.

This chapter examines the benefits of having an independent and active board of directors and discusses the factors to consider in selecting board members. It also summarizes directors' legal responsibilities, which include a duty of loyalty and a duty of care. The chapter discusses board compensation, outlines the types of information that should be provided to directors, and suggests ways to make effective use of directors' time.

The Benefits of Having an Independent Board

Many corporations, large and small, have filpled the positions of directors with agreeable family members or personal friends, rather than selecting an active, outside, and truly independent board. Small-company CEOs and entrepreneurs may be reluctant to have an active, outside board for a variety of reasons. Many CEOs are hesitant to give up any control of the company that they created. The entrepreneur may not feel sufficiently organized to deal with a board. Many entrepreneurs dislike criticism and tend to minimize its sources. The entrepreneur may be reluctant to reveal confidential information, financial or otherwise. CEOs of family businesses may be even more reluctant to invite outsiders into an enterprise where traditionally only family members have been involved. In addition, many CEOs think that outsiders will not understand their business as well as they do. They may feel that their business is unique and that no one else can assist effectively in long-range planning and development of strategy.

Nevertheless, the benefits of an independent board greatly outweigh the drawbacks. A CEO can better assist the company in achieving its full potential when he or she is able to benefit from what often amounts to decades of other people's experience and wisdom. As Clayton Mathile, CEO of the IAMS pet food company, explained, "Your outside board can be your inside sparring partner who tests your strengths and weaknesses before you get to the main arena—the marketplace. Where else can a business owner go to find help from someone he trusts, who is unbiased, and who will help him do the job?"[1]

The reasons for creating an active, outside board are numerous. Board members can bring perspective and experience to the table and provide a set of complementary skills for the CEO. If the prospective directors have been entrepreneurs and CEOs in their own right, they are able to provide vision and insight that insiders cannot supply. The board can help top management recognize the need for long-term planning and can assist the CEO in developing long-range strategies. Boards can provide a framework for control and discipline and give the CEO someone to answer to. Directors can be challenging and objective critics. Securing financial and other information

FROM THE TRENCHES

An entrepreneur founded a company to produce sophisticated software designed to "read" or extract information from form documents, such as insurance claim forms, and to store it digitally. He initially financed the company with money from his father. His board of directors consisted of himself and an industry consultant. After five beta tests proved successful, he decided to seek venture capital funding for the company at a $5 million pre-money valuation. Before starting this process, however, he added two individuals to his board. Both had been venture capitalists before cofounding a company that, after obtaining venture capital financing, had recently gone public. The founder wanted someone at his side who could not only access the venture capital community but could also "walk the walk and talk the talk" when it came to negotiating a deal. The founder reasoned that with their very recent start-up experience, his new directors would also be able to help him deal with the myriad issues that his company would face.

needed by the board can become an internal check for the CEO. Directors can fill the CEO's need for a mentor or a coach. One CEO of a small company explained, "I need a person on the board with whom I can talk very frankly and not be fearful—someone on the board I can tell, 'I don't know.' "[2] Boards can give the CEO the emotional support needed for difficult decision making.

The presence of experienced businesspersons on the board of directors will also lend an air of credibility to the venture that it would not otherwise have. This credibility is particularly important when the enterprise is trying to raise funds. Valuable business connections and introductions can be made through the board. In the case of family corporations, a board of directors with some outside perspective and independence from family politics can ease the often difficult generational transitions.

The Size of the Board

The board of directors should be small enough to be accountable and to act as a deliberative body but large enough to carry out the necessary responsibilities. Most CEOs find that between five and nine directors is a good, manageable size. Many venture-backed companies have five directors.

The outsiders should outnumber the insiders so that the board can reap the benefit of the independent directors. Usually no more than two insiders should sit on the board, although it is common for officers who are not board members to be invited to make presentations to the board and to sit in on certain board discussions.

Frequency and Duration of Board Meetings

The frequency of formal board meetings will be determined in part by how the CEO envisions the role of the board. For a very hands-on board, a meeting every month may be appropriate. But if the board meets formally only to discuss major issues, less frequent meetings may be sufficient. Typically, the CEO should be in touch with each board member between the meetings.

The length of the meetings and the location are also important strategic decisions. Some boards meet for several hours at a time, or for an entire day, with a break for lunch, which facilitates informal discussions among members. The ideal meeting lasts between three and five hours, which is

FROM THE TRENCHES

An entrepreneur who started a bicycle helmet business had a board of directors to satisfy the legal requirements, but it was composed of only himself and two other insiders. For advice, he turned to a business school professor and two retired executives. Every few years, the entrepreneur gathered this unofficial board for a freewheeling discussion of the business and its strategies. Between these infrequent meetings, the entrepreneur called these advisers when he wanted to discuss a problem or an idea. Even as the company grew, the entrepreneur never felt the need to form a board with outsiders and instead continued to use his unofficial board. This practice continued until recently, when he sold his business to a large competitor.

Comment: The ideal situation is to have outside advisers as members of the board of directors. If that is not possible due to liability concerns or time constraints, the next best alternative is to have an outside advisory board that can augment the official board of directors.

long enough to accomplish the necessary work but not so long that the board members cannot continue to give their full attention. Sometimes the board members will get together for several days at a time so that they can concentrate on strategic issues without being distracted by the day-to-day aspects of the business. For example, one company holds a three-day off-site meeting every six months. Although off-site meetings can be very valuable, some companies will find it impossible to schedule them because many directors have full-time jobs, such as running their own companies, and cannot afford to be away from them for so long.

Type of Representation Desired

There are at least two major aspects to consider in building an independent and active board. The first is the combination of functional skills needed to keep the business running smoothly and to bring it to the next level of growth. The second is the mix of personalities. Combining these components, both of which are very important to the successful running of the company, is more an art than a science.[3]

Before selecting board members, the CEO must anticipate the needs of the corporation for the next few years and ask such questions as:

- What is the competitive advantage of the company?
- What will be the demands on the company and the likely changes in the next few years?
- What factors would contribute to the success of the company?
- How much technical expertise is needed to understand the company's products?
- What role does marketing play? Research and development? Customer service?
- What is the company's access to sources of financing?

By inventorying the resources of the company and anticipating its needs, the CEO will be better equipped to choose a board that will unlock the company's inherent possibilities.

The Needed Skills

The goal in putting together the board is to compile a complete combination of abilities. The entrepreneur should assess his or her own weaknesses and strengths and supplement them with complementary talents. These talents should include industry experience, financial expertise, marketing experience, start-up experience, and technical know-how. Although the ideal board member will be familiar with the product, market, and any technologies that may be involved, the entrepreneur should strive to promote breadth on the board. Certainly, if the company is contemplating international expansion, it should consider seeking directors who have had such experience.

In assembling a successful board, the entrepreneur might also want to consider the age, gender, and cultural background of each director. It may be a good idea, especially in a family business, to have at least one director who is of the same generation as the likely successor to the CEO so that when the transition takes place, he or she will have a peer on the board. Many CEOs are choosing directors whose gender and culture are similar to the spectrum of the company's employees and customers. For example, a specialty boutique selling women's clothes would want to have a woman on the board who understands the market.

Although outside representation is important to bring new insights to the company and maintain a truly independent board, the potential benefits of having company insiders on the board are many. Directorships provide a tangible incentive for employees, and insiders often provide invaluable expertise and perspective in a specific area of management.[4]

The entrepreneur should be wary of filling the board with people whose interests may not be aligned with the company's or to whom the company already has access. For example, the interests of the company's commercial banker may not be consistent with the best strategic planning for the company. Although family businesses commonly include corporate counsel or the founder's personal counsel on the board, the result may be the inadvertent waiver of the attorney-client privilege. Consultants of all kinds should be considered carefully. People who already work for the CEO may not be the most appropriate people to challenge him or her.

For companies with venture capital funding, the financing agreement will usually give the investors the right to elect one or more directors. Venture capitalists tend to be very involved and effective board members. They can also be a good source of introductions to other potential board members.

Personality Mix and Board Structure

It is important that the board function cohesively as a group, which means that the board members' personalities must be compatible. Board members need to respect each other; no one person should so dominate the meetings as to preclude others from voicing their opinions. The board's chair should be alert to such an exertion of power, including his or her own. Although a diverse board is ideal, it is important to avoid creating a board that acts like a legislature, with each director focused on championing his or her own constituency.

In selecting board members, the entrepreneur should consider the need for a board that is willing to take a hands-on approach to its job. Board members should include people with practical experience and business savvy, and not just theoretical or technical expertise. At the same time, the board as a whole must understand the difference between meddling with the company's management and maintaining a healthy relationship. The goal is to have a board that will be actively involved in the formulation of long-range planning, will scrutinize the budget, and will question assumptions.

It is often desirable to separate the roles of CEO and chair or to appoint a lead director.[5] Many corporations of all sizes set up compensation, audit, and nominating committees consisting solely or primarily of independent directors.

The Responsibilities of the Board

Legally, the directors of a corporation owe two major responsibilities to a corporation and the shareholders: a duty of loyalty and a duty of care.[6] A breach of either of these duties can lead to multimillion-dollar liability. For example, the directors of Trans Union Corp. were held liable for $23.5 million ($13.5 million in excess of their directors' and officers' liability insurance) because they approved the sale of company stock at $55 a share without first sufficiently informing themselves of the stock's intrinsic value, which the court decided was higher.[7]

Although shareholder suits involving privately held companies are less common than public company suits, they do occur, particularly in the context of a majority shareholder allegedly violating the rights of the minority shareholders. For example, one case involved United Savings and Loan Association, which did not have actively traded shares. The majority shareholders of the association transferred their shares to a new holding company, United Financial Corp. The majority shareholders continued to control the association through the holding company. The association's minority shareholders were not permitted to exchange their association shares for the holding company's shares. The holding company went public, and active trading commenced. In contrast, trading in the association's shares dried up. The minority shareholders of the association successfully sued the majority shareholders and the individuals who set up the holding company for breach of fiduciary duty. The court found that the transaction was not fair because the defendants had misappropriated to themselves the going-public value of the association, to the detriment of the minority shareholders.[8]

Duty of Loyalty

As a fiduciary of the corporation, a director must act in the best interests of the corporation. Personal interests, financial and professional, must be subjugated to the interests of the corporation during decision making. Directors should avoid any hint of self-dealing.

Upholding this duty of loyalty applies to decisions that concern the day-to-day operations of the company, such as executive compensation, as well as strategic decisions, such as a merger. Executive compensation should be determined by those directors with no personal interest in the decision. In addition, a director must not usurp an opportunity that is in the corporation's line of business for himself or herself without first disclosing the corporate opportunity to the other board members and obtaining the board's permission to pursue it.[9]

In determining whether a board of directors is sufficiently disinterested, a relevant factor in some jurisdictions is whether a majority of the board

FROM THE TRENCHES

Digidyne was a venture-backed company founded in the early 1980s to produce minicomputers to emulate a line of Data General products. The founder's family owned approximately 50 percent of the company after the initial round of venture financing at $3.00 per share. The company soon fell on hard times, however. To keep Digidyne alive, the venture capitalists, who controlled the board of directors, invested in several rounds of financing at ever-lower prices per share. The prices were set by the board of directors. The lowest round was at $0.25 per share. The founder's family had the right to participate in the subsequent rounds but didn't because they did not have the money. Eventually, the founder's family's interest was diluted down to approximately 2 percent of the company. Digidyne thereafter won a lawsuit that resulted in a favorable return to all shareholders. The founder's family then sued the venture capitalists, alleging in part that they had violated their fiduciary duty to the minority shareholders by selling themselves stock at too low a price, which had the effect of unfairly diluting the ownership interests of the original shareholders.

After hearing the evidence, the judge granted a verdict for the defendants and did not permit the case to be tried by a jury. Although there was no reported opinion, the judge apparently was influenced by the fact that at every round of financing, the venture capitalists had offered all shareholders the right to purchase their proportionate share (based on existing ownership percentages) of the stock being offered. Accordingly, all shareholders were treated equally, the venture capitalists did not favor themselves at the expense of the other shareholders, and no breach of fiduciary duty was found.

members are outside directors. The fact that outside directors receive directors' fees but not salaries is viewed as heightening the likelihood that they will not be motivated by personal interest when making decisions affecting the company.

Sometimes it is impossible to have a disinterested vote of the directors. When that happens, all the board can do is to try its best to ensure that the directors are informed and that the transaction is fair to the company and all shareholders. If a transaction approved only by interested directors is challenged, the burden of proof is on them to show that the transaction was fair.

Duty of Care and Oversight

A board member must act with the level of care that a reasonably prudent person would use under similar circumstances. To that end, the board member must make a reasonable effort to make informed decisions. In most jurisdictions, the general corporate law authorizes directors to rely on reports prepared by officers of the corporation or outside experts such as investment bankers and consultants. Sometimes, however, passive reliance on these reports without further inquiry when the situation warrants can lead to an insufficiently informed decision.

Board members also have a duty of oversight. They must ensure that adequate procedures are in place to prevent violations of law.[10]

Limitations on Liability and Indemnification

As noted in Chapter 5, many states, including California and Delaware, have adopted legislation that permits shareholders to amend the certificate of incorporation to limit or abolish a director's liability for a breach of duty of care, except for clear cases of willful misconduct or fraud. This can provide a partial substitute for directors' and officers' liability insurance (*D&O insurance*), which is often too costly for private companies. It is appropriate to reduce the potential liability a director faces by amending the corporate charter and entering into agreements that provide for the advancing of legal fees should a director be sued. If it is ultimately found that indemnification is not warranted, the director would be required to reimburse the company for the monies advanced.

BUSINESS JUDGMENT RULE

Challenges to the decisions of a corporation's directors are reviewed using the business judgment rule, which protects directors from having their business decisions second-guessed. If the directors are disinterested and informed, the *business judgment rule* requires the plaintiff to prove that the directors were grossly negligent or acted in bad faith before liability will attach. This high burden of proof protects directors from being liable merely for poor decisions.

The business judgment rule recognizes that all business decisions have inherent risk, and often reasonable decisions can have poor results. Protection under the business judgment rule allows those who might otherwise be deterred from serving on boards to serve without undue fear of being held personally liable for decisions made in good faith.

Compensation of Board Members

Directors receive both tangible and intangible compensation. A person usually does not serve on the board of directors for a private company for the monetary compensation alone, as it normally is not very large. Most directors agree to serve on boards because they enjoy the advisory process and like to keep in touch with what is going on in their industry. Successful entrepreneurs enjoy advising start-ups and sharing their experience.

Intangible Compensation for Directors

Bob Burnett, the former CEO of a large publishing company, has served on the boards of numerous companies, large and small, as well as on the boards of universities and other public institutions. He believes that most CEOs sit on other companies' boards to benefit from the cross-fertilization of ideas, learn, and gain personal fulfillment.

The intangible benefits of board service include the opportunity to learn, through exposure to another company's operations and experiences, strategies or techniques that may prove valuable to the director's own business. Board service provides the opportunity to work collaboratively with colleagues. Often prestige is associated with sitting on the boards of various ventures. Many directors find it satisfying to advise and contribute to a new company. Especially at the early stages, the director can significantly shape the financial and marketing strategy of the business.

Tangible Compensation for Directors

Typically, the company will pay some, if not all, of the expenses related to the directors' attendance at meetings, including travel and meals. It is also a good idea for the entrepreneur to compensate the directors monetarily for their time and effort. This monetary compensation is more a token of appreciation and acknowledgment than a payment to the directors for their time, which many small companies could not afford anyway. Several national executive search firms, including Spencer Stuart, Korn Ferry, and Heidrick & Struggles, routinely publish data about trends in director compensation (broken down by company size) and board structure (such as average number of directors, committees, and frequency of meetings). These reports can provide a useful benchmark for an entrepreneur setting up a board for the first time.

In addition to attending the actual meetings, most effective directors spend at least half a day examining materials sent to them by the CEO to prepare for the board meeting. Also, the directors usually participate in informal discussions with the CEO for a few hours each quarter. They may also meet in committees. Assuming a schedule of quarterly meetings, board work would comprise about eight days of a director's year.[11] As a reflection of time commitment alone, board honoraria could be calculated at 2 to 3 percent of a CEO's annual salary. Yet many small companies cannot afford to pay that in cash.

As a result, many companies compensate directors with equity in the company, such as stock options or restricted stock grants. This form of compensation is effective because it helps to align the directors' incentives with those of the shareholders. Sometimes directors already own shares of the company and view their involvement on the board as a way to protect their financial investment.

In the more informal advisory board setting, monetary compensation may not be discussed at the outset. Although this approach may be appropriate initially, the entrepreneur should raise the issue to avoid future misunderstandings with the advisers, who may be anticipating some monetary or other compensation.

Types of Information Directors Need

Before the board meeting, the company should supply the directors with an agenda of what will be discussed at the meeting so that the directors can prepare effectively. Included in this information packet should be some general statistics on how the company is doing so that the directors can keep abreast of the company in general and alert management to any potential problems. A sample agenda for a board meeting is shown in Exhibit 6.1.

EXHIBIT 6.1

AGENDA

ALTAIR, INC.
BOARD MEETING
THURSDAY, OCTOBER 10, 2002 AT 2:00 P.M.

Agenda

I. Review of September 5 Board Minutes

II. Engineering Update

III. Executive Search

IV. Food and Drug Administration Approval
- Strategy
- Time Lines

V. Business Development
- Company X
- Company Y
- University Z

VI. Financials Review
- Current Financials
- Preliminary Budget—2003

VII. Financing Plans
- Action Items to Be Completed
- Lease Line

VIII. Patent Strategy Review

IX. Competitive Update

X. Approval of Option Grants

Attorney Martin Lipton and Harvard Business School Professor Jay W. Lorsch have suggested that directors be given more information about the longer-term trends of the company. This would include not just information of a financial nature but also information regarding the company's competitive position and organizational health.[12] Efforts should be made to quantify the plans of the company regarding research and development and to set goals for the future.

The types of information that directors need is presented in Exhibit 6.2, arranged by update guidelines.

EXHIBIT 6.2

INFORMATION TO BE PROVIDED TO DIRECTORS

Permanent Information

The vision: Core values and purpose of the corporation[a]

Mission of the corporation

Strategy of the corporation

Certificate of incorporation

Bylaws of the corporation

Directors' curricula vitae

Any director indemnification agreements

Information to Be Updated Annually

Current-year budget

Top competitors

Top 20 customers

Distribution channels

Top 10 vendors

Five- to ten-year balance sheets

History of financial information

Any changes in accounting policy

Insurance coverage, including D&O coverage

continued...

EXHIBIT 6.2 (CONTINUED)

INFORMATION TO BE PROVIDED TO DIRECTORS

Information to Be Updated Annually

Employee benefits, including stock options

Corporate charitable contributions

Organizational chart

List of officers, directors, and key advisers

List of individuals who own more than 1% of stock

Biographies of key executives

Summary of contractual obligations that exceed one year:

- Union contracts
- Patents/intellectual property rights
- Employment agreements
- Customer and supplier agreements

Summary of real estate:

- Long-term leases
- Owned properties

Information to Be Updated Monthly

Current results with variance reports against plan and last year's results (for both month and year-to-date numbers and management's current view of what they will look like at year's end) for:

- Income statement
- Statement of cash flow
- Balance sheet

Summary of financial and operating statistics:

- Return on investment
- Return on assets
- Return on sales

continued...

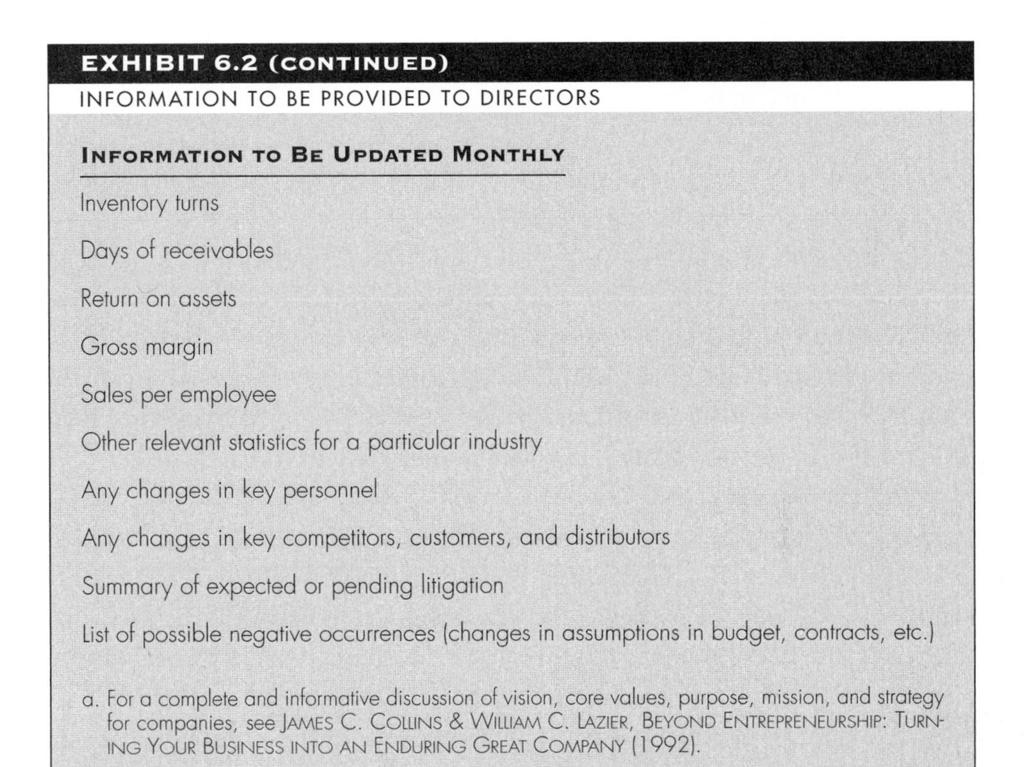

EXHIBIT 6.2 (CONTINUED)

INFORMATION TO BE PROVIDED TO DIRECTORS

INFORMATION TO BE UPDATED MONTHLY

Inventory turns

Days of receivables

Return on assets

Gross margin

Sales per employee

Other relevant statistics for a particular industry

Any changes in key personnel

Any changes in key competitors, customers, and distributors

Summary of expected or pending litigation

List of possible negative occurrences (changes in assumptions in budget, contracts, etc.)

a. For a complete and informative discussion of vision, core values, purpose, mission, and strategy for companies, see JAMES C. COLLINS & WILLIAM C. LAZIER, BEYOND ENTREPRENEURSHIP: TURNING YOUR BUSINESS INTO AN ENDURING GREAT COMPANY (1992).

HOW TO MAKE THE MOST EFFECTIVE USE OF THE BOARD

It is widely believed that most boards do not operate at their maximum effectiveness and, in fact, often function poorly. Management expert Peter Drucker once called the board of directors "an impotent ceremonial and legal fiction."[13] But although Drucker and others may express dismay at the workings of some boards, many academics and practitioners believe that criticism should focus on individuals and circumstances, rather than the inherent nature of the system. In other words, the formation of a board of directors need not automatically convert a talented group of dedicated individuals into an inefficient bureaucratic body.

How, then, does one best use a board of directors? Perhaps by revisiting the most important functions of a board, the CEO can examine and refine the board's priorities. If the board is spending considerable time on company-related activities that do not fall into one of these categories, perhaps the CEO and the board should take a closer look at that activity and ask, How was it delegated to the board? Is it a task that could be more economically handled by management?

The Business Roundtable suggests the following relationship between the CEO and the board: "The relation between board and chief executive officer should be challenging yet supportive and positive. It should be at arm's length, but not adversary. The Board should stimulate management to perform at the peak of its capacity, not by carping, but by setting high standards and providing level-headed encouragement."[14]

Although the Business Roundtable was referring to the large public corporation in this description, the suggestions are equally relevant to small, private companies. The relationship between the board and the CEO can often be fraught with tension. On the one hand, the board of directors lends support to the CEO. On the other hand, the board has the responsibility to oversee the CEO and ensure that his or her performance is satisfactory.[15]

The board should review the performance of the CEO each year and set the CEO's compensation for the coming year.[16] For example, Target is well known for its board's annual review of the CEO, which includes a report card of scores, broken down by area. In all things, the CEO must remain

FROM THE TRENCHES

A lighting-manufacturing company was in poor financial shape after competitive pressures had squeezed its margins. It misjudged the market, requiring it to incur large inventory write-downs. The best solution was to consolidate its product line and lay off part of the workforce. The CEO hesitated to make dramatic changes, but the board pushed him to take the necessary steps. The measures were successful, and three years later the company was sold for a good price.

The board of directors was successful in turning the company around because of the relationship the directors had with the CEO. The key directors were friends of the CEO and had worked with him at another company. Because of their relationship, the CEO respected the directors' business acumen and knew that they were acting in the company's best interest.

accountable to the board. It is also critical for the board to engage in ongoing planning for CEO succession.[17]

Eugene Zuckert, an experienced senior U.S. government official who sat on numerous boards, once said:

> *In the case of boards of directors, our expectations are so extravagant with such high potential for conflict that disappointment is inevitable. For example, we sometimes say that we want a strong board that really runs the business. If pressed, we say that we don't really want the board to run the business because that's a full-time job, and we don't expect the board to operate full time or anything like it. And besides, if we had a board that was too powerful, we probably could not get the strong CEO that we needed.*[18]

Both CEOs and boards can operate effectively, however, if they cooperate with one another. Consultant John Carver succinctly points out that the board has only one employee, the CEO. All other employees are those of the CEO.[19] By considering the activities of the board and CEO in this light, some of the tension is resolved.

The board is charged with outlining long-term planning for the corporation and its purpose, mission, and outlook. At the same time, it monitors the CEO's performance in light of the long-term strategy. If the board is indeed functioning effectively, a CEO will have a clear set of goals to work toward in managing the company and the freedom and autonomy to achieve these goals. In sum, the board is looking toward the future, freeing the CEO to deal with the present.

One of the most important functions of the board is to engage in strategic planning.[20] John Ward has suggested that directors focus on "big picture" questions such as these:

- Is the company meeting its potential? Why or why not?
- Which is our priority, growth or profit? How do we attain this objective?
- What are we learning as an organization? How can we learn more?
- What risks are we currently taking? Do they serve our mission well?

- Are we prepared for political and economic changes that may come suddenly?
- How are we positioned for the next two decades? Can we adapt to a changing world?
- Are we responsible corporate citizens? How can we become more responsible?[21]

Finally, just as the board should formally review the CEO's performance on a regular basis, it should also regularly review its own performance and the performance of its members. The nominating committee should take the results of these reviews into account when deciding whether to renominate an existing director and selecting new directors to fill vacancies.[22]

PUTTING IT INTO PRACTICE

Kendra was painfully aware of her lack of experience in launching a new venture and hoped to find a fourth director who could not only act as her coach and adviser but also bring to the board industry connections, technical expertise, business experience, sound judgment, assistance in predicting future market trends, and, most important, a different perspective from that of the other directors. When Kendra asked Michael Cruz, DataAccelleation's counsel, if he had any suggestions, he thought about it, then suggested Eve Segal, the former head of a research team that had written an important protocol for the Internet. Eve had shrewdly persuaded some of the biggest players in the computer industry to adopt her protocol, and within months, it had become the standard in the field. Eve subsequently left the *Fortune* 500 company for which she had worked to start her own company, which went public in 1999. Eve's latest venture was in the business of selling data compression software for content providers on the Web. Michael said that his firm had handled the initial public offering for Eve's first company but was not representing the new venture. Kendra thought about Michael's suggestion and decided to set up a meeting with Eve.

Before meeting Eve, Kendra wanted to finalize with Michael the compensation that the directors would receive for their service. Michael suggested, and Kendra agreed, that nonemployee directors should receive stock options for each year of service and be paid $750 for each board meeting attended. In addition, the company would purchase a D&O liability insurance policy with $3 million of coverage. DataAccelleation's charter already limited directors' liability and provided mandatory indemnification and advancement of expenses to the maximum extent the law allowed.

Kendra then met with Eve, whom she liked right away. Eve was a very successful entrepreneur and was clearly excited about the prospect of helping Kendra navigate the often difficult waters that had to be crossed to transform a dream into an enduring company and industry leader. In fact, Eve told Kendra that she reminded her of herself when she started her first venture. Eve was friendly but not afraid to speak her mind. Kendra realized that Eve's prior and current experience well positioned her to predict the direction of the Internet industry. In addition, Eve's contacts in the industry,

continued...

continued...

particularly with the larger players, would be invaluable. Kendra then explained the directors' compensation structure and asked Eve if she would be willing to serve as a director. Eve said she would be honored.

Given Philip's right to veto her choice of the fourth director, Kendra realized that it was important to have Philip and Kristine Colgate comfortable with her choice. She arranged a breakfast meeting at Buck's in Woodside so the Colgates could meet Eve. The meeting went well, and the Colgates both thought that Eve would be a valuable addition to the team. Kendra then called Eve to welcome her aboard.

Having filled the board, Kendra, Philip, and Kristine turned their attention to their biggest challenge yet—raising money to launch their venture.

NOTES

1. JOHN L. WARD, CREATING EFFECTIVE BOARDS FOR PRIVATE ENTERPRISE 4 (1991).
2. *Quoted in* Robert Stobaugh, *Voices of Experience: Part One—How Boards Add Value in Small Companies,* DIRECTOR'S MONTHLY, Feb. 1996, at 3.
3. *See* NATIONAL ASSOCIATION OF CORPORATE DIRECTORS, REPORT OF THE NACD BLUE RIBBON COMMISSION ON DIRECTORS' PROFESSIONALISM (1996).
4. *See* MYLES L. MACE, DIRECTORS: MYTH AND REALITY 112–15 (1986).
5. *See* Contance E. Bagley & Richard H. Koppes, *Leader of the Pack: A Proposal for Disclosure of Board Leadership Structure,* 34 SAN DIEGO L. REV. 149 (1997).
6. Directors' duties are discussed in more detail in CONSTANCE E. BAGLEY, MANAGERS AND THE LEGAL ENVIRONMENT: STRATEGIES FOR THE 21ST CENTURY (4th ed. 2002). *See also* AMERICAN BAR ASSOCIATION, CORPORATE DIRECTORS' GUIDEBOOK (2d ed. 1994).
7. Smith v. Van Gorkom, 488 A.2d 858 (Del. 1985).
8. Jones v. H. F. Ahmanson & Co., 460 P.2d 464 (Cal. 1969).
9. *See* BAGLEY, *supra* note 6, at 788.
10. *See In re* Caremark Int'l Derivative Litig., 698 A.2d 959 (Del. Ch. 1996).
11. J.L. Ward & J.L. Handy, *Survey of Board Practices,* 1 FAM. BUS. REV. 289–308 (1988).
12. *See* Martin Lipton & Jay Lorsch, *A Modest Proposal for Improved Corporate Governance,* 48 BUS. LAW. 59, 71 (1992).
13. Peter Drucker, *quoted in* CHARLES A. ANDERSON & ROBERT N. ANTHONY, THE NEW CORPORATE DIRECTORS 1 (1986).
14. THE BUSINESS ROUNDTABLE, THE ROLE AND COMPOSITION OF THE BOARD OF DIRECTORS OF THE LARGE PUBLICLY OWNED CORPORATION (1978).
15. For an excellent description of ways board members can more effectively govern, see JAY W. LORSCH, PAWNS OR POTENTATES: THE REALITY OF AMERICA'S CORPORATE BOARDS 169–93 (1989).
16. *See* NATIONAL ASSOCIATION OF CORPORATE DIRECTORS, REPORT OF THE NACD BLUE RIBBON COMMISSION ON PERFORMANCE EVALUATION OF CHIEF EXECUTIVE OFFICERS, BOARDS, AND DIRECTORS (1995).
17. *See* NATIONAL ASSOCIATION OF CORPORATE DIRECTORS, REPORT OF THE NACD BLUE RIBBON COMMISSION ON CEO SUCCESSION (1998).
18. Eugene Zuckert, *quoted in* ANDERSON & ANTHONY, *supra* note 13, at 2.
19. *See* JOHN CARVER, BOARDS THAT MAKE A DIFFERENCE (1990).
20. NATIONAL ASSOCIATION OF CORPORATE DIRECTORS, BLUE RIBBON REPORT ON THE ROLE OF THE BOARD IN CORPORATE STRATEGY (2000).
21. WARD, *supra* note 1.
22. *See* NATIONAL ASSOCIATION OF CORPORATE DIRECTORS, *supra* note 16, at 19–46.

Chapter 7

Raising Money and Securities Regulation

Raising capital for a new or expanding early-stage company with unknown management and no track record may be one of the greatest challenges facing the entrepreneur. It is likely that loans from commercial banks will be either insufficient for the new company's needs or available only on unacceptable terms. For these reasons, entrepreneurs often must seek alternative funding sources.

This chapter discusses the advantages and disadvantages of several major alternatives, including the sale of stock to private investors, venture capital financing, self-financing, and strategic alliances and joint ventures. (Venture capital is discussed in detail in Chapter 13.) To attract investors, the entrepreneur will need a business plan, and the chapter sets forth the types of information usually contained in such a plan. The chapter concludes with a summary of federal and state securities laws that must be complied with when issuing stock. (Chapter 12 discusses borrowing alternatives and issues raised by loan agreements, as well as bankruptcy.)

Sources of Funds

Several major sources of funds are available to start-up companies: money from private investors, venture capital financing, self-financing and credit, and strategic alliances and joint ventures. Each of these sources of funding has advantages and disadvantages, and more than one source of funding may be suitable for a given company. Before making a final decision on which source to pursue, entrepreneurs should consider the degree of control over the company they wish to retain, the amount of equity dilution (decrease in ownership percentage) they are willing to bear, whether assistance is desired with such tasks as recruiting talent or managing the company, and to what extent a more seasoned company may be interested in a joint venture or strategic alliance with the start-up.

Sometimes an entrepreneur will engage a broker-dealer as a placement agent to help raise money. A *placement agent* distributes a document describing the company and the offering to suitable persons and assists in the private sale of securities. Commissions for placement agents are negotiable and commonly range from 8 to 15 percent of the amount raised. Placement agents are used most often in later-stage rounds.

Private Investors

Private sales of debt or equity securities directly to qualified individual investors (commonly called *angel investors* or *angels*) may be an appropriate way to raise funds, especially if only modest amounts of money are required and the entrepreneur is acquainted with the persons interested in investing in the start-up. The entrepreneur may also want to borrow money from or sell stock to family and friends.

ADVANTAGES Angel financing is often a relatively cheap and quick source of seed capital. It is usually preferable when the management team wants to maintain control and manage the day-to-day business of the enterprise without input from the investors. Private investors are typically primarily interested in a return on their investment and do not seek an active role in the business. They seldom insist on board representation or the right to approve or select key employees. They usually require no more than the right to veto major changes in the business, restrictions on increases in top management's salary, and limits on the amount of equity to be available for incentive programs (such as stock option plans). Also, they generally do not demand as much equity as a venture capitalist, so dilution is minimal.

Offerings to private investors usually take the form of preferred stock, with the company's founders holding shares of common stock. Sometimes the investment is structured as a limited partnership, with the founders as

FROM THE TRENCHES

After graduating from Stanford Law School at the age of twenty-three, Christy Haubegger decided that instead of practicing law, she wanted to publish a high-quality magazine for Hispanic women such as herself. She formed Alegre Enterprises, Inc. One of her first investors was angel Mel Lane. Mel and his brother Bill had just sold their tremendously successful Western lifestyle magazine *Sunset* to Time Warner for about $225 million. Mel not only provided capital but also critiqued drafts of Christy's business plan (including the projections and the assumptions underlying them) and offered advice on how to roll out a successful magazine. Mel was also a great source of encouragement during the tough times when money was in short supply and Christy's "to do" list seemed endless.

Christy's dream became a reality several years later when the first issue of *Latina* magazine hit the newsstands in May 1996. By 2002, *Latina*'s monthly circulation had grown to 250,000 copies.

general partners and the investors as limited partners. Alternatively, a limited liability company may be used. (Factors to consider when choosing an appropriate form of business entity are discussed in Chapter 4.)

DISADVANTAGES Private individual investors usually do not bring as much to the company as venture capitalists do in terms of expertise, talent, and recruitment. They also usually are not willing to invest as much money as a venture capital firm will invest. Moreover, they may be more difficult to find without engaging in prohibited forms of solicitation.

Venture Capital Financing

Venture capital is money provided by professional investors for investment in new or developing businesses. In deciding whether to invest, venture capital firms differ widely in their preferred technologies, products, industries, size of investment, and stage of development of the company in which the investment is made. Reference materials are available that list the names, addresses, and specialties of venture capital funds. Often the entrepreneur's professional contacts, such as attorneys and accountants, can direct him or her to an appropriate firm. (Chapter 13 discusses venture capital in greater detail.)

ADVANTAGES Venture capital firms often have the resources to provide the funds needed to finance research and development and growth. Many venture capital firms work closely with young companies and can assist with formulating business strategy, recruiting additional management talent, assembling a board of directors, and providing introductions in the financial community. They are often able to recommend strategies and approaches that make the company more profitable than the founders alone could have made it.

FROM THE TRENCHES

Jerry Yang and David Filo, the founders of Yahoo! Inc., a leading Internet portal, started the company while they were doctoral students at Stanford University. The pair founded Yahoo! after Filo started keeping track of the cool sites he found while surfing the Net. Initially, they kept the directory on Yang's university workstation, but soon so many people were connecting with Yang's computer that he found it impossible to study. At that point they realized Yahoo! had commercial potential and decided to seek venture capital financing.

They were about to accept a $500,000 valuation from a venture capitalist firm when they received a $1 million buyout offer from America Online, Inc. Yang and Filo went back to the venture capitalists and convinced them to also offer $1 million but for just part of the company. With the funding in hand, Yang and Filo dropped out of their doctoral programs to work full-time on Yahoo!

When the company went public in April 1996, the closing price at the end of the first day valued the company at about $850 million. Yang's and Filo's shares of the company were worth $138 million each.

Source: Todd Copilevitz, On-Line Gold Mine; Surfing Instead of Studying, Yahoo! Team Struck It Rich, Dallas Morning News, Feb. 18, 1996.

DISADVANTAGES In addition to sharing in the equity, most venture capitalists insist on sharing in the control of the company. They may want the right to have one or more representatives on the board of directors. They often require veto power over any major changes to the company's business operations or financial arrangements. They may insist on approving or even selecting candidates to fill key management positions in the company. Venture capitalists also generally desire registration rights, which enable them to liquidate their investment when the company makes a public offering of its stock. (Registration rights are discussed more fully in Chapter 13.)

One of the most troubling decisions for the aspiring entrepreneur is whether to give up autonomy in exchange for the necessary funding for the start-up. Often the entrepreneur has no choice. Losing control of the company may be a prerequisite to financing the cash-starved emerging business. Entrepreneurs are constantly reminded that having a minority position in a well-financed start-up is preferable to being firmly in control of a venture that goes bankrupt because it was underfinanced.

Venture capitalists generally are not interested in investing unless the expected return is in the range of 35 to 45 percent compounded annually.

FROM THE TRENCHES

Brad Jendersee left Pfizer in late 1991 to form Arterial Vascular Engineering (AVE), a company that manufactures and sells coronary arterial stents (metal prostheses designed to hold arteries open) and balloon angioplasty catheters. Because of control and dilution concerns, Brad chose not to pursue venture financing. Instead, he financed AVE with money from angel doctors, many of whom were heart surgeons who understood the need for the company's products. The average price paid by the angels was less than $1 per share. In April 1996, AVE went public at a price of $21 per share. The value of the company at $21 per share was $600 million. Jendersee and his two cofounders together owned approximately 25 percent of AVE's stock at the time of the public offering. AVE was later sold to Medtronic, Inc., for more than $3 billion.

Venture capitalists must produce at least a 20 percent compounded return for their investors, and not all investments will turn out to be winners. In addition, an exit vehicle must be available, usually within five years of the date of the investment, because most venture capitalists invest through funds with only a ten-year life. An *exit vehicle* is a way for investors to get their money back without liquidating the company, such as through the sale of the company to a larger company or through an initial public offering of the company's securities.

Self-Financing and Credit

A few types of businesses, such as distributorships, may be able to self-finance, that is, to generate capital by carefully managing the company's internal funds. For example, a business that sells goods or services may be able to obtain payment within fifteen days of shipment rather than the more customary thirty or forty-five days. The business may even be able to structure contracts with its customers to require advance payments or deposits, although this feature may require price discounts.

In some cases, a business can negotiate favorable trade credit arrangements with its suppliers whereby the suppliers will not require payment until sixty or ninety days after a shipment is received. In addition, the business may be able to eliminate unnecessary expenses, reduce inventories, or improve inventory turnover. To conserve working capital, an entrepreneur may lease equipment rather than purchase it.

Sometimes a finance company will lend money even to a young company if it has current accounts receivable or readily salable inventory. The lender takes a security interest in the accounts receivable and inventory, which serve as collateral; the lender has a right to keep the collateral if the loan is not repaid. (Secured borrowing is discussed more fully in Chapter 12.) Although entrepreneurs have been known to fund start-ups with credit-card debt, that is rarely sufficient.

ADVANTAGES The main advantage of self-financing is that the entrepreneur does not have to share control or the equity of the business. For example, the contractual restrictions and affirmative covenants under an equipment lease may be less restrictive than the rights granted to holders of preferred stock. In addition, because no securities are offered or sold, an equipment lease does not require a disclosure document describing the company.

DISADVANTAGES Self-financing alone may not generate sufficient funds to cover salaries and other overhead expenses. Obtaining favorable trade credit terms is more difficult for a new enterprise than for an established business. Customers may object to making advance payments or deposits.

Experience shows that it is difficult to make self-financing work. Self-financing should be attempted only if the company's business plan contains realistic projections demonstrating that it can be done successfully.

Strategic Alliances and Joint Ventures

A less common source of financing is a collaborative arrangement with an established company that has complementary needs or objectives. In such a strategic alliance or joint venture, the parties commit themselves to sharing resources, facilities, or information, as well as the risks and rewards that may accrue from the alliance.

Strategic alliances can take many forms. A strategic alliance may be structured as a minority investment by the established company in the young company through the creation of a separate joint-venture entity. Alternatively, an established company may agree to fund a young company's research costs in return for the right to market or exploit the product or technology developed. If both parties are required to conduct extensive research, the alliance will often provide that the parties may cross-license each other's technology. With a strategic alliance, the parties generally must accept a substantial loss in autonomy, at least with respect to the project under joint development.

A strategic alliance may be used in any situation in which one party has an essential technology or resource that the other party does not have and cannot readily obtain. For example, if an undercapitalized company is developing a technology that has promising applications in an established company's business, the two companies may agree to collaborate. The established company may provide both financing and access to personnel, equipment, and certain preexisting and future technologies. The young company may correspondingly provide access to its personnel and its preexisting and future technologies.

ADVANTAGES A strategic alliance may provide a young company with less costly financing than a venture capital investor. This advantage is most pronounced when the established company anticipates some synergistic benefit to its existing business from exploiting the new technology. Not only does the young company often benefit from the more mature company's technical and marketing expertise, but it may earn more from the product through a strategic alliance than it would from a licensing agreement.

DISADVANTAGES One difficulty with almost any strategic alliance is that the two companies will have to cooperate and agree on the development and marketing of a product; this situation can give rise to management problems. The respective management teams may be unwilling to give up their autonomy to the extent necessary. Furthermore, because two parallel management groups will be trying to control the same personnel, it may be difficult to manage the alliance effectively without creating a supermanagement group.

Another problem with a strategic alliance is that each party may be liable for the other party's wrongdoing. For example, if one company supplies a technology that takes advantage of a third party's trade secret, the other company will be liable for its use of the misappropriated information, regardless of its intent. This risk can be reduced if each party makes certain representations and warranties, and enters into indemnity agreements, regarding the technology it will supply. The established company will usually want absolute representations and warranties concerning infringements of other parties' intellectual property rights. Nevertheless, it may be possible to get the established company to accept a qualified representation and warranty that "to the best of Party A's knowledge" there is no violation of others' intellectual property rights.

FROM THE TRENCHES

Noah's New York Bagels, Inc., a San Francisco Bay area bagel store chain, sold a 20 percent stake to Starbucks Coffee Co. in March 1995 for $11 million. The money was used to open another twenty-four stores.

The partial sale made sense for a number of reasons. Starbucks and Noah's were a good strategic fit. They shared the same clientele, and bagels and coffee are complementary rather than competitive products. At the time of the purchase, Starbucks and Noah's had two adjacent stores in two areas, with more side-by-side outlets under development. Finally, with the partial sale, Noah's could retain control and would not have to answer to any venture capitalists.

Source: Wendy Sheanin & Kenneth Howe, Starbucks Takes Bite of Noah's Bagels: Coffee Giant Buys Stake in Local Chain, S.F. CHRON. Mar. 7, 1995, at D1.

Strategic alliances also raise antitrust concerns, and experienced counsel should be consulted before talking with competitors or entering into a strategic alliance.

PITCHING TO INVESTORS

The Business Plan

A start-up's success in attracting funds is determined in part by the care and thought the entrepreneur demonstrates in preparing a business plan[1] and presenting it to potential investors. The entrepreneur and his or her colleagues must effectively communicate the nature of the company and its business, markets, and technology; the qualifications of the key members of the management team; the financial goals of the venture; the amount of capital required to achieve these goals; and, in detail, how the required capital will be spent. The business plan should also include such information as the potential market for the company's product, the competition, the barriers to entry, and any research-based projections. Preparation of a formal business plan will help the initial management team to focus its planning efforts and will offer its members the opportunity to discuss goals and set appropriate milestones. Once in place, the business plan will guide management and enable it to measure the company's progress.

Federal and state securities laws prohibit the sale of securities through the use of any misleading or inaccurate information, even if it is only in a business plan. As a result, when preparing the business plan, the entrepreneur should take care to include all material information about the company, its management, and the risks of the investment. The business plan should describe all of the assumptions on which its projections are based, and it should contain only those projections for which management has a reasonable basis. In addition to mentioning the strengths of the enterprise and its products, it is important to point out any material risks or weaknesses. For example, the product may still be in the development stage; there may be a shortage of a raw material or component required for its manufacture; or another company may produce or be able to produce a competing product. It is important to disclose such facts. Often the entrepreneurs are the only ones who really know these details, and they should volunteer such information to the lawyers or other persons preparing or reviewing the offering document.

Requirements of the Business Plan

Set forth below are many of the required components of a business plan. Chapter 13 includes a discussion of business plans prepared specifically for venture capitalists.

DESCRIBE THE COMPANY The business plan should contain a detailed description of the company and its history and goals. The plan should clearly point out the enterprise's limited history and the lack of assurance that the stated goals will be met. A clause similar to the following is sometimes used:

> *The Company is in the development stage and its proposed operations are subject to all of the risks inherent in the establishment of a new business enterprise, including the absence of an operating history. The likelihood of the Company's success must be considered in light of the*

problems, expenses, difficulties, complications, and delays frequently encountered in connection with the formation of a new business, and the competitive and regulatory environment in which the Company will operate. Although forecast revenues and expenses are set forth in this business plan, the actual amounts may vary substantially from those projected and no assurance can be made that the results forecast in this plan will be achieved.

This clause and other sample language in this chapter are for illustrative purposes only. Legal counsel should be consulted in connection with any offering of securities.

DESCRIBE THE PRODUCT AND THE MARKET The business plan should describe the market for the company's product, the technology behind it, how it differs from other products, and how and by whom it will be manufactured and marketed. The business plan should discuss the product's stage of development, the status of any patent or trademark applications, whether and by what means the enterprise has protected its rights to the underlying technology, and any known obstacles to production. A detailed description of the company's market research (if any) should also be included, with projected sales figures for an appropriate period and a discussion of the market for the product, its customer appeal, and competitive strategies. This description should be cautious and factual and should include appropriate disclaimers and information about competitors and competing products.

DISCUSS THE STRATEGIES AND WEAKNESSES OF THE MANAGEMENT TEAM The business plan should contain a detailed discussion of the strengths and the weaknesses of the management team and its members' responsibilities and track records. It should also describe the respective ownership interests of management in the enterprise, the price each person paid for his or her ownership interest, management's salaries and other remuneration, and any existing agreements between members of the management team and the enterprise. If the founders received equity in exchange for noncash consideration (such as rights to ideas or technology), that fact should be disclosed together with a statement about how the consideration was valued.

IDENTIFY THE RISKS The specific elements that make an investment in the enterprise speculative must be clearly stated. These factors may include the lack of operating history and the inexperience of management, as well as the undeveloped status of the company's product. A review of prospectuses prepared for public companies in the same industry (which are available on the Securities and Exchange Commission's EDGAR Web site) may help identify particular industry factors that make the investment risky. Full and prominent disclosure of risk factors can help reduce the likelihood of being sued later for fraud in connection with the sale of securities.

DESCRIBE THE COMPETITION The competition may consist of competing products, other producers of the same or a similar product, and even defensive measures that other producers might take in response to the company's proposed efforts. All of these should be described in detail.

AVOID UNSUPPORTED STATEMENTS It is essential to avoid including statements in the business plan for which there is no evidence. For example, an enterprise should not be referred to as "the only company" that produces an item unless there is tangible evidence to support such an assertion. Entrepreneurs should not refer to their company as "the largest" when it is impossible to be certain that it is the largest. Such statements may be reworded to refer to the enterprise as "one of the largest" or, better yet, to state the actual facts. For example, rather than referring to itself as the "largest owner of privately owned pay telephones in Florida," an enterprise could state the number of such phones it owns and the percentage of the total, citing an industry study as the source for the total.

PREPARE BACKUP FILE It is important to establish a backup or due diligence file that documents the basis for the statements made. For example, if an issuer's business plan states that the company owns the technology behind its product, someone should locate the actual patent or other source of those rights for the file.

FROM THE TRENCHES

One company thought that its founder owned the technology behind its proposed product because the founder had personally conducted the research that led to its discovery and development. The founder had even filed the patent application. In attempting to document the founder's ownership of the technology for potential investors, however, the company discovered that, under the terms of his prior employment contract, he had actually assigned those rights to his former employer. Discrepancies of this nature are best discovered before, rather than after, presenting a proposal to potential investors.

FURTHER REQUIREMENTS The business plan should describe the securities being offered and the intended use of the proceeds from the offering, including any commissions to be paid (for example, to a broker-dealer) for privately placing the securities. Any material litigation involving the issuer must also be disclosed. A supplement to the business plan should be prepared if there is any material change in the information in the plan.

The Private Placement Memorandum

The company seeking funding through the sale of securities may also be required to prepare an offering document (usually called a *private placement memorandum*) that meets the requirements of federal and state securities laws. Although the private placement memorandum is both a selling document and a disclosure document, its primary purpose is to disclose both the benefits and the risks of the investment. Consequently, the memorandum may not be as upbeat as the entrepreneur might like.

The content of the memorandum will be determined by the particular exemption from federal securities registration requirements applicable for the offering. Audited financial statements may be required for some offerings.

State securities laws may also influence the content and format of a private placement memorandum. Because laws requiring disclosure are technical in nature, the entrepreneur should always consult with an attorney before preparing the private placement memorandum and request that the attorney review drafts of it.

In many circumstances, a private placement memorandum is not technically required. Even if not required by the state or federal securities laws relating to the registration or qualification of securities, however, an issuer should disclose all material information and risks associated with the enterprise in a business plan or private placement memorandum. Under the antifraud provisions of the federal and state securities laws (which apply even to offerings exempt from registration, qualification, or any other requirement for approval by a federal or state authority), an issuer is liable if, in connection with the offer or sale of securities, it either makes an untrue statement of a material fact or makes a misleading statement by omitting a material fact. By explaining the company's business and management and the risks of the investment in writing in an offering document, the entrepreneur can avoid a swearing contest later in court about what oral statements were made to the investor.

Issues Related to Investment Securities

Many businesses operate as corporations because of their flexibility and limited liability. Greater discussion of the attributes of corporations can be found in Chapter 4. The investors in a corporation may own shares of one or more classes of stock, and they may have purchased certain debt securities.

Often the type of security to be issued will be determined by the investor. Most investors will desire to purchase preferred stock or some type of convertible debt instrument, such as a promissory note, that can be converted into stock. Some will want warrants (options to acquire stock) or at least a right of first refusal to purchase any new securities that may be issued by the company. Most investors will require the company to make extensive representations and warranties about itself, and many investments will be conditioned on certain corporate changes, such as expansion of the board of directors or the hiring or resignation of certain key persons.

Generally, investors have greater bargaining power than entrepreneurs because there are more start-ups competing for funds than investors looking for deals. Investors are also typically more familiar than entrepreneurs with the form and substance of a financing and the points that are open to negotiation. The percentage of voting power to be acquired by the investors and the price per share are based on the investors' valuation of the company. The extent of board representation granted to the investor, the type of security purchased, and the rights, preferences, privileges, and restrictions afforded to the securities to be purchased are all negotiable. Thus, the entrepreneur needs to know as much as possible about the way a financing works before commencing negotiations. In addition, the entrepreneur should identify the acceptable level of *dilution* (i.e., the amount by which the founders' percentage interest in the company will be reduced); learn the extent to which the principals desire to retain, or relinquish, management and control of the enterprise; identify those persons who will be directors and officers of the corporation; and designate the corporation's accountants, lawyers, bankers, and public relations consultants.

After the founders and investors reach agreement on the terms of the securities and the investment, these terms are memorialized in a term sheet. The *term sheet* allows the parties to agree on the principal terms of the investment before the lawyers proceed to draft a stock purchase agreement and any necessary amendment to the corporate charter.

Equity Financing

CLASSES OF STOCK If all shares of stock have the same rights, then there is only one class of stock, known as *common stock*. If the issuer wishes to give all of the investors the same rights and restrictions, the company should issue only common stock. In this case, the number of votes per share, the shareholders' rights to vote on various decisions, the dividends to shareholders, and their rights to the corporate assets if the corporation is liquidated will be the same on a share-by-share basis for all shareholders.

Many start-up companies issue shares of common stock to their founders. Subsequent investors, however, often require additional rights, such as the right to elect a certain number of directors, the right to approve major corporate changes, and the right to priority of payment if the corporation is liquidated. Such additional rights can be provided by amending the corporation's certificate of incorporation to authorize a second class of stock, called *preferred stock*.

Venture capital firms and institutional investors commonly invest in start-up companies by purchasing *convertible preferred stock,* that is, preferred stock that may be converted into common stock at a specified exchange ratio. In the typical case, outside investors will purchase preferred shares for cash after the company's founders have received shares of common stock in exchange for services, for transferring their rights to technology to the new enterprise, and for modest amounts of cash. Issuing convertible preferred stock to outside investors can create a tax advantage for the founders.

As explained in Chapter 5, a person, such as a founder, who receives stock in exchange for services to the corporation is required to pay income tax on the difference between the fair market value of the stock and the price he or she pays for it. By issuing preferred stock to investors, the founders can argue that they paid less per share than the investors paid because they bought common stock with no special advantages, whereas the investors bought preferred stock with valuable additional rights and protections.

WARRANTS A *warrant* is a right, for a given period of time, to purchase a stated amount of stock at a stated price. The price is often equal to the fair market value of the stock when the warrant is issued, permitting its holder to benefit from any increase in the value of the securities. A warrant differs from a stock option only in that options are granted to the company's employees, whereas warrants are sold to investors. If used in an initial financing, warrants typically will be issued to purchase lower-priced common stock in conjunction with the investor's purchase of higher-priced preferred stock. The warrant in this situation is sometimes called an *equity sweetener* because, if exercised, it lowers the investor's average price paid per share.

EMPLOYEE COMPENSATION PLANS Many start-up companies find it desirable to have an equity compensation plan, usually in the form of a stock option plan, to attract key technical and executive personnel. Such a plan can be a very significant component of employee compensation because the company's stock will appreciate if the company is successful. Employee stock plans are explained further in Chapter 10. Because the equity compensation plan will have tax consequences, legal counsel should be consulted before implementing such a plan.

Rights of Holders of Preferred Stock

State laws impose few requirements on the creation of preferred stock. California law, for example, requires either a dividend preference or a liquidation preference over common shares, without any requirement as to the type of dividend (cumulative or noncumulative) or the amount of the dividend or liquidation preference. Convertible preferred stock gives investors various rights that, depending on the circumstances and the bargaining positions of the parties, may be structured differently in each transaction. (The various rights associated with preferred stock are discussed in detail in Chapter 13.)

LIQUIDATION PREFERENCE If the corporation is liquidated, any assets remaining after payment of all debts and obligations are distributed first to the holders of preferred stock and then to the holders of common stock. Investors buying preferred stock often will require a liquidation preference in an amount at least equal to their original investment plus all accrued and unpaid dividends.

DIVIDEND PREFERENCE Holders of preferred stock are often entitled to a dividend preference, which means that a specified amount of dividends must be paid to holders of the preferred shares before any dividends may be paid on the common shares. These dividend rights are often *cumulative*; in that case, amounts not paid in one year are added to the amounts that must be paid in the following years before any dividends may be paid to common shareholders.

PARTICIPATING PREFERRED Some investors will demand *participating preferred stock*. This entitles them to receive their liquidation preference plus any accrued dividends and then to share the remaining sale proceeds pro rata with the common shareholders as if they had converted their preferred stock into common.

REDEMPTION RIGHTS Redemption occurs when the corporation buys back shares from a shareholder. *Voluntary redemption* rights permit the investor to require the corporation to redeem his or her shares for cash at a specified price, provided that the corporation is not prohibited by law from buying back stock or making distributions to its shareholders. To protect creditors and preferred shareholders against dissipation of corporate assets, the corporation codes of many states, including California, prohibit distributions to shareholders unless the corporation is able to meet certain specified financial tests, often based on retained earnings. Thus, unless a corporation is able to meet such tests, it may be unable to pay a dividend or redeem any of its outstanding shares.

Involuntary redemption rights permit the corporation, at its option, to redeem the shares for a specified price either after a given period of time or upon the occurrence of certain events. This right may have the effect of forcing the investor to convert the shares to common stock to avoid redemption. By forcing conversion, the corporation can eliminate the liquidation and dividend preferences of the preferred stock. Accrued but unpaid dividends, however, generally must be paid upon conversion. In addition, automatic conversion may be triggered by specified events, such as an initial public offering or the company's achievement of stated milestones. The specific events resulting in automatic conversion are a subject of negotiation between the issuer and the investor.

CONVERSION RIGHTS Holders of preferred stock normally have the right to convert their preferred stock into common stock at any time. The preferred stock is usually automatically converted into common stock when the company does an initial public offering. Sometimes conversion can also be required upon the vote of a majority or supermajority of the preferred stock.

ANTIDILUTION PROVISIONS Antidilution provisions adjust the conversion prices at which convertible preferred shares may be exchanged for shares of common stock in the event of certain actions taken by the corporation. *Structural antidilution provisions* come into play when the corporation undergoes structural changes such as stock splits and stock dividends. An antidilution provision can protect against either percentage dilution or the economic dilution of the investor's interest.

Investors in an early-stage start-up are typically looking for protection against percentage dilution. This protection assures the holders of convertible preferred stock that they can exchange their shares for the same percentage of the total common stock after the dilution event as they would have received before the dilution occurred.

In addition to protecting against structural dilution, many investors demand some kind of *price antidilution provision* that is triggered if the corporation issues additional common or preferred shares at a price less than the *conversion price* (typically the per-share price paid by the investor). There are two main types of price antidilution provisions: the ratchet method and the weighted-average method. The *ratchet method* is onerous from the company's point of view because, in the event of a dilutive financing, the conversion price of the protected stock is adjusted downward to the issuance price of the dilutive financing. The *weighted-average method* reduces the conversion price in proportion to the amount that the new, lower-cost stock dilutes the total amount of stock outstanding. Sometimes the company will insist on *pay-to-play provisions,* which require the investors to participate pro rata in certain subsequent financings to retain antidilution protection for their shares.

VOTING RIGHTS Holders of preferred stock usually are entitled to voting rights equal to those of common shareholders and, in addition, are entitled (1) to vote as a separate class on major corporate events, such as amending the corporate charter or selling substantially all of the corporation's assets, and (2) to elect certain members of the board without input from common shareholders. Under the laws of most states, any special voting rights afforded to holders of a class of stock are effective only if they are specified in the corporation's charter.

CHARTER AMENDMENT The rights of the holders of preferred stock must be set forth in detail in the corporate charter. If the certificate of incorporation provides for a class of blank-check preferred stock, then the directors must set out the rights, preferences, and privileges of the securities in a document—often called the *certificate of determination*—that is filed with the secretary of state in the state where the corporation was incorporated. If preferred shares are not authorized, then the certificate of incorporation must be amended to authorize a class of preferred stock with specified rights, preferences, and privileges.

The Stock Purchase Agreement

Investments in shares are governed by a stock purchase agreement signed by the company and the investors. The first draft of the agreement is usually prepared by the company's lawyers after the parties have negotiated the basic terms and reduced them to a term sheet.

DESCRIPTION OF SECURITY The typical stock purchase agreement will begin with provisions concerning the type of security to be purchased, the purchase price per share, the number of shares to be purchased, and the expected date of purchase (the *closing date*).

REPRESENTATIONS AND WARRANTIES The company, and usually the founders as well, will be required to make extensive representations and warranties about such things as the business, financial, and legal condition of the company. Any exceptions to the representations and warranties are listed on a schedule of exceptions attached to the stock purchase agreement. The founders should review the representations and warranties carefully and ensure that the schedule of exceptions accurately states all respects in which the true state of affairs differs from that stated in the standard representations and warranties. Otherwise the company, and perhaps the founders, could be liable for damages to the investors if a representation made in the stock purchase agreement turns out not to have been completely true.

CONDITIONS TO CLOSING The investors' *conditions to closing* are events that must take place before the investors will go forward with the deal, such as an amendment of the corporate charter to authorize the additional class of securities to be purchased or an amendment of the bylaws to provide for an expanded board of directors. The conditions will often include items related to the operation of the business, such as employment contracts (with assignment-of-inventions and confidentiality clauses) with key employees; sometimes the resignation of certain key people is also required. Usually, a legal opinion from the company's counsel is required. If the investment will be made by several persons or entities, a common condition is that a specified minimum amount of capital must be raised.

COVENANTS The typical preferred stock purchase agreement will contain both affirmative and negative covenants on the part of the company. An *affirmative covenant* is a promise to do something; a *negative covenant* is a promise to refrain from doing something. These covenants often remain in effect as long as a substantial portion, such as 25 percent or more, of the securities purchased by the investors remains outstanding. Affirmative covenants may include promises by the company to pay its debts, to meet its obligations under contracts with third parties, to keep its assets in good condition, to deliver specified financial information on a regular basis to the investors, to maintain a certain minimum net worth, and to meet other stated financial tests. Such provisions contractually bind the company to do these things; if it does not, the investors can sue for breach of contract.

Negative covenants may include promises not to increase top management's salaries, to make loans to affiliated persons or entities, to make substantial changes in the company's business, to borrow amounts above a stated level, or to enter into contracts outside the ordinary course of business without the consent of the investors.

INVESTORS' RIGHTS The stock purchase agreement may provide for one or more investor representatives to sit on the board of directors. It may grant the investors a right to participate in future rounds of financing. It may also grant them the right to impose certain controls and restrictions on the company.

Investors make investments in anticipation that the company will appreciate in value and provide an exit vehicle that will enable them to realize that appreciation. Consequently, some investors will require a *right of co-sale,* which means that if one of the founders sells any of his or her shares, the investor is entitled to participate pro rata as a seller. This right protects an investor from being left with an investment in a company whose founders have sold out. (Co-sale agreements are discussed generally in Chapter 5 and in the context of venture capital financings in Chapter 13.)

The stock purchase agreement may also impose obligations on the founder or employees. For example, an officer who is a minority shareholder may be obliged to sell his or her shares to the majority shareholder upon termination of employment.

The stock purchase agreement will frequently grant the investors *registration rights,* that is, the right to require the company to register, under applicable federal and state securities laws, the shares of common stock into which the preferred stock is convertible. These rights permit the investors to sell their stock in a public offering.

INVESTORS' REPRESENTATIONS The stock purchase agreement will contain representations by the investors that the securities are being purchased for investment and not with a view to further distribution. This requirement is necessary for the securities to be exempt from federal and state registration or qualification requirements, which are discussed further below.

FEDERAL SECURITIES REGISTRATION REQUIREMENTS AND EXEMPTIONS

The Securities Act of 1933 (the 1933 Act) was adopted during the Great Depression. In adopting the 1933 Act, Congress sought to give purchasers of securities adequate information relating to the issuer and the offering. The Act requires that promoters of securities offerings register them with the Securities and Exchange Commission (SEC), an agency of the U.S. government, and provide prospective purchasers with a prospectus containing material information about the issuer and the offering, unless the security or the type of transaction is exempt from registration.

Because registered public offerings are very expensive (often costing more than $900,000), sales of securities to private investors or venture capitalists are almost always structured to be exempt from the federal registration requirements. An offering of securities may be exempt if it is a private offering, a limited offering (not more than $5 million), an offering to qualified investors, or an offering confined to a single state. These exemptions are quite technical in nature, and failure to comply can have disastrous consequences. Each purchaser in the offering would have a right to *rescind* (undo) the purchase and get his or her money back or to recover damages. Even if an offering is exempt from registration under the federal securities laws, state securities laws (*Blue Sky laws*) may impose their own registration or qualification requirements.

As noted earlier, even exempt transactions are subject to federal and state antifraud rules. For example, Rule 10b-5 under the Securities Exchange Act of 1934 (the 1934 Act) imposes liability if, in connection with the sale of securities, the issuer makes an untrue statement of a material fact or makes a misleading statement by omitting a material fact. Because federal and state registration requirements and antifraud rules are complicated and subject to strict limitations, it is strongly suggested that the entrepreneur consult with an attorney before soliciting funds.

Private Offerings

Section 4(2) of the 1933 Act provides an exemption for private offerings. In a *private offering* (also called a *private placement*), the securities are offered only to selected qualified investors who can understand and bear the risk of the investment. A private offering can be consummated more quickly and much less expensively than a public offering. To qualify as a private offering, however, the issuer must be able to prove that all offerees, even those that do not eventually purchase the securities, had the ability to comprehend and bear the risk of the investment. This proof requires a pre-offering qualification through an offeree questionnaire that includes questions about the potential offeree's education, investment experience, and financial situation.

Regulation D: Safe-Harbor Exemptions

Regulation D, promulgated by the SEC, provides greater certainty to companies seeking to do private placements by offering them very specific safe-harbor exemptions from registration. An issuer that fails to comply with all the requirements of the applicable rule may still qualify for an exemption if the transaction meets the more burdensome conditions of Section 4(2).

Regulation D contains three separate exemptions from registration. These exemptions are outlined in Rules 504, 505, and 506.

ACCREDITED INVESTORS A key element of Regulation D is the concept of an accredited investor. Offerings to accredited investors are exempted from the registration requirements on the theory that certain investors are so financially sophisticated that they do not need all of the protections afforded by the securities laws.

Rule 501 defines an *accredited investor* as any one of the following:

1. Any national bank.
2. Any private business development company.
3. Any corporation, business trust, partnership (not formed for the purpose of acquiring the offered securities), or charitable organization with total assets in excess of $5 million.
4. Any director, executive officer, or general partner of the issuer.
5. Any natural person who had individual income in excess of $200,000 in each of the two most recent years, or joint income with that person's spouse in excess of $300,000 in each of those years, and who has a reasonable expectation of reaching the same income level in the current year.
6. Any natural person whose individual net worth, or joint net worth with that person's spouse, at the time of the purchase exceeds $1 million.
7. Any trust with total assets in excess of $5 million, not formed for the specific purpose of acquiring the securities offered, whose purchase is directed by a financially sophisticated person.
8. Any entity in which all of the equity owners are accredited investors.

INTEGRATION OF OFFERINGS In calculating the amount raised in a twelve-month period and the number of unaccredited investors, the SEC may combine (*integrate*) certain sales made within a limited period of time; that is, it may deem them to be part of a single sale. This is most likely to happen when the offerings (1) are part of a single plan of financing, (2) are made at or about the same time, (3) involve the same type of consideration and class of security, and (4) are made for the same purpose.

Rule 502(a) provides an integration safe harbor for Regulation D offerings. Offers and sales made more than six months before the start of a Regulation D offering or more than six months after its completion are not considered part of the Regulation D offering, as long as there are no offers or sales of a similar class of securities during those six-month periods. Offerings to employees and others under Rule 701 (discussed later) are not integrated with offerings under Regulation D.

RULE 504: OFFERINGS UP TO $1 MILLION Rule 504 exempts offerings of up to $1 million within a twelve-month period. There is no limit on the number of purchasers, and general solicitation is permitted. Rule 504 is not available to issuers registered under the 1934 Act—known as public reporting companies—or to investment companies such as mutual funds. It is also not available to *blank-check companies*—those that have no specific business except to locate and acquire a currently unknown business.

Because even unsophisticated purchasers can participate in a Rule 504 offering, and there is no prescribed information disclosure requirement, Rule 504 is the exemption most frequently relied on for the sale of securities to the founders and other investors in the initial round of financing. The issuer must file a notice on Form D with the SEC within fifteen days of the first sale of securities.

Because Rule 504 can be used to exempt only $1 million in any twelve-month period, companies must be particularly careful to avoid integration problems. When possible, it is best to take advantage of the SEC's integration safe harbor by refraining from making any offers or sales for six months before and after the Rule 504 offering that, if integrated with the offering under Rule 504, would cause the total offered in any twelve-month period to exceed $1 million.

RULE 505: OFFERINGS UP TO $5 MILLION Rule 505 exempts offerings of up to $5 million within a twelve-month period and limits the number of unaccredited investors to no more than thirty-five. There is no limit on the number of accredited investors. General solicitations and advertising are not permitted in connection with a Rule 505 offering, and the issuer must reasonably believe that there are not more than thirty-five unaccredited investors. Rule 505 is not available to investment companies.

Rule 505 requires that certain specified information (including audited financial statements) be provided to all purchasers (unless all are accredited investors). This information is generally compiled in a private placement memorandum, which should be prepared with the assistance of experienced securities counsel. Rule 505 also requires that purchasers have the opportunity to ask questions and receive answers concerning the terms of the offering. A notice on Form D must be filed with the SEC within fifteen days of the first sale of securities.

RULE 506: UNLIMITED NUMBER OF ACCREDITED INVESTORS AND LIMITED NUMBER OF SOPHISTICATED INVESTORS Rule 506 exempts offerings of any amount to not more than thirty-five unaccredited investors, provided that the issuer reasonably believes immediately prior to making any sale that each investor, either alone or with his or her purchaser representative, has enough business experience to evaluate the merits and risks of the prospective investment (that is, the investor is *sophisticated*). There can be an unlimited number of accredited investors. However, general solicitations and advertising are not permitted in connection with a Rule 506 offering.

Like Rule 505, Rule 506 requires that certain specified information be provided to purchasers (unless all purchasers are accredited investors) and that purchasers have the opportunity to ask questions and receive answers concerning the terms of the offering. Because Rule 506 does not require a complicated offering document if sales are made only to accredited investors and it permits sales in excess of $5 million, it is the exemption most commonly relied on in venture capital financings. A notice on Form D must be filed with the SEC within fifteen days of the first sale of securities.

Intrastate Offerings

Section 3(a)(11) exempts securities offered and sold by an issuer if the issuer and the offerees and purchasers are residents of the same state. The issuer must be domiciled in and doing business in the state in which all of the offers and sales are made.

The issuer must place a legend on the stock certificate stating that the securities have not been registered and cannot be resold for nine months to a nonresident of the state. In addition, the issuer must obtain a written representation from each purchaser indicating his or her residence.

Regulation A

Under Regulation A, a privately held U.S. or Canadian company may offer and sell up to $5 million in a twelve-month period; $1.5 million of the $5 million may be sold by selling security holders. Investment companies, blank-check companies, companies issuing oil, gas, or mineral rights, and companies whose owners have violated the securities laws (designated "bad boys" under Rule 262) cannot rely on Regulation A.

FROM THE TRENCHES

In 1995, Spring Street Brewing Co., a New York–based microbrewer, raised $1.6 million in an offering of shares on the Internet—without incurring the investment banking fees that would normally be paid to the underwriters in a public offering. The company relied on Regulation A and qualified the offering in eighteen states and the District of Columbia. The company could not rely on Rule 505 because the posting of an offer to sell securities on the Internet is an advertisement, which is prohibited under Rule 505.

Source: Constance E. Bagley & John Arledge, SEC Could Ease Offering of Securities Via the Web, 19 NAT'L L.J. B9 (Jan. 13, 1997).

The issuer must file a disclosure document with the SEC and have it qualified before securities are sold.

A testing-the-waters provision permits issuers to solicit indications of interest before filing any required disclosure documents. The issuer need only file a solicitation-of-interest document with the SEC, along with copies of any written or broadcast media ads. There is no prohibition on general solicitation or advertising. Radio and television broadcasts and newspaper ads are permitted to determine investor interest in the offering.

However, no sales can be made or payment received during the testing-the-waters period until after the company has filed Form 1-A with the SEC and the offering statement has been qualified by the SEC. Once the Regulation A offering statement is filed, testing-the-waters activity must cease. In addition, there is a twenty-day waiting period from the time of the last solicitation of interest, during which no sales can be made.

Rule 701: Offerings to Employees

Rule 701 exempts offers and sales of securities by privately held companies (1) pursuant to a written compensatory benefit plan for employees, directors, general partners, trustees (if the issuer is a business trust), officers, consultants, or advisers; or (2) pursuant to a written contract relating to the compensation of such persons. If the benefit plan is for consultants or advisers, they must render bona fide services not connected with the offer and sale of securities in a capital-raising transaction. Exempt compensatory benefit plans include purchase, savings, option, bonus, stock appreciation, profit-sharing, thrift incentive, and pension plans. The issuer must provide each plan participant with a copy of the plan and each contractor with a copy of his or her contract, but no other disclosure document is required by Rule 701.

Rule 701 applies only to securities offered and sold during a twelve-month period in an amount not more than the greater of (1) $1,000,000, (2) 15 percent of the total assets of the issuer, or (3) 15 percent of the outstanding securities of the class being offered and sold. A Form 701 must be filed not later than thirty days after the first sale that brings the aggregate sales under Rule 701 above $100,000, and thereafter a Form 701 must be filed annually within thirty days following the end of the issuer's fiscal year.

Shares issued under Rule 701 can be sold to the public without registration ninety days after the company goes public, without regard to the normal one-year holding period requirement of Rule 144, provided that the seller is not an officer, director, or 10 percent shareholder of the company.

The federal exemptions are summarized in Exhibit 7.1.

Blue Sky Laws

A company offering securities must comply not only with the federal securities laws but with the securities laws of all the states in which the securities are offered or sold. In particular, any offer of securities must be qualified or exempt from qualification in the state where the company is headquartered (and, if different, the state from which the offers are made) and in each state where any of the offerees lives or is headquartered.

If the offer is posted on a Web site, then it is deemed to be made in all fifty states, the District of Columbia, and Puerto Rico. However, several states exempt such an offering from qualification in that state if (1) the offer expressly provides that it is not available to residents of that state and (2) in fact, no sales are made to residents of that state.

Fortunately, many states, the District of Columbia, and Puerto Rico have adopted the Uniform Securities Act, thereby creating some consistency among state laws. Other states, including California, have retained their own securities regulatory schemes.

Like the federal statutes, the Uniform Securities Act emphasizes disclosure as the primary means of protecting investors. However, some states authorize the securities administrator to deny a securities selling permit unless he or she finds that the issuer's plan of business and the proposed issuance of securities are fair, just, and equitable. Even if the state statute does not contain a specific provision to this effect, a state securities commissioner can usually deny registration until he or she is satisfied that the offering is fair. This process is referred to as *merit review.*

EXHIBIT 7.1

KEY ELEMENTS OF CERTAIN FEDERAL EXEMPTIONS FROM REGISTRATION

Type of Exemption	Dollar Limit of the Offering	Limits on the Purchasers	Purchaser Qualifications	Issuer Qualifications
Section 4(2)	No limit	Generally limited to a small number of offerees able to understand and bear risk	Offerees and purchasers must have access to information and be sophisticated investors.	No limitations
Regulation D[a]				
Rule 504[b]	$1 million in 12 months	No limit	No requirements	Not a 1934 Act public reporting company, an investment company, or a blank-check company
Rule 505[c]	$5 million in 12 months	No limit on the number of accredited investors but limited to 35 unaccredited investors	No requirements for unaccredited investors	Not an investment company
Rule 506[c]	No limit	No limit on the number of accredited investors but limited to 35 unaccredited investors	Unaccredited investors must be sophisticated, that is, have sufficient knowledge and experience in financial matters to evaluate the investment.	No limitations

continued...

EXHIBIT 7.1 (CONTINUED)

KEY ELEMENTS OF CERTAIN FEDERAL EXEMPTIONS FROM REGISTRATION

Type of Exemption	Dollar Limit of the Offering	Limits on the Purchasers	Purchaser Qualifications	Issuer Qualifications
Regulation A[d]	$5 million in 12 months, with a maximum of $1.5 million sold by selling security holders	No limit	No requirements	A U.S. or Canadian company, but not a 1934 Act public reporting company, an investment company, a blank-check company, a company issuing oil/gas/mineral rights, or a company disqualified under "bad boy" provisions of Rule 262
Rule 701[e,f]	The greater of $1,000,000 or 15% of the total assets of the issuer or 15% of the outstanding securities of the same class	No limit on the number of employees, directors, general partners, officers, advisers, and consultants	Advisory and consulting services must not be connected with the offer and sale of securities in a capital-raising transaction.	Not a 1934 Act public reporting company or an investment company

a. All issuers relying on these exemptions are required to file notice on Form D with the SEC within fifteen days of the first sale of securities. In addition, for offerings under Rule 505 and Rule 506, solicitations, advertising, and the provision of information are limited.
b. This exemption does not depend on the use of any type of disclosure document.
c. A disclosure document meeting the specified SEC requirements is mandatory if there are any unaccredited investors.
d. The issuer must file a disclosure document with the SEC and have it qualified before securities are sold. Testing the waters is permitted after a solicitation-of-interest document is filed with the SEC.
e. All issuers relying on this exemption must file Form 701 with the SEC within thirty days of the sale of more than $100,000 worth of securities, and annually thereafter. Additional disclosure required if sales exceed $5 million in a 12-month period.
f. Must be pursuant to written compensatory benefit plans or written contracts relating to compensation.

Ignorance of these laws is no excuse. As Judge Easterbrook explained: "No one with half a brain can offer 'an opportunity to invest in our company' without knowing that there is a regulatory jungle out there."[2]

The Capital Markets Efficiency Act of 1996 limits the states' right to regulate certain securities offerings. In the case of offerings exempt pursuant to Rule 506 under Regulation D, states are permitted to require only the type of filing required by the SEC, a consent to service of process, and a filing fee. Accordingly, all pre-offer and pre-sale notice filings and merit review requirements of the states have been preempted in connection with Rule 506 offerings. The law similarly preempts state registration requirements and merit review in connection with most initial public offerings registered with the SEC. The law also provides federal preemption for the issuance of securities to "qualified purchasers," a category of investors to be defined by the SEC at a later time. The Securities Litigation Uniform Standard Act of 1998 limits a shareholder's right to bring a securities fraud case involving a public company traded on a national securities exchange in state court and generally preempts the application of state antifraud laws in such cases.

Exhibit 7.2 outlines some of the main limited-offering exemptions available to entrepreneurs in California, Connecticut, Massachusetts, New York, and Texas. Factors to consider when relying on these exemptions include the number of offerees or purchasers, the type of persons who can be solicited, the time period of the offering, the manner of the offering, the aggregate amount of the offering, the types of securities sold or excluded, notice requirements, and the exemption for offerings coordinated with Regulation D of the Securities Act of 1933. Most of these exemptions are subject to many limitations and requirements, described at greater length in the Blue Sky statutes, regulations, statements of policy, advisories, and interpretations, so an issuer should consult with securities counsel before relying on any exemption.

EXHIBIT 7.2

LIMITED-OFFERING EXEMPTIONS AVAILABLE IN CALIFORNIA, CONNECTICUT, MASSACHUSETTS, NEW YORK, AND TEXAS

State	Exemption	Maximum Number of Purchasers and/or Offerees	Exemption Highlights
CA	Limited-offering exemption: small offers or sales of any security[a]	Sales to no more than 35 persons, inside or outside California[b]	• All offerees must either have a preexisting personal or business relationship with the offeror or any of its partners, officers, directors, controlling persons, or managers (as appointed or elected by the members if the offeror is a limited liability company) or be persons who could be reasonably assumed to have the business and financial experience necessary to protect their own interests in connection with the transaction.[c] • Offer or sale may not be accomplished by the publication of any advertisement.[d] • Each purchaser must be purchasing for the purchaser's own account (or a trust account if the purchaser is a trustee) and not with a view to or sale in connection with any distribution of the security. • Certain individuals are excluded from the count: individuals whose net worth exceeds $1 million, whose individual income exceeds $200,000 per year, whose joint income with their spouse exceeds $300,000 per year, or who purchased $150,000 more of the securities offered in the transaction.[e] • Other excluded categories include: officers, directors, promoters, or affiliates of the issuer, banks, and some other financial institutions.

continued...

EXHIBIT 7.2 (CONTINUED)

LIMITED-OFFERING EXEMPTIONS AVAILABLE IN CALIFORNIA, CONNECTICUT, MASSACHUSETTS, NEW YORK, AND TEXAS

State	Exemption	Maximum Number of Purchasers and/or Offerees	Exemption Highlights
CA	Offers or sales solely to qualified purchasers	No limit on number but can sell only to qualified purchasers (as defined)	• Issuer must be a California business entity (including a partnership) or corporation (or a foreign corporation with more than half of its shares held by persons in California and its business centered in California). • A written general announcement of the proposed offering may be published, but no securities may be sold to any natural persons until a disclosure statement meeting the requirements of Regulation D is provided to the prospective purchasers. • Each purchaser must be purchasing for the purchaser's own account (or a trust account if the purchaser is a trustee) and not with a view to or sale in connection with any distribution of the security. • Notice of transaction must be filed with the Commissioner of Corporations concurrently with the publication of a general announcement of a proposed offering or at the time of the initial offer of securities, whichever occurs first. A second filing must be made within ten days of the close of the offering but no later than 210 days from the date of the initial filing. Failure to file the notices precludes one from using the exemption.

continued...

EXHIBIT 7.2 (CONTINUED)

LIMITED-OFFERING EXEMPTIONS AVAILABLE IN CALIFORNIA, CONNECTICUT, MASSACHUSETTS, NEW YORK, AND TEXAS

State	Exemption	Maximum Number of Purchasers and/or Offerees	Exemption Highlights
CA	Offers or sales of voting common stock by a corporation	Sales to no more than 35 persons total[b]	• After sale and issuance, there can be only one class of the corporation's stock outstanding, which is owned beneficially by not more than 35 people. • No promotional payments or selling expenses can be paid in connection with the sale or offering.[f] • Offer or sale may not be accomplished by publication of any advertisement.[d] • Each purchaser must be purchasing for purchaser's own account, and not with a view to or sale in connection with any distribution of the security. • A notice signed by an active member of the State Bar of California must be filed not later than ten days after receipt of payment for the stock.
CT	Limited offering	Sales to no more than ten purchasers	A non-Regulation D sale by the issuer to not more than ten purchasers of all securities of the issuer provided that[b]: • No advertisement or general solicitation is used to procure the sale. • No commissions are paid.[f] • Total expenses do not exceed 10% of the total sales price.

continued...

EXHIBIT 7.2 (CONTINUED)

LIMITED-OFFERING EXEMPTIONS AVAILABLE IN CALIFORNIA, CONNECTICUT, MASSACHUSETTS, NEW YORK, AND TEXAS

State	Exemption	Maximum Number of Purchasers and/or Offerees	Exemption Highlights
CT	Connecticut uniform limited-offering exemption: Regulation D, Rule 504[a]	Total of nonaccredited investors in Connecticut cannot exceed 35	If the transaction is exempt from federal registration in reliance on Rule 504, it is exempted under Connecticut law provided that: • Each offeree is given a written disclosure statement. • Commission, discount, or other remuneration in connection with the sale does not exceed 15% of the initial offering price.[g] • A pre-offering notice is filed.
CT	Connecticut uniform limited-offering exemption: Regulation D, Rule 505 or Rule 506[a]	No limit on the number of accredited investors, but no more than 35 nonaccredited investors	If the transaction is exempt from federal registration in reliance on Rule 505 or Rule 506, it is exempted under Connecticut law provided that: • If issuer sells to any nonaccredited investor, then the disclosure requirements of Rule 502 apply to all purchasers in Connecticut regardless of their accreditation. • Commission, discount, or other remuneration in connection with the sale cannot exceed 15% of the initial offering price.[g] • A pre-offering notice must be filed for Rule 505 transactions.
CT	Accredited investor offering	Unlimited sales to accredited investors	• Each purchaser must be purchasing for purchaser's own account, and not with a view to or sale in connection with any distribution of the security. • A general announcement is required.

continued...

EXHIBIT 7.2 (CONTINUED)

LIMITED-OFFERING EXEMPTIONS AVAILABLE IN CALIFORNIA, CONNECTICUT, MASSACHUSETTS, NEW YORK, AND TEXAS

State	Exemption	Maximum Number of Purchasers and/or Offerees	Exemption Highlights
			• Solicitation is permitted if directed solely to accredited investors. • Notice filing required along with general announcement.
MA	Limited-offering exemption	25 nonexcluded offerees within a 12-month period[b,h]	• Excluded categories: certain investment entities with assets in excess of $5 million, banks, non-profit corporations, and other financial institutions • Only offers that are part of the same offering will be counted in the 25-purchaser total.[b,h] • Offer or sale may not be accomplished by the publication of any advertisement.[d] • The seller must reasonably believe that all buyers in Massachusetts are purchasing for investment purposes. • Requires notice to the Secretary of the Commonwealth if there is any commission or other remuneration involved in the solicitation of the transaction, and registration of such person as a broker-dealer or an agent in the state. Failure to file the notice within ten days prior to receipt of any consideration or the delivery of a subscription agreement may preclude one from using the exemption.
NY	General limited-offering exemption	No more than 40 offerees wherever located[b]	• Requires a pre-offering written offering statement (unless sales are to accredited investors only) and a notification filing.

continued...

EXHIBIT 7.2 (CONTINUED)

LIMITED-OFFERING EXEMPTIONS AVAILABLE IN CALIFORNIA, CONNECTICUT, MASSACHUSETTS, NEW YORK, AND TEXAS

State	Exemption	Maximum Number of Purchasers and/or Offerees	Exemption Highlights
NY	Offerings exempt from federal provisions	No limit	• Transactions that are exempt from the federal provisions because they are New York intrastate offerings are excluded from this exemption.
TX	General limited-offering exemption: a sale of any security by the issuer	Total number of security holders cannot exceed 35 within a 12-month period.	• No advertising may be published in connection with the transaction.[d] • The issuer must reasonably believe purchasers are either sophisticated, well-informed investors who can protect themselves or well-informed investors who have a relationship with the issuer such that there is trust between the two parties.[c] • Each purchaser must be purchasing for investment.
TX	General limited-offering exemption: a sale of any security by issuer	Sales cannot exceed 15 purchasers everywhere within a 12-month period, excluding purchasers who are purchasing securities under other exemptions.[b]	• No advertising may be published in connection with the transaction.[d] • The issuer must reasonably believe purchasers are either sophisticated, well-informed investors who can protect themselves or well-informed investors who have a relationship with the issuer such that there is trust between the two parties.[c] • Buyers must be purchasing securities for their own account and not with a view to distributing the security.

continued...

EXHIBIT 7.2 (CONTINUED)

LIMITED-OFFERING EXEMPTIONS AVAILABLE IN CALIFORNIA, CONNECTICUT, MASSACHUSETTS, NEW YORK, AND TEXAS

State	Exemption	Maximum Number of Purchasers and/or Offerees	Exemption Highlights
TX	Limited-offering exemption: Rule 505 or Rule 506[a]	Unlimited number of purchasers, but dollar amount limited by Rule 505 or Rule 506	If the transaction is exempt from federal registration in reliance on Rule 505 or Rule 506, it is exempt under Texas law provided that: • No advertising may be published in connection with the transaction.[d] • The issuer must reasonably believe purchasers are either sophisticated, well-informed investors who can protect themselves or well-informed investors who have a relationship with the issuer such that there is trust between the two parties.[c] • Buyers must be purchasing securities for their own account and not with a view to distributing the security. • No commissions may be paid. • Notice must be filed.
TX	Intrastate limited-offering exemption	Not more than 35 new security holders who became security holders during the 12-month period ending with the date of sale[a]	• All offers and sales must be pursuant to an offering made and completed solely within the state of Texas. • No advertising may be published in connection with the transaction.[d] • The 35 new security holders must be either sophisticated, well-informed investors who can protect themselves or well-informed investors who have a relationship with the issuer such that there is trust between the two parties.[c]

continued...

EXHIBIT 7.2 (CONTINUED)

LIMITED-OFFERING EXEMPTIONS AVAILABLE IN CALIFORNIA, CONNECTICUT, MASSACHUSETTS, NEW YORK, AND TEXAS

State	Exemption	Maximum Number of Purchasers and/or Offerees	Exemption Highlights
			• Sales may be made to other well-informed, accredited investors, bringing the total number of security holders beyond 35. • A pre-offering notice must be filed ten business days before any sale (unless sales are to accredited investors only) by issuers that are not registered as securities dealers or who do not sell securities through registered securities dealers.

a. For the California, Connecticut, and Texas uniform limited-offering exemptions, a notice must be filed with the state commissioner/director, but failure to file on time does not necessarily preclude reliance on the exemption.
b. For purposes of these totals, a husband and wife count as one person.
c. Keep in mind that the ultimate goal of the state in assessing business and personal relationships between issuers and purchasers is to ascertain the purchaser's ability to protect his or her interests in connection with the transaction. Factors considered in determining the sophistication of an investor include financial capacity, total commitment in relation to net worth, and knowledge of finance and securities generally.
d. The states' prohibition on the use of advertising for purposes of these exemptions is very broad. Publication of any advertisement includes any written or printed communications (mailers, posters), any recorded and publicly broadcast communications (on television, radio, or otherwise), recorded phone messages, and even seminars or meetings that are publicly advertised. Most states encourage sellers to circulate disclosure materials only to individuals who are believed to be interested in purchasing or to individuals who meet the purchaser requirements.
e. Individuals purchasing $150,000 or more of the securities may be excluded only if they have the capacity to protect their own interests, or if they can bear the economic risk of the transaction, or if the investment does not exceed 10 percent of the individual's net worth or joint net worth with that person's spouse.
f. This means there must not be any payments incurred or made to individuals who organized or founded the enterprise or who helped bring about the sales of the security.
g. Legal, printing or accounting fees are excluded. This limitation does not apply when a document itemizing such remuneration is filed in Connecticut prior to the first sale and distributed to each purchaser in Connecticut.
h. The number of offerees can be increased to the number of offerees to whom the offering was actually made if:
(1) the number of purchasers within Massachusetts is no greater than ten;
(2) there is no discount, fee, or remuneration for the seller connected with the transaction; and
(3) there was no general solicitation or advertisement connected with the sale.

Putting it into Practice

Once Kendra and her cofounders decided to go forward with DataAccelleation, they needed to determine how to finance it. In choosing a finance structure, they had no hard-and-fast rules to follow—just guidelines. DataAccelleation's attorney, Michael Cruz, outlined seven ways that Kendra could finance her venture.

First, Kendra could approach CSS and ask for financial support. Kendra had already given CSS 15 percent of the equity in exchange for CSS transferring all of its rights in the SDB technology to DataAccelleation. Kendra could now approach the CSS management and discuss with them the possibility of getting funding to help her develop the product in exchange for more equity. Many mature companies, especially in the high-tech area, realize that some of their best and brightest employees have an entrepreneurial spirit. One way for a mature company to renew its own high-growth nature is to subsidize new ventures, typically by providing seed money. Alternatively, a corporate partnership could be set up.

Second, she could seek financing or a corporate partnership with a company other than CSS. Kendra had the expertise and could offer an equity partnership in a business that could generate significant revenues. This method of financing had the advantage that it did not give one company (such as CSS) too much control over DataAccelleation. The downside, however, was that bringing in another company would require Kendra to keep an additional major shareholder informed and happy. Also, CSS might object.

Third, Kendra could approach family and friends. If Kendra could get some short-term support from them, she could obtain the necessary capital to develop her business while still holding out for a higher valuation at a later stage.

Fourth, Kendra could find an angel investor or a group of angel investors willing to make a significant investment in DataAccelleation in return for an equity stake. However, finding angel investors willing to invest at a reasonable price is often difficult.

Fifth, Kendra could obtain venture capital funding. Venture capital funding is more prevalent in some parts of the country than in others and more appropriate in some circumstances than in others. In deciding whether

continued...

continued...

this was a viable funding method, Kendra first had to decide whether DataAcceleation was the type of business a venture capitalist would want to finance. Given the high risk of failure, a venture capitalist needs a high rate of return to satisfy investors and typically looks for a company that will generate at least a 40 percent annual return on its investment in a period of three to five years.

Sixth, Kendra could try to secure a bank loan. Because DataAccelleation did not yet have a product to ship and thus had no accounts receivable or inventory, a bank would not be willing to lend DataAccelleation any substantial amount of money, unless Kendra could demonstrate personal wealth and personally guarantee the loan. In addition, DataAccelleation would not generate cash flow for a while, so it would have no way to pay interest and principal on a bank loan.

Seventh, Kendra might be able to self-finance her company. This would allow her to continue to develop the business without diluting the equity share of the founders. Kendra might, for example, be able to secure 50 percent prepayment from DataAccelleation's customers for certain orders. This would help cover the cost of materials. This type of self-financing would work if Kendra had a client base that would enable her to identify customers with a prior relationship with her and the necessary confidence to prepay. This financing structure might be beneficial to the customer as well because, with an identified customer, the product could be developed to suit the particular customer's need. As for using her credit cards, Kendra was still paying off her student loans and was very reluctant to incur any more personal credit-card debt.

Kendra decided not to approach CSS for funding because she would have had to give CSS an even larger share of the equity. If she allowed CSS to become a major shareholder, Kendra could lose control or find herself pressured to take actions that were favorable to CSS.

Although going to another company in the industry would prevent CSS from gaining too much influence, Kendra and DataAccelleation would then have to answer to not one but two corporate shareholders. In addition, Kendra doubted that CSS would want a potential competitor to have an equity stake in DataAccelleation.

continued...

continued...

Kendra knew that she wanted to get venture capital financing at some point, but she planned to wait until the product was further developed so that she could obtain a higher valuation for the company. She decided to borrow a small sum of money from her family and friends to start the business.

Kendra finished a detailed business plan that included five-year projections and the assumptions underlying them. Then, with the help of Michael, she found an angel investor named Billy Barnett, a retired executive who was willing to contribute $50,000 in return for a 5 percent stake in the company.

DataAccelleation sold Series A Preferred Stock to Billy pursuant to Rule 506 and the corresponding exemption in California. As Billy was an accredited investor, DataAccelleation was not required to provide a disclosure document that went beyond Kendra's business plan. Even so, she was careful to fully disclose to Billy all the risks and uncertainties concerning the venture of which she was aware.

Kendra hoped that these funds would be sufficient to support the business's operations for six months. She was now ready to focus her attention on securing office space.

NOTES

1. For an excellent discussion of business plans, see William A. Sahlman, *Some Thoughts on Business Plans, in* THE ENTREPRENEURIAL VENTURE 138 (Sahlman et al. eds., 2d ed. 1999), and Stanley R. Rich & David E. Gumpert, *How to Write a Winning Business Plan, supra,* at 177.
2. Mueller v. Sullivan, 141 F.3d 1232 (7th Cir. 1998).

Chapter 8

Contracts and Leases

A *contract* is a legally enforceable promise or set of promises. Without contract law, entrepreneurs would find themselves providing services and merely hoping to get paid. Banks would not lend them money because the borrower's promise to repay would not be enforceable. Investors would be reluctant to invest without an enforceable stock purchase agreement. An entrepreneur might find that the storefront on which he or she made a deposit is occupied by a new tenant who is an old friend of the landlord. Contracts enable entrepreneurs to increase predictability[1] and to expressly allocate risk. By understanding the principles of contract law, entrepreneurs can read intelligently the agreements drafted by others and, in some cases, can create the first drafts of their own agreements.

This chapter first explains some of the basic concepts of contract law, including the elements necessary to form a contract. Next, the chapter deals with the different ways to form a contract and discusses the enforceability of electronic contracts. General contract terms to consider are identified, and a checklist for contract analysis is provided.

The chapter then explains the remedies that may be available if a contract is breached. Remedies can be monetary, but in some situations, money may not be adequate. In that case, a court might order someone to do what that person agreed to do under the contract (i.e., order specific performance). The more limited remedies available under the doctrines of promissory estoppel and quantum meruit are also discussed.

The chapter concludes with a description of three types of contracts the entrepreneur is likely to see and their special characteristics: leases, contracts for the purchase of real property, and loan agreements.

There are two sources of contract law: common law and the Uniform Commercial Code (UCC). Most contracts, such as those involving the rendering of services or the purchase of real estate, are governed by common law rather than by statute. Common law is law developed by judges in court cases. The UCC is a body of statutes, enacted by the legislature in some form in every state, that is designed to codify certain aspects of the common law applicable to commercial contracts and to free those engaging in commercial transactions from some of the more onerous requirements of the common law. Article 2 of the UCC governs the sale of goods, such as computers, automobiles, and sacks of flour.

Unless otherwise specified, the principles of contract law presented in this chapter are generally accepted common-law principles. Chapter 9 discusses contracts for the sale of goods under Article 2 of the UCC, as well as international sales contracts governed by the Convention on Contracts for the International Sale of Goods and contracts governed by the Uniform Computer Information Transactions Act. Employment agreements are discussed in Chapter 10, and licensing agreements are discussed in Chapter 14. Contracts for the sale or acquisition of a business are discussed in Chapter 16.

Choice of Law

Each individual state has its own governing body of law that will be used in determining whether a contract existed and, if so, what the terms were, whether a breach occurred, and what remedies are available. A written contract will often include a choice-of-law provision, which specifies which state's law is to govern the contract. In the absence of such a provision, the governing law will be the law of the state that has the strongest relationship with the substance of the contract and the parties and the greatest governmental interest in having its law apply.

Elements of a Contract

Contracts can be written, oral, or implied. Although most contracts are enforceable even if they are not in writing, the statute of frauds (discussed below) requires certain types of contracts to be in writing to be enforceable.

An *implied contract* is a contract that is not explicitly articulated and is held to exist based on certain circumstances or on the conduct of the parties. An entrepreneur is most likely to encounter an implied contract in connection with employees who argue that they were promised that they would not be terminated without cause. Implied employment contracts are discussed in Chapter 10.

There are four basic requirements for a contract: (1) there must be an agreement between the parties formed by an offer and acceptance; (2) the parties' promises must be supported by something of value, known as consideration; (3) both parties must have the capacity to enter into a contract (i.e., not be mentally incompetent or a minor); and (4) the contract must have a legal purpose.

An *offer* is a statement by a person (the *offeror*) that indicates a willingness to enter into a bargain on the terms stated. *Acceptance* occurs when the person to whom the offer was addressed (the *offeree*) indicates a willingness to accept the offeror's proposed bargain. *Consideration* is anything of value that is exchanged by the parties. It can be money, property, a promise to do something a person is not otherwise legally required to do, or a promise to refrain from doing something a person would otherwise be legally entitled to do.

For example, assume Angela owns a software consulting company. Zany, a friend who is starting her own travel business, asks Angela to design a software package to keep track of her clients. Angela (the offeror) says she would be willing to design the software for $2,000. Zany (the offeree), familiar with the high quality of Angela's work, immediately agrees to pay her $2,000 for the software. The agreement, casual though it may seem, incorporates all the basic requirements of a contract: (1) an offer to design the software for a certain price; acceptance, which includes a promise to pay for the work done; (2) consideration—the exchange of promises by each party, one to design the software and the other to pay; (3) parties who have capacity to enter into a contract—neither is a minor or mentally incompetent; and (4) a legal purpose—the creation of a software package.

Offer and Acceptance

Under the common law, the acceptance must be the mirror image of what is being offered; otherwise, there is no meeting of the minds. There must also be intent to be bound.

If the offeror proposes that something be done, but the offeree does not accept the proposal, then there is no contract. For example, in one case, a person with insurance asked his insurance agent to increase the coverage limits on his existing policies. The agent, who had no authority to bind the insurers, wrote to the insurers, asking whether they

FROM THE TRENCHES

Irwin Schiff, a tax protester, appeared on the CBS News program *Nightwatch* in 1983. Schiff offered a $100,000 reward to anyone calling the show who could cite a section of the Internal Revenue Code that required an individual to file a tax return. No one called in with the code section during the show, but the next morning CBS replayed a two-minute segment that included Schiff's $100,000 reward offer. John Newman then called CBS and cited the relevant code provisions; he also sent a letter to CBS repeating the citations. Schiff refused to pay the $100,000 reward, and Newman filed suit for breach of contract.

The court ruled that Schiff's statement that he would pay a $100,000 reward constituted a valid offer and that if anyone had called in during the original broadcast with the correct code sections, then a contract would have been formed and Schiff would have been obligated to pay the reward. However, the court held that Schiff's offer had expired at the end of the *Nightwatch* show and that the morning newscast's rebroadcast of the segment did not renew or extend the offer. Therefore, although there was an offer, there was no acceptance while the offer was open, and thus no contract was formed.

Source: Newman v. Schiff, 778 F.2d 460 (8th Cir. 1985).

would be willing to increase coverage in the specified amounts. He received no answer. Because there was no express or implied acceptance by the insurance companies of the insured's offer to buy increased coverage, the court found that there was no meeting of the minds between the insured and the insurer, and thus no additional coverage.[2]

Unless the parties specifically agree otherwise, an offer is usually considered open for acceptance for a reasonable time, unless it is revoked or becomes void. What is considered reasonable depends on the circumstances and practices in the industry. If the offeree waits beyond a reasonable time to accept an offer, no contract will result.

To keep an offer open for a longer time, parties can enter into a separate agreement, called an *option contract*, that requires the offeree to pay something to the offeror for the privilege of having the offer left open. Option contracts are often used when real estate or businesses are sold. Without a separate option contract, the offer would no longer stand if the offeror revoked it before the offeree had accepted or relied upon it.

Counteroffers

If the offeree does not accept the terms specified in the offer but instead offers different terms, that constitutes a *counteroffer*, not an acceptance. No contract is formed unless the initial offeror accepts the different terms proposed by the offeree. A counteroffer extinguishes the original offer, so if the counteroffer is rejected, the person making the counteroffer cannot go back and accept the initial offer. Many business negotiations involve several rounds of counteroffers before a contract is formed.

Authority

When a contract is entered into with an entity, such as a partnership, limited liability company (LLC), or corporation, it is important to make sure that the person who signs the agreement has the authority to do so. Normally, a general partner will have the authority to bind a partnership, as will the managing member of an LLC. In the case of an LLC, however, some major transactions may have to be approved by the members.

A contract with a corporation must be signed by a duly authorized officer. The president of the corporation has the authority to enter into most contracts relating to the operation of the business, but contracts for the issuance of stock must be authorized by the board of directors. Thus, an agreement granting stock options must be authorized by the board of directors. When dealing with persons besides the president, it is prudent to verify their authorization, perhaps by requesting a copy of the board of directors' resolution on the subject or the section of the corporation's bylaws that spells out the authority of different officers. Some contracts, such as an agreement to sell substantially all of the corporation's assets, must be approved by both the board and the shareholders.

When entering into a contract with a governmental body, special care should be taken to ensure that the contract is authorized under state or other applicable law and is signed by the proper official. In addition, it is important to determine whether the governmental entity can be sued if it breaches the contract, or if it has contractual immunity.

Consideration

Consideration is a legal concept that means a bargained-for exchange. This requirement is met when one party gives up something of value in exchange for the other party's giving up something of value. Value has many meanings and can include the exchange of things with monetary worth, as is found in money or property, or the exchange of things with intrinsic worth, as is found in the performing of a service or the making of a promise to do something or to refrain from doing something. Even if the value exchanged is small, there will still be consideration.

The relative value of the promises exchanged is irrelevant to the issue of whether a contract has been formed. For example, in our software example, had Angela offered to design the software for a fee of $10, and had Zany accepted that offer, a contract would have been formed, despite the wide disparity between the value of the fee and the work done.

FROM THE TRENCHES

Shortly before he died, Elvis Presley was engaged to be married to Ginger Alden. Presley offered to give Alden's mother, Jo Laverne Alden, $40,000 to pay off the mortgage on the Alden home. Presley died several months later without paying off Alden's mortgage. Presley's estate informed Alden that it would not assume the liability for her mortgage, and Alden sued to enforce Presley's promise.

The court held that Presley's promise was not supported by consideration and therefore was not binding. The court refused to apply the doctrine of promissory estoppel (discussed later in the chapter) because Alden failed to show that her reliance on Presley's promise was reasonably justified.

Source: Alden v. Presley, 637 S.W.2d 862 (Tenn. 1982).

Whenever the original contract is modified, additional consideration must be provided for the modification to be enforceable. For example, if a landlord agrees to reduce the rent and the tenant gives nothing in exchange, then the landlord's promise to reduce the rent would be unenforceable by the tenant. Even modest consideration, such as the tenant's agreement to pay $100 in exchange for the reduction in rent, would be enough to make the landlord's promise binding.

ILLUSORY PROMISES An *illusory promise* does not result in a contract; it occurs when one party fails to provide anything of value. In a classic case involving a supplier and a distributor, a coal company agreed to sell coal to a lumber company for a certain price regardless of the amount ordered. The lumber company, in contrast, was obligated only to pay for the amount it ordered. The court found the agreement to be an illusory promise lacking consideration because the lumber company had the option to buy coal from another supplier and thus had not bound itself to any promise.[3]

Had the lumber company agreed to order all of the coal it needed from the coal company, then even if it wound up needing no coal at all, there would have been adequate consideration because the lumber company would have agreed to refrain from buying coal from anyone else. A buyer's agreement to purchase all of a specified commodity it needs from a particular seller is called a *requirements contract.* A seller's agreement to sell all of its output to a particular buyer is an *output contract.*

Unilateral Contract

The examples discussed above are considered *bilateral contracts,* meaning that in each case one promise was exchanged for another promise. Another, equally valid, type of contract is a *unilateral contract,* in which a promise is exchanged for the performance of a certain act. Acceptance of a unilateral contract takes place when the offeree has completed the required act.

To illustrate, a pharmaceuticals company offered to provide a one-year free supply of an experimental drug to patients who participated in the drug's clinical trials, which included submission to intrusive and necessarily uncomfortable testing for one year. Patients were free to drop out of the study before the end of the trials, but if they did, they were not eligible to receive the one-year posttrial free supply. When the patients who stayed the course through the end of the trials requested their free supply, the company refused to provide it, arguing that the patients had given no consideration as they could have voluntarily dropped out of the study. The court disagreed, holding that this was a classic example of a unilateral contract, which the patients accepted when they remained in the study until the end.[4]

Oral Agreements and the Statute of Frauds

Sometimes an entrepreneur will not want to spend the time or money needed to reduce a deal to writing and will instead decide to rely on an oral exchange of promises. Before moving ahead with an oral agreement, it is important to make sure that it will be enforceable in a court of law. Most types of contracts are enforceable even if they are oral and not set forth in writing. However, individual states have adopted a type of legislation—called a *statute of frauds*—that requires parties to put certain types of contracts in writing.

The Statute of Frauds

Although the exact requirements vary from state to state, the following types of business contracts are usually subject to the statute of frauds and therefore must be in writing to be enforceable: (1) contracts that cannot be performed within one year; (2) contracts that involve the transfer of interests in real property (including options to purchase real property and leases); (3) contracts by which someone agrees to assume another person's debt; (4) prenuptial contracts whereby a man and woman who are going to be married agree how assets are to be allocated if they divorce; and (5) contracts for the sale of goods for $500 or more (which are governed by the UCC's statute of frauds). Failure to put a contract in writing in accordance with the statute does not make the contract void, but it will render the contract unenforceable in court if the other party asserts that the contract should have been in writing.

Even if a contract's terms do not clearly indicate that it cannot be performed within one year, a court may still hold that the contract is subject to the statute of frauds. For example, in a case that involved a partnership agreement to purchase and develop properties throughout the country, the court held that because the agreement was not intended to be performed within a year, it was subject to the statute of frauds. In deciding that the contract would take longer than one year to complete, the court looked at the intent of the parties, as inferred from surrounding circumstances and the goal of the contract.[5] To avoid the possibility of having an agreement ruled unenforceable, the parties should put in writing any contract that might take more than one year to perform.

The agreement does not have to be very formal to satisfy the requirements of the statute of frauds. In general, all that is required is a signed writing setting forth the essential terms, as determined from the overall context of the agreement. Initialed notes on the back of an envelope or on a napkin will suffice.

The writing must be signed by the party against whom enforcement is sought. If an agent is signing a contract that must be in writing to be enforceable, then the agent's authority to sign on behalf of the principal must itself be evidenced by a writing signed by the principal. For example, a real estate agent cannot enter into an enforceable lease on behalf of a tenant unless the tenant has signed a power of attorney or similar document authorizing the agent to sign on the tenant's behalf.

Advantages of Putting a Contract in Writing

Even if the oral agreement in question does not come within the statute of frauds, the entrepreneur should still be wary. Oral agreements, by their nature, are difficult to enforce. For this reason, even if a writing is not legally

FROM THE TRENCHES

Two struggling semiconductor capital equipment manufacturers merged in search of synergy. Company A, an established but somewhat anemic venture-backed firm, was looking for a chief executive officer. Company B, a start-up, had a CEO and potential new technology but no access to venture capital. The merger agreement referred to and incorporated by reference a business plan for the merged company, created by Company B's CEO. The business plan stated the intention of the merged company to raise "up to $1 million, a large portion of which has been committed by the current venture capital investor." When the merged company was unable to attract new financing or to build its new product, it failed. The Company B investors then sued the venture backers of Company A for breach of contract and fraud.

The lawsuit resulted in a six-week jury trial. After two days of deliberation, the jury found the venture capitalists not liable. The jury concluded that the business plan and merger documents did not constitute an enforceable promise to supply funding but rather signaled an intent to assist the merged company in obtaining financing—an intent that was frustrated by problems of the merged company's own making.

Comment: Although the venture capitalists were vindicated, the case highlights the importance of communicating funding expectations in clear and unambiguous language and ensuring that the expectations of all parties to a deal are clearly understood and put in writing.

required, it is advantageous to put the terms of the deal on paper. Putting a contract in writing helps prevent later misunderstandings by forcing the parties to articulate their intentions and desires. A clearly drafted contract provides a written record of the terms agreed to and is more reliable evidence of the parties' intentions than the faded memories of what was said. The act of signing an agreement reinforces the fact that a contract gives rise to legal rights and duties. The drafting process sometimes identifies misunderstandings or unclear points that might otherwise come to the surface only in the event of a later dispute that could lead to an expensive lawsuit.

When negotiations have been drawn out or are complicated, the parties can avoid ambiguity about what they finally agreed to by including a clause to the effect that "this agreement constitutes the entire agreement of the parties and supersedes all prior and contemporaneous agreements, representations, and understandings of the parties." This is called an *integration* or *merger clause.*

The parties can also include an explicit *nonreliance clause,* whereby both parties confirm that they have not relied on any representations or promises that might have been made during the course of the negotiations other than those set forth in the written contract. Such a clause can be helpful in defending a claim of fraudulent inducement, when one party claims that its decision to enter into the contract was based on its reliance on oral statements made during the course of negotiations that are not reflected in the written contract. Similarly, the parties can prevent ambiguities with regard to discussions taking place after the contract has been signed simply by providing that "no supplement, modification, or amendment of this agreement shall be binding unless executed in writing by both parties."

Despite the advantages of having a written contract that clearly sets forth the parties' respective rights and obligations, many businesspersons find themselves relying on a handshake or signing contracts that are riddled with ambiguities or otherwise do not protect their interests. Many entrepreneurs, after working cooperatively with another party to reach a mutually advantageous agreement, find it awkward and sometimes even impolite to ask the other party to put it in writing.

Ironically, this seemingly cooperative approach to doing business may actually hinder the formation of a clearly understood agreement between

FROM THE TRENCHES

Twenty-seven years after the release of the 1969 hippie-biker film *Easy Rider* (which made famous the Steppenwolf song "Born to Be Wild," played while a group of longhairs on motorcycles roared side by side cross-country), the two lead actors, Dennis Hopper and Peter Fonda, were involved in a lawsuit over how the profits should be divided and who should get credit for creating the now-classic film. In keeping with the hippie themes of free love and drugs, the actors never wrote down the terms of their profit-sharing agreement. Although Peter Fonda told the *Wall Street Journal* that he has "an extraordinarily accurate memory," the lawsuit could have been avoided entirely if Hopper and Fonda had put down on paper the agreed-upon split and credits.

Source: Hey, Man, See You in Court: "Easy Rider" Gets a New Epilogue, Wall St. J., Feb. 9, 1996, at A1.

the parties. Studies have shown that people tend to be unrealistically optimistic about the future of their personal relationships. Because the parties believe it is unlikely that misunderstandings will arise, they spend little time addressing them in the process of drafting a carefully worded contract. Also, many businesspersons tend to overestimate the strength of memory. During negotiations, some issues may seem so obvious that no one even thinks to include them in the contract. As time passes and memories fade, however, the parties to the contract may find themselves differing as to what they thought they had originally agreed on.

Preparing Written Contracts

Drafting Language

The strength of contract law lies in carefully drafted written agreements. By using clear, specific language to state their understandings, the parties can often avoid misunderstandings later. But precise contracts do not come without costs. An entrepreneur must balance the time and expense of having a lawyer draft or review an agreement against the costs of litigating the problems that can stem from a poorly drafted contract and the value of the benefits that might not be attained if the contract does not accurately reflect the entrepreneur's needs.

Written contracts do not need to be in a particular form or to use stylized language such as "party of the first part." All that is required is a writing that is signed by all parties and contains such information as the identities of the parties, the subject matter of the agreement, and the basic (what is basic depends on the particular situation) terms and conditions.

Contractual wording is very literal. "All" means everything; "shall" means it must be done; and "may" means it is permitted but not required. The term "and/or" should be avoided, as it tends to be ambiguous. "And" means that both elements must be satisfied, whereas "or" means that satisfying either element is sufficient.

A careful entrepreneur will be wary of rushing to sign an incomplete or poorly worded contract. The pressure of a deadline is often used as a stratagem by the other party when negotiating a contract. The entrepreneur may feel compelled to sign a contract without understanding it or being in complete agreement with it. It is important to resist these pressures.

The contract should set forth all aspects of the relationship or agreement that the entrepreneur believes are important to the needs of the business. For example, a new café owner preparing to negotiate a lease in a strip mall might decide that having adequate parking for customers and a restriction on other cafés in the strip mall are considerations worth paying a higher rent to obtain. By carefully considering priorities in advance, the owner minimizes the chances that something important will be excluded in the final agreement.

Form

Written contracts come in a variety of forms.

CUSTOMIZED LONG-FORM AGREEMENTS Certain transactions, such as the purchase and sale of substantially all the assets of a business (discussed in Chapter 16), require heavily negotiated, customized agreements prepared by experienced attorneys. The officer signing such agreements should read them before signing and make sure that he or she understands what they mean. It is often very helpful to ask one's counsel to prepare a memorandum summarizing the agreement's key terms and flagging any unusual provisions.

LETTERS OF AGREEMENT One format often used to organize a simple agreement between parties is the *letter of agreement*. Typically, one of the parties drafts this letter. The drafter first includes a statement to the effect that the letter constitutes a contract between the parties and will legally bind them, then lists all of the important terms and conditions of the agreement. The end of the letter invites the recipient to indicate his or her approval of the terms by signing it, inserting the date after the word "Accepted" typed at the bottom of the page, and returning the letter to the drafter. Official acceptance takes place when the letter is mailed or otherwise sent by the offeree to the drafter-offeror.

STANDARD-FORM CONTRACTS Another commonly used format is a generic printed form (a *standard-form contract*). Standard-form contracts can be used for many business purposes, including leases and promissory notes. If the entrepreneur decides to use one, he or she should obtain an industry-specific sample. Because a standard form will be used frequently, the entrepreneur should have an attorney review it.

A good standard-form contract enhances rather than obscures the understanding between the parties. Therefore, the drafter should write clearly and concisely, using simple language and short sentences.

Even with a preprinted contract, many of the terms and conditions remain negotiable. The wise entrepreneur will assess his or her needs and rank them, rather than settling for a cursory review of a preprinted contract. Any changes, modifications, additions, and deletions (which can be handwritten in the margin, if necessary) should be signed or initialed and dated by both parties, so that neither party can later claim that one party made the changes without the assent of the other.

The law generally holds those entering contractual relationships responsible for reading and understanding the contracts they sign. This is known as the *duty to read*. Nevertheless, people sometimes claim that they should not be bound by the promises they made in a contract because they were not aware of what they signed. Small print or a crowded format can lend credence to this claim. Besides writing clearly and using a readable type size, the entrepreneur can take other steps to counter this problem. For example, if some of the terms and conditions are printed on the reverse side of the page, the drafter can state in bold letters: "This contract is subject to terms and conditions on the reverse side hereof." Leaving a blank for the signer's initials next to certain terms or conditions can also help to prove later that the signer was aware of those terms.

ATTACHMENTS Attachments may also be used to supplement a written agreement. Attachments are ideal when the additional terms are too extensive to note in the margins of the agreement. For example, a caterer might use a general form contract for customers that contains not only printed terms and conditions but blank spaces in which the caterer can fill in such information as the quantity of hors d'oeuvres required, the date of the function, and the price. Additional issues not covered in the form contract can be addressed in a simple attachment that both parties sign and date at the same time they sign the main document. To ensure that the attachment is treated as part of the contractual agreement (in other words, that the meeting of the minds incorporates both documents), the drafter should name the attachment (e.g., "Attachment A") and include a clause in the main contract clearly stating that the main agreement and the named attachment are incorporated into one contract.

ADDENDA Like attachments, *addenda* provide a way for the parties to modify the main agreement. They differ in that attachments are used at the time the main contract is approved by both parties, whereas addenda are used *after* the main contract has been signed by both parties. Typically, the parties note changes to an already approved contract by crossing out words and writing in new ones, then initialing the revisions. If the modifications are extensive, however, an addendum may be drawn up instead.

Each addendum should include an explicit reference to the main contract. For example, "This is an addendum to the contract dated May 17, 2002, between Karen Wells and Juliet Tyler for the purchase of . . . ." The addendum should also spell out the relevant changes and state clearly that, if the terms of the original agreement and the addendum conflict, the addendum's terms should prevail. It is also wise to provide that "the parties agree to the above changes and additions to the original contract" and "in all other respects, the terms of the original contract remain in full effect."

It is important to ensure that each party gives some consideration for the modifications or addendum. This is not an issue when both parties are giving up rights or assuming new or different duties, but it can arise if one party makes a unilateral concession.

Electronic Contracts

With the rise of e-commerce, more and more transactions have been taking place electronically. Until recently, many states did not give contracts executed electronically the same legal effect as physical paper contracts. Moreover, laws governing electronic transactions varied widely from state to state. National legislation providing for the enforcement of most electronic contracts became effective on October 1, 2000.

The Uniform Electronic Transactions Act

In 1999, the National Conference of Commissioners on Uniform State Laws (NCCUSL) adopted the Uniform Electronic Transactions Act (UETA) to address the issue of whether electronic contracts and signatures are legal contracts. UETA serves as a model for state legislatures, but its adoption is not mandatory. As of January 2002, more than thirty-eight states had enacted UETA.

UETA sets forth four basic rules regarding contracts entered into by parties that agree to conduct business electronically: (1) a record or signature may not be denied legal effect or enforceability solely because it is in electronic form; (2) a contract may not be denied legal effect or enforceability solely because an electronic record was used in its formation; (3) an electronic record satisfies a law that requires a record to be in writing; and (4) an electronic signature satisfies a law (such as the statute of frauds) that requires a signature.

Under UETA, almost any mark or process intended to sign an electronic record will constitute an electronic signature, including a typed name at the bottom of an e-mail message, a faxed signature, and a "click-through" process on a computer screen whereby a person clicks on "I Agree" on a Web page. The essential element necessary to determine the validity of an electronic signature is whether the person intended the process or mark provided to act as a signature and whether it can be attributed to that person.

The E-Sign Act

In an effort to ensure more uniform treatment of electronic transactions across the United States, Congress enacted the Electronic Signatures in Global and National Commerce Act, more commonly known as the E-Sign Act, effective October 1, 2000. Consistent with UETA, the E-Sign Act provides that "a signature, contract, or other record . . . may not be denied legal effect, validity, or enforceability solely because it is in electronic form." The provisions of the E-Sign Act are very similar to those of UETA, except that UETA, where enacted, applies to intrastate and interstate transactions, whereas the E-Sign Act governs only transactions in interstate and foreign commerce. (Congress limited application of the E-Sign Act to transactions involving interstate and foreign commerce because the power given Congress under the U.S. Constitution's Commerce Clause does not extend to purely intrastate commerce.) Moreover, the provisions of the E-Sign Act are mandatory.

The E-Sign Act resolves the problem of inconsistency among states that have or have not enacted UETA by expressly preempting all state laws inconsistent with its provisions. For states that have adopted UETA, however, the E-Sign Act does allow state law "to modify, limit, or supersede" its provisions to the extent such variations are not inconsistent with the E-Sign Act. What variations will ultimately be considered "inconsistent" is not entirely clear and may have to be determined by the courts.

To protect those who choose not to conduct business electronically or do not have access to computers, the E-Sign Act and UETA require that the use or acceptance of electronic records or electronic signatures be voluntary. Moreover, under the E-Sign Act, if a business is legally bound to provide information to a consumer in writing, electronic records may be used only if the business first secures the consumer's informed consent.

Notwithstanding, the broad scope of the E-Sign Act and UETA, several classes of documents are not covered by their provisions and thus may not be considered fully enforceable if executed electronically. Both UETA and the E-Sign Act exclude the following:

- Wills, codicils, and trusts.
- Contracts or records relating to adoption, divorce, or other matters of family law.
- Contracts governed by certain provisions of the Uniform Commercial Code in effect in each state.

Unlike UETA, the E-Sign Act also excludes the following:

- Court orders and notices and other official court documents.
- Notices of cancellation or termination of utility services.
- Notices regarding credit agreements secured by, or rental agreements for, a primary residence (for example, eviction notices).
- Notices of cancellation or termination of health or life insurance benefits.
- Notices of recall.
- Documents required to accompany the transport of hazardous materials, pesticides, or toxic materials.

Of course, a national standard governing electronic transactions does not resolve inconsistencies in laws of other countries. Some form of international coordination will be necessary to ensure that electronic transactions are consistently enforced across national borders.

General Contract Terms to Consider

Exactly what should be included in a written contract varies from situation to situation, but without question any contract should include certain provisions that identify the parties, establish the existence of a contractual relationship, and verify the intent of the parties to be bound by a contract. Other provisions more specifically address the important terms of the agreement, timing, and allocation of risk.

Identification

Contracts should explicitly state the names and addresses of the parties. Corporations, partnerships, and other entities should be identified as such, together with an indication of the state under whose laws they were formed.

Signatures

A contract that is subject to the statute of frauds can be enforced only against the party or parties who have signed it. Sole proprietors may sign on their own behalf, making them personally responsible for fulfilling the terms of the agreement. A general partner should sign on behalf of a general or limited partnership. This is done by setting forth the name of the partnership and then on a separate line writing the name of the person signing:

[NAME OF PARTNERSHIP]
By ______________________
[name of person signing]
Its ______________________
[title]

By making it clear that the contract is being entered into by the partnership, the general partner can require the other party to exhaust the partnership's assets first before going against the general partner's personal assets.

The officer of a corporation or a manager of a limited liability company is not personally responsible for the obligations of the entity as long as the officer or manager makes it clear that he or she is signing only in a representative capacity. This is done by setting forth the name of the corporation or LLC and then on a separate line writing the name of the person signing:

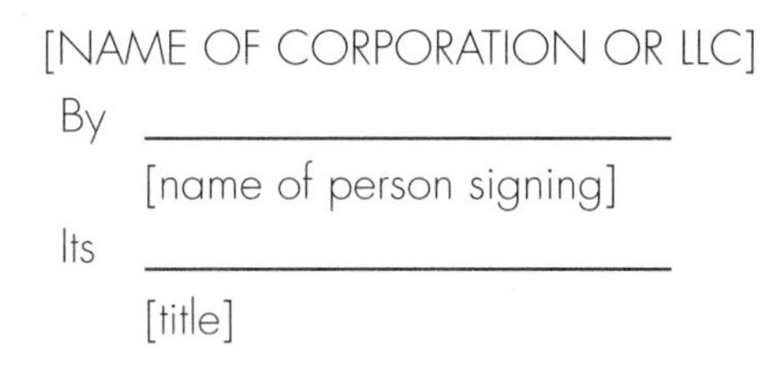
[NAME OF CORPORATION OR LLC]
By ______________________
[name of person signing]
Its ______________________
[title]

Ideally, the parties should produce two identical copies of the agreement and sign both copies, so that each party may retain an original. However, under the *best evidence rule,* duplicate photocopies, facsimiles, or photographs may be substituted for the original in court unless (1) a genuine question is raised as to the authenticity of the original, or (2) circumstances suggest that it would be unfair to admit the duplicate in place of the original. If possible, all parties should sign on the same signature page. If this is not possible (e.g., if one party is located out of town), then the agreement should expressly provide for the signing of counterparts. When using *counterparts,* each party signs a copy of the signature page, and all signature pages taken together are deemed to be one original.

Establishing Intent to Enter into a Contract

EXISTENCE OF AN AGREEMENT AND INTENT TO BE BOUND Some disputes over contractual relationships center on the question of original intent or even the very existence of a contract. Because an arbitrator or court might later have to determine the parties' intentions, it is useful to have an explicit preamble or statement summarizing the parties' intentions (called the *recitals*) drafted at the time the parties enter into the agreement.

DATE It is important to establish when the meeting of the minds took place. If the parties all sign the agreement on the same date and want it to be effective immediately upon signing, then the agreement should provide:

"This Agreement is executed and entered into on [date]." If the parties sign on different days, then the agreement might provide that it is "made and entered into as of the later of the two dates on the signature page." If the agreement is to be effective as of a date other than the date it is signed, then the agreement should provide: "This Agreement is executed and entered into as of [date]."

Terms of the Agreement

The following types of provisions are the heart of the agreement and determine the parties' contractual obligations to one another.

REPRESENTATIONS AND WARRANTIES Any key assumptions or understandings upon which the agreement rests should be explicitly stated as representations and warranties. For example, "Party A represents and warrants that the hardware when installed meets the specifications on Schedule A for use in the production of computer chips." If such a representation were not included in the contract, Party A could later claim that it was under the impression that the equipment was to be installed under less stringent specifications or for a different use.

Representations and warranties are also used to contractually guarantee that certain facts are true. For example, an investor will want assurance that the company owns all of its intellectual property and that it is not violating any other person's rights. The investors can sue for breach of contract if it later turns out that someone else—such as a prior employer of the founder or a university where the founder was a graduate student—owns key technology.

CONDITIONS The fulfillment of some contractual obligations may be conditioned on the occurrence of certain events (called *conditions*), such as the approval of a loan application by a third party, or on the other party's performance of a particular obligation, such as the procurement of insurance. Normally, a party's obligation to perform under a contract is conditional on the representations and warranties being true and correct in all material respects.

The only restriction on the use of conditions is that one party's obligation may not be made conditional upon some occurrence exclusively within the control of that same party. If one party to an agreement had complete control over the occurrence of a condition, that party's obligation would effectively be negated, reducing an otherwise valid contract to an illusory promise.

The condition should be stated clearly, using simple, straightforward language such as "if," "only if," "unless and until," or "provided that." For example, a stock purchase agreement will usually include language to this effect: "The investors shall have no obligation to purchase the shares and to pay the purchase price unless all conditions set forth in Section 4 are satisfied."

LOGISTICAL CONSIDERATIONS Such details as performance requirements, delivery and installation instructions, risk of loss allocation, and the procurement of insurance should be discussed in advance and included in the written agreement.

PAYMENT TERMS Payment terms should specify both when and in what form payment must be made. If payment is to be made in installments, the seller can attempt to deter a buyer from missing payments by including an acceleration clause in the written agreement. An *acceleration clause* specifies that all remaining installments (and interest, if applicable) become immediately due and payable if the buyer is late in paying any installment. Some acceleration clauses take effect automatically upon default, but in many contracts (especially when long-term relationships are a factor), it may be preferable to make the exercise of the acceleration clause optional at the creditor's discretion.

NOTICE AND OPPORTUNITY TO CURE Especially when the evaluation of performance is subjective, it is helpful to include a provision requiring written notice of a failure to comply with the contract and some opportunity to cure the default.

TIMING ISSUES The parties should agree in advance on such crucial questions as the duration, termination, and renewal of the contract, as well as specifying when their obligations to each other must be fulfilled.

Duration and Notice of Termination Regardless of the original intent of the parties, contracts lacking a specific duration may be construed later as terminable at-will by either party. It is better to avoid this ambiguity by including a clause stating that the contract is terminable at-will or indicating its duration.

Furthermore, a contract terminable at-will should be drafted so as to avoid providing either party with an absolute right of termination, which might cause a court to find an illusory promise and thus no contract. For example, the drafter can stipulate that a party or parties must give notice of intent to terminate the contract a set amount of time before actual termination. It is also wise to outline specific rules as to how proper notice shall be effected.

When Performance Must Be Completed Special deadlines or time requirements should be stated explicitly. For example, if time is of the essence (performance being completed on time is especially important), that fact should be noted in the contract. The entrepreneur may want to reserve the right to terminate the contract in the event the other party fails to perform on time. This would be appropriate, for example, when a florist is ordering a certain number of Easter lilies from a grower in anticipation of filling customers' orders before Easter; lilies delivered a week late will be of no use to the florist, who will have to find another source.

Another method of discouraging tardiness is to build in a specific amount that one party will pay the other party if it does not perform its obligations by the deadline. In drafting such a *liquidated damages* clause, the drafter must take care not to build the wrong incentives into the contract. Finishing the job safely and properly should not be subordinated to finishing it on time. To realign performance with values such as safety and quality, the drafter may want to include a separate clause that, for example, requires a third party's approval of the completed performance before payment is due. This arrangement is often used in construction contracts. In addition, determining the amount to be paid as liquidated damages may be difficult. The amount should reflect the parties' best estimate of the actual damage that would result from the delay in performance. Moreover, the amount should be high enough to influence the party's behavior but not so high as to constitute a penalty. Courts generally are unwilling to enforce penalties.

Renewability of the Contract The contract may be automatically renewable, meaning that the contract is automatically extended for a certain period unless one of the parties gives notice of its intention not to renew within a stated period of time before expiration of the contract. Or the contract may be renewable dependent on prior notice of intention to renew. Either way, the drafter should take care to leave an out, so that the contract cannot be construed as perpetual.

ALLOCATING RISK The parties to a contract should decide what events would relieve one or more parties of their obligations under the contract. For example, the occurrence of certain natural disasters (known as *acts of God*), such as an earthquake, fire, or flood, that make performance impossible or commercially impracticable may release the parties from their contractual obligations. Similarly, an unanticipated governmental action (such as an international embargo) or *force majeure* (literally translated as *superior force* but used to designate problems beyond the reasonable control of a party) may excuse the parties from performance if it makes performance impossible or commercially impracticable.

Courts are very reluctant to find *commercial impracticability*, however. The event must have been both unforeseen and unforeseeable, and the party asserting impracticability must not have expressly or implicitly assumed the risk of the occurrence. It is not enough that performance becomes unprofitable or more costly. For example, when political turmoil in the Middle East resulted in the closing of the Suez Canal in 1967, shipping companies had to detour around the Cape of Good Hope. Although the companies incurred substantial losses as a result, most were unsuccessful in nullifying the contracts they had entered into before the Suez Canal was closed.

It is often advisable to draft an exculpatory clause listing the many potentially disastrous events that could prevent the party or parties from fulfilling their obligations under the contract. For example:

> *Party A will not be liable for any loss, including, without limitation, the loss of Party B's prospective profits, resulting from events outside of Party A's control. Examples of occurrences outside of Party A's control include, but are not limited to, strikes, lockouts, fires, floods, mud slides, earthquakes, machine breakdowns, lack of shipping space, carrier delays, governmental actions, and inability to procure goods or raw materials.*

Although persuading the other party to accept such a wide-ranging exculpatory clause may be a challenge, it is worth the effort to include as many potential problems as possible. Despite the wording "but not limited to," any events that are not listed in the clause may be subjects of dispute in an action for breach of contract. Also, it should be noted that the inclusion of such a clause does not automatically release the party from liability under the circumstances listed. If a court concludes that a contingency could have been reasonably guarded against, it may decide not to excuse the party from liability for the resulting loss.

In some instances, the parties may consciously want to shift the risk of certain events occurring to one party. For example, a customer might want its supplier to insure against certain risks, such as fire, that might make delivery impossible or commercially impracticable. Similarly, a customer might want its supplier to buy futures or forward contracts to ensure the supply of raw materials. If this is the parties' intent, then the contract should expressly state that occurrence of the specified events shall not excuse nonperformance.

Arbitration and Mediation Despite the best intentions of both parties, misunderstandings and disputes do arise. One way to avoid the expense, tension, delay, and publicity of litigation, and the vagaries of a jury trial, is to resolve the issue through arbitration. In arbitration, the parties take their dispute to one or more persons given the power to make a final decision that binds the parties. Unless the parties agree in advance to employ arbitration for conflicts that arise, they are likely to wind up in litigation in the event of a dispute. Often, once a dispute has arisen, one of the parties feels it has a strong case and is unwilling to concede its advantage by seeking an equitable solution through arbitration.

The American Arbitration Association (AAA) suggests inserting a clause similar to this:

> *Any controversy or claim arising out of or relating to this contract, or the breach thereof, shall be settled by arbitration in accordance with the Commercial Rules of the American Arbitration Association, and judgment upon the award rendered by the Arbitrator(s) may be entered in any court having jurisdiction thereof.*

Like any other provision in a contract, an arbitration clause will not be enforced if it is *unconscionable*, that is, if it would shock the conscience of the court to enforce it.

The parties may want to specify which arbitration service will be used. Some industries have special arbitration agencies that perform this service for members of their trade; some do not, forcing the parties to rely on a private arbitration firm or a branch of the AAA itself. The parties may

FROM THE TRENCHES

Circuit City required all applicants for employment to sign the "Circuit City Dispute Resolution Agreement," which required employees to agree to submit all claims and disputes to binding arbitration but did not require Circuit City to arbitrate any claims against employees. The agreement restricted the amount of damages available to employees and specified that an employee would have to split the cost of arbitration (including the daily fees of the arbitrator, the cost of a reporter to transcribe the proceedings, and the expense of renting the room where the arbitration would be held), unless the employee prevailed and the arbitrator ordered Circuit City to pay the employee's share of the costs.

After the U.S. Supreme Court ruled that mandatory arbitration of employment claims (including those for discrimination in violation of federal statutes) was permissible unless the agreement to arbitrate was invalid under ordinary contract law, the U.S. Court of Appeals for the Ninth Circuit ruled that Circuit City's agreement to arbitrate was an unconscionable contract of adhesion under California law because it "functions as a thumb on Circuit City's side of the scale should an employment dispute ever arise between the company and one of its employees." The appeals court held that a mandatory arbitration agreement will not be valid unless there is some "modicum of bilaterality." Because the employer was not bound to arbitrate its claims (with no apparent justification for the lack of mutual obligations) and the agreement did not allow full recovery of the statutory damages for which the employee would be eligible in a court of law, the agreement was both procedurally and substantively unconscionable. As a result, the employee could not be compelled to arbitrate his claims against Circuit City but could instead litigate them in court.

Sources: Circuit City Stores, Inc. v. Adams, 532 U.S. 105 (2001); Circuit City Stores, Inc. v. Adams, 279 F.3d 889 (9th Cir. 2002).

also wish to spell out in which jurisdiction the case should be arbitrated and who will pay the resulting fees. If the two parties will be doing business with each other on a continual basis, the clause can be drafted to cover all of their dealings.

Sometimes the parties are not willing to submit disputes to arbitration. In such cases, it is helpful to include a *mandatory mediation clause.* Such a clause requires the parties to discuss their claims with a mediator before filing a lawsuit. The mediator, who is often a lawyer, does not have the power to make a final decision. Rather, a mediator facilitates the settlement discussions and works with the parties to craft a mutually acceptable resolution. If the mediation fails to result in a binding settlement agreement, the parties are free to go to court.

CHOICE OF LAW AND FORUM The contract should specify where disputes are to be adjudicated and which jurisdiction's law is to be applied. It is almost always advantageous to require that litigation be commenced in the city and county where the entrepreneur does business. This gives the entrepreneur the home-court advantage and increases the likelihood of finding a sympathetic jury. If local law governs the contract, the entrepreneur's lawyers will not have to learn another jurisdiction's law or hire counsel in the other state. Traveling expenses are also minimized. Because a court generally has personal jurisdiction only over persons with at least some minimal contacts with the jurisdiction in which the court sits, the contract should expressly state that all parties submit to the jurisdiction of the courts in the designated locale.

ATTORNEYS' FEES If the contract does not include a clause requiring the loser to pay the winner's attorneys' fees, then each party must pay its own. Typically, a clause will specify that the losing party shall pay the prevailing party's reasonable attorneys' fees and court costs.

CHECKLIST FOR CONTRACT ANALYSIS

The following is a checklist of questions to consider when drafting or signing a contract and when assessing claims that a contract has been breached or that performance is excused:

- Is this contract void because it is illegal or violates public policy? A contract to do something illegal or immoral is void.
- Is this contract being entered into freely? Unlawful explicit or veiled threats to induce a party to enter an agreement (referred to as *duress*) make it unenforceable.
- Is this contract unconscionable? Sometimes a contract is unconscionable because onerous terms (such as a limitation of liability or release of claims) are buried in fine print, thereby creating an element of surprise. Other times a party may be aware of the terms but will agree to a totally unfair exchange because he or she lacks bargaining power.
- Has performance become impossible or commercially impracticable? If so, then nonperformance will be excused unless the event making performance impossible or impracticable was foreseeable or one party assumed the risk of its occurrence. Although a several-fold increase in costs usually will not be enough to find commercial impracticability, a ten-fold increase has been held sufficient to excuse performance.
- Is the contract clearly worded and structured to prevent ambiguity? If a contract is worded in such a way that its terms are subject to different interpretations, it may be voidable by the party that would be hurt by the use of a particular interpretation. This is true only when (1) both interpretations would be reasonable, and (2) either both parties or neither party knew of both interpretations when they contracted with each other. If one (but not both) of the parties knew of the existence of the differing interpretations, a court would find in favor of the party who was unaware of the ambiguity. Some courts will resolve any ambiguity by finding against the person who drafted the contract.
- Was there a mistake of fact that rendered this contract voidable? A *mistake of fact* occurs when the parties make a mistake about the actual facts of the transaction. To determine whether a mistake of fact calls for the undoing of the contract, courts consider three things: (1) whether the mistake had a material effect on one or both of the parties, (2) whether either party allocated the risks of such a mistake to itself, and (3) whether the party alleging mistake did so promptly after discovering

it. In determining whether there was a mistake of fact, the courts will often look at the recitals in the beginning of the agreement to determine the intent of the parties. A classic case involved a contract for the purchase of 125 bales of cotton to be brought by the seller from India to England on a ship named *Peerless*. Two ships named *Peerless* were sailing out of Bombay that year, however. The buyer meant the one sailing in October, while the seller meant the one sailing in December. When the cotton arrived on the later ship, the buyer refused to complete the purchase. The seller then sued for breach of contract. The court found for the buyer, holding that this was a case of mutual mistake of fact so there was no meeting of the minds and thus no contract.[6]

- Did a party make a mistake of judgment? Unlike a mistake of fact, a mistake of judgment is not grounds for undoing a contract. A mistake of judgment differs from a mistake of fact in that a *mistake of judgment* occurs when the parties make an erroneous assessment about the value of some aspect of what is bargained for. For example, if a developer buys an apartment building in the belief that real estate values in that location will soon skyrocket, but two years later prices have not risen, the contract is still valid. The mistake was in the developer's own judgment, not in the character of the subject of the bargain, the apartment building. Similarly, a court held that a contract to sell a stone for $1 was enforceable when neither party knew at the time that the stone was in fact a diamond.[7] It should be noted, however, that sometimes distinguishing between mistakes of fact and mistakes of judgment is very difficult.
- Was there a breach of contract by one party that resulted in damages to the other party? Breaches of contract are usually not punished in and of themselves. Some substantial damage to the other party must result for a court to provide a remedy for breach of contract.
- Did the party claiming injury mitigate the damages? When a breach of contract has taken place that causes injury to one party, the injured party has a common-law duty to ensure that the injury does not become worse or, in some cases, to attempt to lessen the injury. If the

party does not mitigate its damages, a court may order the defendant to pay only the damages that would have occurred had the plaintiff used reasonable efforts to limit the damage resulting from the defendant's breach.

EFFECT OF BANKRUPTCY

The entrepreneur should understand what happens if a party to a contract goes into voluntary or involuntary bankruptcy. As will be explained in detail in Chapter 12, when a party enters bankruptcy, the law provides for an *automatic stay,* which means that creditors are barred from taking any legal action to enforce the contract or to collect money owing under it. A company that has a contract with the bankrupt party (the *debtor*) may neither foreclose on collateral nor stop performing its obligations under the contract without first receiving permission from the bankruptcy court. A provision in a contract that purports to give a party the right to terminate the contract if the other party goes into bankruptcy (a *bankruptcy clause*) is not enforceable.

The penalty for willful violation of an automatic stay is stiff. The debtor may recover lost profits and punitive damages. An entrepreneur who has a contract with a party in bankruptcy, or in danger of entering bankruptcy, should consult with a lawyer before taking any action to enforce or terminate the contract.

In addition to having the benefit of the automatic stay, a debtor may also choose which contracts it wishes to maintain and which it wants to reject. If the debtor rejects a contract, then the other party becomes an unsecured creditor of the debtor for an amount equal to the damage caused by the breach of contract. This often means that the nonbreaching party either receives only cents on the dollar or nothing if all of the debtor's assets are mortgaged or otherwise have been used as collateral for secured loans. On the other hand, if the debtor chooses to affirm a contract (as would happen with a lease with a below-market rent or a favorable supply contract in a tight market), then the other party must continue to perform it in accordance with its terms.

Remedies

When a breach of contract occurs, remedies can be monetary, or if monetary compensation would not be adequate, they can take the form of specific performance or an injunction. In some cases where there is no contract, the courts may grant limited relief under the theory of promissory estoppel or provide compensation for the services rendered under the doctrine of quantum meruit, both of which are discussed later in this chapter.

Monetary Damages

If one party breaches a contract, the nonbreaching party is usually entitled to monetary damages. Damages can take one of three forms: expectation damages, reliance damages, and restitution. Sometimes more than one remedy is appropriate; in that case, the plaintiff may ask for remedies measured by each of the three types of damages. In some cases, consequential and liquidated damages may also be available.

EXPECTATION DAMAGES *Expectation damages* compensate the plaintiff for the amount it lost as a result of the defendant's breach of contract; in other words, the damages put the plaintiff in the position it would have been in if the contract had not been breached. For example, suppose that Angela agrees to design Zany's software for $2,000 (payable on delivery) and that Zany has a contract to resell the software for $3,000, which will net her $1,000. If Angela fails to deliver the software, then subject to the duty to mitigate damages discussed below, she will be liable for expectation damages in the amount of $1,000. This is the amount required to put Zany in the position she would have been in had Angela completed the job.

RELIANCE DAMAGES A second measurement of damages is *reliance,* which compensates the plaintiff for any expenditures made in reliance on a contract that was subsequently breached. Instead of giving the plaintiff the benefit of the bargain (expectation damages), reliance damages return the plaintiff to the position that he or she was in before the contract was formed. For example, suppose that Jim agrees to sell Frank a mainframe computer system, and Frank invests in renovating a room to allow for proper ventilation and cooling of the computer. If Jim then sells the computer to someone else, Jim will be required to reimburse Frank for the renovation expenses.

RESTITUTION Restitution is similar to reliance damages, but whereas reliance damages look at what the plaintiff has lost, restitution looks at what both parties have gained from the transaction. *Restitution* puts both parties back in the same position they were in before the contract was formed. For example, if Zany paid Angela $2,000 when she commissioned the programming, but Angela never wrote the program, Angela has benefited by receiving the $2,000. Thus, Zany's restitution damages are $2,000.

MITIGATION The nonbreaching party is required to make reasonable efforts to minimize damages in the event of a breach. This is called *mitigation of damages.*

Thus, if the supplier fails to deliver goods in accordance with the contract, the buyer must try to procure them elsewhere. Using our software example, if Zany learns that Angela will be unable to fulfill the contract, Zany is required to try to find someone else to provide the software. If Zany is able to hire another programmer to write the software at the cost of $2,200, then Angela will be liable for only $200—the additional amount Zany was required to pay to get the software written. If Zany could have hired someone else but didn't, then a court probably would award Zany only $200, which is the additional amount she would have paid had she properly mitigated her damages.

Similarly, suppose that Christina's company has a contract to sell 10,000 game pieces to a game manufacturer on a certain schedule. If she doesn't meet her obligations under this contract, Christina will lose a great deal of money and the possibility of future contracts with that company. Christina has a contract with Trevor's company for production and delivery of certain chemicals used in the production of the game pieces. Two weeks before she must deliver her first installment of game pieces, Trevor informs Christina that his regular shipment of chemicals will be late, which Christina knows will delay her shipment unacceptably. In this case, Christina has a duty to mitigate the damages caused by Trevor's breach, perhaps by calling other suppliers or by substituting another chemical. She may not simply sit back, lose her contract with the game manufacturer, and then sue Trevor for the loss of her profit on the contract.

If an employee is fired in violation of an employment agreement, the employee must try to find comparable work. If the employee fails to take a comparable job elsewhere, then (unless the employment contract explicitly provides that the employee has no duty to seek other employment) the employee will be able to recover only the difference between what would have

FROM THE TRENCHES

Actress Shirley MacLaine and Twentieth Century-Fox Film Corp. signed a contract for MacLaine to appear in the musical motion picture *Bloomer Girl* in 1966. Before production began, the studio decided not to produce *Bloomer Girl* and instead offered MacLaine a role in a dramatic Western called *Big Country.* MacLaine declined the offer and sued the studio for the compensation due under the contract. The studio conceded that a valid contract had been breached but contended that MacLaine had failed to properly mitigate damages by unreasonably refusing to accept the studio's offer of the leading role in *Big Country.*

The court ruled for MacLaine, finding that the *Big Country* lead was both different from and inferior to the role in *Bloomer Girl*. The court reasoned that *Bloomer Girl* was a musical to be produced in Los Angeles that would have called upon MacLaine's talents as a dancer and an actress. *Big Country,* on the other hand, was a Western requiring a straight dramatic role and was to be filmed in Australia. The court said that the role of dramatic actress in a Western is not equivalent or substantially equivalent to the lead in a song-and-dance production, and therefore MacLaine was not obligated to accept the role as mitigation.

Source: Parker v. Twentieth Century-Fox Film Corp., 474 P.2d 689 (Cal. 1970).

been paid under the employment agreement and what he or she could have earned at the comparable job.

CONSEQUENTIAL DAMAGES AND LIQUIDATED DAMAGES Consequential damages are damages that the plaintiff is entitled to as compensation for losses that occur as a foreseeable result of a breach. Consequential damages can include harm resulting from the loss of future business. For example, if Zany loses a future contract worth $5,000 because of Angela's failure to deliver the software on time, Zany may be entitled to consequential damages of $5,000. To be recoverable, the damages must be reasonably foreseeable. Consequential damages will be awarded only if the breaching party knew, or should have known, that the loss would result from a breach of contract. In our software example, Zany will be entitled to consequential damages only if Angela knew, or should have known, that the successful delivery of the software would allow Zany to receive a future contract worth $5,000. Angela will not be liable for consequential damages if Zany mitigates and receives the future contract, or if she fails to mitigate properly and loses the contract as a result. But, if Zany tries to mitigate but cannot find another programmer to write the software, then Angela will be liable for the damages that were reasonably foreseeable.

The nonbreaching party is entitled to receive consequential damages based on lost future profit only if he or she can demonstrate that the profit would have been earned had the other party not breached the contract. This requirement can be a problem for entrepreneurs who seek to recover lost profits for a business that either never got started or ran for only a short time.

One way to address this problem is to provide for liquidated damages in the contract. A liquidated damages provision, agreed on ahead of time, will specify a set figure that the breaching party will pay the injured party in the event of breach. The figure should be the parties' best estimate of what their expectation damages would be. If the specified amount exceeds this reasonable estimate, the court may consider it a form of punishment, which is not permissible under contract law, and refuse to enforce the liquidated damages provision.

Nonmonetary Equitable Remedies

SPECIFIC PERFORMANCE AND INJUNCTIONS Sometimes granting monetary damages to a plaintiff is neither appropriate nor suitable compensation for the defendant's contract breach. In such cases, the court may exercise its discretionary, equitable powers to grant *specific performance,* that is, order the defendant to do exactly what it promised. Specific performance is used if (1) the item involved in the contract was unique (e.g., a sculpture); (2) the contract involved real property; or (3) the calculation of monetary damages would likely be difficult to do accurately, making it unfair to do so.

Injunctions are court orders to do something or to refrain from doing something. For example, although specific performance by an employee may never be required in a case for breach of an employment contract (individuals may not be forced to work), courts can enjoin the employee from working for the injured party's competitor. Before a case goes to trial, a court sometimes will issue a temporary restraining order (*TRO*) or preliminary injunction to preserve the status quo. Courts usually will not issue a TRO or preliminary injunction unless the plaintiff proves that it will be irreparably damaged if the defendant does not halt certain conduct (e.g., disclosure of trade secrets in violation of a nondisclosure agreement).

RESCISSION In some situations, such as mistake or misrepresentation, in which enforcing the contract would be unfair, a court may exercise its equitable powers and *rescind* (cancel) the contract and order restitution. For example, Geert, an importer, paid $7,500 for a very rare desk that turned out to be a reproduction worth only $2,000. If the seller misled the importer and told him that the desk was genuine when the seller knew it to be a reproduction, then the court could rescind the contract, and each party would return the benefit it received up until that point. Geert would return the desk in exchange for the return of his $7,500.

PROMISSORY ESTOPPEL

Under certain circumstances, a court will invoke an equitable doctrine called *promissory estoppel* to give limited relief to a person who has reasonably and foreseeably relied, to his or her detriment, on the promises of another. This is most likely to occur when a person relies on promises made in the course of negotiations that break down before there is a meeting of the minds on all essential terms.

A party may recover under promissory estoppel only if four conditions are met: (1) there must be a promise, (2) reliance on the promise must be genuine and justifiable, (3) the actions taken in reliance must be *reasonably foreseeable* to the person making the promise, and (4) grave injustice must result if no relief is given. If all four requirements are met, then the court may require the person who made the promise to pay to the person who relied to his or her detriment damages in an amount equal to the out-of-pocket loss the plaintiff suffered by relying on the promise.

For example, in a landmark case, Hoffman had been negotiating with Red Owl Stores for two years, trying to secure a franchise for a Red Owl grocery store. During the two-year period, Hoffman relied on the promise Red Owl had made that he could get a franchise for a stated price. In reliance on that and other promises, he moved, bought a small grocery store to gain experience, sold a bakery that he had previously owned, and borrowed money from his family. Negotiations broke down when the chain insisted that Hoffman's father-in-law sign a document stating that the money he was advancing was an outright gift. Hoffman sued Red Owl for damages based on its failure to keep promises that had induced Hoffman to act to his detriment. The court held that the doctrine of promissory estoppel applied and awarded Hoffman reliance damages equal to the amount he was out-of-pocket because of his reliance on Red Owl's promises.[8]

Quantum Meruit

Quantum meruit can be used to recover the value of products or services provided in the absence of a contract in a situation in which the products or services clearly were needed but the party receiving the benefit could not agree to purchase them. For example, if Fiona is unconscious on the side of the road, and paramedics pick her up and take her to the emergency room, then Fiona will be required to pay the paramedics, the hospital, and the physician treating her the value of the

FROM THE TRENCHES

Michigan passed several statutes allowing municipalities to provide tax exemptions for businesses to encourage the creation and maintenance of jobs. In 1988, General Motors Corp. (GM) announced that it would build a new vehicle, the Chevrolet Caprice, at its plant in Willow Run, Michigan. GM applied for and received a twelve-year, 50 percent reduction in its property taxes for its $75 million project. In 1991, after suffering record losses, GM announced its intention to close its Willow Run manufacturing plant in Michigan and instead build its Chevrolet Caprice models exclusively at its plant in Arlington, Texas.

Michigan and the county and township where the plant was located sued GM to prevent it from closing the Willow Run plant. The plaintiffs claimed that GM had breached a contract created by the tax abatement and that, even if a contract did not exist, GM should be prevented from closing the plant under the doctrine of promissory estoppel.

The trial court ruled that although there was no contract, GM was bound by promissory estoppel to continue operations at the Willow Run plant as long as the company continued to manufacture the Caprice model. The trial court stated that the citizens of the surrounding area had given up millions of tax dollars, which could have been used for education and government services, in return for the plant. Therefore, the trial court reasoned, it would be a gross inequity and patently unfair to allow GM to close the plant and lay off 4,500 workers just because it thought it could make the same cars more cheaply somewhere else.

The appellate court, however, overturned the trial court decision, holding that promissory estoppel did not apply. GM had merely taken advantage of a statutory opportunity, and GM's abatement application did not constitute a promise or an assurance of continued employment.

Source: Charter Township of Ypsilanti v. General Motors Corp., 506 N.W.2d 556 (Mich. Ct. App. 1993).

services provided, even though she did not ask for them and did not agree to pay for them.

Similarly, suppose that an entrepreneur asks an advertising agency to place an advertisement. The advertising agency contracts with an industry publication to place the advertisement but fails to pay for it. Under the doctrine of quantum meruit, the advertising agency's default on payment for the advertisement will render the entrepreneur liable to the publication for the value of the benefit the entrepreneur received (the advertisement). The entrepreneur must pay the publication even though there was no contract between the entrepreneur and the publication.

LEASES

Entrepreneurs who do not work out of their homes may need to lease a place in which to conduct the business. A *lease* is a contract between a landlord (also called a *lessor*) and tenant (also called a *lessee*). Usually, the landlord presents a preprinted contract with language favoring his or her interests. It is then up to the tenant to try to negotiate better terms.

The best way for a potential tenant to approach a lease negotiation is to determine which issues are important and rank them. By systematically considering all options in advance, the tenant minimizes the possibility that important interests will be overlooked.

For example, when negotiating a lease for a restaurant, securing a good location is the primary concern. For example, it is more important for Bruce to locate his rotisserie chicken restaurant in the vacant slot next to the anchor tenant, a well-known video rental store, than to pay $300 per month less in rent for a vacant space at the far end of the mall. Without carefully considering his business's ultimate needs, Bruce might have bargained away thousands of dollars of income each month just to save $300.

A tenant should carefully think through all aspects of what he or she wants in a lease. For example, in rental negotiations for the restaurant space, Bruce might seek a provision by which the landlord promises not to rent space to another take-out restaurant in the same half of the mall. Other issues to consider include the landlord's provision of janitorial services; snow and trash removal; maintenance of plumbing and electrical systems; repair, maintenance, or even remodeling of the interior of the rental property; payment of utilities and property taxes; guaranties against environmental hazards; indemnification provisions; and maintenance of the building's common areas (such as lobbies and hallways). If the lessee is a start-up, it is not uncommon for the lessor to demand a personal guarantee by the major shareholder.

It is also important to make sure that the lessee's contemplated use of the property does not interfere with anyone else's property rights. In one situation, the entrepreneurs' neighbors threatened to sue them for using the alleyway. They claimed that the entrepreneurs were violating their easement. The entrepreneurs ended up buying some of the neighbors' space to appease them.

Two important elements that appear in almost every commercial lease merit some discussion: (1) the rental charge and (2) restrictions on subleasing the space or assigning the lease to a third party. Often the rental charge is a flat monthly or yearly rate. Sometimes, however, the landlord may require some percentage of the tenant's gross sales, in addition to the flat rate. For example, Bruce might be charged a $3,000 flat rate, plus 7 percent of his gross sales above $100,000 each year, not to exceed $20,000 per year. In such a situation, Bruce would be wise to clearly define what is meant by gross sales, carefully excluding such things as sales tax, which are not really a part of his income.

Subleasing and assignment of a lease to a third party are very important issues for entrepreneurs setting up a new business. Should they find themselves in an unprofitable location or even on the verge of going out of business, they will not want to be responsible for the entire duration of the lease. A landlord may agree to permit the tenant to sublet the

FROM THE TRENCHES

When they started renovating, several entrepreneurs found asbestos in the building they were leasing. The lease did not specify who was responsible for remedying preexisting environmental problems. The tenants had to negotiate with the landlord after the fact to establish who was responsible for removing the asbestos.

space to a responsible third party, if necessary, with the tenant remaining ultimately responsible for the payment of the rent. The landlord may not agree to a tenant's request for the right to assign the remainder of the lease to a third party, because an assignment would eliminate the original tenant's involvement completely and potentially leave the landlord in the position of trying to extract rent from an uncooperative or insolvent new tenant.

In fact, landlords often attempt to forestall the possibility of subletting or lease assignment completely by allowing the tenant to sublet the space or assign the lease only with the landlord's prior written consent. In practice, requiring the landlord's consent means that the tenant has no such right. Tenants can even the playing field a bit by negotiating a sentence into the contract that states, "The landlord's consent shall not unreasonably be withheld." Even when subletting or assignment is permitted, the landlord may require that the tenant share with the landlord any excess rent the subtenant or assignee pays the original tenant over and above the rent specified in the original lease.

Contracts for the Purchase of Real Property

The laws governing the acquisition of real property, such as an empty lot or a building, are highly technical and vary markedly from one state to another. An entrepreneur should never enter into a contract to buy real property without first consulting an experienced real-property lawyer in the state where the property is located.

One particularly dangerous trap for the unwary is liability for the cleanup of hazardous waste. Under the Comprehensive Environmental Response, Compensation, and Liability Act (CERCLA), the current owner or operator of real property can be liable for the cleanup of all hazardous waste on the property even if it was dumped there by a previous owner. To avoid liability, the purchaser must be able to prove that it acquired the facility after the hazardous substances were disposed of and without any knowledge or reason to know that hazardous substances had previously been disposed of at the facility. To establish that it had no reason to know that hazardous substances were disposed of at the facility, the purchaser

FROM THE TRENCHES

A partnership that ran a local newspaper planned to buy a small building. Before doing so, one of the partners consulted with an experienced lawyer, who suggested that they hire an environmental auditing firm to obtain and analyze soil and water samples. The audit revealed the existence of hazardous waste underground. Armed with their report, the partners were able to negotiate a more favorable purchase price.

must show that, prior to the sale, it undertook all appropriate inquiry into the previous ownership and uses of the property consistent with good commercial or customary practice. This can be very difficult to prove, and counsel experienced in environmental law should be consulted to help devise an appropriate environmental audit.

Loan Agreements

Loan agreements, which are discussed in more detail in Chapter 12, are usually long, standardized agreements, carefully designed to ensure that the lender's money will be repaid (to the extent it is possible to ensure such a thing). Loan agreements are also characterized by many technical clauses regarding calculation of interest, interest rates, special repayment terms, and so forth. As with all contracts, the parties have a duty to read, and therefore be responsible for, the agreement. However, this duty is especially important with loan agreements, which may contain substantial obligations for the borrower buried in technical language. An entrepreneur should not sign a loan agreement without first consulting with counsel.

Four particular loan agreement provisions require the borrower's special scrutiny:

1. *Logistical details of receiving the loan,* such as whether the money will be wired or sent by check, and whether the amount will be transferred in full or in installments.

2. *Conditions precedent,* which are all the conditions that must be met by the borrower (or, in some cases, a third party) before the lender is obligated to fund the loan.

3. *Covenants,* which are promises made by the borrower to the lender that, if breached, will result in an event of default and a termination of the loan, usually thereby accelerating payment of all amounts due.

4. *Repayment terms,* including any rights to cure an event of default due to a late or missed payment.

In addition, if the loan is secured by a mortgage or deed of trust on real property or by a security interest in other collateral, it is critical that the borrower understand what happens to the collateral if there is an event of default and whether the creditor has recourse to all assets of the borrower or only the collateral. (Secured lending is discussed in Chapter 12.)

Putting it into Practice

Kendra knew that she needed to negotiate and sign several contracts to keep DataAccelleation on the fast track. DataAccelleation had outgrown Kendra's basement, so the first order of business was renting office space. After a week of searching for an appropriate location, Kendra found one that both met DataAccelleation's needs and was affordable. But the landlord refused to lease the premises to DataAccelleation unless Kendra personally guaranteed the payments due under the lease. At first Kendra balked at doing this, but after she checked around, she discovered that a personal guaranty by the key shareholder was customary when start-ups rented space. She wanted to limit her exposure, though, so she negotiated a two-year lease, with three one-year options.

After reading the proposed lease and going over it with Sanjay Datar, Kendra had some other concerns as well. The first issue was employee parking. Because the proposed space was downtown, parking would be both scarce and expensive. She knew that the landlord owned an adjacent parking lot and proposed that DataAccelleation be given five free spaces. The landlord balked and countered with an offer of one free space and the guaranteed right to rent an additional space at the lowest available market rate. After some haggling, Kendra and the landlord agreed that the lease would provide for two free spaces and the right to rent an additional two spaces at the lowest rate charged any other person.

The second issue was outside lighting. Kendra and the other programmers were likely to work late many nights, and she was concerned about the lack of lighting in the area. She raised the issue with the landlord, who said that he too had been unhappy with the street lighting. The landlord agreed to install several external lights.

The final lease issue was a provision prohibiting an assignment of the lease or the subleasing of the space. The landlord explained that he prohibited lease assignments because the party assuming the lease might not be creditworthy, and he was very selective about the type of tenants he allowed. After some discussion, Kendra agreed to the no-assignment provision in exchange for the right to sublease. In the event of a sublease, Kendra and DataAccelleation agreed that they would be liable for the rental payments if the sublessee failed to make them and that any remaining one-year options would be extinguished.

With the lease in hand, Kendra and the Colgates worked furiously to finish the product in preparation for its upcoming launch.

NOTES

1. *See* HOWARD H. STEVENSON, DO LUNCH OR BE LUNCH 150 (1998).
2. Engleman v. General Accident, Fire & Life Assurance Corp., 250 F.2d 202 (9th Cir. 1957).
3. Wickham & Burton Coal Co. v. Farmers' Lumber Co., 179 N.W. 417 (Iowa 1920).
4. Dahl v. HEM Pharms. Corp., 7 F.3d 1399 (9th Cir. 1991).
5. Dwight v. Tobin, 947 F.2d 455 (11th Cir. 1991).
6. Raffles v. Wichelhaus, 159 Eng. Rep. 375 (Exch. 1864).
7. Wood v. Boynton, 25 N.W. 42 (Wis. 1885).
8. Hoffman v. Red Owl Stores, Inc., 133 N.W.2d 267 (Wis. 1965).

Chapter 9

E-Commerce and Sales of Goods and Services

Many entrepreneurs are in the business of selling goods. Entrepreneurs providing services will almost certainly buy goods as part of their business. Sometimes goods delivered pursuant to a contract do not live up to the buyer's expectations. The buyer may sue the seller for breaching an express or implied warranty that the goods sold would have certain qualities or would perform in a certain way. Alternatively, if the product has a defect or did not contain proper warnings, the plaintiff may sue in tort for strict product liability, which imposes liability regardless of the seller's fault. Often advertisements will include claims about the quality of a service or a product's performance. False or misleading advertising is illegal, as is unfair competition, in connection with the sale of goods or services.

The chapter begins with a brief discussion of Article 2 of the Uniform Commercial Code (UCC), which governs the sale of goods, and identifies several important differences between Article 2 and the common law of contracts discussed in Chapter 8. It then discusses express and implied warranties under the UCC. The Uniform Computer Information Transactions Act (UCITA), a model statute designed to regulate software licenses and computer information, is summarized, as is the Convention on Contracts for the International Sale of Goods (CISG). Exhibit 9.1 identifies some of the key differences between the UCC, the common law of contracts, UCITA, and CISG. The chapter examines strict liability in tort for defective products and describes the important role played by administrative agencies in regulating the advertising and sale of certain products and services. Online and offline consumer privacy issues are addressed along with laws banning deceptive advertising and unfair competition. The chapter concludes with a detailed analysis of the various jurisdictional and choice-of-law issues associated with sales of goods and services on the Internet.

Sales of Goods Under Article 2 of the UCC

Definition of "Goods"

Article 2 of the UCC governs the sale of goods. Section 2-105 defines *goods* as "all things (including specially manufactured goods) which are movable at the time of identification to the contract for sale." Identification to the contract means the designation—by marking, setting aside, or other means—of the particular goods that are to be supplied under the contract. It is important to know whether a product is a good, because it affects both the liability of the manufacturer under the UCC's warranties and the exposure of firms in the chain of distribution to suits for strict product liability in tort.

FROM THE TRENCHES

Jasmine Bell was driving with her two children on a highway. Nearby, a van struck a telephone pole, causing it to break and the lines to sag over the highway. Bell's car was caught in the lines, lifted off the ground, and landed on its back. One of the children died. Jasmine Bell sued the telephone pole manufacturer, alleging a defective product. The case centered on whether the telephone pole was a product or a fixture on real property. The court held that it could be both and permitted the product liability case to proceed.

Source: Bell v. T.R. Miller Mill Co., Prod. Liab. Rep. (CCH) ¶ 15,743 (Feb. 4, 2000).

EXHIBIT 9.1

COMPARISON OF THE UCC, COMMON LAW, UCITA, AND CISG

	Scope	Battle of the Forms	Warranties	Statute of Frauds
UCC	Sale of goods	Contract even if acceptance has additional or different terms	1. Implied warranties of merchant-ability and fitness for a particular purpose 2. Any express warranties made	Sales of $500 or more
Common Law	1. Provision of services 2. Contracts for sale of land or securities 3. Loan agreements	Mirror-image rule	Any express warranties made	1. Transfer of real estate 2. Contract that can't be performed within one year 3. Prenuptial agreement 4. Agreement to pay debt of another
UCITA	Computer information (including software, computer games, and online access)	Contract even if acceptance has additional or different terms unless acceptance materially alters the offer	1. Warranty of noninterference and noninfringement 2. Implied warranties of merchantability of computer program, informational content, fitness for licensee's particular purpose, and fitness for system integration 3. Any express warranties made	Contracts for $5,000 or more

continued...

EXHIBIT 9.1 (CONTINUED)

COMPARISON OF THE UCC, COMMON LAW, UCITA, AND CISG

	Scope	Battle of the Forms	Warranties	Statute of Frauds
CISG	Sale of goods by merchants in different countries unless parties opt out	In practice, mirror image rule	1. Implied warranties of merchantability and fitness for a particular use 2. Any express warranties made	None

Contract Formation

Although the UCC's requirements of offer, acceptance, and consideration parallel the common-law requirements, the code is more liberal in some respects. For example, the UCC presumes the existence of a contract if the parties act as if there is one, such as when a seller has shipped goods and the buyer has paid for them. This is the case even if material terms are omitted. To determine the exact terms of the contract, a court will examine whatever writings existed between the parties, identify the provisions on which the writings agree, and fill in the rest of the terms based on the circumstances, industry practice, and certain rules set forth in Article 2 (called *gap fillers*).

The UCC abolishes the mirror-image rule and provides that a contract can be formed even if the acceptance contains terms that are in addition to, or even in conflict with, those in the offer. If the parties intended to close a deal, then there is definitely a contract. Should a party wish to avoid a contract, it should make this explicit by using the language of the UCC: "This acceptance is expressly made conditional on offeror's assent to all additional or different terms contained herein. Should offeror not give assent to said terms, there is no contract between the parties." Less direct language has been held to be an acceptance.

As under the common law, however, there still must be a meeting of the minds. If there is a mistake of fact, then no contract will result.

FROM THE TRENCHES

ProCD compiled information from more than 3,000 telephone directories into a single database at a cost of more than $10 million. It sold this database on CD-ROM under the name SelectPhone. Each CD-ROM package contained a *shrink-wrap* license, that is, a license that customers couldn't read when they bought the product but were deemed to have accepted by opening the wrapping around the envelope containing the disks or clicking on the "I Accept" box of their computer screens. The shrink-wrap license prohibited the unauthorized resale of the database. Zeidenberg purchased the SelectPhone CD-ROM and made the information available on the Internet through Silken Mountain Web Services, Inc. He charged a price less than the cost of SelectPhone for access to the database. ProCD sued Zeidenberg for violating the license agreement.

The U.S. Court of Appeals for the Seventh Circuit upheld the shrink-wrap agreement and held that the terms were binding on the buyer, unless they were objectionable under contract law in general. The court drew an analogy with airline tickets or concert tickets, where the buyer accepts the terms by using the ticket. The UCC permits contracts to be formed by any manner sufficient to show agreement, including the conduct of the parties. ProCD had made an offer that Zeidenberg could accept by reading the contract at leisure after purchasing the box; and he had accepted it because the software would not let him proceed without clicking the "I Accept" box. Had he found the terms objectionable, or the overall contract to be worth less than the purchase price, he could have avoided the contract by returning the package. Refusing to apply the terms of the agreement would make buyers worse off in the long run by increasing the cost of products.

Source: ProCD, Inc. v. Zeidenberg, 86 F.3d 1447 (7th Cir. 1996).

Like other contracts, a supply agreement details who the parties are and the general terms of the relationship. If the supplier is doing something new and innovative for the entrepreneur, the entrepreneur needs to ensure that this privilege is protected, especially if the two parties have worked together in developing the product.

When goods or services are being purchased on credit through a sales representative, the seller may afford itself some flexibility by including an approval clause in the sales order specifying that the order, although signed

FROM THE TRENCHES

Spokane Computer Systems was planning to purchase a surge protector to protect its computers from damage caused by electrical surges. The employee in charge of investigating the various products found several units priced between $50 and $200. The employee also contacted Konic International Corp., whose salesman quoted a price of "fifty-six twenty." The salesman meant $5,620, but the Spokane employee thought he meant $56.20.

The discrepancy was not discovered until after the equipment was installed and the invoice was received. Spokane asked Konic to remove the equipment, but Konic refused and sued Spokane for nonpayment.

The court ruled that because both parties attributed a different meaning to the same ambiguous term "fifty-six twenty," there was no meeting of the minds, and thus no valid contract was formed. The court relieved Spokane of its debt.

Source: Konic Int'l Corp. v. Spokane Computer Sys., Inc., 708 P.2d 932 (Idaho Ct. App. 1985).

by the sales representative, is not a valid contract until it has been approved by either the home office or a corporate officer above a specified level. In this way, the sales representative is free to take orders without unknowingly binding the company to an unauthorized buyer.

The UCC permits merchants to enter into enforceable option contracts for the sale of goods without the payment of consideration. However, the option cannot be in effect for more than three months. Section 2-104 of the UCC defines *merchant* as:

> *[A person who deals in goods of the kind involved in the transaction or] otherwise by his occupation holds himself out as having knowledge or skill peculiar to the practices or goods involved in the transaction or to whom such knowledge or skill may be attributed by his employment of an agent or broker or other intermediary who by his occupation holds himself out as having such knowledge or skill.*

Thus, a casual seller with no special knowledge or skill peculiar to the goods involved is not a merchant.

FROM THE TRENCHES

Two entrepreneurs collaborated with their supplier to develop a uniquely flavored tortilla. They didn't realize what a success it would be and later had to negotiate with the supplier to ensure that the supplier would not start selling the tortilla to others. They stated, "We worked long and hard with our supplier to develop a special recipe for a flavored tortilla. Ideally you make sure you agree in advance with the supplier that he can't go off and distribute the product to the competitor."

Battle of the Forms

Because the UCC makes it possible for a contract to exist even if the parties exchange confirmation forms that contain additional or conflicting terms that are advantageous to the sender, the question arises as to which terms govern the sale. If there is an acceptance with additional terms, the terms of the contract depend on whether both parties are merchants. If one of the parties is not a merchant, then the additional terms are deemed proposals and are not considered part of the contract unless they are expressly approved by all parties. If, however, all parties are merchants, then the additions are automatically considered part of the contract unless (1) any of the parties expressly objects to them within a reasonable time, (2) they materially alter the original offer (e.g., substitute a different product) or (3) the original offer contains a clause expressly limiting acceptance to the terms of the offer.

If the acceptance contains different terms, the answer is not clear. Most courts, however, apply the *knock-out rule,* whereby the conflicting terms knock each other out, and a UCC gap filler is substituted in their place.

Statute of Frauds

Section 2-201 of the UCC is a *statute of frauds* that provides that contracts for the sale of goods for $500 or more are unenforceable unless at least

FROM THE TRENCHES

Ionics, on three separate occasions, purchased thermostats from Elmwood for use in its water dispensers, sending purchase orders that contained various provisions in small type. One of the provisions stated that remedies would be in addition to those provided in law or equity, and another read: "Acceptance by the seller of this order shall be upon the terms and conditions set forth in [the order]. Said order can be so accepted only on the exact terms herein and set forth." Ionics also sent Elmwood a letter stating that the terms of the purchase order were extremely important to it and that any variations Elmwood desired would have to be discussed with Ionics.

Elmwood responded to each order with an acknowledgment form that had provisions in small type stating that the sale was only on the terms set forth therein as a counteroffer and that "[b]uyer shall be deemed to have accepted such counteroffer unless it is rejected in writing within ten (10) days of the receipt [thereof]." Among the terms and conditions of the acknowledgment form was a warranty provision that guaranteed the goods to be free of defects in materials and workmanship for a period of ninety days after purchase by the buyer or eighteen months since the date of manufacture, whichever should be longer. The form further provided: "There is no implied warranty of merchantability and no other warranty, expressed or implied, except such as is expressly set forth herein." The form went on to disclaim liability for consequential and incidental damages and for negligence.

Elmwood's products allegedly caused fires, and Ionics sued for a breach of the implied warranty of fitness. Elmwood asserted that its language disclaiming any implied warranties should control. The trial court ruled that the conflicting terms should be stricken and that the UCC warranty terms should be inserted in their place.

The U.S. Court of Appeals for the First Circuit affirmed, reasoning that where clauses on confirming forms conflict, each party is assumed to object to the conflicting clause of the other. As a result, the conflicting terms do not become part of the agreement. The contract consists of the terms originally expressly agreed to, the terms on which the confirmations agree, and the default terms provided by the UCC to substitute for the terms that conflicted. In this case, the default terms of the UCC provided an implied warranty of fitness.

Source: Ionics, Inc. v. Elmwood Sensors, Inc., 110 F.3d 184 (1st Cir. 1997).

partially in writing. It requires that only three elements be in writing: (1) a *statement* recognizing that an agreement exists, (2) the *signature* of the party against whom enforcement is sought, and (3) an indication of the *quantity of goods* being sold. If the contract is between merchants, then the contract can still be enforced against the party who has not signed it if the other party sent a written confirmation that the first party did not respond to within ten days. If a party goes to court to enforce a contract that specifies quantity but has other terms missing, the court will fill in the rest of the terms (including price) based on general tradition and practice within the particular industry.

ELECTRONIC CONTRACTS

E-Sign Act and Uniform Electronic Transactions Act

As explained in Chapter 8, the Electronic Signatures in Global and National Commerce Act (the E-Sign Act) provides that in transactions involving interstate or foreign commerce, "a signature, contract or other record relating to such transaction may not be denied legal effect, validity, or enforceability solely because it is in electronic form." The Uniform Electronic Transactions Act (UETA), which has been adopted by more than thirty-eight states, provides that electronic contracts may not be denied effect solely because they are in electronic form. As a result, electronic signatures will satisfy the UCC's statute of frauds in most cases.

Almost any mark or process intended to sign an electronic contract or record will constitute a valid electronic signature. These include a name typed at the bottom of an e-mail message and a "click-through" process on a computer screen whereby a person clicks on "I Agree" on a Web page. The E-Sign Act does not address the situation where the person to whom an electronic signature is attributed denies it. Digital signatures add cryptography and other security measures to electronic signatures. These include smart cards, thumbprints, retinal scans, and voice-recognition tests.

UETA does address the question of how mistakes and errors in electronic contracting should be handled. It requires a party transacting business on the Web to offer its counterpart the opportunity either (1) to confirm its assent to the terms by other means or (2) to revoke consent if it claims there was a mistake.

UNCITRAL

The United Nations Commission on International Trade Law (UNCITRAL) has promulgated a Model Law on Electronic Signatures and was deciding in early 2002 whether to pursue a proposed global treaty on electronic contracting that would focus primarily on contract formation. A draft document prepared by the UNCITRAL secretariat entitled "Legal aspects of electronic commerce—Electronic contracting provisions for a draft convention" would address such issues as (1) where an electronic contract is created (which can have important implications for jurisdiction and choice of law); (2) where the parties are located (where they have brick and mortar or where their servers are located); (3) how a party expresses consent in an electronic environment and what happens when a party disputes a signature imputed to it or claims that an electronic contract contains errors or mistakes; (4) at what time a contract is formed; and (5) whether displays of goods on a Web site are offers or just invitations to deal akin to newspaper advertisements. Other UNCITRAL initiatives are discussed at the end of this chapter.

UCC Article 2 Warranties

There are three types of warranties under Article 2: an express warranty, an implied warranty of merchantability, and an implied warranty of fitness for a particular purpose.

Express Warranty

An *express warranty* is an explicit guarantee by the seller that the goods will have certain qualities. Two requirements must be met to create an express warranty. First, the seller must make a statement or promise relating to the goods, provide a description of the goods, or furnish a sample or model of the goods. Second, the buyer must have relied on the seller's statement, promise, or sample in making the purchase decision. The seller has the burden of proving that the buyer did not rely on the representations.

Sellers of goods should be very careful about how they represent the qualities of their products. If a seller has made a representation about the product's qualities that is then relied on by the buyer in choosing to purchase that

FROM THE TRENCHES

A man wishing to buy his wife a diamond bracelet for Christmas consulted a jeweler, who offered to sell a specific bracelet for $15,000. The jeweler described the diamonds as "nice," but his appraisal letter, enclosed for insurance purposes, described the diamonds as "v.v.s. grade," which is one of the highest ratings in the quality classification system used by jewelers and gemologists. The customer purchased the bracelet and gave it to his wife.

Four months later, another jeweler looking at the bracelet informed the customer that the diamonds were not v.v.s. quality. The customer asked the original jeweler to replace the bracelet with one containing v.v.s. diamonds. The merchant refused but offered to refund the $15,000 purchase price in exchange for the return of the bracelet. Because the price of diamonds had appreciated during the four-month period, the customer rejected the offer and filed suit against the dealer for breach of express warranty.

The court found that the diamonds were substantially less than v.v.s. grade. The jeweler, however, contended that the appraisal letter was intended for insurance purposes only and that, in any case, it was merely an opinion. The court ruled that only the appraised value listed in the letter was for insurance purposes and that the description of the bracelet in the letter should be treated like any other statement that the jeweler made about the bracelet. The court also ruled that the jeweler's writing that the diamonds were v.v.s. quality was more than a mere opinion. When a person with superior knowledge makes a statement about goods and does not qualify the statement as a mere opinion, the statement will be treated as a statement of fact. Therefore, the jeweler's letter constituted an express warranty that the diamonds were v.v.s. quality, which the jeweler breached.

Source: Daughtrey v. Ashe, 413 S.E.2d 336 (Va. 1992).

product, the buyer can sue for breach of express warranty if the product does not live up to that representation. A warranty may be found even though the seller never uses the word "warranty" or "guarantee" and has no intention of making a warranty. For example, the statement "this printer prints seven color pages per minute" is an express warranty.

PUFFING If a seller is merely *puffing*, that is, expressing an opinion about the quality of the goods, then the seller has not made a warranty. For example, a statement that "this is a top-notch car" is puffing, whereas a factual statement such as "this car gets twenty-five miles to the gallon" is an express warranty. Unfortunately, the line between opinion and fact is difficult to draw. Much turns on the circumstances surrounding the representation, including the identities and relative knowledge of the parties involved.

If the seller asserts a fact of which the buyer was ignorant, the assertion is more likely to be a warranty. If, however, the seller merely states a view on something about which the buyer could be expected to have formed his or

FROM THE TRENCHES

Doug Connor, the president of Connor, Inc., a land-clearing business, purchased a large commercial grinding machine from Proto-Grind, Inc. The brochure for the machine stated that it could grind timber stumps and railroad ties into mulch. During a demonstration of the machine, Connor spoke to Protos, the president of Proto-Grind, and told him that he needed a machine that would grind palmettos as well as palm and other trees. Protos assured him that the machine was capable of doing this. Connor purchased the machine for $226,000 pursuant to a contract that provided for a two-week trial period to try the machine out. Connor waived this trial period for a discount of $5,500. He had problems with the machine, however, and sued for breach of express oral warranties that the machine would grind organic materials effectively, that the machine would be free from defects for a period of six months, and that Proto-Grind would fix the machine. Proto-Grind asserted that Connor had waived the express warranties when he waived the trial period.

continued...

FROM THE TRENCHES

continued...

The Florida Court of Appeal first ruled that only implied warranties may be waived when the buyer refuses an opportunity to inspect the product prior to purchase. Proto-Grind then argued that the statements were mere puffing or opinion and were not specific enough to rise to the dignity of an express warranty. The court found that Proto-Grind's statements could amount to more than sales talk. There was enough for the finder of fact to conclude that the alleged oral promises were more than mere puffing, that the product failed to meet the promise that it would sufficiently grind palm trees and palmettos, that Connor relied on these affirmations, and that because the deficiency of the product was not cured, Proto-Grind had breached this express warranty.

Source: Connor, Inc. v. Proto-Grind, Inc., 761 So. 2d 426 (Fla. Ct. App. 2000).

her own opinion, and the buyer can judge the validity of the seller's statement, then the seller's statement is an opinion.

Implied Warranty of Merchantability

The *implied warranty of merchantability* guarantees that the goods are reasonably fit for the general purpose for which they are sold and that they are properly packaged and labeled. The warranty applies to all goods sold by merchants in the normal course of business. This warranty is implied even if the seller makes no statements and furnishes no sample or model.

To be merchantable, the goods must (1) pass without objection in the trade under the contract description; (2) be fit for the ordinary purpose for which such goods are used; (3) be within the variations permitted by the agreement; (4) be of even kind, quality, and quantity within each unit and among all units involved; (5) be adequately contained, packaged, and labeled as the agreement may require; and (6) conform to the promises or affirmations of fact made on the container or label, if any.

The key issue in determining merchantability is whether the goods do what a reasonable person would expect of them. The contract description is crucial. Goods considered merchantable under one contract may

FROM THE TRENCHES

A hotel operator building a new hotel purchased blue carpet for its single rooms and mauve carpet for its double-occupancy rooms. Although the rate of occupancy in the blue-carpeted rooms had exceeded that of the mauve-carpeted rooms, within ninety days the mauve carpet was so badly worn that it was unsightly and needed to be replaced. The blue carpet, on the other hand, had maintained its original appearance.

An agent of the carpet manufacturer looked at the mauve carpet and agreed that the mauve carpet needed to be replaced. Nevertheless, the carpet manufacturer refused to replace it. The hotel operator sued for breach of an implied warranty of merchantability. The carpet manufacturer claimed that the carpet damage was due to excessive cleaning by the hotel operator and also misuse because the carpet was classified as "residential."

The court ruled for the hotel operator. The mauve carpet had been put on the same cleaning schedule as the blue carpet. Even though the carpet had been classified as residential, it had not been subjected to particularly heavy use during the period. In addition, the blue carpet had also been classified as residential but had not lost its original condition. The court held that the mauve carpet was not fit for any of its ordinary uses at the time of delivery; therefore, the carpet manufacturer had breached the implied warranty of merchantability.

Source: Meldco, Inc. v. Hollytex Carpet Mills, Inc., 796 P.2d 142 (Idaho Ct. App. 1990).

be considered not merchantable under another. For example, a bicycle with a cracked frame and bent wheels is not fit for the ordinary purpose for which bicycles are used, but it will pass under a contract for the sale of scrap metal.

Implied Warranty of Fitness for a Particular Purpose

The *implied warranty of fitness for a particular purpose* guarantees that the goods are fit for the particular purpose for which the seller recommended them. Unlike the implied warranty of merchantability, this warranty does not arise in every sale of goods by a merchant. It will be implied only if four elements are present: (1) the buyer had a particular purpose for the goods; (2) the seller knew or had reason to know of that purpose; (3) the buyer relied on the seller's expertise; and (4) the seller knew or had reason to know of the buyer's reliance. Although a warranty of fitness for a particular purpose can be created by any seller, typically the seller must be a merchant because the seller must purport to be an expert regarding the goods, and the buyer must have relied on the seller's expertise.

A seller may prove that a buyer did not rely on the seller's expertise by showing that (1) the buyer's expertise was equal to or superior to the seller's, (2) the buyer relied on the skill and judgment of persons hired by the buyer, or (3) the buyer supplied the seller with detailed specifications or designs that the seller was to follow.

Limiting Liability and Disclaimers

Subject to certain federal and state-law restrictions, the seller can limit its liability under any of these warranties. First, the seller need not make any express warranties. This may be difficult to do, however, because even a simple description of the goods may constitute a warranty. Second, a seller may disclaim any warranties of quality if it follows specifically delineated rules in the UCC designed to ensure that the buyer is aware of, and assents to, the disclaimers. A seller can exclude all implied warranties by using expressions such as "AS IS, WITH ALL FAULTS," or other language that in common understanding calls the buyer's attention to the exclusion of warranties and makes plain that there is no implied warranty. (Capital letters are used to fulfill the UCC's requirement that waivers of warranties be prominently displayed.) If this language is used, the buyer assumes the entire risk as to the quality of the goods involved. To avoid creating a warranty of fitness for a particular purpose, the seller can refrain from professing expertise with respect to the goods and can leave the selection to the buyer.

More commonly, the seller limits responsibility for the quality of the goods by limiting the remedies available to the buyer in the event of breach. A typical method is to include a provision limiting the seller's responsibility for defective goods to repair or replacement. It should be noted that some state laws limit the ability of sellers to disclaim warranties and to limit remedies in consumer contracts.

FROM THE TRENCHES

Walker Farms purchased a herbicide, ASSERT, produced by American Cyanamid Co. to use on crops of grain and potatoes. A Cyanamid representative told Walker that ASSERT was safe and posed no risk to potatoes even if sprayed directly on the plants. The label also stated that potatoes could be planted in rotation after applying ASSERT on certain grain crops. There was also a disclaimer on the label that stated:

> *Any damages arising from breach of this warranty shall be limited to direct damages and shall not include consequential commercial damages such as loss of profits or values or any other special or indirect damages. American Cyanamid Company makes no express or implied warranty, including other express or implied warranty of FITNESS or MERCHANTABILITY.*

Walker applied ASSERT to crops in 1988 and 1989 and then harvested potato crops on those same fields in 1989 and 1990. The crops were irregular and substandard. Walker sued Cyanamid on numerous theories, including breach of express warranty. Walker claimed that the limitation of liability provision on the label was unconscionable. The trial court found the provision unconscionable, and the jury awarded $3,428,703 in damages.

The Idaho Supreme Court upheld the verdict. The court found that Cyanamid had advised Walker that ASSERT was safe for his operation, that Walker proceeded under this premise, and that his assessment of risks was influenced by the representation. Cyanamid had greater knowledge regarding ASSERT. The provision on the label was ambiguous: it was logical to think direct damages would be the value of the potatoes, but the second clause seemed to suggest otherwise. Cyanamid's superior knowledge and its assertions that ASSERT was safe, coupled with the ambiguous label and Walker's lack of bargaining power concerning the limitation of liability, supported a finding of procedural unconscionability. Because a reasonable consumer would read the provision as not eliminating liability for damages like those to Walker's crops, the element of unfair surprise supported substantive unconscionability.

Source: Walker v. American Cyanamid Co., 948 P.2d 1123 (Idaho 1997).

Magnuson-Moss Warranty Act

The Magnuson-Moss Warranty Act is a federal law that protects consumers against deception in warranties. The Act provides that if a seller engaged in interstate or foreign commerce makes an express warranty to a buyer, then the seller may not disclaim the warranties of merchantability and fitness for a particular purpose.

Although no seller is required to make a written warranty under this Act, if the seller does make a written promise or affirmation of fact, then it must also state whether, for example, the warranty is a full or a limited warranty. A *full warranty* has to satisfy three requirements. First, it must give the consumer the right to free repair of the product within a reasonable time period or, after a reasonable number of failed attempts to fix the product, permit the customer to elect a full refund or replacement of a defective product. Second, the warrantor may not impose any time limit on the warranty's duration. Third, the warrantor may not exclude or limit damages for breach of warranty unless such exclusions are conspicuous on the face of the warranty. Any warranty that does not meet these minimum federal standards must be designated as *limited.*

Uniform Computer Information Transactions Act

As discussed further in Chapter 14, the Uniform Computer Information Transactions Act (UCITA) is a model statute promulgated by the National Conference of Commissioners on Uniform State Laws. Its goal is to provide a uniform commercial contract code for software licenses and other computer information transactions. As of January 2002, only Maryland and Virginia had adopted UCITA.

UCITA governs transactions in *computer information,* defined as "information in electronic form which is obtained from or through the use of a computer or which is in a form capable of being processed by a computer." Accordingly, it covers contracts to license or buy software, contracts to create computer programs, contracts for online access to databases, and contracts to distribute information over the Internet. It also governs custom software development and the acquisition of various rights in multimedia products.

Offer and acceptance under UCITA follow the common law. UCITA generally upholds shrink-wrap and click-wrap agreements as long as the buyer (or licensee) has the opportunity to review the terms before manifesting assent. In the absence of express assent to the license terms, the buyer (or licensee) must continue to use the product in order for the license agreement to be enforceable.

UCITA provides for several express and implied warranties that are not recognized under common law. The licensor must expressly warrant that the information furnished under the agreement will conform to any fact, promise, or description made by the licensor to the licensee. Under the warranty of *noninterference and noninfringement,* which is applicable only to licensors who are merchants, the licensor warrants that the information will be delivered free of the rightful claim of any third person by way of infringement or misappropriation.

Under the *implied warranty of merchantability of a computer program,* which is applicable only to licensors who are merchants, the licensor warrants to the end user that the program is fit for the ordinary purpose for which such computer programs are used. Under the *implied warranty of informational content,* which also is applicable only to licensors who are merchants, a licensor that is in a special relationship of reliance with a licensee and collects or provides data warrants that there is no inaccuracy caused by the merchant's failure to perform with reasonable care.

If a licensor has reason to know that the information is required for a particular purpose and that the licensee is relying on the licensor for expertise, then under the *warranty of fitness for the licensee's particular purpose,* the licensor warrants that the information will be fit for that purpose. If an agreement requires a licensor to provide a system consisting of computer programs and goods, and the licensor has reason to know that the licensee is relying on the licensor's skill or judgment to select the components, then under the *implied warranty of system integration,* the licensor warrants that the components will function together as a system.

Critics

Critics of UCITA (including the American Bar Association) charge that it goes too far in upholding software vendors' right to use click-wrap and other contracts to restrict user activities that would otherwise be permitted by the fair use exception to the copyright laws. Another controversial aspect of UCITA is a damages provision allowing self-help. UCITA provides that upon cancellation of a license, the licensor has the right to possess all copies of the licensed information held by the licensee and to prevent continued use. The licensor can do this through self-help if it does not breach the peace or damage property. Electronic self-help (through placing bugs or disabling time bombs) must meet the requirements of UCITA, which include obtaining the licensee's assent to the term authorizing use of electronic self-help and providing notice to the licensee prior to exercising self-help. As of March 2002, UCITA's widespread adoption by the states was in doubt.

International Sale of Goods and the Convention on Contracts for the International Sale of Goods

The UCC applies only to transactions within the United States. International sales of goods are outside its scope. The Convention on Contracts for the International Sale of Goods (CISG), promulgated under the United Nations, became effective in 1988. Many of the world's largest economies, including Canada, China, France, Germany, Russia, Singapore, and the United States, have ratified the convention.

CISG sets out substantive provisions of law to govern the formation of international sales contracts between merchants and the rights and obligations of buyers and sellers. CISG does not apply to sales of goods bought for personal, family, or household use, unless the seller neither knew nor should have known that the goods were for such use.

CISG is the default provision that applies if a sales contract involving merchants from different countries that are signatories to CISG is silent as to applicable law. In other words, if merchants from different signatory countries fail to specify that another law should govern their dealings, then CISG will automatically apply. Parties can vary the terms of CISG or elect to be governed by another set of laws if they expressly agree to do so.

CISG has no statute of frauds provision, so oral contracts for the sale of goods are fully enforceable. CISG also differs from the UCC in its treatment of the battle of the forms. Under CISG, a reply to an offer that purports to be an acceptance, but contains additional terms or other modifications that materially alter the terms of the offer, is deemed to be a rejection and counteroffer. In such a case, there is no contract. If the modifications do not materially alter the terms and the offeror fails to object in a timely fashion, then there is a contract, which will include the terms of the offer with the modifications stated in the acceptance. Price, payment, quality and quantity of goods, place and time of delivery, extent of one party's liability to the other, and settlement of disputes are all considered material topics. As a result, as a practical matter, CISG largely applies the mirror-image rule.

CISG also provides that there shall be regard for the "observance of good faith in international trade," which can limit a party's right to insist on *perfect tender,* that is, the delivery of goods that are exactly in accordance with the contract on the exact date specified. This contrasts with the UCC's perfect tender rule, which entitles a buyer to insist that the delivery of goods meet all of the requirements of the contract. For example, under the UCC a buyer would be entitled to reject goods delivered on June 2, if the contract specified delivery on June 1. Under CISG, if the one-day delay caused no harm to the buyer, then the buyer could not reject the goods on June 2.

CISG holds sellers liable for implied warranties of merchantability and fitness for particular use and for any express warranties they make. The implied warranty of merchantability does not attach if the buyer knew that the goods were not fit for ordinary use.

Strict Liability for Defective Products

Even if the seller makes no warranties, it may still be liable under the theory of strict product liability if the goods are defective. Product liability extends to anyone in the chain of distribution, including manufacturers, wholesalers, distributors, and retailers.

Most states have adopted strict product liability, whereby an injured person does not need to show that the defendant was negligent or otherwise at fault, or that a contractual relationship existed between the defendant and the injured person. The injured person merely needs to show that (1) the defendant was in the chain of distribution of a product sold in a defective condition, and (2) the defect caused the injury. For example, a person who is injured by a product purchased from a retail store can sue the original manufacturer.

A plaintiff injured by a product can also sue for negligence if he or she can prove that the defendant failed to use reasonable care in its design or manufacture. If the defendant made a warranty to the plaintiff, the plaintiff could also sue for breach of warranty. Proving negligence by the defendant allows the plaintiff to receive punitive damages, however, whereas a plaintiff can receive only compensatory damages for breach of warranty or strict product liability.

In the service industries, there is no strict liability (unless the service involves an ultrahazardous activity), only liability for negligence. In some cases, it is unclear whether an injury was caused by a defective product or a negligently performed service. For example, a person may be injured by a needle used by a dentist or the hair solution used by a beautician. Some courts apply strict liability in these situations. Other courts will not, saying the use of the product was incidental to the provision of a service.

Defective Product

An essential element for recovery in strict liability is proof of a defect in the product. The injured party must show that (1) the product was defective when it left the hands of the defendant, and (2) the defect made the product unreasonably dangerous. Typically, a product is dangerous if it does not meet the consumer's expectations as to its characteristics. For example, a consumer expects a stepladder not to break when someone stands on the bottom step.

Certain laws and regulations set minimum safety standards for products. Compliance with a regulatory scheme is not a conclusive defense, however. The regulatory standards are often considered minimal requirements, and compliance with them will not shield a manufacturer from liability in all circumstances. However, failing to comply with them is often a *prima facie* case of a defective product or negligence *per se* (that is, negligence without the proof of anything else).

A product may be dangerous because of a manufacturing defect, a design defect, or inadequate warnings, labeling, or instructions.

MANUFACTURING DEFECT A *manufacturing defect* is a flaw in the product that occurs during production, such as a failure to meet the design specifications. A product with a manufacturing defect is not like the others rolling off the production line. For example, suppose that the driver's seat in an automobile is designed to be bolted to the frame. If the worker forgets to tighten the bolts, the loose seat will be a manufacturing defect.

DESIGN DEFECT A *design defect* occurs when, even though the product is manufactured according to specifications, its inadequate design or poor choice of materials makes it dangerous to users. Typically, there is a finding of defective design if the product is not safe for its intended or reasonably foreseeable use. A highly publicized example was the Ford Pinto, which a jury found to be defectively designed because the car's fuel tank was too close to the rear axle, causing the tank to rupture when the car was struck from behind.

FAILURE TO WARN A product must carry adequate warnings of the risks involved in normal use. In the absence of such warnings, the product is defective due to *failure to warn.* For example, the manufacturer of a prescription drug must warn the user of possible side effects. A product must also include instructions on its safe use. For example, sellers have been found liable for failing to provide adequate instructions about the proper use and capacity of a hook and the assembly and use of a telescope and sun filter.

A warning will not shield a manufacturer from liability for a defectively manufactured or designed product. For example, an automobile manufacturer cannot escape liability for defectively designed brakes merely by warning that "Under certain conditions this car's brakes may fail." On the other hand, a plaintiff can win a suit for failure to warn even if there was no manufacturing or design defect.

FROM THE TRENCHES

John Potter and his fellow plaintiffs were shipyard workers injured through the extended use of pneumatic tools manufactured by the defendant. They used the tools to chip, grind, and smooth metal surfaces at General Dynamics for approximately twenty-five years. The plaintiffs developed permanent vascular and neurological impairment of their hands and were unable to continue their employment. They claimed that the tools were defectively designed. The defendant appealed a jury verdict for the plaintiffs, claiming that the plaintiffs were required to prove that there was a reasonable alternative design.

Because this was a defective design case, the Connecticut Supreme Court decided to apply the consumer expectations test, under which a product is unreasonably dangerous if it is more dangerous than would be contemplated by an ordinary consumer who purchased it, with the ordinary knowledge common to the community as to its characteristics. The court acknowledged that, in some instances, a product may be unreasonably dangerous to the user, and thereby give rise to product liability, even if no feasible alternative design is available. In this case, however, because the employer had substantially modified the tools, the court vacated the verdict against the manufacturer and ordered a new trial.

Comment: In applying the consumer expectations test, the Connecticut Supreme Court expressly rejected the proposed standard contained in the Restatement (Third) of Torts: Product Liability, which requires the plaintiff in a defective design case to prove the existence of a reasonable alternative design.

Source: Potter v. Chicago Pneumatic Tool Co., 694 A.2d 1319 (Conn. 1997).

Who May Be Liable?

In theory, each party in the chain of distribution may be liable. Manufacturers of component parts are frequently sued as well.

MANUFACTURERS A manufacturer will be held strictly liable for its defective products regardless of how remote it is from the final user of the product. The only requirements are that the manufacturer be in the business of selling the injury-causing product and that the product be defective when it left the manufacturer. Thus, occasional sellers, such as a typesetting company selling an unused computer, are not strictly liable. The manufacturer may be held liable even when the distributor makes final inspections, corrections, and adjustments of the product.

WHOLESALERS Wholesalers are usually held strictly liable for defects in the products they sell. In some jurisdictions, however, a wholesaler is not liable for latent or hidden defects if the wholesaler sells the products in exactly the same condition that it received them.

RETAILERS A retailer may also generally be held strictly liable. Several jurisdictions, however, will not hold a retailer liable if it did not contribute to the defect and played no part in the manufacturing process.

SELLERS OF USED GOODS Sellers of used goods usually are not held strictly liable because they are not in the original chain of distribution of the product. In addition, the custom in the used-goods market is that there are no warranties or expectations relating to the quality of the products (although some jurisdictions have adopted rules requiring warranties for used cars). However, a seller of used goods is strictly liable for any defective repairs or replacements that it makes.

COMPONENT-PART MANUFACTURER A maker of component parts to manufacturers' specifications is not liable if the specifications for the entire product are questioned, as this is considered a design defect. For example, if an automaker's specifications for a car's fuel injection system prove defective because the system fails to provide the engine sufficient power to change lanes safely on a freeway, the maker of the fuel injection system will not be liable. Makers of component parts are liable for manufacturing defects in their components, however.

Successor Liability

As explained further in Chapter 16, a corporation purchasing or acquiring the assets of another is liable for its debts (including product liability) if there is (1) a consolidation or merger of the two corporations or (2) an express or implied agreement to assume such obligations. Even if a transaction is structured as a sale of assets with no assumption of liabilities, there will still be successor liability if (1) the purchasing corporation is merely a continuation of the selling corporation, or (2) the transaction was entered into to escape liability. Thus, the acquiring corporation can be liable to a party injured by a defect in a product sold by the acquired business prior to the acquisition.

Defenses

The defendant in a product liability case may raise the traditional tort defenses of assumption of risk and, in some jurisdictions, a variation of comparative negligence, known as comparative fault. In addition, some defenses apply only to product liability cases, such as the state-of-the-art defense available in some jurisdictions. Availability of the following defenses varies from state to state.

COMPARATIVE FAULT Contributory negligence by the plaintiff is not a defense in a strict liability action. However, the damages may be reduced by the degree to which the plaintiff's own negligence contributed to the injury. This doctrine is known as *comparative fault.*

ASSUMPTION OF RISK When a person voluntarily and unreasonably assumes the risk of a known danger, the manufacturer is not liable for any resulting injury. For example, if a toaster bears a conspicuous warning not to insert metal objects into it while it is plugged in, and a person sticks a metal fork into it anyway and is electrocuted, the toaster manufacturer will not be liable. Similarly, if a person goes to a baseball game and is injured by a foul ball, the baseball club will not be liable.

Courts are reluctant to find assumption of risk, and some jurisdictions have eliminated it as a defense in tort cases except where the injured party contractually agreed to assume the risk. For example, one court found no assumption of risk when a grinding disc exploded and hit a person in the eye.[1] The court reasoned that, although the injured person should have been wearing goggles, he could not have anticipated that a hidden defect in the disc would cause it to explode. By not wearing goggles, the injured person assumed only the risk of dust or small particles of wood or metal lodging in his eyes.

FROM THE TRENCHES

During a cable installation project, Hollenbach struck a buried gas line and caused a leak. The neighborhood was evacuated, and Washington Gas dispatched a repair crew. Crews, the foreman of the repair crew, was severely injured when the gas ignited. Crews sued Hollenbach and his employer. The defendants argued that the claim was barred by Crews's assumption of the risk. The Maryland court agreed, reasoning that Crews (1) had knowledge of the risk of danger, (2) appreciated the risk, and (3) voluntarily exposed himself to it. Other courts, however, have held that employees do not assume a risk they are forced to take as a result of their employment.

Source: Crews v. Hollenbach, 751 A.2d 481 (Md. 2000).

OBVIOUSNESS OF THE RISK If the use of a product carries an obvious risk, the manufacturer will not be held liable for injuries that result from ignoring the risk. For example, a Volkswagen microbus was held not defective even though the shortened front end resulted in more serious injuries in a collision.

MISUSE OF THE PRODUCT A manufacturer or seller is entitled to assume that its product will be used in a normal manner. The manufacturer or seller will not be held liable for injuries resulting from abnormal use of its product. However, an unusual use or a misuse that is reasonably foreseeable may still result in liability. For example, operating a lawn mower with the grass bag removed was held to be a foreseeable use, and the manufacturer was liable to a bystander injured by an object that shot out of the unguarded mower.[2]

STATE-OF-THE-ART DEFENSE The state-of-the-art defense is based on a manufacturer's compliance with the best available technology (which may or may not be synonymous with the custom and practice of the industry). The *state-of-the-art defense* shields a manufacturer from liability if no safer product design is generally recognized as being possible. For example, one statute provides: "It is a defense that the design, manufacture, inspection, packaging, warning, or labeling of the product was in conformity with the generally recognized state of the art at the time the product was designed, manufactured, packaged, and labeled." Another provides that, if the defendant can prove that the dangerous nature of the product was not known and could not reasonably be discovered at the time the product was placed in the stream of commerce, then the defendant will not be held liable for failure to warn.

PREEMPTION Under certain circumstances, federal law will preempt claims based on state-law product liability. In some instances (such as product liability for tobacco or cigarettes), Congress has explicitly preempted state law. In others, federal preemption is implied.

FROM THE TRENCHES

While driving a 1987 Honda Accord, Geier crashed into a tree and was seriously injured. He sued American Honda under state-law product liability for failing to install an airbag. The Federal Motor Vehicle Safety Standard 208, promulgated pursuant to the National Traffic and Motor Vehicle Safety Act, required auto manufacturers to equip 10 percent of their national fleet of cars with passive restraints but did not require airbags. The U.S. Supreme Court held that the federal statute directly preempted state-law tort claims alleging defective products for lack of an airbag. The Act gave manufacturers a choice among passive restraint systems. If the product liability claim were valid, it would mean that manufacturers have a duty to use airbags under state law. That would conflict with the federal statute, so the suit was dismissed.

Source: Geier v. American Honda Motor Co., 529 U.S. 861 (2000).

THE CONSUMER PRODUCT SAFETY COMMISSION AND OTHER ADMINISTRATIVE AGENCIES

The Consumer Product Safety Commission (CPSC) is charged by Congress with protecting the public against unreasonable risks of injury associated with consumer products and assisting consumers in evaluating the comparative safety of such products. To that end, the CPSC is authorized to set consumer product safety standards, such as performance or product-labeling specifications.

Any interested person may petition the CPSC to adopt a standard and may resort to judicial remedies if the Commission denies the petition. The CPSC itself can begin a proceeding to develop a standard by publishing a notice in the *Federal Register* inviting any person to submit an offer to do the development. Within a specified time limit, the CPSC can then accept such an offer, evaluate the suggestions submitted, and publish a proposed rule. The issuance of the final standard is subject to notice and comment by interested persons.

It is unlawful to manufacture for sale, offer for sale, distribute in commerce, or import into the United States a consumer product that does not conform to an applicable standard. Violators are subject to civil penalties, criminal penalties, injunctive enforcement and seizure, private suits for damages, and private suits for injunctive relief.

If a product cannot be made free of unreasonable risk of personal injury, the CPSC may ban its manufacture, sale, or importation altogether. The supplier of any already-distributed products that pose a substantial risk of injury may be compelled by the CPSC to repair, modify, or replace the product or refund the purchase price.

Before implementing a mandatory safety standard, the CPSC must find that voluntary standards are inadequate. One obvious concern for the Commission is that producers motivated solely by short-term profits may not be willing or able to self-regulate. Any standards that the CPSC issues must also be reasonably necessary to eliminate an unreasonable risk of injury that the regulated product presents. To determine whether a standard is reasonably necessary, the Commission weighs the standard's effectiveness in preventing injury against its effect on the cost of the product.

The National Highway Traffic Safety Administration has the power to establish motor vehicle safety standards. The Federal Drug Administration monitors the production and sale each year of $1 trillion worth of food, drugs, cosmetics, and medical devices. The U.S. Department of Agriculture regulates the slaughtering or processing and labeling of meat, poultry, and egg products. The Federal Trade Commission has primary responsibility for regulating the packaging and labeling of all commodities other than food, drugs, medical devices, and cosmetics. Broadcasting and telecommunications are regulated by the Federal Communications Commission.

Congress has given these and other administrative agencies the power to adopt and enforce regulations that can profoundly affect businesses in particular industries. Before enacting regulations, administrative agencies must publish their proposed rules and solicit public comment. It is important for companies to participate in the public notice and comment period when agencies are proposing rules that might affect their operations. Emerging or small companies usually do not have the resources to devote to a government relations function, so it is important for founders and executives to keep abreast of regulatory developments (including enforcement actions) by working with trade associations, Chambers of Commerce, local lawmakers, and the like.

Consumer Privacy

One of the hottest areas of consumer protection is privacy. In particular, under what circumstances may a company collect and sell identifiable personal information (such as names, e-mail addresses, or home addresses) without first obtaining the customer's consent? The ease with which such information can be collected online through the use of "cookies" and other devices that keep track of the Web sites visited by customers, as well as marketers' ability to collect, process, and combine data on specific consumers, has sparked calls for new federal and state privacy legislation.

Legislation

The Children's Online Privacy Protection Act of 1998 prohibits the collection of personal information from children under the age of thirteen without first receiving parental consent. The Gramm-Leach-Bliley Financial Services Modernization Act of 1999 requires financial services firms to notify consumers in writing regarding what personal information is being collected, how it is being used, and with whom it is shared. They must also give consumers the opportunity to opt out of having such information shared with other affiliated or unaffiliated entities. The law applies to banks, debt collectors, credit counselors, retailers, and travel agencies. As discussed in Chapter 10, the Health Insurance Portability and Accountability Act (HIPAA) and the privacy regulations issued by the Health and Human Services Department under the HIPAA require health care providers and others with personal medical information to implement appropriate policies and procedures (including the appointment of a privacy officer) to ensure that medical information is kept private.

Efforts in Congress to legislate new online privacy laws stalled in 2001. After several states (including California) proposed tough new privacy legislation in 2001, IBM and others pushed for limited federal legislation that would preempt any tougher state legislation. Amazon.com indicated to the Senate Commerce Committee that it could support federal legislation that required privacy notices with an opt-out option but would oppose giving individuals the right to sue companies for privacy violations.[3]

Meanwhile, several states have enacted privacy legislation, and state attorneys general have prosecuted companies for violating state requirements. For example, TOYS Я US, Inc. agreed to pay the State of New Jersey $50,000 for allegedly obtaining and transmitting personally identifiable information about consumers who accessed its Web sites in violation of the New Jersey Consumer Fraud Act.[4]

FTC and FCC Regulation

As of January 2002, the Federal Trade Commission (FTC) did not require companies to adopt or publish privacy policies. If, however, a company elects to publish a policy, then it must abide by it. Failure to do so is prosecuted as an "unfair or deceptive trade practice" under Section 5 of the Federal Trade Commission Act.

FROM THE TRENCHES

From March 2000 through June 2001, Eli Lilly and Co. offered, through its Prozac.com Web site, a service called "Medi-Messenger," which enabled its subscribers to receive individualized e-mail reminders from Lilly concerning their Prozac antidepressant medication or other matters. On June 27, 2001, Lilly sent a form e-mail to subscribers to the service, which inadvertently disclosed all of the subscribers' e-mail addresses to each individual subscriber by including all of their addresses within the "To:" entry of the message.

The FTC sued Lilly, claiming that its representation that it employs measures and takes steps appropriate under the circumstances to maintain and protect the privacy and confidentiality of personal information obtained from or about consumers through its Prozac.com and Lilly.com Web sites was false or misleading and constituted unfair or deceptive acts or practices in violation of Section 5(a) of the Federal Trade Commission Act. The FTC claimed that Lilly had not, in fact, employed such measures or taken such steps. For example, Lilly failed (1) to provide appropriate training for its employees regarding consumer privacy and information security; (2) to provide appropriate oversight and assistance for the employee who sent out the e-mail, who had no prior experience in creating, testing, or implementing the computer program used; and (3) to implement appropriate checks and controls on the process, such as reviewing the computer program with experienced personnel and pretesting the program internally before sending out the e-mail. Lilly's failure to implement appropriate measures also violated certain of its own written policies.

In January 2002, the FTC and Lilly agreed (subject to public comment) on a consent order that would prohibit Lilly from misrepresenting the extent to which it maintains and protects the privacy or confidentiality of any personally identifiable information collected from or about consumers. It also would require Lilly to implement a four-stage information security program designed to establish and maintain reasonable safeguards to protect consumers' personal information against unauthorized access, use, or disclosure. In particular, Lilly agreed to:

1. Designate appropriate personnel to coordinate and oversee the program.
2. Identify reasonably foreseeable internal and external risks to the security, confidentiality, and integrity of personal information, including any such risks posed by lack of training, and address these risks in each relevant area of its operations, including (a) management and training of personnel; (b) information systems for the processing, storage, transmission, or disposal of

continued...

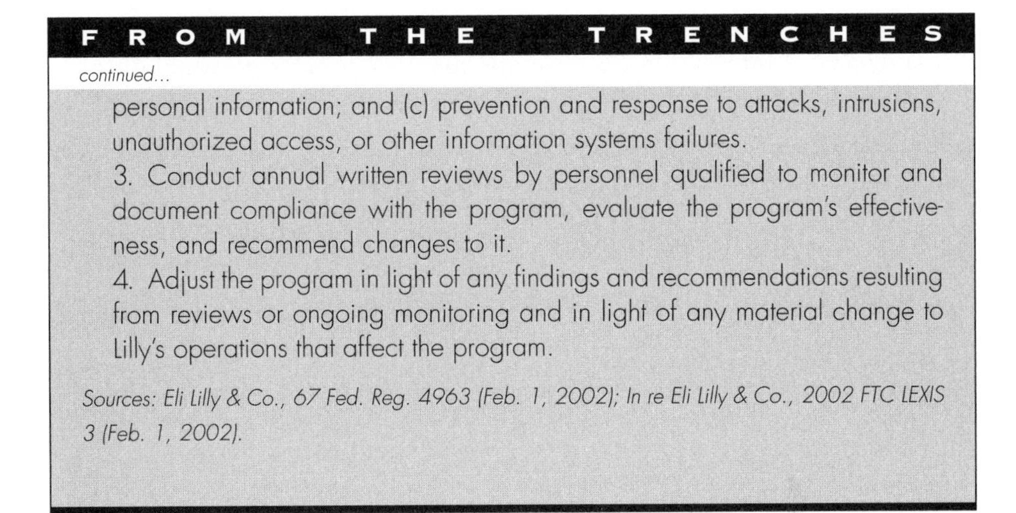

FROM THE TRENCHES

continued...

personal information; and (c) prevention and response to attacks, intrusions, unauthorized access, or other information systems failures.

3. Conduct annual written reviews by personnel qualified to monitor and document compliance with the program, evaluate the program's effectiveness, and recommend changes to it.

4. Adjust the program in light of any findings and recommendations resulting from reviews or ongoing monitoring and in light of any material change to Lilly's operations that affect the program.

Sources: Eli Lilly & Co., 67 Fed. Reg. 4963 (Feb. 1, 2002); In re Eli Lilly & Co., 2002 FTC LEXIS 3 (Feb. 1, 2002).

FEDERAL COMMUNICATIONS COMMISSION In 1998, the Federal Communications Commission (FCC) promulgated regulations requiring telecommunications firms to obtain customer consent (opt-in) before marketing or otherwise disclosing any individually identifiable customer proprietary network information (such as the time, date, and duration of calls and the numbers called). In 1999, the U.S. Court of Appeals for the Tenth Circuit struck down the opt-in requirement as a violation of free speech.[5] As of January 2002, the FCC was in the process of reconsidering its privacy regulations in light of public comments from industry groups, state attorneys general, and others.

European Privacy Directive

The European Union's Data Protection Directive (95/46/EC), which went into effect in 1998, requires its member states to safeguard the privacy of personal data by (1) giving notice to individuals regarding how their information will be used; (2) offering a choice when disclosing information to a third party (with an opt-in consent required for sensitive information); (3) maintaining the security of personal information; (4) ensuring that the data are reliable, accurate, and current; and (5) giving individuals access to examine, correct, and delete information about them. The Directive also prohibits the export of personal information from European Union member states to countries that do not "adequately" protect personal data.

Self-Regulation

In an effort to forestall tougher governmental regulation, a number of companies have started to institutionalize their privacy policies and practices by (1) appointing privacy officers, (2) adopting online and offline privacy policies, (3) conducting privacy risk assessments to evaluate how personal information is used and collected, (4) establishing a formal complaint-resolution program for consumers, (5) training employees, (6) conducting privacy audits, and (7) creating a formal privacy assessment process for new products and services.[6] As of 2002, U.S. firms employed approximately 500 privacy officers; the number increases to 1,000 if persons with significant responsibilities beyond privacy are included.[7] Brent Saunders, the founder of the Privacy Officers Association and an attorney and privacy consultant with PricewaterhouseCoopers, points out that some companies:

> *see privacy as a market differentiator, as a way of getting and keeping customers. . . . For these companies, it's not just a matter of doing something because they have to or because someone is telling them to. It's more a matter of building a foundation of trust with customers that is crucial to the success of their business.*[8]

ADVERTISING

Sellers of goods and services will usually want to advertise. Three main bodies of law regulate advertising; the purpose of each is to protect consumers against false or deceptive advertising.

Common Law

A traditional common-law approach provides two remedies for a consumer who has been misled by false advertising. First, a consumer may be able to sue for breach of contract. Proving the existence of a contract is often difficult, however, because courts usually characterize advertisements as merely offers to deal. A consumer might also sue for the tort of deceit. Deceit requires the proof of several elements, including knowledge by the seller that the misrepresentation is false. The misrepresentation must be one of fact and not opinion, which is a difficult distinction to make in the context of advertising. (Deceit, also called fraudulent misrepresentation, and other business torts are discussed in Chapter 11.)

Statutory Law

Both the UCC and the federal Lanham Act may protect consumers from false advertising. As explained above, under Article 2 of the UCC, any statement, sample, or model may constitute an express warranty if it is part of the basis of the bargain. Sometimes advertisement of a product may be construed as an express warranty. If so, the buyer can recover for breach of warranty under the UCC.

A federal law called the Lanham Act forbids the use of any false "description or representation" in connection with any goods or services. It provides a claim for any competitor (rather than consumer) who might be injured by any other competitor's false claims. The purpose of the Act is to ensure truthfulness in advertising and to eliminate misrepresentations of quality regarding one's own product or the product of a competitor.

For example, the Coca-Cola Co., maker of Minute Maid orange juice, sued Tropicana Products, Inc. in the early 1980s under the Lanham Act. At issue was a television commercial in which athlete Bruce Jenner squeezed an orange while saying, "It's pure, pasteurized juice as it comes from the orange," and then poured the juice into a Tropicana carton. Coca-Cola claimed that the commercial was false because it represented that Tropicana cartons contain unprocessed, fresh-squeezed juice when in fact the juice is heated (pasteurized) and sometimes frozen before packaging. The court agreed that the representation was false because it suggested that pasteurized juice comes directly from oranges and enjoined Tropicana from continuing to use the advertisement.[9]

A number of states permit consumers to bring suits for deceptive trade practices under state statutes. For example, purchasers of Kenner Corp.'s Easy Bake Oven brought a class action under California law. The plaintiffs alleged that it took children twenty-nine to thirty-four minutes to bake a treat, not the less than ten minutes claimed by Kenner Corp. The case was settled under a confidentiality agreement in 1995.[10]

Both companies and consumers can handle disputes privately and more cheaply by turning to a private court run by the National Advertising Division of the Council of Better Business Bureaus. This option is particularly attractive to growing companies that are cash constrained.

Regulatory Law: The FTC

Unfair or deceptive acts or trade practices, including false advertising, are illegal. As noted earlier, the Federal Trade Commission has the authority to prevent unfair and deceptive trade practices in violation of Section 5 of the Federal Trade Commission Act. Among the areas the FTC has addressed are deceptive price and quality claims as well as false testimonials and mock-ups.

DECEPTIVE PRICE Deceptive pricing is any practice that tends to mislead or deceive consumers about the price they are paying for a good or service. Deceptive pricing practices include offers of free merchandise with a purchase, or two-for-one deals, in which the advertiser recovers the cost of the free merchandise by charging more than the regular price for the merchandise bought.

Another example of deceptive pricing, *bait and switch* advertising, is banned by the FTC. An advertiser violates FTC rules if it refuses to show an advertised item, fails to have a reasonable quantity of the item in stock, fails to promise to deliver the item within a reasonable time, or discourages employees from selling the advertised item.

QUALITY CLAIMS Advertisements often include quality claims. These claims imply that the advertiser has some reasonable basis for making the claim. Under the FTC's general view, quality claims made without any substantiation are deceptive. On the other hand, obvious exaggerations and vague generalities are considered puffing, and they are not deemed to be deceptive because they are unlikely to mislead consumers.

FALSE TESTIMONIALS AND MOCK-UPS Testimonials and endorsements in which the person endorsing a product does not, in fact, use or prefer it are deceptive and violate the law. Additionally, it is deceptive for the endorser to imply falsely that he or she has superior knowledge or experience of the product. It is also illegal to show an advertisement that purports to be an actual product demonstration but, in fact, is a mock-up or simulation.

For example, television and print ads from an October 1990 ad campaign showed a Volvo automobile withstanding the impact of a giant-tired "monster truck" named *Big Foot* that flattened the rest of a line of cars. What was not readily apparent from the advertisement was that the Volvo's roof had been reinforced and that some of the other vehicles' supports had been weakened. In response, the FTC, for the first time, required, the advertising firm (and not just the advertiser) to pay a fine for the deceptive ad. The carmaker and its New York advertising firm each agreed to pay a $150,000 penalty, though neither admitted violating laws against false advertising.[11]

Unfair Competition

A number of states have adopted statutes prohibiting *unfair competition;* these laws are designed to prevent unlawful, false, deceptive, unfair, and unauthorized business practices, particularly in the areas of sales and advertising. Certain types of unfair competition may also violate federal laws, including the Federal Trade Commission Act and the Lanham Act. Many of these practices will strike the average businessperson as simply unfair, but some of them are close calls. Courts are willing to find certain kinds of anticompetitive behavior actionable if the activities complained of seem egregious to the court. For example, the improper use of trade secrets and customer information of prior employers is often found to be unfair competition, as is destroying a business by hiring away all of its employees.

Types of Unfair Competition

There are many types of unfair competition. Some of the most common are outlined below.

Passing off involves attempting to fool customers into believing that one's goods are actually those of a competitor. In one case, the publisher of *National Lampoon* successfully sued ABC when the network used the word "lampoon" in the title of a television series without permission, after having attempted to negotiate for use of the name. The court held that ABC was trying to use the reputation of *National Lampoon* for its own benefit. Passing off often involves improper use of another's trademark or trade name or of a confusingly similar mark or name.

As noted earlier, *false advertising* occurs when untrue, unsupported, or deceptive claims are made in advertising. For example, Campbell Soup Co. engaged in false advertising when it used in its advertisements photographs of bowls of soup into which clear glass marbles had first been placed to make the solid ingredients rise to the surface, thereby making the soup appear more appetizing.[12]

Disparagement includes untrue claims about a competitor that would tend to damage its business. Disparagement frequently arises when disgruntled former employees make untrue but damaging statements about their former employer's business.

As discussed further in Chapter 14, *dilution* involves using another's trade name or trademark to promote noncompeting goods if the consumer might be confused about the true origin of the goods.

Right of publicity is the exclusive right to exploit commercially one's name or likeness. Typically, these cases involve unauthorized attempts to use a sports or entertainment celebrity's name or likeness for commercial gain. For example, Bette Midler successfully sued an automobile manufacturer that used a sound-alike singer in television advertising.[13]

Remedies

A victim of unfair competition may be entitled to a court order to stop the activity, as well as to actual and punitive damages. Some types of unfair competition also carry criminal penalties.

Jurisdiction, Choice of Forum, and Choice of Law in E-Commerce Disputes

Up to this point, this chapter has for the most part focused on U.S. laws governing the sale of goods and services without factoring in the complexities introduced when those sales are effected using the Internet, which is inherently global and multijurisdictional. Because most countries have laws akin to those described in this chapter, the international regulation of electronic commerce is complex and subject to rapid change.

Resolving Online Disputes in an Offline Court

As the World Intellectual Property Organization explains: "Users can access the Internet from almost any place on Earth. Because of packet-switching technology and the complex weave of digital networks and telecommunications infrastructure, digitized information may travel through various countries and jurisdictions, each with its own legal system, in order to reach its destination."[14]

Key issues arising from the use of this international medium in a world of geographically discrete countries with physical borders include (1) which country (or in the case of disputes between U.S. parties from different states, which state) has the authority to require a defendant to adjudicate a dispute at a particular location (i.e., what will be the forum or *situs*); (2) what law will govern the dispute (choice of law or conflict of law); and (3) when a court will recognize and enforce a judgment rendered in a foreign jurisdiction.[15] Although these three issues are present in any transaction involving parties from different countries:

> *In electronic commerce, these issues are complicated by the fact that one or more of the parties involved (or processes used) in the commercial activities—including Internet users, service and content providers, buyers, sellers, businesses (and their assets), technology systems and computer servers—may be located in different countries. Not only may uncertainty arise as to where the relevant activities are taking place, but the activities themselves can have intended and unintended consequences all over the globe, resulting in uncertainty when it comes to questions of localizing the dispute, determining the applicable law, and the practicalities of pursuing enforcement or adequate dispute-settlement alternatives.*[16]

For example, suppose that a consumer in Germany uses the Internet to order a physical product built in and shipped from France that proves defective and injures the German consumer. It is clear that the consumer could sue the French manufacturer in France for product liability. But could the consumer require the French company to try the case in a German court applying German law? The European Union and a number of countries have been wrestling with these issues.

FROM THE TRENCHES

On November 20, 2000, Judge Jean-Jacques Gomez of the Superior Court of Paris ordered California-based Yahoo! to block French Internet surfers from accessing the English-language Yahoo.com Web site to view (1) auctions of Nazi memorabilia or (2) Web pages displaying text, extracts, or quotations from Adolf Hitler's *Mein Kampf*. Yahoo! was also ordered to remove from all browser directories accessible in France certain index headings used by "negationists" to deny existence of the Holocaust. The French-language portal www.yahoo.fr did not carry the auctions, but Web surfers in France could easily access the U.S. site and view the Nazi items for sale. Judge Gomez called the auctions "an offence to the collective memory of the country" and held that they violated the French law against exhibiting or selling objects with racist overtones.

Critics of the decision argued that it "is an alarming example of a foreign court's willingness to impose its national law on the activities of a U.S.-based Web site."[a] They claimed that under Judge Gomez's logic, "any Web site with global reach could be subject to the jurisdiction of every nation on earth."[b] Supporters of the court's ruling called it "perfectly reasonable under the circumstances" and "a welcome harbinger of things to come."[c]

Although Yahoo! announced in early 2001 a new policy of prohibiting the auctioning of items glorifying groups or individuals known principally for hateful or violent acts (such as Nazis and the Ku Klux Klan), it still offered some items for sale and permitted access to some sites that appeared to violate the French order.

Yahoo! claimed that because it lacked the technology to block French citizens from accessing the Yahoo.com site to view materials that violate the French order, it could not comply with the order without banning Nazi-related material from Yahoo.com altogether. Yahoo! contended that such a ban would infringe impermissibly upon its rights under the First Amendment to the U.S. Constitution and sought a declaratory judgment from the U.S. District Court for the Northern District of California that the French court's orders were neither cognizable nor enforceable under the laws of the United States.

The U.S. court identified the issue as being "whether it is consistent with the Constitution and laws of the United States for another nation to regulate speech by a United States resident within the United States on the basis that such speech can be accessed by Internet users in that nation." The court noted that "in a world in which ideas and information transcend borders and the Internet in particular renders the physical distance between speaker and audience virtually meaningless, the implications of this question go far beyond the facts of this case."

continued...

FROM THE TRENCHES

continued...

The court ruled that the U.S. Constitution and U.S. laws governed the determination of whether the French order could be enforced in the United States. The French order's content and viewpoint-based regulation of the Web pages and auction site "clearly would be inconsistent with the First Amendment if mandated by a court in the United States. What makes this case uniquely challenging is that the Internet in effect allows one to speak in more than one place at the same time." The court acknowledged that "France has the sovereign right to regulate what speech is permissible in France" but held that "the First Amendment precludes enforcement within the United States of a French order intended to regulate the content of its speech over the Internet."

a. *Carl S. Kaplan, Ruling on Nazi Memorabilia Sparks Legal Debate, N.Y. Times, Nov. 24, 2000.*
b. *Id.*
c. *Id.*

Source: Yahoo!, Inc. v. La Ligue Contre Le Racisme et L'Antisemitisme, 169 F. Supp 2d 1181 (N.D. Cal. 2001)

The U.S. Approach to Jurisdiction

As a general matter, a court sitting in a state in the United States cannot require an out-of-state defendant to submit to its jurisdiction unless the defendant either (1) has agreed to do so (for example, by consenting to jurisdiction in a contract) or (2) has sufficient minimum contacts with the state "such that the maintenance of the suit does not offend 'traditional notions of fair play and substantial justice.' "[17] This generally means that the nonresident defendant must either (1) have done some act or consummated some transaction in the forum in which it is being sued or (2) have purposefully availed itself of the privilege of conducting activities in the forum, thereby invoking the benefits and protections of the forum's laws.

In the case of companies doing business over the Internet, the U.S. courts have generally held that a state does not have personal jurisdiction over a nonresident defendant merely because the defendant has a Web site accessible to users in that state.[18] On the other hand, a state clearly does have personal jurisdiction over a nonresident defendant that knowingly and repeatedly uses the Internet to transact business in the state.[19] For example, if a corporation based in Arizona intentionally targets Utah users or repeatedly sells products or services to a Utah resident, then the Arizona company can be sued in the Utah courts for breach of warranty or product liability. The Utah resident can then invoke the Full Faith and Credit Clause of the U.S. Constitution to require the courts in Arizona to enforce the Utah judgment. Courts tend to resolve cases between these two extremes, which often involve interactive Web sites, on an ad hoc basis.[20]

In Search of Global Rules

The European Commission's proposed Regulation on Jurisdiction and Enforcement of Judgements in Civil and Commercial Matters (the Brussels Regulation) [21] went into effect on March 1, 2002. It gives consumers the right to sue a foreign defendant in the consumer's home country if the defendant "pursues commercial or professional activities in the Member State of the consumer's domicile or, by any means, directs such activities to that Member State...and the contract falls within the scope of such activities." Thus, consumers have the right to bring a lawsuit relating to any contracts executed via the Internet in their home country. Mere advertisement on a Web site might be enough to establish personal jurisdiction in the consumer's home country if the legal claim relates to teh advertised product, even if the consumer purchased the product while in the vendor's country of domicile. A number of international bodies are working to promulgate uniform rules for electronic commerce. Efforts include the United Nations Commission on International Trade Law's Model Law on Electronic Commerce, Model Law on Electronic Signatures, and the proposed convention on electronic contracting alluded to earlier;[22] the Hague draft Convention on Jurisdiction and Foreign Judgments in Civil and Commercial Matters;[23] and the Organization for Economic Cooperation and Development's proposed findings and research agenda.[24]

Although as of 2002 it was far from clear whether these efforts will succeed or what form any global rules might take, there seems to be a general inclination to permit parties to use private contract law and to choose their own set of rules regarding jurisdiction, choice of forum, and choice of law, except in cases involving consumers, who often lack adequate bargaining power to effectively negotiate the terms proposed in a seller's click-wrap agreement. It seems likely, therefore, that consumers will be permitted to sue in their home court under local law if the seller shipped products (including bits transmitted electronically) to the consumer's home state.

What to Do

Given all this uncertainty, what should an emerging company that plans to use the Internet to sell goods or services do about these issues? First, to the extent possible, a company should try to include in its contracts explicit provisions addressing jurisdiction, choice of forum, and applicable law, while understanding that they may not be enforceable against consumers. Second, a firm should assume that if it regularly sells products or services in a state or country or makes direct offers directly to persons in a particular state or country, then it will be subject to that jurisdiction's laws and can be required to litigate in that jurisdiction all claims brought by residents of that state arising out of such sales or offers. Finally, a company should keep in mind that any presence in a jurisdiction, other than a passive Web site accessible there, may be enough to make the company subject to that jurisdiction's laws and answerable in its courts.

PUTTING IT INTO PRACTICE

With its products ready for launch, DataAccelleation enlisted the aid of an advertising agency to create a marketing campaign. The agency produced several thirty-second commercials showing DataAccelleation's products in action. Kendra liked the commercials but sensed that something wasn't quite right with the product demonstrations. Although the SDB would allow information to be obtained in a matter of seconds, the programs in the commercial were retrieving information almost instantaneously.

She asked the ad's designer about it. "Oh yeah, we filmed the program and sped up the tape by a factor of three," the designer replied. "We thought it looked better accelerated." Kendra nodded her head but knew she would have to check with Michael Cruz to see whether this was all right.

"I'm glad you thought to ask," said Michael. "The ad must either show the program at its normal speed or have a disclaimer flashed on the screen telling viewers that the demonstration has been accelerated. Otherwise DataAccelleation could be guilty of false advertising and subject to FTC sanctions."

Kendra discussed the alternatives with the Colgates. After some deliberation, they decided that the ad program should be shown in real time and that the several-second lag could easily be filled with conversation between the actors.

Kendra was also concerned that DataAccelleation might face ruinous liability if it could be held responsible for any damage caused to a client's database. She discussed the matter with Michael, who suggested that the SDB software include a feature whereby a buyer could not purchase and download the software unless the buyer first scrolled through a software license agreement and checked a box on the screen indicating that the buyer agreed to be bound by the terms and conditions of the software license agreement. Michael said that the license should explicitly disclaim all implied warranties under the UCC and, if applicable, the UCITA and expressly limit DataAccelleation's liability. He cautioned, however, that some states curtail a seller's ability to limit its liability. To reduce the chance that any such limitation would be deemed procedurally or substantively unconscionable, he encouraged Kendra to be as explicit as possible in the documentation and advertising about any risks SDB posed to the integrity of the client's underlying database.

continued...

continued...

Michael and Sanjay Datar prepared a license agreement that included the following provisions:

1. **License.** This DataAccelleation License Agreement grants you the nonexclusive right to install and use one copy of the accompanying software and documentation on a single computer for your own internal use. You may use the software on a different computer only if you first delete the software from all computers on which it has previously been installed.
2. **Limited Warranty.** DataAccelleation warrants that the software will be free from defects for a period of ninety days from the date of purchase. If defects are present, DataAccelleation's entire liability and your exclusive remedy shall be limited to the replacement of the defective software or, at DataAccelleation's option, refund of the purchase price.
3. **No Other Warranties.** THE WARRANTIES OF SECTION 2 ABOVE ARE THE ONLY WARRANTIES MADE BY DATAACCELERATION UNDER THIS AGREEMENT. TO THE MAXIMUM EXTENT PERMITTED BY APPLICABLE LAW, DATAACCELLEATION EXPRESSLY DISCLAIMS ALL OTHER WARRANTIES, BOTH EXPRESS AND IMPLIED, INCLUDING BUT NOT LIMITED TO IMPLIED WARRANTIES OF MERCHANTABILITY, FITNESS FOR A PARTICULAR PURPOSE, ACCURACY, RESULTS, NON-INFRINGEMENT OR EFFORTS, WITH RESPECT TO THE SOFTWARE AND DOCUMENTATION. DATAACCELLEATION DOES NOT WARRANT THAT THE SOFTWARE WILL MEET YOUR NEEDS OR THAT OPERATION OF THE SOFTWARE WILL BE UNINTERRUPTED OR ERROR FREE.
4. **Limitation of Liability.** To the maximum extent permitted by applicable law, DataAccelleation shall not under any circumstances, including its own negligence, be liable for any incidental, special, exemplary or consequential damages relating to this agreement or that otherwise result from the operation of or inability to use the software or documentation, whether in contract, in tort, or otherwise, including, without limitation, lost profits, lost sales, or any damage to your database, even if DataAccelleation has been advised of the possibility of such damages.

Kendra then scheduled a meeting with Michael to discuss DataAccelleation's hiring and personnel policies.

NOTES

1. Haugen v. Minnesota Mining & Mfg. Co., 550 P.2d 72 (Wash. Ct. App. 1976). *See also* Salinas v. Vierstra, 695 P.2d 369 (Idaho 1985).
2. LaPaglia v. Sears, Roebuck & Co., 531 N.Y.S.2d 623 (App. Div. 1988).
3. *Regulatory Proposals in E-Commerce Field Face Strong Opposition in 2002,* 7 Electronic Com. & L. Rep. 105–06 (Jan. 30, 2002).
4. *In re* TOYS Я US, 1 Privacy & Security L. Rep. 48 (Jan. 14, 2002).
5. U.S. West v. Federal Communications Comm'n, 182 F.3d 1224 (10th Cir. 1999).
6. *See Pressure from Legislators, Firms Are Turning to "Privacy Officers,"* 7 Electronic Com. & L. Rep. 9 (Jan. 30, 2002).
7. *Id.*
8. *Id.* at 93.
9. Coca-Cola v. Tropicana Prods., Inc., 690 F.2d 312 (2d Cir. 1982).
10. *See* Jeff Barge, *Advertising Was Heating Up,* A.B.A. J., Apr. 1996, at 32–33.
11. *F.T.C. Accord on Volvo Ads,* N.Y. Times, Aug. 22, 1991, at D19.
12. *See* 77 F.T.C. 664 (1970).
13. Midler v. Ford Motor Co., 789 F.2d 460 (9th Cir. 1988), *cert. denied,* 506 U.S. 1080 (1993).
14. World Intellectual Property Organization, Primer on Electronic Commerce and Intellectual Property Issues 10 (WIPO/OLOA/EC/PRIMER) (May 2000), available at <http://ecommerce.wipo.int>.
15. *Id.* at 10.
16. *Id.* at 11.
17. International Shoe Co. v. Washington, 326 U.S. 310, 316 (1945).
18. *See, e.g.,* GTE New Media Series, Inc. v. Bellsouth Corp., 199 F.3d 1343 (D.C. Cir. 2000).
19. *See, e.g.,* Zippo Mfg. Co. v. Zippo Dot Com, Inc., 952 F. Supp. 1119 (W.D. Pa. 1997).
20. *See, e.g.,* iAccess, Inc. v. WEBcard Techs., Inc., 182 F. Supp. 2d 1183 (D. Utah 2002).
21. Council of Europe Regulation No. 44/2001, *Jurisdiction and the Regulation and Enforcement of Judgments in Civil and Commercial Matters*, 2001 O.J. (L 012) 1-23 (Dec. 22, 2000).
22. UNCITRAL, *Model Law on Electronic Commerce with Guide to Enactment* (1996 & 1998), and UNCITRAL, *Model Law on Electronic Signatures* (2001), both available at <http://www.uncitral.org/en-index.htm>.
23. The text of the preliminary draft is available at <http://www.hcch.net/e/work prog/jdgm.html> (Oct. 30,1999).
24. *See* Organization for Economic Co-operation and Development, *The Economic and Social Impacts of Electronic Commerce: Preliminary Findings and Research Agenda* (1999).

Chapter 10

MARSHALING HUMAN RESOURCES

Hiring and retaining motivated and talented workers are key to the success of virtually any venture. Yet employers face a sometimes bewildering array of overlapping state and federal statutes, regulations, and common-law principles governing the employment relationship. Failure to appreciate how these laws affect everything from a company's prehiring practices to its decision to terminate an employee can result in time-consuming and expensive litigation and government investigations, which can consume precious cash and divert management attention from execution of the business plan.

This chapter addresses some of the more prevalent laws, with an emphasis on federal statutes of nationwide application. For example, Title VII of the Civil Rights Act of 1964 is one of the most important employment statutes, prohibiting employment discrimination based on race, color, religion, sex, or national origin. The Age Discrimination in Employment Act guards against age-discriminating employment practices. The Americans with Disabilities Act prohibits discrimination against individuals with disabilities. The Family and Medical Leave Act gives certain employees a right to up to twelve weeks of unpaid medical or family leave per year. The Fair Labor Standards Act regulates the minimum wage, overtime pay, and use of child labor. The Occupational Safety and Health Act was designed to reduce workplace hazards and improve safety and health programs for workers. The National Labor Relations Act gives employees the right to organize unions. In addition to these federal laws, state laws may impose additional employment requirements, which may vary widely from state to state.

A company may decide to hire a worker as an independent contractor rather than as an employee. A worker, such as a painter, who provides unsupervised, specialized work that is needed only sporadically is the most clear-cut example of an independent contractor. How a worker should be classified is often unclear, however. Many times, the worker is trying to claim the status of employee to qualify for the legal protections afforded employees at the same time the employer is classifying him or her as an independent contractor. Often, the Internal Revenue Service (IRS) asserts that a person is an employee to recover Social Security payments (plus penalties) from the employer and to force the employer to withhold income taxes from the worker's pay. Misclassification can create serious legal problems, including audits of the entire workforce by federal and state tax authorities.

Furthermore, a worker's status can affect the rights of the employer to any copyrightable works or patentable inventions created by the worker. As explained more fully in Chapter 14, the employer generally is deemed to be the author of (and therefore the owner of the copyright for) any works created by an employee acting within the scope of employment, even in the absence of an express assignment of copyright. Similarly, the employer is the owner of any invention created by an employee "hired to invent," even in the absence of an assignment of inventions. In contrast, a company commissioning a work by an independent contractor will not own the copyright unless there is either a written contract stating that it is a "work made for hire" or a written assignment of the copyright. Similarly, independent contractors own their inventions (and any patents thereon) absent a written assignment of inventions.

Because the application of many employment statutes hinges on the distinction between employees and independent contractors, this chapter begins with a discussion of what differentiates an employee from an independent contractor. The chapter continues with a summary of certain key employment legislation and then discusses employment at-will and wrongful discharge. It concludes with an outline of what should be contained in certain key employment agreements, including stock option agreements.

Employees Versus Independent Contractors

Workers may be classified into two legal categories: employee and independent contractor. The distinction between them is crucial. From the employer's standpoint, considerable money can be saved by classifying a worker as an independent contractor. An employer who hires a worker as an independent contractor, rather than as an employee, does not have to provide workers' compensation insurance, unemployment compensation, or job benefits (such as health insurance and a retirement savings plan). More important, when an independent contractor is hired, the employer is not required to pay any portion of his or her Social Security and Medicare taxes. The penalties under federal and state tax laws for misclassification can be severe.

Although IRS guidelines and various employment statutes differ as to what constitutes employee status, two primary criteria distinguish independent contractors from employees. First, independent contractors agree upon the desired work product and then control the means and manner of achieving the outcome. Second, independent contractors offer services to the public at large, not just to one business.

The following criteria have been used by various courts in determining whether an employment relationship existed:

1. The nature and degree of control or supervision retained or exercised by the employer.
2. The extent to which the services in question are an integral part of the employer's business.
3. Whether the employer provides the training.
4. The amount of the worker's investment in facilities and equipment.
5. The kind of occupation.
6. The worker's opportunities for profit or loss.
7. The method of calculating the payment for the work (by time worked or by the job).
8. The skill, initiative, and judgment required for the independent enterprise to succeed.

9. The permanence and duration of the work relationship.
10. Whether annual or sick leave is given.
11. Whether the worker accumulates retirement benefits or is given medical benefits.
12. Whether the employer pays Social Security taxes.
13. The intention of the parties, including any written agreement between the parties, regarding independent contractor or employee status.

Employee status is more likely to be found for workers who are lower paid, are lower skilled, lack bargaining power, have a high degree of economic dependence on their employer, and are subject to regular supervision.

Misclassification of a worker can result in very serious consequences for an employer. Thus, every attempt should be made to determine proper status prior to the commencement of the work relationship. An employer who wishes to hire an independent contractor must ensure that this status will be upheld in case of a dispute. Although a provision in a written

FROM THE TRENCHES

A court concluded in 2000 that approximately 10,000 current and former Microsoft software testers and writers of technical manuals were employees for purposes of participation in Microsoft's benefit plans, even though the workers' contracts specified that they were independent contractors responsible for their own federal taxes and benefits. The court was particularly influenced by the fact that some workers had worked exclusively for Microsoft for years doing work that was supervised by the same Microsoft supervisors who supervised employees doing similar work in the same offices. In 2000, Microsoft agreed to pay $97 million to misclassified workers who had not been permitted to participate in employee benefit plans.

Source: Vizcaino v. Microsoft Corp., 173 F.3d 713 (9th Cir. 1999), cert. denied, 528 U.S. 1105 (2000); Vizcaino v. Microsoft Corp., 97 F.3d 1187 (9th Cir. 1996), aff'd on reh'g, 120 F.3d 1006 (9th Cir. 1997), cert. denied, 522 U.S. 1099 (1998).

agreement between the two parties specifying the worker's status is given significant weight, it is not determinative. To withstand challenge, a worker with independent contractor status (1) should not perform tasks that are central to the employer's primary business and (2) should retain sufficient control and autonomy with respect to the manner and means of his or her performance. Ideally, the worker would be associated with a separate company and would perform the services for the employer on behalf of that company.

Establishing Nonemployee Status

Even though an employer can never guarantee that a worker will be legally determined to be an independent contractor, the employer can take certain steps to help establish nonemployee status. A written contract spelling out the intent of the parties and detailing the worker's duties and the terms and conditions of his or her service will provide some support for finding independent contractor status. The agreement should clearly lay out the responsibilities of the contractor, describing the services to be performed, the time frame in which they will be completed, and the payment that will be given in consideration for these services. The contract should specify what is expected of the contractor (e.g., the contractor will supply all necessary tools, equipment, and supplies). Unless all work must be done by the contractor alone, the contract should give the contractor the right to hire any assistants, at his or her own expense. The contractor should be responsible for carrying his or her own liability and workers' compensation insurance and for paying his or her own taxes and benefits. (An example of an agreement between a company and an independent contractor is set forth in "Getting It In Writing" at the end of this chapter. Before using any form, the entrepreneur should consult with legal counsel to ensure that the form agreement complies with all applicable federal, state, and local legal requirements and meets all of the entrepreneur's needs.)

The more the employer can establish the independent economic viability of the worker, the better. Thus, a file should be kept containing, for example, the worker's business card, references, and stationery samples. When feasible, it is best to retain contractors who are incorporated and have their own business offices and equipment. That way, more of the work can be completed off the employer's premises. It is also important to make it clear that the independent contractor is free to offer services to other businesses as well.

The existence of an independent contractor agreement is essential from an entrepreneur's standpoint, but it may not be dispositive. When courts

FROM THE TRENCHES

A transportation engineering firm obtained a contract from a city to measure ridership on the city's bus routes. The firm needed a large number of short-term workers to ride buses and count passengers. The firm entered into independent contractor agreements providing for minimum wages with more than fifty persons (most of whom were unemployed at the time) who had responded to a newspaper advertisement. The firm carefully explained to each worker the nature of the independent contractor agreement, which specified that no workers' compensation or unemployment benefits were included. The firm gave each worker a schedule of routes to ride and provided each worker with forms to fill out, pens, clipboards, and manual counters to aid in filling out the forms.

Each worker rode the buses alone without supervision. The workers each worked approximately fifty hours per week. Upon completion of the project, the firm informed each worker that the agreement was terminated. Thereafter, several of the workers filed claims for unemployment benefits with the state unemployment department, asserting that they had been employees rather than independent contractors.

Notwithstanding the written agreements, the state unemployment department awarded the workers benefits, which were charged to the firm's account. The state unemployment department reasoned that the firm exercised control over the workers by specifying the form to be filled out and by providing the tools to complete the forms. The state unemployment department, which also had responsibility to ensure that employers withheld amounts for state income tax, issued an assessment against the firm, requiring it to pay the amounts that should have been withheld for all fifty-plus workers, plus penalties. The firm unsuccessfully appealed these rulings and was ultimately required to pay unemployment benefits to the relatively small number of workers who filed claims and to pay withholdings for all fifty-plus workers. Once the workers realized they had been misclassified, they also successfully brought a claim against the firm for overtime pay and penalties for failure to pay wages in a timely manner.

or agencies weigh the interests of relatively low-paid workers against those of employers, in close cases the workers' interests usually prevail.

Temporary Workers

A variation of the independent contractor versus employee dichotomy is a hybrid worker, often called a *temporary worker.* Many companies turn to temporary personnel agencies for short-term staffing solutions. Because a temporary personnel agency typically hires, fires, pays, and provides benefits to the temporary worker, it is likely to be considered an employer of the temporary worker. Unlike the relationship with an independent contractor, however, the client company usually retains the right to direct temporary workers and manage their duties while they are on site. Depending on the amount of control the client company and the temporary agency exert over

FROM THE TRENCHES

A biotech company had been using temporary workers hired through a temporary personnel agency to perform lab tests. The temporary workers worked at the company's site for more than a year and were supervised directly by a company manager who supervised other company employees as well. The temporary workers attended the same training as the employees and were given the same forms to complete, which stated that they were for "employees" (e.g., Employee Proprietary Information & Inventions Agreement; Employee Handbook; Employee Acknowledgment of Receipt of Handbook). One temporary worker requested a family medical leave from the company, which the company denied on the theory that the worker was not a company employee. The worker sued the company for violation of the Family and Medical Leave Act on the theory that he was a common-law employee of the company and therefore was entitled to rights under the Act. The company lost the case and was required not only to reimburse the worker for the cost of providing care to his family member but also to pay liquidated damages for its willful failure to provide the family medical leave. The company had no recourse against the temporary personnel agency because it did not have an agreement governing its relationship with the agency.

the temporary workers and the work performed, the temporary arrangement may make the client company either a sole or a joint employer. If found to be joint employers, both the company and the personnel agency will be held liable under most employment laws, such as nondiscrimination laws, wage and hour laws, laws governing employee benefits, and family medical leave laws. One precautionary measure is for the client company to seek an agreement with the temporary personnel agency under which the agency indemnifies the employer from all employment-related liabilities.

MAJOR EMPLOYMENT LEGISLATION

Title VII of the Civil Rights Act of 1964

All businesses, public and private, with fifteen or more employees are covered by Title VII of the Civil Rights Act of 1964 (Title VII). Title VII protects employees from discrimination based on race, color, religion, sex, or national origin. Congress later amended Title VII to expand the coverage of sex discrimination to include discrimination on the basis of pregnancy, childbirth, or related medical conditions, as well as discrimination against married women. Of all the civil rights legislation, Title VII has had the greatest impact on the recruitment, hiring, and other employment practices of American businesses. Many states have adopted comparable legislation, some of which is broader in scope and applies regardless of the number of employees employed by the business. Title VII does not apply to independent contractors, and because of this, a worker's status can be a contentious point in Title VII litigation.

Before the enactment of the Civil Rights Act of 1991, damages under Title VII were limited to compensation for lost salary and benefits (*back pay*), injunctive relief such as reinstatement, and pay for a limited period of time in lieu of reinstatement (*front pay*). Compensatory damages (e.g., for emotional distress or damage to reputation) and punitive damages were not available. The Civil Rights Act of 1991 expanded the remedies under Title VII to include compensatory and punitive damages subject to caps based on the size of the employer. Specifically, in addition to amounts for back pay and front pay (which are not capped), the 1991 Act allows combined amounts of compensatory and punitive damages not to exceed $50,000 against employers with between 15 and 100 employees; not to exceed $100,000 against employers with between 101 and 200 employees; not to exceed $200,000 against employers with between 201 and 500 employees; and not to exceed $300,000 against employers with more than 500 employees.

Litigation under Title VII has produced two distinct legal theories of discrimination: disparate treatment and disparate impact.

DISPARATE TREATMENT A plaintiff claiming *disparate treatment* must prove that the employer intentionally discriminated against him or her by denying employment or a benefit or privilege of employment because of his or her race, color, religion, sex, or national origin. The U.S. Supreme Court has established a three-step analysis of proof in such cases. First, the employee must make a prima facie case. This means that the employee must prove that (1) he or she is a member of a class of persons protected by Title VII and that (2) he or she was denied a position or benefit that he or she sought and was qualified for and that was available. If the employee proves this prima facie case, the employer then must present evidence (but need not prove) that it had legitimate, nondiscriminatory grounds for its decision. If the employer meets this burden of producing evidence, the employee then must prove that he or she was unlawfully discriminated against and that the grounds offered by the employer were only a pretext for this discrimination. In certain circumstances, proof that the employer's explanation for its decision is false may in itself be sufficient evidence to prove intentional discrimination.[1]

For example, an employee who is a member of a minority ethnic group may claim that he was fired because of his race. He would do this by showing that he is a member of the ethnic group, that he was fired, and that he possessed at least the minimum qualifications for the job. Some courts may require that he also show that his job was not eliminated but was filled by someone else after his termination. Once he proves this, his employer might present evidence that the employee was terminated for excessive absenteeism. The employer might produce the employee's attendance records and a supervisor's testimony that his attendance record was unacceptable.

The employee may then attempt to prove pretext in a number of ways. He may show that his supervisor uttered racial slurs from time to time. He may show that his employer's attendance policy requires a written warning about poor attendance before an employee can be terminated on that ground, and that he received no such warning. He may show that nonminority employees with similar attendance records were not fired. Or he may show that his employer's claim of excessive absenteeism is false. The employee has the burden of proving that his employer fired him because of his race, not because of his attendance record.

DISPARATE IMPACT The *disparate impact* theory arose out of Title VII class actions brought in the 1970s against large employers. These suits challenged testing and other employment selection procedures, claiming they systematically excluded women or particular ethnic groups from certain types of jobs. In a disparate impact case, it is not necessary to prove intentional discrimination. Discrimination can be established simply by proving that an employment practice, although neutral on its face, had a disparate impact on a protected group.

For example, suppose an employer has a policy that for security guard positions, it will hire only persons who are 5 feet 8 inches or taller, weigh 150 pounds or more, and can pass certain agility tests. This policy would appear to be neutral. It does not, for example, expressly exclude women or some Asian males. However, if the number of women or Asian males who are refused employment is proportionately greater than the number of white males refused employment, then that policy has a disparate impact.

To prove disparate impact, the plaintiff must demonstrate that the specific employment practice, policy, or rule being challenged has, in a statistically significant way, disproportionately affected a certain protected group and that he or she is a member of that group. The employer then has the burden to produce evidence that the challenged practice, policy, or rule is job related for the position in question and consistent with business necessity. Inconvenience, annoyance, or expense to the employer will not suffice.

For example, a Latina applicant who is denied employment because she failed an English-language test may challenge the language requirement. If she has applied for a sales job, the employer may be able to justify the requirement on the grounds that ability to communicate with customers is an indispensable qualification. On the other hand, if she has applied for a position on the production line, where communication may be a less critical part of the job, that justification may not suffice. As with disparate treatment analysis, the ultimate burden of proof rests with the plaintiff.

Historically, disparate impact analysis has been limited to objective selection criteria, such as tests and degree requirements. However, the Supreme Court has ruled that disparate impact analysis may also apply to subjective bases for decisions, such as interviews and supervisor evaluations. For example, if an employer makes hiring decisions on the basis of interviews alone, and if the percentage of qualified women or African Americans hired differs significantly from the percentage of qualified women or African Americans in the relevant labor pool, then a rejected applicant may claim that this process is unlawful under Title VII. The issue then will be whether the process is justified by business necessity.

STATUTORY DEFENSES UNDER TITLE VII Title VII sets forth several statutory defenses to claims of discriminatory treatment. Statutory defenses absolve the employer even if the employee can prove that discrimination occurred. Of these defenses, the one most frequently cited is bona fide occupational qualification.

Bona Fide Occupational Qualifications Title VII provides that an employer may lawfully hire an individual on the basis of his or her religion, sex, or national origin if religion, sex, or national origin is a *bona fide occupational qualification (BFOQ)* reasonably necessary to the normal operation of that particular business. This is known as the *BFOQ defense*. The BFOQ defense is never available if discriminatory treatment is based on a person's race or color. Because BFOQ is an affirmative defense, the employer has the burden of showing a reasonable basis for believing that persons in a certain category (e.g., women) excluded from a particular job were unable to perform that job.

The BFOQ defense has been narrowly construed. For example, regulations promulgated by the Equal Employment Opportunity Commission provide that gender will not qualify as a BFOQ if a gender-based restriction

FROM THE TRENCHES

Johnson Controls, Inc., a battery manufacturer, adopted a policy barring all women from working in the manufacturing plant at jobs involving actual or potential lead exposure above a certain level. The policy was intended to protect fetuses from unsafe levels of lead exposure. The only exception to the policy was for women whose infertility was medically documented. A class action suit was filed on behalf of female employees affected by the policy. They claimed that the policy constituted sex discrimination in violation of Title VII.

The U.S. Supreme Court held that the policy was illegal discrimination under Title VII. First, the Court found that the policy was discriminatory against women on its face because it did not apply to men even though there was evidence that lead exposure was also harmful to the male reproductive system. Because the policy involved disparate treatment through explicit discrimination, the Court evaluated the policy under the bona fide occupational qualification (BFOQ) standard.

The Court rejected the BFOQ defense because the capacity of a woman to become pregnant does not affect her ability to perform on the job and because fertile women can participate in the manufacture of batteries as efficiently as men. Finally, the Court said that the potential tort liability should not change the result because it doubted the company would be liable for harm to a woman or her fetus so long as it fully informed the women of the potential risk and did not act negligently.

Source: International Union v. Johnson Controls, Inc., 499 U.S. 187 (1991).

is based on (1) assumptions of the comparative employment characteristics of women in general (such as the assumption that women have a higher turnover rate than men); (2) stereotyped characterizations of the sexes (e.g., that men are less capable of assembling intricate equipment than women); or (3) the preferences of coworkers, employers, or customers for one sex over the other. Gender may, however, be considered a BFOQ if physical attributes are necessary for the position (as with a wet nurse) or for purposes of authenticity (as with actors) or if a gender-based restriction is necessary to protect the rights of others to privacy (as with rest room attendants).

Sexual discrimination suits can be brought by men as well as women. For example, in the 1970s, a group of men successfully sued Southwest Airlines over its policy of hiring only female flight attendants. The court reasoned that the airline could not make gender a BFOQ merely because it wished to exploit female sexuality as a marketing tool. Because the main business of the company was transportation, not entertainment, the court ruled that Southwest Airlines could not bar males from becoming flight attendants.

In contrast, Playboy Enterprises was permitted to hire only women to serve as Playboy "bunnies" in Playboy Clubs because the main purpose of the clubs was to provide male entertainment. Several other courts have similarly held that gender, specifically being female, is a BFOQ in some entertainment and fashion jobs.

Seniority and Merit Systems Under Title VII, an employer can lawfully apply different standards of compensation, or different terms or conditions of employment, pursuant to a bona fide seniority or merit system. A seniority or merit system is considered to be "bona fide" as long as there has not been purposeful discrimination in connection with the establishment or continuation of the system. This is considered an exemption from Title VII rather than an affirmative defense. Consequently, the plaintiff has the burden of proving that the seniority or merit system has a discriminatory intent or illegal purpose. Moreover, although a system's disproportionate impact may indicate some evidence of a discriminatory intent, such an impact is not in itself sufficient to establish discriminatory intent.

SEXUAL HARASSMENT Sexual harassment has emerged as one of the more complex and emotional issues in antidiscrimination law. Early on, the courts recognized that a specific, job-related adverse action (such as denial of promotion) in retaliation for a person's refusal to respond to a supervisor's sexual advances was a violation of Title VII. Such retaliation is referred to as *quid pro quo harassment*. *Quid pro quo harassment* also occurs when a supervisor makes submission to sexual conduct a condition for receiving employment benefits.

In 1986, the U.S. Supreme Court ruled that the creation of a hostile work environment by sexual harassment is also a form of discrimination barred

FROM THE TRENCHES

Teresa Harris, a manager, sued her former employer for sexual harassment under Title VII, claiming that the conduct of the company's president, Charles Hardy, created an abusive work environment. Hardy often insulted Harris because of her gender and subjected her to unwanted sexual innuendos. At one point Hardy suggested that he and Harris "go to the Holiday Inn to negotiate [her] raise." Hardy also sometimes asked Harris and other female employees to take coins from his front pants pocket and would throw objects on the ground in front of Harris and ask her to pick them up.

Eventually, Harris complained to Hardy about his conduct. Hardy claimed he was only joking and apologized. A few weeks later, however, he resumed his insulting behavior. Shortly thereafter, Harris quit and sued the company.

A lower court dismissed the case because the conduct in question was not so egregious as to cause Harris psychological damage. The U.S. Supreme Court reversed the decision and held that although merely offensive behavior would not constitute an abusive work environment, conduct may be actionable under Title VII even if it does not seriously affect the psychological well-being of, or cause injury to, the plaintiff. In the words of the Court, "Title VII comes into play before the harassing conduct leads to a nervous breakdown." Instead, the Court took a middle ground, ruling that as long as the environment would be reasonably perceived, and was perceived by the plaintiff, as hostile or abusive, the conduct violates Title VII.

Source: Harris v. Forklift Sys., Inc., 510 U.S. 17 (1993).

by Title VII.[2] An employee can establish a case of *hostile work environment harassment* by showing that (1) he or she was subjected to sexual conduct (such as sexual advances); (2) the conduct was unwelcome; and (3) the conduct was sufficiently severe or pervasive as to alter the conditions of the victim's employment and create an abusive working environment.[3] An illegal hostile work environment can exist even if the employee does not lose a tangible job benefit (e.g., is not terminated).

Both men and women can sue for sexual harassment, and Title VII applies to same-sex harassment regardless of whether the conduct is motivated by sexual desire.[4] An employer may also be liable for nonsexual, gender-related conduct if it causes a discriminatory or hostile work environment.

The employer is liable for hostile environment harassment by a supervisor, coworker, or customer if it knew or should have known of the sexual harassment and failed to take prompt and reasonable steps to prevent or remedy it. For example, Pizza Hut was found liable when a rowdy male customer grabbed a waitress and put his mouth on her breast. Before this incident, the waitress had informed the manager that the customer and his companion had made offensive comments to her and pulled her hair, but the manager had ordered her to continue waiting on them saying: "You wait on them. You were hired to be a waitress. You waitress."[5]

Under certain circumstances, the employer may be liable for sexual harassment in the workplace even if the employer was not aware of the conduct and had no reason to be aware of it. For example, an employer is absolutely liable for a supervisor's *quid pro quo* harassment. The employer is also absolutely liable for a supervisor's hostile work environment harassment—even if the employer had no reason to be aware of the harassment—if the supervisor took adverse employment action against the employee (such as discharge, demotion, or undesirable reassignment). However, when no adverse action is taken against the employee, the employer has an affirmative defense against liability for a supervisor's hostile work environment harassment when the following two requirements are satisfied: (1) the employer exercised reasonable care to prevent and promptly correct any sexually harassing behavior, and (2) the employee unreasonably failed to take advantage of any preventive or corrective opportunities provided by the employer. Thus, employers should always promulgate and distribute an antiharassment policy, including an effective complaint procedure that specifies company officials other than the employee's direct supervisor to whom complaints can be made.

FROM THE TRENCHES

Beth Ann Faragher, a lifeguard, sued her former employer, the City of Boca Raton, for hostile environment sexual harassment under Title VII. She claimed that over a period of five years, her immediate supervisors, Bill Terry and David Silverman, repeatedly subjected her and other female lifeguards to uninvited and offensive touching and lewd remarks. For example, Faragher alleged that Terry had put his hand on her buttocks and that Silverman had once told her that, but for a physical characteristic he found unattractive, he would readily have sex with her.

Faragher never complained to higher management about the harassment, and she filed her lawsuit two years after resigning from her position. The U.S. Supreme Court concluded that the harassing conduct of Terry and Silverman was sufficiently serious to alter the conditions of Faragher's employment and create an abusive working environment. The Court ruled that, under the aided-in-the-agency-relation theory, the City was liable for Terry and Silverman's conduct even though the City had no reason to know what they were doing. Although Terry and Silverman were acting outside the scope of their employment when harassing the female lifeguards, it was the authority that the City gave them as supervisors that made the harassment possible. As the Court explained: "When a fellow employee harasses, the victim can walk away or tell the offender where to go, but it may be difficult to offer such responses to a supervisor" with the power to hire, fire, and set work schedules and pay raises.

The Court indicated that the City could have avoided liability if it had exercised reasonable care to prevent and promptly correct any sexually harassing behavior, and if it had shown that Faragher had unreasonably failed to take advantage of the preventive and corrective opportunities provided by the City. However, the Court ruled as a matter of law that the City did not exercise reasonable care to prevent the supervisors' harassing conduct. The City had failed to disseminate its policy against sexual harassment among the beach employees; its policy did not include a sensible complaint procedure because it did not provide any assurance that the harassing supervisors could be bypassed in registering complaints; and its officials made no attempt to keep track of the conduct of supervisors, even though the supervisors were given virtually unchecked authority over subordinates who were completely isolated from the City's higher management.

Source: Faragher v. City of Boca Raton, 524 U.S. 775 (1998).

Age Discrimination in Employment Act

The Age Discrimination in Employment Act (ADEA) applies to all companies that affect interstate commerce and have at least twenty employees. (Some states have adopted comparable legislation that applies regardless of the number of employees employed by the business.) The ADEA prohibits employers, employment agencies, and labor unions from age-discriminating employment practices. The Act covers workers age forty and older, and it applies to applicants for employment as well as to current employees. Independent contractors are excluded from ADEA coverage.

If an employee age forty or older is fired, he or she can state a claim under the ADEA by showing that he or she was replaced by someone substantially younger. The burden then shifts to the employer to present evidence that it had legitimate, nondiscriminatory grounds for its decision. The burden then shifts back to the employee to prove that there was discrimination and that the grounds offered by the employer were only a pretext for unlawful discrimination.

ADEA claims generally involve allegations of disparate treatment. In 2001, the U.S. Supreme Court agreed to hear a case in which the employee sought recovery based on the theory of disparate impact.[6]

WAIVERS Often an employer will require an employee who is terminated or laid off to waive all employment discrimination claims as a condition to receiving extra severance benefits (such as additional severance pay). If the employee is age forty or older, then an employee release of age discrimination claims will be effective only if the employer meets all the requirements for a special ADEA waiver.

For an ADEA waiver to be valid when *one* employee is discharged, the waiver must (1) be understandable; (2) specifically refer to the employee's rights under the ADEA; (3) not require the employee to waive rights or claims that might arise after the date the waiver is executed; (4) waive rights and claims only in exchange for something of value to which the employee is not otherwise entitled (e.g., additional weeks of severance pay); (5) advise the employee to consult with an attorney prior to signing the waiver; (6) provide the employee with twenty-one days to consider the waiver; and (7) provide the employee with seven days after signing the waiver to revoke his or her consent.

ADEA waiver requirements are similar when *two or more* employees are discharged at the same time in a layoff, except that in these situations the waiver must also (1) contain separate lists of the ages and job titles of all employees in the same organizational unit who are (a) being retained and (b) being discharged and (2) provide the employee with forty-five days (instead of twenty-one days) to consider the waiver. The U.S. Supreme Court has made it clear that employers must strictly comply with these requirements for an ADEA waiver to be effective.

Americans with Disabilities Act

The Americans with Disabilities Act (ADA) covers all employers with fifteen or more employees who work at least twenty or more calendar weeks in a year. (Several states have adopted comparable legislation that applies regardless of the number of employees employed by the business.) The ADA prohibits discrimination against qualified individuals with disabilities in employee job application procedures, hiring, promotions, training, compensation, and discharge. It also requires the employer to provide reasonable accommodations so that the disabled employee can perform his or her job, unless doing so would constitute an undue hardship for the employer. Available remedies for a violation of the ADA include back pay, reinstatement or hiring, and reimbursement of attorneys' fees and court costs.

The ADA protects only employees and prospective employees. Because strict compliance with the ADA can be costly, an employer may have an incentive to try to avoid falling under its purview by hiring independent contractors. However, any attempt to alter the characterization of existing employees solely to avoid compliance with the ADA will be viewed by the courts as a clear violation of the Act. The choice to use independent contractor services must be made prior to the start of a working relationship. Thus, the use of any contractual arrangements to circumvent the Act will be considered an ADA violation if the effect is to screen out qualified individuals with a disability.

Definition of Disability A *disability* is defined under the ADA as (1) a mental or physical impairment that substantially limits one or more of a person's major life activities, (2) a record of such an impairment, or (3) being regarded as having such an impairment. Physical impairments generally include any physiobiological disorder or condition, cosmetic disfigurement, or anatomic loss affecting a person's skin or a person's neuromuscular, musculoskeletal, cardiovascular, reproductive, digestive, lymphatic, endocrine, or sensory (including speech organs) body systems. If the physical or mental impairment is corrected by medication or other measures (such as eyeglasses for someone with myopia), then the person will not be deemed to be disabled.[7] Some states (such as California) define disability much more broadly.

Major life activities are "those activities that are of actual importance to daily life"[8] and include walking, seeing, hearing, procreating, and working. A person will not be considered disabled unless the impairment substantially limits a major life activity. Thus, a person claiming that he or she is disabled because of inability to work must be able to show an inability to work in a broad range of jobs, rather than a specific job.[9]

Similarly, a person with an impairment affecting his or her ability to perform manual tasks will not be considered disabled unless the impairment (1) prevents or severely restricts the individual from doing activities that are of central importance to most people's lives and (2) has a permanent or long-term impact.[10] Such activities include doing household chores, bathing, and brushing one's teeth. It is not enough that an impairment might limit manual tasks unique to any particular job; it must severely restrict activities of central importance to most people's daily lives. Accordingly, the U.S. Supreme Court ruled that a woman who worked on an automotive assembly line and developed carpal tunnel syndrome and related impairments that limited her ability to do "repetitive work with both hands and arms extended at or above shoulder levels for extended periods of time" was not disabled as a matter of law because "she could still brush her teeth, wash her face, bathe, tend her flower garden, fix breakfast, do laundry and pick up around the house."[11]

Employers must exercise caution regarding any employee health issues that might be deemed to be disabilities because of the broad way the term "disabilities" is defined under the ADA. For example, the U.S. Supreme Court ruled that a woman who was HIV-positive but asymptomatic was a qualified individual with a disability.[12] The Court reasoned that procreation qualified as a major life activity within the statutory definition of a disability. Even though a woman's HIV-positive status did not preclude her from bearing children, it substantially limited her ability and willingness to do so because of the risk of infecting her partner or baby.

An employer considering disciplining an employee for missing work should ensure that the absences are not related to a disability requiring reasonable accommodation. For example, courts have found that employees with psychological conditions, such as obsessive-compulsive disorder, deserved ADA protection depending on the particular circumstances. At the same time, courts have held that if a person has a disability that makes it impossible for the person to come to work, even with reasonable accommodation, then the person will not be deemed qualified for the job.

REASONABLE ACCOMMODATION The ADA requires an employer to provide reasonable accommodations for an employee's disability, unless doing so would cause the employer undue hardship. Thus, even if a disability precludes an individual from performing the essential functions of the position, or presents a safety risk, the employer is required to assess whether there is a reasonable accommodation that will permit the individual to be employed despite the disability. The ADA includes a nonexhaustive list of what might constitute reasonable accommodation, including (1) making work facilities accessible; (2) restructuring jobs or modifying work schedules; (3) acquiring or modifying equipment or devices; (4) modifying examinations, training materials, or policies; and (5) providing qualified readers or interpreters or other similar accommodations for individuals with disabilities.

UNDUE HARDSHIP Reasonable accommodation is not required if it would impose an undue hardship on the employer. The ADA defines *undue hardship* to mean an activity requiring significant difficulty or expense when considered in light of (1) the nature and cost of the accommodation needed; (2) the overall financial resources of the facility, the number of persons employed at the facility, the effect on expenses and resources, or any other impact of the accommodation on the facility; (3) the overall financial resources of the employer and the overall size of the business with respect to the number of employees and the type, number, and location of its facilities; and (4) the type of operation of the employer, including the composition, structure, and functions of the workforce, the geographic separateness, and the administrative or fiscal relationship of the facility in question to the employer.

ESTABLISHING A NONDISCRIMINATORY REASON FOR TERMINATION An employee with a disability may still be terminated if the reason for the termination is unrelated to the individual's disability. For example, an assistant football coach at the University of Tennessee was terminated because of a well-publicized incident in which he was arrested for driving under the influence of alcohol. The coach was an alcoholic, a disability expressly protected under the ADA. However, the court found that the coach was not terminated because of his disability, but rather because of his criminal conduct and behavior and the significant amount of bad publicity surrounding him and the school.[13] Similarly, the ADA will not protect individuals disabled due to drug addition who sell illegal drugs on company property.

Other courts have found that absenteeism unrelated to an individual's disability can provide the grounds for disciplinary action up to and including discharge. However, where an employee's absenteeism is directly related to a disability, some courts have found that an absenteeism policy may be suspended as a reasonable accommodation.

Family and Medical Leave Laws

The federal Family and Medical Leave Act (FMLA) requires employers with fifty or more full-time employees to provide eligible employees up to twelve weeks of unpaid leave per year if such leave is requested in connection with (1) the birth of a child; (2) the placement of an adopted or foster child with the employee; (3) the care of a child, parent, or spouse; or (4) a serious health condition that renders the employee unable to do his or her job. To be eligible, an employee must have worked for the employer for at least twelve months and for at least 1,250 hours per year. Under some circumstances, leave may be taken intermittently, in increments of as little as one hour at a time until the twelve weeks is exhausted. Some states require employers with fewer than fifty employees to grant family and medical leave.

Under the FMLA, an employer must expressly designate leave taken by an employee as FMLA leave. The employer must also continue providing health care coverage for the employee on the same terms as if the employee was actively working.

The Act requires the employer to restore the employee to the same position, or one with equivalent benefits, pay, and other terms and conditions of employment, following the expiration of the leave, unless the employee is a key employee (among the top 10 percent based on salary) and substantial and grievous injury will result from reinstatement. As soon as the employer determines that reinstatement would cause such injury, the employer must notify the employee that the company intends to deny job restoration and give the employee a reasonable time to return to work.

An employee cannot contract out of his or her right to leave time under the FMLA. However, the employer may require the employee, or an employee may choose, to substitute any or all accrued paid leave for the leave time that is provided for under the Act. The Act should be considered a floor, not a ceiling, as to what employers can provide their employees in terms of a leave option. In addition, the FMLA may interact with other leave laws, such as state pregnancy leave statutes or state and federal disability discrimination statutes, which may entitle an employee to leave greater than the twelve weeks provided by the FMLA.

Summary of Federal Civil Rights Legislation

Exhibit 10.1 summarizes the major federal statutes barring various kinds of employment discrimination. As noted already, many states have passed their own fair employment acts, which apply to employees working in the state and, in some instances, provide greater protection than their federal counterparts.

EXHIBIT 10.1

MAJOR PIECES OF FEDERAL CIVIL RIGHTS LEGISLATION

Statute	Major Provisions	Employers Subject To Statute	Comments
Civil Rights Act of 1866 (Section 1981)	Prohibits racial discrimination by employers of any size in the making and enforcement of contracts, including employment contracts.	All public and private employers	The bar against racial discrimination applies not only to hiring, promotion, and termination but also to working conditions, such as racial harassment, and to breaches of contract occurring during the term of the contract.
Equal Pay Act of 1963	Mandates equal pay for equal work without regard to gender.	All public and private employers with twenty or more employees (including federal, state, and local governments)	
Title VII of the Civil Rights Act of 1964 (Title VII)	Prohibits discrimination in employment on the basis of race, color, religion, national origin, or sex. Later amended to provide that discrimination on the basis of sex includes discrimination on the basis of pregnancy, childbirth, or related medical conditions.	All public and private employers with fifteen or more employees	

continued...

EXHIBIT 10.1 (CONTINUED)

MAJOR PIECES OF FEDERAL CIVIL RIGHTS LEGISLATION

Statute	Major Provisions	Employers Subject To Statute	Comments
Age Discrimination in Employment Act of 1967 (ADEA)	Protects persons forty years and older from discrimination on the basis of age. The ADEA was amended in 1990 by the Older Workers' Benefit Protection Act, which prohibits age discrimination in providing employee benefits and establishes minimum standards for waiver of one's rights under the ADEA.	All public and private employers with twenty or more employees	
The Vietnam Era Veteran's Readjustment Assistance Acts of 1972 and 1974	Prohibits discrimination and requires affirmative action to employ disabled Vietnam-era and other war veterans.	Employers holding federal contracts of $25,000	Enforced by U.S. Department of Labor.
Vocational Rehabilitation Act of 1973	Prohibits discrimination against the physically and mentally disabled and requires affirmative-action efforts	Employers holding federal contracts of $10,000	Enforced by U.S. Department of Labor. This legislation was the precursor to and guided the development of the Americans with Disabilities Act.
Veterans Re-Employment Act of 1974	Gives employees who served in the military at any time the right to be reinstated in employment without loss of seniority benefits and the right not to be discharged without cause for one year following such reinstatement.	All public and private employers	

continued...

EXHIBIT 10.1 (CONTINUED)

MAJOR PIECES OF FEDERAL CIVIL RIGHTS LEGISLATION

Statute	Major Provisions	Employers Subject To Statute	Comments
Immigration Reform and Control Act of 1986	Prohibits discrimination against applicants or employees based on national origin or citizenship status.	All private employers with four or more employees	If employer has fifteen or more employees, plaintiff must file national-origin discrimination claims under Title VII.
Americans with Disabilities Act of 1990 (ADA)	Prohibits discrimination in employment on the basis of a person's disability. Also requires businesses to provide "reasonable accommodation" to the disabled, unless such an accommodation would result in "undue hardship" on business operations.	All private employers with fifteen or more employees	The ADA is the most sweeping civil rights measure since the Civil Rights Act of 1964.
Civil Rights Act of 1991	Legislatively overruled several parts of prior Supreme Court rulings that were unfavorable to the rights of plaintiffs in employment-discrimination cases. Also extended coverage of the major civil rights statutes to the staffs of the president and the Senate.	Varies	

continued...

EXHIBIT 10.1 (CONTINUED)

MAJOR PIECES OF FEDERAL CIVIL RIGHTS LEGISLATION

Statute	Major Provisions	Employers Subject To Statute	Comments
Family and Medical Leave Act of 1993	Designed to allow employees to take time off from work to handle domestic responsibilities, such as the birth or adoption of a child or the care of an elderly parent. Employees are guaranteed job security despite familial responsibilities.	Private employers with fifty or more employees at work sites within a seventy-five mile radius.	Part-time employees are excluded from the Act's coverage and are not counted in calculating the fifty employees necessary for an employer to be covered by the Act.

Fair Labor Standards Act

The federal Fair Labor Standards Act (FLSA) covers all employers who participate in interstate commerce, regardless of the size of the business or the number of people employed. The FLSA was enacted in 1938 with the primary goal of regulating the minimum wage, overtime pay, and the use of child labor. All nonexempt employees must be paid a minimum wage, which as of January 1, 2002, was $5.15 per hour, for all hours worked as specified by federal law. If the applicable state minimum wage is higher than the federal rate, the worker is entitled to the higher of the two rates. Under the FLSA, the employer must pay for hours worked in excess of forty in a workweek at a rate equal to one and one-half times the regular rate of pay.

Some types of employees (such as outside salespersons and professional, executive, administrative, and highly skilled computer professional employees) are exempt from the minimum-wage and overtime provisions of the FLSA. In general, to be exempt, the employee must have job responsibilities that he or she fulfills without supervision and must meet other statutory criteria. Independent contractors are not covered by the statute.

In addition to the federal statute, most states and several cities have adopted their own provisions regulating wages and overtime pay. Some states (such as California) require that overtime be paid for work performed over eight hours in a day and for work performed over forty hours in a week. Some states also hold managers personally liable for certain violations of the wage and hour laws. Generally, if there is a discrepancy between the federal and state statutes, the employer must abide by the law that is more favorable to the employee.

Workers' Compensation

Workers' compensation statutes require most employers to obtain insurance for income and medical expenses for employees who suffer work-related accidents or illnesses. These statutes, which generally exclude independent contractors, are based on the principle that the risks of injury in the workplace should be borne by industry. Coverage applies to accidents as well as to gradual onset conditions, such as carpal tunnel syndrome, and illnesses that are the gradual result of work conditions, such as heart disease or emotional illness. The workers' compensation system is no-fault, and an injured employee is entitled to receive insurance benefits regardless of the level of safety in the work environment and the degree to which the employee's carelessness contributed to the incident. In exchange for the no-fault nature of the system, the monetary awards available to employees are generally restricted and lower than those that might be obtained in lawsuits for negligence and other torts. This arrangement is commonly referred to as the workers' compensation bargain.

Workers' compensation insurance can be provided in one of three ways. Some states allow an employer to self-insure by maintaining a substantial cash reserve for potential claims. This is an unrealistic option for many small businesses. Some states require an employer to purchase insurance through a state fund. Other states give the employer the choice of purchasing insurance through a state fund or from a private insurer. State funds and private insurance companies have attorneys who usually resolve legal questions of whether an employee is entitled to coverage.

A properly implemented workers' compensation program provides employers with a basis for arguing that workers' compensation insurance should be the exclusive remedy for workplace injuries. If a workers' compensation program is not properly implemented, an injured employee may have a right to claim potentially unlimited damages in a lawsuit against his or her employer (as opposed to the restricted payments available under the workers' compensation scheme). Additionally, some states may impose substantial fines or shut down companies that fail to obtain workers' compensation insurance properly. Accordingly, it is very important for employers to ensure that they are in full compliance with the applicable workers' compensation statute and that all eligible employees are properly insured. Not having legally sufficient workers' compensation insurance can be very costly for the employer.

FROM THE TRENCHES

Jon Fretland, a county employee hurt on the job, sued his employer for employment discrimination and intentional infliction of emotional distress. He claimed that as a result of his physical injury, his coworkers falsely accused him of theft, vandalized his car, and left obscene and threatening telephone messages for him.

The employer moved to dismiss Fretland's emotional distress claim, arguing that it was barred by the exclusive remedy provisions of the workers' compensation law. The California Court of Appeal disagreed, ruling that the workers' compensation statute does not preempt all emotional distress claims against the employer, "but only those based on conduct that is a normal risk of the employment relationship." The court reasoned that because intentional, injury-related harassment is not a normal risk of the employment relationship, Fretland's emotional distress claims were not barred by the workers' compensation exclusivity rule.

Source: Fretland v. County of Humboldt, 69 Cal. App. 4th 1478 (1999).

Occupational Safety and Health Act

Businesses must comply with the federal Occupational Safety and Health Act, known as *OSHA*, as well as its state-law counterparts. OSHA requires employers to establish a safe and healthy working environment for their employees. OSHA applies to all employers engaged in interstate commerce but does not apply to state or federal employees.

An employer governed by OSHA must provide a place of employment that is free from recognized hazards that are causing or are likely to cause death or serious physical harm to employees. What constitutes a recognized hazard is not entirely clear, but its reach is broad and includes anything from sharp objects to radiation. Employers regulated by OSHA are also subject to regulations promulgated by the Occupational Safety and Health Administration (the OSHA agency). The OSHA agency is authorized to issue standards regarding a variety of workplace issues, including exposure to hazardous chemicals, first aid and medical treatment, noise levels, protective gear, fire protection, worker training, and workplace temperatures and ventilation.

Businesses regulated by the OSHA agency are subject to many requirements. For example, businesses with ten or more employees are required to maintain an injury-and-illness log, medical records, and training records. The only types of businesses exempt from these record-keeping requirements are certain low-hazard retail, service, real estate, insurance, and finance businesses. The OSHA agency may conduct surprise inspections at work sites. If a violation is found, the employer must correct the problem immediately. The OSHA agency may seek a court order to ensure compliance. The OSHA agency may also impose fines for more egregious violations. Serious violations resulting in the death of an employee may lead to criminal prosecution of the company's management.

National Labor Relations Act

The National Labor Relations Act (NLRA) covers all enterprises that have a substantial effect on commerce. The NLRA protects employees from adverse employment action because of their union activities or nonunion concerted activities for mutual benefit (e.g., signing a petition for better compensation and benefits). The NLRA requires employers to negotiate with labor unions representing the employees and governs employment policies limiting union solicitation and policies prohibiting an employee from disclosing his or her own salary. The NLRA provides a remedy for an unlawfully discharged employee by mandating reinstatement and payment of back pay for the time off work. However, its protection extends only to employees, not to supervisors or independent contractors.

Entrepreneurs sometimes face union organizing among their employees in response to the employer's failure to comply with basic employment regulations out of a misguided desire to minimize expenses or streamline operations. Lack of compliance with employment regulations may cause employees to believe that banding together in a union is the best way to protect themselves. If an entrepreneur decides to oppose union-organizing efforts, doing so may require hiring labor consultants or attorneys; the process itself can be a major disruption to normal business operations. Thus, failure to comply with the law or to address employee-relations issues at the outset may cause a long-term problem in the form of union-organizing efforts.

Equal Employment Opportunity Commission

The *Equal Employment Opportunity Commission* (*EEOC*) is the federal administrative agency created for the purpose of enforcing Title VII and other federal antidiscrimination statutes. An individual with a grievance must first follow (*exhaust*) the administrative procedures of the EEOC before filing a lawsuit under Title VII or related federal statutes. Because many employment disputes involve promotions, pay raises, and other issues regarded as less extreme than termination of employment, the theory is that the administrative process of the EEOC may help to resolve employment discrimination issues without the parties involved having to resort to time-consuming and expensive litigation.

Exhaustion of the EEOC process requires that an individual file a sworn document called a charge of discrimination, which lists the particulars of the alleged discrimination, harassment, or retaliation. The EEOC then investigates the charge, typically by sending to the employer a copy of the charge, a request for a written response to the charge, and any documentation regarding the allegations in the charge. The EEOC is authorized to make a finding that reasonable cause exists to believe that a violation has occurred and, if so, to attempt to resolve the charge by the informal process of conciliation and persuasion.

Prehiring Practices

Job Advertisements

Many employers begin the recruitment process by posting or publishing a "Help Wanted" notice. Title VII, the ADEA, and the ADA prohibit employers from publishing or printing job notices that express a preference or limitation based on race, color, religion, sex, national origin, age, or disability, unless such specifications are based on good-faith occupational qualifications. These limitations apply to traditional media, such as print or radio advertising, as well as to job openings posted on a company's Web site or intranet.

For example, an advertisement for a "waitress" implies that the employer is seeking a woman for the job. If there is no bona fide reason why the job should be filled by a woman rather than a man, the advertisement would be considered discriminatory. Similarly, terms such as "young woman" or "girl" should never be used because they discourage job candidates from applying for positions because of their sex or age.

Many state laws also prohibit discriminatory advertisements, and some states may prohibit references to additional protected classifications. For example, Massachusetts and Ohio prohibit references to ancestry, and California prohibits references to sexual orientation.

Word-of-mouth recruitment practices can also be discriminatory. Word-of-mouth recruiting normally takes the form of current employees informing their family and friends of job openings. When information is disseminated in this way, it may tend to reach a disproportionate number of persons of the same ethnicity as the employer's current employees. Thus, reliance on word-of-mouth recruiting practices may perpetuate past discrimination. If word-of-mouth recruiting is used, it should be supplemented with other recruiting activities that are designed to reach a broader spectrum of people.

Employers advertising for jobs should avoid placing advertisements in publications with sex-segregated help-wanted columns. They should indicate that the employer is an equal-opportunity employer and should use media designed to reach people in both minority and nonminority communities.

Applications and Interviews

Employers use the application and interview process to gain information about an individual's personal, educational, and employment background. Unless there is a valid reason, an employer should avoid making inquiries relating to the protected characteristics of a job candidate on an application form, during a preemployment interview, or in some other manner. Although federal laws do not expressly prohibit preemployment inquiries concerning an applicant's race, color, national origin, sex, marital status, religion, or age, such inquiries are disfavored because they create an inference that these factors will be used as selection criteria. These inquiries may be expressly prohibited under state law.

Often the line between permissible and impermissible areas of inquiry is not clear. Because the actions of recruiters, interviewers, and supervisors can expose an employer to legal liability, it is crucial that they understand which questions should and should not be asked. As a general rule, recruitment personnel should ask themselves, "What information do I really need to decide whether an applicant is qualified to perform this job?"

SEX Any preemployment inquiry that explicitly or implicitly indicates a preference or limitation based on an applicant's sex is unlawful unless the inquiry is justified by a bona fide occupational qualification. In rare cases, a candidate's sex may be a valid criterion for a job, as in the case of actors, actresses, or fashion models. Normally, however, questions concerning an applicant's sex, marital status, or family should be avoided. For example, application forms and interviewers should not inquire about the following:

- Whether an applicant is male or female.
- The number or ages of an applicant's children.
- How an applicant will arrange for child care.
- An applicant's views on birth control.
- Whether an applicant is pregnant or plans to become pregnant.
- Whether a female applicant prefers to be addressed as Mrs., Miss, or Ms.
- The applicant's maiden name.

In addition, an interviewer should not direct a particular question, such as whether the applicant can type, to only female or only male applicants for the same job.

Some of this information eventually will be needed for benefits, tax, and EEOC profile purposes, but it usually can be collected after the applicant has been hired. There are exceptions to this general rule, however. For example, state law may require employers to collect data regarding the race, sex, and national origin of each applicant and the job for which he or she has applied. Certain federal or state government contractors are also obligated to collect applicant-flow data. Such data are collected for statistical and record-keeping purposes only and cannot be considered by the employer in its hiring decision. In general, if an employer is required to collect such data, the employer should ask applicants to provide self-identification information on a form that is separate or detachable from the application form.

AGE Application forms and interviewers should not try to identify applicants aged forty and older. Accordingly, job candidates generally should not be asked their age, their birth date, or the date that they completed elementary or secondary school. An employer can inquire about age only if (1) age is a bona fide job requirement, as for a child actor; or (2) the employer is trying to comply with special laws, such as those applying to the employment of minors. The fact that it may cost more to employ older workers as a group does not justify differentiation among applicants based on age.

RACE Employers should not ask about an applicant's race. Questions concerning complexion, skin color, eye color, or hair color should be avoided, and applicants should not be asked to submit photographs.

NATIONAL ORIGIN AND CITIZENSHIP An interviewer should not ask an applicant about nationality or ancestry because Title VII prohibits discrimination on the basis of national origin. In addition, the Immigration Reform and Control Act of 1986 (IRCA) makes it unlawful for an employer with four or more employees to discriminate against applicants or employees on the basis of either their national origin or their citizenship status. (If the employer has fifteen or more employees and therefore is covered by Title VII, charges of national-origin discrimination must be filed under Title VII, not the IRCA.)

The IRCA also makes it unlawful for an employer of any size to knowingly hire an individual not authorized to work in the United States. Violators can face civil and criminal penalties. However, employers cannot discriminate against persons solely because they have a foreign appearance or speak a foreign language. The Act specifies the correct procedure for determining whether an applicant is authorized to work.

Under the IRCA, any newly hired employee is required to complete Immigration and Naturalization Service Form I-9, certifying that he or she is authorized to work in the United States and has presented documentation of work authorization and identification to the employer. After examining the documents presented, the employer must complete the remainder of the form, certifying that the documents appear genuine, relate to the employee, and establish work authorization. Form I-9 must be completed within a prescribed period of time.

RELIGION An employer generally should not ask questions regarding an applicant's religion. An employer can tell an applicant what the normal work schedule is and ask the applicant whether he or she will be able to work this schedule, but the employer should not ask which religious holidays the applicant observes or whether the applicant's religion will interfere with his or her job performance. Title VII's ban on religious discrimination encompasses more than observance of the Sabbath. It applies to all conduct motivated by religion, such as dress or maintenance of a particular physical appearance. Title VII imposes a duty on employers to make reasonable accommodation for their employees' religious practices as long as such accommodation will not cause undue hardship to the employer's business.

An employer may ask about a candidate's religious beliefs if the beliefs are a bona fide occupational qualification. For example, a school that is owned, supported, or controlled by persons of a particular religion may require that its employees have a specific religious belief. In an extreme case, a federal district court ruled that a helicopter pilot could be required to convert to the Muslim religion in order to fly over certain areas of Saudi Arabia that are closed to non-Muslims. The court ruled that the requirement was a bona fide occupational qualification justified by safety considerations because Saudi Arabian law prohibited non-Muslims from entering Mecca, and non-Muslims who did so risked being beheaded if caught.[14]

DISABILITY AND PHYSICAL TRAITS The Americans with Disabilities Act prohibits all discrimination on the basis of disability and prohibits employers from questioning applicants about their general medical condition or any disabilities. After an employer has described a job's requirements, the employer may ask the applicant if he or she will be able to perform the job, with or without accomodation. If the applicant discloses a disability, then the employer should ask if there is any way to accommodate the applicant's limitation. An applicant may also be told that the offer is contingent on passing a job-related medical exam, provided that all candidates for the same position must also pass the exam.

Applicants generally should not be asked questions regarding their height or weight. Height and weight requirements have been deemed unlawful where such standards disqualify physically disabled persons, women, and members of certain ethnic or national origin groups, and the employer could not establish that the requirements were directly related to job performance.

CONVICTION RECORD Although employers may ask applicants if they have ever been criminally convicted, this question should be followed by a statement that the existence of a criminal record will not automatically bar employment. Because in many geographic areas a disproportionate number of minorities are convicted of crimes, automatically excluding applicants with conviction records may have a disparate effect on minorities and therefore may be unlawful. Some state laws further restrict what an employer may ask concerning criminal convictions.

Consideration of a criminal record generally will be lawful only if the conviction relates to the requirements of the particular job. For example, an employer may be justified in rejecting an applicant convicted of theft for a hotel security position. When a job applicant has been convicted of a crime involving physical violence, the employer may be faced with a delicate problem. Some courts have held the employer liable where an employee with a record of violent behavior later assaulted another employee or a third party. Liability is based on the theory that the employer was negligent in its duties to protect the health and safety of the injured person by hiring such an employee. If the employer is operating in a jurisdiction that recognizes this negligent-hiring theory, a policy against hiring any person with a criminal conviction for a violent act is justified.

Although employers should exercise caution in asking about criminal convictions, there may be compelling reasons to ask about them nonetheless. Asking about convictions may have the benefit of providing a basis for defending claims of wrongful termination of employment if an employee fails to disclose the conviction when asked during the hiring process.

Employers generally should not ask applicants if they have ever been arrested. Some states, such as California, Washington and Illinois, prohibit or restrict employers from asking applicants about arrests or detentions that did not result in conviction.

EDUCATION AND EMPLOYMENT EXPERIENCE Employers may ask applicants questions regarding their education and work experience, but all requirements, such as possession of a high school diploma, must be job related. Inflated standards of academic achievement, language proficiency, or employment experience may be viewed as a pretext for unlawful discrimination or may have a disparate impact on individuals in certain protected classifications.

FROM THE TRENCHES

A husband and wife worked in support positions for a law firm that had asked them during the hiring process if they had been convicted of a felony. The husband and wife said they had not. The law firm did business with government agencies that required the firm to certify that it had no employees who had been convicted of felonies as a condition of contracting with the agency. The law firm so certified based on the false statements of the husband and wife. When their employment was terminated for performance reasons, the husband and wife sued for wrongful termination.

During the course of the litigation, the law firm discovered their felony convictions and their earlier false statements denying that they had been convicted. The court held that the husband's and wife's false statements denying that they had been convicted acted as a total bar to their claims. The court reasoned that their unclean hands prevented them from seeking relief in court regardless of whether their terminations were wrongful.

Source: Camp v. Jeffer, Mangels, Butler & Marmaro, 41 Cal. Rptr. 2d 329 (Cal. App. 1995).

CREDIT REFERENCES Rejection of an applicant because of a poor credit rating may be unlawful unless the employer can show that the decision not to hire the applicant was due to business necessity. Because the percentage of minority-group members with poor credit ratings generally is higher than that of nonminority-group members, rejection of applicants on this basis can have a disparate impact on minority groups. If a third-party investigator is retained to conduct a credit or background check, then consent from the job applicant may be required under federal or state fair credit laws.

EMPLOYEE PRIVACY, MONITORING OF EMPLOYEE E-MAIL, AND LIMITATIONS ON THE USE OF EMPLOYEE HEALTH INFORMATION

Employee privacy issues can arise in a variety of contexts, including employer monitoring of employee e-mail and computer use and employer access to confidential employee medical information.

E-Mail

Employers are increasingly concerned that employees are wasting company time by using the Internet for personal reasons during working hours. For example, people spend 70 percent more time visiting financial Web sites on the job than they do at home.[15] Employers also are rightfully concerned about their potential liability for unlawful, offensive, and defamatory statements sent via the corporate e-mail system. For example, the New Jersey Supreme Court ruled in 2000 that Continental Airlines could be liable for hostile environment and sexual harassment if senior management knew or should have known that offensive messages posted on the company e-mail system were part of a pattern of harassment taking place in the workplace and in settings related to the workplace.[16]

In response, more and more employers are checking employee e-mail. Most courts have upheld the right of private employers to monitor and regulate workplace e-mail and use of computers on the grounds that the employees could not prove that they had a reasonable expectation of privacy in workplace e-mails or computer use. To bolster their right to examine employee e-mail, employers should adopt explicit, written policies on the proper and improper use of e-mail and office computers, and they should conduct employee training on the subject. The electronic systems policy should make it clear that the company's computer and electronic systems are the company's property and that employees have no reasonable expectation of privacy in those systems. It should also reserve to the employer the right to access, review, monitor, disclose, and intercept communications sent or received on those systems.

Medical Information

On April 14, 2001, the U.S. Department of Health and Human Services finalized its regulations, under the Health Insurance Portability and Accountability Act, on maintaining the privacy of personal medical information.[17] Covered entities must comply by April 14, 2003, except for small health plans with annual receipts of $5 million or less, which must comply by April 14, 2004.

At first blush, the regulations apply only to health-care providers (such as doctors, hospitals, and nurses), group health plans (such as health maintenance organizations and self-insured plans that have fifty or more participants or are administered by an entity other than the employer that established and maintained the plan), and health-care clearinghouses that process claims. Yet, upon a closer reading, it becomes clear that, in fact, almost all employers that provide health-care coverage to their employees will be affected by the privacy regulations and required to develop privacy policies and procedures to safeguard protected health information.[18] *Protected health information* includes any information relating to a person's health that (1) was created by a health-care provider, health plan, employer, or health-care clearinghouse and (2) identifies the person to whom the health information relates. For example, if, as is usually the case, the employer acts as the plan sponsor, then the employer must establish "fire walls" to ensure that private health information is used only for purposes of plan administration and not for any other employment-related decisions, such as termination of employment.

Employment At-Will and Wrongful Discharge

Employers are generally advised to hire employees on an at-will basis. *At-will* means that an employee is not guaranteed employment for a fixed period of time. Rather, both the employee and the employer remain free to terminate the employment relationship at any time for any reason, with or without cause or advance notice. In most of the United States, workers are deemed to be employed at-will unless (1) there is an employment agreement setting a specific term of employment, (2) they are covered by a collective-bargaining agreement, or (3) they are public employees subject to a civil service system.

Wrongful Discharge

Significant inroads on the traditional doctrine of employment at-will have been made as a result of judicial decisions as well as legislation. Employers are usually well advised to consider whether the reasons for any termination will pass muster as good cause.

THE PUBLIC-POLICY EXCEPTION Even if an individual is employed on an at-will basis, in most states the person cannot be discharged for a reason that violates public policy. In other words, an at-will employee can be discharged for *no* reason but not for a *bad* reason. For example, an employee cannot be lawfully discharged for (1) refusing to commit an unlawful act, such as perjury or price-fixing, at the employer's request; (2) alleging that the company has violated a law; (3) taking time from work to serve on a jury or for military leave; (4) filing a workers' compensation claim; or (5) joining a union. An employee terminated in violation of public policy may be able to recover both contract and tort damages, including damages for pain and suffering and, in egregious cases, punitive damages. For example, in Michigan, an employee discharged for refusing to manipulate the sampling results for state pollution reports was entitled to damages because the dismissal violated public policy.[19]

Although most states recognize a public-policy exception to at-will employment, several states (including New York, Alabama, Mississippi, and Florida) do not. For example, the Georgia Supreme Court ruled that an at-will employee could not sue in tort for wrongful discharge based on age discrimination because the Georgia age discrimination law provided no civil remedy for violations.[20]

Even in states recognizing a public-policy exception, the courts have shown restraint in defining what constitutes a public policy. For example, the California Supreme Court ruled that an employee could be fired for reporting to his superiors that his incoming supervisor was under investigation by the FBI for embezzlement from a former employer because no fundamental public policy was involved.[21] Courts in California,[22] Michigan,[23] and Pennsylvania[24] have limited the sources of public policy to statutory or constitutional provisions designed to protect society at large. In contrast, the Supreme Court of Colorado held that the rules of professional conduct for accountants could be the source of a public-policy wrongful-termination claim by an in-house accountant who was fired.[25]

The judicially created cause of action for discharges in violation of public policy exists alongside a number of specific statutory provisions that prohibit retaliatory discharge. For example, the Fair Labor Standards Act prohibits discharge for exercising rights guaranteed by its minimum-wage and overtime provisions. The Occupational Safety and Health Act prohibits discharge of employees in retaliation for exercising rights under the Act, such as complaining about work procedures or health and safety violations in the workplace. Many state acts contain similar provisions. Also, many states (including New York) have adopted whistle-blower protection statutes, which prohibit an employer from discharging or retaliating against an employee who has exercised the right to complain to a government agency about the employer's violation of law.

IMPLIED CONTRACTS The second judicial exception to the at-will rule arises from the willingness of courts to interpret the parties' conduct as implying a contract limiting the employer's right to discharge without good cause, even though no written contract exists. Such a contract is known as an *implied contract.* Some of the factors that can give rise to an implied obligation to discharge the employee only for good cause are that (1) he or she had been a long-term employee; (2) the employee had received raises, bonuses, and promotions throughout his or her career; (3) the employee was assured that employment would continue if he or she did a good job; (4) the employee had been assured before by the company's management that he or she was doing a good job; (5) the company had stated that it did not terminate employees at his or her level except for good cause; and (6) the employee had never been formally criticized or warned about his or her conduct. A personnel manual, together with oral assurances, may give rise to a reasonable expectation that an employee will not be terminated except for good cause.

IMPLIED COVENANT OF GOOD FAITH AND FAIR DEALING The third prong in the developing law of wrongful discharge is the recognition of an implied covenant of good faith and fair dealing in the employment relationship. In one case, the court found that termination of a twenty-five-year employee without good cause in order to deprive him of $46,000 in commissions was not in good faith and was a breach of contract.[26] A start-up that fired an employee on the eve of the date his or her stock was due to vest might be found to have violated the implied covenant of good faith and fair dealing. This is one reason why many companies vest stock monthly after some initial period (usually six months to one year).

The Employment Agreement

Employers should memorialize the terms of the employment relationship in a written document—either an offer letter or a formal employment agreement. (For ease of discussion, both the offer letter and the employment agreement will be referred to as the *employment document.*) The employment document will clarify the terms and conditions of the employment relationship and will serve as an indispensable tool if a dispute later arises concerning the employment or its termination. Although there are numerous terms that an employer may wish to include, the following terms are essential.

Duties

The employment document should briefly describe the employee's duties. The description should be general enough that the company retains the flexibility to expand or modify the employee's duties and responsibilities as necessary. If the employee works on an hourly basis (and is therefore eligible for overtime under the wage and hour laws), the regular work schedule should be described. If the employee is salaried and exempt from overtime laws, that fact should be stated in the agreement.

Compensation and Benefits

The employee's base salary should be stated in the employment document. If the employee is eligible for a bonus, the employment document should clarify whether the granting of a bonus is at the employer's discretion or is pegged to a specific formula or performance milestone. If possible, milestones should be described in objectively measurable terms to limit future misunderstandings or disputes.

The employment document should also briefly describe the benefits an employee may be entitled to receive, such as health, dental, and life insurance; retirement benefits; vacation; sick leave; stock options; and an automobile allowance. It need not provide too much detail, however, as the terms and conditions of coverage should be delineated in separate, formal benefit plan documents. To avoid future confusion and litigation, the employment document should expressly state that the benefits are subject to the applicable plan documents, which are controlling.

The employment document should also state that the company reserves the right to modify compensation and benefits from time to time as it deems necessary or appropriate. This provision helps prevent the company from being locked into certain compensation and benefit levels if circumstances change.

Stock Options and Stock Grants

It is important that the employment document specifically state that the terms of any stock option grants are subject to the company's stock option plans and a separate stock option agreement and that the stock options are subject to a vesting schedule. This provision helps prevent litigation over whether an outright grant of unrestricted stock was intended, as opposed to a stock option, which is usually subject to forfeiture if the employee leaves before the end of the vesting period. Companies should also consider including clauses in their stock option documents stating that nothing in these documents shall be construed to alter the terms of employment set forth in each employee's employment agreement or in any employment handbook or personnel manual.

FROM THE TRENCHES

An employee of a software company sued the company for more than $1 million upon termination of his employment. He alleged that the stock he had been granted was not subject to a vesting schedule, but rather that the company had issued him an outright grant of stock. The company had neither an employment agreement nor an option agreement stating that the stock he was receiving was subject to a vesting schedule. The company could have avoided hundreds of thousands of dollars in both legal fees and settlement costs had it used a written employment agreement that expressly referred to the company stock option plan and the terms (including the vesting schedule) on which the stock was granted.

Duration and Termination of Employment

Employment should be guaranteed for a specified period of time only in extenuating circumstances and only after consultation with legal counsel. If an employer desires to obtain the services of an employee for a specified period of time, the employer should state both the anticipated term of employment and the circumstances under which the employer may terminate the employment relationship prior to the end of the contemplated term. The employer may elect to provide the employee with a severance benefit if it terminates the employment relationship without cause (as defined in the employment document) prior to the end of the contemplated term. An employer cannot force an employee to work (the Thirteenth Amendment to the U.S. Constitution abolished involuntary servitude), but the employer may be able to prohibit an employee subject to a valid employment agreement from working for someone else before the term of the agreement expires.

Right to Work in the United States

As required by federal immigration laws, the employment document should require the employee to verify that he or she has the right to work in the United States by virtue of citizenship, permanent residency, or a work visa.

Proprietary Information and Inventions Agreements

All employees, at all levels of the company, should be required to sign detailed, proprietary information and inventions agreements, sometimes called nondisclosure and invention assignment agreements. Such agreements provide broad protection for the company's proprietary information by prohibiting employees from the unauthorized use or disclosure of any proprietary information and by requiring them to assign to the company all rights and title that they might have to works and inventions created during the period of employment. Accordingly, the employment document should state that the employee is required to sign the employer's standard proprietary information and inventions agreement as a condition of employment. Chapter 14 describes the provisions usually contained in such agreements, as well as the other steps employers should take to protect their intellectual property and ensure that they own their employees' inventions, writings, and other work product. Under the doctrine of work made for hire, under certain circumstances an employer will be treated as the author of a copyrightable work created by an employee, and thus the owner of the copyright, even in the absence of an express copyright assignment by the employee. Chapter 14 explains these circumstances and also discusses the employer's right to own and patent inventions created by employees expressly hired to invent.

Noncompetition Clauses and Nonsolicitation Agreements

Employers often desire to include noncompetition clauses in employment documents to prohibit an employee from competing with the company both during and for some period of time after the termination of employment. As explained in Chapter 2, although noncompetition covenants are enforceable during the term of employment, the enforceability of postemployment noncompetition covenants varies from state to state. It is, therefore, advisable to consult legal counsel prior to attempting to preclude a prospective or current employee from engaging in postemployment competitive activities.

Nonsolicitation provisions—under which a former employee agrees not to solicit his or her former employer's employees or customers—are narrower than noncompetition agreements, but they serve a similar purpose of protecting the former employer's business from unfair competition. Because nonsolicitation agreements place fewer restrictions on a former employee's ability to earn a living, such agreements tend to be enforced more frequently than noncompetition agreements. The enforceability of nonsolicitation agreements varies from state to state, however, so again consultation with local legal counsel is essential.

Entire Agreement

The employment document should contain an integration clause stating that the document (and any exhibits attached to the document) constitute the entire agreement with regard to the employment relationship and that the employee is not relying on any prior or contemporaneous oral or written promises that are not delineated in the document. This provision will help a company defeat a later claim that certain promises or commitments were made regarding terms and conditions of employment. Without such a provision, the employee may later claim that the company orally promised a promotion after six months or guaranteed a year-end bonus.

Mandatory Arbitration of Employment Disputes

Increasingly, employers are requiring employees to sign a document in which they agree that they will not sue the company but rather will submit all work-related disputes to binding arbitration or nonbinding mediation. Mandatory arbitration protects the employer from the often unpredictable results of a jury trial, and it may provide a faster and less costly way to resolve disputes. Although mandatory arbitration deprives employees of their day in court before a jury of their peers, the U.S. Supreme Court has upheld the mandatory arbitration of employment claims, even those based on federal statutes (such as Title VII).[27]

Absent a clear agreement to arbitrate, employees generally cannot be forced to forgo their right to go to court.[28] If execution of an agreement requiring arbitration is required as a condition of employment, then the employer's agreement to hire the employee will be adequate consideration for a binding contract. If, however, an existing employee is requested to sign an arbitration agreement, then it is important for the employer to provide some new value, such as a one-time cash bonus, as consideration for the employee's agreement to arbitrate.

Under some state laws, arbitration agreements between employers and employees are not enforceable unless they contain certain safeguards designed to protect the rights of employees, such as a requirement that there be a neutral arbitrator. For example, the California Supreme Court declared unconscionable, and therefore invalid, an arbitration agreement that required arbitration of employee (but not employer) claims and limited the employee's damages to less than what would be available in court.[29]

Employers should consider whether to require arbitrations to be conducted confidentially. Unless agreed to by the parties, there is no reason why an employee might not attempt to publicize the fact that an arbitration is pending or the result of an arbitration.

Foreign Employees

Foreign Nationals and U.S. Citizens Working Abroad

Companies hiring foreign nationals or U.S. citizens to work outside the United States should arrange for the employee to sign a detailed employment agreement. Employment laws in countries vary widely, and employment relationships are often heavily regulated by statute. For example, the U.S. antidiscrimination laws (such as Title VII) apply to all persons working in the United States (regardless of their nationality) and to all U.S. citizens working outside the United States if the employer is either based in the United States or is controlled by a U.S. employer. A company cannot rely on a standard American employment document or standard American employment practices to provide sufficient protection or to ensure that it is in compliance with foreign law. It is advisable to engage foreign legal counsel prior to entering into relationships that involve employees residing in foreign countries.

Similarly, it is crucial to have the company's nondisclosure and invention assignment agreements reviewed by foreign counsel to ensure that the employee is both contractually and legally obligated to assign his or

FROM THE TRENCHES

A Texas company was opening sales offices in several European and Asian countries and planned to hire foreign nationals to help staff the offices. The company wanted to use its standard employment agreements. After quickly researching the employment law of these countries, however, the company learned that provisions in its standard employment agreements relating to the amount of notice to be given prior to terminating an employee's employment and the obligation to make severance payments would violate the statutes of two of the countries. Had the company used its standard employment agreements, it would have been in violation of the statutes and might have been subject to government fines and penalties.

her rights to company inventions and to refrain from making unauthorized use or disclosure of the company's proprietary information.

Foreign Nationals Working in the United States

Employers wishing to hire foreign nationals to work in the United States must comply not only with the U.S. antidiscrimination laws but also with U.S. immigration laws and procedures prior to hire. In most situations, the employer must file a visa petition with the Immigration and Naturalization Service and obtain approval on behalf of the foreign national desiring employment in the United States. These employment-based visas range from temporary nonimmigrant visas to immigrant visas. Immigration laws are very specific, and at times complex, and they require the expertise of an immigration specialist. Thus, employers are well advised to consult with an immigration attorney prior to promising employment to foreign nationals.

EQUITY COMPENSATION

Compensating employees in a start-up company has special challenges and opportunities. Cash is a precious commodity in a start-up company and is typically best used in product research and development efforts. Therefore, base salaries are usually significantly lower than those talented individuals could earn doing comparable work for a mature business. Benefits, such as health insurance or a retirement package, are not used to attract and retain employees because, for the most part, purchasing these benefits would require the company to use its cash.

At the same time, many individuals join an entrepreneurial company because of the opportunity to receive equity incentives, such as stock options. As a result, to attract good employees, companies must use their own stock as compensation. There are a number of advantages to using company stock as an integral part of the business's total compensation strategy. First, using stock rather than cash helps conserve cash for research and development. Second, compensating with stock aligns the interests of employees with those of investors in a collaborative effort to produce value for everyone's stock holdings.

Third, use of stock compensation is a signaling device that helps attract individuals who are willing to make shorter-term financial sacrifices in exchange for the opportunity to succeed financially along with the business—the very type of individuals a start-up business needs. As a result, the significant use of stock helps to reinforce the typical start-up company's strategic business objectives of rapid product development for commercial success.

Equity compensation can take a bewildering variety of forms, but, as explained in Chapter 5, for most employees in entrepreneurial companies, the opportunity to acquire a stake in the business will usually come in the form of a stock option. The most important terms of an option are (1) the number of shares that may be purchased, (2) whether the option will be a tax-advantaged incentive stock option or not, (3) the exercise price, (4) the maximum duration of the option, (5) the permissible form or forms of payment, and (6) any contractual restrictions on the purchase or transfer of stock.

Number of Shares in Option Pool

Typically, a start-up business will establish a collective pool of shares under a formal stock option plan that has been approved by the shareholders; options to purchase the stock may then be granted from this pool. For an individual award, the only formal limit is the number of uncommitted shares left in this pool. As a practical matter, however, a business will need to manage its share reserve pool carefully to ensure adequate grants for all employees and other personal service providers (such as nonemployee directors, consultants, and advisers). A reasonable rule of thumb is to earmark about 20 percent of a business's shares for issuance to employees and other service providers. In making this calculation, the number of shares in the option pool is included in the total number of shares; any convertible securities (such as preferred stock that is convertible into common) are treated as if they had been converted; any other outstanding options or warrants are treated as if they had been exercised; and stock issued to the founders upon the formation of the business is generally excluded.

Types of Stock Options

Two types of options may be granted to eligible individuals: *incentive stock options* and *nonqualified stock options*. Although a stock option plan may be designed to grant one type of options, most will provide for the grant of both types of options. As explained in Chapter 5, the difference between these two types of options relates to their income tax attributes.

Exercise Price

Most options in a start-up business are generally granted at an exercise price equal to 100 percent of the fair market value of the stock that may be acquired, valued as of the date of the option's grant. A plan may be designed to allow the grant of options with a lower exercise price (a so-called *discounted stock option*). However, the use of discounted stock options is limited to selective situations because of adverse tax implications for employees, accounting charges for the employer, and securities law restrictions.

Maximum Duration

Incentive stock options may not be granted with a term longer than ten years. Optionees owning more than 10 percent of the corporation are covered by a special rule that reduces the maximum term for incentive stock options to five years. Most plans provide for options with a maximum term of ten years. Many companies have found through bitter experience that five years can be too short a period of time if the business does not develop as rapidly as originally projected. Extending the term of an option due to expire may incur accounting charges for the company and cause the loss of incentive stock option treatment for outstanding options.

A related issue is under what circumstances an option will terminate prior to the expiration of its term. Most plans provide for expiration of an option only upon the termination of an individual's service with the company. Typically, individuals have one to three months after termination of service within which to exercise their options. This period is typically extended to six to twelve months if the termination of service is attributable to disability and to twelve to eighteen months if it is attributable to death.

Permissible Forms of Payment

Stock option plans allow optionees to use four basic forms of payment to purchase stock when exercising their options: (1) cash or cash equivalents, such as checks; (2) shares of the company's stock already owned by the optionee; (3) proceeds from the immediate sale of stock upon the exercise of an option (which, as a practical matter, is available only to companies with publicly traded stock); and (4) a promissory note. Most plans permit the use of all four forms of payment, or a combination of those forms, but the standard agreement by which the option is actually granted will typically limit the permissible forms of payment to either cash and cash equivalents or previously owned shares of the company's stock.

Vesting and Contractual Restrictions on the Purchase or Transfer of Stock

Most option plans provide that an optionee must continuously perform services for a period of time in order to acquire a contractually unrestricted right to purchase stock upon the exercise of an option. Shares that are not subject to contractual restrictions in favor of the company are called *vested shares*. Although the exact features of vesting schedules differ among plans, a typical vesting period is four years, with no vesting for the first twelve months (called *cliff vesting*) and vesting in equal monthly increments thereafter over the remainder of the vesting period.

Some companies tie vesting to the achievement of performance goals. The use of performance vesting is limited, however, because it has the potential for adverse financial accounting consequences. Under current accounting rules, if the vesting restrictions imposed on a stock option disappear with the passage of time and continued service, and if the option is granted with an exercise price of at least 100 percent of the fair market value of the company's stock on the date of grant, then accountants routinely will not calculate any charge to earnings for financial accounting purposes. If the vesting restrictions on an option are performance based, however, then the accountants will wait to calculate any possible charge to earnings for financial accounting purposes until the time that the performance objective has been satisfied, if at all. As a result, a company will have difficulty managing these charges to its earnings for financial accounting purposes because it cannot determine in advance the fair market value of its stock at the time a performance objective is achieved.

A stock option plan may be designed to permit an individual to exercise an option immediately, even if the optionee would acquire only unvested shares. Alternatively, an option plan may permit optionees to acquire only vested shares. It is administratively simpler to restrict the exercise of options to vested shares, and most stock option plans sponsored by private companies do exactly that.

For certain optionees, however, the ability to exercise options on unvested shares may produce some tax advantages. For example, the spread on the exercise of an incentive stock option is included for purposes of calculating an individual's alternative minimum tax; an early exercise typically results in a smaller spread that is potentially subject to this tax. More significantly, optionees acquiring *qualified small business stock* within the meaning of Section 1202 of the Internal Revenue Code can generally exclude 50 percent of any capital gains recognized upon sale if they have held the stock for at least five years. An option providing for early exercise permits the optionee to initiate that five-year holding period sooner. In addition, if a company's stock becomes publicly traded, immediately exercisable options may provide officers and directors of the company, who are subject to various securities law restrictions, greater flexibility in acquiring and disposing of the stock.

A company designing a stock option plan needs to decide whether it will give itself the right to reacquire even fully vested shares owned by an optionee that the optionee wishes to transfer at a time when the company's stock is not publicly traded. As discussed in Chapter 5, most companies do provide for a right of first refusal in favor of the company. Often this right is extended to the other shareholders if the company itself does not exercise the right in full.

A company that wishes to maintain tight control over the ownership of its shares while the stock is not publicly traded may retain the right to reacquire even vested shares upon an individual's termination of service. A repurchase right enables a company to restrict ownership of shares acquired through its stock option plan to current service providers, but such a repurchase provision can also entail disadvantages. To repurchase vested shares, the company generally pays the greater of the individual's purchase price or the stock's fair market value on the date of termination. Problems can arise because making a determination of the stock's fair market value for such a repurchase may set a benchmark as to the stock's fair market value for other purposes (e.g., for awarding future stock options). In addition, a repurchase provision for vested shares produces an economic disincentive for the optionee.

Other Employee Benefits

Although for most start-up businesses most of an employee's total compensation will be provided in the form of base salary and performance incentives (usually through stock options), broad-based employee benefits are a necessary part of a well-designed, competitive total compensation strategy.

Health Coverage

The broad-based employee benefit that is most important to employees is adequate health insurance. Small businesses generally should not self-insure, so they will typically buy health coverage from an insurance company or health maintenance organization through an insurance broker or consultant. The health-care services industry has gone through some wrenching changes, so it is important that the business owner spend some time identifying a knowledgeable and responsive broker to help the company select appropriate health coverage. As discussed earlier, any employer that provides health care to its employees and/or their dependents (whether through insurance or a self-insured arrangement) must comply with the health information privacy regulations promulgated by the Department of Health and Human Services unless the health benefit consists solely of a group health plan with fewer than fifty participants that is self-administered by the employer that established it.

Tax law also creates an incentive for businesses to deliver health-care coverage to their employees because the receipt of these benefits does not create taxable income for the employees (except for partners in a partnership, members of a limited liability company, or greater than 2 percent shareholders in a Subchapter S corporation). In addition, the cost of employee health coverage is tax deductible by the company as a business expense.

Even with these tax advantages, given the stubborn persistence of health-care inflation, businesses continue to look for ways to control their health-care costs. As a result, most businesses share the cost of health-care coverage with their employees, particularly the cost of covering an employee's family. A popular way of reducing the after-tax cost of the employee's share of the cost of health-care coverage is for the business to adopt a pre-tax premium plan. Such a plan allows employees to pay their share of health-care costs with before-tax, rather than after-tax, dollars. Having these costs paid through a pre-tax premium plan can produce income and employment tax savings of up to about 50 percent of the employee's before-tax cost. The business can reap tax savings as well, as these payments generally are not subject to payroll taxes such as Social Security taxes.

Retirement Benefits

How young businesses provide retirement benefits to their employees is perhaps the best illustration of the overall strategy that many businesses with limited cash employ in offering employee benefits in general. Start-ups cannot afford expensive employer-funded benefits, so instead they offer flexible tax-advantaged plans that permit employees to decide how to split their pay between taxable cash compensation and tax-deferred or tax-exempt employee benefits.

In the area of retirement benefits, the primary type of plan that offers this flexibility coupled with tax advantages is the *Section 401(k) plan.* Such a plan allows employees to authorize nontaxable contributions to a special tax-exempt trust account through payroll withholding. The contributions are invested in the trust account without tax liability to permit a more rapid accumulation of retirement assets. The employee may withdraw those accumulated assets at a later time (typically upon retirement) and will not incur a tax liability until the time of distribution. Meanwhile, the business is entitled to take an immediate tax deduction at the time the employee authorizes contributions to the trust account. Although the tax treatment is basically the same as for other types of tax-qualified retirement plans, Section 401(k) plans offer employees a high degree of flexibility in determining the level of their contributions subject to an annual maximum (generally $11,000 for calendar year 2002, with an additional $1,000 permitted for employees attaining age fifty in that year) and certain other legal limitations. (For companies with twenty-five or fewer employees, an even simpler and less expensive 401(k) plan look-alike, known as a *salary reduction SEP,* is available.)

In the simplest form, a business makes no contributions to the Section 401(k) plan, so its only costs are for establishing and administering the plan. Employees make all contributions through authorized payroll withholding. However, companies may find that plans funded solely through payroll withholding may not pass relevant nondiscrimination tests imposed by federal tax law. In particular, one test limits the permissible contributions for the benefit of highly compensated employees in relation to those made for the benefit of all other employees. To safeguard the tax-qualified status of the plan in this situation, companies commonly introduce a matching contribution designed to encourage enough lower-paid employees to authorize sufficient contributions through payroll withholding to enable the plan to pass the nondiscrimination test. Recent surveys indicate that a typical matching contribution is $0.50 for each $1.00 contribution, up to a maximum matching contribution of 2 to 4 percent of a participant's base pay. The proper matching contribution formula for a particular company's Section 401(k) plan is likely to differ from this typical formula, as the appropriate formula is affected by workforce demographics, actual contribution rates, and other variables.

At a later stage in development, some companies also consider making performance-oriented profit-sharing contributions to their tax-qualified retirement plans. Frequently, these contributions take the form of contributing a portion of the company's annual incentive bonus to the plan for the benefit of employees, rather than paying it to them directly in cash. The contribution may also be made in shares of company stock. In deciding whether to divert some of its bonus payout to the plan, however, the company must consider various tax law requirements on important issues, such as which employees must be eligible to share in these contributions and how the contributions must be allocated (requirements that cash bonuses paid directly to employees need not satisfy). Many companies with broad-based profit-sharing plans with contributions based on a formula find that they can make contributions to their retirement plan while preserving the basic integrity of the incentives built into their annual cash-incentive bonus plan. Furthermore, many employees, particularly more highly compensated employees concerned about generating an adequate retirement income, appreciate having a portion of their bonus contributed to the plan instead of being paid to them directly in cash. To encourage employees to stay with the company, these company contributions may be conditioned on satisfying vesting requirements similar to those imposed on stock options.

Other Benefits

Even if a young company offers basic health and retirement benefits, it typically will refrain from introducing significant additional benefits so that it can save its cash for more important purposes. Of course, some vacation and holiday time off is usually provided from the outset, as well as some basic level of group-term life insurance (at least to take advantage of the tax law that allows businesses to provide their employees with up to $50,000 of life insurance coverage without creating any taxable income for the employees). The next benefit introduced that has a significant cost is disability insurance. Companies may either pay for this benefit themselves or arrange for employees to pay for some or all of the cost through a pre-tax premium plan; in that case, any disability benefits are taxable income when received. Alternatively, if employees pay for these benefits with after-tax dollars, any disability benefits ultimately received are not taxed at all. The use of a pre-tax premium plan in this fashion gives employees a measure of flexibility in determining the tax treatment of their disability premiums and benefits, at least within the confines of some rather broad nondiscrimination tax requirements governing these types of plans.

Eligibility

As explained earlier, the misclassification of employees as independent contractors can result in the employer being held liable retroactively for the employee benefits previously denied to such workers. To avoid such unexpected retroactive liability, a company should make sure that its benefit plans (e.g., 401(k), health, disability, and life insurance) specifically exclude workers classified as independent contractors, even if a government agency or court subsequently reclassifies such workers as employees.

Employer Liability for Employees' Acts

An employer is liable for his or her own negligence in supervising or hiring an employee. As explained in Chapter 11, the employer may also be vicariously liable for the employee's wrongful acts, even if the employer had no knowledge of them and in no way directed them, if the acts (1) were committed while the employee was acting within the course and scope of his or her employment or (2) the employee was aided in the agency relation. For example, an employer will be liable for an auto accident caused by an employee driving on a work-related errand and for the creation of a hostile environment by a supervisor who takes adverse employment action against a subordinate.

As explained in Chapter 8, an employer is bound by a contract entered into by an employee with authority to enter into it. Authority can be actual or apparent. An employee has *actual authority* when the employer expressly or implicitly authorizes the employee to enter into the agreement. Even if an employee does not have actual authority, he or she can still bind the employer if the employer engages in conduct (e.g., leaving the employee alone or giving the employee the title "manager" in a store) that would reasonably lead a third party to believe that the employee has authority. This is known as *apparent authority.* Thus, it is extremely important to delineate to employees and to third parties the acts that an employee or an independent contractor may undertake so that misunderstandings regarding the scope of a worker's authority are kept to a minimum.

Reducing Litigation Risk

An employer can minimize misunderstandings, decrease the likelihood of work-related disputes or union-organizing efforts, and increase the chances of winning a wrongful discharge or discrimination lawsuit by taking certain simple steps. Such steps may also increase productivity and decrease turnover.

Select Employees Carefully

Every employer should exercise care in selecting employees. Companies in a growth mode sometimes fall victim to the tendency to hire individuals quickly to satisfy a compelling need, rather than hiring individuals thoughtfully and deliberately regardless of how long the process may take. Many employment lawsuits stem from a lack of care in hiring. To the extent possible, companies should know whom they are hiring, based on thorough screening, interviewing, and reference checks.

Companies may wish to retain an outside service to conduct comprehensive background checks on candidates for employment. Background checks, while potentially informative, are governed by an array of federal and state laws, including the federal Fair Credit Reporting Act. A company should retain a reputable consumer reporting agency if it wishes to have background checks conducted, and it should consult employment law counsel to make sure that all applicable legal requirements are met. Offers of employment should be made contingent on the satisfactory results of any such background check.

Document the Relationship

Once the employer decides whether a worker is an employee or an independent contractor, the employer should formalize the working relationship in a written document signed by both the contractor/employee and the employer. As discussed earlier, the writing should delineate most, if not all, of the working conditions and benefits. For an employee, this includes job title, duties, and hours; term of employment or at-will language; compensation, benefits, and stock options; and the company's right to modify job duties and compensation. For an independent contractor, the document should include the project description and milestones, fees, a recitation of the independent contractor relationship, assignment of inventions and protection of proprietary information, indemnification, and language regarding the contractor's right to control the manner and means of performing the work. An employment or independent contractor agreement should also contain an integration clause that provides that the agreement is the sole and exclusive statement of the parties' understanding, and supersedes all prior discussions, agreements, or understandings. It is also advisable to state that the agreement can be modified only by a written agreement signed by both parties.

FROM THE TRENCHES

A consumer-products company terminated one of its executives in 1995. The company and the executive signed a letter of agreement that was intended to cover outstanding issues, such as severance pay and vesting of stock options. Due to a number of technical glitches, however, the agreement had to be reworked several times. Once the former executive got wind of the company's plans to do an initial public offering (IPO), progress on ironing out the details of the settlement became slower and slower—and eventually stopped altogether. It became apparent to the company that the former executive had decided to stall the settlement in the hope that the company's reluctance to disclose the dispute in its prospectus would drive up the value of his claim. Litigation ensued.

Comment: Unfortunately, this situation is typical. Claims against companies often materialize "out of the woodwork" as the filing date for an IPO nears. Companies are well advised to recognize and resolve potential claims as early as possible to avoid the actual or perceived leverage that comes with an imminent public filing.

Implement Good Policies and Practices

Employers should implement good employment policies and practices. Although a lengthy employee handbook is not legally required or even always advisable, every employer should have a few essential written policies, including an at-will employment policy; a policy prohibiting unlawful harassment, discrimination, and retaliation that creates an effective mechanism for employees to report and seek redress for any such conduct; an electronic systems policy to protect the employer's computer and electronic systems against improper or illegal use; a proprietary information and inventions policy; policies governing eligibility for and use of leaves of absence; an insider trading policy (if applicable); and a policy reserving the company's unilateral right to revise its policies and benefits as it deems appropriate. Employees should also be required to sign an acknowledgment form confirming that they have read and will abide by such company policies. Once the company adopts such policies, they should be adhered to and applied consistently.

Employers should also implement practices that ensure that employees are treated in a fair and nondiscriminatory manner at every stage of the employment relationship. The employer should ensure that all of its recruiting materials accurately describe job requirements and omit non-job-related criteria. The company must then hire or promote the candidate who best fits the criteria for the job, without respect to age, race, or any other protected classification. When evaluating an employee's perfor-mance, the supervisor must be timely, honest, specific, and tactful. Evaluation criteria must be objective and job related. A copy of all performance appraisals should be signed by the employee and kept in his or her personnel file. Performance problems should be documented and communicated to the employee as they arise.

If an employee complains about a failure to promote or about harassment or discrimination of any kind, the employer must promptly and thoroughly investigate the circumstances surrounding the claim. The company should choose an appropriate investigator—preferably one whom the employee trusts. A supervisor should document the results of the investigation and report the results to the employee. If harassment or discrimination has occurred, immediate and effective action must be taken to remedy the situation and to prevent it from occurring again.

Terminate with Care

If a company has to fire an employee, it should do so with care. The employee should be paid his or her final pay within the time required by state law, which in some states is on the last day of work. The employment agreement should be reviewed to make sure that all amounts due to the employee are paid on the termination date. The employee should be reminded of the obligation to keep the employer's proprietary information and trade secrets confidential and should be required to return all company property and information before leaving. An exit interview may be useful to air the departing employee's grievances, collect all company property, and explain exit compensation and benefits issues.

When a high-level or complaining employee is terminated, it is often desirable to enter into a written separation agreement. Generally, severance should not be paid to the employee without obtaining a signed release of all claims as part of the agreement.

PUTTING IT INTO PRACTICE.

When Kendra hired workers to create the beta-test version of the Saturn Data Booster (SDB), she had to decide whether to hire them as independent contractors or employees. From an economic perspective, she preferred to engage contractors, rather than hire employees, because the contractor, not the employer, is liable for taxes. Classifying workers as independent contractors would also allow DataAccelleation to escape paying for unemployment insurance, workers' compensation insurance, and other employee-related expenditures. However, Kendra knew that the government favors classifying workers as employees, not independent contractors, and that substantial fines and penalties might be assessed against DataAccelleation for misclassifying workers.

After reviewing the relevant criteria for classifying workers with Sanjay Datar, Kendra decided to hire them as employees. Although several workers would be using their own computers and working at home, the programming was central to DataAccelleation's business and was subject to coordination and supervision by Kendra, Philip, and Kristine. Also, the programmers would be working exclusively for DataAccelleation for a substantial period of time.

Kendra worked with Sanjay to prepare a standard at-will employment agreement, which each of the workers signed. The agreement provided for a salary but no extra pay for overtime. Because she fully expected the programmers to work more than forty hours per week, Kendra had checked with Sanjay to confirm that the programmers were exempt employees under the federal and California Fair Labor Standards Acts. They concluded that the programmers' status as well-paid professionals doing largely unsupervised tasks over which they had substantial decision-making authority caused them to be exempt from the hourly wage and overtime requirements applicable to nonexempt employees.

Kendra was then faced with two more problems. The first involved Gracie Lu, a forty-one-year-old Chinese-American employee who had been laid off due to her inability to write efficient code. Although Gracie's code worked, it required too much computer memory and ran too slowly because it was poorly written. Gracie had been warned of the need for improvement, but despite extensive tutoring by fellow employees, her code was still not acceptable. Finally, she was dismissed for poor job performance.

continued...

continued...

About three months later, Kendra was served with papers from Gracie's lawyer alleging employment discrimination. The lawsuit claimed that Gracie was fired in violation of Title VII because of her race, national origin, and gender and in violation of the ADEA because of her age.

Kendra immediately called Michael Cruz, who initiated a conference call with Jill Calderon, a senior employment litigator in his firm. Jill explained that Gracie could establish a prima facie case by proving that she was a member of a protected group (by means of her race, national origin, gender, and age) and had been fired from a job for which she was arguably qualified. The burden would then shift to DataAccelleation to present evidence that it had legitimate, nondiscriminatory grounds for its decision.

Fortunately, Gracie's poor code writing was well documented. Kendra had given her timely and honest feedback based on objective and job-related criteria. Copies of all performance appraisals were signed by Gracie and kept in her personnel file. Nevertheless, Jill warned that there was a subjective element to the determination that Gracie failed to write elegant code. Gracie might argue that this was a pretext for firing her and try to prove that the real reason she was fired was because she was a forty-one-year-old Asian woman.

Because there was no evidence that Gracie had in fact been discriminated against (no one had complained of her Chinese accent, for example), Jill believed that DataAccelleation would ultimately prevail if the case went to trial. However, it would be expensive and time-consuming to litigate her claims. Jill explained that this was a typical strike suit and that it was likely that Gracie would settle for a small but significant amount of money. Kendra and Jill agreed that Jill would contact Gracie's attorney to try to negotiate a settlement.

A week later, Jill called Kendra to report that Gracie's attorney had offered to settle all claims for $10,000. Jill recommended that Kendra accept the offer because the legal fees to fight the suit would be a multiple of that amount, and even more if the case went to trial. Although Kendra hated to settle because she knew she was in the right, she could not afford the distraction a lawsuit would cause. So she decided to simply chalk the settlement up to the cost of doing business.

continued...

continued...

The second problem was potential sexual harassment by a female supervisor named Brooke Barnes of an employee named Alan Raskovich. Brooke, who had just moved from Atlanta, frequently called Alan "babe" and made comments about his physique. One day Brooke grabbed Alan's arm, squeezed his biceps, and cooed, "I like my men with muscles." After this last incident, Alan came to Kendra to complain.

Alan said that Brooke's ongoing behavior embarrassed him and made him feel uncomfortable. He was afraid his coworkers might get the wrong idea. He was also concerned that Brooke was becoming more aggressive and felt that it was just a matter of time before she propositioned him. Kendra asked Alan if he would like to have a different supervisor, and he said that he would.

Kendra thanked Alan for coming to her and assured him that she would take care of the problem. Kendra next spoke with several of Alan's coworkers, who confirmed the incident. Kendra then called Brooke into her office to discuss Alan's complaints. Brooke's face became flushed, and she said that she had not meant anything by her comments, noting that everyone in her former firm in Atlanta called each other "babe." Kendra said that that was no excuse for inappropriate behavior that, in California at least, created a hostile environment for an employee. Kendra told Brooke that a reprimand letter would be placed in her personnel file and warned her that she would be fired if she engaged in similar conduct with Alan or any other employee in the future. Kendra concluded by telling Brooke that Alan would no longer report to her as she was being shifted to a different programming group. Brooke apologized and assured Kendra that it would never happen again.

After settling the lawsuit with Gracie Lu and resolving Alan Raskovich's complaints, Kendra decided that it was time to sit down with Michael Cruz to review the adequacy of DataAccelleation's liability insurance policies and to establish internal procedures designed to ensure compliance with applicable laws and reduce the risk of operational liabilities.

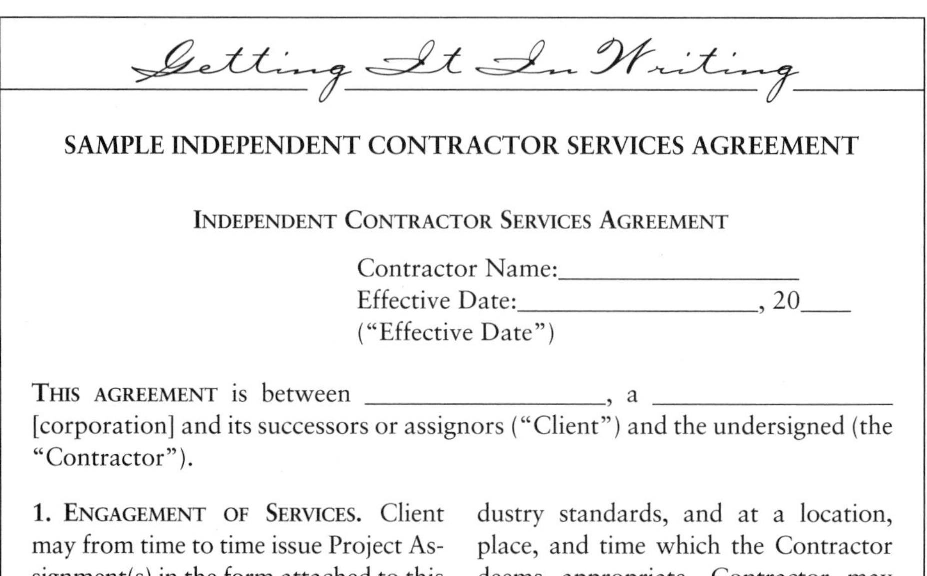

Getting It In Writing

SAMPLE INDEPENDENT CONTRACTOR SERVICES AGREEMENT

INDEPENDENT CONTRACTOR SERVICES AGREEMENT

Contractor Name:__________________
Effective Date:__________________, 20____
("Effective Date")

THIS AGREEMENT is between __________________, a __________________ [corporation] and its successors or assignors ("Client") and the undersigned (the "Contractor").

1. ENGAGEMENT OF SERVICES. Client may from time to time issue Project Assignment(s) in the form attached to this Agreement as <u>Exhibit A</u>. Subject to the terms of this Agreement, Contractor will, to the best of its ability, render the services set forth in Project Assignment(s) accepted by Contractor (the "Project(s)") by the completion dates therein. The manner and means by which Contractor chooses to complete the Projects are in Contractor's sole discretion and control. Contractor agrees to exercise the highest degree of professionalism, and to utilize its expertise and creative talents in completing such Projects. In completing the Projects, Contractor agrees to provide its own equipment, tools, and other materials at its own expense. Client will make its facilities and equipment available to Contractor when necessary. Contractor shall perform the services necessary to complete the Projects in a timely and professional manner consistent with industry standards, and at a location, place, and time which the Contractor deems appropriate. Contractor may not subcontract or otherwise delegate its obligations under this Agreement without Client's prior written consent. **If contractor is not a natural person, then before any Contractor employee or consultant performs services in connection with this Agreement, the employee or consultant and Contractor must have entered into a written agreement expressly for the benefit of Client and containing provisions substantially equivalent to this section and to Section 4 below.**

2. COMPENSATION. Client will pay Contractor a fee for services rendered under this Agreement as set forth in the Project Assignment(s) undertaken by Contractor. [Contractor shall be responsible for all expenses incurred in performing services under this Agreement.] [Contractor will be reimbursed for any reasonable expenses incurred

continued...

continued...

in connection with the performance of services under this Agreement provided Contractor submits verification of such expenses as Client may require.] Upon termination of this Agreement for any reason, Contractor will be paid fees and expenses on a proportional basis as stated in the Project Assignment(s) for work which is then in progress, up to and including the effective date of such termination. Unless other terms are set forth in the Project Assignment(s) for work which is in progress, Client will pay the Contractor for services and will reimburse the Contractor for previously approved expenses within thirty (30) days of the date of Contractor's invoice.

3. INDEPENDENT CONTRACTOR RELATIONSHIP. Contractor's relationship with Client will be that of an independent contractor and nothing in this Agreement should be construed to create a partnership, joint venture, or employer-employee relationship. Contractor is not the agent of Client and is not authorized to make any representation, contract, or commitment on behalf of Client. Contractor will not be entitled to any of the benefits which Client may make available to its employees, such as group insurance, profit sharing, or retirement benefits. Contractor will be solely responsible for all tax returns and payments required to be filed with or made to any federal, state, or local tax authority with respect to Contractor's performance of services and receipt of fees under this Agreement. Client will regularly report amounts paid to Contractor by filing Form 1099-MISC with the Internal Revenue Service as required by law. Because Contractor is an independent contractor, Client will not withhold or make payments for Social Security; make unemployment insurance or disability insurance contributions; or obtain workers' compensation insurance on Contractor's behalf. Contractor agrees to accept exclusive liability for complying with all applicable state and federal laws governing self-employed individuals, including obligations such as payment of taxes, Social Security, disability, and other contributions based on fees paid to Contractor, its agents, or employees under this Agreement. Contractor hereby agrees to indemnify and defend Client against any and all such taxes or contributions, including penalties and interest.

4. TRADE SECRETS—INTELLECTUAL PROPERTY RIGHTS.

4.1 Proprietary Information. Contractor agrees during the term of this Agreement and thereafter to take all steps reasonably necessary to hold Client's Proprietary Information in trust and confidence. By way of illustration but not limitation **"Proprietary Information"** includes (a) trade secrets, inventions, mask works, ideas, processes, formulas, source and object codes, data, programs, other works of authorship, know-how, improvements, discoveries,

continued...

continued...

developments, designs, and techniques (hereinafter collectively referred to as **"Inventions"**); and (b) information regarding plans for research, development, new products, marketing and selling, business plans, budgets and unpublished financial statements, licenses, prices and costs, and suppliers and customers; and (c) information regarding the skills and compensation of other employees of the Client. Notwithstanding the other provisions of this Agreement, nothing received by Contractor will be considered to be Client Proprietary Information if (1) it has been published or is otherwise readily available to the public other than by a breach of this Agreement; (2) it has been rightfully received by Contractor from a third party without confidential limitations; (3) it has been independently developed for Contractor by personnel or agents having no access to the Client Proprietary Information; or (4) it was known to Contractor prior to its first receipt from Client.

4.2 Third Party Information. Contractor understands that Client has received and will in the future receive from third parties confidential or proprietary information (**"Third Party Information"**) subject to a duty on Client's part to maintain the confidentiality of such information and to use it only for certain limited purposes. Contractor agrees to hold Third Party Information in confidence and not to disclose to anyone (other than Client personnel who need to know such information in connection with their work for Client) or to use, except in connection with Contractor's work for Client, Third Party Information unless expressly authorized in writing by an officer of Client.

4.3 No Conflict of Interest. Contractor agrees during the term of this Agreement not to accept work or enter into a contract or accept an obligation inconsistent or incompatible with Contractor's obligations under this Agreement or the scope of services rendered for Client. Contractor warrants that to the best of its knowledge, there is no other existing contract or duty on Contractor's part inconsistent with this Agreement, unless a copy of such contract or a description of such duty is attached to this Agreement as Exhibit B. Contractor further agrees not to disclose to Client, or bring onto Client's premises, or induce Client to use, any confidential information that belongs to anyone other than Client or Contractor.

4.4 Disclosure of Work Product. As used in this Agreement, the term **"Work Product"** means any Invention, whether or not patentable, and all related know-how, designs, mask works, trademarks, formulae, processes, manufacturing techniques, trade secrets, ideas, artwork, software, or other copyrightable or patentable works. Contractor agrees to disclose promptly in writing to Client, or any person designated by Client, all Work Product which is solely or jointly conceived, made, reduced to practice, or

continued...

continued...

learned by Contractor in the course of any work performed for Client (**"Client Work Product"**). Contractor represents that any Work Product relating to Client's business or any Project which Contractor has made, conceived, or reduced to practice at the time of signing this Agreement (**"Prior Work Product"**) has been disclosed in writing to Client and attached to this Agreement as Exhibit C. If disclosure of any such Prior Work Product would cause Contractor to violate any prior confidentiality agreement, Contractor understands that it is not to list such Prior Work Product in Exhibit C but it will disclose a cursory name for each such invention, a listing of the party(ies) to whom it belongs, and the fact that full disclosure as to such Prior Work Product has not been made for that reason. A space is provided in Exhibit C for such purpose.

4.5 Ownership of Work Product. Contractor shall specifically describe and identify in Exhibit C all technology which (a) Contractor intends to use in performing under this Agreement, (b) is either owned solely by Contractor or licensed to Contractor with a right to sublicense, and (c) is in existence in the form of a writing or working prototype prior to the Effective Date (**"Background Technology"**). Contractor agrees that any and all Inventions conceived, written, created, or first reduced to practice in the performance of work under this Agreement shall be the sole and exclusive property of Client.

4.6 Assignment of Client Work Product. Except for Contractor's rights in the Background Technology, Contractor irrevocably assigns to Client all right, title, and interest worldwide in and to the Client Work Product and all applicable intellectual property rights related to the Client Work Product, including, without limitation, copyrights, trademarks, trade secrets, patents, moral rights, contract, and licensing rights (the **"Proprietary Rights"**). Except as set forth below, Contractor retains no rights to use the Client Work Product and agrees not to challenge the validity of Client's ownership in the Client Work Product. Contractor hereby grants to Client a nonexclusive, royalty-free, irrevocable, and worldwide right, with rights to sublicense through multiple tiers of sublicenses, to make, use, and sell Background Technology and any Prior Work Product incorporated or used in the Client Work Product for the purpose of developing and marketing Client products **[but not for the purpose of marketing Background Technology or Prior Work Products separate from Client products]**.

4.7 Waiver of Assignment of Other Rights. If Contractor has any rights to the Client Work Product that cannot be assigned to Client, Contractor unconditionally and irrevocably waives the enforcement of such rights, and all claims and causes of action of any kind against Client with respect to such rights, and agrees, at Client's request

continued...

continued...

and expense, to consent to and join in any action to enforce such rights. If Contractor has any right to the Client Work Product that cannot be assigned to Client or waived by Contractor, Contractor unconditionally and irrevocably grants to Client during the term of such rights an exclusive, irrevocable, perpetual, worldwide, fully paid, and royalty-free license, with rights to sublicense through multiple levels of sublicensees, to reproduce, create derivative works of, distribute, publicly perform, and publicly display by all means now known or later developed such rights.

4.8 Assistance. Contractor agrees to cooperate with Client or its designee(s), both during and after the term of this Agreement, in the procurement and maintenance of Client's rights in Client Work Product and to execute, when requested, any other documents deemed necessary by Client to carry out the purpose of this Agreement. Contractor agrees to execute upon Client's request a signed transfer of copyright to Client in the form attached to this Agreement as Exhibit D for all Client Work Product subject to copyright protection, including, without limitation, computer programs, notes, sketches, drawings, and reports. In the event that Client is unable for any reason to secure Contractor's signature to any document required to apply for or execute any patent, copyright, or other applications with respect to any Client Work Product (including improvements, renewals, extensions, continuations, divisions, or continuations in part thereof), Contractor hereby irrevocably designates and appoints Client and its duly authorized officers and agents as its agents and attorneys in fact to act for and in its behalf and instead of Contractor to execute and file any such application and to do all other lawfully permitted acts to further the prosecution and issuance of patents, copyrights, mask works, or other rights thereon with the same legal force and effect as if executed by Contractor.

4.9 Enforcement of Proprietary Rights. Contractor will assist Client in every proper way to obtain, and from time to time enforce, United States and foreign Proprietary Rights relating to Client Work Product in any and all countries. To that end Contractor will execute, verify, and deliver such documents and perform such other acts (including appearances as a witness) as Client may reasonably request for use in applying for, obtaining, perfecting, evidencing, sustaining, and enforcing such Proprietary Rights and the assignment thereof. In addition, Contractor will execute, verify, and deliver assignments of such Proprietary Rights to Client or its designee. Contractor's obligation to assist Client with respect to Proprietary Rights relating to such Client Work Product in any and all countries shall continue beyond the termination of this Agreement, but Client shall compensate Contractor at a reasonable rate after such termination for the time actually spent by Contractor at Client's request on such assistance.

continued...

continued...

In the event Client is unable for any reason, after reasonable effort, to secure Contractor's signature on any document needed in connection with the actions specified in the preceding paragraph, Contractor hereby irrevocably designates and appoints Client and its duly authorized officers and agents as its agent and attorney in fact, which appointment is coupled with an interest, to act for and on its behalf to execute, verify, and file any such documents and to do all other lawfully permitted acts to further the purposes of the preceding paragraph with the same legal force and effect as if executed by Contractor. Contractor hereby waives and quitclaims to Client any and all claims, of any nature whatsoever, which Contractor now or may hereafter have for infringement of any Proprietary Rights assigned hereunder to Client.

5. CONTRACTOR REPRESENTATIONS AND WARRANTIES. Contractor hereby represents and warrants that (a) the Client Work Product will be an original work of Contractor and any third parties will have executed assignment of rights reasonably acceptable to Client; (b) neither the Client Work Product nor any element thereof will infringe the Intellectual Property Rights of any third party; (c) neither the Client Work Product nor any element thereof will be subject to any restrictions or to any mortgages, liens, pledges, security interests, encumbrances, or encroachments; (d) Contractor will not grant, directly or indirectly, any rights or interest to third parties whatsoever in the Client Work Product; (e) Contractor has full right and power to enter into and perform this Agreement without the consent of any third party; (f) Contractor will take all necessary precautions to prevent injury to any persons (including employees of Client) or damage to property (including Client's property) during the term of this Agreement; and (g) should Client permit Contractor to use any of Client's equipment, tools, or facilities during the term of this Agreement, such permission shall be gratuitous and Contractor shall be responsible for any injury (including death) to any person or damage to property (including Client's property) arising out of use of such equipment, tools, or facilities, whether or not such claim is based upon its condition or on the alleged negligence of Client in permitting its use.

6. INDEMNIFICATION. Contractor will indemnify and hold harmless Client, its officers, directors, employees, sublicensees, customers, and agents from any and all claims, losses, liabilities, damages, expenses, and costs (including attorneys' fees and court costs) which result from a breach or alleged breach of any representation or warranty of Client (a **"Claim"**) set forth in Section 5 of this Agreement, provided that Client gives Contractor written notice of any such Claim and Contractor has the right to participate in the defense of any such Claim at its expense. From the date of written notice from Client to Contractor of any such Claim, Client shall have the right to withhold from any payments due Contractor under this Agreement the amount of any defense costs, plus additional reasonable amounts as security for Contractor's obligations under this Section 6.

continued...

continued...

Contractor, at its sole cost and expense, shall maintain appropriate insurance with Commercial General Liability Broad Form Coverage, including Contractual Liability, Contractor's Protective Liability and Personal Injury/Property Damage Coverage in a combined single limit of not less than $3,000,000. A Certificate of Insurance indicating such coverage shall be delivered to Client upon request. The Certificate shall indicate that the policy will not be changed or terminated without at least ten (10) days' prior notice to Client, shall name Client as an additional named insured, and shall also indicate that the insurer has waived its subrogation rights against Client.

7. TERMINATION.

7.1 Termination by Client. Client may terminate this Agreement at its convenience and without any breach by Contractor upon fifteen (15) days' prior written notice to Contractor. Client may also terminate this Agreement immediately in its sole discretion upon Contractor's material breach of Section 4 or Section 7.3.

7.2 Termination by Contractor. Contractor may terminate this Agreement at any time that there is no uncompleted Project Assignment in effect upon fifteen (15) days' prior written notice to Client.

7.3 Noninterference with Business. During and for a period of two (2) years immediately following termination of this Agreement by either party, Contractor agrees not to solicit or induce any employee or independent contractor to terminate or breach an employment, contractual, or other relationship with Client.

7.4 Return of Client Property. Upon termination of the Agreement or earlier as requested by Client, Contractor will deliver to Client any and all drawings, notes, memoranda, specifications, devices, formulas, and documents, together with all copies thereof, and any other material containing or disclosing any Client Work Product, Third Party Information, or Proprietary Information of the Client. Contractor further agrees that any property situated on Client's premises and owned by Client, including disks and other storage media, filing cabinets, or other work areas, is subject to inspection by Client personnel at any time with or without notice.

8. GOVERNMENT OR THIRD PARTY CONTRACTS.

8.1 Government Contracts. In the event that Contractor shall perform services under this Agreement in connection with any Government contract in which Client may be the prime contractor or subcontractor, Contractor agrees to abide by all laws, rules, and regulations relating thereto. To the extent that any such law, rule, or regulation requires that a provision or clause be included in this Agreement, Contractor agrees that such provision or clause shall be added to this Agreement and the same shall then become a part of this Agreement.

continued...

continued...

8.2 Security. In the event the services of the Contractor should require Contractor to have access to Department of Defense classified material, or other classified material in the possession of Client's facility, such material shall not be removed from Client's facility. Contractor agrees that all work performed under this Agreement by Contractor which involves the use of classified material mentioned above shall be performed in a secure fashion (consistent with applicable law and regulations for the handling of classified material) and only at Client's facility.

8.3 Ownership. Contractor also agrees to assign all of its right, title, and interest in and to any Work Product to a Third Party, including without limitation the United States, as directed by Client.

9. GENERAL PROVISIONS.

9.1 Governing Law. This Agreement will be governed and construed in accordance with the laws of the State of California as applied to transactions taking place wholly within California between California residents. Contractor hereby expressly consents to the personal jurisdiction of the state and federal courts located in _____ County, California for any lawsuit filed there against Contractor by Client arising from or related to this Agreement.

9.2 Severability. In case any one or more of the provisions contained in this Agreement shall, for any reason, be held to be invalid, illegal, or unenforceable in any respect, such invalidity, illegality, or unenforceability shall not affect the other provisions of this Agreement, and this Agreement shall be construed as if such invalid, illegal, or unenforceable provision had never been contained herein. If, moreover, any one or more of the provisions contained in this Agreement shall for any reason be held to be excessively broad as to duration, geographical scope, activity or subject, it shall be construed by limiting and reducing it, so as to be enforceable to the extent compatible with the applicable law as it shall then appear.

9.3 No Assignment. This Agreement may not be assigned by Contractor without Client's consent, and any such attempted assignment shall be void and of no effect.

9.4 Notices. All notices, requests, and other communications under this Agreement must be in writing, and must be mailed by registered or certified mail, postage prepaid and return receipt requested, or delivered by hand to the party to whom such notice is required or permitted to be given. If mailed, any such notice will be considered to have been given five (5) business days after it was mailed, as evidenced by the postmark. If delivered by hand, any such notice will be considered to have been given when received by the party to whom notice is given, as evidenced by the written and dated receipt of the receiving party. The mailing address for notice to either party will be the address shown on the signature page of this Agreement. Either party may change its mailing address by notice as provided by this section.

continued...

continued...

9.5 Legal Fees. If any dispute arises between the parties with respect to the matters covered by this Agreement which leads to a proceeding to resolve such dispute, the prevailing party in such proceeding shall be entitled to receive its reasonable attorneys' fees, expert witness fees, and out-of-pocket costs incurred in connection with such proceeding, in addition to any other relief it may be awarded.

9.6 Injunctive Relief. A breach of any of the promises or agreements contained in this Agreement may result in irreparable and continuing damage to Client for which there may be no adequate remedy at law, and Client is therefore entitled to seek injunctive relief as well as such other and further relief as may be appropriate.

9.7 Survival. The following provisions shall survive termination of this Agreement: Section 4, Section 5, Section 6, and Section 7.3.

9.8 Export. Contractor agrees not to export, directly or indirectly, any U.S. source technical data acquired from Client or any products utilizing such data to countries outside the United States, which export may be in violation of the United States export laws or regulations.

9.9 Waiver. No waiver by Client of any breach of this Agreement shall be a waiver of any preceding or succeeding breach. No waiver by Client of any right under this Agreement shall be construed as a waiver of any other right. Client shall not be required to give notice to enforce strict adherence to all terms of this Agreement.

9.10 Entire Agreement. This Agreement is the final, complete, and exclusive agreement of the parties with respect to the subject matter hereof and supersedes and merges all prior discussions between us. No modification of or amendment to this Agreement, nor any waiver of any rights under this Agreement, will be effective unless in writing and signed by the party to be charged. The terms of this Agreement will govern all Project Assignments and services undertaken by Contractor for Client.

IN WITNESS WHEREOF, the parties have caused this Independent Contractor Services Agreement to be executed by their duly authorized representative.

Client:

____

(Printed Name)

By:
Title:
Address:

Contractor:

____

(Printed Name)

By:
Title:
(if applicable)
Address:

For copyright registration purposes only, Contractor must provide the following information:

Date of Birth:
Nationality or Domicile:

EXHIBIT A

PROJECT ASSIGNMENT

SERVICES MILESTONES

Payment of Fees. Fee will be: (cross out inapplicable provisions)

A fixed price for completion of $ ______________________.

Based on a rate per hour of $ ______________________.

Other, as follows: ____

____.

If this Project Assignment or the Independent Contractor Services Agreement that governs it is terminated for any reason, fees will be paid based on: (cross out inapplicable provisions)

Contractor time spent

The proportion of the deliverables furnished Client, as determined by Client.

Other, as follows: ____

____.

Expenses. Client will reimburse Contractor for the following expenses:

____.

NOTE: This Project Assignment is governed by the terms of an Independent Contractor Services Agreement in effect between Client and Contractor. Any item in this Project Assignment that is inconsistent with that Agreement is invalid.

Signed: ______________________ ______________________
for Client Contractor

Dated: ______________________

EXHIBIT B

CONFLICT OF INTEREST DISCLOSURE

EXHIBIT C

PRIOR WORK PRODUCTS DISCLOSURE

1. Except as listed in Section 2 below, the following is a complete list of all Prior Work Products that have been made or conceived or first reduced to practice by Contractor alone or jointly with others prior to my engagement by Client:

_____ No inventions or improvements.

_____ See below:

_____ Additional sheets attached.

2. Due to a prior confidentiality agreement with, and the proprietary rights and duty of confidentiality Contractor owes to, the following party(ies), Contractor cannot complete the disclosure under Section 1 above with respect to the inventions or improvements generally listed below:

INVENTION OR IMPROVEMENT	PARTY(IES)	RELATIONSHIP
1.____________________	__________	__________
2.____________________	__________	__________
3.____________________	__________	__________

__________ Additional sheets attached.

BACKGROUND TECHNOLOGY DISCLOSURE

The following is a list of all Background Technology that Contractor intends to use in performing under this Agreement:

EXHIBIT D

ASSIGNMENT OF COPYRIGHT

For good and valuable consideration that has been received, the undersigned sells, assigns, and transfers to Client, a _____ **[corporation]**, and its successors and assigns, the copyright in and to the following work, which was created by the following indicated author(s):

Title: ______________________________

Author(s): ________________________

Copyright Office Identification No. (if any): ___________________________

and all of the right, title, and interest of the undersigned, vested and contingent, therein and thereto.

Executed this _____ day of _____, 20 __.

Signature: ______________________________

Printed Name: __________________________

NOTES

1. Reeves v. Sanderson Plumbing Prods., Inc., 530 U.S. 133 (2000).
2. Meritor Savings Bank, FSB v. Vinson, 477 U.S. 57 (1986).
3. Faragher v. City of Boca Raton, 524 U.S. 775 (1998).
4. Oncale v. Sundowner Offshore Serv., Inc., 523 U.S. 75 (1998).
5. Lockard v. Pizza Hut, Inc., 162 F.3d 1062 (10th Cir. 1998).
6. Adams v. Florida Power Corp., 255 F.3d 1322 (11th Cir. 2001), *cert. granted,* 122 S. Ct. 643 (2001).
7. Sutton v. United Air Lines, Inc., 527 U.S. 471 (1999).
8. Toyota Motor Mfg., Ky., Inc. v. Williams 534 U.S. 184 (2002).
9. Sutton v. United Air Lines, Inc., 527 U.S. 471 (1999).
10. *Toyota Motor Mfg.,* 534 U.S. 184.
11. *Id.*
12. Bragdon v. Abbott, 524 U.S. 624 (1998).
13. Maddox v. University of Tenn., 62 F.3d 843 (6th Cir. 1995).
14. Kern v. Dynalectron Corp., 577 F. Supp. 1196 (N.D. Tex. 1983), *aff'd,* 746 F.2d 810 (5th Cir. 1984).
15. Simon J. Nadel, *Employers Have Good Reason to Be Bearish, as Online Trading by Their Employees Increases Thirty-Seven Percent During Company Time,* CORP. COUNS. WKLY., Oct. 13, 1999, at 6. *See also* Muick v. Glenayre Electronics, 280 F.3d 741 (7th Cir. 2002) (company's computer use policy reserving the employer's right to inspect computers assigned to employees negated any reasonable expectation of privacy by employee and was also reasonable because "the abuse of access to workplace computers is so common (workers being prone to use them as media of gossip, titillation, and other entertainment and distraction).").

16. Blakey v. Continental Airlines, Inc., 751 A.2d 538 (N.J. 2000).
17. Health Insurance Portability & Accountability Act of 1996, Privacy Regulations, 45 C.F.R. §§ 160–164 (2000).
18. *See generally* Linda Abdel-Malek, *HIPAA Privacy Rules Impact Employers,* N.Y. L.J., May 14, 2001, at 5.
19. Trombetta v. Detroit, Toledo and Irontown R.R. Co., 265 N.W.2d 385 (Mich. 1978).
20. Reilly v. Alcan Aluminum Corp., 528 S.E.2d 238 (Ga. 2000).
21. Foley v. Interactive Data Corp., 765 P.2d 373 (Cal. 1988).
22. Green v. Ralee Eng'g Co., 960 P.2d 1046 (Cal. 1998).
23. Suchodolski v. Michigan Consol. Gas Co., 316 N.W.2d 710 (Mich. 1982).
24. McLaughlin v. Gastrointestinal Specialists, 750 A.2d 283 (Pa. 2000).
25. Rocky Mountain Hosp. & Med. Serv. v. Mariani, 916 P.2d 519 (Colo. 1996).
26. Fortune v. National Cash Register Co., 364 N.E.2d 1251 (Mass. 1977).
27. Circuit City Stores, Inc. v. Adams, 532 U.S. 105 1302 (2001).
28. *See, e.g.,* Rosenberg v. Merrill Lynch, Pierce, Fenner & Smith, Inc., 170 F.3d 1 (1st Cir. 1999). *Contra* Haskins v. Prudential Ins. Co. of America, 230 F.3d 231 (6th Cir. 2000).
29. Armendariz v. Foundation Health Psychcare Servs., Inc., 6 P.3d 669 (Cal. 1999).

Chapter 11

Operational Liabilities and Insurance

A fledgling business faces a range of legal liabilities, stemming from various aspects of its business. The law of torts is the source of the most wide-ranging civil liability. A *tort* is a civil wrong that injures a person, property, or certain economic interests and business relationships. Torts range from negligence to intentional interference with contract. The injured party is entitled to recover damages from the responsible party. A company is always liable for the torts it commits. In addition, companies are vicariously liable for torts committed by employees acting within the scope of their employment.

It is important that entrepreneurs understand a company's potential tort exposure so that they can minimize the potential risk. Tort liability and its ensuing litigation can threaten a new business venture's viability. The risk of tort liability is a major reason for incorporating or otherwise properly structuring a company to shield the owners from personal liability.

In addition to torts, a company may face statutory liabilities stemming from state unfair business statutes and a variety of federal statutes imposing both civil and criminal liability for antitrust violations, environmental cleanup costs, bribery, and various types of fraud. As with torts, corporations are vicariously liable for crimes committed by their employees acting within the scope of their employment. Under some circumstances, a supervisor may be held civilly and criminally liable for the misdeeds of subordinates.

The chapter first introduces the tort of negligence, its elements, and its defenses. It then describes a variety of intentional torts that protect people, property, and certain economic interests and business relationships. The chapter next addresses strict liability for ultrahazardous activities. Product liability, false advertising, and unfair competition are discussed in Chapter 9. The chapter continues with a discussion of an employer's liability for torts committed by its employees.

Next, antitrust laws, particularly the Sherman Act and its prohibition against horizontal price-fixing agreements, are discussed. Federal environmental liability, bans on bribery under the Foreign Corrupt Practices Act, tax fraud, and mail and wire fraud are also addressed. Insurance, which can cover many types of liability and losses, is also discussed. The chapter concludes with suggestions for risk management.

NEGLIGENCE

Negligence is conduct that involves an unreasonable risk of causing injury to another person or damage to another person's property. To establish liability for negligence, the plaintiff must show that (1) the defendant owed a duty to the plaintiff to act reasonably under the circumstances; (2) the defendant breached that duty by failing to use the care that a reasonably prudent person would have used; (3) there is a reasonably close causal connection between the defendant's breach and the plaintiff's injury; and (4) the plaintiff suffered an actual loss or injury.

Duty

A person with a legal duty to another is required to act reasonably under the circumstances to avoid harming the other person. Duty exists in a variety of contexts, including those discussed below.

DUTY OF LANDOWNER OR TENANT A processor of land (such as a tenant) or its owner has a legal duty to keep the property reasonably safe. Such a person can be liable for injury that occurs outside, as well as on, the premises. For example, a person may be liable for harm caused if water from his or

FROM THE TRENCHES

In 1995, a truck bomb exploded outside a federal building in Oklahoma City, killing 168 and injuring hundreds more. Victims sued ICI Explosives, the manufacturer of the ammonium nitrate used to make the bomb. The plaintiffs alleged that ICI negligently mislabeled its explosive-grade ammonium nitrate as fertilizer grade, allowing it to reach the hands of the eventual bombers.

The causal chain between an act of negligence and injury can be broken by a supervening cause. A *supervening cause* must be (1) independent of the original act, (2) adequate to bring about the injury, and (3) not reasonably foreseeable. If the intervening act is intentionally tortious or criminal, then it is reasonably foreseeable if the negligent party realized or should have realized that its negligent conduct created a situation that afforded the third party the opportunity to commit the crime. The criminal acts of a third party are reasonably foreseeable if the situation provides a temptation to which a recognizable percentage of persons would yield, or if the temptation is created at a place where persons of a peculiarly vicious type are likely to be.

Because only one ammonium nitrate bomb had been exploded in the last twenty-eight years, and the complexity involved in creating and detonating such a bomb limited the number of people capable of doing so, the court found that there were not enough people to comprise a recognizable percentage. The bombers' criminal activities were a supervening cause; therefore, ICI Explosives's failure to properly label the ammonium nitrate was not the proximate cause of the plaintiff's injuries.

Source: Gaines-Tabb v. ICI Explosives USA, Inc., 160 F.3d 613 (10th Cir. 1998).

her cooling tower floods the highway, or if sparks from improperly maintained machinery start a fire on adjacent property.

Generally, landowners are not liable for harm caused by natural conditions on their property, such as uncut weeds that obstruct a driver's view, the natural flow of surface water, or falling rocks. Landowners may be liable, however, if they have altered the natural state of the land, for example, by building a dam that floods a highway or erecting a sign or planting trees that obstruct a motorist's view.

FROM THE TRENCHES

Robert Gadams, a school administrator at Livingston School, allegedly molested Randi W., a thirteen-year-old student at Livingston. As part of his application to Livingston, Gadams had submitted letters of recommendation from schools where he had previously worked. He had been accused of sexual misconduct at each of the school districts where he had worked, but the letters of recommendation omitted these facts and instead were quite positive. Randi sued the letter writers and the school districts, alleging negligent misrepresentation. The key issue was whether the letter writers had a duty to students at the school or just to the recipients of the letters.

The California Supreme Court upheld the claim. The defendants had a duty to the students because the defendants could reasonably foresee that (1) Livingston's officers would rely on the defendants' letters in hiring Gadams; (2) that if they did not unqualifiedly recommend Gadams, he would not be hired; and (3) that Gadams might molest or injure a Livingston student, such as Randi. The court also rejected the defendants' claim that this was mere nondisclosure. By omitting material information necessary to qualify the statements made in the letter, the defendants made misleading half-truths, which constituted negligent misrepresentation.

Source: Randi W. v. Muroc Joint Unified Sch. Dist., 929 P.2d 582 (Cal. 1997).

In a few jurisdictions, landowners have a duty to maintain sidewalks immediately adjacent to their property. In all jurisdictions, landowners have a general duty to inspect a building on their land and keep it in repair, and they may be liable if a showroom window, a downspout, a screen, or a loose sign falls and injures someone.

Under traditional analysis, landowners' duty to a person on their land varied, depending on the person's reasons for being on the property. The duty owed ranged from almost no duty to someone who was a trespasser (present on the property without permission) to an affirmative duty to protect a person who entered the premises for business purposes (an *invitee*). A customer is clearly an invitee and is accordingly owed the highest duty of care. A mere social guest (called a *licensee*) is owed a lesser duty.

The more modern approach, adopted by several states (including New York), is to impose a duty to use reasonable care under the circumstances.

Under this standard, courts require all landowners to act in a reasonable manner with respect to entrants on their land, with liability hinging on the foreseeability of harm.

DUTY OF EMPLOYER TO THIRD PARTIES As discussed later in this chapter, an employer is liable for any torts committed by employees acting within the scope of their employment, where the scope of employment is liberally defined. Under certain circumstances, employers have a legal duty to protect strangers from injuries caused by their employees even when the employees are off-site and are clearly not acting within the scope of their employment.

For example, the Texas Supreme Court ruled that an employer was potentially liable for an automobile accident in which an intoxicated employee sent home by his supervisor killed someone while driving home.[1] The Arizona Court of Appeals reached the opposite result in a case with similar facts.[2] An employer may also be responsible for the safe passage home of an employee who is not intoxicated but is tired from working too many consecutive hours.[3]

DUTY OF PROFESSIONALS TO THIRD PARTIES Accountants, lawyers, architects, and other professionals have a duty to their clients to use reasonable care when rendering their services. Failure to do so can result in liability for negligence (commonly referred to in this context as *malpractice*). But under what circumstances can a third party who has relied on the professional's opinion sue the professional for negligence?

For example, suppose that an accounting firm prepares audited financial statements for a retailer that submits them to a bank as part of an application for an unsecured loan. The bank relies on the audited statements when deciding to make the loan and discovers after the borrower defaults that the accountants had negligently failed to require the retailer to write off obsolete inventory. Can the bank hold the accountants liable for negligence? The answer will vary depending on which state's law governs the suit. A few states (including New York) require that there be a contractual relationship (*contractual privity*) between the professional and the person suing for negligence. A few others will permit a third party to sue for negligence if the professional knew that the

FROM THE TRENCHES

Pursuant to the Securities Investor Protection Act (SIPA), broker-dealers must file annual audit reports with the Securities and Exchange Commission (SEC), and they must use independent public accountants for the audit. A.R. Baron & Co., a registered broker-dealer, retained BDO Seidman to serve as its independent certified public accountant and to conduct its audits. A number of Baron's managers were engaging in fraud in connection with the sale of securities. Customers of Baron sued Seidman for negligence, alleging that it had (1) negligently misrepresented Baron's financial condition, (2) failed to disclose Baron's inadequate internal fraud controls, and (3) failed to follow proper audit procedures.

A key issue was whether Seidman had a duty to Baron's customers. The U.S. Court of Appeals for the Second Circuit, applying New York's high threshold for suits against accountants by third parties, upheld the district court's dismissal of the claim. Under New York law, a plaintiff suing an accountant with which it has no contractual tie for negligence must show that (1) the accountant must have been aware that the reports would be used for a particular purpose, (2) in furtherance of that purpose a known party was intended to rely, and (3) some conduct by the accountant "linked" him or her to the known party. This has come to be known as a requirement of *near privity.*

Here, the reports were prepared for the SEC and the National Association of Securities Dealers, not for customers of Baron. Knowing that customers might rely on the information is not sufficient, because they are not known to the accountant. Furthermore, there was no linking behavior, such as direct contact or communication between the accountants and Baron's customers.

Source: Securities Investor Protection Corp. v. BDO Seidman, LLP, 223 F.3d 63 (2d Cir. 2000).

client intended to give the opinion to a third party that the professional knew would rely on it when deciding whether and on what terms to enter into a transaction with the client.[4]

Standard of Conduct

A person is required to act as a reasonable person of ordinary prudence would act under the circumstances. The standard of care is not graduated to include the reasonably slow person, the reasonably forgetful person, or the reasonable person of low intelligence. On the other hand, a person who is specially trained to participate in a profession or trade will be held to the higher standard of care of a reasonably skilled member of that profession or trade. For example, the professional conduct of a doctor, architect, pilot, attorney, or accountant will be measured against the standard of the profession.

The fact that one has complied with the law is not a defense if a reasonably prudent person would have done more than the law required. Thus, for example, a tugboat operator who does not have a radio could still be found negligent even though a radio is not legally required, if a prudent tugboat operator would have installed one. In most jurisdictions, however, failing to follow a law is a *prima facie* case of negligence, or negligence *per se,* if the harm that follows is of the type that the law sought to prevent. For example, if the law requires a school bus to have side mirrors of a certain size and a bus company fails to repair a broken mirror, which results in the death of a child walking behind the bus, then the bus company is negligent *per se,* without the need to prove anything further.

Defenses to Negligence

In some jurisdictions, the defendant may absolve itself of part or all of the liability for negligence by proving that the plaintiff was also partly at fault.

Contributory Negligence

Under the doctrine of *contributory negligence,* if the plaintiff was also negligent in any manner, he or she cannot recover any damages from the defendant. Thus, if a plaintiff was 5 percent negligent and the defendant was 95 percent negligent, the plaintiff's injury would go unredressed. Most courts have replaced the doctrine of contributory negligence with that of comparative negligence.

Comparative Negligence

Comparative negligence allows the plaintiff to recover the proportion of his or her loss attributable to the defendant's negligence. For example, if the plaintiff was 5 percent negligent and the defendant was 95 percent negligent, the plaintiff can recover 95 percent of the loss. Some jurisdictions permit plaintiffs to recover for the percentage the defendant is at fault only if the plaintiff is responsible for less than 50 percent of his or her own injuries. Thus, in these jurisdictions, if the plaintiff is found 51 percent negligent and the defendant 49 percent negligent, the plaintiff cannot recover at all. These are called *modified comparative negligence jurisdictions.*

INTENTIONAL TORTS

A number of business torts require an intent to harm the plaintiff, the plaintiff's property, or certain economic interests and business relationships. A person intends a result when he or she subjectively wants it to occur or knows that it is substantially certain to occur as a result of his or her actions. A person is automatically liable for intentional torts without regard to duty.

Torts That Protect Persons

Several business torts are designed to protect individuals from physical and mental harm. These include battery, false imprisonment, intentional infliction of emotional distress, defamation, invasion of privacy, and appropriation of another's likeness. A single set of facts may give rise to claims under more than one theory.

BATTERY *Battery* is a harmful or offensive contact with the plaintiff's body or something (such as a coat) touching it. Putting poison in a person's food constitutes battery.

FALSE IMPRISONMENT *False imprisonment* is intentional restraint of movement, imposed against someone's will by physical barriers, physical force, or threats of force. False imprisonment has also been found when the plaintiff's freedom of movement was restricted because of force applied to the plaintiff's valuable property. For example, a court found false imprisonment when a store's clerk confiscated a shopper's purchase after the shopper had paid for it.[5] Most states have legislation exempting shopkeepers from false imprisonment claims if it can be

FROM THE TRENCHES

A customer in a supermarket was stopped by a store security guard and accused of stealing a bottle of aspirin that he had in the top pocket of his sweater. The guard told the customer that he had been under surveillance and had been seen taking the aspirin. The customer explained that he had bought the aspirin elsewhere and was just comparing prices.

The security guard notified the store manager that he had apprehended a shoplifter. While the manager called police, the security guard took the customer to a stockroom in the rear of the store, searched him, and handcuffed him to a large metal container.

The man protested his innocence to the security guard, to the store manager, and to the police who arrived to arrest him. The customer suggested that if they counted the aspirin, they would find that he had already taken two, and if they went to the drugstore where he had bought the aspirin, they would find the box for the aspirin in a trash can in front of the store. Neither the security guard nor the manager complied with the customer's request. After the police left with the customer, the store manager searched the supermarket unsuccessfully for the aspirin box that the guard claimed that the customer had ditched.

The customer sued the owner of the supermarket, alleging false imprisonment and several other intentional torts. A jury awarded the customer $400 in actual damages and $175,000 in punitive damages. The appellate court upheld the actual and punitive awards on the grounds that the store manager's conscious indifference and refusal to attempt to ascertain the truth as to whether the aspirin had been purchased elsewhere justified the award.

Source: Colonial Stores, Inc. v. Fishel, 288 S.E.2d 21 (Ga. App. 1981).

shown that the shopkeeper acted in good faith and the detention was made in a reasonable manner, for a reasonable time, and was based on reasonable cause.

INTENTIONAL INFLICTION OF EMOTIONAL DISTRESS The tort of *intentional infliction of emotional distress* protects the right to peace of mind. In most jurisdictions, to prove intentional infliction of emotional distress, a plaintiff must show that (1) the defendant's conduct was outrageous,

(2) the defendant intended to cause emotional distress, and (3) the defendant's actions caused severe emotional suffering.

For the tort to arise, the plaintiff's emotional distress must be foreseeable, and the defendant's acts must have been outrageous or intolerable. Insulting, abusive, profane, or annoying conduct is not in itself a tort. Everyone is expected to be hardened to a certain amount of abuse. In determining outrageousness, courts will consider the context of the tort, as well as the relationship of the parties. For example, in the workplace, the plaintiff can expect to be subjected to evaluation and criticism, and neither criticism nor discharge is in itself outrageous. Furthermore, in most jurisdictions, the plaintiff must have sought counseling. Merely being upset or depressed is insufficient.

The entrepreneur is most likely to encounter claims of intentional infliction of emotional distress in situations in which an employee complains to a supervisor about racial or sexual harassment and the employer fails to investigate the claim and take appropriate remedial action. This could also lead to claims of negligent infliction of emotional distress.

FROM THE TRENCHES

Leta Fay Ford won a suit against cosmetics manufacturer Revlon, Inc. for intentional infliction of emotional distress after company officials failed to stop ongoing harassment by her supervisor, Karl Braun.

The harassment began in April 1980 after Braun invited Ford to dinner, supposedly to discuss business. At the end of the evening, when Ford tried to leave, Braun told her to stay because he planned to spend the night with her. When she rejected his advances, he told her, "You will regret this." This was only the first of several incidents in which Braun harassed Ford, including one a month later at a company picnic where Braun held Ford in a choke hold, fondled her, and made lewd comments to her.

Although Ford had not reported the first incident to Revlon's management, after the company picnic incident she initiated a series of meetings with several members of Revlon's management to report her complaints. She told them that she was afraid of Braun, that she wanted help, and that the strain of dealing with Braun and his advances was making her sick.

continued...

FROM THE TRENCHES

continued...

The harassment continued throughout 1980 with Braun threatening to destroy Ford and promising her that as long as she worked for him she was never going to go anywhere. When Revlon's management still had taken no action by December 1980, Ford contacted the manager to whom she had complained earlier. The manager told Ford that the situation was too hot to handle and that she should put the matter in the back of her mind and try to forget about it. During the time of the harassment, Ford developed high blood pressure, a nervous tic in her left eye, chest pains, rapid breathing, and other symptoms of emotional distress.

In February 1981, Ford requested a job transfer and met with a personnel representative to try to resolve her grievance. Not until three months later did the personnel representative submit a report on Ford's complaint to a Revlon vice president. The report confirmed Ford's charge of sexual assault and recommended that Braun be censured. In May 1981, a full year and a month after Braun's initial act of harassment, Revlon issued Braun a letter of censure.

In October 1981, Ford attempted suicide. Later that month, Revlon fired Braun. In April 1982, Ford sued both Braun and Revlon for assault and battery and for intentional infliction of emotional distress.

The Arizona Supreme Court upheld a jury verdict against Revlon. Revlon's conduct in ignoring Ford's situation for months was outrageous and extreme and thus fulfilled the requirements for intentional infliction of emotional distress.

In an interesting turn on the situation involved in the Revlon case, Rajiv Malik was hired in the executive training program at Carrier Corp. During the program, several female coworkers complained that he made inappropriate sexual comments to them and that he often turned the conversation to sexual topics. Carrier investigated the sexual-harassment claims. Malik was not disciplined, but a letter of record regarding the complaints was placed in his personnel file. Malik failed to secure a position at the end of the program and was let go. He then sued Carrier for intentional infliction of emotional distress.

The court acknowledged that being accused of sexual harassment could generate a great deal of emotional distress; however, it pointed out that an employer's decision to undertake an investigation is not optional but is mandated by federal law banning sexual harassment in the workplace. Although some investigations will be baseless, to impose liability in a situation like this would undermine the federal policies underlying the requirement that employers investigate claims of sexual harassment. Malik's claim for intentional infliction of emotional distress was dismissed.

Sources: Ford v. Revlon, Inc., 734 P.2d 580 (Ariz. 1987); Malik v. Carrier Corp., 202 F.3d 97 (2d Cir. 2000).

FROM THE TRENCHES

An impostor opened numerous accounts with Internet service provider Prodigy under the false name of Alexander Lunney. The impostor then sent vulgar, obscene, and threatening e-mail messages and posted offensive material on electronic bulletin boards. Prodigy notified the real Lunney that it was closing one of his accounts due to transmission of obscene and threatening material. Lunney sued Prodigy, alleging that it was negligent in allowing accounts to be opened in his name and was responsible for defamation.

The New York Court of Appeals decided that since e-mail was the "evolutionary hybrid of traditional telephone line communications and regular postal service mail," Prodigy could not be considered a publisher, much as a telephone company is not considered a publisher of phone calls. It exercises no discretion or control over the communication and assumes no responsibility for it. Even if the service provider could be characterized as a publisher, it was entitled to the same qualified privilege available to telephone and telegraph companies. Prodigy was, therefore, not liable for defamation.

Source: Lunney v. Prodigy Serv. Co., 723 N.E.2d 539 (N.Y. 1999), cert. denied, 529 U.S. 1098 (2000).

DEFAMATION *Defamation* is the communication (often termed *publication*) to a third party of an untrue statement of fact that injures the plaintiff's reputation. *Libel* is written defamation, and *slander* is spoken defamation.

Claims of defamation in the business context often arise out of adverse comments about a former employee's performance. Fear of such claims causes many employers to refuse to act as references for former employees other than to confirm dates of employment, title, and salary.

INVASION OF PRIVACY Individuals are protected against inappropriate invasions of privacy, including public disclosure of private facts and intrusion. *Intrusion* is objectionable prying, such as eavesdropping or unauthorized rifling through files. For intrusion to be tortious, the plaintiff must have a reasonable expectation of privacy in whatever has experienced the intrusion.

FROM THE TRENCHES

In the process of putting together an exposé about contaminated blood products being shipped to Japan, a reporter for NHK, Japan's only public broadcasting corporation, arrived unexpectedly at Clyde McAuley's house and secretly taped McAuley's responses to questions with a microphone hidden under his tie. McAuley sued for invasion of privacy. The appeals court explained that an invasion of privacy has two elements: (1) intrusion into a private place, conversation, or matter (2) in a manner highly offensive to a reasonable person. It held that McAuley could reasonably expect privacy against the electronic recording of his comments, even though he had no reasonable expectation that the content of the conversation would be kept private.

The Supreme Court of California has held that when a workplace is open to regular intrusion by the public or the press, objection to press recording is less likely to be deemed reasonable.

Sources: Alpha Therapeutic Corp. v. Nippon Hoso Kyokai, 199 F.3d 078 (9th Cir. 1999); Sanders v. American Broad. Co., 978 P.2d 67 (Cal. 1999).

Torts to Protect Interests in Property

A number of torts are designed to protect interests in property. These include trespass to land, nuisance, conversion, and trespass to personal property.

TRESPASS TO LAND *Trespass to land* is an intentional invasion of real property without the consent of the owner. For example, a person driving a truck onto land belonging to another person commits trespass even if the land is not injured. The intent required is the intent to enter the property, not the intent to trespass. Thus, a person who intentionally stands on land believing that it is owned by a friend who has given consent is still liable for trespass if the land is, in fact, owned by someone else who has not given consent. The mistake as to ownership is irrelevant.

Trespass may occur both below the land's surface and in the airspace above it. Throwing something, such as trash, onto the land or shooting bullets over it may be a trespass, even though the perpetrator was not standing on the plaintiff's land.

Refusing to move something that at one time the plaintiff permitted the defendant to place on the land may be a trespass. For example, if the plaintiff gave the defendant permission to leave a forklift on the plaintiff's land for one month, and it was left for two, the defendant may be liable for trespass.

NUISANCE *Nuisance* is a nontrespassory interference with the use and enjoyment of real property, for example, by an annoying odor or noise. *Public nuisance* is unreasonable and substantial interference with the public health, safety, peace, comfort, convenience, or utilization of land. A public nuisance action is usually brought by the government. It may also be brought by a private citizen who experiences special harm different from that suffered by the general public.

Private nuisance is unreasonable and substantial interference with an individual's use and enjoyment of his or her land. Discharge of noxious fumes into the air, the pollution of a stream, or playing loud music late at night in a residential neighborhood can constitute a private nuisance.

To determine whether the defendant's conduct is unreasonable, the court will balance the utility of the activity creating the harm and the burden of preventing it against the nature and the gravity of the harm. For example, hammering noise during the remodeling of a house may be easier to justify than playing loud music purely for pleasure.

CONVERSION *Conversion* is the exercise of dominion and control over the personal property, rather than the real property, of another. This tort protects the right to have one's personal property left alone. It prevents the defendant from treating the plaintiff's property as if it were his or her own. Conversion is the tort claim a plaintiff would assert to recover the value of property stolen, destroyed, or substantially altered by the defendant.

The intent element for conversion does not include a wrongful motive. It merely requires the intent to exercise dominion or control over goods, inconsistent with the plaintiff's rights. The defendant need not know that the goods belonged to the plaintiff. If someone takes a box of computer hardware from the back of a store without paying for it, puts it in his or her car, and drives away, that is conversion.

TRESPASS TO PERSONAL PROPERTY If personal property is interfered with but not converted, there is a *trespass to personal property* (sometimes referred to as *trespass to chattels*). No wrongful motive need be shown. The intent required is the intent to exercise control over the plaintiff's personal property. For example, an employer who took an employee's car on a short errand without the employee's permission would be liable for trespass to personal property. However, if the employer damaged the car or drove it for several thousand miles, thereby lowering its value, he or she would be liable for conversion.

FROM THE TRENCHES

Bidder's Edge, Inc. (BE) is an auction aggregation site that allows online auction buyers to search for items across numerous online auction sites. Online auction leader eBay originally permitted BE to crawl the eBay site to collect information but later revoked that permission when license negotiations fell through. The eBay User Agreement expressly prohibits the use of "any robot, spider, other automatic device, or manual process to monitor or copy our web pages or the content contained therein without our prior expressed written permission." After briefly ceasing its actions, BE resumed crawling the eBay site without authorization. eBay sued for an injunction, alleging among other things, a trespass to chattels. To prevail on a trespass claim based on access to computer systems, the plaintiff must show that (1) the defendant intentionally and without authorization interfered with the plaintiff's possessory interest in the computer system, and (2) the defendant's unauthorized use proximately resulted in damage to the plaintiff.

Even though eBay's site is accessible to the public, the user agreement explicitly forbids the type of access BE engaged in. California law recognizes a trespass where the defendant exceeds the scope of the consent. The quality or value of personal property may be diminished even if it is not physically damaged by the defendant's conduct. The searches used only a very small portion of the capacity of eBay's servers but nonetheless deprived eBay of its ability to use that portion. BE was enjoined from crawling eBay's site.

Source: eBay, Inc. v. Bidder's Edge, Inc., 100 F. Supp. 2d 1058 (N.D. Cal. 2000).

Torts That Protect Certain Economic Interests and Business Relationships

Several torts are designed to protect certain economic interests and business relationships. These torts include fraudulent misrepresentation, interference with contractual relations, interference with prospective business advantage, and unfair competition.

FRAUDULENT MISREPRESENTATION The tort of *fraudulent misrepresentation,* also called *fraud* or *deceit,* protects economic interests and the right to be treated fairly and honestly. Fraud requires proof that the defendant knowingly and intentionally misled the plaintiff by making a material misrepresentation of fact on which the plaintiff justifiably relied. It also requires that the plaintiff suffer injury as a result of the reliance. For example, if entrepreneurs tell an investor that they developed certain key technology and own all rights to it when, in fact, they know that it belongs to their former employer, that is fraudulent misrepresentation.

Fraud can also be based on the defendant's omission of a material fact when he or she has a duty to speak because of a special relationship of trust with the plaintiff (a *fiduciary duty*). For example, in one case, the owner of an auto dealership, who had relied on a bank for several years for financial advice, consulted the bank about purchasing a second dealership. The bank recommended that he purchase a certain dealership but failed to tell him that the dealership was in financial straits and owed the bank money. The plaintiff took the bank's advice and bought the troubled dealership. The plaintiff suffered great financial hardship and eventually lost both dealerships after the bank refused to extend financing. The plaintiff sued the bank for fraudulent misrepresentation and won a $4.5 million verdict.

INTERFERENCE WITH CONTRACTUAL RELATIONS The tort of *interference with contractual relations* protects the right to enjoy the benefits of legally binding agreements. It provides a remedy when the defendant intentionally induces another person to breach a contract with the plaintiff. Interference with contractual relations requires that the defendant know that there is a contract.

Perhaps the most famous case involving tortious interference with a contract was *Pennzoil v. Texaco.* A jury assessed Texaco $10.5 billion in damages for interfering with Pennzoil's contract to buy Getty Oil. Texaco offered Getty

Oil a better price and agreed to indemnify Getty Oil if it was sued by Pennzoil for breach of contract.[6] The case was ultimately settled for $3 billion.

In some jurisdictions, interference with contractual relations requires an unacceptable purpose; if good grounds exist for the interference, the defendant is not liable. For example, if a manager of a corporation is incompetent, a shareholder of a corporation may be able to induce breach of the employment agreement between the manager and the corporation. The shareholder's motive would be to protect his or her investment. On the other hand, a defendant may not interfere with another person's contract in order to attract customers or employees away from that person.

INTERFERENCE WITH PROSPECTIVE BUSINESS ADVANTAGE Courts are less willing to award damages for interference with prospective contracts than they are to protect existing contracts. A party still engaged in negotiating a contract has fewer rights not to have a deal disturbed than a party that has already entered into a contract.

To prove *interference with prospective business advantage,* the plaintiff must prove that the defendant unjustifiably interfered with a relationship the plaintiff sought to develop and that the interference caused the plaintiff's loss. The interference must be intentional. In rare cases, however, courts have permitted recovery if the defendant was merely negligent.

Interference with prospective business advantage is usually committed by a competitor or at least by one who stands to benefit from the interference. However, it is not a tort to compete fairly. Most jurisdictions recognize a privilege to act for one's own financial gain.

UNFAIR COMPETITION Courts are willing to find certain kinds of anticompetitive behavior actionable if the activities complained of seem egregious and predatory to the court. These cases fall under the rubric of *unfair competition.* The improper use of trade secrets and customer information of prior employers often is found to constitute unfair competition. Also, destroying a business by hiring away all of its employees has been deemed unfair competition. Unfair competition is discussed more fully in Chapter 9.

FROM THE TRENCHES

Two employees of AMCOA, the general manager and the chief engineer from two divisions, left the company to join a competitor. Prior to leaving, one had prepared a list showing all jobs bid by AMCOA that totaled more than $10,000. He also had prepared a list of recently completed jobs, showing customers, type of materials, and dollar amount. During the two days immediately following the resignations, the two former employees called virtually all of the sales representatives of AMCOA throughout the country to inform them of their resignation and to tell them that either the competitor would buy AMCOA or the two former employees would start their own company. Sales representatives were informed that a majority of the representatives were canceling their contracts with AMCOA and signing on with the competitor. The competing firm placed bids on jobs on which the former employees had prepared preliminary specifications for AMCOA. Additionally, the former employees contacted key personnel of AMCOA on behalf of the competitor. The former employees informed the key personnel that AMCOA was a sinking ship and would not be in business long, and they expressed the belief that they would be able to hire away AMCOA's entire sales force for the competitor.

AMCOA sued the competitor and the two former employees. The court held that the destruction or substantial injury of a business, by attracting away all or a large percentage of the personnel on whom the business depends, is unfair competition and compensable, even in the case of at-will employees, especially if other circumstances, such as misrepresentation of the plaintiff's solvency to the plaintiff's employees or customers or misappropriation of confidential information, are involved.

Source: Architectural Mfg. Co. v. Airotec, Inc., 166 S.E.2d 744 (Ga. App. 1969).

Strict Liability

Strict liability is liability without fault, that is, without negligence or intent. Strict liability is imposed in product liability cases and for ultrahazardous activities. (Strict liability for defective products is discussed in Chapter 9.)

Ultrahazardous Activities

If the defendant's activity is *ultrahazardous,* that is, so dangerous that no amount of care could protect others from the risk of harm, the defendant is strictly liable for any injuries that result from the activity. Courts have found the following activities to be ultrahazardous: (1) storing flammable liquids in quantity in an urban area, (2) pile driving, (3) blasting, (4) crop dusting, (5) fumigation with cyanide gas, (6) emission of noxious fumes by a manufacturing plant located in a settled area, (7) locating oil wells or refineries in populated communities, and (8) test-firing solid-fuel rocket motors. However, courts have considered parachuting, drunk driving, maintaining power lines, and letting water escape from an irrigation ditch not to be ultrahazardous. A court is more likely to consider a dangerous activity ultrahazardous when it is inappropriate to the particular location.

Under strict liability, once the court determines that the activity is abnormally dangerous, it is irrelevant that the defendant observed a high standard of care. For example, if the defendant's blasting injured the plaintiff, it is irrelevant that the defendant took every precaution available. Although evidence of such precautions might prevent the plaintiff from recovering under a theory of negligence, it does not affect strict liability. Strict liability for ultrahazardous activities makes it imperative that a company have liability insurance covering such activities.

Toxic Torts

Since the 1970s, tort law has been evolving in response to sustained social and political concern over toxic substances and their potential for personal injury and environmental and property damage. A *toxic tort* is a wrongful act that causes injury by exposure to a harmful, hazardous, or poisonous substance. Modern industrial and consumer society uses these substances in a variety of ways, creating countless opportunities for toxic tort claims.

Potential toxic tort defendants include manufacturers (1) that use substances that may injure an employee, a consumer, or a bystander; (2) whose processes emit hazardous by-products into the air or discharge them into a river; (3) whose waste material goes to a disposal site if the waste could migrate to the groundwater and contaminate nearby wells; and (4) whose products contain or create substances that can injure. Liability is not limited to manufacturers, however. Everyday activities of governmental agencies, distribution services, and consumers may provide a basis for toxic tort claims. Some substances once thought to be safe, such as asbestos, have resulted in ruinous litigation when it was later established that they were harmful. Owners of so-called sick buildings have been sued for negligence because of substances present in their buildings. Even financial institutions can be caught in the toxic tort net by becoming involved in the operations of a company handling hazardous materials or by foreclosing on contaminated land held as collateral and continuing to hold it for an unreasonably long period of time.

Open-ended claims for punitive damages are commonplace in toxic tort cases. When pursuing a toxic tort claim, plaintiffs typically allege intentional torts, such as trespass, intentional infliction of emotional distress, and outrageous or despicable conduct, as well as negligence.

Vicarious Tort Liability and *Respondeat Superior*

Under the doctrine of *respondeat superior*—"let the master answer"—an employer is vicariously liable for the torts of an employee acting within the scope of his or her employment. The employer is liable even if the employer had no knowledge of the actions or had instructed the employee not to do the wrongful act. For example, a pizza company will be liable if its delivery person hits someone while speeding to deliver a pizza on time, even if the manager had instructed the employee not to speed.

Scope of the Employment

Activities within the scope of employment are activities closely connected to what the employee is employed to do or reasonably incidental to it. Generally, an employee's conduct is considered within the scope of employment if it (1) is of the nature that he or she was employed to perform; (2) is within the time and space limitations normally authorized by the employer; and (3) furthers, at least in part, the purpose of the employer.

On the other hand, an employer is generally not vicariously liable if an employee commits a tort while engaged in an activity solely for his or her own benefit. Unfortunately, it is often unclear whether the employee's act was entirely outside the employer's purpose.

The law draws a distinction between a frolic and a detour. A *frolic* occurs when an employee goes off and does something for himself or herself that is unrelated to the employer's business. A *detour* occurs when an employee temporarily interrupts his or her work to do something for himself or herself. Although the law holds an employer responsible for an employee's torts occurring during a detour, an employer is not responsible for a frolic. For example, if an employee leaves work to run a personal errand and in the process hits someone with his or her car, it is a frolic. If, however, the employer sends the employee to drive and pick something up and the employee runs a personal errand along the way, then it is a detour, and the employer will be liable for any torts committed by the employee, including those committed during the portion of the trip relating to the personal matter.

If an employee intentionally causes injury to the plaintiff or the plaintiff's property, an employer may still be liable if the wrongful act in any way furthered the employer's purpose, however misguided the manner of furthering that purpose. For example, if an employee of a financially troubled company misrepresents the company's financial condition to obtain a bank loan needed for working capital, the employer will be liable for fraud.

Aided-in-the-Agency-Relation Doctrine

Under the *aided-in-the-agency-relation doctrine,* an employer can be vicariously liable for a tort committed by an employee acting outside the scope of employment if the authority of the employer made it possible for the employee to commit the tort. For example, as discussed further in Chapter 10, if a supervisor fires a subordinate because the subordinate rejected the supervisor's sexual advances, then the employer is liable for sexual harassment even if the employer had no reason to know that the supervisor was harassing the subordinate.

FROM THE TRENCHES

Bucher was employed as a priest by the Franciscan Friars of California, Inc. and the Archdiocese of Portland, Oregon. While acting as a youth pastor, he committed a series of sexual assaults on Fearing, a minor. Fearing later sued the Archdiocese for sexual assault. The assaults were clearly outside the scope of Bucher's employment, but the Oregon Supreme Court held that the Archdiocese could still be liable if acts within the scope of Bucher's employment resulted in the acts causing the plaintiff's injury. Because Bucher's role as pastor and spiritual guide enabled him to gain the family's trust and confidence and to spend large quantities of time alone with the minor, a jury could infer that his employment as a pastor was a necessary precursor to the sexual assaults. As a result, the Archdiocese could be held liable for Bucher's sexual assaults.

Comment: In 2001 and 2002, the Archdiocese of Boston was rocked by a series of lawsuits against priests accused of molesting young boys. As of mid-2002, the Archdiocese had paid or agreed to pay more than $100 million to settle the cases.

Sources: Fearing v. Bucher, 977 P.2d 1163 (Or. 1998); Walter V. Robinson, Diocese, Plaintiffs Settle Suit, Boston Globe, Mar. 12, 2002, at A1.

Tort Remedies

Tort damages are intended to compensate the plaintiff for the harm caused by the defendant. In egregious cases, the plaintiff may be able to recover punitive damages as well as compensatory damages. If monetary damages are not sufficient, then a court may impose equitable relief.

Actual Damages

Actual damages, also known as *compensatory damages,* are based on the cost to repair or replace an item, or the decrease in market value caused by the tortious conduct. Actual damages may also include compensation for medical expenses, lost wages, and pain and suffering.

Punitive Damages

Punitive damages (also called *exemplary damages*) may be awarded to punish the defendant and deter others from engaging in similar conduct. Punitive damages are awarded only in cases of outrageous misconduct. The amount of punitive damages may properly be based on the defendant's wealth and, in most jurisdictions, must be proportional to the actual damages. Several states have limited punitive damage awards to situations in which the plaintiff can prove by clear and convincing evidence that the defendant was guilty of oppression, fraud, or malice.

Equitable Relief

If a money award cannot adequately compensate for the plaintiff's loss, courts may grant *equitable relief*. For example, the court may issue an

FROM THE TRENCHES

In a well-publicized case that has become the poster child for tort reform, an eighty-two-year-old woman was awarded almost $2.9 million by a jury for the third-degree burns she suffered after spilling her McDonald's coffee in her lap while she was a passenger in a car stopped at a McDonald's drive-thru window. The verdict consisted of $160,000 in compensatory damages and $2.7 million in punitive damages. The trial judge subsequently reduced the punitive damages to $480,000.

McDonald's served its coffee at between 180 and 190 degrees on the advice of a coffee consultant, who claimed that coffee tastes best at that temperature. Coffee brewed at home is typically between 135 and 140 degrees. McDonald's acknowledged that it had previously received 700 complaints of scalding. After the parties reached an out-of-court settlement for an undisclosed amount, McDonald's lowered the temperature of its coffee. The *Wall Street Journal* faulted McDonald's for, among other things, failing to offer the apology the plaintiff had requested early on.

Sources: Coffee Spill Burns Woman; Jury Awards $2.9 Million, Wall St. J., Aug. 19, 1994, at B3; Coffee Case a Hot Topic; Facts Cool Debate, Hartford Courant, Apr. 10, 1995, at A5.

injunction, that is, a court order, prohibiting the defendant from continuing in a certain course of activity. This remedy is particularly appropriate for torts such as trespass or nuisance, when the plaintiff wants the defendant to stop doing something. The court may also issue an injunction ordering the defendant to do something. For example, a newspaper found liable for defamation could be ordered to publish a retraction.

Tort Liability of Multiple Defendants

The plaintiff may name numerous defendants in a liability action. In some cases, the defendants may ask the court to join, or add, other defendants. As a result, when a court determines what liability exists, it must grapple with the problem of allocating the losses among multiple defendants.

Joint and Several Liability

Under the doctrine of *joint and several liability,* multiple defendants are jointly (i.e., collectively) liable and also severally (i.e., individually) liable. This means that once the court determines that multiple defendants are at fault, the plaintiff may collect the entire judgment from any one of them, regardless of that defendant's degree of fault. Thus, a defendant who played a minor role in causing the plaintiff's injury might be required to pay all the damages. This is particularly likely when only one defendant is solvent and able to pay.

Joint and several liability often is imposed in toxic tort cases when a number of companies might have contributed to the contaminated site, such as a landfill or a river. Frequently, the company with deep pockets ends up having to pay for all the harm done the plaintiff. Some states have adopted statutes to limit the doctrine of joint and several liability.

Contribution and Indemnification

The doctrines of contribution and indemnification can mitigate the harsh effects of joint and several liability. *Contribution* distributes the loss among several defendants by requiring each to pay its proportionate share (often based on their relative fault) to the defendant that discharged the joint liability. *Indemnification* allows a defendant to shift some of its individual loss to other defendants whose relative blame is greater. These other defendants can be ordered to reimburse the one that has discharged the joint liability.

The right to contribution and indemnification is worthless to a defendant, however, if all the other defendants are insolvent or lack sufficient assets to contribute their share. In such a case, the defendant with money must still pay the plaintiff the full amount of damages awarded even though the other defendants will not be able to reimburse the solvent defendant for their share of the damages.

Antitrust Violations

Section 1 of the Sherman Act provides that "[e]very contract, combination in the form of trust or otherwise, or conspiracy, in restraint of trade or commerce among the several States, or with foreign nations, is declared to be illegal." Although Section 1 appears to prohibit any and all concerted activity that restrains trade, the courts have construed Section 1 to prohibit only those restraints of trade that *unreasonably* restrict competition. Violations of Section 1 may be prosecuted as felonies. In addition, private plaintiffs or state attorneys general acting on behalf of citizens in their states can recover treble damages in civil cases.

Contract, Combination, or Conspiracy

Agreements can be *horizontal,* that is, between firms that directly compete with one another, such as two automakers; or *vertical,* that is, between firms at different levels of production or distribution, such as a retailer and a manufacturer. In general, courts view horizontal agreements much more harshly than vertical agreements, because they reduce *interbrand competition,* that is, competition among manufacturers selling different brands of the same product. As a result, they are more likely to result in higher prices for consumers. In contrast, a vertical restraint, such as a manufacturer's requirement that a distributor sell the manufacturer's products in only a particular geographic location, may limit *intrabrand competition* (that is, competition among distributors selling the same brand product) but increase interbrand competition (and thereby reduce prices) by creating a stronger distribution network.

Per se Violations of Section 1

Per se analysis condemns practices that are considered completely void of redeeming competitive rationales. This is appropriate when the practice always or almost always tends to restrict competition and harm consumers. Once identified as *illegal per se,* a practice need not be examined further for its impact on the market, and its procompetitive justifications will not be considered. Law and Economics scholars have argued, however, that very few practices are inherently anticompetitive. Because the U.S. Supreme Court has generally been receptive to this scholarship, the number of truly *per se* violations of the antitrust laws has declined.

HORIZONTAL PRICE-FIXING The classic example of a *per se* violation of Section 1 is horizontal price-fixing. *Horizontal price-fixing agreements* include agreements between competitors (1) setting minimum prices; (2) setting the terms of sale, such as customer credit terms; and (3) setting the quantity or quality of goods to be manufactured or made available for sale. *Bid rigging,* agreements between or among competitors to rig contract bids, is also a form of horizontal price-fixing.

Even start-ups are prohibited from engaging in horizontal price-fixing. It is illegal *per se* even if none of the parties involved has a significant share of the market. The U.S. Justice Department views price-fixing as "hard crime" to be punished by prison sentences.

HORIZONTAL MARKET DIVISION *Market divisions,* whereby competitors divide up a market according, for example, to a class of consumers or geographic territory, are *per se* violations of Section 1. Market division is prohibited even if it is intended to enable small competitors to compete with larger companies and to foster interbrand competition.

GROUP BOYCOTTS An agreement among competitors to refuse to deal with another competitor—a *group boycott*—is also a *per se* violation of Section 1. An agreement between or among competitors that deprives another com-

FROM THE TRENCHES

A recent example of horizontal price-fixing involved the world's leading auction houses, Christie's International PLC and Sotheby's Holding. The two colluded to enter into economic agreements, including identical sliding-scale fee commission structures. Christie's and Sotheby's agreed to pay $537 million to settle civil suits by former sellers. Sotheby's former chairman, Alfred Taubman, and the former chairman of Christie's, Sir Anthony J. Tennant, were indicted in May 2001. Tennant escaped prosecution because he lives in England, where only companies, not individuals, can be charged with price-fixing. Seventy-eight-year-old Taubman was found guilty and sentenced to one year and a day in prison and $7.5 million in fines. Sotheby's chief executive, Diana D. Brooks, pled guilty to one felony count of conspiring to fix prices but received a reduced sentence of three years' probation (including six months of home confinement), a $350,000 fine, and 1,000 hours of community service because she testified against Taubman.

Source: Ex-President of Sotheby's Gets Probation, L.A. Times, April 30, 2002, at 12.

petitor of something it needs to compete effectively is considered so inherently anticompetitive that no economic motivation may be offered as a defense. For example, manufacturers of different brands of appliances could not agree with a particular distributor's competitors to refuse to sell their appliances to the distributor or to do so at a higher price.

Restraints on Trade Subject to the Rule of Reason

If the plaintiff has not proved that a restraint on trade is a *per se* violation, then the activity will be evaluated under the rule of reason. The objective of the *rule of reason* is to determine whether, on balance, the activity promotes or restrains competition or, to put it differently, whether it helps or harms consumers. In making this determination, the court will consider the structure of the market as well as the defendant's conduct. The court will analyze the anticompetitive and procompetitive effects of the challenged practice. Activity that has a substantial net anticompetitive effect is deemed an unreasonable restraint of trade and hence is unlawful.

FROM THE TRENCHES

The Chicago *Daily Herald* sued the *Chicago Tribune* for entering into an agreement with the New York Times News Service, whereby the *Chicago Tribune* was given the exclusive right to publish the *New York Times* crossword and certain other features in the Chicago area for a period of one year. The U.S. Court of Appeals for the Seventh Circuit applied the rule of reason and concluded that the exclusive distributorship arrangement was not an unreasonable restraint of trade. It was of short duration, and other (albeit less famous) crossword puzzles were available to the *Daily Herald*. Exclusive stories and features help newspapers differentiate themselves and thereby better compete with one another. The court noted that the *Herald* had never tried to make a better offer to obtain the right to carry the *New York Times* features and suggested that it "should try to outbid the *Tribune* and *Sun-Times* in the marketplace, rather than to outmaneuver them in court."

Source: Paddock Publ'g, Inc. v. Chicago Tribune Co., 103 F.3d 42 (7th Cir. 1996), cert. denied, 520 U.S. 1265 (1997).

For example, although minimum price-fixing is *per se* illegal, maximum price-fixing is subject to the rule of reason. Vertical restraints are also judged by the rule of reason. *Exclusive dealing arrangements*, whereby a party agrees to sell its products only to select buyers, are also subject to the rule of reason. As a general matter, such arrangements are more likely to be upheld if they are of limited duration and do not foreclose a major share of the market.

Monopolization

Section 2 of the Sherman Act prohibits monopolization or attempts to monopolize. A firm does not violate Section 2 merely by having a major share of the market; that may be the result of the firm's superior business foresight, skill, or acumen. To violate Section 2, a firm must have *market power* (generally defined as the ability to raise prices without losing market share) and have engaged in anticompetitive acts (such as predatory pricing or exclusive dealing).

FROM THE TRENCHES

Responding, in part, to substantial encouragement and support from Netscape (creator of the first widely used Internet browser Netscape Navigator) and other companies in Silicon Valley, the U.S. Justice Department and nineteen states brought a wide-ranging suit against Microsoft Corp. for (1) maintaining a monopoly in the market for Intel-compatible personal computer (PC) operating systems; (2) attempted monopolization of the Internet browser market; and (3) illegal tying of two separate products, Windows and Microsoft's Internet Explorer.

On appeal, the U.S. Court of Appeals for the District of Columbia Circuit upheld the finding that Microsoft had illegally maintained its monopoly of the Intel-compatible PC operating system market. The appeals court rejected the finding of attempted monopolization of the browser market and ordered the trial court to reconsider the tying claim under a much tougher test for liability that required the plaintiffs to prove, under the rule of reason, that the anticompetitive costs to consumers of impairing their ability to make direct price/quality trade-offs in the browser market outweighed the procompetitive advantages of product integration. The appeals court also rejected the trial court's remedy, which would have required the breakup of Microsoft into two companies—one to produce and license Windows and the other to produce and license the applications software, such as Microsoft Office and Internet Explorer.

Thereafter, the U.S. Justice Department and a majority of the states involved in the suit agreed to drop their request for the breakup of Microsoft and instead sought so-called conduct remedies designed to prevent Microsoft from engaging in illegal practices in the future. As of February 2002, the case was back in the hands of U.S. District Court Judge Colleen Kollar-Kotelly to fashion a suitable remedy.

On the strength of the factual findings by the trial court and the conclusions of law and fact upheld by the appeals court, several of Microsoft's competitors brought private civil antitrust suits in early 2002, seeking treble damages as well as injunctive relief. Foremost among them was Netscape, now a part of AOL TimeWarner. Sun Microsystems, creator of the Java programming language, has sued for potentially billions of dollars in damages and is also requesting sweeping controls over the conduct of various aspects of Microsoft's operations, including an injunction requiring Microsoft to disclose technical information earlier so that competitors can make compatible programs and enjoining Microsoft from bundling certain products.

continued...

FROM THE TRENCHES

continued...

Sources: United States v. Microsoft Corp., 253 F.3d 34 (D.C. Cir. 2001); Lee Gomes & Nicholas Kulish, Sun Fights Microsoft in Court Yet Again, Wall St. J., Mar. 11, 2002, at B5. See also Constance E. Bagley, Note on Application of the Antitrust Laws to the New Economy: An Analysis of United States v. Microsoft Corporation, Harvard Business School Note No. 802-090 (Sept. 20, 2001). For an interesting analysis of the financial performance of Microsoft during the period it was found to have exercised undue market power, see William A. Sahlman, Financial Analysis of Microsoft, Harv. Bus. Sch. Note No. N9–802–194 (Mar. 1, 2002).

Although most young firms do not have sufficient market power to be monopolists, they may well be competing against larger firms that do have market power. If the larger firm also engages in anticompetitive acts, then its smaller rivals may be able to invoke Section 2 to require the larger rival to compete more fairly.

Environmental Liabilities

CERCLA

As mentioned in Chapter 8, the Comprehensive Environmental Response, Compensation and Liability Act (CERCLA) provides that certain "responsible parties" are strictly liable for the cleanup of hazardous waste, namely, (1) the current owners or operators of a facility, (2) the owners or operators at the time the hazardous substances were disposed of, (3) the transporters of hazardous substances to a facility if they selected the facility, and (4) persons who arranged for treatment or disposal of hazardous substances at a facility.

Owners include the current fee owners and past owners at the time of disposal. Most importantly, owners can include lessees with attributes of ownership. The term *operators* also may include lessees with authority to control the facility, but liability extends only to the portion they lease.[7]

In the absence of any of the defenses outlined below, these parties are liable for response costs, including investigation and cleanup costs, administrative costs, legal costs, and prejudgment interest to the government.

The cleanup liabilities are retroactive, strict (that is, without fault), and generally joint and several. As one can imagine, an assessment and action by the Environmental Protection Agency (EPA) under CERCLA can be financially crippling to a new venture.

For example, suppose a start-up signs a triple net lease with the owner of a warehouse to rent space in the warehouse. A *triple net lease* requires the lessee to pay all taxes, insurance, and maintenance costs. The lease is sufficient to give the start-up the attributes of ownership. If it turns out that the warehouse site contains hazardous substances and the EPA designates the site for cleanup, then the EPA can sue the start-up as well as the owner of the building for the response costs and can collect all of them from the start-up under joint and several liability.

Defenses

There are three defenses to liability: an otherwise responsible party is not liable if the contamination was caused by (1) an act of God, (2) an act of war, or (3) the act of a third party. The first two are self-explanatory and rarely available. To establish the third-party defense (also referred to as the *innocent landowner defense*), a defendant must have taken precautions and used due care. In particular, an owner may be relieved of cleanup liability if (1) the owner acquired the property after the disposal occurred, (2) had no actual knowledge of the contamination when it acquired the property, and (3) had no reason to know of the contamination after conducting all appropriate inquiry into the previous ownership and uses of the property consistent with good commercial or customary practice in an effort to minimize liability.

In evaluating the adequacy of the landowner's due diligence, courts consider (1) the specialized knowledge or experience of the landowner, (2) the relationship of the purchase price to the property's value if uncontaminated (be wary of too good a deal), (3) commonly known or reasonably ascertainable information about the property, (4) the obviousness of the contamination, (5) the ability to detect contamination by appropriate inspection, and (6) the levels of inquiry conducted at the time the property was acquired.

Before buying property or entering into a net lease, the company must conduct some investigation into the site in accordance with ASTM International standards. For sites without any known industrial or commercial use, a simple questionnaire based on a site visit, interviews, and government records checks by nonprofessionals may suffice. If there has been known industrial or commercial use, then a Phase I Environmental Site Assessment (ESA) is called for. A Phase I is performed by an environmental professional, who conducts record searches, site reconnaissance, and interviews and then prepares a report. If the Phase I ESA does not identify a Recognized Environmental Condition (REC), then a Phase II ESA may not be required. If there is a potential problem, however, a Phase II ESA should be conducted.

In a Phase II, a qualified professional does media sampling to investigate RECs identified in the Phase I. If the professional states that there is no reasonable basis for suspecting a disposal or release, then the innocent landowner defense should be available.

Failure to follow these standards will not automatically cripple a defense. Instead, courts will analyze the factors identified above. Companies should also purchase pollution legal liability (PLL) insurance to cover the risk of CERCLA liability.

RCRA

Any person who generates hazardous waste has "cradle to grave" responsibility for its ultimate proper disposal under the Resource Conservation Responsibility Act (RCRA). Potentially liable parties include (1) the generators of the waste; (2) the persons who arrange for its transport, treatment, or disposal; (3) the transporters of the waste; and (4) the persons who treat and dispose of it.

Personal Liability of Operators

Under both CERCLA and RCRA, the individuals responsible for operating a facility that generates hazardous waste are potentially personally liable for violations. This means that they can be fined or even sent to prison for knowing violations. In some cases, courts will apply the *responsible corporate officer doctrine* and hold an officer liable for the misdeeds of a subordinate. This makes appropriate training of personnel and monitoring all the more important.

Bribery and the Foreign Corrupt Practices Act

Bribes

The Foreign Corrupt Practices Act (FCPA) prohibits any payments by a U.S. company or a non-U.S. company controlled by a U.S. company, or its employees or agents, to a foreign government official or a foreign political party for the purpose of improperly influencing government decisions. The statute is violated even if the bribe is only offered and is never paid. It is also illegal to make a payment to a private party with actual knowledge, or willful disregard of the fact, that it will be funneled to a foreign government official or a foreign political party.

An exception is made for payments to low-ranking officials who merely expedite the nondiscretionary granting of a permit or license. A second exception is made for payments to foreign businesses, subject to the funneling caveat mentioned above.

Record-Keeping Provisions

The FCPA has record-keeping provisions that apply to all public companies that file periodic reports with the Securities and Exchange Commission under the Securities Exchange Act of 1934. Every public company must keep records that accurately reflect the dispositions of the company's assets and implement internal controls to ensure that its transactions are completed as authorized by management. Failure to maintain the appropriate records is a violation, irrespective of whether a bribe is paid.

Even a purely domestic public company that is not engaged in foreign trade must comply with the FCPA's record-keeping requirements, which are designed to prevent companies from setting up a slush fund and then accounting for questionable payments as legitimate business expenses.

Tax Fraud

Certain violations of the Internal Revenue Code are subject to criminal penalties. The strictest penalties are found in Section 7201, which prohibits willful attempts to evade taxes imposed under the code, including employee withholding requirements. Section 7206 forbids any false statements in a tax return, and Section 7207 prohibits the willful delivery of a fraudulent return to the secretary of the treasury.

Section 6672 imposes civil liability for a penalty equal to the amount of a corporation's unpaid federal employment taxes on those with the power and responsibility for seeing that the taxes withheld from various sources are remitted to the government in a timely fashion. The bottom line for entrepreneurs is that they should never use the taxes withheld from employees' paychecks to meet a cash crunch. The penalties can be severe and personal.

Wire and Mail Fraud

The Wire and Mail Fraud Acts prohibit (1) a scheme intended to defraud or to obtain money or property by fraudulent means and (2) the use of the mails or of interstate telephone lines in furtherance of the fraudulent scheme. The U.S. Supreme Court has broadly construed fraud to encompass everything designed to defraud by representations as to the past or present, or suggestions and promises as to the future.[8] Almost all white-collar criminal prosecutions include a count for violation of these Acts. This strengthens the plea bargaining power of the government and increases the likelihood of a conviction on at least one count.

Computer Crime and the CFAA

Computer fraud is the use of a computer to steal company or government funds. This type of theft generally involves improper or unauthorized access to the computer system and the creation of false data or computer instructions.

The Computer Fraud and Abuse Act (CFAA) prohibits (1) accessing a computer without authorization, if by such access the user obtains in-

FROM THE TRENCHES

Wayne T. Schmuck, a used-car distributor, purchased used cars, rolled back their odometers, and sold them to Wisconsin retail dealers at prices artificially inflated by the low mileage readings. The unwitting dealers, relying on the altered readings, resold the cars to customers at inflated prices. The dealers consummated their transactions by mailing title application forms to the state authorities on behalf of the buyers. The U.S. Supreme Court held that mailing the title forms satisfied the mailing element of mail fraud even though the mailings were merely incidental to the scheme to defraud.

Source: Schmuck v. United States, 489 U.S. 705 (1989).

formation from any protected computer and if the conduct involves an interstate or foreign communication; or (2) knowingly transmitting a program, information, code, or command that results in intentionally causing "damage" without authorization to a protected computer. *Damage* is defined as any impairment to the integrity or availability of data, a program, a system, or information. If the computer fraud perpetrated by the defendant was committed for commercial advantage or private gain, or if the value of the information obtained by the fraud exceeds $5,000, the defendant is subject to up to five years of imprisonment and/or a fine of up to $250,000 or up to twice the amount of the defendant's gross gain or the victim's gross loss for the offense. Violations that result in obtaining information worth less than $5,000 are misdemeanors.

The CFAA also makes it illegal to knowingly transmit computer viruses. A *computer virus* is a computer program that can replicate itself into other programs without any subsequent instruction, human or mechanical. A computer virus may destroy data, programs, or files, or it may prevent user access to a computer (*denial-of-service attacks*). The proliferation of computer networks has created millions of entry points for viruses, and they can be quite destructive. Even if a virus is benign or temporary, knowingly transmitting it is illegal.

Computer piracy is the theft or misuse of computer software in violation of the licensing agreement. Congress amended the Copyright Act in 1980 to cover computer software. Most states have made the theft of computer software a crime as well. Entrepreneurs should be sure they have purchased the software they use on their networks and are in compliance with any end user licensing agreements.

INSURANCE

The insurance markets have evolved to a point where entrepreneurs can insure against most risks (other than fraud or other intentional wrongdoing) if they are willing to pay a premium to a sophisticated insurer. Entrepreneurs should make certain that the company's insurance broker adequately understands the risks associated with the business and has put in place insurance sufficient to cover those risks. Insurance is generally divided between first-party insurance and third-party insurance, and it is prudent for a new business to carry both.

First-Party Insurance

First-party insurance protects the policyholder in the case of damage or loss to the insured or its property. For example, a standard property owner's policy insures against loss due to fire, theft, or flood but not against structural damage due to termite infestation. Business interruption insurance insures against lost revenues and profits resulting from an earthquake or other event that interferes with the normal conduct of business.

Liability Insurance

A *third-party* or *liability policy* typically insures against liabilities arising out of the conduct of the business, such as damages arising out of slip-and-fall cases, automobile accidents, or product defects. At a minimum, it is recommended that entrepreneurs carry third-party insurance for product liability and premises liability. The publisher of a newspaper would most likely also insure against lawsuits for defamation.

Typically, a liability policy will provide that the insurance company will also bear the costs of defending any tort litigation against the insured and will pay damages up to the limits of the policy. As a matter of public policy, however, punitive damages are uninsurable because they are intended to punish a party for its practices.

Directors and officers might be provided insurance to protect them against claims by shareholders and others for breach of fiduciary duty or negligence. Certain claims are often excluded, such as claims under ERISA, the legislation dealing with employee pension plans. Sometimes special endorsements are available, such as coverage for employment-related claims (such as wrongful termination, discrimination, or sexual harassment) or for securities law claims arising out of a public offering.

Liability policies are usually either "claims based" or "occurrence based," and the distinction can make the difference between coverage and no coverage. Under a claims-based policy, the insured must report the claim to the insurance carrier while the policy is still in effect. Claims made after the end of the policy period are not covered. An occurrence-based policy covers claims arising out of events that occurred during the policy period even if a claim is not asserted until after the policy expired. For example, suppose that a customer slipped and fell on an icy sidewalk on January 2, 2002, but did not inform the property owner until May 15, 2002. If the property owner had a claim-based policy terminating on May 2, 2002, there would be no coverage. By the same token, if the property owner had an occurrence-based policy commencing May 1, 2002, there would be no coverage because the accident giving rise to the claim occurred before that date. Under certain circumstances, it is possible to purchase "tail coverage," which extends the period of time during which claims may be asserted.

Implied Duty of Good Faith and Fair Dealing

Entrepreneurs should be wary of insurance company tactics when the suit is for an amount far greater than the policy size. The insurance company may have little incentive to settle for an amount at the policy cap because it is going to pay the maximum it faces anyway. Hence, the insurance company may be inclined to roll the dice and let the case go to trial because, in the event of

FROM THE TRENCHES

Plaintiff Pavia sued for injuries from an auto collision caused by the defendant who was insured by State Farm. The plaintiff offered to settle the case for the full policy limit of $100,000 if settlement occurred within thirty days. State Farm, which was defending on behalf of the defendant, missed the deadline but subsequently offered to settle for the full policy amount. The plaintiff then refused to settle for the $100,000 amount, went to trial, and won a verdict that was later reduced to $3.8 million. The defendant had no assets to satisfy the excess $3.7 million verdict and so assigned his tort claim against the insurance company to the victorious plaintiff, who then sued State Farm for refusing to settle in "bad faith." The court found that the proper test was not negligence, because it was likely the insurance company was negligent in failing to settle, or sinister motives. The proper legal standard was "gross disregard" for the insured; thus, to win the bad-faith claim, the plaintiff had to establish that the defendant insurer engaged in a pattern of behavior evincing a conscious or knowing indifference to the probability that the insured would be held personally accountable for a large judgment if a settlement offer within the policy limits was not accepted. The court found that State Farm's conduct in this case did not rise to that level.

Source: Pavia v. State Farm Mutual Auto. Ins. Co., 626 N.E.2d 24 (N.Y. 1993).

an adverse verdict, it is liable for the damages only up to the policy cap. The insured is on the hook for the rest of the damages. Consequently, the interests of the insured and the insurer may diverge during settlement discussions. Most jurisdictions impose on insurance companies an implied duty of good faith and fair dealing. Failure to satisfy that duty can result in punitive damages. Jurisdictions vary in what they consider sufficiently egregious behavior by an insurance company to constitute a violation of this duty. Courts in California are far more likely to find a breach of the duty and award punitive damages than courts in most other states.

Risk Management

A program of overall risk management and reduction is essential to reduce potential tort and regulatory liability. It is often desirable to designate one person to be in charge of risk management. That person will keep track of all claims and determine what areas of company activity merit special attention. The head of risk management should be free to report incidents and problems to the chief executive officer and the board of directors, in much the same way as an internal auditor reports directly to the independent directors on the audit committee. This protocol enhances independence and reduces the fear of reprisals if the risk manager blows the whistle on high-ranking officers.

Reducing Tort Risks

The entrepreneur should implement ongoing programs of education and monitoring to reduce the risks of tort liability. Because torts can be committed in numerous ways, the programs should cover all possible sources of liability. For example, if a company's management does not respond satisfactorily to an allegation of racial discrimination, the managers may be liable for intentional infliction of emotional distress. False statements made by representatives of a company about a competitor can constitute defamation.

In addition to preventing intentional torts such as these, employers should work to prevent their employees from committing acts of negligence, which can lead to large damage awards against the company. Any tort prevention program must recognize that, under the principle of *respondeat superior,* employers will be held liable for any torts their employees commit within the scope of their employment. Thus, it is crucial to define the scope of employment clearly.

Entrepreneurs should use care to avoid committing torts that are related to contractual relations and competition with other firms. For example, a company may be held liable for interference with contractual relations if it intentionally induces an employee to breach an enforceable covenant not to compete with a prior employer.

Although competition itself is permissible, intentionally seeking to sabotage the efforts of another firm is not. Managers should consult counsel when they are unsure whether their activity has crossed the line from permissible competition to tortious interference with a prospective business advantage.

In the toxic torts area, companies should adopt a long-term policy to protect employees, customers, and the environment from excess toxic exposure. They should identify any hazardous toxic substances used in their business activities or products or released into the environment. When appropriate, companies should test and monitor to determine levels of exposure. Often it is necessary to obtain an expert assessment of the hazards of toxicity of these substances. In some cases, companies can reduce their possible toxic tort exposure by substituting less hazardous materials.

Putting it into Practice

Kendra was sitting in her office feeling pleased with the success of the product launch. Her thoughts were interrupted by a knock on her open door. She turned and saw Shawn Gersich, one of DataAccelleation's licensing representatives, poke his head into her office. "Do you have a minute to talk?" Shawn asked.

"Sure, what's up?" Kendra replied. She watched Shawn, a former football lineman, sheepishly walk into her office and slouch into a chair. "I messed up," Shawn said. "And now someone is threatening to sue me and the company." "Uh-oh," Kendra muttered. "Start from the beginning, and tell me everything."

Shawn explained that he had been meeting with James Ward, an employee from WebRunner, a start-up that had developed an innovative search engine DataAccelleation was interested in licensing. The negotiations had been difficult, but Shawn and James had finally reached an agreement, at which point James offered to write up a term sheet. When James gave the term sheet to Shawn, however, Shawn discovered that James had incorporated all of DataAccelleation's concessions but none of WebRunner's. Enraged, Shawn ripped the term sheet in half and hurled it at James, striking him in the chest. James rose to leave, but Shawn moved quickly to block his exit.

"No, you don't," Shawn said. "Neither of us is leaving until we write up a term sheet that reflects our agreement." After two hours, both Shawn and James initialed a revised draft of the term sheet, and James left without saying a word.

The next day Shawn received a phone call from an attorney representing James, threatening to sue him and DataAccelleation for assault, battery, and false imprisonment. It was at this point that Shawn had gone to talk with Kendra.

As Shawn finished the story, Kendra shook her head and sighed. "Well, thank you for telling me about this," she said. "Let me look into it and we'll talk about this later."

The moment Shawn left her office, Kendra picked up the phone, called Michael Cruz, and said, "Michael, I have a problem." After hearing her story, Michael replied, "You're right, Kendra, you do." Michael explained

continued...

continued...

that under the doctrine of *respondeat superior,* DataAccelleation was liable for the actions of its employees as long as they were acting within the scope of employment. Shawn's actions, although out of line, were within the scope of his employment because he was working on DataAccelleation's behalf. Michael said that DataAccelleation was probably liable for battery and false imprisonment and that the damages could easily reach $100,000.

Although Kendra had purchased a liability policy for DataAccelleation that would cover the damages, she didn't want to use it because she knew the premiums would then go up. At the same time, DataAccelleation didn't have an extra $100,000 or even the tens of thousands of dollars that would be needed for legal fees if the case went to trial. Michael suggested that Kendra call James and invite him to discuss the matter to see whether there was some alternative to litigation.

Kendra called James and invited him to meet with her the following day. After listening carefully to his story, Kendra told James that she agreed that what Shawn had done was wrong. She then apologized for his actions. Kendra assured James that she would sternly warn Shawn about his behavior and put a memorandum describing the incident in his personnel file. She also said that she would assign a different licensing representative to deal with WebRunner in the future. James appreciated the apology and told Kendra that he was satisfied with her handling of the situation and would drop the matter.

Kendra then walked down the hall to meet with Randy Short, DataAccelleation's Vice President, Sales. Randy told Kendra that several cities were requesting bids on data mining software. In addition to a number of very large firms expected to bid, Randy had been told by a buddy who worked for a small competitor, Interseek, that they intended to put in a bid for two cities in northern California and two in southern California.

Over beers at the end of a trade show held a few weeks before Randy's conversation with Kendra, Randy and his buddy had chatted about how tough it was to compete against the big players. Randy agreed and told his buddy that "We little guys have to watch out for each other."

Randy proposed to Kendra that DataAccelleation submit what it knew to be overly high bids for the two cities in northern California in exchange

continued...

continued...

for Interseek doing the same for the two cities in southern California. Neither firm was guaranteed to be the lowest bidder, but at least this way the two little guys wouldn't be cutting each others' throats.

Kendra rebuked Randy for having discussions with direct competitors that could be construed as price-fixing or bid rigging. When Randy responded that it was all pretty harmless because both companies had almost no market share, Kendra explained that that was irrelevant. Any agreement with a direct competitor to fix prices or rig bids was per se illegal and could result in fines and prison time for the parties involved. She told Randy that if the question of price or terms of sale or any aspect of competitive bids ever came up again at a trade show or anywhere else where Randy was likely to see his counterparts at competing firms, he should immediately leave the room and do something memorable, such as spilling his drink, in the course of leaving so that if any allegations of price-fixing or bid rigging arose out of the meeting, the participants would remember that he had left as soon as the discussions began.

Kendra went back to reworking her budget to try and avoid running out of cash before the next round of financing closed. Although she was tempted to draw on the account containing the income tax withheld from employees' salaries, Michael had warned her not to do so. Because Kendra was authorized to write checks on that account, she would be personally liable if the employee taxes were not remitted to the Internal Revenue Service on time.

NOTES

1. Otis Eng'g Corp. v. Clark, 668 S.W.2d 307 (Tex. 1983).
2. Riddle v. Arizona Oncology Servs., Inc., 924 P.2d 468 (Ariz. App. 1996).
3. Robertson v. LeMaster, 301 S.E.2d 563 (W. Va. 1983).
4. *See, e.g.*, Petrillo v. Bachenberg, 655 A2d 1354 (N.J. 1995) (property seller's attorney liable to the buyer for providing incomplete inspection reports in the case of a sale of land when seller's attorney knew or should have known that the nonclient buyer would rely on his professional capacity).
5. Burrow v. KMart Corp., 304 S.E.2d 460 (Ga. App. 1983).
6. Texaco, Inc. v. Pennzoil Co., 729 S.W.2d 768 (Tex. App. 1987).
7. Nurad, Inc. v. Hooper & Sons Co., 966 F.2d 837 (4th Cir. 1991).
8. Durland v. United States, 161 U.S. 306, 313 (1896).

Chapter 12

Creditors' Rights and Bankruptcy

Although entrepreneurs hope to raise sufficient capital to weather any financial difficulties, they are not always successful in doing so. Unanticipated events can result in the new company being unable to pay its bills in a timely manner. Unless the enterprise can access additional sources of funding in such a financial crisis, the company will need strategies for working with creditors and other constituencies. Bankruptcy is one of those strategies. These strategies are best understood by considering the types of creditors a company may have. In particular, founders should be familiar with the basics of secured lending, in which the lender is given the right to foreclose against company assets, because a secured lender is often at the center of a financial crisis.

The impact bankruptcy may have on the founders personally will be affected by the form of business entity selected for the enterprise and the extent to which the founders have personally guaranteed any of the enterprise's obligations. Although the bankruptcy of a corporation or limited liability company (LLC) generally will not put the personal assets of shareholders at risk, a bankruptcy by a general partnership usually will expose each general partner's personal assets to liability for the partnership's debts. In addition, if an individual involved in a corporation or LLC has given a personal guaranty for any of the enterprise's debts, the creditor holding that guaranty may pursue the individual directly if the enterprise is unable to pay.

This chapter first describes the different types of loans available to an entrepreneur and reviews issues raised in obtaining credit on a secured basis. It then gives an overview of the types of creditors and others implicated in a financial crisis. After exploring various strategies for responding to a financial crisis, the chapter goes on to discuss bankruptcy in more detail.

Types of Loans

A borrower may require funds to meet everyday working capital needs, to finance an acquisition of assets or a business, to finance a real estate construction project, or for a wide variety of other reasons. These reasons will dictate whether the loan should be a term loan or a revolving loan. Additionally, the borrower may also have to consider the implications of a secured loan.

Term Loans

Funds required for a specific purpose, such as an acquisition or a construction project, are generally borrowed in the form of a *term loan.* A specified amount is borrowed, either in a lump sum or in installments. It is either to be repaid on a specified date—known as the *maturity date*—or *amortized,* that is, paid off over a period of time. For example, in an acquisition, the buyer may be required to pay the purchase price up front and thus will require a lump-sum loan. By contrast, the owner of a construction project will require a loan to be disbursed in installments as scheduled progress payments become due. Amounts repaid under a term loan cannot be reborrowed.

Revolving Loan

A borrower may project its working capital needs for a given period but desire flexibility as to the exact amount of money borrowed at any given time. A *revolving loan* or *revolving line of credit* allows the borrower to borrow whatever sums it requires, up to a specified maximum amount.

The borrower may also reborrow amounts it has repaid (hence the term *revolving*). The lender will require a *commitment fee* as consideration for its promise to keep the commitment available, because it receives no interest on amounts not borrowed.

Secured Loans

Most start-ups are not able to qualify for a bank loan and instead rely on equity investments from the various sources described in Chapter 7. Nevertheless, understanding the basics of secured lending is critical. Not only will most young companies develop to a point at which a bank loan is sought for additional capital, but the many other funding sources that may be considered will often seek to invest on a secured note basis in addition to, or as an alternative to, equity.

In making a loan, the lender relies on the borrower's cash flow, the borrower's assets, or the proceeds of another loan as sources of repayment. If the lender relies solely on the borrower's promise to repay the loan, the lender's recourse for nonpayment is limited to suing the borrower. Moreover, even if the lender does sue the borrower, the lender stands in no better position than other *general creditors* of the borrower (those who have no special claim to any specific assets of the borrower as a source of repayment). Because of this risk, many lenders are often unwilling to make loans without something more than the borrower's promise of repayment. Lenders usually require *collateral,* that is, property belonging to the borrower that will become the lender's if the loan is not repaid. A loan backed up by collateral is known as a *secured loan.* Unsecured loans, if available at all, are priced at a higher rate to reflect the greater credit risk to the lender.

If the borrower fails to repay a secured loan, the lender, in addition to being able to sue for return of the monies lent, may *foreclose* on the collateral (that is, take possession of it) and either sell it to pay off the debt or keep it in satisfaction of the debt. However, under some *antideficiency* and *one form of action laws,* lenders seeking remedies against real property security may be restricted from suing the borrower personally. Furthermore, in cases in which a lender has recourse to the borrower or to other property of the borrower, and exercises such rights, the lender may be precluded from foreclosing on real estate mortgaged by the borrower. These laws, some of which date back to the Great Depression, are designed to protect borrowers from forfeiting their real estate to overzealous lenders.

Loan Agreements

Given the variety of loans described above, the basic structure of loan agreements is surprisingly standard. Lenders are concerned about the administration of the loan, their ongoing relationship with the borrower, and the rights they have if the borrower breaches his or her promises. At times these concerns must be addressed in specially tailored documentation; however, banks generally use a collection of standard forms, which are distributed to loan officers along with instructions for their use.

Secured Transactions Under the UCC

Both the mechanics of taking a security interest in personal property and fixtures (property attached to real property, such as light fixtures and built-in bookcases) and the consequences of taking such a security interest are governed by Article 9 of the Uniform Commercial Code (UCC), which has been adopted, with certain variations, in all states. Article 9 of the UCC provides a unified, comprehensive scheme for all types of *secured transactions,* that is, loans or other transactions secured by collateral put up by the borrower. With certain exceptions, Article 9 applies to any transaction (regardless of its form) that creates a security interest in personal property or fixtures by contract, including goods, documents, instruments, general intangibles, chattel paper, or accounts.

Article 9 of the UCC also sets forth the rights of the secured party as against other creditors of the debtor; the rules for perfecting a security interest, that is, making it prior to the rights of other creditors of the debtor; and the remedies available to a secured party if a debtor defaults.

Terminology

The UCC uses the single term *security interest* to signify any interest in personal property or fixtures put up as collateral to secure payment or the performance of an obligation. The parties to a secured transaction are the debtor and the secured party. The *debtor* is the person who has an interest in the collateral (other than a security interest or lien) whether or not such person owes payment or performance of the obligation secured. The *secured party* is the lender, seller, or other person in whose favor there is a security interest. A *security agreement* is an agreement that creates or provides for a security interest.

Scope of Article 9

Article 9 provides a single source of reference for most consensual security interests, but some security interests are outside its scope. Article 9 does not apply to liens on real property. Various state and federal laws preempt the UCC in the areas of ship mortgages, mechanic's liens, and aircraft liens. Notices of security interests in trademarks and patents are commonly filed in the U.S. Patent and Trademark Office in addition to being perfected as general intangibles under the UCC. Generally speaking, Article 9 does not apply to security subject to a landlord's lien, to a lien given by statute or other rule of law for services or materials, or to a contractual right to deduct the amount of damages from the amount of money otherwise due (a *right of setoff*).

Formal Requisites

The UCC also prescribes the formal requisites for creating an enforceable security interest and describes the rights of the parties to a security agreement. If the secured party takes possession of the collateral, an oral agreement is sufficient to create a security interest; otherwise, an authenticated security agreement containing a description of the collateral is required. A security agreement is *authenticated* if it is manually signed or some other symbol or process is used to adopt or accept the agreement (such as executing a record that is stored in an electronic or other medium and is retrievable in perceivable form). For a security interest to be enforceable, value must be given in exchange for it, and the debtor must have rights in the collateral. These requirements do not have to be fulfilled in any particular order. When all of the requirements have been met, a security interest is said to have *attached*.

Security Agreements

A security agreement identifies the parties and the property to be used as collateral. It may also specify the debtor's obligations and the lender's remedies in case of default.

Parties

Security agreements typically use the UCC terminology to identify the parties. In a loan transaction, the secured party is the lender. The debtor owns the collateral and is also the obligor if it owes payment or other performance of the obligation. The debtor also may simply be the owner who has authorized the obligor to use the property for collateral. If a third party acts as a guarantor of the borrower's obligation, he or she may also be referred to as the obligor.

Granting Clause

Unless the security interest is a possessory interest, whereby the lender takes possession of the collateral (traditionally called a *pledge*), the security agreement must be signed or otherwise authenticated by the debtor and must expressly grant a security interest in some specified property. The standard operative words are, "The debtor hereby grants to the secured party a security interest in. . . ." The UCC does not require a precise form, but the collateral must be described.

Description of the Collateral

The description of the collateral need not be specific as long as it reasonably identifies the property. Loans to finance the purchase of specific property, such as an equipment loan, will typically be secured by the property purchased, and the security agreement will contain a specific description of the property.

For example, a working capital loan may be secured by receivables and inventory. The inventory may be described as "any and all goods, merchandise, and other personal property, wherever located or in transit, that are held for sale or lease, furnished under any contract of service, or held as raw materials, work in process, supplies, or materials used or consumed in the debtor's business." Frequently, a secured party will take a security interest in all the assets of the debtor—not only fixed assets, inventory, and receivables but also trademarks, trade names, patents, licenses, goodwill, books, and records. In such cases, the collateral may be described as "all tangible and intangible property which, taken together, is intended to preserve the value of the debtor as a going concern." Such a security interest is also known as a *blanket security interest* because it covers all of the debtor's assets.

After-Acquired Property

After-acquired property is property that the debtor acquires after the execution of the security agreement. After-acquired assets may be specified in the security agreement either in addition to, or as replacements of, currently owned assets. A security interest in after-acquired collateral will attach when the debtor acquires rights in the collateral, assuming that the other prerequisites for attachment have previously been met. For example, a lender financing a car dealership's inventory would take a security interest in all cars currently owned by the dealership and all cars acquired later. When a car is sold and a new one purchased, the security interest automatically covers the new car. This feature makes a security interest created under Article 9 a *floating lien.*

FROM THE TRENCHES

When one software start-up was two months from a "cash cliff," it returned to its venture capital investors for a further round. The venture capitalists, unwilling to make another investment in return for equity, made the capital infusion in the form of a secured bridge loan. To secure repayment, they required a blanket security interest, including a security interest in the venture's intellectual property. The company used the much-needed cash to fund operations, continued to develop its business plan, and a year later paid off the bridge loan with proceeds from a further equity venture round, as a prelude to an initial public offering.

Proceeds

The UCC provides that the attachment of a security interest in collateral gives the secured party rights to proceeds of the collateral. If the collateral is sold, leased, licensed, exchanged, or otherwise disposed of, the security interest continues unless the secured party authorized the disposition free of the security interest.

Debtor's Obligations

Under most secured loans, the debtor will be obligated to repay the debt and to pay interest and related fees, charges, and expenses. In addition, the debtor likely will have nonmonetary obligations, such as obligations to maintain prescribed standards of financial well-being, measured by net worth, cash flow, and *leverage* (the ratio of debt to equity). These obligations are typically set forth in detail in a loan agreement or a promissory note, although occasionally they may be found in a security agreement.

Cross-Collateralization

The collateral for one loan may be used to secure obligations under another loan. This is done by means of a *cross-collateralization* provision—sometimes called a *dragnet clause*—in the security agreement. For example, a lender extending an inventory and receivables line of credit to a borrower may insist that the line be secured not only by inventory and receivables but also by equipment owned by the borrower and already held by the lender as collateral for an equipment loan. Thus, if the lender *forecloses on* (sells) the equipment, any proceeds in excess of the amounts owed under the equipment loan will be available to pay down the inventory and receivables line of credit. Likewise, if the equipment loan is cross-collateralized with collateral for the inventory and receivables line of credit, any proceeds realized from foreclosure of the inventory and receivables in excess of what is owed under the line of credit will be available to pay down the equipment loan.

Remedies for Default

The remedies described in a security agreement track the rights and procedures set forth in Article 9. After default, the secured party has the right to take possession of the collateral without judicial process, if this can be done without breach of the peace. The secured party must then dispose of the collateral at a public or private sale or propose to retain the collateral in satisfaction of the debt (sometimes called *strict foreclosure*). If there is a surplus from the sale of the collateral, the secured party is required to return it to the debtor. If there is a deficiency, the debtor remains liable for that amount. The proceeds from the sale must be applied in the following order:

1. To the reasonable expenses of foreclosure and, if provided for in the agreement, reasonable attorneys' fees and legal expenses.
2. To the satisfaction of the obligations secured.
3. To the satisfaction of any indebtedness secured by a subordinate security interest or to another secured party that is a consignor of the collateral, if an authenticated demand for satisfaction is received in a timely manner.

Although the UCC establishes a framework within which the lender may exercise its remedies, certain details should be provided for by contract. For example, the parties may agree to apply the proceeds of a foreclosure sale to attorneys' fees and legal expenses. They may also agree that the debtor will assemble the collateral and make it available to the secured party at a designated place. In any event, after default a secured party may require the debtor to assemble the collateral. All such provisions are subject to the requirement that the secured party's disposition of the collateral must be commercially reasonable.

The UCC contains guidelines regarding what constitutes a commercially reasonable disposition of collateral by a secured party. The secured party and the debtor are also free to fashion a mutually acceptable standard of commercial reasonableness, if the standard is not manifestly unreasonable. Security agreements typically contain a description of such standards.

Perfecting a Security Interest

To protect its rights in the collateral, a lender must ensure that its security interest is *perfected,* that is, prior to the rights of other secured creditors of the debtor; to the rights of certain buyers, lessees, and licensees of the collateral; and to the rights of a trustee in bankruptcy and other lien creditors of the debtor. The UCC does not define perfection; instead, it describes the situations in which an unperfected security interest will be *subordinated* to, or put below, the rights of third parties. For example, generally speaking, a security interest is subordinate to the rights of a person who becomes a lien creditor before the security interest is perfected. (A *lien creditor* includes a creditor that has obtained a lien by attachment, levy, or the like.) Subordination to lien creditors essentially means that the security interest is not enforceable in bankruptcy.

Generally speaking, security interests can be perfected by possession of the collateral, by filing a financing statement, by taking control of the collateral, and automatically.

By Possession

A security interest in money is perfected only by the secured party's taking possession of the collateral. A security interest in goods may be perfected either by possession or by filing a form known as a *UCC-1 Financing Statement*. For example, when a person goes to a pawnshop and surrenders possession of a wristwatch in exchange for a loan, the pawnshop acquires a perfected security interest in the wristwatch. A security interest in negotiable documents, instruments, or tangible chattel paper may also be perfected either by possession or by filing a financing statement. A security interest in certificated securities may be perfected by taking delivery of the certificates under Article 8 of the UCC.

By Filing

For most other types of collateral, perfection is accomplished by filing a UCC-1 Financing Statement. Standard printed forms are widely available for this purpose.

By Control

A security interest in investment property, letter-of-credit rights, or electronic chattel paper may be perfected by control of the collateral. A security interest in a deposit account must be perfected by control. One way for the secured party to obtain control over a deposit account is to enter into a control agreement with the debtor and the bank with which the deposit account is maintained. Under the control agreement, the parties agree that the bank will comply with instructions originated by the secured party directing disposition of the funds in the deposit account without further consent by the debtor.

Automatic Perfection

Some security interests require neither possession nor filing for perfection. For example, a *purchase-money security interest* (a security interest taken by the seller at the time of purchase to secure payment of the purchase price) in consumer goods is automatically perfected. Under certain circumstances, a security interest in certificated securities, instruments, or negotiable documents is temporarily perfected without filing or possession. Automatic perfection of a security interest in such collateral is of limited duration, however, and must be followed by possession or filing if perfection is to survive for a longer period.

FILING PROCEDURE

The fundamental concept behind perfection by filing is to provide notice to the world that assets of one person are subject to the security interest of another. When a security interest is perfected by filing, the collateral typically remains in the debtor's possession and control. This happens, for example, when the collateral is intangible (as with accounts receivable) or when possession by the secured party is impractical (as in the case of inventory). A centralized system gives effective public notice that property in the possession and under the apparent control of the debtor is actually subject to the rights of another. The filing system enables a prospective creditor to determine whether, in claiming its rights to such assets, it will be competing with other creditors. It also enables a purchaser of goods to determine whether the seller's creditors have any claims against the goods. (It should be noted that, under certain circumstances, a purchaser of goods is protected from liens on such goods created by the seller. For example, consumers are protected from inventory liens on a seller's goods.)

What to File

To perfect a security interest in personal property by filing, a UCC-1 Financing Statement must be filed. The financing statement merely gives notice that a financing transaction is being or is about to be entered into; the statement does not describe the transaction. It need only contain the names of the parties to the transaction, their mailing addresses, and a description of the kinds of collateral in which a security interest has been or may be granted. When a financing statement covers goods that are or are to become fixtures, the UCC also requires a legal description of the land involved; if the debtor does not have an interest of record in the real property, the financing statement must also provide the name of a record owner.

When to File

A financing statement may be filed in advance of the transaction or the signing of the security agreement. Timing is important because, under the UCC, conflicting perfected security interests rank according to priority in time of filing or perfection. Thus, provided that the security interest has attached, the first secured party to file has priority over other parties with security interests in the same debtor's property, unless special priority rules apply, as in the case of purchase-money security interests.

Where to File

Generally, the proper place to file to perfect a security interest is in the office of the secretary of state in the state where the debtor is located. A corporate debtor is located in the state of its incorporation; a noncorporate debtor is generally located at its chief executive office; and an individual debtor is located at the individual's principal residence. A security interest in collateral closely associated with real property (such as fixtures, timber, or minerals) must be filed in the office where a deed of trust or mortgage on the real estate would be recorded, usually the county recorder's office in the county where the property is located.

TYPES OF CREDITORS AND THEIR RIGHTS

A lender with a security interest represents just one of several types of creditor. Other creditors of an entrepreneurial venture may include a bank, a venture capitalist acting as a lender, a seller of goods or services, an equipment lessor, a taxing authority, or an employee. The law gives certain creditors priority over other creditors, depending on the nature of the contract or relationship with the debtor. The number of creditors with priority positions, the amount of their claims, and the nature of their priority will affect the strategy selected by the company to deal with a financial crisis.

Secured Creditors

As discussed above, the secured party under a UCC security interest is known as a secured creditor. Generally, the first secured creditor to perfect has priority in payment over all other types of creditors, at least with respect to repayment from its collateral.

Equipment Lessors

Young companies often need equipment, ranging from computers to manufacturing equipment to copy machines. Many companies prefer to rent or to finance the equipment rather than use existing capital to purchase it. Although many dealers will offer to lease specific equipment, a separate segment of the financial industry has developed to provide equipment financing. Known as *equipment lessors,* these entities finance leases and provide extended financing for the lease or purchase of equipment.

In a *true lease* of equipment, the lessor retains ownership of the equipment. If the company defaults, the lessor is entitled to repossess the leased equipment and has an unsecured claim for the balance of the payments owed. In a bankruptcy, if the payments due under the lease equal the entire economic value of the equipment, then the lease may be recharacterized as a financing arrangement, or *finance lease,* rather than a true lease. In the event of such a recharacterization, the lessor will be treated as an unsecured creditor rather than as the owner of the equipment. To protect themselves against this outcome, equipment lessors commonly require a security interest in the equipment being leased and file a financing statement on the equipment. Then, if the lease is recharacterized as a financing arrangement, the equipment lessor will at least be treated as a secured creditor in bankruptcy.

Taxing Authorities

The Internal Revenue Service (IRS) and state taxing authorities have certain special creditors' rights. These include the right to place liens on a taxpayer's property for unpaid taxes and even to seize property. *Withholding taxes* (those taxes required to be withheld from employees' paychecks and paid to the IRS) are considered *trust fund taxes* and must be paid on a timely basis. If they are not paid on time, then the officers of a corporation may be held personally liable for 100 percent of the unpaid taxes. Obviously, withheld funds should be paid in a timely manner to the taxing authorities and should not be used to pay other debts or operating expenses of the company.

Employees

An employee's claim for wages, salary, vacation, or sick leave pay is generally treated as an unsecured claim. In a bankruptcy, however, each employee is given a *priority claim* (entitling him or her to payment after secured creditors but before unsecured creditors) for up to $4,650 of compensation earned but unpaid in the ninety days prior to a bankruptcy filing or the cessation of business, whichever is earlier. State law may give employees additional remedies. For example, in California, the labor commissioner can assist unpaid employees in collecting their wages and may issue fines or penalties against the employer for nonpayment of employees. In addition, an employee with an unsatisfied judgment for wages or salary can petition a court to require the employer to post a bond to pay the employee's wages or be ordered to cease doing business in California.

Unsecured Trade Creditors

Most of a new company's creditors will be unsecured creditors. *Unsecured creditors* have no security interest in any collateral but only a general claim against the company for payment. If debts remain unpaid, these creditors often first resort to telephone calls and letters to obtain payment. If these measures are unsuccessful, the claim is turned over to a collection agency or an attorney.

If an attorney becomes involved, he or she generally will file a lawsuit on behalf of the creditor. In California and a few other states, the creditor may attempt to obtain a *prejudgment attachment* of the company's assets to secure payment for the claim. If an attachment is allowed before judgment, or if the creditor obtains a judgment against the company, then the creditor has the right to attempt to *levy* on the attachment or judgment. This involves seizing bank accounts and other assets of the company. A creditor that obtains an attachment or judgment also can file a lien similar to a UCC-1 Financing Statement against the company's equipment, inventory, and certain other types of non-real-estate assets and can record an abstract of the judgment against any real estate the company owns. When creditors take these more aggressive actions, they often precipitate a financial crisis that forces the company to pursue a workout strategy or to file a bankruptcy.

Personal Guaranties

Some creditors, typically landlords and banks, may demand that an enterprise's founder or officers personally guarantee repayment of the credit extended. If given, a personal guaranty exposes the individual's home and other assets to the creditor's claim in the event the company does not pay the debt. Generally, a personal guaranty gives the creditor the right to sue the individual directly, regardless of whether the creditor has sued the company or whether the company is in bankruptcy. In addition, even though bankruptcy may provide the company with certain benefits (e.g., capping the extent of a landlord's damages from breach of a lease), those protections may not be available to an individual guarantor. For these reasons, an individual should obtain legal advice before giving a personal guaranty.

Strategies for Responding to a Financial Crisis

A young company's specific responses to a financial crisis will depend largely on the nature of the crisis, including the kinds of creditors involved and the amount and type of their claims. In almost every crisis, however, conserving cash and gaining additional time are critical. The company needs to be able to use its cash for essential business purposes and needs time to allow its business plan (or revised business plan) to develop. These objectives require methods for restructuring the company's liabilities. Although bankruptcy always remains an option, alternatives for restructuring or *working out* a company's debts short of bankruptcy can be less expensive and buy additional time, even if a bankruptcy is ultimately required. The discussion below provides only an overview of some of the alternative strategies. Because a financial crisis has many complexities, the company should obtain specific legal advice from an insolvency attorney.

General Considerations

As part of a workout strategy, the company may consider hiring a financial consultant or *turnaround expert,* who has experience in refocusing business plans, analyzing financial data, and preparing budgets and other reports helpful in persuading creditors that the venture can work its way out of the financial crisis. In some cases, the turnaround expert can serve as a management consultant or even as chief executive officer until the company has resolved the crisis. Retaining a turnaround expert can also help build credibility with creditors, an asset often in short supply as payment terms become stretched out or shifted to a cash-on-delivery (C.O.D.) basis.

If they desire, three or more creditors with claims aggregating $11,625 can file a petition to force the company into an involuntary bankruptcy. Trade creditors frustrated by a lack of payment often use this threat. It can become a major distraction for management because in some cases the threat can become real. Generally, however, creditors shy away from taking such a drastic step because the Bankruptcy Code permits a company to recover damages against creditors that are unsuccessful in forcing it into an involuntary bankruptcy. Moreover, if an out-of-court workout is under way, and most creditors are observing a collection-action moratorium, the company may be able to persuade a bankruptcy court to refrain from hearing a petition for involuntary bankruptcy filed by a few dissatisfied creditors. However, the possibility of involuntary bankruptcy only emphasizes the need to address a company's financial problems aggressively. (Involuntary bankruptcy is discussed more fully below.)

If the enterprise's founder has given a personal guaranty of any of the company's debts, the financial crisis may prompt the holder of the guaranty to demand payment on the personal guaranty and file a lawsuit to collect. Likewise, if the enterprise is a partnership, the individual general partners are personally liable for the partnership's debts and may face lawsuits for collection. Individual entrepreneurs in these situations should obtain personal legal advice about their own exposure caused by the enterprise's financial crisis.

In addition, as discussed below, when a company becomes *insolvent*—when the sum of its debts exceeds the fair value of its assets—officers and directors of the company are generally held to owe expanded fiduciary duties, not just to shareholders but also to the creditors of the company. This expanded fiduciary duty means that in conducting the company's business, officers and directors must take special care to work in the interests of both shareholders and creditors and must not take steps that unduly favor shareholders at the expense of creditors or that prefer insiders to noninsider creditors.

Out-of-Court Reorganization

One workout method involves contacting creditors, individually or as a group, to request a payment moratorium or an agreement to some other payment terms the young company can afford. If a company has only a few large creditors, and they are willing to extend their payment terms, the immediate crisis may be avoided. If a company has many creditors, then a letter to creditors reporting on the company's difficulties and requesting new payment terms may be necessary. Although creditors have the legal right to ignore the request, most will assess the proposal to determine whether they will realize more from agreeing to new terms than they would if the company filed for bankruptcy. Because bankruptcy generally means no payments to unsecured creditors for months or years, if at all, creditors often are willing to accept an offer if it means that they will be paid on terms more favorable than the bankruptcy alternative would likely provide.

Secured creditors may also be willing to work with a company in financial trouble and overlook defaults on *financial covenants,* such as financial ratios, particularly if the company can keep current on its payments. Even if the company cannot, secured creditors often want to avoid the expense and likely financial loss associated with a foreclosure or a potentially prolonged bankruptcy case, and they will evaluate a serious restructuring proposal on its merits. If the secured creditors are venture capitalists, they may have even more flexibility to work with the company, although they may also demand a greater equity stake.

If the company has lost credibility with its creditors, as often happens when honest promises to pay cannot be fulfilled, the workout may have a better chance of success if an intermediary is used. Credit associations, such as the Credit Managers Association of California (CMAC), facilitate workouts by organizing a meeting of creditors at which a creditors committee is formed to work with the company in trouble. The company and its creditors committee then enter into discussions in an attempt to negotiate a workout agreement. To convince the creditors to agree to a workout, the company will need to provide the creditors committee with financial reports and information on its current and projected performance. Confidentiality agreements can be entered into with the creditors committee members to protect the company's business information.

Once a workout agreement is reached, the intermediary will distribute the workout agreement with a consent form. The consent form asks each creditor to list the amount of its claim and to agree to abide by the moratorium on collection actions generally provided for in the workout agreement. If the consent form is signed, the creditor is contractually bound to honor the moratorium and will receive payments according to the workout agreement. Disputes over the amount of a claim must be worked out between the company and the creditor before the creditor receives any payment, which enhances the company's leverage in resolving the dispute. The workout agreement generally specifies a minimum percentage of creditors that must accept the terms of the agreement for it to become effective, although the percentage may be adjusted depending on the overall reaction of the creditors. The creditors committee will thereafter require financial reports from the company, to be discussed at periodic meetings, as well as reports on the company's progress.

To protect the creditors, the creditors committee usually will require the company to provide the intermediary, acting as a stakeholder on behalf of all of the creditors, with a security interest in all of the company's assets. The security interest can also protect the company from collection actions by creditors that refuse to agree to the moratorium, because any attachment or judgment lien obtained after the security interest is perfected will be junior and subject to the security interest given to the intermediary on behalf of the other creditors. If a company has one or more senior secured creditors, it should disclose its intention to give the intermediary a junior security interest. Many secured creditors will permit the granting of such a security interest, although it generally violates the terms of their own security agreements, to enable the company to work out its overall financial problems. If not, the company may attempt to reach a workout agreement without granting the intermediary a security interest, or else the company may be forced to file bankruptcy.

Out-of-Court Liquidation

When a company has more severe problems, and especially if a non-revenue generating company cannot raise additional capital, liquidation of the company's assets may be required. Although filing for bankruptcy is one vehicle, a nonbankruptcy liquidation may result in higher payments to creditors. Like a reorganization outside bankruptcy, liquidation can be done by the company itself or with the help of outside organizations.

If the company is not faced with creditors levying on attachments or judgments, it generally can wind down its business operations over a period of time, liquidate its assets through sales of technology and other assets, close its doors, and distribute the proceeds on a pro rata basis according to the legal priorities of its creditors (secured creditors first, then unsecured creditors). If a company has long-term equipment or facilities leases, it may attempt to negotiate termination of those leases on terms that limit claims for the remaining years on the leases. Because bankruptcy offers the ability to cap a landlord's damages, the company often can use a threat of bankruptcy as leverage in these negotiations. The situation can also be complicated by the presence of agreements called *executory contracts* under which the company has continuing performance obligations other than or in addition to payment. The company may need to negotiate an assignment of these obligations to an asset purchaser or an amicable termination of the company's obligations.

When a liquidation is not feasible without an intermediary, two alternatives may be considered. The first involves hiring an organization, such as CMAC, that will work at the direction of the company and act as a liquidator. Much as with the reorganization effort described above, the intermediary will send a notice to creditors and organize a creditors meeting where a collection-action moratorium will be requested and a creditors committee will be formed. The creditors committee, with or without its own counsel, will oversee the company's liquidation effort and help resolve disputes over creditors' claims. The company pays the fees of counsel for the creditors committee out of the liquidation proceeds.

FROM THE TRENCHES

When a start-up company's primary customer failed to place expected orders, the company found itself without sufficient cash to continue in business. It asked CMAC to organize a meeting of its trade creditors and granted CMAC a security interest in its assets. At the meeting, the creditors in attendance agreed to an interim collection-action moratorium and formed a creditors committee. Two months later, the company and its creditors committee reached a workout agreement, which continued the collection-action moratorium in return for the company's promise to repay its creditors over time. Many creditors returned consent forms agreeing to the workout agreement; others simply stopped calling the company for payment. When one aggressive creditor levied on one of the company's bank accounts to enforce a judgment, CMAC filed a third-party claim objecting to the levy and invoked its rights under the prior security interest it had been granted. The funds were released back to the company, enabling it to continue in business.

If the company is willing to cede control over the liquidation to a liquidator it selects, a second alternative is to make a *general assignment for the benefit of creditors.* In this formal legal procedure, the company appoints an individual to act as assignee and to take possession and control of the company's assets. The assignee then liquidates the assets and distributes the proceeds, much as a bankruptcy trustee does in a liquidation under Chapter 7 of the U.S. Bankruptcy Code. Also, like a bankruptcy trustee, the assignee can in some states (including California) sue creditors for recovery of preferential payments and fraudulent transfers. If insiders or other creditors have received substantial payments from the company on old debt, they may be subject to such preference lawsuits, as explained more fully below.

One major difference between bankruptcy and this form of liquidation involves loans, leases, or other contracts that provide for automatic termi-

FROM THE TRENCHES

When a dot-com company ran out of cash and its investors were unwilling to provide additional funds, the company entered into negotiations to sell its principal assets and customer base to another company. Due to concerns over possible successor liability and fraudulent transfer risks, the purchaser was unwilling to buy these assets directly from the dot-com company. Although a purchaser of assets can obtain protection from fraudulent transfer claims by acquiring assets from a company in bankruptcy, in this case bankruptcy was not a feasible option because obtaining an order from a bankruptcy court approving the sale would likely have required too much time.

The dot-com company instead contacted an experienced liquidation professional, who agreed to serve as the assignee for the benefit of creditors. The professional became involved in the sale negotiations, and ultimately, just before the parties were ready to close the sale, the dot-com company made a general assignment for the benefit of creditors to the professional. The professional then finalized the sale agreement with the purchaser, and the sale closed with almost no interruption in service to the customers. The purchase price was paid to the professional in the capacity as assignee for the benefit of the dot-com company's creditors. The assignee then wound up the affairs of the dot-com company, sending notices to its creditors and administering its remaining assets for their benefit.

nation upon the making of an assignment for the benefit of creditors. Such provisions are unenforceable in bankruptcy, but they may be enforced if a general assignment for the benefit of creditors is made (subject to a limited right of the assignee to stay termination of a lease of real property for up to ninety days by continuing to pay rent). In addition, many personal guaranties make a general assignment for the benefit of creditors by the company an event of default, triggering personal exposure for the guarantor. For these reasons, the company's business should be carefully reviewed before choosing this liquidation option.

Secured Creditors and Foreclosure

If the company has obtained financing by giving a security interest in some or all of its assets, consideration of reorganization and liquidation options must start with the secured creditor. If a liquidation is chosen, then the secured creditor may simply prefer to repossess its collateral and foreclose through a public or private sale or by retaining the collateral in lieu of the debt. If the secured creditor has a blanket security interest, this may result in disposal of all of the company's assets. Alternatively, the secured creditor may support a liquidation by the company itself, or a liquidation through an intermediary or by a general assignment for the benefit of creditors, with the secured creditor receiving a priority distribution of the proceeds. If an out-of-court reorganization is desired, the company must reach some form of forbearance agreement or debt restructure with the secured creditor, as the secured creditor has the immediate right to foreclose on its collateral if the company defaults. If a forbearance agreement cannot be reached, a bankruptcy, with its automatic stay of foreclosure efforts, may be the only alternative.

TYPES OF BANKRUPTCY

Bankruptcy is a final alternative strategy for a young company in a financial crisis. A company that chooses to file a voluntary bankruptcy gains an immediate respite from creditor actions, including foreclosure, by virtue of the automatic stay, discussed below. By filing under Chapter 11 of the U.S.

Bankruptcy Code, a company can retain possession of its assets, propose a plan to restructure its debts to creditors, and, in successful cases, emerge from bankruptcy in better financial shape.

Although bankruptcy gives a company the opportunity to reorganize in an orderly fashion, it also imposes many obligations. The company's finances become an open book, as it must file a full schedule of its assets and liabilities, as well as a statement of its financial affairs, soon after the bankruptcy is filed. The company's officers are subject to questioning about every aspect of its business at deposition-style examinations, and approval of the bankruptcy court is required for any business decision outside the ordinary course of business. For these reasons, bankruptcy should be considered a last resort, although its unique benefits may make it the only viable strategy for solving the most severe financial crises.

The following discussion assumes that the company has been organized as a corporation, the most common form of business organization, but also generally applies to limited liability companies. Enterprises organized as partnerships can raise different issues because individual general partners are liable for a partnership's debts.

Chapter 11 Reorganization Versus Chapter 7 Liquidation

A Chapter 11 reorganization bankruptcy offers a company the tools to propose a plan for restructuring its debts and emerging from bankruptcy as a going concern. When the financial problems become too severe, the company may file a Chapter 7 liquidation bankruptcy, also known as *straight bankruptcy.* In a *Chapter 7* bankruptcy, a bankruptcy trustee is automatically appointed to liquidate all of the company's assets for ultimate distribution to creditors. The company's management must turn over possession to the bankruptcy trustee, and no reorganization is attempted. A bankruptcy trustee is also under a fiduciary duty to pursue recovery of preferences and fraudulent transfers. Because the goal of most companies in a bankruptcy is to reorganize and maintain ownership of the enterprise, this chapter focuses primarily on Chapter 11 bankruptcy.

Voluntary Versus Involuntary Bankruptcy

When a company chooses to file for bankruptcy, it is known as *voluntary bankruptcy.* When three or more creditors holding claims totaling at least $11,625 jointly petition to force a company into bankruptcy, the result is involuntary bankruptcy. An *involuntary bankruptcy* is started by filing a petition, which is similar to a complaint in regular litigation. However, an involuntary bankruptcy petition seeks to have the bankruptcy court order that the company be placed into bankruptcy.

An involuntary bankruptcy can be filed as either a Chapter 11 or a Chapter 7 bankruptcy. An involuntary Chapter 11 filing is often coupled with a request for appointment of a Chapter 11 bankruptcy trustee. In a Chapter 7 bankruptcy, appointment of a bankruptcy trustee is automatic. The company can respond to an involuntary bankruptcy petition by (1) objecting to the effort, in which case further litigation will ensue until the bankruptcy court makes its decision, or (2) consenting to the bankruptcy by filing its own voluntary Chapter 11 or Chapter 7 bankruptcy petition.

If the involuntary bankruptcy petition is successful, the company will officially be placed in bankruptcy with an order for relief. If the involuntary bankruptcy petition fails, then the involuntary case will be dismissed, and the company may be able to recover its costs and attorneys' fees from the petitioning creditors. If the petition was filed in bad faith, the company may even be awarded compensatory and punitive damages. The potential exposure to liability for damages inhibits many creditors from actually filing an involuntary bankruptcy petition. It does not, however, stop creditors from threatening such a filing in an attempt to intimidate the company into paying their claims. An involuntary bankruptcy is more likely in those cases in which creditors suspect a company has engaged in fraudulent activity, is dissipating or concealing its assets, or has announced its inability to pay creditors but has failed to propose a credible workout plan.

THE CHAPTER 11 BANKRUPTCY PROCESS

Chapter 11 of the U.S. Bankruptcy Code is designed to permit a company to reorganize its business by changing the terms on which its debts must be paid. A reorganization is accomplished through a plan of reorganization, which is proposed by a debtor company and considered by the bankruptcy court according to specific substantive requirements set forth in the Bankruptcy Code. Chapter 11 can also preserve the *going-concern* economic value of an operating company, which is the enhanced value of the company's assets functioning together as an ongoing enterprise. This enhanced value is lost when the debtor company is liquidated piecemeal or torn apart by individual creditors foreclosing on security interests or levying on judgments. When a Chapter 11 bankruptcy is filed, the debtor company, through its existing management, generally stays in possession and control of its assets. The company serves as a *debtor-in-possession* instead of having a bankruptcy trustee appointed to take control of the assets.

Costs of Bankruptcy

Aside from the potential negative impact on customer or vendor confidence and the possible stigma associated with a company that filed bankruptcy, a very real cost of bankruptcy is attorneys' and other professional fees. A Chapter 11 bankruptcy for a relatively small company can cost anywhere from $100,000 to $250,000 or more in attorneys' fees; in more complex cases, attorneys' fees can be substantially higher. In addition, given the company's financial condition, most bankruptcy attorneys require these funds to be paid up-front as a prepayment retainer. When a creditors committee is active and retains its own attorneys, the company will be required to pay those fees as well. Similarly, if an investment banker, accountant, or other financial consultant is needed, their fees will also be charged to the company. Thus, although bankruptcy can offer significant relief, it can also be expensive.

Automatic Stay

Immediately upon filing a bankruptcy petition, a company is protected by an *automatic stay* preventing its creditors from pursuing collection of debts. The automatic stay operates as a statutory injunction that prohibits a creditor from continuing litigation against the debtor (but not against others), sending dunning notices or taking other collection steps, or attempting to exercise control over the debtor's property (e.g., through repossession, foreclosure, or termination of contracts).

Although the automatic stay is one of the most powerful aspects of bankruptcy relief, it is subject to being lifted by the bankruptcy court. If the debtor does not have equity in specific property over and above the claims of secured creditors and its reorganization prospects are doubtful, or if the court finds that other good cause exists, then the court may terminate the automatic stay to permit certain creditor actions, including foreclosure.

Types of Creditor Claims in Bankruptcy

Every creditor of a company in bankruptcy has the right to file a proof of claim in the bankruptcy case. The *proof of claim* is the creditor's statement of its own claim. A deadline known as a *bar date* is established, and all creditors (with some exceptions) must file their claims by that date or be barred from recovering anything in the bankruptcy. The debtor company must file a schedule of assets and liabilities that lists each creditor and the amount owed according to the company's books. The company then categorizes the creditors' claims as appropriate. A claim is designated *disputed* if the company believes the claim is not valid, *contingent* if the company believes the claim will be valid only if some event does or does not occur, and *unliquidated* if the company believes the amount of the claim has not been established. If the company has designated a creditor's claim as disputed, contingent, and/or unliquidated, then the creditor must file a proof of claim. Otherwise, a creditor in a Chapter 11 bankruptcy may rely on the statement of the claim shown in the company's schedules.

Payment Priority

Creditor claims in a bankruptcy are paid in an order of priority established by the Bankruptcy Code. A secured creditor holds a *secured claim* to the extent of the value of that creditor's collateral. Thus, if, for example, a secured creditor is owed $100,000 and its collateral is worth $200,000, then that creditor is *fully secured.* If the same creditor's collateral is worth only $60,000, however, then the creditor is referred to as *undersecured;* the creditor has a secured claim to the extent of the $60,000 value of the collateral and an *unsecured claim* for the $40,000 balance. Secured creditors have the highest priority in a bankruptcy case and are entitled to certain specified, favorable treatment.

Creditors that are not secured by any collateral can file either priority claims or general unsecured claims, depending on the circumstances. Certain claims are entitled to priority over claims of other unsecured creditors and thus are called *priority claims*. These claims may relate to the expenses of administering the bankruptcy case (*administrative claims*), which receive first priority after secured creditors. Administrative claims include the claims of the debtor's attorneys and accountants and postbankruptcy filing (known as *postpetition*) claims for business expenses, including wages and salaries for employees for work performed postpetition, postpetition raw material and office expenses, and postpetition payments for equipment and facilities leases. Prebankruptcy (*prepetition*) claims of employees for unpaid salaries, wages, severance, vacation, and sick leave, earned within the ninety days prior to the bankruptcy filing, are entitled to a third priority to the extent of $4,650 per employee. (Claims of ordinary business creditors that arise in the gap between the filing of an involuntary bankruptcy petition and an order for relief putting a company in bankruptcy get the second priority.) Other common creditors with priority claims include consumer deposits for personal or household goods (sixth priority) and certain prepetition income and other taxes (eighth priority).

The claims of creditors not entitled to any priority are known as *general unsecured claims*. These claims include employee claims other than those claims entitled to the $4,650 priority, trade creditors, damage claims in litigation, and creditors whose executory contracts or leases have been rejected in the bankruptcy (discussed below). Exhibit 12.1 summarizes these payment-priority rules.

If a creditor files a proof of claim but the debtor company (or another party) believes the claim is invalid or in an improper amount, it can file an *objection* to the claim. If the creditor disputes the objection, it will file papers with the bankruptcy court so stating and requesting a hearing on its claim. Ultimately, the bankruptcy court will establish a procedure for resolving the objection to the claim, often by holding a short trial. If the

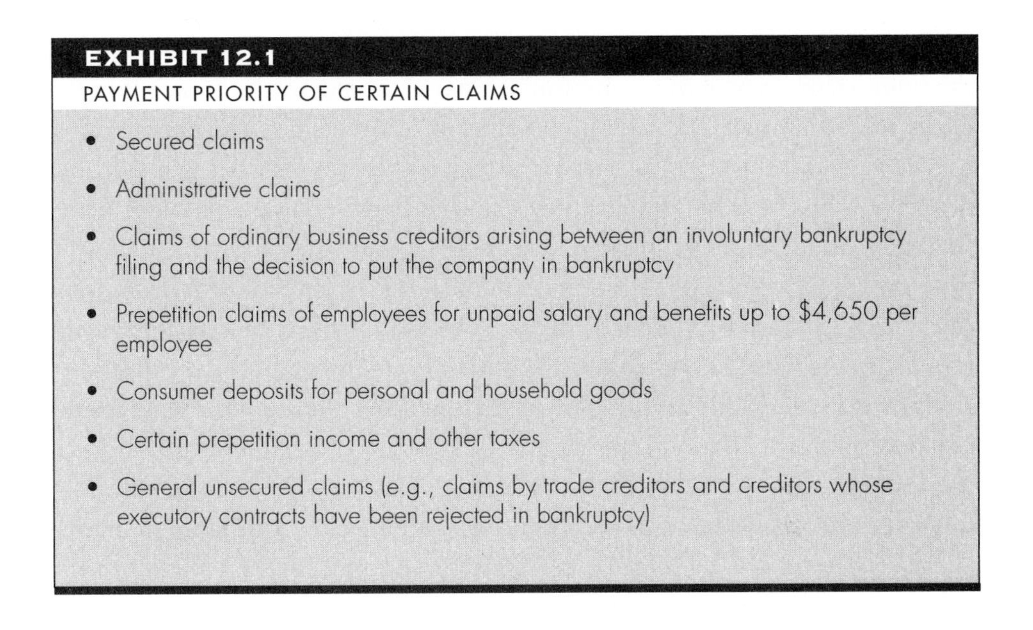
EXHIBIT 12.1

PAYMENT PRIORITY OF CERTAIN CLAIMS

- Secured claims
- Administrative claims
- Claims of ordinary business creditors arising between an involuntary bankruptcy filing and the decision to put the company in bankruptcy
- Prepetition claims of employees for unpaid salary and benefits up to $4,650 per employee
- Consumer deposits for personal and household goods
- Certain prepetition income and other taxes
- General unsecured claims (e.g., claims by trade creditors and creditors whose executory contracts have been rejected in bankruptcy)

court decides the claim is valid (or valid but in a different amount), it will allow the claim in the amount it finds appropriate, and the claim will be paid according to the terms of a plan of reorganization or the Bankruptcy Code. If the court decides the claim is not valid, the claim will be disallowed and will not be entitled to payment in the bankruptcy case.

Executory Contracts and Leases

An *executory contract* is an agreement in which both parties to the contract have continuing obligations to perform. Typical examples include joint development agreements, manufacturing agreements, and licenses in which each party has an ongoing, affirmative performance obligation. In bankruptcy, a debtor company has the right to terminate the active performance obligations in executory contracts by *rejecting* the contracts. The debtor also has the right to terminate unfavorable leases for real property, including stores, facilities, and offices, by rejecting such leases. The rejection is treated as a breach of the contract and must be approved by the bankruptcy court. However, the court usually defers to management's business decision.

The other party to an executory contract or lease that has been rejected has the right to file a proof of claim for its damages caused by the breach, but the claim will be treated only as a prepetition unsecured claim (unless the other party to the contract was granted a security interest). When a lease of real property is involved, the Bankruptcy Code gives the company another benefit: The amount of the landlord's unsecured claim for unpaid rent under the lease is capped at the greater of one year's rent or 15 percent of the total rent owed, not to exceed three years' worth of rent. This can be a major benefit to a company with a long-term lease at high rental rates. In some cases, a serious threat of bankruptcy can motivate a landlord to renegotiate lease terms.

The company also has the right to assume, or assume and assign to another person, the executory contract or lease, generally regardless of whether the nondebtor party consents. When the company in bankruptcy *assumes* the executory contract or unexpired lease, it expressly agrees to continue to perform all of its obligations under the contract or lease. Before being permitted by the bankruptcy court to assume an executory contract or lease, the debtor must (1) cure any defaults; (2) compensate for any pecuniary losses suffered by the nondebtor party, which may include attorneys' fees incurred in responding to the bankruptcy case; and (3) provide the nondebtor party with adequate assurances of the debtor's ability to perform under the contract or lease in the future. When the debtor company seeks to *assume and assign* an executory contract or unexpired lease, these same three requirements must be met, except that the party taking over the contract or lease from the debtor must itself provide adequate assurances of future performance.

A few types of contracts cannot be assigned to a third party without the nondebtor's consent and, in certain jurisdictions, cannot even be assumed without the nondebtor's consent. These include contracts for personal services and nonexclusive patent licenses where the debtor company is the licensee. For example, the U.S. Court of Appeals for the Ninth Circuit (which includes California, Oregon, and Washington) ruled that a debtor in Chapter 11 may not assume a nonexclusive patent license even though the debtor, not a third-party assignee, would in fact continue to be the licensee.[1] The First Circuit (which includes Massachusetts) had reached the opposite result on similar facts.[2]

FROM THE TRENCHES

After the dot-com bubble burst in 2000, hundreds of dot-coms filed for bankruptcy. In a number of cases, the debtor's most valuable asset was a below-market lease for office space. For example, Boo.com North America, Inc., an Internet retailer of brand name sportswear that filed under Chapter 11 on October 31, 2000, sought to assign its unexpired lease for 9,043 square feet of office space in New York City at a rent of $27.50 per square foot to Radical Media for $350,000. Given that market rent had risen to $50.00 a square foot, the lessor opposed the assignment. Even though the lease prohibited assignment without the lessor's consent and further provided that, even if consent were given, the lessee was required to pay over to the lessor any profit realized on the assignment, the bankruptcy court ruled that Boo.com had the right to assign the lease over the lessor's objections and to keep the $350,000 profit.

Source: In re Boo.com North America, Inc., 2000 Bankr. LEXIS 1559 (Bankr. S.D.N.Y. Dec 15, 2000).

Preference and Fraudulent Transfer Claims

The Bankruptcy Code provides that the debtor, a bankruptcy trustee if one is appointed, or, in some cases, a creditors committee may pursue recovery of preferential or fraudulent transfers made by the debtor prior to the bankruptcy. *Preferences* are transfers made by the debtor, when insolvent, to or for the benefit of a creditor on account of preexisting debt in the ninety days prior to the filing of the bankruptcy petition. The ninety-day *reach-back period* means that potentially all payments made to a creditor during the ninety days prior to the bankruptcy filing may be recoverable. If such a transfer is made to an *insider* (such as an officer, director, or affiliate of the debtor company) within one year prior to the filing of the bankruptcy petition, it is also a recoverable preference if the debtor was insolvent at the time.

The Bankruptcy Code provides creditors with certain defenses, including those for payments made in the ordinary course of business or for C.O.D. or other contemporaneous exchanges. In addition, creditors can

FROM THE TRENCHES

When a large Internet service provider (ISP) filed for bankruptcy, among its creditors was one of the licensors of mission-critical software. When the ISP sought to assign the software license to the proposed purchaser of the ISP's assets, the software licensor objected. The licensor asserted that under recent bankruptcy decisions, the ISP could not assign the software license to the proposed purchaser because such copyright licenses were personal and could be assigned only with the licensor's consent. Negotiations then ensued between the ISP, the proposed purchaser, and the software licensor. As a condition to giving its consent, the software licensor was able to require payment of the amounts that the ISP had failed to pay and to impose limitations on the license granted to the purchaser.

offset against payments the amount of new value provided on an unsecured basis (credit or shipments) after each payment was received. Thus, despite the preference law, creditors may be able to keep certain payments made within ninety days of bankruptcy.

Preference payments can be recovered not only from the recipient but also from those for whose benefit the payments were made. When an officer or founder of a company gives a personal guaranty to a bank or other creditor, payments that reduce the company's debt also reduce the individual's exposure on the guaranty. Thus, in a bankruptcy, the company (or more likely a bankruptcy trustee if one is appointed) may sue the guarantor to recover payments made by the company to the bank that indirectly benefited the guarantor. Because the guarantor is an insider, the reach-back period is one year, not ninety days. The company or bankruptcy trustee can recover the payments only once, however, and often it will sue the recipient of the payments as well.

Fraudulent transfers include transfers made by the debtor with actual intent to hinder, delay, or defraud creditors. They also include transfers made by the debtor when financially impaired and for which the debtor did not receive reasonably equivalent value in return. Thus, if a company in need of cash sells a major line of its business for substantially

FROM THE TRENCHES

A creditor of a company filed suit for collection of a past due account. The creditor obtained a prejudgment attachment of the company's assets and went so far as to post a sheriff's deputy in the company's offices. The company, unable to do business under these conditions, settled with the creditor by paying the creditor with a cashier's check. Approximately eighty days later, the company filed for bankruptcy. Some time later, the debtor filed a preference lawsuit against the creditor, seeking return of the funds paid by cashier's check. The company ultimately negotiated a settlement with the creditor, recovering 75 percent of the money. Because of the extraordinary collection actions taken, the creditor had no ordinary-course-of-business defense to the preference and agreed to settle on terms favorable to the debtor company.

less than its market value, then the buyer may be subject to a lawsuit by the company, a bankruptcy trustee, or a creditors committee seeking to *avoid* (i.e., set aside) the transfer or seeking damages for what is claimed to be the true value of the assets. Unlike the ninety-day rule for preferences, the reach-back period for fraudulent transfers generally extends back to transfers made four years before bankruptcy or even earlier in some circumstances.

Creditors Committee

The Bankruptcy Code provides for the appointment of a committee of unsecured creditors, generally including as members the debtor's largest unsecured creditors. In appropriate cases, committees can also be appointed for bondholders, equity security holders, or others. The United States Trustee, a division of the U.S. Justice Department overseeing bankruptcy cases, appoints the committee, usually in the first month after the case is filed. The committee may employ attorneys and financial advisers, whose fees and expenses are paid out of the debtor's assets (estate) as a priority administrative expense.

Running a Business in Bankruptcy

When a company is in bankruptcy, court approval is not necessary for transactions in the ordinary course of business. However, notice to parties in interest and court approval are required prior to, among other things, (1) using, leasing, or selling property of the estate outside the ordinary course of business; (2) borrowing money on a secured or superpriority basis; (3) rejecting or assuming prepetition contracts; and (4) entering into new contracts or settlement agreements that affect property of the estate.

The court will generally defer to the business judgment of the company's management with respect to affairs related to its everyday business operations, such as whether to assume or reject a contract or lease. Business decisions become subject to closer judicial scrutiny, however, as they begin to address core reorganization issues.

Cash Collateral

When a secured creditor's collateral includes cash or cash proceeds of other collateral, the company in bankruptcy may not use the cash collateral unless the company adequately protects the creditor or obtains its consent. If a debtor cannot provide the secured creditor with adequate protection or obtain the creditor's consent, then the debtor cannot use the cash collateral. Generally, this means the debtor cannot spend any cash and may be forced to close its business. Although a secured creditor will have a security interest in the debtor's prepetition assets, the Bankruptcy Code generally provides that a secured creditor's security interest will not extend to *postpetition assets,* or those assets created after the bankruptcy petition is filed. Thus, adequately protecting a secured creditor often means giving the secured creditor a *replacement lien* on the same type of assets in postpetition collateral as the secured creditor has in prepetition collateral. Adequate protection can take a number of forms, including periodic cash payments, a replacement lien on additional types of assets, or both.

If the value of a secured creditor's collateral more than covers the outstanding debt owed, then the *equity cushion* of collateral value over debt generally will itself provide adequate protection. However, if the secured creditor is undersecured, with the outstanding debt exceeding the value of its collateral, some other form of adequate protection must be provided. This is particularly true for a *junior secured creditor* (a secured creditor whose priority position is behind one or more senior secured creditors), who may be undersecured given the outstanding debt owed a secured creditor with a higher-priority security interest in the same collateral.

Postpetition Financing

In many Chapter 11 cases, the debtor will need an additional credit line to continue operations. Under the Bankruptcy Code, a debtor may obtain *postpetition* or *debtor-in-possession financing* (often referred to as *DIP financing*) on such terms as the bankruptcy court approves. Generally, with DIP financing, the new, postpetition lender receives an administrative claim that is ahead of all other administrative expenses, including attorneys' and other professionals' fees (known as *superpriority administrative expense treatment*). Alternatively, the postpetition lender may receive a security interest in the debtor's postpetition assets. If the value of the debtor's assets is sufficiently high, the bankruptcy court can even approve a *priming* or *first-priority lien,* which gives the DIP lender a first-position lien on all of the debtor's prepetition and postpetition assets, even ahead of a prepetition lender.

CHAPTER 11 PLAN OF REORGANIZATION

When a debtor (or other party) proposes a plan of reorganization, the Bankruptcy Code provides for a procedure to determine whether the plan will be considered. Along with a plan, the plan proponent must file a disclosure statement. The *disclosure statement* functions much like a prospectus, informing creditors and equity security holders of material financial and business information to be used to evaluate the proposed plan of reorganization. The court must conclude that the disclosure statement contains adequate information before the plan itself can be considered. (Securities offered pursuant to a bankruptcy court–approved plan of reorganization are generally exempt from registration under the

Securities Act of 1933.) Once approved, the disclosure statement is sent to all creditors along with the plan and a ballot for voting on the plan. After the ballots are tabulated, the court holds a hearing on *confirmation* or approval of the proposed plan of reorganization.

Exclusivity Period

During the first 120 days after a bankruptcy petition is filed, the debtor has the exclusive right to propose a plan of reorganization, unless the bankruptcy court extends or reduces this period for cause. This precludes other parties in interest in the bankruptcy case (generally creditors) from proposing a plan that might dispossess the debtor and its management from control.

If exclusivity is terminated or expires, any creditor or party in interest in the bankruptcy case can file a proposed plan of reorganization. Sometimes creditors file plans to liquidate a debtor's assets, force a sale to a third party, or effect a corporate takeover. Thus, a creditor's plan can pose significant risks for a debtor's management, in addition to the potential litigation expense of opposing the plan.

Classification of Claims

Every plan of reorganization must classify creditors into classes. Usually, each secured creditor is placed in its own class, and general unsecured creditors are placed in a separate class. Equity security holders are also placed in a separate class based on the type of securities held. Depending on the circumstances, subordinated debenture holders may be placed in a separate class or grouped with unsecured creditors if they have no security interest in collateral.

Classes must be designated as impaired or unimpaired, depending on their treatment under the plan. If the plan provides that a particular class will not receive all of its state-law rights (e.g., the plan provides that a secured creditor's loan is to be extended for two years), then the class will be deemed *impaired*. If the plan provides a class all of its state-law rights (e.g., a secured creditor is to receive full payment pursuant to existing terms of a promissory note), then the class will be deemed *unimpaired*. Impaired classes are entitled to vote on the plan, but unimpaired classes do not vote and are deemed to have accepted the plan.

Unasserted, Contingent, and Unliquidated Claims

In many cases, a debtor may have creditors or potential creditors that have contingent or unliquidated claims or even unasserted claims. If a creditor has a claim and learns of the bankruptcy (either through formal notice or otherwise) but fails to file a proof of claim, then its claim can be barred from any recovery against the debtor and *discharged,* that is, deemed satisfied by the bankruptcy proceeding.

A debtor may have one or more creditors holding a contingent or unliquidated claim, the fixing or liquidation of which would unduly delay reorganization. In such an event, the debtor may seek intervention by the court to estimate the claim for purposes of the bankruptcy case. Thus, a creditor with an uncertain claim, which otherwise might take several years of litigation to establish, may have its claim estimated in a short evidentiary hearing or trial; thereafter, the creditor is limited to the amount of the estimated claim. This procedure enables a debtor company to reorganize even if it faces significant contingent or unliquidated claims.

FROM THE TRENCHES

A technology company had entered into a manufacturing agreement with a more established company to make products incorporating the technology company's key technology. When the technology company filed bankruptcy, it rejected the manufacturing agreement, which was an executory contract. The nondebtor party filed a proof of claim stating a multimillion-dollar claim, which the debtor company could not have paid under its proposed plan of reorganization. Because the damages claimed were unliquidated, the debtor company filed a motion with the bankruptcy court to have the claim estimated for all purposes, including for payment under the proposed plan. Even though a full trial of the claim could have taken months outside bankruptcy, the bankruptcy court scheduled only three days for the estimation hearing. The nondebtor party, fearing that its claim might be estimated at an unrealistically low figure, settled the claim prior to the estimation hearing, thereby permitting the debtor to confirm its plan of reorganization.

Plan Voting Requirements

Under the Bankruptcy Code, certain voting requirements must be met before a plan of reorganization can be confirmed. Fundamentally, at least one impaired class must vote to accept the proposed plan of reorganization. If that happens, the plan proponent may attempt to *cram down* the plan on any classes of creditors or equity security holders that oppose it; in that case, the proponent seeks court confirmation of the plan without the consent of each of the classes. In contrast, if all impaired classes vote to accept the plan, confirmation is much more easily obtained. For voting purposes, the votes of the debtor's insiders (such as officers, directors, and controlling shareholders) are not counted.

For a class to accept the plan, two-thirds of the dollar amount of the claims actually voting on the plan, and a majority in number of the creditors actually voting on the plan, must vote to accept it. For example, assume a class of creditors has thirty members and $2 million of claims. Only seventeen creditors, representing total claims of $1 million, vote. In this case, at least nine of the seventeen creditors voting will have to vote in favor of the plan, and they will have to represent at least $666,666 in claims. If the class vote does not satisfy these requirements, the class will be deemed to have rejected the plan, and the plan proponent will have to attempt to cram down the plan on that nonaccepting class.

If the debtor files an objection to a creditor's proof of claim, absent further action, the creditor will not be permitted to vote. However, the creditor can file a motion seeking temporary allowance of its claim for purposes of voting only, with the actual allowance of its claim being subject to a later determination. The court will determine whether, or in what amount, the claim should be allowed for voting purposes.

Cramdown Issues and the Absolute Priority Rule

If a plan is accepted by at least one impaired class of claims but is rejected by one or more other classes, the plan proponent can seek confirmation of its plan under the *cramdown* rules. These Bankruptcy Code provisions are designed to provide objecting classes with fair and equitable treatment. Although some variations exist, the plan must provide that a secured creditor retains its lien on its collateral and receives deferred cash payments (periodic cash payments over time with an appropriate discount rate of interest) equal to the creditor's allowed secured claim (i.e., the value of the collateral or the amount of the claim, whichever is less).

For unsecured creditors to be crammed down, either they must be paid in full with interest, or all junior classes must be precluded from receiving any property on account of their claims. Generally, this means that equity security holders (preferred or common shareholders) may not receive anything by reason of their ownership of shares if unsecured creditors are not being paid in full with interest. Their shares would be canceled under such a plan. This requirement implements the *absolute priority rule* of bankruptcy, which provides that, absent consent, each senior class of creditors must be paid in full before any junior class may receive anything under a plan. Thus, if secured creditors are not being paid in full, unsecured creditors and equity security holders can receive nothing. Or, as just described, if unsecured creditors are not being paid in full, equity security holders cannot retain their stock.

Some courts recognize what is known as a new value exception to this absolute priority rule. The *new value exception* permits a junior class, generally shareholders, to retain their shares if they contribute to the debtor substantial new value in the form of money or property that is essential to funding a reorganization. Other courts do not recognize this exception, however, and even when the exception is recognized, satisfying its requirements can be difficult. In particular, equity holders cannot be given an exclusive right to contribute new capital in exchange for equity in the reorganized entity free from competition from other bidders and without the benefit of a market valuation to ensure that the old equity holders pay full value for the new equity.[3]

Instead of relying on the new value exception, equity holders usually work to negotiate a plan of reorganization in which all impaired classes vote in favor of the plan. If all impaired classes vote in favor of the plan, neither the cramdown rules nor the absolute priority rule applies, and equity holders may retain whatever percentage of ownership they are able to negotiate.

Considerations in the Negotiation and Proposal of a Chapter 11 Plan

Generally, a plan must adhere to the priority scheme of the Bankruptcy Code, including the requirement that the interests of shareholders become subordinated to those of creditors. During the first 120 days, when the debtor has the exclusive right to propose a plan, a debtor's management and board must remember their fiduciary duty to all constituents, including creditors. When the venture's reorganization value is insufficient to pay all creditors in full, favoring equity holders over creditors can pose fiduciary duty problems for officers and directors.

The Bankruptcy Code also requires disclosure of which officers, directors, and other insiders will be employed or retained under the plan and the nature of any compensation to be paid to insiders by the reorganized debtor.

Discharge of Claims

A corporate debtor that successfully confirms a plan of reorganization and remains in business can receive a discharge of all of its debts. This means that creditors must accept the property being distributed under the plan as full satisfaction on their claims and cannot pursue the corporation thereafter on those claims. A discharge injunction, similar to the automatic stay, is issued to prevent creditors from taking action inconsistent with the confirmed plan of reorganization. As discussed above, equity holders will either have been able to negotiate a plan in which they retain ownership of some or all of the company's stock, have successfully used the new value exception to the absolute priority rule to retain ownership even in a cramdown case, or have been wiped out.

PREPACKAGED BANKRUPTCY AND PLANS OF REORGANIZATION

It can often take a debtor months or years to propose a plan, obtain approval for a disclosure statement, and finally win confirmation of the plan. Consequently, the Bankruptcy Code permits a debtor to prepare a disclosure statement and plan, circulate the statement and plan to its creditors, and actually solicit and complete voting on the plan—all before filing a bankruptcy petition. This process is known as a *prepack-*

aged bankruptcy. When a case has been prepackaged, the debtor typically files its disclosure statement, plan of reorganization, ballot, and ballot report on the day it files for bankruptcy. The debtor then seeks an expedited hearing both to approve the adequacy of the information in the disclosure statement and to confirm the plan of reorganization. If the court finds that the disclosure statement was inadequate, a new one must be prepared and sent to creditors along with new ballots for voting. Because many companies filing bankruptcy hope for a quick (and successful) exit from bankruptcy, prepackaged bankruptcy has become popular. Nevertheless, it is very difficult to achieve, particularly for operating companies.

Assuming sufficient votes are received to permit the plan to be confirmed, a prepackaged bankruptcy can speed up a debtor's emergence from bankruptcy. An out-of-court workout can be structured as a prepackaged bankruptcy, with a disclosure statement and plan instead of simple notices and a workout agreement. If sufficient majorities support the workout for confirmation of a bankruptcy plan, but too many holdouts refuse to consent to the workout to make it practical without a bankruptcy, a prepackaged bankruptcy can be filed to bind the holdout creditors to the plan. The formality of the documentation required unfortunately adds to the cost of the out-of-court workout. In appropriate cases, however, this approach can be used.

In a variant of the prepackaged bankruptcy, called a *prenegotiated bankruptcy,* the debtor meets with its creditors and negotiates the terms of the plan of reorganization prior to filing bankruptcy but solicits votes only after the case is filed and the disclosure statement is approved. If the groundwork is laid with the creditor body, the prenegotiated plan can shorten a company's time in bankruptcy. Also, because a formal disclosure statement and plan are drafted only if a bankruptcy case is needed, it involves lower up-front costs.

Although a prenegotiated bankruptcy can be useful for some companies, a true prepackaged bankruptcy is most effective for corporations with large amounts of public bond or debenture debt that they seek to restructure. This type of bankruptcy also works best for corporations that have few or insignificant disputed, contingent, or unliquidated claims and have no major litigation pending.

FROM THE TRENCHES

When Southland Corp., owner of the 7-Eleven convenience store chain, needed to restructure its high-yield public bond debt, it first solicited votes for a nonbankruptcy restructuring of the bonds. It placed advertisements in national newspapers and engaged in rounds of negotiations, all in an attempt to get bondholders to exchange their bonds for Southland stock and bonds at lower interest rates. In the end, Southland could get approval from only 80 percent of the bondholders, not the 95 percent it needed.

Because Southland used a disclosure statement and a plan of reorganization as part of its bond restructuring documents, however, it used the votes it did obtain (which were sufficient for bankruptcy plan confirmation) to file a Chapter 11 bankruptcy case, along with the disclosure statement, plan, and ballots. Southland hoped that the bankruptcy court would approve its disclosure statement and confirm its plan based on those documents alone, but other creditors that were dissatisfied with the proposed plan objected to the disclosure statement and ballot process. The bankruptcy court ruled that defects in the process from a bankruptcy perspective meant that Southland had to redraft its disclosure statement and resolicit votes. Although this was done at considerable additional cost and delay, ultimately Southland did confirm a plan of reorganization restructuring its bond debt in far less time than would have been required if it had simply filed bankruptcy without any prepackaging.

Business Combination Through Chapter 11 Bankruptcy

It is possible to accomplish a merger between a debtor corporation and another corporation through a Chapter 11 plan of reorganization. Similar to a plan of merger outside bankruptcy, a Chapter 11 plan may set forth the terms of a merger and provide that the stock of the debtor is to be sold to the acquiring corporation, that a new corporation is to be formed into which the debtor and the acquiring corporation are merged, or that some other form of transaction is to be implemented.

The principal disadvantage of a stock merger with a debtor corporation is that the acquiring corporation generally will become liable for all debts of the debtor. Because creditors have priority over shareholders, it may also be very difficult to direct that the debtor's shareholders receive the proceeds of the merger. If a plan proposes to pay the proceeds to the debtor's shareholders, it otherwise would have to meet the Chapter 11 plan requirements, potentially including the cramdown and absolute priority rule of bankruptcy.

An alternative to a stock merger is a sale of a debtor company's assets, free and clear of liens, with the proceeds to be paid into the bankruptcy estate. Such a sale may be done either through a Chapter 11 plan or as a separate asset sale after notice to creditors and court approval pursuant to Section 363 of the Bankruptcy Code. The acquiring corporation purchases those assets free and clear of existing liens and debts but often assumes selected debts (usually those associated with the ongoing business). The purchase price is distributed in the debtor's bankruptcy pursuant to a Chapter 11 plan or in a Chapter 7 liquidation if the case is converted from Chapter 11. If the debtor is insolvent, however, its shareholders will most likely not receive any of the proceeds. These "363 sales" are a common use of Chapter 11 bankruptcy.

Fiduciary Duties of the Officers and Directors of an Insolvent Company

When a company becomes insolvent, the fiduciary duty of its directors and officers extends beyond the shareholders to include the company's creditors as well. Accordingly, officers and directors must be careful not to approve or take actions that favor shareholders at the expense of creditors. Management, officers, and directors have expanded fiduciary duties triggered by insolvency even if the company has not yet filed bankruptcy. They are required to act as trustees of the company's property for the benefit of creditors, shareholders, and other parties in interest, subject to the provisions of the Bankruptcy Code. If anything, a director's duty to shareholders after a bankruptcy is filed weakens in comparison with his or her duty to the creditors because shareholders are at the bottom of the totem pole in bankruptcy. Balancing the interests of shareholders and creditors can be difficult. Nevertheless, bankruptcy actually provides a forum conducive to resolution of conflicts among competing interests because the contest is judicially supervised, and constituencies can form committees and seek to be represented at the expense of the company.

Continuation of prepetition management with prepetition levels of compensation ordinarily does not require court approval. Management and the board can continue to run the debtor company, and shareholders can continue to meet and vote their shares, absent intervention from the court.

Effect of Bankruptcy on Director and Officer Litigation and Indemnification

Although the filing of a bankruptcy case immediately protects the debtor from further litigation on prepetition claims due to the automatic stay, there is no stay of litigation against anyone other than the debtor. For example, litigation against the debtor's directors and officers will not be stayed, even if it directly relates to the company's business. Under rare circumstances, a bankruptcy court can issue an injunction prohibiting further litigation against nondebtor officers or directors. This power is rarely used absent a compelling showing that the litigation would be so disruptive to management that, without an injunction, the debtor would not be able to reorganize.

Indemnification claims arising from prepetition services and based on a prepetition contract may be treated as prepetition unsecured claims even if the duty to indemnify arose postpetition. For example, if a director of the debtor company has a prepetition contractual right to be indemnified by the company for any liability arising out of board service, and the director is sued after the bankruptcy petition is filed, his or her claim for indemnification is a prepetition unsecured claim. However, indemnification claims arising from prepetition services but based on an executory employment contract that the debtor has obtained the bankruptcy court's approval to assume should constitute postpetition administrative claims. If directors' and officers' (D&O) insurance policy proceeds are payable directly to the officer and director beneficiaries, the proceeds likely will not be deemed property of the bankruptcy estate and may be so paid. The automatic stay may prevent insurance companies from canceling a company's D&O policies after a bankruptcy is filed.

Loss of Control and Other Risks in Bankruptcy

In a typical Chapter 11 case, a debtor company's management remains in possession and control, subject to replacement by the board of directors. However, creditors or others in a Chapter 11 case can file a motion seeking appointment of an independent Chapter 11 trustee to take possession of all of the debtor's assets. The most common grounds for such a motion are fraud or gross mismanagement by the debtor-in-possession. Accordingly, although a debtor's management generally will not be replaced by a Chapter 11 trustee, replacement remains a risk of filing a bankruptcy.

Another risk of filing a Chapter 11 case is that at some point the court may convert the case to a Chapter 7 liquidation, with the accompanying automatic appointment of a Chapter 7 trustee, or may decide to dismiss the Chapter 11 case altogether. Conversion or dismissal can be ordered for cause, including inability to effectuate a plan of reorganization, unreasonable delay prejudicial to creditors, failure to meet any court-imposed deadlines for filing a plan, or other failure to comply with court orders.

EXHIBIT 12.2

PROS AND CONS OF FILING BANKRUPTCY

Advantages	Disadvantages
• Automatic stay of creditor actions	• Expensive
• Power to reject unfavorable executory contracts and limit damages on leases	• Court approval required for all decisions outside the ordinary course of business
• Power to force restructure of debts on nonconsenting creditors	• Potential loss of customer or vendor relationships
• Ability to recover preferences and fraudulent transfers	• Possible loss of control through conversion to Chapter 7 or appointment of trustee
• Opportunity to preserve going-concern value of company	• Risk that shareholders' equity position will be wiped out in favor of creditors

Bankruptcy Pros and Cons

Obviously, filing or not filing bankruptcy can be a life-or-death decision for a company. Although bankruptcy offers significant and often unique advantages, there are major risks. Exhibit 12.2 lists some of the major advantages and disadvantages of filing bankruptcy.

PUTTING IT INTO PRACTICE

Although things started out well for DataAccelleation, the money raised from Billy Barnett and family and friends proved insufficient. Over the past three months, the company had experienced an increasingly serious shortfall in cash. At first, Kendra was able to pay the landlord and other operating expenses by delaying some payments to less critical vendors. As the cash flow problems became worse, payments to some more important creditors were delayed even further. Calls from creditors began to increase, and several threatened legal action if they were not paid. Kendra paid the most vocal creditors but lacked the cash to pay all of them. Eventually, two vendors sued DataAccelleation for breach of contract. Kendra called Michael Cruz for advice.

Michael involved his insolvency partner, Pete Bengal, who filed answers on DataAccelleation's behalf to the two complaints and asked Kendra for a package of financial information on the company. After reviewing it, Pete asked Kendra for her most conservative projections of DataAccelleation's financial situation and an assessment of its business plan in light of the current financial problems. Pete pressed Kendra to be certain that these projections were realistic, and he warned that a failure to keep promises to creditors could seriously damage DataAccelleation's credibility if problems got worse.

Mindful of her personal guaranty of the lease and the additional costs an unlawful detainer (eviction) action would involve, Kendra made sure that funds were available to pay the landlord. After their discussions, however, Kendra concluded that DataAccelleation needed the ability to stretch out payments to its creditors for another three months or so. If the creditors agreed, DataAccelleation probably could avoid a more formal workout effort.

Kendra made a list of the largest creditors, the amounts owed each, and how delinquent DataAccelleation was on payments. She then personally called each of the major creditors and explained DataAccelleation's financial condition. She asked that DataAccelleation be allowed to pay 20 percent of the normal payment for the next two months, at which point DataAccelleation projected it would be able to resume ordinary payment terms. She told these creditors that DataAccelleation would completely catch up on payments within six months.

continued...

continued...

Although several creditors refused these terms, most accepted Kendra's proposal, with the proviso that DataAccelleation be caught up in five months. Building on the progress made with some of DataAccelleation's largest creditors, Kendra again called the creditors who had not agreed. She named some of DataAccelleation's creditors that had agreed to the terms and again asked for cooperation. After several more rounds of discussions, Kendra finally was able to work out a less favorable, but still feasible, arrangement. Fortunately, the next few months proved to be close to Kendra's projections, and DataAccelleation was able to work its way out of the immediate crisis. The litigation with the two vendors continued during this period, and DataAccelleation later settled both cases by paying the full debt owed but without additional interest or attorneys' fees.

After several more months of successful operations, Kendra felt it was time to seek additional financing. She decided to investigate venture capital financing.

NOTES

1. *In re* Catapult Enter., Inc., 165 F.3d 747 (9th Cir. 1999), *cert. denied*, 528 U.S. 924 (1999).
2. Institut Pasteur v. Cambridge Biotech Corp., 104 F.3d 489 (1st Cir. 1997), *cert. denied*, 521 U.S. 1120 (1997).
3. Bank of America NT & SA v. 203 North LaSalle St. Partnership, 526 U.S. 434 (1999).

Chapter 13

VENTURE CAPITAL

The most common sources of capital for start-up enterprises are the entrepreneur and the entrepreneur's family and friends. For the most part, institutional investors have little interest in investing in start-up companies. One notable exception is the investment funds that comprise the venture capital industry. In the past forty years, venture capitalists have grown some of the nation's leading companies, including Intel, Sycamore Networks, Cisco, Genentech, Staples, and Microsoft. Indeed, the 2,000 plus publicly traded, venture-backed firms created between 1972 and 2000 have an aggregate market capitalization of more than $2.7 trillion, almost one-third of the total market value of all public companies in the United States.[1]

In 2000, the venture capital industry invested more than $90 billion in more than 5,000 financings, according to VentureOne, a San Francisco firm that researches the industry. Despite a drop in both the number of financings and the amount of money invested in 2001 to just over 2,700 deals with approximately $32 billion invested, venture capital money continues to be available as never before to fund the dreams of entrepreneurs.

This chapter first discusses the pros and cons of seeking venture capital, then outlines strategies for finding it, and provides tips for preparing business plans to present to venture capitalists. It then highlights factors to consider when selecting a venture capitalist. Next comes a discussion of how the parties reach agreement on a valuation for the company, and thus the percentage of the equity the venture capitalists will receive in exchange for their investment. The chapter then analyzes the rights and protections normally given venture capitalists buying preferred stock. These include the liquidation preference, the dividend preference, redemption rights, conversion rights, antidilution provisions (including preemptive rights and price-protection provisions), voting rights, registration rights, information rights, and co-sale rights. The chapter concludes with a brief description of the vesting requirements normally imposed by venture capitalists and their expectations with respect to the granting of employee stock options.

Certain aspects of the topics covered in this chapter were introduced in previous chapters. This chapter will build on those discussions and develop them further in the context of an entrepreneur seeking venture capital.

Deciding Whether to Seek Venture Capital

The first question the entrepreneur should consider in deciding whether to pursue venture capital is whether the new venture will meet the criteria used by most venture capitalists (often referred to as VCs). Generally, a venture capitalist will want to invest a substantial amount of money, usually more than $500,000 and often more than $1 million. However, a few funds will do seed investing for a new start-up at a lower level. Venture capitalists are usually looking for an enterprise that has the potential to grow to a significant size quickly and to generate an annual return on investment in excess of 40 percent over a period of three to five years. Venture capitalists need to target that rate of return to realize the compounded returns of at least 20 percent per annum expected by their investors.

For the most part, venture capitalists have focused on the information-technology industry, which includes computer hardware and software, scientific instruments, telecommunications, multimedia, and, more recently, cyberspace. Venture-backed public companies include Akamai, eBay, Yahoo!, Amazon.com, and Juniper Networks. The second largest concentration of venture capital investing has been in life science companies, including those focusing on biotechnology, medical devices, diagnostics, and therapeutics. Genentech and Amgen were both venture-backed. Although venture capital investment remains most concentrated in these two fields, venture capitalists are financial investors seeking an optimal rate of return, and they have invested successfully in other areas such as retail, consumer products, new materials, health services, and environmental technology.

As discussed briefly in Chapter 7, venture capital financing can be an attractive funding source for a number of reasons. Venture capital may allow the entrepreneur to raise all of the capital from one source or from a lead investor who can attract other venture funds. Venture capitalists have experience with the challenges of start-ups and know how to grow a company to an initial public offering, sale of the business, or other liquidity event. Experienced venture capitalists have a large network of contacts who can help the company succeed. Venture capitalists are often able to provide valuable assistance in recruiting other members of the management team. Venture capitalists are usually excellent board members. Being venture-backed gives an enterprise a certain cachet, which can open doors to other financing and resources.

Venture backed firms tend to raise more money, grow more quickly, secure more patents, and have substantially higher market shares than companies not backed by venture capital.[2] Ninety percent of new entrepreneurial businesses that do not attract venture capital fail within three years. This contrasts with a 33 percent failure rate for venture-backed companies.[3] Venture-backed firms also perform significantly better after they go public than similar non-venture-backed firms.[4]

Most venture capitalists look for companies that can provide liquidity in three to five years. If an entrepreneur is looking for a longer time horizon—a factor that should be discussed with any investor—the enterprise may not be suitable for venture capital. Other reasons to avoid using venture capital funding include the following: (1) venture investors are more sophisticated and may drive a harder bargain on the pricing and terms of their investment than friends or family; (2) venture investors may be more likely to assert their power in molding the enterprise than more passive investors; and (3) venture investors may be more interested than passive investors in taking control of the enterprise if the entrepreneur stumbles.

At some point, most entrepreneurs face the choice between raising the initial (or additional) funds from family and friends and *angels* (wealthy individuals who invest in start-ups) and obtaining venture capital financing. Family and friends and angels may be willing to invest at a lower price (i.e., to accept a higher valuation of the company at the time they invest) and tend to require less onerous investment terms and conditions than venture capitalists, but they often bring little else to the table. Perhaps more importantly, these sources may be limited after an initial investment, leaving the ongoing business high and dry. Venture capitalists may demand a lower valuation but will almost always bring many intangibles that can help the company to grow faster and to be more successful. Often this decision is referred to as the choice between "dumb money" and "smart money."

There are a number of sources of printed and electronic information on the venture industry. An entrepreneur may wish to consult published guides such as *Pratt's Guide to Venture Capital* and *West Coast Venture Capital;* magazines that cover the industry such as *Fast Company, Upside,* and *The Red Herring;* and reports from information-gathering organizations such as VentureOne Corp., Venture Economics, and Securities Data Corp. *The Money of Invention: How Venture Capital Creates New Wealth,* by Harvard Business School Professors Paul A. Gompers and Josh Lerner, provides an excellent overview of the venture capital industry and the mechanisms venture capitalists use to achieve success. An entrepreneur may also want to use West Law, Lexis-Nexis, or a similar online service to cull news articles on particular companies or venture capitalists. Some information may also be available on the World Wide Web, including the Web sites of venture capital firms.

FINDING VENTURE CAPITAL

Sending unsolicited business plans to a venture capital firm is almost certainly a formula for failure. Venture capitalists receive dozens of unsolicited plans each week. Very few of these plans are read thoroughly, if at all, and even fewer lead to financing.

A good way to get a venture capitalist's attention is to arrange an introduction by someone who knows the venture capitalist. If the entrepreneur has friends who have obtained venture capital financing, they may be able to provide the introduction. Similarly, individuals working at universities, government labs, and other entities that license technology to venture-backed companies may have connections worth pursuing. Accountants and bankers

FROM THE TRENCHES

eBay, Inc., the pioneer of online person-to-person trading, was formed as a sole proprietorship in 1995 by Pierre M. Omidyar. eBay's business model called for bringing together buyers and sellers of a wide range of goods in an efficient and entertaining Web-based auction format. eBay remained a sole proprietorship until it was incorporated in 1996. In June 1997, eBay raised $3 million in a financing led by Benchmark Capital. The venture capitalists helped recruit key employees and directors, provided valuable direction on the development of the business plan, and introduced the company to potential investment bankers. In August 1998, a group of investment bankers led by Goldman, Sachs & Co. took eBay public, raising approximately $60 million.

who do business with venture-backed companies also are good sources for introductions, as are money managers at pension funds, insurance companies, universities, and other institutions that invest in venture funds.

Perhaps the best way to find venture money is to engage a lawyer who works primarily in the venture capital field as a business attorney. Although many lawyers may have done a venture capital deal, fewer than a dozen law firms nationwide truly specialize in representing venture-backed companies. More than half of these law firms are located in or near northern California's Silicon Valley or in other technology centers in the United States.

In choosing a law firm, an entrepreneur should ask for information about the venture funds that the law firm has formed, the number and identity of venture funds the firm has represented in investments, and the venture-backed companies the firm represents. A law firm that specializes in this area will have lists of these clients readily available. Less experienced firms may speak in generalities.

A firm that specializes in this area will also have lawyers with the experience to give information and advice and to ensure that negotiations with the venture capitalists go smoothly. Although deal making in the venture capital industry is not rocket science, it is a bit clubby, and it helps to have an attorney who knows the club rules.

Because the most experienced firms represent venture capitalists as well as venture funds, it is likely that the entrepreneur's lawyer may have represented, or may be currently representing, the venture capitalist in other matters. The legal code of ethics requires that the attorney disclose his or her involvement in other transactions to both parties and obtain appropriate consents. An entrepreneur may wish to explore with the attorney his or her relationships with the venture capitalists to whom the entrepreneur is being introduced.

Because attorneys in this industry work with a large number of venture capitalists, they should be able to introduce the entrepreneur to those venture capitalists who would be most interested in this particular deal. Most venture capitalists specialize in particular industries; thus, it does not make much sense to present an Internet deal to a venture capitalist who specializes in medical device companies. Venture capitalists also tend to prefer to invest at a particular stage of development: *seed* (raw start-up), *early stage* (product in beta testing or just being shipped), *later stage* (product is fully developed or is being sold and generating revenue), or *mezzanine* (the financing round before the anticipated initial public offering).

Selecting a Venture Capitalist

Generally, an entrepreneur begins the process of seeking venture capital by preparing a business plan, although many deals have been done without a plan. (The preparation of business plans and offering memoranda is discussed generally in Chapter 7.)

Business Plans

Business plans prepared for venture capitalists should be more concise and less legalistic than plans prepared for other investors. Venture capitalists are very sophisticated and do not need, or expect, the type of disclosure mandated by federal and state securities laws for sales to less experienced investors.

The business plan prepared for circulation to venture capitalists usually describes the product or service concept and the opportunity for investors.[5] Typically, the plan includes sections describing the industry, the market, the means for producing the product or delivering the service, the competition, the superiority of this product or service over existing products or services, the marketing plan, the proprietary position (such as patents) that will provide barriers to entry by competitors, and the strengths of the management team. Projections and the assumptions on which they are based are generally included. The entrepreneur should prepare an executive summary, keeping in mind that many venture capitalists will not read beyond the first paragraph of that summary. Therefore, the compelling reason to make the investment should appear at the top of the executive summary and should be borne out by the remainder of the plan. An experienced lawyer can assist in editing the business plan.

Most venture capitalists will focus on the viability of the concept, the size of the opportunity, and the quality of the management team. To the extent that there are holes in the team (e.g., the team has technicians but no experienced managers, or the team lacks a strong CFO or VP of Marketing), the entrepreneur should acknowledge these weaknesses in discussions with venture capitalists and ask them for assistance in finding the right people. More than one venture capitalist has said that the three most important factors in making an investment are "people, people, and people." The right team can fix a flawed concept, but a flawed team cannot get a brilliant concept to market.

Venture capitalists comment that certain weaknesses appear again and again in the plans they review. Common pitfalls include:

- ***The plan is too long.*** Most venture capitalists have little tolerance for reading more than fifteen or twenty pages. Details such as projections, financials, press clips, detailed biographies, detailed schematics, and detailed market analysis can be shortened, eliminated (for now, but presented later to those really interested), or moved into appendices for the most interested reader.

- ***The executive summary is too long.*** The executive summary should be one page and should concisely describe (1) the market; (2) the unmet need in the market; (3) the compelling solution offered by the entrepreneur; (4) the strategy for connecting the need, the solution, and the customers; (5) the technology or other proprietary aspects of the solution that will give this venture an edge over the competition; (6) the experience of the team that demonstrates that the plan can be implemented; and (7) how much money is being raised and what will be accomplished with the funding.

- ***The opportunity is too small.*** Many good business opportunities are too small for venture investors because of their need to earn a high return on investment. Although other investors might be willing to put up $2 million to grow a company into a $25 million business with net income of 10 percent of sales in five years, these returns are too low to interest most venture capitalists.
- ***The plan is poorly organized.*** A poorly organized plan suggests that the team may be incapable of taking on the larger task of organizing a company. There is no set formula, but a plan should have a logical progression and should not be overly focused on one area at the expense of others. For example, many plans drafted by engineers devote substantial pages to explaining the technology in minute detail but fail to adequately describe the market, the competition, or the strategy for connecting customers and the product.
- ***The plan lacks focus.*** Many plans call for a company to pursue multiple opportunities simultaneously in multiple markets. The more complex the story, the harder it is to sell to venture capitalists. Great opportunities are conveyed in few words (e.g., remember "plastics" from the movie *The Graduate*). Focus on the greatest opportunity. The other opportunities can be discussed later or handled in a very brief section toward the back of the plan.

Courtship Process

Once introductions are made, venture capitalists will follow up with meetings if they are interested in investing. This begins a courtship process that typically takes two to three months. For this reason, it is a good idea to engage a number of venture capitalists in discussions simultaneously, rather than serially. Generally, venture capitalists will be quick to let a company know if they are interested. Follow-up meetings are an expression of interest, and many venture capital funds hold weekly internal meetings to discuss the status of various prospects.

As a part of this courtship, the venture capitalists will perform due diligence. *Due diligence* is the process through which venture capitalists will examine a company's concept, product, potential market, financial health, and legal situation. Due diligence is typically conducted by venture capitalists or consultants with financial and technical expertise and by lawyers. Often a technical or industry expert will be sent to meet with the entrepreneur and take a close look at the technology or concept. The venture capitalist may also talk with potential customers to help gauge the size of the potential market for the product.

As the courtship continues, the entrepreneur should also perform due diligence on the venture capitalist. Much information can be gathered conversationally. Appropriate questions include the following:

- What other companies within this industry has the venture fund invested in?
- What deals has this particular venture capitalist done?
- On what boards does the venture capitalist sit?
- How many more years does the fund that will be making the investment have to run?
- Will the venture capitalist be willing and able to participate in the next round of financing?
- Are there other venture capital firms that the venture capitalist thinks should be invited into the deal?
- Would the venture capitalist be willing to work alongside other venture capitalists with whom the entrepreneur is in discussions?
- How has the venture capitalist handled management changes in the past?
- Are there any founders who were pushed aside or pushed out?
- What is the time horizon for this investment?
- What if there is no exit event providing liquidity by that date?
- What kind of return does the venture capitalist need to make on this investment?

The entrepreneur should ask the venture capitalist to provide introductions to other founders of companies in which he or she has invested and then should contact those founders to obtain insight on the kind of partner the venture capitalist is likely to be.

Multiple Investors

If it is possible to attract and accommodate more than one venture capitalist in a round, it can be to the company's advantage to do so. Although working with more than one venture investor may be a bit more complicated, it does increase the network of resources available to the company. In addition, another venture capitalist may be able to serve as a counterbalance if the entrepreneur and the first venture capitalist end up at loggerheads on some issue. Such venture capitalists are often excellent partners. However, some venture capitalists will not participate in a deal unless they are the only investor or the only lead investor.

In raising money during the next round of venture capital, the company will want to be able to tell new investors that the prior-round investors are stepping up to invest more. Typically, the lead venture capitalist in the prior round will allow the new investor(s) to take the lead in negotiating with the company the price of the stock in the subsequent round. Once the price is set, the lead investors from the prior round will indicate how much stock they will buy. If there is more than one venture capitalist in the initial round, the company stands a better chance that at least one of the existing investors will invest in the next round. Also, if there are several venture investors in the initial round, the entrepreneur is more likely to have an ally who can coax further investment from the group if the company underperforms.

Determining the Valuation

Eventually, a venture capitalist will indicate that he or she is ready to make the investment, and the discussion will turn to valuation. In essence, this is a discussion of price: How much will the venture capitalist pay for what percentage of the company?

FROM THE TRENCHES

Polly President, the founder of a traditional multimedia company, bootstrapped her company into a leader in its nascent industry. The company, which had been financed by family and friends, had modest earnings. With the growth of the Internet, Polly decided to raise $2.5 million in venture capital to move into cyberspace. By chance, she was introduced to Joe Venture, a venture capitalist who had just set up a new fund for Internet investing. Polly had little time to devote to fund-raising. Because the discussions with Joe were going so well, she decided not to seek introductions to any other venture capitalists.

After weeks of discussion, Joe and Polly agreed on a valuation, and Joe sent over a term sheet. Unbeknownst to Polly, Joe was previously employed in the banking industry, and he had only recently moved into the bank's venture fund, which did only mezzanine investing (the financing round before an anticipated public offering). The term sheet Joe presented looked more like a complex loan deal than a venture deal, due both to his background in banking and to the focus of mezzanine-round investors on protecting against the downside (due to the limited upside of a mezzanine deal). It took more than five months to conclude a deal with Joe, and the ultimate deal contained highly unusual downside protection for Joe's fund. Although Joe had the right industry focus for Polly's company, an inquiry about his experience would have revealed that he was the wrong investor for this stage of investment.

Comment: Had Polly pursued multiple investors and selected a more appropriate venture capitalist, she would have saved time and been able to negotiate a less onerous deal.

Pricing Terminology

The venture capitalist's offer is often communicated in an arcane shorthand that is unfathomable to the uninitiated. For example, a venture capitalist might say,

- "I'll put in $2 million based on three pre-money."
- "I'm thinking two-thirds based on three pre-; that will get you to five post."

- "I'm looking for two-fifths of the company post-money, and for that I'll put up the two."
- "It's worth $3 million pre-money, and I want to own 40 percent of it after we close."

What does all this mean? This is exactly the question the entrepreneur needs to ask to make sure that there is no misunderstanding about the price being offered.

Each of the above statements is a different way of expressing exactly the same proposal. The venture capitalist is willing to invest $2 million in the company. The terms *pre-money* and *post-money* refer to the valuation that is put on the company before and after the investment. The venture capitalist is proposing that the company is worth $3 million before the investment of $2 million and is therefore worth $5 million immediately after the investment. The ownership share being requested is an amount equivalent to 66⅔ percent of the equity based on the pre-money number (i.e., $2 million/$3 million), which is 40 percent of the company measured immediately after the closing of the deal (i.e., $2 million/$5 million). It is a very good idea to ask what dollar amount is to be invested and what the percentages of the equity are that translate into pre- and post-money.

If the investor knows the number of shares the company has outstanding, he or she may give the entrepreneur a per-share price. It is relatively easy to translate valuations based on share prices into pre- and post-money company valuations, and vice versa. For example, if 6 million shares are outstanding, the company will need to issue 4 million shares at $0.50 per share for a venture capitalist to invest $2 million and end up owning 40 percent of the company.

If the percentage the investor wants to own after the deal closes is known, the following two equations can be used to work back to the number of shares that will need to be issued:

(1) Shares outstanding post-money = Shares outstanding pre-money divided by 1 minus the percentage to be owned by investor post-money

(2) Shares to be issued = Shares outstanding post-money minus shares outstanding pre-money

Accordingly, if 6 million shares are outstanding pre-money and the venture capitalist wants to end up owning 40 percent of the company, then 6 million divided by 60 percent (i.e., 1 minus .40) tells us that 10 million shares need to be outstanding after the offering. Therefore, the company will need to issue 4 million new shares.

Negotiating Price

Often there is some negotiation during pricing discussions. A venture capitalist may ask what valuation the company is seeking or may volunteer a ballpark figure for pricing. Valuing a company is never easy. It is especially difficult with a start-up, which has no operating history. Venture capitalists will often base their valuations on management's own projections and on other deals done in the industry by other companies. Obtaining information on comparable companies that have received venture financing can help the entrepreneur establish the right valuation.

The entrepreneur should press the venture capitalist on how the reservation of shares for future stock issuances to employees will work or, alternatively, propose to the venture capitalist how it will work. For example, if the venture capitalist's offer of $2 million is for 40 percent of the company including the reservation of 1 million shares for options, then he or she is saying that there are in effect 7 million shares outstanding or reserved (not 6 million). Therefore, under the formulas set forth above, the venture capitalist would be entitled to 4.667 million shares (not 4 million) for the $2 million investment. Applying the formulas:

$$11.667 \text{ million} = \frac{7 \text{ million}}{.60}$$

$$4.667 \text{ million} = 11.667 \text{ million} - 7 \text{ million}$$

If this is not what the entrepreneur has in mind, the company should propose that the 1 million reserved shares not be taken into account in the valuation. If they are not, then the venture capitalist will be issued 4 million shares, as we calculated above. In that case, the holders of the 6 million old shares and the venture capitalist holding the 4 million new shares will jointly bear the dilution for the 1 million reserved shares in a ratio of 60/40, rather than having the holders of the 6 million old shares bear all of the dilution.

When the entrepreneur is confident that an offer is about to be made, or immediately after an offer is made, he or she will want to inform the other potential venture capitalists and ask any that remain interested for their offers. Provided that they have had a chance to do some due diligence and to discuss the investment with their colleagues within the fund, other venture capitalists who are interested in the deal will generally put their valuation offers on the table fairly quickly. These valuations may differ substantially, and the entrepreneur may attempt to use the higher offers to persuade others to pay a higher price.

The venture capitalist willing to pay the highest price is not necessarily the person whom the entrepreneur should most want in the deal. Another venture capitalist who is not willing to pay quite as much may be a better partner in growing the business or in attracting investors for future rounds. Some firms are better than others at standing behind an entrepreneur who stumbles. The entrepreneur should undertake due diligence in the form of reference checks to determine who the best partners might be.

An entrepreneur who has more than one offer should be pleased and should move quickly to choose the investors and finalize the deal. Indeed, if the entrepreneur is extremely comfortable with the venture capitalist with whom he or she has been primarily negotiating, the entrepreneur may decide not to shop the offer to other venture capitalists after reviewing the initial offer but may simply proceed to a closing.

Although it may seem like a good idea to get all the suitors into a room to negotiate the price, this approach should be resisted. Those offering the higher valuation have little incentive to talk the lower offerors into offering more, and the lower offerors may convince those willing to pay a higher price that they are paying too much.

The final price will depend on whom the entrepreneur wants to have in the deal, how much money needs to be raised, and the nonprice terms (discussed below). For tax reasons and for fairness, generally just one price is paid for the stock in a round.

Once the valuation is agreed upon, it is unusual to revisit the issue, unless there is a material adverse change in the business before the closing, or material adverse information is discovered. Although most venture capitalists will not attempt to renegotiate the price absent those kinds of developments, there are always some who feel that all items are negotiable before the deal is closed. To avoid these types of partners, the entrepreneur should find out all he or she can about each venture capitalist.

By far the most important issue in these negotiations will be price. Nonetheless, some of the most time-consuming and difficult negotiations may still lie ahead—determining the other terms and conditions of the investment.

Rights of Preferred Stock

As explained in Chapter 4, for tax reasons, most venture funds are precluded by their pension fund and other tax-exempt limited partners from investing in a tax pass-through vehicle such as an S corporation, a limited partnership, a general partnership, or a limited liability company. Therefore, when venture capitalists make an investment, it is almost always in preferred stock of a C corporation.

Most of the nonprice terms of the deal will relate to rights that attach to the preferred stock. These rights will be spelled out in the company's certificate of incorporation. Certain other rights may not be contained in the company's charter but will be established in one or more contracts.

Traditional preferred stock issued by large, publicly traded companies carries a preference on liquidation, pays a higher dividend than common stock, and is often set up to be redeemed at a certain date. It is usually not convertible into common stock, and it is often nonvoting. In many ways, it functions like debt.

Venture capital preferred stock is a very different beast. It does have a preference on liquidation. It also has a dividend preference but traditionally only if and when the directors declare dividends, and everyone expects none to be declared.

Venture capital preferred stock is convertible at any time at the election of the holder and automatically converts upon the occurrence of certain events. It votes on an as-if-converted-to-common basis and may have special voting rights with respect to certain events and the election of directors. It may have a mandated redemption provision, requiring the company to buy back the stock at a set price on a given date in the future. Even if it does have a redemption provision, however, the ability of a start-up company to make the redemption is often far from certain.

Downside and Sideways Protection

Over the years, a number of bells and whistles have been added to the preferred stock issued to venture capitalists. At first, this was done to differentiate it from the common stock and to bolster the argument that it has a higher value for tax purposes. As explained in Chapter 5, this allows the common stock to be sold to the founders and employees at a much lower price than the preferred stock. Later, many features were added to increase the rights and protections provided to the preferred investors in the event that the company ran into difficulty.

When negotiating the rights and privileges afforded the preferred stock, entrepreneurs should keep in mind that if all goes well and the venture performs as projected, the venture capitalists will convert their preferred stock into common stock (upon an initial public offering or, in some cases, upon a successful sale of the company). Upon conversion, most, if not all, of the bells and whistles go away. As a result, if the company is successful, all the protective devices will have had little or no effect on the return to the founders and the other holders of common stock. But, if the company goes down in value or moves *sideways* (that is, earns a modest return on capital invested), then the venture capitalists will not convert their preferred stock, and they will rely on their rights and preferences to augment their return. Unfortunately for the holders of the common, this reduces their share of the pie.

Since the market downturn of 2000–2001 and the burst of the dot-com bubble, many investors are seeking better protection against falling valuation. It is, however, still the case that new money sets the terms of each new round of investment. As a result, the new investor may require the investors who participated in earlier rounds to give up many of their protective provisions to get the deal done.

FROM THE TRENCHES

The first-round investor's rights in an investment in a telecommunications company included the right to put the stock back to the company if the company did not make its projections, the right to add directors and control the board if milestones were missed, a full-ratchet antidilution provision, and a right to buy all of any future issuance. Extending these rights to additional investors would have created misaligned incentives and created rivalry within the investor group.

When the company lined up its second-round investors, it went back to the first-round investor and explained that it had investors ready to put in $4 million. The company also explained that if these rights stayed in place, the new investors would either seek the same rights or would want a deep discount on the true value of the company. The first-round investor agreed to carve back its rights to those found in a conventional deal so that the company could have the greatest opportunity for success.

Comment: This entrepreneur was fortunate in being able to convince subsequent investors to take lesser rights and to restructure the rights of the earlier round to be less onerous. The better practice is to consider carefully the rights to be given to a round of investors on the assumption that investors in follow-up rounds will expect rights at least as great.

Many seasoned venture capitalists will tell you that no investor has ever made any significant money from these downside or sideways protection features and will argue that they receive far too much attention in the negotiation of a venture deal. Under this line of reasoning (which an entrepreneur should embrace in the negotiations), once the valuation is set, the preferred stock needs to have only a liquidation preference and a dividend preference (if declared). The preferred stock should otherwise function as common stock so that all investors are on essentially the same terms going forward. By having all shareholders aligned in this manner, the entrepreneur and the outside investors will focus only on what will create value for the company, rather than on special circumstances that may afford one or the other greater leverage or returns. If the preferred stock gets special rights and downside protection, the stock begins to look like debt rather than equity. If it functions like debt, the argument goes, it should have a fixed return (like a loan) rather than the unlimited upside of equity in a high-growth venture.

Other venture capitalists will argue that the special rights of preferred stock are necessary because the investors are putting up most of the cash for the enterprise and will not be managing company affairs on a day-to-day basis. If there are difficulties down the road, the preferred investors may need to assert certain rights to protect their investment from mismanagement or abuse by the founders, who hold common stock.

This debate over what rights the preferred stock requires and whether these rights will create misalignment in the shareholders' incentives as the company goes forward often arises as the various terms of the investment are discussed and negotiated. If the entrepreneur and the venture capitalist are equally optimistic about how successful the venture is likely to be, then the venture capitalist will be less insistent on tough protective provisions. The greater the difference in their levels of optimism, the tougher the terms are likely to be.[6]

Entrepreneurs should bear in mind that most venture capitalists have completed far more venture investment deals than have the entrepreneurs with whom they negotiate. It helps to have an adviser who has seen dozens of these transactions from different perspectives. An entrepreneur should also be skeptical about any term that is described as "standard." What is "standard" for one venture fund may be unusual for another.

Another very important issue for entrepreneurs to remember is that the company is likely to need subsequent rounds of financing. In deciding what rights to give first-round investors, the company must also consider how the rights granted to these investors will affect negotiations with investors in subsequent rounds. It is highly unusual for investors in a subsequent round to accept fewer rights than were granted in a prior round.

Each round of investors is likely to receive a slightly different type of preferred stock (usually differentiated at least by price). Each round typically receives what is called a different *series* of preferred stock. By convention, the first round purchases a security called "Series A Preferred Stock"; each subsequent series follows alphabetically: "Series B Preferred," "Series C Preferred," and so on.

The next sections of this chapter review the typical rights sought by venture capitalists investing in preferred stock. The discussion begins with the simplest type of deal and then proceeds with an outline of the different bells and whistles that may be added and the reasons raised for and against such additions.

Liquidation Preference

Simply put, the *liquidation preference* provides that upon a liquidation or dissolution of the company, the preferred shareholders must be paid some amount of money before the common shareholders are paid anything. The definition of a liquidation is typically broad enough to include any sale of the business or sale of substantially all of the company's assets. In the simplest case, the preference amount is equal to the amount initially paid for the stock.

For example, if the Series A Preferred is sold to the investors at a price of $.50 per share, it will be given a liquidation preference of $.50 per share. This means that if the preferred shareholders invested $2 million for 40 percent of the company, then the first $2 million to be distributed to shareholders will go to the preferred shareholders. The remainder will then go to the common shareholders. If the company is to be liquidated for more than $5 million, it would make sense for the holders of the preferred stock to convert to common stock immediately prior to the liquidation. For example, if the company is to be liquidated for $9 million, the preferred shareholders would be better off converting to common stock and abandoning their liquidation preference (because 40 percent of $9 million is $3.6 million as opposed to the $2 million liquidation preference).

Dividend Preference and Cumulative Dividends

Typically, the preferred stock is to earn a dividend at some modest rate (6 to 8 percent), when and if declared by the board of directors of the company. In most cases, the venture capitalist does not expect the dividend to be declared; nevertheless, this provision bolsters the argument for tax purposes that the preferred stock is worth more than the common stock purchased by the founders at a lower price.

Often the liquidation preference will equal the original purchase price plus any accrued and unpaid dividends. If no dividends are declared, then this language normally has little effect. In some deals, however, there will be a mandatory annual (or quarterly) dividend that, if not paid, will cumulate (a *cumulative dividend*). Usually, the sole purpose of this cumulation is to build up the liquidation preference over time. Everyone expects that the dividend will never be paid if the company does well and the preferred stock converts (on a public offering or a high-priced sale of the company if the preferred is nonparticipating).

The provision is included to ensure that the preferred investors receive some rate of return on the investment ahead of the common shareholders if the company does not do well. Sometimes, rather than having dividends cumulate (which may require an accounting footnote of explanation), the same objective is achieved by having the liquidation preference increase annually by some rate (often 6, 7, or 8 percent but sometimes higher).

The venture capitalist who seeks either a cumulative dividend or an increasing liquidation preference will argue that the hard-money investors are entitled to receive at least a money market rate of return before the common shareholders are paid on their very cheaply priced common stock. The entrepreneur may want to resist this argument by pointing out that this transaction is not a loan deal with a guaranteed rate of return and no other upside. Instead, the entrepreneur will argue that all of the investors should be focused on what brings the greatest value for the company, rather than on creating a situation in which some investors may push to sell the company because a particular deal provides a better return on their series of stock than available alternatives. The entrepreneur will also argue that although the common stock may have been sold cheaply, it is as "hard dollar" as the preferred stock when the value of the "sweat equity" of the entrepreneur is taken into account.

Participating Preferred

Another typical twist on the liquidation preference concept is called participating preferred. If an investor holds *participating preferred stock,* then after the preferred stock is paid its liquidation preference, it receives, in addition, its pro rata share of what remains as though the preferred stock had converted to common stock. If the preferred shareholder is not participating, all proceeds in excess of the liquidation preference go to the common shareholders.

The investor's argument here is similar. If the founders have paid only pennies for their stock (as is typically the case) and the preferred investors have paid hard dollars, then there are prices for the company at which the preferred stock would sensibly convert to common stock but would still earn only a relatively modest internal rate of return on the investment. In contrast, the common shareholders who paid little for their stock would earn huge internal rates of return.

For example, if the company is sold after five years for $8 million and the preferred stock converts into common stock to get its $3.2 million return (40 percent of $8 million) on its $2 million investment, then the venture capitalist's internal rate of return is only about 11 percent, which is a disappointment in a venture portfolio. The founder team, on the other hand, which may have paid less than $100,000 for its common stock, is able to split the remaining $4.8 million for a large return. So, the argument goes, the preferred shareholders should both receive their preference (commonly referred to as *getting the bait back*) and be allowed to participate in the common-stock share. Thus, with participating preferred, the investors would receive their original $2 million investment back (plus any cumulative dividends) and then would receive 40 percent of the remaining $6 million of sales proceeds, for a total payout of $4.4 million. The common shareholders would receive the $3.6 million remaining.

The entrepreneur can argue that the preferred shareholder is trying to double-dip and should either take its preference or convert into common. Founders can become quite emotional about this issue because the holders of common stock have invested not just their cash but also years of sweat equity in building the company. If the preferred shareholder is to participate, one could argue, then the founders should receive back pay at the market rate.

A typical compromise is to "cap" the liquidation preference. Caps are often set at an amount three to four times the preferred holders' original investment plus either accrued but unpaid dividends or a set percentage increase over time. For example, with a three times cap, the preferred

FROM THE TRENCHES

An entrepreneur and a venture capitalist had agreed on a $10 million post-money valuation for a storage device company but were at loggerheads over whether the venture capitalist's preferred stock should be participating. The entrepreneur appreciated the venture capitalist's point that if the company turned out to be only modestly successful (often referred to as a sideways deal), the venture capitalist's return on its investment would be quite small. However, the entrepreneur could not understand why, in a successful deal, the venture capitalist should be entitled not only to share in the upside enjoyed by the common shareholders but also to receive a return of its capital. To solve the impasse, the entrepreneur and the venture capitalist agreed that the preferred stock would be participating but that the participating feature would be capped at two times the amount of the original investment plus accrued but unpaid dividends.

holders are entitled to receive their liquidation preference (including any accrued cumulative dividends) and to share the remaining proceeds pro rata with the common shareholders up to the point where they have received three times their original investment plus accrued dividends. If the preferred holders would be entitled to more than the capped amount if they converted into common, then they will forgo their liquidation preference and convert. In other words, if the company is a home run, then the holders of the preferred will convert it to common and share the sale proceeds on a pro rata basis with the common shareholders with no cap on their upside return. But if the company is only moderately successful, the preferred investors will want both their liquidation preference *and* a share of the remaining proceeds.

Rights of Subsequent Series

When a subsequent series of preferred stock is issued, one matter that will need to be addressed is whether one series will come before the other in a liquidation or whether all series will be treated equally (in legal terms, *pari passu*) with a pro rata allocation based on what is available to satisfy the liquidation preferences of all the series of preferred stock prior to any distribution to the common stock. The new money has the greatest negotiating leverage for being paid out first (otherwise it may not invest), but to maintain good relations among preferred investors (and to set the precedent for the next round), the new investors may consent to having payouts to the preferred be pari passu.

Redemption Rights

Some venture investors will ask for the right to force the company to repurchase (i.e., *redeem*) its own stock at some point in the future (a *voluntary redemption right*). The investors may argue that they are minority shareholders and need some mechanism to ensure that they will have a way to exit from the investment in the future. In asking for a redemption right, the venture capitalists are concerned that if the company does not perform well enough to be a public offering or acquisition candidate, they may have no effective way to achieve any liquidity.

Although redemption requests seem reasonable on their face—and are increasingly granted—they can cause difficulties for companies both in raising future rounds of capital and in meeting redemption requirements. If a redemption right is granted, the next round of investors may be legitimately concerned that the money they are putting into the company may be used to redeem the earlier-round investors rather than to grow the company. Also, once a redemption right is granted, it is likely that future investors will want one as well.

The company can argue that no redemption rights should be given and that the investors should rely on the judgment of the board of directors on liquidity matters. The board will seek a liquidity opportunity for all investors but should not be forced into making a poorly timed decision because of a looming redemption deadline. Another strong argument against redemption rights is that they may turn out to be meaningless if the company has no money. Of course, a counterargument is that if they are so meaningless, then there is no harm in granting them.

Another tactic to use in resisting redemption rights is to suggest that if the investors are to have what is in essence a *put* on the stock (i.e., the right to sell the stock back to the company at a set price by a given date in the future), then it is only fair that the company should have a right to *call* the stock (the right to force the investors to sell the stock back to the company at a set price by a given date in the future). However, this strategy is of little benefit to the company. In reality, a fast-growing company is probably not going to want to use its limited cash to exercise the call. In addition, the put-and-call approach could end up pitting different investor groups against one another, as their own interests will no longer be aligned with what creates the most value for the company as a whole.

DURATION If redemption rights must be granted, the entrepreneur will want to push them as far into the future as possible. Redemption rights that are seven years out are not as threatening as those that kick in after five years. Similarly, it might be worthwhile to specify that the actual payment of the

FROM THE TRENCHES

One San Francisco Bay area venture fund is particularly fond of redemption rights and insists on them in every deal. The fund does a fair amount of investing outside the technology industry, where it is less likely to run into companies with advisers who are familiar with typical venture deals. In one such deal, the venture capitalists requested a redemption right that kicked in after three years at a price equal to twice the initial investment. The venture capitalists explained that, without the redemption right, they would receive an internal rate of return of less than 25 percent, which would be deemed a bad investment in the venture industry. In addition, they argued that the company should be willing to honor their request because its own projections showed a much higher rate of return. The entrepreneurs responded that they had no doubt that the company was a good long-term investment but that they could not accurately predict every bump in the road toward success. The company could not take the risk of being caught in a cash-short position if the venture capitalists exercised the redemption right at an inopportune time. After much haggling, the parties agreed to a redemption right at any point after the seventh year for the then fair market value of the stock as determined by an appraiser.

redemption price be spread over two or three years so that it will have as little impact as possible on the company's cash flow. The period in which redemption can be requested should be quite limited so that the threat to cash flow is not an ongoing concern. Any redemption rights should terminate upon an initial public offering.

REDEMPTION PRICE The redemption price is another matter for negotiation. Often venture capitalists will want the stock to be redeemed at its liquidation preference plus any accumulated but unpaid dividends. If the sole purpose is to give the investors liquidity, however, an argument can be made that the redemption price should be based on the fair market value of the company's stock at the time (which may be less than the investment plus unpaid dividends). If the company and the investors cannot agree on the fair market value, it may be determined by an appraisal process, which the entrepreneur will argue should apply appropriate discounts for any lack of liquidity of the stock and the lesser value of a minority interest.

Conversion Rights

RIGHT TO CONVERT Holders of preferred stock in venture deals normally have the right to convert their preferred stock into common stock at any time. The ratio at which preferred stock is converted into common stock is typically determined by dividing the initial purchase price of the preferred stock by a number called the *conversion price,* which is adjusted upon certain events. Initially, the conversion price is equal to the purchase price of the preferred stock, so the preferred stock converts into common stock on a one-to-one basis.

AUTOMATIC CONVERSION The preferred stock usually is automatically converted into common stock upon certain events. Typically, these events are the vote of some specified percentage of the preferred stock or an initial public offering that meets certain criteria. The company would like the preferred stock to convert as soon as possible to eliminate its special rights and to clean up the balance sheet for the initial public offering.

Often an affirmative vote of a majority or a supermajority of the preferred stock is required to force an automatic conversion of all of the preferred stock. A high threshold requirement ensures that no one investor controls the preferred stock. The entrepreneur should favor a simple majority or as small a supermajority as possible and should resist any language that gives one investor the right to block a conversion if the other investors believe it is in the company's best interest. If the deal involves only a few investors, or if one investor holds a majority of the preferred stock, it may be difficult to avoid having an investor with a blocking right.

The criteria for automatic conversion on an initial public offering generally include the following: (1) the offering must be firmly underwritten (i.e., the underwriters must have committed to placing the entire offering, rather than adopting the best-efforts approach common in penny stock offerings); (2) the offering must raise a certain amount of money for the company; and (3) (often) the offering price must be at a certain minimum (e.g., three to four times the conversion price of the preferred stock).

EFFECT OF CONVERSION ON RIGHTS Upon any conversion of the preferred stock, the rights associated with it (i.e., liquidation preference, dividend preference, antidilution protection, special voting rights, and redemption provisions) cease to exist. Some contractual rights, such as *registration rights* (the right to force the company to register the holder's stock), usually survive, although others, such as *information rights* (the right to certain ongoing financial information about the company) and *preemptive rights* (the right to buy stock issued by the company), often will terminate upon an initial public offering.

Antidilution Provisions

STRUCTURAL ANTIDILUTION Any equity issuance to another person can be considered dilutive to existing shareholders because it reduces their percentage ownership stake. All shareholders are customarily entitled to protection against the dilution caused by certain issuances. For example, when common stock is issued as a stock dividend, a pro rata dividend is given to each common shareholder, not just to some of them.

Preferred stock is also customarily given antidilution protection against stock dividends, stock splits, reverse splits, and similar recapitalizations. The conversion price is adjusted to ensure that the number of shares of common stock issuable upon conversion of the preferred stock represents the same percentage of ownership (on a converted-to-common basis) as existed prior to the stock dividend, stock split, reverse split, or recapitalization. For example, when there is a five-to-one stock split, the conversion price is reduced to one-fifth of its prior amount. Thus, if the conversion price was $1.25 prior to the split, it will be $0.25 after the split. In this way, the number of shares of common stock issuable upon the conversion of the preferred stock increases proportionately with the effect of the split.

FROM THE TRENCHES

Structural antidilution provisions are important for the company as well as for the preferred shareholders. One company learned this the hard way. Financial Performance Corporation issued warrants that entitled the investors to purchase 1,698,904 shares of common stock at a price of $0.10 per share. The company effected a five-to-one reverse stock split, thereby reducing the number of common shares outstanding to one-fifth of the original number outstanding. As a consequence, each shareholder owned one-fifth of the original number of shares with the value of each share increased fivefold. Because the company failed to include structural antidilution provisions, the New York Court of Appeals ruled that the investors were entitled to exercise their warrants for the original number of shares at the original price. So, instead of having the right to acquire 1,698,904 shares (or *x* percent of the company) for $0.10 per share (or a total of $169,890.40), the investors became entitled to acquire 5*x* percent of the company for $169,890.40.

Source: Reiss v. Fin. Performance Corp., 715 N.Y.S. 2d 29 (N.Y. 2001).

This type of *structural antidilution protection* from stock dividends, stock splits, and reverse splits is the most basic kind of antidilution provision and is nearly always included in venture capital financings. When venture capitalists say they want protection against dilution, they may be referring to this basic type of protection, or they may have in mind some of the more complex provisions discussed below.

PREEMPTIVE RIGHT AND RIGHT OF FIRST REFUSAL Another type of antidilution provision is called a right of first refusal or preemptive right. A *right of first refusal* or *preemptive right* entitles any shareholder to purchase its pro rata share in any subsequent issuance to ensure that the shareholder maintains its percentage ownership. In venture deals, this type of provision, if adopted, usually is a contractual right that terminates upon an initial public offering. The right can, however, be attached to the preferred stock if it is included in the certificate of incorporation. In its most extreme form, a preemptive right can require the company to give the venture group first refusal on all shares of subsequent offerings, not merely on sufficient shares to maintain their pro rata ownership interest.

Although a pro rata preemptive right appears reasonable on its face, in many circumstances a company may want to sell stock to a particular investor without being required to first offer it to every current investor. For that reason, if this right is included, it usually exempts stock issued to employees, directors, consultants, strategic partners, those providing leases or loans to the company, and acquisition targets.

Waiting for a right-of-first-refusal time period to expire (or soliciting waivers of such rights) can be time-consuming and can prevent a deal from closing. An entrepreneur may want to avoid giving up the company's flexibility to choose to whom it sells stock in the future. For example, the company may want to bring in a new venture capitalist or corporate investor but may find that, due to the exercise of preemptive rights, there is not enough stock to meet the new investor's minimum investment criteria. Also, if there is no such right, investors who want to be invited to buy in future rounds have an incentive to remain on good terms with the company. Finally, a preemptive right, if exercised by a large shareholder, may force other investors either to buy into the offering or to risk losing control of the company.

PRICE PROTECTION One could argue that the two types of antidilution provisions discussed above (protection from stock splits and the like, and the right to participate in future offerings) should be sufficient protection for an investor. Nevertheless, most venture deals feature a third type of antidilution protection known as price protection. *Price protection* gives the venture capitalist some protection from subsequent financing rounds in which stock is issued at a lower share price than the investor paid.

The theory behind price protection is that the valuation of a company at the time venture capitalists purchase stock is open to debate, and the investors are entitled to a price adjustment if the company was overvalued. As it is impractical to give back a portion of the venture capitalists' money, more shares are issued to the investors to make them whole.

Full Ratchet The simplest form of price protection (although by no means the fairest) is called full ratchet antidilution protection. If the venture capitalist has *full ratchet antidilution protection,* then if stock is sold at a lower price per share in a subsequent round, the ratio for converting the preferred stock into common stock is adjusted so that an investor in a higher-priced earlier round gets the same deal as it would have gotten had the purchase been made in a later lower-priced round. The mechanics of the adjustment are straightforward: the conversion price of the prior round is adjusted to the purchase price of the new round.

Consider an example. Acorn Enterprises issues Series A Preferred Stock based on a pre-money valuation of $9 million. Acorn issues shares resulting in a 25 percent ownership interest to investors for $3 million (i.e., post-money valuation of $12 million). Assuming that there are 4.5 million shares of common stock outstanding (which the founders may have bought in the early days of the company for pennies a share or more recently for $0.20 a share), the Series A investors will purchase 1.5 million shares at $2.00 per share. The shares convert into common stock based on the original price, so $3 million of preferred stock at $2.00 per share will convert into 1.5 million shares of common stock. It is said to initially convert on a one-to-one basis.

Business does not go according to plan, and when Acorn tries to raise another $2 million, it finds it can obtain a pre-money valuation of only $10 million. It may seem counterintuitive that the second round could have a valuation lower than the post-money valuation of the first round, but it does happen. Typically, this situation occurs either when the earlier round was overvalued or when the business has not met the projections in its plan.

The second-round Series B venture capitalists buy their preferred stock at $1.67 per share (i.e., the $10 million pre-money valuation divided by the 6 million total shares already outstanding). At this valuation, the second-round investors will receive 1.2 million shares of Series B Preferred stock for the $2 million second-round investment. After the first and second rounds, the capitalization will be as set forth in Exhibit 13.1.

The Series A venture capitalists will be none too pleased about having overpaid for their Series A stock compared to the Series B investors. If the Series A investors have full ratchet antidilution protection, their conversion price will be reset to the lower sale price of the Series B stock. The result will be as though the Series A investors were able to purchase at the most recent price. Now the Series A investors are able to convert the Series A stock they purchased for $3 million into 1.8 million shares of common stock. As a result of the lower-priced dilutive issuance, additional stock will be issued to the Series A investors upon conversion of their preferred stock, and the capitalization will be as set forth in Exhibit 13.2.

EXHIBIT 13.1

CAPITALIZATION TABLE WITH NO ANTIDILUTION PROTECTION

	Number of Shares	Percentage of Company
First Round		
Common	4.5 million	75.00%
Series A	1.5 million	25.00
Second Round (with no adjustment for dilution)		
Common	4.5 million	62.50%
Series A	1.5 million	20.83
Series B	1.2 million	16.67

EXHIBIT 13.2

CAPITALIZATION TABLE WITH FULL RATCHET PROTECTION

	Number of Shares	Percentage of Company
Second Round (with full ratchet protection)		
Common	4.5 million	60.00%
Series A	1.8 million	24.00
Series B	1.2 million	16.00

Full ratchet appears simple and fair on its face, but it is rarely used for more than a brief period of time. It is widely viewed as unfair because it pushes most of the dilution onto the common shareholders; in an anomaly, the Series B investors end up buying less of the company than they bargained for (which can push down their price even further). Perhaps most unfairly, all of the Series A stock is repriced regardless of the size of the issuance of Series B stock.

Although the ratchet formula is used much less often than the weighted average formula discussed next, a ratchet may be appropriate under some limited circumstances. For example, if a venture capitalist uncovers a fact in due diligence that suggests that a company is overvalued and may need a cash infusion sooner than was anticipated, the company might agree to a ratchet for six or twelve months to give the investors some assurance that there will not need to be a subsequent financing at a lower price per share than the price paid in the previous financing (a *down-priced financing*). Similarly, if some event may occur within the next year that will have a dramatic effect on valuation (such as the issuance of a patent), the venture capitalists may seek a ratchet as protection in case the event does not occur and more money must be raised at a lower valuation. Also, investors in a mezzanine round might be concerned about the company being overvalued and about a down-priced financing if the public market window closes. They too might seek a ratchet for a limited period. In such cases, when the ratchet period expires, the weighted average method typically becomes applicable.

Weighted Average Today almost all venture deals use a weighted average antidilution formula, which attempts to calibrate the repricing based on the size and price of the dilutive round, or they use a full ratchet for a brief period and then a weighted average. *Weighted average antidilution* sets the new conversion price of the outstanding preferred stock as the product of (a) the old conversion price multiplied by (b) a fraction in which (1) the numerator is the sum of (x) the number of shares outstanding before the issuance plus (y) the quotient of the amount of money invested in this round divided by the old conversion price, and (2) the denominator is the sum of (x) the shares outstanding before this round and (y) the shares issued in this round. Algebraically,

$$NCP = OCP \times \frac{OB + \frac{MI}{OCP}}{OB + SI}$$

where *NCP* is the new conversion price, *OCP* is the old conversion price, *OB* is the number of shares outstanding before the issuance, *MI* is the amount of money invested in the current round, and *SI* is the number of shares issued in the current round. The weighted average formula adjusts the conversion price based on the relative amount of the company that is being sold at the lower price.

Applying this formula to the example above, the new conversion price is calculated as follows:

$$NCP = 2.00 \times \frac{6 \text{ million} + \frac{2 \text{ million}}{2.00}}{6 \text{ million} + 1.2 \text{ million}}$$

$$NCP = \$1.944$$

Under weighted average antidilution, the capitalization table for the example given earlier would be as set forth in Exhibit 13.3. No longer does the Series A stock convert on a one-to-one basis; each share of Series A stock now converts into 1.029 shares of common ($2.00/1.944) based on the new conversion price.

The weighted average formula is fairly standard in venture capital financings, but there are some variations. The most common variation in-

EXHIBIT 13.3

CAPITALIZATION TABLE WITH WEIGHTED AVERAGE PROTECTION

	Number of Shares	Percentage of Company
Second Round (with weighted average protection)		
Common	4,500,000	62.13%
Series A	1,542,860	21.30
Series B	1,200,000	16.57

volves how options are counted—whether as issued or unissued common stock. Although counting the options adds the same amount to both the denominator and the numerator in the weighted average formula, including them broadens the base so that it absorbs more dilution and keeps the conversion price from falling as quickly. Often shares reserved for options already granted are counted, but those reserved for future grants are not. This issue is a minor negotiating point, as it tends to have a negligible effect unless the option pool is unusually large.

Carve-Outs Certain issuances will often be carved out from the price-protection antidilution provisions. Often the issuances exempted from price protection mirror those exempted from the preemptive rights mentioned earlier in this chapter. For example, it is usually anticipated that additional members of the management team will have to be hired and that it will be necessary to offer those employees stock options or low-priced common stock. Over time, other members of management may need to have their incentives revitalized (following dilutive venture rounds) with additional stock options. For this reason, options to be granted under stock option plans and other equity arrangements with employees are generally excluded from the price-protection formula. Often there is a cap on the aggregate amount of stock that a board can allocate under this carve-out (typically between 10 and 30 percent of the stock for equity incentive programs) without obtaining the approval of the investors. Similarly, any outstanding rights to purchase shares at a lower price that were granted prior to the issuance of the preferred stock are usually excluded. Shares of common stock issued upon conversion of preferred stock into common stock are also excluded.

Pay to Play Some venture capitalists and entrepreneurs like to add a pay-to-play provision. With a *pay-to-play provision,* holders of preferred stock get the benefit of price-protection antidilution only if they buy their pro rata share of any subsequent down-priced round. An investor who does not participate at least pro rata in a down-priced round is automatically converted into a different series of preferred stock that is identical to the original series in all respects except that there is no price protection. Pay-to-play provisions are intended to encourage all investors to step up and help the company in difficult times; therefore, entrepreneurs generally favor them, as do some venture capitalists. Although prominent in discussions of types of antidilution provisions, in practice, pay-to-play provisions are atypical.

Voting Rights

The preferred stock issued to the venture capitalist votes on most matters on an as-converted-to-common basis (i.e., one vote for each common share into which the preferred can be converted). On most matters the preferred and common shareholders vote together as one class.

PROTECTIVE PROVISIONS There may be certain matters for which the company must obtain the approval of the preferred stock voting as a separate class. These matters generally include any change in the certificate of incorporation that would adversely affect the rights, preferences, and privileges of the preferred shareholders. For example, the liquidation preference cannot be changed without the consent of the preferred shareholders. There is often a separate prohibition on the issuance of any security senior to (or even on a par with) the existing preferred stock, as well as separate provisions prohibiting changes in the liquidation preference, dividend rights, conversion rights, voting rights, or redemption rights of the preferred shareholders (even though all of these rights might be considered to fall within the general prohibition on adverse change to the preferred shareholders).

When investors control a larger percentage of a particular series than of the preferred stock as a whole, they will want these protective provisions to require the approval of holders of each series of preferred stock, with each series voting separately. Avoiding a series vote is in the company's best interest because doing so will give the company greater flexibility and lessen the likelihood that any single investor will have blocking power. Even if some investors end up with blocking power, the fewer who have this power, the better for the company.

Another common protective provision is a prohibition on the redemption of stock, other than redemptions provided for in the certificate of incorporation and repurchases from departed employees, consultants, and directors pursuant to the contractual arrangements made when stock was sold to such persons (but often still subject to some cap on the number of shares that can be redeemed). There may be a prohibition on any sale of substantially all of the assets of the company or a merger in which the surviving entity is not controlled by shareholders of the company prior to the merger. Any increase in the authorized number of shares of stock may be prohibited. If there is an agreement on how the board is to be elected, changes in the number of directors or the designation of who elects a stated number of directors may also require approval by the preferred shareholders.

Some preferred investors may try to expand the number of items requiring their approval to include the types of matters often found in bank loan covenants, such as (1) investing in any other enterprise, (2) establishing subsidiaries, (3) incurring certain levels of indebtedness, (4) making loans to others, and (5) exceeding certain levels for capital expenditures. Generally, the company should vigorously resist such provisions. Rather than forcing such matters to be delayed by a shareholder vote, the investors should rely on the company's board of directors to do what is prudent.

BOARD ELECTIONS As discussed in Chapter 6, the board of directors is charged with the management of the company's business affairs, and it appoints the officers to carry out board policies and handle day-to-day operations. In America's version of shareholder democracy, as reflected in the corporation laws of the fifty states, the shareholders elect the board to run the company. At the same time, the shareholders are permitted to vote on a limited number of matters (e.g., amendments to the certificate of incorporation, decisions about selling the business, certain merger transactions, and dissolution). Control of the company is determined by the persons with the power to elect the board of directors, along with the directors themselves.

Generally, the lead venture capitalist in a round will expect a board seat. Sometimes each venture capitalist would like a board seat. As the number of venture investors increases over time, the board can become too large and be completely dominated by financial investors.

At the time of the first venture round, the founders will likely retain a majority of the company and be permitted to elect a majority of the board. If the round involves only one venture fund, it is not unusual for it to request two board seats.

Usually, the founders and the investors will enter into a voting agreement or will designate in the certificate of incorporation that a certain number of seats are to be elected by the common shareholders, that another number of seats are to be elected by the preferred shareholders, and perhaps that the balance are to be elected by the shareholders at large. Control of the board is likely to shift over time as subsequent financings occur.

The founders may wish to establish from the outset that they want to be able to look to the board as a repository of business experience and advice. To this end, the founder group may decide to limit itself to just two founders on the board, with one or two seats reserved for venture investors and two or three seats reserved for industry leaders who are respected by the venture capitalists and the founders. With this type of board composition, no one group controls the board, and the board can focus on the best interest of the company rather than the best interest of any particular group. (Chapter 6 further discusses board composition issues.)

Milestones

Sometimes venture capitalists will require the company to achieve certain goals (*milestones*) within a specified time. These milestones might include reaching certain stages in product development or attaining certain levels of sales or profitability. The rationale for milestones is that they protect the venture capitalist from overvaluing the company to a greater degree than price antidilution provisions. Sometimes the achievement of milestones will trigger an obligation by the venture capitalist to make a follow-on investment in the company at a previously determined price per share. In some cases, failure to meet the milestones will permit the investor to purchase shares at a much lower price. In other cases, the conversion price of the venture capitalist's preferred stock may be adjusted downward, thereby increasing the venture capitalist's ownership of the company. In still other cases, an investor will suggest that control of the board should shift to the investors if the management team fails to achieve the milestones.

The company should resist any milestones that would result in a change of control. Business is filled with risks, and the unexpected can occur. When that happens, all shareholders in the company need to pull together and not split into groups trying to use the company's difficulty to their own advantage. Although milestones associated with subsequent rounds of investment are not quite as onerous, they too may cause misalignment of incentives among shareholders. For example, some may want the company to fall short so that they will be relieved of a further investment obligation (or, more likely, be in a position to purchase stock cheaply or renegotiate the deal). Similarly, milestones that trigger ownership adjustments put the venture capitalist and the founders on different sides of the table, which is hardly where the parties should or want to be. Finally, milestones of any kind in a deal may distort the behavior of the entrepreneur, who may focus too much on the milestone and not enough on the actions or expenditures that are in the best interest of the business. For these reasons, many venture capitalists avoid using milestones.

Registration Rights

The parties will devote a fair amount of discussion to the subject of registration rights. A *registration right* is the right to force the company to register the holder's stock with the Securities and Exchange Commission (SEC) so that it can be sold in the public markets. Often when a company goes public, the underwriters are unwilling to permit existing shareholders to sell in the initial public offering, as such sales will adversely affect the marketing of the new issuance of stock being sold by the company to raise capital.

If a shareholder has held unregistered stock for more than *one* year and the company is public at the time the shareholder wants to sell, then the holder is permitted to sell a limited amount of stock (up to the greater of 1 percent of the outstanding stock and the average weekly trading volume in the preceding four weeks) in any three-month period under Rule 144. If the selling shareholder is not an *affiliate* of the company (that is, an officer, director, or owner of more than 5 to 10 percent of the outstanding shares), then it can freely resell any shares that it has owned for at least *two* years (regardless of whether the company is privately held or public and without regard to volume or manner of sale) under Rule 144(k). If the holder is unable to sell under Rule 144(k) (for example, because it is an affiliate or has held the shares for less than two years) but cannot meet the requirements of Rule 144 (for example, because it is an affiliate of a private company), then it may need to register the shares to exit from the investment. Because venture capitalists are often directors of their portfolio companies and often own more than 10 percent of the outstanding shares (and are accordingly affiliates), they usually cannot sell under Rule 144(k). If the company has not gone public, then Rule 144 will be unavailable as well. Similarly, if the shareholder has not held the shares for at least one year or wishes to sell more than is permitted by Rule 144, then registration may be required.

TYPES OF REGISTRATION RIGHTS Venture investors are likely to request three types of registration rights: demand rights, S-3 rights, and piggyback rights.

A *demand right* is a right to demand that the company file a registration statement on SEC Form S-1 to sell the holder's stock. The company uses this form for an initial public offering; it requires a prospectus with extensive information about the company and the offering. (Initial public offerings are discussed further in Chapter 17.) A company generally will want to limit this right as it can be expensive and time-consuming. It can also adversely affect the company's own capital-raising plans. Generally, the investor group will receive only one or two demand rights, with limits on when they can be exercised.

The company will especially resist granting demand rights that can be used to force the company to go public. The argument is that if the company is not yet ready, its management team should not be forced to find underwriters, do the road show required for the offering, and try to make the offering successful. (During the *road show*, the company's managers and investment bankers travel around the country and make presentations

FROM THE TRENCHES

One venture fund was quite thankful that it had obtained a demand registration right exercisable five years after it invested in a consumer products company, which became very successful. The founder decided that he liked running a profitable private company and had no desire to take it public. He was also unwilling to sell the company or to find some other path to liquidity at a high enough valuation to satisfy the investor. The investor insisted on a public offering and threatened to exercise its demand right. Because the company had a well-known brand and was not a development-stage technology company, it appeared that a fairly successful offering could be consummated even without an enthusiastic management team. Faced with the investor's threat, the founder and management agreed that the company should go public and completed a successful offering, which gave the investor the desired liquidity.

to potential investors.) The investors will seek such a right, arguing that an initial public offering may be their only path to liquidity, especially if the founders are content with the lifestyle afforded by running a successful private company.

An S-3 right is actually another type of demand right. An *S-3 right* allows the investor to force the company to register the investor's stock on Form S-3. This form is part of a simpler procedure that can be used by most companies that have been public for at least twelve months with a *public float* (market value of securities held by nonaffiliates) of at least $75 million. Form S-3 permits the registration statement to incorporate by reference information already on file with the SEC, so the preparation of the registration statement is simpler, less time-consuming, and cheaper than the preparation of a Form S-1 registration statement. S-3 rights granted to venture capitalists tend to be unlimited in quantity but are available only once or twice per year and may expire at some point.

A *piggyback right* is the right to participate in an offering initiated by the company. Piggyback rights are generally subject to cutback or elimination by the offering's underwriter, if the underwriter determines, based on market conditions, that a sale by shareholders will adversely affect the company's capital-raising effort. The venture capitalist will seek rights that may not be completely cut back except in connection with the company's initial public offering. Piggyback rights granted to venture capitalists are generally unlimited in number but often expire three to five years after the company's initial public offering or after a certain percentage of the venture investors have sold their shares. Unless the rights expire, the company must notify all holders of the rights every time the company has a public offering and perhaps include a portion of the holders' shares in the offering.

Information Rights

Holders of significant blocks of preferred stock may be granted the rights to certain information, such as monthly financial statements, annual audited financial statements, and the annual budget approved by the board. These rights should expire upon an initial public offering, when the investors will be able to rely on SEC filings.

Some investors may seek more expanded rights, such as the right (1) to review the company's auditor's letter to management concerning the audit of the financial statements and any weaknesses in internal controls, (2) to make on-site inspections and inquiries of officers or employees, and (3) to observe board meetings. Generally, these additional information rights should be resisted. They can be disruptive to the company's operations and conflict with the board's performance of its duties. Investors who maintain good relations with the company will be able to obtain sufficient information to monitor their investment without placing undue burdens on the start-up enterprise.

Co-Sale Rights

Venture capitalists often ask for a co-sale right. Typically, a *co-sale right* binds some of the key founders of the company and gives the investors a contractual right to sell some of their stock alongside a founder's stock if the founder elects to sell stock to a third party. A co-sale right protects the investors from a situation in which the founder transfers control of the company by selling his or her stock to another person. In such a circumstance, the investor is looking for the opportunity to consider exiting as

FROM THE TRENCHES

One venture fund learned the hard way the merits of a co-sale right. The fund led a $2 million financing of a company that distributed toys and video games. The key founder resisted any effort to put vesting on his shares, arguing that the company was more than two and a half years old and that he had earned his shares. He also argued successfully that a co-sale right was not needed, because he had no reason to transfer his shares as the company could not make it without him and the shares represented most of his net worth. He also persuaded the venture capitalist that it was fundamentally unfair to put restrictions on his right to transfer his shares. Within twelve months of the closing, the entrepreneur transferred his shares to a competitor for more than $1 million and left the company. The company was unable to compete effectively without the entrepreneur, and the venture capitalist's investment became virtually worthless.

well. Mechanically, a co-sale right usually gives the investor the right to replace a portion of the stock the founder planned to sell with the investor's stock. The portion is usually the pro rata share of the investor's total holdings compared with the founder's total holdings.

It is reasonable for a founder to resist a co-sale right except in situations when a substantial portion of the stock held by all the founders is being sold. Founders may insist on exceptions to permit a sale of some of their stock for liquidity purposes (e.g., for estate planning purposes, to make a down payment on a house, or to pay college tuition) as well as carve-outs for dispositions upon death or upon termination of employment. Founders may also ask for a reciprocal co-sale right so that they can obtain some liquidity if the venture capitalist seeks to sell its shares. This reciprocal right usually is not given.

Drag-Along Rights

Some investors (historically, especially those based on the East Coast) will request *drag-along rights,* which basically give the investors the right to force the founders to sell their shares on the same terms and conditions on which the investors have decided to sell their shares. Founders will usually vigorously resist granting drag-along rights or at least will insist that they not be exercisable for a substantial period of time.

Relationship Between Price and Rights of the Preferred Stock

Experienced venture capitalists are acutely aware of the economic value of the rights and preferences of the stock they agree to buy. If an entrepreneur insists on a valuation that the venture capitalist considers to be at the high end of acceptable, then the venture capitalist may agree to the price but insist on tough terms, such as board control, participating preferred with no cap, a high cumulative dividend rate, mandatory redemption rights exercisable at an early date, and ratchet price protection.

OTHER PROTECTIVE ARRANGEMENTS

Vesting

The venture investors will often request that the founders subject their stock, and all other common stock to be sold to employees, to a vesting schedule if they have not already done so. As explained in Chapter 5, the vesting schedule is usually four years, with cliff vesting for the first year and then monthly or quarterly vesting for the next three years. If the vesting schedule is not put in place until the venture round closes, the founders may want to commence the vesting period on an earlier date, such as the day the founders first acquired stock or joined the company.

Employees whose stock is subject to repurchase should almost always file a *Section 83(b) election* with the Internal Revenue Service. As explained in Chapter 5, this election allows the stock to be taxed at the time it is acquired (when there is no tax, assuming the employee paid fair market value) rather than on the date the vesting is complete (when it may have increased dramatically in value over the original purchase price). The 83(b) election must be filed within thirty days of the commencement of the vesting arrangement. It is extremely important that the election be filed on time; a missed or late filing can result in a very large tax bill at a time when the shareholder has no money because the stock is not liquid.

Options

As discussed in Chapter 5, common stock is typically issued to founders at the earliest stages of a company. Soon thereafter, many companies set up stock option plans as additional equity incentives for employees. Venture capitalists understand well the need for such programs and support them as long as they are not excessively generous.

Options provide employees with an opportunity to share in the equity upside of the business without having to invest any of their own money until a future date. Incentive stock options (ISOs) are particularly popular because they permit an employee to purchase cheap common stock at a future date without triggering a taxable event. After a company goes public, ISOs become less important because there is liquidity in the stock, and an option holder can buy the stock and then sell enough to pay taxes on the gain within the same tax period.

An entrepreneur will want to reserve (at least mentally) a certain percentage of the company for future equity incentives to new and existing employees. Generally, somewhere between 10 and 30 percent of the stock (measured on a post-financing basis) is reserved for this purpose. A generous plan will dilute the holders of the common stock and the preferred stock alike, so such options should be granted with some care. Nonetheless, a healthy pool of options will likely be advisable to enable the young company to attract the talent necessary for success. Options generally vest over four or five years (although credit is sometimes given in the initial grant for prior service to the company). Unlike stock, which vests by the repurchase right lapsing, options vest by the exercise right extending to a greater proportion of the grant over time.

The entrepreneur should reach agreement with the venture capitalist on the scope of any option plan prior to the closing of the financing. If the company later wishes to exceed this scope, the entrepreneur may be required to obtain the written approval of the investors. Alternatively, the investors may agree that the scope can be exceeded as long as their representatives on the board vote in favor of the option grants. Typically, the number of shares in a company's option plan is reevaluated and readjusted at each venture financing.

Putting it into Practice

Kendra talked with Michael Cruz about venture capital funding. Because DataAccelleation, Inc. had successfully validated the technology and had modest overhead needs, Kendra figured that DataAccelleation was worth about $1.2 million and would need only about $600,000 in an initial round. This would result in one-third ownership by the venture capitalists. Michael suggested bumping that figure up to $800,000 to reflect unanticipated delays and expenses and to allow a venture capitalist to buy 40 percent of the company. Kendra agreed, particularly in light of her earlier miscalculation of cash needs. Also, she hoped that some of the extra money could be used to buy out Billy Barnett, who had become dissatisfied with his $50,000 investment during DataAccelleation's earlier financial crisis. Michael liked this idea, because it meant that the new investors would be able to purchase Series A Preferred Stock rather than a Series B, thus simplifying the capital structure.

Kendra had already prepared a business plan for Michael's review. She worked with Sanjay Datar to pull together all of the company's material agreements and information on its technology so that once an investor was selected, the investor could proceed quickly with its due diligence investigation.

Michael suggested approaching Centaur Partners, a venture capital group looking for software opportunities, which he thought would be a good investor. Michael told Kendra that he was obligated to disclose that his firm had represented Centaur Partners in the past and would continue to do so in the future. He said that he personally always represented the issuer in venture capital financings and that his firm would not represent Centaur in any business relating to DataAccelleation. Michael told Kendra that he would understand, however, if she wanted to seek other representation for the transaction. Kendra said she was comfortable with Michael continuing to represent DataAccelleation, and she asked Michael to contact Centaur on her behalf.

Michael set up an initial meeting between Kendra and Centaur's managing partner. That meeting went well, and Kendra used the opportunity to discuss her thoughts on valuation and to sound out Centaur on such issues as its vision for the company, its willingness and ability to step up for other rounds,its assessment of the company's weaknesses, and its ability to assist the company in addressing those weaknesses. Kendra also performed her own due

continued...

continued...

diligence investigation of Centaur, keeping in mind that Centaur was not just a source of needed capital but was about to become her partner in one of the most important undertakings of her life.

After several more successful meetings, including meetings involving all three Centaur general partners and the Colgates, Centaur agreed to invest in DataAccelleation, pending a satisfactory due diligence review. Kendra, along with Michael and Sanjay, met with Centaur and its counsel to hammer out a term sheet.

After much negotiation, the two parties agreed on a term sheet that reflected the $1.2 million pre-money valuation that Kendra was seeking. (A sample venture capital term sheet is set forth in "Getting It in Writing" at the end of this chapter.) Centaur agreed to use $60,000 of its investment to purchase Billy Barnett's 50,000 shares, which would then be folded into the new Series A Preferred Stock to be issued by DataAccelleation.

Michael negotiated a provision that would allow DataAccelleation, with Centaur's permission, to bring in another venture firm for up to $200,000 of the $800,000 financing. After the meeting, Michael suggested gently to Kendra that she might want to talk to a few other firms and to select one to be another voice in the investor group. However, Kendra was comfortable with Centaur being the only investor because of the rapport she had established with the Centaur partners and the smoothness of the negotiations. Michael pointed out that other venture funds could be part of the next round, as Centaur had agreed to a limited preemptive right of 50 percent of future financings.

During negotiations with Centaur Partners, all parties agreed that the board would consist of five directors. The stock purchase agreement specified that the holders of the Series A Preferred Stock (the investors), voting as a class, would elect two directors. The holders of the common stock (the founders) would also elect two directors, one of whom would be Kendra. The second management director was to be chosen by a vote of the common shareholders. The fifth seat was to be filled by an independent director, preferably someone with significant experience in the computer industry. The stock purchase agreement specified that the fifth director had to be approved by both the common and the preferred shareholders, with each class holding veto.

continued...

continued...

Kendra instructed Michael to immediately draft and circulate documents for closing the transaction. Although the attorneys for Centaur, Michael, and the principals were able to reach agreement on the documents within three weeks, Centaur did not complete its due diligence until a month after the principals had agreed to the term sheet. As no problems were found, Centaur proceeded to invest $800,000.

After the DataAccelleation board members were elected, Kendra began to work closely with Centaur's two designated board representatives to make sure they were kept in the loop on activities at the company. Kendra planned to brief Centaur's representatives prior to board meetings so that board discussions could be as thoughtful as possible and surprises could be kept to a minimum. Centaur would play a critical role in helping the company raise money in subsequent rounds, and her relationship with the Centaur board representatives was central to the success of their partnership.

Kendra next turned to issues surrounding the protection of DataAccelleation's intellectual property.

Getting It In Writing

SAMPLE VENTURE CAPITAL TERM SHEET

DATAACCELLEATION, INC.
SALE OF SERIES A PREFERRED STOCK
SUMMARY OF TERMS

Issuer:	DataAccelleation, Inc. (the "Company").
Amount of Financing:	$800,000.
Type of Security:	666,667 shares of Series A Convertible Preferred Stock (the "Series A Preferred"), initially convertible into an equal number of shares of the Company's Common Stock (the "Common Stock").
Price:	$1.20 per share (the "Original Purchase Price").
Resulting Capitalization:	The Original Purchase Price represents a post-financing valuation of $2 million, based on fully diluted outstanding common stock of 1,666,667 shares as of the Closing.
Purchaser(s):	Centaur Partners, L.P. as lead investor will purchase at least $600,000 and up to $800,000 of Series A Preferred. The Company may seek other investors (together with the lead investor, the "Investors") to invest up to $200,000, subject to the approval of the lead investor.
Anticipated Closing Date (the "Closing"):	March 5, 2002.

continued...

continued...

Terms of Series A Preferred Stock

Dividends:	The holders of the Series A Preferred shall be entitled to receive cumulative dividends in preference to any dividend on the Common Stock at the rate of 7 percent of the Original Purchase Price per annum, when and as declared by the Board of Directors. The Series A Preferred will participate pro rata in dividends paid on the Common Stock.
Liquidation Preference:	In the event of any liquidation or winding up of the Company, the holders of the Series A Preferred shall be entitled to receive in preference to the holders of the Common Stock an amount equal to the Original Purchase Price plus any accrued but unpaid cumulative dividends (the "Liquidation Preference"). After the payment of the Liquidation Preference to the holders of the Series A Preferred, the remaining assets shall be distributed ratably to the holders of the Common Stock and the Series A Preferred until the Series A Preferred holders have received three times their original investment. All remaining assets shall be distributed ratably to the Common Stock. A merger, acquisition, or sale of substantially all of the assets of the Company in which the shareholders of the Company do not own a majority of the outstanding shares of the surviving corporation shall be deemed to be a liquidation.
Conversion:	The holders of the Series A Preferred shall have the right to convert the Series A Preferred, at any time, into shares of Common Stock. The initial conversion rate shall be 1:1, subject to adjustment as provided below.

continued...

continued...

Automatic Conversion:	The Series A Preferred shall be automatically converted into Common Stock, at the then applicable conversion price, (i) in the event that the holders of at least 50 percent of the outstanding Series A Preferred consent to such conversion, or (ii) upon the closing of a firmly underwritten public offering of shares of Common Stock of the Company at a per share price not less than $3.60 per share (as presently constituted) and for a total offering of not less than $10,000,000 (before deduction of underwriters' commissions and expenses).
Antidilution Provisions:	The conversion price of the Series A Preferred will be subject to a weighted average adjustment to reduce dilution in the event that the Company issues additional equity securities (other than employee, director, and consultant shares approved by the Board of Directors) at a purchase price less than the applicable conversion price. The conversion price will also be subject to proportional adjustment for stock splits, stock dividends, recapitalizations, and the like.
Redemption at Option of Investors:	Commencing on the fifth anniversary of the Closing, at the election of the holders of at least 50 percent of the Series A Preferred, the Company shall redeem the outstanding Series A Preferred in three equal annual installments. Such redemption shall be at the Original Purchase Price plus any unpaid cumulative dividends.

continued...

continued...

Voting Rights:	The Series A Preferred will vote together with the Common Stock and not as a separate class except as specifically provided herein or as otherwise required by law. Each share of Series A Preferred shall have a number of votes equal to the number of shares of Common Stock then issuable upon conversion of such share of Series A Preferred.
Board of Directors:	The size of the Company's Board of Directors shall be changed to five. The holders of the Series A Preferred, voting as a separate class, shall be entitled to elect two members of the Company's Board of Directors. The holders of the Common Stock shall be entitled to elect two directors. The fifth director must be approved by both the Common Stock and Preferred Series A holders, voting separately.
Protective Provisions:	For so long as at least 300,000 shares of Series A Preferred remain outstanding, consent of the holders of at least 50 percent of the Series A Preferred shall be required for any action which (i) alters or changes the rights, preferences, or privileges of the Series A Preferred, (ii) increases or decreases the authorized number of shares of Series A Preferred, (iii) creates (by reclassification or otherwise) any new class or series of shares having rights, preferences, or privileges senior to or on a parity with the Series A Preferred, (iv) results in the redemption of any shares of Common Stock (other than pursuant to employee agreements), or (v) results in any merger, other corporate reorganization, sale of control, or any transaction in which all or substantially all of the assets of the Company are sold.

continued...

continued...

Information Rights:	So long as an Investor continues to hold shares of Series A Preferred or Common Stock issued upon conversion of the Series A Preferred, the Company shall deliver to the Investor audited annual and unaudited quarterly financial statements. So long as an Investor holds not less than 120,000 shares of Series A Preferred, the Company will furnish the Investor with monthly financial statements and will provide a copy of the Company's annual operating plan within thirty (30) days prior to the beginning of the fiscal year. Each Investor shall also be entitled to standard inspection and visitation rights. These provisions shall terminate upon a registered public offering of the Company's Common Stock.
Registration Rights:	*Demand Rights:* If Investors holding at least 50 percent of the outstanding shares of Series A Preferred, including Common Stock issued on conversion of Series A Preferred ("Registrable Securities"), request that the Company file a Registration Statement for at least 30 percent of the Registrable Securities having an aggregate offering price to the public of not less than $5,000,000, the Company will use its best efforts to cause such shares to be registered; provided, however, that the Company shall not be obligated to effect any such registration prior to the third anniversary of the Closing. The Company shall have the right to delay such registration under certain circumstances for two periods not in excess of ninety (90) days each in any twelve (12) month period.

continued...

continued...

Registration Rights (cont.):	The Company shall not be obligated to effect more than two (2) registrations under these demand right provisions, and shall not be obligated to effect a registration (i) during the ninety (90) day period commencing with the date of the Company's initial public offering, or (ii) if it delivers notice to the holders of the Registrable Securities within thirty (30) days of any registration request of its intent to file a registration statement for such initial public offering within ninety (90) days. *Company Registration:* The Investors shall be entitled to "piggyback" registration rights on all registrations of the Company or on any demand registrations of any other investor subject to the right, however, of the Company and its underwriters to reduce the number of shares proposed to be registered pro rata in view of market conditions. If the Investors are so limited, however, no party shall sell shares in such registration other than the Company or the Investor, if any, invoking the demand registration. No shareholder of the Company shall be granted piggyback registration rights that would reduce the number of shares includable by the holders of the Registrable Securities in such registration without the consent of the holders of 50 percent of the Registrable Securities. *S-3 Rights:* Investors shall be entitled to two (2) demand registrations on Form S-3 per year (if available to the Company) so long as such registered offerings are not less than $500,000.

continued...

continued...

Registration Rights (cont.):	*Expenses:* The Company shall bear registration expenses (exclusive of underwriting discounts and commissions) of all such demands, piggybacks, and S-3 registrations (including the expense of a single counsel to the selling shareholders, which counsel shall also be counsel to the Company unless there is a conflict of interest with respect to the representation of any selling shareholder or the underwriters otherwise object). *Transfer of Rights:* The registration rights may be transferred to (i) any partner or retired partner of any holder that is a partnership, (ii) any family member or trust for the benefit of any individual holder, or (iii) any transferee who acquires at least 100,000 shares of Registrable Securities; provided the Company is given written notice thereof. *Termination of Rights:* The registration rights shall terminate on the date five years after the Company's initial public offering. *Other Provisions:* Other provisions shall be contained in the Stock Purchase Agreement with respect to registration rights as are reasonable, including cross-indemnification, the period of time in which the Registration Statement shall be kept effective, and underwriting arrangements
Right of First Refusal:	The Investors shall have the right in the event the Company proposes to offer equity securities to any person (other than securities issued to employees, directors,

continued...

continued...

Right of First Refusal (cont.):	or consultants, or pursuant to acquisitions, etc.) to purchase up to 50 percent of such shares (on a pro rata basis among the Investors). Such right of first refusal will terminate upon an underwritten public offering of shares of the Company.
Purchase Agreement:	The investment shall be made pursuant to a Stock Purchase Agreement reasonably acceptable to the Company and the Investors, which agreement shall contain, among other things, appropriate representations and warranties of the Company, covenants of the Company reflecting the provisions set forth herein, and appropriate conditions of closing, including an opinion of counsel for the Company. The Stock Purchase Agreement shall provide that it may only be amended and any waivers thereunder shall only be made with the approval of the holders of 50 percent of the Series A Preferred. Registration rights provisions may be amended or waived solely with the consent of the holders of 50 percent of the Registrable Securities.
EMPLOYEE MATTERS	
Stock Vesting:	Unless otherwise determined by the Board of Directors, all stock and stock equivalents issued after the Closing to employees, directors, and consultants will be subject to vesting in accordance with the vesting provisions currently in place under the Company's stock option plan.
Proprietary Information and Inventions Agreements:	Each officer and employee of the Company shall enter into acceptable agreements governing nondisclosure of proprietary information and assignment of inventions to the Company.

continued...

continued...

Co-Sale Agreement:	The shares of the Company's securities held by Kendra Commodore, Philip Colgate, and Kristine Colgate shall be made subject to a co-sale agreement (with certain reasonable exceptions) with the holders of the Series A Preferred such that they may not sell, transfer, or exchange their stock unless each holder of Series A Preferred has an opportunity to participate in the sale on a pro rata basis. This right of co-sale shall not apply to and shall terminate upon the Company's initial public offering. In addition, such co-sale agreement will contain a right of first refusal such that Commodore, Colgate, and Colgate may not sell, transfer, or exchange their stock without first offering to the Company and then to each holder of Series A Preferred the opportunity to purchase such stock on the same terms and conditions as those of the proposed sale.
Key-Person Insurance:	As soon as reasonably possible after the Closing, the Company shall procure key-person life insurance policies for each of Kendra Commodore, Philip Colgate, and Kristine Colgate in the amount of $1,000,000 each, naming the Company as beneficiary.
OTHER MATTERS	
Finders:	The Company and the Investors shall each indemnify the other for any finder's fees for which either is responsible.
Legal Fees and Expenses:	The Company shall pay the reasonable fees, not to exceed $25,000, and expenses of one special counsel to the Investors.

NOTES

1. PAUL A. GOMPERS & JOSH LERNER, THE MONEY OF INVENTION: HOW VENTURE CAPITAL CREATES NEW WEALTH 5, 12 (2001).
2. *Id.*
3. *Id.* at 10–11
4. *Id.* at 28.
5. For an excellent discussion of business plans and factors to consider in evaluating opportunities, see William A. Sahlman, *Some Thoughts on Business Plans, in* THE ENTREPRENEURIAL VENTURE 158 (Sahlman et al. eds., 2d ed. 1999).
6. Thanks to Professor Jay O. Light, of the Harvard Business School, for this insight.

Chapter 14

INTELLECTUAL PROPERTY AND CYBERLAW

According to a recent study, intellectual property represents approximately 70 percent of an average firm's value (up from less than 40 percent in the past).[1] As the *New York Times* observed, "Intellectual property has been transformed from a sleepy area of law and business to one of the driving engines of a high technology economy."[2] Nevertheless, many entrepreneurs assume that intellectual property issues are important only to mature, high-technology companies with large scientific staffs. In fact, virtually all businesses, even start-ups, have knowledge and information that are important to competitive success. Does the company have a name or a logo? Advertising materials? Product literature? Customized software? A new invention? A training video? A new way of doing things? A customer list? These may be among a company's most valuable assets. Intellectual property laws can help protect these assets.

In addition, all businesses need to take precautions to avoid violating others' intellectual property rights. Even unintentional violations can result in time-consuming and costly litigation that can ruin a business. For example, Kodak had to pay Polaroid $920 million in damages, shut down its instant camera business, and destroy approximately $1 billion in inventory after a court concluded that Kodak's products infringed certain of Polaroid's patents.[3]

The law of intellectual property is vast and complex. Obviously, no general businessperson can or should try to grasp all of its subtleties and nuances. Still, every entrepreneur needs to understand the basic rights that can be protected and the limitations on the protections available under the law. This basic understanding is critical to knowing when experienced help is needed.

Protecting intellectual property assets, and avoiding infringement of others' rights, requires the entrepreneur and his or her employees to act to prevent missteps. Experienced counsel can provide guidance, but the ultimate responsibility rests with the company itself. This chapter will give the entrepreneur an important leg up in meeting these challenges.

The chapter begins with a discussion of the important area of trade secrets. Trade secret law can help to protect confidential business information that is vital to competitive success. Trade secrets can protect broad classes of information, but concrete steps must be taken to preserve confidentiality.

Next, the chapter addresses copyrights. Copyrights have moved beyond their traditional role of protecting published literary works, musical compositions, and works of art into the realm of computer software and the digital distribution of music and other works on the Internet. Challenging new issues arising out of the Digital Millennium Copyright Act are addressed. The discussion then moves to patents, which can protect inventions ranging from gene-sequencing techniques to business processes. A patent gives an inventor very powerful rights that last for twenty years from the date the patent application is filed. The chapter next outlines the basics of trademarks and service marks, which are important tools to protect logos, brand names, slogans, and other identifying symbols. The use of domain names in a company's Internet address and protection for trade dress are also discussed.

The chapter then outlines the steps companies should take to ensure that they own the intellectual property created by their employees and describes the provisions commonly included in employee proprietary information and inventions agreements. Finally, the chapter presents an overview of key business and legal issues for transactions involving intellectual property. This discussion includes both licenses and acquisitions of intellectual property rights in the course of larger transactions, such as the sale of an entire business, and the use of open source software.

TRADE SECRET PROTECTION

Most businesses have important confidential information that helps them to compete in the marketplace. Such information may take the form of business and marketing plans, customer lists, financial statements, supplier terms, product formulas, custom software, and key contracts. Once competitors gain access to these company secrets, their value is often destroyed. Thus, the law of trade secrets can help to preserve a company's business secrets when patent and copyright protection cannot.

Trade secret disputes most often arise when an employee leaves a company to join a competitor and is suspected of taking valuable competitive information with him or her. For example, suppose that a recent hire in a medical equipment firm brings to her new job a presentation she created for her former employer that outlines an as-yet-undisclosed marketing strategy for a new diagnostic medical instrument. Even if the new hire merely intends to show her new boss the presentation to demonstrate her skill in creating effective presentations, her actions may well constitute misappropriation of her former employer's trade secrets. Violations of trade secret rights, both inadvertent and intentional, are common and are often costly.

What Is a Trade Secret?

GENERAL DEFINITION Although trade secret laws vary somewhat from state to state, the general principles are quite similar. A *trade secret* is (1) any information, including any formula, pattern, compilation, program, device, method, technique, or process, that (2) provides a business with a competitive advantage from not being generally known by a company's current or potential competitors or readily discoverable by them through legitimate means, and (3) is the subject of reasonable efforts to maintain its secrecy. A trade secret is protected for as long as each of these criteria is met.

TYPES OF INFORMATION THAT CAN BE PROTECTED Virtually any type of information can be protected as a trade secret as long as the requirements listed above are met. Sales and marketing plans, customer lists and data, software, computer files, manufacturing techniques, formulas, recipes, research and development results, survey information, sales data, secrets embodied in products, circuits on computer chips, and almost any other type of information can qualify as long as the information provides the business with some competitive advantage from not being generally known. Thus, it is crucial to think in the broadest possible terms when assessing what information may qualify as a trade secret. The biggest risk is failing to take appropriate measures to protect less obvious forms of trade secrets and thereby losing trade secret protection.

TRADE SECRETS MUST NOT BE GENERALLY KNOWN OR DISCOVERABLE Information that is generally known or discoverable through proper means by competitors cannot constitute a trade secret. Thus, trade secret protection does not extend to information that is in the public domain or is otherwise generally available to customers or competitors. This includes information contained in a company's own product and promotional materials (even technical specifications) that are distributed to the public. It also includes information that is disclosed by mistake, such as when a document is left on top of a desk in plain view of a visitor to the company's offices, or when an employee in an elevator is overheard by a customer. In addition, trade secret protection is unavailable for information that competitors or others obtain through legitimate reverse engineering of a hardware product. (Reverse engineering is the process of deconstructing a product and examining its inner workings.) Thus, once a product containing trade secrets is released for sale, trade secret protection is often lost. However, if the trade secret cannot be ascertained from examination of the product, as is the case with the formula for Coca-Cola, for example, then release of the product will not cause the loss of trade secret protection. In addition, prototypes and information destined for public release can still be protected as trade secrets before they are released.

REASONABLE EFFORTS TO MAINTAIN SECRECY Simply stated, a court will not protect trade secrets unless the owner does also. It is not necessary to take every conceivable precaution, but the owner must make reasonable efforts under the circumstances. In assessing reasonableness, courts examine the value of the information, the resources available to the company to protect its trade secrets, the difficulty and expense required for a competitor to develop the information on its own, and how broadly the information is known, both inside and outside the company. Elements of a sample trade secret protection program are discussed below.

Enforcing Trade Secret Rights

Legal remedies can protect the owner of a trade secret against improper disclosure and use by others. Improper means of acquiring trade secrets include theft, misrepresentation, bribery, breach of contract, and espionage. Perhaps more important, improper disclosures also include disclosures that violate a duty of confidentiality owed to the owner of the trade secret. This duty of confidentiality may arise because an employee, customer, consultant, independent contractor, banker, or other person has signed a *nondisclosure agreement* (also referred to as a *confidentiality agreement*) with the trade secret owner, in which the person to whom trade secrets are disclosed promises not to disclose them to others or to use them. A duty of confidentiality may also arise by operation of law, that is, merely because of a person's status as an officer, director, or employee of a company owning the trade secret.

When a person discloses or uses a trade secret in violation of a duty of confidentiality, the trade secret owner can use the courts to protect its trade secret rights. Just as important, if a company acquires a trade secret from someone, such as an ex-employee of a competitor, and knows or has reason to know that the ex-employee was violating a duty of confidentiality in disclosing the information, then the company must refrain from using the trade secret. Note, however, that if no duty of confidentiality exists, legal protections generally will not be available, unless the secret was obtained by improper means (such as theft). This is why confidentiality agreements are so important.

Legal relief can include a court order preventing disclosure or use of the trade secret information, money damages, and, in some cases, punitive damages. The government may also bring criminal charges under the federal Economic Espionage Protection Act. Although criminal charges are

FROM THE TRENCHES

The long-running legal battle over Avanti Corp.'s alleged misappropriation of trade secrets from Cadence Design Systems ended abruptly when Avanti and several of its executives pled no contest in July 2001 to the charges during the criminal trial. In addition to prison terms, the court imposed fines and a restitution award in excess of $220 million. Avanti founder Stephen Wuu was sentenced to two years in prison and led away in handcuffs.

Source: William Rodarmor, Prosecution Complex, Calif. Law (Dec. 2001) at 22.

relatively rare in trade secret cases, increasing recognition that trade secrets are valuable company property (often far more valuable than physical property) may lead to greater use of criminal sanctions in trade secret theft cases. If trade secret rights may have been violated, it is prudent to contact an attorney immediately.

Even when trade secrets become public in violation of the owner's rights, once they are public, they cease to be trade secrets. This is true even though the owner is entirely innocent. Damages may be available, but winning them requires victory at trial, which is never a certainty. Even with a victory at trial, court-awarded damages may not provide full compensation for the harm to the business. If the wrongdoers are unable to pay the damages, there may be no effective remedy. Thus, an entrepreneur's best course is to take steps to prevent both improper and inadvertent trade secret disclosures. A trade secret protection program should form the centerpiece of this effort.

Establishing a Trade Secret Protection Program

Taking reasonable steps to protect trade secrets is legally necessary to secure the protection provided by the trade secret laws. Developing a program to protect company secrets usually makes good business sense as well. The company's trade secret policies should be in writing, be made available to all employees and contractors, and be discussed thoroughly with every employee and contractor who has access to trade secrets. In the end, knowledgeable and conscientious employees are the most important line of defense against trade secret disclosure.

An experienced attorney should help develop the trade secret protection program, but ultimately the entrepreneur is responsible for seeing that the program is carried out by all employees and contractors. The plan should be comprehensive but not so complex and burdensome that employees or contractors refuse to implement it or are unable to do so. What constitutes a reasonable trade secret protection program that meets the legal standard necessary to enforce trade secret rights will vary from business to business. An entrepreneur in a start-up business need not take the same precautions as IBM. Again, an attorney can help craft a balanced, effective plan that meets the legal requirements for a particular business. Because many elements of a trade secret protection program are quite similar across businesses, such legal advice should not be too expensive.

Although every business's circumstances are different, most trade secret protection programs will contain most of the following elements.

IDENTIFYING TRADE SECRETS The program should include guidance as to what constitutes a trade secret. The head of a small business is likely to be aware of many, but not all, of the company's important trade secrets. Employees and contractors must also shoulder responsibility for helping to identify a company's trade secrets. The trade secret protection plan should spell out general categories of information that are likely to be particularly important to the business. For a software company, this could be source code, sensitive computer files, and documentation; for a telemarketing company, it could be customer data. In addition, the plan should include appropriate catchall categories, such as any information that is not known outside the company and might have value to competitors.

The plan should require employees to mark all documents that contain trade secrets as "Confidential." However, it is important not to treat all company information as trade secrets. If every document is marked "Confidential," a court is likely to conclude that the company is not taking the notion of confidentiality seriously and may refuse to grant any trade secret protection, even for those items that truly are confidential.

SECURING EMPLOYEE COMMITMENT Securing employee commitment to protecting trade secrets is essential. Employees are the biggest source of trade secret disclosure, both accidental and otherwise. Steps to achieve employee commitment include the following.

Preemployment Clearance As noted above, trade secret disputes commonly arise when an employee leaves one company to work for a competitor and takes sensitive information along. When hiring an employee away from a competitor, it is important to stress that no trade secrets from the former employer are to be used on the job or shared with others in the company. In sensitive cases, an applicant should be required to sign an agreement to that effect as part of the recruiting process. The employer should make sure that the new employee has not brought documents, computer disks, or other papers containing trade secrets to the job. The employer should require promises to this effect in the employee's employment or nondisclosure agreement. It is also prudent to review any employment or nondisclosure agreement that the new employee had with the former employer. Finally, conducting a broad search for a new hire to fill a vacant job, rather than merely offering the position to a competitor's employee, can help show that a new hire was not singled out with the specific intent to acquire trade secrets from his or her former employer.

Nondisclosure Agreements Many authorities consider nondisclosure agreements to be the single most important element in a company's trade secret protection program. In brief, a nondisclosure agreement contains a promise by the employee to avoid unauthorized use or disclosure of the company's trade secrets and to use care to prevent unauthorized use and disclosure from occurring. In addition to strengthening the employer's legal rights, the agreement impresses upon the new employee the seriousness with which the company guards its trade secrets.

Although a nondisclosure agreement may be a stand-alone document or be included in a more comprehensive employment agreement or an invention assignment agreement, it is usually preferable for companies to include the nondisclosure obligations in a standard employee proprietary information and inventions agreement. Proprietary information and inventions agreements are discussed further below.

Middle- and upper-level management, engineers, technical employees, secretaries, janitors, clerks, and all others with access to trade secrets, even as only an incidental part of their jobs, should be required to sign a nondisclosure agreement before beginning work. Experience suggests that most new employees will readily sign a nondisclosure agreement. If an employee was not required to sign a nondisclosure agreement as part of the hiring process, the employer should offer some consideration other than just continued employment in exchange for the employee's agreeing to sign such an agreement later.

Noncompetition Agreements Some companies use noncompetition agreements (also called covenants not to compete) to prevent employees who leave the company from using trade secrets and other sensitive information on behalf of a competitor. The key advantage of a noncompetition agreement is that it avoids the often difficult task of proving that a former employee actually stole and used trade secrets to help a competitor. For example, a former employee might use general knowledge of a company's long-range strategic plans to design a strategy for his or her new company. In such a case, proving that the former employee actually divulged trade secrets in designing the new strategy might be virtually impossible. With a noncompetition agreement, the employee is simply prevented from working for the competitor at all. Typically, only senior managers and technical staff are asked to sign noncompetition agreements, which usually have a limited duration, often one to three years.

The chief difficulty with noncompetition agreements is that in many states, including California, such agreements are generally unenforceable (except when executed in connection with the sale of a business, as discussed more fully in Chapter 2). In states in which noncompetition agreements are generally enforceable, many employees refuse to sign them. If a noncompetition agreement is desired, however, experienced counsel should draft the contract to maximize the likelihood that it will be held to be fully enforceable.

Employee Education All employees should be provided basic information about the company's trade secret protection program. Periodic reminders in newsletters and at companywide functions will help to keep employees aware of the need to protect trade secrets. For example, Synopsys, Inc., a Silicon Valley software firm, created a sinister-looking caricature of a spy and put it up on walls and in newsletters as a vivid reminder of the importance of trade secret protection. Company executives even performed a brief skit at a companywide meeting to show how easily sensitive information can accidentally be divulged. Educational efforts should also stress to employees the dangers of improperly using others' trade secrets. Companies should require employees to acknowledge annually all of the company's policies, including its trade secret program. Unintentional trade secret disclosures are common, and employee education is a key to safeguarding confidential information.

Other Protective Measures Other recommended measures to protect trade secrets include the following:

- Marking as "Confidential" documents that contain trade secrets.
- Disclosing confidential information within the company on a need-to-know basis.
- Keeping confidential information on-site whenever possible.
- Using appropriate passwords and security codes to protect sensitive computer files.
- Encrypting e-mail and other sensitive electronic transmissions.
- Maintaining a clean-desk policy and locking offices and file cabinets.
- Protecting prototypes and other physical products that contain trade secrets.
- Avoiding the discussion of sensitive topics when visitors are present, over unsecured telephone lines (especially cellular phones), and in public, especially in airplanes, elevators, restaurants, and other places where competitors could possibly be present.
- Advising employees to use extra caution at trade shows, scientific conferences, and professional gatherings, where competitors are almost always present and the temptation is great to boast about new but confidential developments at informal social gatherings (especially in bars).
- Using a shredder or otherwise destroying discarded confidential information before putting it in the trash.
- Prohibiting personal software and personal computer files at work.
- Keeping records of what software was checked out to whom and when.
- Using appropriate precautions when working at home or away from the office.

Precautions such as these cost little and are good business practice, but too many companies fail to implement them, often with unpleasant consequences.

Technically oriented companies should have a policy of reviewing engineers' and scientists' speeches and publications in advance to prevent inadvertent disclosures of company trade secrets. (Disclosures in publications and speeches may also have implications for the company's patent rights, which is another reason why review of such material is critical.) This review can be especially important because many scientists and engineers are justifiably proud of their new discoveries and are eager to share their findings with colleagues.

Exit Interview/Exit Agreement Exit interviews should be conducted to ensure that departing employees recognize, and agree to abide by, their duty to refrain from taking any materials containing trade secrets. Personal files, computer disks, and other items that employees wish to remove should be inspected for company trade secrets, and the company should confirm with employees that all such materials have been deleted from hard drives in home or laptop computers. Companies should try to get all departing employees to acknowledge these matters in writing. If the departing employee never signed a confidentiality agreement, this becomes even more important. If an employee is leaving to work for a competitor, the company should consider having its lawyer send a letter to the new employer, informing it that the employee had access to valuable trade secrets and warning it against using any trade secrets that may be brought into its possession by the new employee.

DEALING WITH OUTSIDERS A trade secret protection program should also include precautions for dealing with outsiders, such as independent contractors and potential investors.

Nondisclosure Agreements Before disclosing confidential information to consultants, independent contractors, potential investors or business partners, and other outsiders with access to trade secrets, a company should require them to sign a nondisclosure agreement. Without such an agreement, these persons may have no duty to refrain from disclosing or using a company's trade secrets. (For an example of such a provision, see Section 4 of the Independent Contractor Services Agreement in "Getting It In Writing" at the end of Chapter 10.)

Building Security Security measures may range from steps as simple as keeping unattended doors locked, maintaining a visitor sign-in log, and providing employee escorts to steps as elaborate as providing fully guarded and electronically protected access. In addition, many of the suggested employee precautions noted above can also help to prevent inadvertent leaks to outside visitors.

International Considerations

Although most industrialized countries provide some protection for trade secrets, trade secret laws differ from country to country. The preceding discussion covers only U.S. trade secret law. If confidential business information is to be used or kept abroad, the company should consider retaining foreign counsel. An experienced U.S. attorney can help to determine whether the often considerable expense of hiring a foreign attorney is justified and may be able to provide referrals.

COPYRIGHTS

Copyrights are critical to companies operating in the software, publishing, journalism, movie, entertainment, music, multimedia, and Internet industries, among others. Copyrights are also important to artists, writers, musicians, photographers, and architects. Indeed, virtually all businesses have some materials that can be protected through copyright law. This is especially true today when most businesses have a presence on the Internet. A company's Web site is a copyrightable work.

What Is a Copyright?

A *copyright* gives the owner of an original work of authorship the exclusive legal right to obtain certain economic benefits from the work, including the right to prevent reproduction and distribution of the work. In particular, the copyright owner has the exclusive rights (1) to reproduce copies of the work; (2) to develop derivative works based on the copyrighted work; (3) to distribute copies of the work; (4) to perform the work publicly; and (5) to display the work publicly. These exclusive rights can be used to prevent others from using, copying, distributing, performing, or displaying the copyrighted work or any derivative works.

For example, the owner of a copyright for a book or a piece of software has the exclusive rights to create later editions, versions, or sequels to the work. Generally, if another person reproduces or distributes copyrighted material without permission, or exercises any of the copyright owner's other exclusive rights without permission, then the copyright owner can obtain legal relief.

What Can Be Protected by a Copyright?

Copyrights protect a wide range of works. In addition to protecting books, works of art, musical recordings, magazines, plays, dramatic performances, and movies, copyrights can also protect software, Web pages, advertisements, photographs, videos, games, instruction manuals, sales presentations and client proposals, original labels, diagrams, architectural drawings, financial tables, business plans, and many other forms of creative work.

Copyrights can also be used to protect derivative works and some compilations. A *derivative work* is a work that is based on another work. Derivative works can include adaptations and modifications of previous works, such as a translation of the original work into another language.

Facts are not copyrightable. A database or other compilation of facts is protected only if the author used some degree of originality and creativity in selecting and presenting the information.[4] For example, a selective listing of high-quality auto repair shops sorted by geographic location

FROM THE TRENCHES

Pro CD, which compiled information from more than 3,000 telephone directories into a single database, sold a version of the database on CD-ROM. Each CD-ROM package contained within it a "shrink-wrap" and "click-wrap" license agreement prohibiting unauthorized resale of the database; customers were deemed to accept the agreement when they opened the wrapping around the envelope containing the disks or clicked on the "I Accept" box on the computer screen. Even though the database was probably not eligible for copyright protection, the U.S. Court of Appeals for the Seventh Circuit held that the restrictions in the license agreement were binding on the purchaser.

Source: Pro CD, Inc. v. Zeidenberg, 86 F.3d 1447 (7th Cir. 1996).

could be copyrighted, although the individual names of the shops themselves would not be copyrightable. Even if a factual compilation is not eligible for copyright protection, the compiler may be able to require the purchaser of the database to agree by contract not to reproduce the information contained in the database.

Copyrights Do Not Protect Ideas

Copyright cannot be used to protect an idea or a certain way of performing some function; copyright protects only the particular way the idea or function is expressed in a tangible medium (such as printed on paper, recorded on tape, or coded on a disk). For example, this book is protected by copyright, but the ideas contained in it are not. A business plan may be copyrighted, but that does not prevent another person from developing a business that uses the ideas contained in the plan. However, such ideas may be protectable as trade secrets if appropriate steps are taken to keep them confidential.

If an idea and the way it is expressed are inseparably bound, the idea and the expression are said to *merge,* and no copyright protection is available. For example, the maker of a karate video game cannot obtain a copyright on the karate moves made by the action figures in the game because the expression of the karate moves in the video game is inseparable from the moves performed in actual karate. The "H" pattern for a manual transmission cannot be copyrighted because it is inseparable from the basic functioning of the gearshift pattern employed in most manual transmissions.

In practice, it can be very difficult to separate an idea from its tangible expression, so the degree of protection afforded by a copyright is often hard to predict with precision. In general, the more ways an idea can be expressed, the more likely the work is to be copyrightable. For example, a court held that the use of the "+" sign to indicate addition in a computer spreadsheet program is not copyrightable because there really is no other logical and feasible way to express the notion of addition on a computer keyboard. On the other hand, a basic literary plot such as love triumphing over adversity is capable of so many unique expressions that many different stories expressing the same basic idea can be copyrighted.

Fair Use

Even if material does qualify for copyright protection, the law permits others to make limited use of copyrighted materials, including making copies for certain purposes, under the doctrine of fair use. *Fair use* purposes include criticism, comment, news reporting, scholarship, and research. Under the copyright statute, four factors are considered in determining whether a use is fair use: (1) the purpose and character of the use (including whether it is commercial or not), (2) the nature of the copyrighted work, (3) the amount and substantiality of the portion used, and (4) the effect of the use upon the potential market or value of the copyrighted work. Whether an unauthorized use of a copyrighted work constitutes protected fair use is fact specific. In very general terms, though, if the use is transformative—if it adds new information, insights, and understandings to the copyrighted work—it is more likely to qualify as a fair use. On the other hand, if it is commercial and diminishes the value of the copyright to the owner, the use is less likely to qualify as a fair use.

Courts sometimes interpret the fair use exception quite broadly. For example, one court held that using another's drawings of film frames of the assassination of President Kennedy in a book qualified as fair use because the

FROM THE TRENCHES

Determining what is fair use often requires a subjective judgment, and courts do not always agree. When, for example, a publisher began promoting a book called *The Wind Done Gone* based on the novel *Gone with the Wind,* the owners of the copyright in the famous novel filed suit. A federal district court concluded that the new book would infringe *Gone with the Wind* and ordered the publisher not to publish the book. The appeals court, however, finding that *The Wind Done Gone* was a parody, vacated the lower court's order and allowed publication of the book. In another case, courts disagreed over the unauthorized use of an art poster on a television program. The lower court found that briefly displaying the poster was fair use, particularly because the display was unlikely to hurt sales of the poster. Because the copyright owner had been denied the right to license the work, however, the appeals court ruled that unauthorized use of the poster was not fair use but copyright infringement.

Source: Ringgold v. Black Enter. Television, Inc., 126 F.3d 70 (2d Cir. 1997).

public interest was served by making available information about the assassination. The U.S. Supreme Court held that the use of the copyrighted song "Pretty Woman" in a parody by rap group 2 Live Crew was fair use as long as, in making fun of "Pretty Woman," the parody used no more of the lyrics and music of the original work than was necessary to make it recognizable.[5]

Many commercial uses of copyrighted information are not permitted under the doctrine of fair use. For example, Kinko's Graphics Corp. violated the copyrights of Basic Books, Inc. and other publishers when it copied without permission and sold portions of copyrighted works selected by professors to be used in student course readers. The court rejected Kinko's fair use claim, noting that Kinko's involvement was for the purpose of obtaining profits, even though the copied materials were used for educational purposes.[6] Similarly, the copying of articles in scientific and technical journals by a scientist at Texaco, Inc. for his own files was held not to be fair use.[7] In a highly publicized lawsuit discussed further below, Napster unsuccessfully argued that its users' sharing of MP3 files constituted fair use of copyrighted songs.[8]

Reverse Engineering Unauthorized reverse engineering of a computer program can be fair use. Copying unprotectable aspects of a work, such as facts and ideas, does not constitute infringement. Given the nature of computer code, however, if a competitor wishes to identify the unprotectable elements in a software program, it sometimes must copy and then decompile the object code. Copying and reverse engineering for this purpose have been held to be fair use.[9]

Similarly, in a case involving the popular Sony PlayStation games, a court ruled that it was fair use for a company to decompile Sony's software program in order to create a new program that allowed the games to be played on a Macintosh computer. The court reasoned that the new program did not merely take the place of the Sony program but transformed it into something new and different.[10]

The Digital Millennium Copyright Act (DMCA) prohibits circumventing access-control mechanisms, which could limit a developer's ability to reverse engineer. Although the DMCA contains an exception for reverse engineering necessary to achieve interoperability, it is not yet clear how broadly or narrowly courts will apply this exception. In addition, many software licenses expressly prohibit reverse engineering. Before implementing any reverse engineering program, a company should consult with experienced legal counsel.

Duration of Copyrights

A key advantage of copyrights is that protection typically lasts far longer than is needed for most commercial uses. The copyright for an individual creator lasts for the life of the creator plus 70 years. For a work made for hire (discussed below), the duration is 95 years from the year of publication or 120 years from the year of creation, which ever occurs first.

Requirements for Obtaining Copyright Protection and Suing for Copyright Infringement

To be eligible for copyright protection, a work of authorship must meet three basic requirements. First, the work must be fixed in a tangible medium of expression (e.g., written down, saved on a computer disk or hard drive, or recorded on tape). Almost any medium from which the idea can be retrieved will qualify. Second, the work must be original; that is, it must have been created by the author claiming the copyright. The work does not need to be unique, novel, or of high quality. Third, the work must contain some minimal level of creativity. The standard of creativity required is quite low—no particular merit is required. Thus, the white pages of the telephone directory would not qualify, but the "Yellow Pages" with ads and text displayed would. Directions for how to use a beauty product displayed on a product label would also qualify. Thus, almost any original work of authorship developed for a business can qualify for copyright protection.

No action is required to obtain copyright protection. It automatically arises when an original work of authorship is first fixed in a tangible medium of expression. Nevertheless, steps can be taken to strengthen copyright protections. It is always advisable to display a copyright notice, even though it is not legally required. This puts others on notice that the work is copyrighted and can prevent a third party from attempting to avoid liability by asserting innocent infringement. This notice should be in the form of the word "Copyright" or a "c" enclosed in a circle (©), followed by the name of the author and the year of publication and the phrase "All rights reserved." The notice should be displayed prominently.

To file an infringement suit in the United States, the owner of the copyright must have registered it with the Register of Copyrights in Washington, D.C. Although the right to sue can be secured by registration after an infringement occurs, statutory damages and attorneys' fees are available only if the copyright is registered within three months of the date that the work is first published. Statutory damages are remedies provided by the Copyright Act and currently are limited to $30,000 for ordinary infringement of each copyrighted work and $150,000 for each willful infringement. Statutory damages are typically sought when the actual damages suffered are less than these amounts or are very difficult to prove in court. Because a start-up often cannot prove actual damage given its short operating history, the availability of statutory damages becomes particularly important. A plaintiff who made a timely copyright registration can seek actual damages or statutory damages, but not both. Actual damages awarded in copyright cases can be much greater than these statutory amounts.

Registration is a relatively simple and inexpensive procedure and should be considered for any significant works of authorship. Registration requires filing a copy of the work, which is available to the public, but special rules may be invoked to help protect valuable software code.

Proving Copyright Infringement

Direct proof that a work was copied is not required to prove copyright infringement. All that is needed is a showing that the alleged infringer had access to the copyrighted work and that his or her work is substantially similar to the copyrighted work. To make it easier to prove that software was copied, useless pieces of software code are often embedded within a program; if another program contains the useless code, it is almost certain that the original code was copied.

In cases other than literal copying, determining whether protected expression was copied can be highly fact specific and costly to litigate. A company should contact an experienced attorney immediately if infringement of an important copyright is suspected.

There are three basic types of copyright infringement—direct, vicarious, and contributory.

DIRECT COPYRIGHT INFRINGEMENT Direct copyright infringement occurs when a person, without the consent of the copyright holder and outside the scope of fair use, violates at least one exclusive right granted to the copyright holder. For example, if a person buys a version of Microsoft XP, burns a copy, and sells that copy, he or she has directly infringed Microsoft's exclusive right to copy, distribute, and sell its copyrighted program. Similarly, if a company uses copyrighted music or art on its Web site without permission from the copyright owner then the company will be liable for direct infringement.

VICARIOUS COPYRIGHT INFRINGEMENT Liability for vicarious copyright infringement attaches to a person who has the right and ability to supervise a direct copyright infringement and who has a direct financial interest in the infringement. For example, courts have held that swap meet organizers vicariously infringed when they knowingly created and administered a market where bootleg music was sold and where the organizers were paid a flat fee for admission.[11]

CONTRIBUTORY COPYRIGHT INFRINGEMENT Contributory copyright infringement occurs when a person knowingly induces or causes the directly infringing conduct. For example, if a company creates and maintains a Web site that it knows or should know that users are using to post and download games without the consent of the copyright owners, then the company will be liable for contributory infringement.

Ownership of Copyrights and Works Made for Hire

As a general rule, the author of a work owns the copyright. However, under the doctrine of *work made for hire,* the employer owns works created

FROM THE TRENCHES

Napster, a wildly popular start-up, enabled users to share MP3 music files with each other. As Napster's user base expanded rapidly, the major record labels sued, alleging that Napster both vicariously infringed their copyrights and contributed to its users' direct infringement. Napster argued that it did not infringe the labels' copyrights because, as in the landmark Sony Betamax case, its technology was capable of "substantial non-infringing uses." In the earlier case, the U.S. Supreme Court had held that Sony did not engage in contributory copyright infringement when it sold its Betamax video recorders. Although Betamax made it possible for users to copy copyrighted movies, the Court concluded that "time shifting"—users' ability to record a program broadcast on television and play it back at a later time—was fair use. Napster also argued that it did not directly copy any copyrighted songs—all MP3 files were owned and possessed by its users.

The U.S. Court of Appeals for the Ninth Circuit found Napster's arguments unpersuasive and upheld a preliminary injunction that required Napster to remove from its directory every title to which a record company could establish a legitimate copyright. The injunction essentially crippled Napster, slashing its user base and forcing it to convert to a paid subscription service.

Sources: A&M Records, Inc. v. Napster, Inc., 239 F.3d 1004 (9th Cir. 2001); Sony Corp. v. Universal City Studios, Inc., 464 U.S. 417 (1984). See also Constance E. Bagley & Michael J. Roberts, Napster, Harv. Bus. Sch. Case No. 9-801-219 (Mar. 29, 2001).

by its employees in the scope of their employment. The courts consider the following factors in determining whether an employee created a particular work within the scope of employment:

- Right to control—whether the employer had the right to direct and to supervise the manner in which the work was being performed.
- Who initiated the creation of the work.
- At whose expense the work was created.
- Time spent on the project.

- Who owned the facilities where the work was created.
- The nature and amount of compensation received by the employee for the work.

If the court finds that no employment relationship existed and that the creator of the work was an independent contractor, then, absent a work-made-for-hire agreement or an express assignment of the copyright, the creator (not the employer) will be granted the copyright ownership of the work. For example, the U.S. Supreme Court held that the copyright to a sculpture was owned by the sculptor who created it and not by the organization that commissioned it.[12] The Court observed that the sculptor used his own tools, worked in his own studio, had only one project that lasted a short period of time, and had total discretion in hiring and paying assistants.

The company that pays for work created by an independent contractor will own the work as a work made for hire only if (1) there is a written agreement that states that the work is a work made for hire, and (2) the work falls into one of nine legal categories of specially commissioned works made for hire (none of which expressly includes computer software). Because not all copyrighted works fit within the statutory categories of works made for hire, independent contractors are typically asked to sign agreements assigning to the company that hires them all of their rights to any works they produce during their service and the copyrights related thereto. Such an agreement is particularly crucial for works such as computer software that do not clearly fall within one of the nine listed categories. Without such a written assignment, the independent contractor will own his or her works, and the party that paid for them may be entitled to only a single copy.

Copyright ownership disputes can often arise between parties when their relationship is not clear. Such disputes can occur in relation to musical compositions, trade catalogs and pamphlets, pictorial illustrations, scientific and technical writings, photographs, works of art, and translations of foreign literary works. To avoid possible problems, the parties should enter into a written contract that specifies their intentions and relationship and that assigns to the employer the right to the copyright ownership of the work to be created. (See, for example, Section 4.6 of the Independent Contractor Services Agreement in "Getting It In Writing" at the end of Chapter 10.)

FROM THE TRENCHES

The New York Times Co. (which owns *The New York Times*) obtained licenses from freelance journalists giving the company the right to copy and sell their articles to LexisNexis, a company that operates a computerized database of news articles, and University Microfilms International (UMI), which produces CD-ROM products featuring news articles. Six freelance journalists who had written articles for those publications then sued The New York Times Co. for contributory copyright infringement. The writers argued that, while The New York Times Co. owned the copyright to the actual newspapers and magazines containing their freelance works, it did not—in the absence of the writers' assignment of their copyrights—have the right to sell each article individually. The New York Times Co. argued that its sale of articles to LexisNexis and UMI was merely a "revision" of the newspapers and magazines to which it held the copyrights. Because the Copyright Act authorizes copyright holders to "revise" collective works, the company claimed it was well within its rights when it sold the freelance articles.

The U.S. Supreme Court ruled in favor of the freelance authors. In finding copyright infringement, the Court reasoned that "the database [and CD-ROM] no more constitutes a 'revision' of each constituent edition than a 400-page novel quoting a sonnet in passing would represent a 'revision' of that poem."

Source: New York Times Co. v. Tasini, 533 U.S. 483 (2001).

As discussed in Chapter 10, it is not always clear whether a worker is an employee or an independent contractor and whether an employee is acting within the scope of his or her employment. Thus, both employees and independent contractors who create copyrighted works should be required to sign an agreement assigning any rights they may have in their works to their employer.

Copyright in Cyberspace and the Digital Millennium Copyright Act

The Digital Millennium Copyright Act was enacted in 1998 to provide copyright protection for books, music, videos, software, and other creative works transmitted in digital form over the Internet. Modifying the statutory scheme for licensing sound recordings, the DMCA sets forth a number of specific conditions, including the payment of royalties to the artist, that an Internet music service must satisfy to qualify for a statutory license to Web cast sound recordings.

The DMCA makes it a crime to circumvent technological antipiracy measures designed to control access to a copyrighted work. It also outlaws the manufacture, distribution, or sale of technologies and devices that enable consumers to circumvent these measures. The DMCA does, however, permit the cracking of copyright protection devices to conduct encryption research, to test computer security systems, and to access products to achieve interoperability. The DMCA also makes it illegal to intentionally remove or tamper with certain "copyright management information," data identifying the title of a copyrighted work, the author, and the copyright owner. The DMCA also makes it a crime to provide false copyright management information. Armed with the DMCA's legal protections and the criminal penalties it provides, copyright owners have stepped up their development of technology-based protection schemes designed to control the flow and use of copyrighted content.

The DMCA contains several safe-harbor provisions that protect certain computer bulletin board services and other Internet service providers from

FROM THE TRENCHES

The anticircumvention provisions of the DMCA have raised the hackles of legal scholars, librarians, and journalists, who argue that these provisions outlaw legally protected fair use copying. In 2001, Dmitry Sklyarov; a twenty-six-year-old Russian computer programmer, found himself at the center of this controversy when he was arrested by the FBI during a visit to a trade show in Las Vegas. His Moscow-based employer, ElcomSoft Co., Ltd., had been selling a computer program Sklyarov had written that allowed purchasers of Adobe Systems' ebooks to bypass Adobe's encryption software and make backup copies. After a firestorm of protest, Adobe dropped the charges and Sklyarov was released. As of January 2002, the charges against ElcomSoft were still pending.

copyright infringement liability when they innocently store or transmit infringing materials posted by their users. Several of the safe harbors require that the service provider take active steps to qualify, such as (1) registering designated agents with the Copyright Office, (2) following specified notice and take-down procedures to remove infringing materials, (3) adopting a policy for terminating users who are repeat infringers, and (4) taking steps to inform users of the policy. In addition, a service provider must accommodate and not interfere with "standard" technical measures used by copyright owners to identify and protect copyrighted works. Given the DMCA's many limitations and exclusions, an entrepreneur should seek the advice of qualified counsel for help in complying with it if it could be relevant to his or her business.

International Issues

Unlike most other forms of intellectual property protection, U.S. copyrights generally are valid overseas through a treaty (the Berne Convention) signed by most major countries. Nevertheless, enforcing copyrights in other countries may be far more difficult and costly than enforcing them in the United States. In some countries, enforcement of copyrights may not be practical at all. However, recent U.S. government initiatives to promote protection for U.S. intellectual property overseas (including pressure on China to stop software copying) have led some experts to conclude that enforcing copyrights in many foreign nations will become easier in the future.

The World Intellectual Property Organization (WIPO) Copyright Treaty represents a step toward that end. Drafted in 1996, the treaty extends traditional Berne Convention copyright protections to cover computer programs and electronic databases. Importantly, the treaty imposes on each ratifying nation the obligation to provide legal protection and effective legal remedies to combat the circumvention of copyright-protecting measures and the removal of digital rights management information.

PATENTS

Any entrepreneur whose business involves the creation of new products or manufacturing or business processes must understand the basics of patent law. Patents can provide powerful protections for new products, inventions, and processes. Patents can also give a young business a legal monopoly over a new technology and, with it, enormous advantages over even the largest competitors. For example, in 1994 Stac Electronics won a $120 million jury verdict against Microsoft Corp. for infringement of Stac's data compression software patents. Although Stac later settled the case for $43 million cash and the purchase by Microsoft of $40 million of Stac nonvoting preferred stock, the award was a monumental victory for Stac. Patents can also give a new business instant prestige and quick revenues from licensing fees, and they may make it easier to raise venture capital.

Another benefit is that patents can be used defensively as bargaining chips in patent disputes. If a competitor claims that a company's product violates a patent, it is very helpful if the company can claim that the competitor is violating one of the company's patents. This often results in a cross-licensing agreement whereby each party is permitted to use the other's patented technology, often on a royalty-free basis.

The government does not grant these exclusive rights readily. Obtaining a patent is often a complex and costly undertaking, and violating another's patent rights, even innocently, can result in crushing damage awards. Savvy competitors use patents in strategic ways, such as securing patents for improvements on another company's patents. Recent legal develop-

FROM THE TRENCHES

In 1994, Johnson & Johnson introduced and patented the first stent—a heart-repair device used to prop open arteries after blockages have been cleared. After the Johnson & Johnson device had dominated the market for three years, Boston Scientific Corp. introduced its own stent. Johnson & Johnson sued Boston Scientific, claiming patent infringement. In 2000, a federal jury ruled in favor of Johnson & Johnson and ordered Boston Scientific to pay $324.4 million in damages. Boston Scientific has asked a federal judge to set aside the verdict.

Source: Ron Winslow & Laura Johannes, Johnson & Johnson Wins $324.4 Million in Patent Suit Against Boston Scientific, Wall St. J., Dec. 18, 2000, at B4.

ments (especially the creation of the U.S. Court of Appeals for the Federal Circuit to hear all patent cases) favor the enforcement of patents, and patent law is becoming more critical in many industries, including software, biotechnology, and medical devices.

One note of caution: Patent law is a subspecialty within the legal specialty of intellectual property. (Even within the subspecialty of patent law, attorneys often focus on a single industry, such as biotechnology, software, or telecommunications.) Patent law is particularly complex and technical. If patent issues arise, a company should consult a patent attorney. The following discussion presents an overview that will help in assessing when to contact patent counsel.

What Is a Patent?

A *patent* is an exclusive right granted by the federal government that entitles the inventor to prevent anyone else from making, using, selling, or offering to sell the patented process or product in the United States for a specified period of time. There are two main types of patents: utility patents and design patents. (Patents for certain plants are a third type.)

The patent application must contain a detailed description of the invention sufficient to allow someone else who is skilled in the technical field to make and use it. For inventions for which patent protection is sought only in the United States, the patent application remains confidential until the patent is issued so that trade secret protection continues until the patent protection begins. If the U.S. patent application has a foreign counterpart, however, the U.S. Patent and Trademark Office (PTO) will publish the application eighteen months after filing. After the patent protection period lapses, anyone can use the information in the patent application to make or use the invention.

Types of Patents and Patentable Subject Matter

Utility patents can protect several kinds of inventions. Utility patents can cover a machine, such as a machine for making auto parts, or a process, such as the process for filling an aerosol can or fabricating a computer chip. Utility patents can also protect articles of manufacture, such as an intermittent windshield wiper or a plastic paper clip. Utility patents can also cover new compositions of matter, such as a new chemical compound or a formula for mouthwash. Human-made microorganisms are also patentable. Improvements to any of these types of inventions can also be protected with a utility patent.

If an invention falls into one of these categories (i.e., machine, process, article of manufacture, or composition of matter), it qualifies as patentable subject matter. The requirements and procedures for obtaining a utility patent are discussed in greater detail on the following pages, but the range of inventions that can be patentable is broad. Examples of nonpatentable subject matter include natural phenomena (such as photosynthesis), abstract ideas (such as pure algorithms not applied to any useful purpose), and laws of nature (e.g., $E = mc^2$).

A *design patent* can be used to protect ornamental (as opposed to useful) designs that are both novel and original. Design patents can protect the shape or appearance of items, such as computer icons, furniture, or a pair of running shoes. Design patents have become more popular in recent years. For example, Reebok International, Ltd. successfully sued L.A. Gear, Inc. for violation of a design patent on its running shoe design.

Although methods of doing business used to be considered unpatentable abstract ideas, recent cases have recognized that business processes can be patentable, particularly when implemented using computers.[13] For example, Priceline.com obtained a utility patent for its method of using the Internet and credit cards to conduct a variation on a reverse auction that permits customers to bid for airline tickets and the like. When the Microsoft spin-off Expedia began offering a similar service, Priceline sued Microsoft and Expedia. The case later settled when Expedia agreed to pay Priceline an undisclosed amount of money to license Priceline's patented process.[14]

Requirements for Obtaining a Patent

Not all new inventions qualify for patent protection. First, as noted above, the invention must fall within a class of patentable subject matter. Second, the invention must be useful. This is rarely a problem because most companies will not invest the time and expense of seeking a patent for a useless invention. Third, the invention must be *novel.* An invention is

FROM THE TRENCHES

In December 1999, J. M. Smucker obtained patent protection for a decidedly "low-tech" invention—the peanut butter and jelly sandwich. Smucker's crustless culinary creation—the "Uncrustable"—apparently represented a breakthrough in PB&J production. As noted by Smucker's attorneys, "there is currently no method or device for baking bread without having an outer crust. Hence there is a need for a convenient sandwich which does not have an outer crust and which is not prone to waste of the edible outer crust portions." The PTO agreed, granting Smucker U.S. Patent 6,004,596.

Source: Seth Shulman, PB&J Patent Punch-up, Tech. Rev., May 2001, at 37.

considered to be novel if, among other things, (1) it has not been patented, or known, or used by others in the United States, and (2) it has not been previously patented or described in a printed publication in another country. Fourth, even if the invention is novel, it cannot be merely an obvious extension of previously existing technology (whether or not that technology is actively used today or is patented).

The Statutory Bar

A patent will also be denied if the invention is disclosed to the public more than one year before the date that the patent application is filed. For this purpose, "disclosed" means that the invention has been publicly used or sold in the United States or was described in a written publication anywhere in the world. This limitation on an inventor's ability to file a patent application is known as the *statutory bar.* Scientists and engineers frequently are eager to publish their results and share their learning with others, but doing so before a patent is filed can render the invention unpatentable. Similarly, even beta testing (trial use by select customers to ascertain product performance) can undermine patentability unless adequate safeguards are taken, particularly if the beta tester is to pay any money for the use of the product.

Equally troubling, no other major country has even a one-year grace period. Thus, in other countries, *any* publication of the invention before filing may result in a loss of patentability. For example, if a scientist presents a technical paper describing a patentable invention to a conference in Tokyo before the patent is filed in Japan, then the invention may no longer be patentable in Japan. A Japanese patent will not be issued if there has been disclosure in Japan or to a Japanese national outside Japan prior to the filing of the patent application. Disclosing the invention anywhere in the world is enough to prevent the invention from being patentable in most European countries, unless a U.S. patent application was filed prior to disclosure and a European patent application is filed within one year thereafter. Thus, to preserve foreign patentability, it is usually best to file a U.S. patent application before allowing any public disclosure or sale of the invention.

Duration of Patents

Rights to utility patents (the most important and most common type) last for twenty years from the date the patent application is filed. Rights to design patents last for fourteen years from the date the design patent is issued. Patent rights can be extended beyond these periods only under special circumstances defined in the patent statute. These special circumstances include cases where examination of a patent application is delayed by the PTO.

Overview of Procedures for Obtaining a Patent

THE APPLICATION The procedures for obtaining a patent are usually time-consuming and expensive. A complex application must be filed with the PTO. The application must describe the invention in detail and include a diagram or illustration of it. Most inventions contain both patentable and unpatentable elements. For example, Polaroid Corp. obtained many patents for its instant cameras, but elements of these cameras, such as the lens and the shutter, were not themselves patentable. The application must set forth in detail the specific claims of the patent, that is, the precise elements of the invention for which patent protection is sought. These patent claims must be written in highly stylized language. Skill and experience are required to draft claims that are sufficiently broad to achieve meaningful protections yet narrow enough to withstand scrutiny from a patent examiner. Thus, an experienced patent attorney should prepare the patent claims. The inventor usually understands the novel aspects of the invention better than anyone else, though, so legal costs can often be reduced if the inventor works with patent counsel to prepare an initial draft of the patent claims.

SEARCH FOR PRIOR ART In addition, before filing a patent application, it is advisable for the applicant to conduct a search for prior art. *Prior art* refers to earlier inventions that may undercut the applicant's claims that the invention is novel and nonobvious. Prior art includes both patented and nonpatented technology that is in the public domain, whether incorporated in existing products or described in written materials. Searching for prior art is essential to avoid wasting time and money trying to patent an invention that is not novel. It also helps the inventor anticipate the PTO's response. The patent attorney uses the search results to craft the patent claims to avoid the prior art, and the patent examiner at the PTO uses them to help determine whether a

FROM THE TRENCHES

Amazon.com (Amazon) sued barnesandnoble.com (BN) for infringing its patented "1-click" system, which, using previously stored user data, enabled users to purchase selected items with one click of their mouse. BN, in turn, challenged the validity of Amazon's patent, arguing that 1-click was obvious in light of prior art and thus unpatentable. In February 2001, Amazon moved to preliminarily enjoin BN from using its potentially infringing version of 1-click until a full trial on the merits. The U.S. Court of Appeals for the Federal Circuit did not grant Amazon's motion. The court reasoned that although Amazon appeared likely to succeed against BN on its infringement suit, BN had raised substantial evidence of prior art that might invalidate Amazon's patent at trial. Litigation was still pending in early 2002.

Source: Amazon.com, Inc. v. Barnesandnoble.com, Inc., 239 F.3d 1343 (Fed. Cir. 2001).

patent should be issued. The applicant is required to disclose in the patent application all material prior art of which it is aware. Although online databases can be accessed by anyone, it is usually advisable to have a professional search firm conduct the search. Failing to uncover prior art leads to wasted time and expense if the examiner (or a person challenging the patent's validity) later discovers relevant prior art that was missed in the search.

THE PATENT EXAMINATION Once the application is submitted, a patent examiner will be assigned to determine whether the invention is patentable. The patent examiner will conduct his or her own search for prior art and frequently will seek to modify the claims of the patent. Very few applications are approved without modification. This back-and-forth process between the applicant and the examiner (called *prosecution*) usually takes at least a year and often more than two years. In many cases, an inventor will want to begin using or selling the invention before the patent application is approved to achieve time-to-market advantages.

COSTS Patents usually represent a major expense for a small business. However, many patent attorneys will provide a free initial consultation to determine whether pursuing a patent application makes sense. Although a definite answer to the question of patentability is unlikely to emerge from a single consultation (unless the answer is a clear "no"), the entrepreneur can usually get a better idea of whether it is practical to pursue the patent process further.

As of January 2002, the filing fee for individuals and companies with fewer than 500 employees was $370, with an additional fee of $640 due if and when the patent is issued. Fees are higher for large companies. Additional fees are required over the life of the patent to keep it in force. Total PTO fees currently amount to approximately $4,000, and these have been rising as the PTO attempts to overcome staffing shortages. Attorney and search firm fees can bring the total cost of filing an application, including government fees, to $13,000 or more depending on the complexity of the application and the level of modifications sought by the patent examiner. Over the life of the application, the total cost may be $25,000 or more. In assessing whether a patent is worth the cost, it is important to remember that having a strong patent portfolio may make it easier to raise money from outside investors.

OTHER CONSIDERATIONS There are several other important points to note about the patent process. First, although patent examiners usually have some relevant training, many patent applicants have been frustrated by the unfamiliarity of examiners with pertinent technology and the slowness of the proceedings. Applicants should be prepared for frustrations and delays.

Second, patents are frequently challenged and overturned. The granting of a patent is not always the end of the story. Patents can be reviewed and invalidated by the PTO and the courts. This can happen when prior art is uncovered (often by a competitor seeking to undermine the patent) that was not revealed in the initial patent search. Perhaps the best-known recent case of a patent being overturned involved Compton's NewMedia, Inc. Compton's was granted a patent that, if upheld, was widely seen as giving it a monopoly over much of the then emerging multimedia field. Competitors complained to the PTO, which took the unusual step of reexamining the patent. The PTO subsequently withdrew the patent on the basis that it lacked novelty and failed the nonobviousness test in view of the prior art.

Third, it is important to obtain a written transfer of ownership rights in inventions from employees and independent contractors. Absent an agreement, all employees and independent contractors (except those falling into the narrow category of employees "hired to invent") will personally own the patentable inventions they create. It is therefore crucial to have any employee involved with inventions sign a written agreement assigning any rights in the inventions to the employer.

Competing Claims for a Patent

If two inventors independently develop essentially the same patentable invention, the U.S. patent system awards the patent to the first person to invent the invention, not necessarily the first person to file the patent application. Determining who was the first to invent can be difficult. For example, in 1989 Calgene, Inc. was granted a patent covering a genetic engineering process to improve the flavor and shelf life of tomatoes. In 1992, another company, Zeneca Group PLC, won an opportunity for review of the patent, arguing that it had invented the process first. Although the dispute was settled in 1994, Zeneca would not have had a winning argument in a first-to-file country because it had filed its patent application two weeks after Calgene. Other countries in the world award the patent to the first person to file the application, and some have proposed that the United States move to a first-to-file system.

If two or more inventors file for patent protection at about the same time, then the first to invent gets the rights to the patent, unless he or she was not diligent in reducing the invention to practice. *Reduction to practice* occurs when an inventor (1) produces a working prototype or (2) files a patent application that includes the required description of the invention in sufficient detail to enable someone else to reproduce it.

Thus, documenting the dates of invention and reducing the invention to practice can be critical for securing patent rights. To document dates of invention and reduction to practice, scientists, engineers, and others working on the invention must keep detailed records of their progress. Often this information is kept in lab books. These records must be signed and dated by both the inventor and another witness not involved in the development process. Inventors often resent the paperwork, but these records can be the difference between securing a valuable patent and losing it to a competitor. An attorney can provide more detailed advice on setting up an effective invention record-keeping program. In addition, it is always wise to file the patent application promptly.

Patent Infringement

The unauthorized making, use, or sale of, or offer to sell, a patented item or process constitutes patent infringement. This is true whether or not the infringer was aware of the patent at the time of the infringement. Infringement can also occur if someone intends to induce another to infringe a patent or knowingly contributes to another's infringement. The damages that can be awarded are often substantial and may include all profits earned with the infringing product. Courts can triple damage awards for intentional infringement and can also award attorneys' fees. In recent years, courts have been increasingly willing to find infringement and uphold substantial damage

FROM THE TRENCHES

According to the American Intellectual Property Law Association's *2001 Economic Survey,* total patent litigation costs through the close of discovery were as follows:

FOR CASES WITH $25 MILLION OR LESS AT RISK:

Median cost—$1,499,000

75th percentile—$2,497,000

25th percentile—$802,000

FOR CASES WITH MORE THAN $25 MILLION AT RISK:

Median cost—$2,992,000

75th percentile—$4,507,000

25th percentile—$1,700,000

claims, some running into the hundreds of millions of dollars. For example, Hewlett-Packard agreed to pay Pitney Bowes $400 million to settle a lawsuit over patents involving laser printer technology.

Under the American Inventor Protection Act of 1999, inventors can obtain reasonable royalties from others who make, use, sell, or import the invention during the period between the time the patent application is published and the patent is granted. This new right may be invaluable during the formulation stage of new businesses and for independent inventors in need of investments. Investors are entitled to royalties under this provision only when the invention as claimed in the issued patent is substantially identical to the invention claimed in the published patent application. Filers can also request that applications be published earlier than eighteen months, which would give inventors provisional rights at an earlier stage. Thus, it may be worth monitoring published applications as well as issued patents.

FROM THE TRENCHES

In 1990, both the California Air Resources Board and a consortium of several major U.S. oil companies initiated research aimed at developing cleaner gasoline to satisfy California's toughening environmental standards. Although the oil companies agreed to collaborate on the research and not to seek patents on behalf of the consortium as a whole, no individual oil company promised to refrain from patenting its own findings.

During the course of the research, Unocal—a member of the consortium and then the ninth-largest U.S.-based oil producer—isolated certain combinations of chemical properties that could reduce smog-causing emissions from gasoline. Unocal shared portions of this research with the consortium; it also secretly filed a patent application.

While the PTO processed its patent application, Unocal tried to persuade the air board to adopt clean-fuel requirements consistent with its pending patent. It did not disclose the pending patent to the board or to the other oil companies. As it received information from the air board detailing the upcoming clean-fuel requirements, Unocal continually modified its secret patent application. When the PTO finally approved the patent in 1994, Unocal's patented combinations of chemical properties closely matched those needed to meet the new California standards.

Balking at the prospect of paying royalties for the right to produce gasoline with Unocal's patented chemical combinations, five major oil companies jointly filed suit in federal court, trying to invalidate Unocal's patent. Unocal countersued, claiming that each of those companies had violated its patent by selling low-emission gasoline in California.

In 1997, a federal jury upheld Unocal's patent and also awarded Unocal $69 million in damages. In 2001, a federal appeals court upheld the verdict. In addition to the initial patent, Unocal has since obtained four additional patents related to low-emission gasoline. The value of Unocal's intellectual property has grown quickly—as of August 2001, about a third of the nation had adopted California's tougher emissions standards.

Source: Alexei Barrionuevo, A Patent Fracas Pits Unocal Corp. Against Big U.S. Oil Producers, Wall St. J., Aug. 17, 2000, at A1.

When Does It Make Sense to Pursue a Patent?

Because of the time and cost required to obtain a patent, the decision to file a patent application merits careful thought. Some experts suggest that, before seeking a patent, the entrepreneur first evaluate the core technologies that are key to the business's success. For a small business, technologies outside this core area are probably not worth the expense of patenting (unless the patent is being obtained for strategic reasons, as discussed below). If the technology is such that better-established competitors could review the patent and design a different invention that would not infringe the patent but would still convey the same benefits, then a patent may be of little value.

Experts caution against overlooking improvements to existing inventions. If an improvement is nonobvious and otherwise meets the standards of patentability, the improvement itself can be patented. However, such a patent will give the inventor only the right to exclude others from using the improvement—not rights to practice the invention. Nevertheless, this right provides a powerful negotiating chip when seeking a license to the earlier invention.

In deciding whether to seek patent protection, the entrepreneur should also consider other, less costly forms of protection. For example, trade se-

FROM THE TRENCHES

Xerox has been a great technology innovator, but until recently many of its patents lay dormant and unused. Xerox's Rick Thoman formed a business unit to optimize its intellectual property assets, including its portfolio of over 800 patents, and thereby increased license revenues from $8.5 million to $180 million in just three years. Patent behemoth IBM, which proudly claims the largest patent portfolio in the world, earns $1 billion a year in patent royalties—one-ninth of its pretax profit. After a trial in which a Texas jury found that Hyundai Electronics had infringed patents owned by Texas Instruments, Hyundai agreed to a patent license that will generate approximately $1 billion in revenues for Texas Instruments over its ten-year term.

cret protection may be adequate for some inventions, particularly those that involve a process employed in making a product rather than a product that is sold to the public. Unlike patents, however, trade secrets cannot protect against a competitor that independently develops similar technology, even through reverse engineering. Patentable software can also benefit from copyright protection. Consulting an experienced patent attorney, particularly one with knowledge of the field in which the patent is sought, is usually advisable to assess the best strategy in the face of these complicated trade-offs.

Strategic Aspects of Patents

Because the rights granted through patents are so powerful, it is not surprising that patents are often used strategically, particularly by larger businesses. These strategic uses often affect small businesses. For example, in one practice, known as *bracketing*, a large company will systematically review patent issuances and seek to obtain patents on improvements to the issued patents. With its patent on the improvement, the company may seek either to exact a royalty-free cross-license from the company that holds the initial patent or to block use of the improvement altogether. In some instances, it may be worthwhile to pursue additional patents to block potential bracketers.

Competitors frequently review patents with an eye to designing around a patent, that is, coming up with a functionally similar invention that does not legally infringe the patent's claims. This is another reason why an experienced patent attorney is needed to precisely tailor the claims of the patent. Large companies can often beat entrepreneurs by designing around the patent and then using superior sales and marketing resources to capture the market. But, as in the Stac Electronics–Microsoft case noted earlier, the big guy doesn't always win.

Companies with foreign operations also review U.S. patents. If the U.S. inventor does not promptly file in other countries, another company can use the details of the U.S. patent to seek a patent in foreign jurisdictions.

On the other hand, patents can provide added benefits to small companies. Patents often convey prestige and can be used to help promote the image of a technologically innovative company. The familiar phrase "Patent Pending" on some products is thought to convey an image of technical superiority that can be useful in marketing. A strong patent portfolio can also make it easier to raise money from venture capitalists and other outside investors who are looking for a proprietary technology that creates a barrier to others who might otherwise enter the market. As noted earlier, having a portfolio of patents that can be cross-licensed gives a company something to trade in a patent dispute.

Even if a young company is successful in obtaining one or more patents, it is important to remember that a patent rarely will be enough to create an impenetrable barrier to entry by other firms. It may give the patent holder a head start, but usually that early lead will be sustainable only if the company keeps a stream of new inventions flowing through the pipeline.

Understanding Competitors' Patents

Gaining knowledge of others' patented inventions can yield substantial benefits. The search for prior art conducted in the course of preparing a patent application can reveal important competitive information. Some companies that do not plan to file for patent protection nonetheless undertake a patent search to uncover competing technology and to reduce the risk of inadvertent patent infringement. If the search uncovers a competitor's patent for a different invention that achieves superior results, pursuing a patent may make little sense. If the patent for that superior technology is owned by a company that is not a direct competitor, however, then a licensing arrangement, whereby the entrepreneur gets the right to use the invention for a noncompeting product, can frequently be worked out. Competitors' patent filings can also provide clues about future product and development directions. Search results have even been known to spark creative ideas in the minds of inventors, helping them come up with new noninfringing inventions. Indeed, that is the purpose of the patent system: to promote the useful arts by encouraging public disclosure of new inventions in exchange for the right to exclude others from making the invention for a limited period.

International Issues

U.S. patents do not protect inventions in foreign countries, although they will prevent a foreign company from importing into the United

States a product that includes features that violate the U.S. patent. An inventor should consider obtaining patents in each foreign country where the patent may yield meaningful benefits. Each country usually requires a separate patent filing, but a single filing in the European Patent Office can provide protection in the nations in the European Union. In addition, as noted earlier, many countries will not grant a patent if the invention is disclosed before the patent application is filed in that country. Costs to prepare and file a foreign patent currently average about $5,000 per country, assuming that a U.S. patent application has already been completed. Even if a patent is granted, foreign patents may be difficult or impossible to enforce in some countries.

Most foreign countries publish patent applications eighteen months after the patent application is filed. Given the time required to process a patent, the information contained in the patent application usually becomes public before the patent is issued. Once such information is public, trade secret protection is lost. As noted earlier, a patent application filed in the United States will remain confidential until the patent is issued only if the applicant attests in its U.S. filing that it has not and will not file an application for the same invention in a foreign country that requires publication eighteen months after filing. In all other cases, the United States publishes U.S. patent applications eighteen months after the U.S. filing date.

The decision to obtain foreign patents is an important strategic issue that should be discussed with a patent attorney if the invention may be used abroad. Even if the company has no plans for overseas use, it may still be worth the considerable expense to block foreign competitors from gaining access to the invention.

Trademarks

All businesses strive to develop a positive image in the minds of their customers. Many companies spend lavishly to build reputations for quality, reliability, innovation, performance, and value. These reputations and positive images can be among a business's most valuable assets. Trademarks like Mercedes Benz, the Nike swoosh, "Intel Inside," and McDonald's "Golden Arches" all carry with them images and associations that boost sales and contribute to the bottom line. If a low-quality automaker could freely use the name "Mercedes," or something confusingly similar such as "Mircedes," or the familiar circled three-point-star hood ornament, consumers could be fooled into thinking that they were buying a genuine Mercedes. DaimlerChrysler AG's sales and reputation could deteriorate as consumers wrongly concluded that Mercedes Benz had let its quality and performance slip. Trademark law helps to protect both trademark owners and consumers from the confusion that can result when different companies use the same or confusingly similar identifying marks, either intentionally or unintentionally.

Trademarks used in connection with a service business are called service marks. *Service marks* identify a service, such as American Express Travel Services, rather than a product. Because the principles and laws relating to service marks are virtually identical to those of trademarks, the remainder of this section should be read as applying to service marks as well.

Trademarks are not the exclusive province of large, established manufacturing companies. Local businesses also develop goodwill in their markets, which can be embodied in trademarks. Selecting good trademarks early in the life of a business can help to ensure that those marks will not need to be changed later on, perhaps at great expense.

A *trade name* is a business's formal, legal name, which typically must be registered with either local or state authorities. A company's trade name is most often also a trademark because the company typically uses its trade name in connection with its products and services. In fact, a company's trade name may well be the most important trademark it owns. For example, Apple is a trademark of the company whose trade name is Apple Computer Co. A company's domain name may also incorporate its trademark, and in today's business world, securing the domain name is often a critical step in choosing a company name.

Definition of a Trademark

A *trademark* is any word (or phrase), name, symbol, sound, or device that identifies and distinguishes one company's products from those

FROM THE TRENCHES

A small Florida company named Dreamwerks Production Group, Inc., which was in the business of organizing conventions (mostly with a Star Trek theme), sued SKG Studio, a large Hollywood motion picture production company, over SKG's use of the business name "DreamWorks." Although DreamWorks was much larger and better known, Dreamwerks had registered its trademark first and had been using its name longer. Dreamwerks claimed that DreamWorks was causing confusion in the marketplace by using a similar name for similar goods and services. DreamWorks moved for summary judgment and won at the district court level, but the U.S. Court of Appeals for the Ninth Circuit reversed and remanded for trial. The court said that there were material issues of fact as to whether the goods and services of Dreamwerks, which included science-fiction merchandise such as movie and TV collectibles and memorabilia, and those of DreamWorks, which included movies as well as related merchandise, were sufficiently similar to create a likelihood of confusion among consumers. In its opinion, the court specifically pointed out that DreamWorks had discovered the Dreamwerks name while conducting trademark searches and said that the dispute could have been avoided if DreamWorks had been more careful or creative in selecting its name.

Source: Dreamwerks Prod. Group, Inc. v. SKG Studio dba DreamWorks SKG, 142 F.3d 1127 (9th Cir. 1998).

made or sold by others. The key requirement is that the mark must identify and distinguish the product from those of competitors. "It's the real thing" is a trademark of the Coca-Cola Co., and the distinctive AT&T "bong" is a trademark of AT&T. The "swoosh" is a trademark of Nike, and "Visa" is a service mark relating to credit card services offered by Visa International Services Association. Trademarks can also protect trade dress, such as packaging, which is purely ornamental. For example, Coca-Cola has a trademark for its "old-fashioned" six-ounce bottle. Even a distinctive color can serve as a trademark when the public has come to associate a color with a product, such as pink with Owens Corning insulation. The U.S. Supreme Court has held that the universe of things that can qualify as a trademark should be viewed "in the broadest possible terms."[15]

Establishing a Trademark

SEEK DISTINCTIVENESS The first step in selecting a trademark is to consider marks that are distinctive and thus will serve uniquely to identify the company in its field of business. The degree of protection available under trademark law is determined by how distinctive the trademark is: the more distinctive, the better. The basic idea is that the more distinctive the mark, the more it uniquely identifies the products as belonging to a single company. Generic terms such as "plane," "software," and "designer" are not protectable trademarks for the products they describe. Many businesspeople choose their own marks, but professional advice from advertising agencies or marketing firms may be worth the cost, particularly for consumer goods.

Inherently distinctive marks are the strongest form of trademark. These marks have no meaning within an industry before their adoption by a company in that industry. There are three main types of inherently distinctive marks. *Fanciful marks* include made-up words such as "Exxon" for gasoline and "Kodak" for cameras. *Arbitrary marks* are real words that have nothing to do with the product category, such as "Apple" for computers. Note, however, that neither Apple nor Macintosh could be trademarks for a company that sells apples. *Suggestive marks* suggest something about the product but do not describe it. Examples include "Chicken of the Sea" for tuna and "Gleem" for toothpaste.

Descriptive marks are not considered to be inherently distinctive. A mark that indicates characteristics of the product it identifies is a descriptive mark. Examples include "Rapid Seal" for a paint sealant and "cc:Mail" for an electronic mail program. Laudatory terms such as "Gold Medal" are also considered descriptive. Marks that indicate the geographic origin of the product, such as "California Lumber" and "Albany

Roofing," are considered descriptive. Marks derived from a proper name, such as "Hilton Hotels," are also considered descriptive.

Descriptive marks are not immediately protectable but may become fully protectable once they acquire secondary meaning in the marketplace. *Secondary meaning* is acquired when a significant number of people come to associate the mark with a particular company or product. For example, in 1995 Microsoft was successful in registering "Windows" as a trademark for its PC operating system in part because the word had acquired secondary meaning; consumers had come to associate Windows with Microsoft's operating system and did not use it as a descriptive term for any software that generated "windows" on a computer screen. If a dispute over the ownership of a descriptive trademark arises, it can be expensive to establish the existence of secondary meaning in court.

PERFORM A TRADEMARK SEARCH The second step in acquiring a trademark is to perform a trademark search to ensure that someone else has not already established rights in the proposed mark or one confusingly similar to it. The search should include both federal searches and state searches in any states where business will be conducted. Computerized databases exist for conducting both federal and state trademark searches. LexisNexis can be used to search for unregistered trademarks that are still entitled to protection under the common law. If the trademark is to be used in countries outside the United States, the search should also include foreign countries where the mark may be used.

Although hiring an attorney to conduct a trademark search is not necessary, it is often a good idea. A preliminary search can usually be performed for less than $200. An attorney can usually have a full search performed and assess the risk that the proposed mark infringes confusingly similar marks for less than $2,500. At the very least, the entrepreneur should review online trademark databases and search the Internet, including the domain name registries. A careful search reduces the risk of infringing another's mark and can limit any infringement damages by helping to show that the infringing use was undertaken in good faith.

CREATE RIGHTS IN THE TRADEMARK The final step in establishing a trademark is to create rights in the trademark. Certain rights are obtained merely by using the trademark in business. Attaching the trademark to goods for sale and using the mark in advertising and promotional materials constitute use. The use must be in good faith, meaning that the user must be unaware of anyone else with prior rights to the mark or a confusingly similar mark. Note that every user is deemed by the law to be aware of every valid federal trademark registration, so failure to conduct a proper trademark search is not a defense.

In the United States, if the trademark is inherently distinctive, the first person to use the mark becomes the owner. If the mark is a descriptive mark, using the mark merely begins the process of developing the secondary meaning necessary to create full trademark rights. For both inherently distinctive and merely descriptive marks, greater use generally leads to stronger rights as the mark becomes more closely identified with a single business.

Creating Additional Trademark Rights: Trademark Registration

Although mere use can establish rights to a trademark in the United States under common law, federal registration of the trademark on the Principal Register of the U.S. Patent and Trademark Office offers important benefits. First, registration is evidence of ownership that can be useful if the trademark is ever contested. Second, everyone is presumed by law to be aware of a registered trademark, so no infringing use can be in good faith. This makes it easier to stop trademark infringers and can also make it possible to collect damages. Third, after five years of continuous use, the trademark can be declared incontestable, making it far more difficult for anyone to challenge it. Fourth, registration enables the owner to prevent importation of articles bearing the trademark. In general, federal trademark registration is strongly recommended for all important trademarks.

If a person genuinely intends to use a trademark in the future, he or she can file an intent-to-use application. Once this application is filed, the owner secures the filing date as his or her priority date and thus will be able to prevent others from subsequently adopting or registering the identical mark for the same or similar goods. Before a registration will issue, the owner must use the mark in business. If the mark is approved, the owner has six months to begin using it; this period can be extended for up to a total of three years for good reason.

Not all trademarks are eligible for federal registration on the Principal Register. In particular, descriptive marks are generally not eligible. This is yet another reason to avoid using them. However, separate filing procedures for descriptive marks do exist that can offer some protections. An attorney can provide additional advice about protecting descriptive marks.

The process of obtaining federal trademark registration can be complex, and it is usually advisable to consult with an experienced attorney before proceeding. After the application is filed, a trademark examiner at the U.S. PTO will search for prior filings of confusingly similar marks and will decide whether the trademark is sufficiently distinctive to qualify for trademark protection. The process can be drawn out and involve multiple filings; sometimes it takes many months after the initial filing for a federal registration to issue. In the interim, it may be advisable to file a state registration.

Loss of Trademark Rights

Federal trademark registration currently lasts for ten years but can be renewed indefinitely. Once a trademark has been obtained, however, the owner must take certain steps to ensure that the trademark rights are not lost. Failure to use a trademark for two years may create a presumption of abandonment. Trademark protection can also be lost if a trademark becomes generic, thereby losing its distinctiveness. "Escalator," "yo-yo," "aspirin," and "cornflakes" were all once trademarks; they lost their protected status because their owners failed to police their use.

Trademark Infringement

To prove trademark infringement, the trademark owner must prove, among other things, a likelihood that the allegedly infringing mark could create confusion in the minds of potential customers. Such a showing is easy in the case of counterfeit goods displaying another's trademark. If the marks are not identical, however, determining whether another's mark is confusingly similar is a highly factual matter that can be expensive and time-consuming to prove in court. If infringement can be proved, remedies may include a court order barring the infringer from using the infringing mark and the assessment of damages. In addition, some foreign governments appear to be treating trademark infringement more seriously than in the past.

Holders of "famous marks," that is, registered marks that have become strongly associated with a particular company, can prevent others from using marks that would dilute the value of the famous mark. *Dilution* involves using another's trademark on noncompeting goods if the use harms the reputation of the mark's owner (*tarnishment*) or lessens the distinctiveness of the mark (*blurring*). For example, Tiffany & Co. could successfully sue to stop a tire manufacturer from using "Tiffany" as a trademark for its tires, even though the average consumer would not confuse Tiffany jewelry with Tiffany tires.

FROM THE TRENCHES

Palm Computing, Inc., the early predecessor of Palm, Inc. and the maker of the popular handheld computers, was sued by Pilot Pen Corp. over Palm's use of the name "Palm Pilot" for its products. Among other things, Pilot Pen claimed that Palm's practice of separately selling replacements for the Palm Pilot's stylus pointing device created a likelihood of confusion among consumers because the styluses were similar to pens and were sold at comparable prices. Although U.S. law provided Palm with defenses that might have been successful, Pilot Pen's affiliates in France and other countries also sued Palm for trademark infringement. The defenses available under U.S. law were not necessarily available under the laws, customs, and practices of those countries. Rather than face uncertainty over possible disruption or inconsistency in its global marketing campaign, Palm dropped the "Pilot" part of its product name as part of a settlement agreement.

International Issues

Trademarks, like patents, must be registered in each country where protection is sought. Although the United States gives priority to the first to *use* the trademark, most other countries give priority to the first to *file* an application to register the mark. Early registration in foreign countries is important for companies planning to offer products or services abroad.

DOMAIN NAMES

With the growth of electronic commerce, most firms want to use their trademark plus a suffix, such as ".com," as their Internet domain name. But domain names are given on a first-come, first-served basis with no field-of-use restrictions. There is only one Ford.com, for example, although both Ford Motor Co. and the Ford Modeling Agency might own the registered trademark "Ford" for use in connection with cars and trucks and for modeling services, respectively. In addition, even if only one firm owns a trademark, having a trademark does not automatically translate into a right to use the mark as a domain name.

Seizing on the opportunity created by a system that gave domain names to the first to apply, so-called cybersquatters registered domain names containing trademarks and then tried to sell them to the owners of the trademarks. In response, Congress passed the Anticybersquatting Consumer Protection Act of 1999 to make it illegal for a person to register or

FROM THE TRENCHES

When Timberland Co. decided to export its shoes to Brazil, it discovered that a Brazilian generic shoe manufacturer already owned the trademark "Timberland." Timberland Co. was able to secure rights to the trademark in Brazil, but only after suing on the basis that its copyright and trade name rights overcame the generic manufacturer's trademark rights.

FROM THE TRENCHES

In 1996, Virtual Works, Inc. (VWI) registered the domain name vw.net. At the time, two of the company's principals recognized the possibility that some Internet users might mistakenly associate vw.net with Volkswagen. VWI used vw.net for the next two years, at which point Volkswagen approached VWI about purchasing the domain name. In a voicemail to Volkswagen, one of VWI's principals stated that he owned the rights to the domain name; he said that unless Volkswagen purchased the domain name from VWI within twenty-four hours, VWI would sell it to the highest bidder.

Volkswagen subsequently sued VWI under the 1999 Anticybersquatting Consumer Protection Act. Volkswagen claimed that VWI had acted in bad faith by registering vw.net knowing that it could be confused with the Volkswagen trademark and intending to reap financial gain from that confusion. The U.S. Court of Appeals for the Fourth Circuit ruled for Volkswagen. The court held that Volkswagen had established bad faith because it had presented evidence that (1) VWI knew at the time it registered its domain name that the name was confusingly similar to that of Volkswagen and (2) intended to profit from that confusion.

Source: Legitimate Use of Domain Name Does Not Establish Good Faith Intent, 69 U.S.L.W. 1462 (2001).

use a domain name, with a bad-faith intent to profit from the name, if the domain name is (1) identical or confusingly similar to a distinctive trademark or (2) identical or confusingly similar to or dilutive of a famous trademark.

The Internet Corporation for Assigned Names (ICANN) has established an arbitration procedure that all domain name registries follow. The ICANN arbitration procedure is a relatively fast and inexpensive way to pursue a cybersquatter.

TRADE DRESS

In addition to protecting registered trademarks, courts have extended the protections of the Lanham Act to include *trade dress,* that is, the packaging or dressing of a product as it relates to a company's overall

FROM THE TRENCHES

Seeking to cash in on the success of the Taco Cabana restaurant chain, another company established a competing restaurant chain called Two Pesos that copied the design, decor, and product offerings of Taco Cabana. Taco Cabana sued Two Pesos for infringement of trade dress. An expert witness testified that the restaurants were nearly identical. The jury found for Taco Cabana and awarded it $306,000 for lost profits and $628,000 for lost income. The district court found the infringement to be deliberate, doubled the damage award, and further awarded attorneys' fees of $937,550. To drive home the point, the judge also ordered Two Pesos to display for one year a prominent sign in front of each of its restaurants acknowledging that it had unfairly copied Taco Cabana's restaurant concept. The U.S. Supreme Court affirmed the decision.

Source: Two Pesos, Inc. v. Taco Cabana, Inc., 505 U.S. 763 (1992).

image in the marketplace. Unregistered trade dress is not entitled to protection unless it is distinctive or has acquired secondary meaning.[16] Second, even if a feature has acquired secondary meaning, it will not receive trade dress protection if the feature is functional rather than ornamental. The existence of an expired utility patent is "strong evidence" that the design features claimed in it are functional and thus not entitled to trade dress protection.[17]

Employee Proprietary Information and Inventions Agreements

As explained earlier, all employees at all levels of the company should be required to sign detailed proprietary information and inventions agreements, sometimes called nondisclosure and invention assignment agreements. Such agreements both provide broad protection for the company's proprietary information (including trade secrets) and ensure that the company will be entitled to all rights and title that an employee may have to inventions created during the period of employment.

Nondisclosure and Nonuse of Proprietary Information

The nondisclosure provisions should obligate the employee to refrain from unauthorized disclosure and unauthorized use of the company's proprietary information. The agreement should also state that the obligation to refrain from unauthorized use or disclosure of the company's proprietary information continues indefinitely after the employee terminates his or her employment with the company.

A company may also wish to include the following provisions in its nondisclosure agreement:

- A broad definition of proprietary information, which includes personnel information about employees.
- A commitment not to disclose or use third-party proprietary information, including information from joint venture partners or previous employers.
- An agreement that precludes the employee from participating in business activities other than those activities that the employee is performing for the company.
- A commitment to return all company materials upon termination of employment with the company, including any embodiment of proprietary information such as notes or computer-recorded information.
- An acknowledgment that signing the nondisclosure agreement does not breach any other agreement that the employee may have with other entities.
- An acknowledgment that employment with the company is at-will.
- An agreement not to solicit coworkers for a defined period after leaving the company.

Assignment of Inventions

The assignment-of-inventions agreement should require the employee to assign to the company all rights to any invention that results from work performed for the employer or work that relates to the employer's current business or demonstrably anticipated research or development. Any invention made on the employer's time, or using the employer's materials, equipment, or trade secrets, should also be assigned to the company. The assignment agreement should be as broad as the law allows. In some states, such as California and Washington, statutes have carved out an exception for inventions unrelated to the employer's business that the employee develops on his or her own time and without use of the employer's material, equipment, or trade secrets. Such carve-outs should be expressly referenced in the agreement.

It is important that the agreement include an actual assignment of inventions (e.g., "I hereby assign to the company . . .") rather than an agreement to assign (e.g., "I agree that I *will* assign to the company . . ."). Although this distinction may seem to be a mere technicality, an agreement to assign suggests that some further act is necessary to document the assignment; as a result, the employee can allege, at some point in the future, that the actual assignment never took place.

Disclosure of Preemployment and Postemployment Inventions

The assignment-of-inventions agreement should require the employee to identify preexisting inventions to which the employee claims ownership

FROM THE TRENCHES

SoftPro employed a software engineer to develop source codes for various software products. In her free time and using her own equipment, the engineer developed a source code for a different, but related, software product that, unbeknownst to her, SoftPro had research and development plans to design. The engineer, believing she owned the new source code, resigned from SoftPro to start her own company, CopiPro. SoftPro initiated legal action against the engineer and CopiPro, claiming ownership rights to the new source code. SoftPro's invention assignment agreement, signed by the engineer, specifically stated that the engineer agreed to assign any invention she developed while she was employed by SoftPro (excluding certain narrow exceptions). As a result of its strong position, SoftPro negotiated a very favorable resolution to the matter.

rights. This will help eliminate disputes regarding employee claims to ownership of an invention allegedly made prior to joining the company. To ensure that inventions belonging to the company do not sneak out the door, the agreement should also obligate the employee to disclose all of his or her inventions created during employment, as well as those invented for a specified period of time after employment (e.g., six months or one year). This provides the company with an opportunity to determine whether a particular invention rightly qualifies as the company's property.

Comparison of Types of Protection

As explained in this chapter, different types of intellectual property protection are available and appropriate in different settings. The advantages and disadvantages of the four basic types of protection are summarized in Exhibit 14.1.

Licensing Agreements and Other Transfers of Intellectual Property

Like most other forms of property, intellectual property rights can be bought, sold, and transferred. This is often done by granting a license. A *license* gives a person the right to do something he or she would not otherwise be permitted to do. For example, a movie theater ticket is a license giving the holder permission to enter the theater. Licensing agreements are often used to grant limited, specified rights to use intellectual property. For example, an inventor who owns a patent that has uses in several different industries might license the rights to use the patent in the medical field to one company, license the rights to use it in the chemical industry to another company, and retain the rights to use the patent in all other fields. Because of their great flexibility, licenses are a popular way to transfer intellectual property rights. Some of the most important and heavily negotiated terms of a typical license agreement are discussed below.

Transfers of intellectual property also occur in less obvious situations. When one company acquires another, patents, trademarks, and copyrights may be among the most valuable assets in the transaction. Many employ-

EXHIBIT 14.1

ADVANTAGES AND DISADVANTAGES OF DIFFERENT TYPES OF INTELLECTUAL PROPERTY PROTECTION

	TRADE SECRET	COPYRIGHT	PATENT	TRADEMARK
Benefits	Very broad protection for sensitive, competitive information; very inexpensive	Prevents copying of a wide array of artistic and literary expressions, including software; very inexpensive	Very strong protection; provides exclusive right to make, use, and sell an invention	Protects corporate image and identity by protecting marks that customers use to identify a business; prevents others from using confusingly similar identifying marks
Duration	For as long as the information remains valuable and is kept confidential	Life of author plus 70 years; for works made for hire, 95 years from year of first publication or 120 years from year of creation, whichever is shorter	20 years from date of filing the patent application	Indefinitely as long as the mark is not abandoned and steps are taken to police its use
Weaknesses	No protection from accidental disclosure, independent creation by a competitor, or disclosure by someone without a duty to maintain confidentiality	Protects only the particular way an idea is expressed, not the idea itself; apparent lessening of protection for software; hard to detect copying in digital age	High standards of patentability; often expensive and time-consuming to pursue (especially when overseas patents are needed); must disclose invention to public	Can be costly if multiple overseas registrations are needed

continued...

EXHIBIT 14.1 (CONTINUED)

ADVANTAGES AND DISADVANTAGES OF DIFFERENT TYPES OF INTELLECTUAL PROPERTY PROTECTION

	TRADE SECRET	COPYRIGHT	PATENT	TRADEMARK
Required Steps	Take reasonable steps to protect—generally, a trade secret protection program	None required. However, notice and registration can strengthen rights.	Detailed filing with U.S. Patent and Trademark Office, which performs a search for prior art and imposes hefty fees	Only need to use mark in commerce. However, filing with U.S. Patent and Trademark Office is usually desirable to gain stronger protections.
U.S. Rights Valid Internationally?	No. Trade secret laws vary significantly by country, and some countries have no trade secret laws.	Generally, yes	No. Separate patent examinations and filings are required in each country; however, a single filing in the European Patent Office can cover a number of European countries.	No. Separate filings are required in foreign jurisdictions, and a mark available in the United States may not be available overseas.

ment and consulting agreements require the worker to transfer intellectual property rights to the company funding the work. In all of these situations, the entrepreneur must understand exactly what rights are being conveyed.

Equally important, the entrepreneur must carefully evaluate the role played by the people—inventors, technicians, and others—who work with and understand the technology. Acquiring the rights to a patent without securing the services of the inventors may be next to worthless if the inventors' experience and expertise are necessary to exploit the technology.

Transferring Rights to Intellectual Property

Trademarks, copyrights, and patents can be transferred in several ways. An *assignment* is typically used to transfer all of one's interests in an item of intellectual property to a new owner. For example, an inventor wishing to sell a patent to a corporation will transfer all of his or her "right, title and interest" in the patent to the new corporation through an assignment document. After the assignment, the inventor will have no rights to the patent, and the corporation can sue the inventor for infringement if he or she uses any elements of the patent. Employment and independent contractor agreements frequently contain assignments that convey to the company paying for the work to be done all intellectual property rights developed in conjunction with the work. Assignments are also used to transfer intellectual property when a company sells some or all of its assets to another company.

When an owner wishes to retain some rights to or control over its intellectual property, a license agreement is commonly used. For example, software developers will typically license, not sell, their software to the customer. The license agreement often contains many restrictions on how and by whom the software may be used. These restrictions can become extremely detailed. McDonald's licenses rights to its many trademarks, such as the "Golden Arches" and "Big Mac," to its franchisees, but the licenses provide that McDonald's can take back the rights to use the trademarks if the franchisees use them improperly. Indeed, to protect the rights to its trademarks, the owner must police their use by others who are licensed to use them. Imagine the damage to McDonald's reputation if a franchisee were to operate a dirty restaurant with McDonald's trademarks displayed prominently throughout.

Key Terms in Licensing Agreements

The potential variety and complexity of licensing agreements are limited only by the ingenuity and business needs of the parties. Agreements can range from a few pages to several hundred pages in length. Because license agreements are so flexible, the entrepreneur should take an active role in structuring the arrangements.

Patent, trademark, and copyright licenses all have differing provisions that are of particular importance to each type of intellectual property. What follows is a very brief overview of key considerations common to many intellectual property licenses. One bit of terminology: The *licensor* is the party granting the license; the *licensee* is the party receiving the license.

SPECIFICATION OF WHAT IS TO BE LICENSED The *specification* sets forth the precise description of the intellectual property covered by the license. The licensee does not obtain rights to anything not included in the description. Developing the specification can be straightforward, but traps abound. The licensee must be sure that the license conveys all rights the licensee needs to meet its business objectives. For example, are all necessary trademarks conveyed? If a developer of multimedia products licenses the rights to use scenes in a movie, does the license include the right to use the accompanying music in the soundtrack? Major issues in many software license agreements are whether the license includes improvements or enhancements to the licensed technology made by the licensor after the license agreement is signed and whether these will be provided free of charge or require an additional fee.

SCOPE OF LICENSE The *scope* of the license is the most important provision in many license agreements. This provision describes what the licensee may do with the licensed intellectual property and spells out any limitations on the rights granted in the licensed intellectual property. Matters to address include the following:

- Is the license exclusive or nonexclusive? If the license is nonexclusive, the licensor can grant the same rights to another licensee.
- Is the license limited to certain geographic regions? To particular markets or products?
- Does the license include the right to modify or improve the licensed technology? To sublicense it to others? To share the license with affiliated corporations?
- How long does the license last?

- Does the license set performance criteria such as minimum sales requirements that, if not met, result in a termination of the license?
- On what terms, if any, can the license be renewed?

These and many other limitations on the use of the licensed intellectual property are contained in the scope-of-license provision.

Licensors must be careful to restrict the licensing of valuable rights to only those rights that the licensee truly needs. Otherwise, revenue opportunities may be lost. For example, if a licensor grants to a distributor exclusive rights to sell a patented invention throughout the United States, but the distributor has no operations in the Southwest, then the licensor may lose revenues that could have come from granting a separate license to a Southwest distributor.

The licensee must also consider what rights it needs to meet its objectives, both now and in the future. For example, geographic restrictions can impede future growth. If the license does not cover improvements to the licensed technology made by the licensor, the licensee could end up with an exclusive right to obsolete technology. Lawyers can craft careful language to implement a deal, but the businesspeople themselves must carefully consider the scope of the license.

PAYMENTS Payments are most often in the form of up-front lump sums, installment payments, royalties, or some combination of these. Sometimes a licensor will accept equity in the licensee in exchange for the license grant. Royalties can be based on many different measures, including unit sales, percentage of gross revenues, or percentage of profits. Careful consideration must be given to how royalties are calculated because the method chosen will affect licensee behavior. For example, a license based on the number of units sold will give the licensee an incentive to sell fewer units but at a higher price than would be the case under a percentage-of-gross-revenues calculation. Similarly, basing royalties on a percentage of profits may require specifying exactly how profits are to be calculated because financial accounting principles allow for some leeway, especially in such areas as allocation of overhead across products. Many agreements include minimum royalty payments and sliding-scale royalties, under which the per-unit royalties decrease as sales increase.

FROM THE TRENCHES

A producer of boxing videos signed license agreements with five top former heavyweight champions, including Muhammad Ali, to use film footage of the boxers in a video. Each license included in the boilerplate a so-called most-favored-nations clause. Under this clause, if the producer agreed to an improved financial deal for any one of the boxers, the producer would have to offer the same deal to each of the other boxers. Some time later, Ali's representatives negotiated a highly favorable deal that gave him 20 percent of the revenues from the video. When the other boxers learned of this deal, they each invoked the most-favored-nations clause, obligating the producer to pay over to each of the five boxers 20 percent of the revenues from the video. Thus, the producer was left with none of the revenues.

REPRESENTATIONS, WARRANTIES, AND INDEMNIFICATION The licensee wants to be sure that the licensor actually possesses all of the rights that the agreement requires it to transfer to the licensee and that performing the agreement will not infringe the rights of any other person. The licensee also wants to ensure that the licensor is not bound by any restrictions that prevent it from carrying out its obligations under the license agreement. The representations and warranties set forth the licensor's statements on these (and many other) matters.

In computer software licenses, the indemnification provisions commonly require the licensor to defend the licensee against claims by third parties that the licensed software infringes the third parties' intellectual property rights and to pay any resulting damages and costs. Licensors are often reluctant to give unlimited indemnification, especially for patent infringement, which can happen innocently. As a result, the indemnification provisions often specify a maximum total amount that can be recovered. The obligation to indemnify usually terminates after a stated period of time.

Similarly, the licensor will often demand representations, warranties, and indemnification from the licensee. For example, a licensor may demand assurances that the licensee is financially sound and is not under any contractual or other restrictions that could prevent it from performing its duties under the license agreement. These provisions are also intensely negotiated.

COVENANTS Covenants are promises by a party to the license agreement to do (or not do) certain things. For example, in a trademark license, the licensee must agree to use the trademarks in ways that maintain their value as symbols of goodwill for the business. In a patent license, one party will usually promise to make the additional payments necessary to keep the patents in force for the term of the agreement.

Rather than requiring a party to make an absolute promise to do something, covenants sometimes require the party to use reasonable or best efforts to accomplish a task. Such covenants are frequently used when the party making the promise does not have complete control over the outcome. For example, a party may be required to use its best efforts to obtain patent protections in certain foreign jurisdictions. Because the party cannot force the patent examiners to issue the required patents, the party will not have breached the covenant if it did everything legally possible to obtain the patents.

The licensee should be aware, however, that many courts interpret "best efforts" literally and will require a party under a best-efforts obligation to use extraordinary and costly measures if necessary to achieve the promised result. A reasonable-efforts standard requires the party to operate with diligence but introduces an element of cost-benefit analysis into the determination of whether the party has lived up to its promise. Extreme care should be exercised in agreeing to any best-efforts obligation.

Shrink-Wrap and Click-Wrap Licenses

Except for custom-produced software, virtually all software is licensed, not sold outright. Software license agreements come in many varieties: end-user, distribution, beta, development, VAR (value-added reseller), and others. Licensing permits the program's owner to retain important controls over the software's use and transferability. In addition, software vendors usually use license agreements to limit their warranties and liabilities.

Most mass-market software is sold without a signed license agreement under what are known as shrink-wrap licenses. *Shrink-wrap licenses* are included with the software along with a statement to the purchaser that by opening the software packaging (i.e., tearing off the shrink wrap), the purchaser agrees to be bound by the terms of the included shrink-wrap license agreement. A more sophisticated version—the *click-wrap license agreement*—requires the user to scroll through the license agreement on a computer screen and to indicate acceptance of its terms by clicking on an "I Accept" icon (or typing words to that effect) before being able to download or install the program. As described earlier, the U.S. Court of Appeals for the Seventh Circuit upheld a shrink-wrap license prohibiting resale of a database contained on a CD-ROM.[18]

On the other hand, the federal district court in the Southern District of New York refused to enforce a license agreement for software available for downloading on the licensor's Web site when the license agreement was available for viewing on the Web site, but the user was not required to click on an "I Accept" button, or even view the license terms, before downloading.[19] Vendors should continue to seek appropriate legal advice when implementing mass-market license programs.

Under the recently completed Uniform Computer Information Transactions Act (UCITA), which as of January 2002 had been adopted only in Maryland and Virginia, most mass-market software licenses, such as shrink-wrap and click-wrap licenses, would be enforceable, provided that they meet certain requirements, including giving the user the right to return the software for a refund if the license terms are not acceptable. UCITA covers a wide range of other issues relating to software and information licensing, and vendors in jurisdictions where it has been adopted should give this statute careful consideration.

Importance of Due Diligence

Although a well-crafted license or technology-sale agreement can provide many protections, it is no substitute for thoroughly investigating the technology and the other party to the transaction—*due diligence* in legal jargon. The amount of due diligence necessary often varies, depending on the representations, warranties, and indemnities provided and the financial condition of the licensor. For example, if IBM gives full indemnification for any intellectual property problems, the licensee will have less need to conduct extensive due diligence.

A company acquiring technology must investigate whether the seller or licensor actually has all the rights in the technology that the agreement requires it to transfer. Sometimes another party (such as an inventor or another licensee) may have rights to the technology that the seller or licensor has no right to transfer. The acquiring company should also analyze whether the patents, trademarks, and copyrights to be conveyed fully cover all technology that is truly important to the acquiror. Too often a buyer or licensee will assume that just because a company has some patents, all of its key technologies are fully owned and protected. Frequently, this is not the case. The financial condition and reputation of the seller or licensor should also be investigated. This is particularly important if the relationship is expected to last for a long period of time.

A licensor should also thoroughly investigate the licensee, including an analysis of the licensee's financial strength, reputation, and future prospects. This is particularly important if the licensee is required to pay royalties based on the level of sales or if the payments are to be made over a number of years. The licensee's technological and marketing capabilities to develop and sell products using the technology, as well as the strength of the licensee's desire to exploit the technology, are also critical. An ill-equipped or undermotivated licensee is unlikely to generate substantial royalty revenue.

Technology and Human Capital

People are often key to making an acquisition of technology competitively successful. Technology changes so rapidly that the success of a technology acquisition often depends on whether the acquiror also gains the services of technical experts who can help bring products to market quickly and can improve and enhance the acquired technology to meet new market pressures. Frequently, companies acquiring technology will also hire key personnel who were involved in its development. Often these key personnel are asked to sign employment agreements with the acquiring company to ensure that their know-how will be available for a period of time. Acquiring the rights to use or sell technology may be of little value if a company does not have the expertise to develop it fully.

Use of Open Source Software

In recent years, open source software has become increasingly popular. *Open source software* is software that is typically distributed in source code form (rather than in object code or compiled form) under a license agreement that gives the licensee broad rights to use, copy, distribute, and modify the licensed software. Open source software is also typically distributed at no charge or for a nominal charge. Many useful software programs and utilities are available as open source.

Although open source software can save a company time, work, and money in its development efforts, entrepreneurs should be cautious when utilizing open source code. Several problems can arise, especially for entrepreneurs who plan to incorporate the open source code in their products.

First, open source software is typically distributed without warranty or support from the developer. Thus, the entrepreneurs must either be confident that they will be able to fix bugs in the software and support it or be prepared to purchase support separately, perhaps from someone other than the licensor. The absence of warranties also means that if the open source software is not, in fact, owned by the licensor and infringes the intellectual property rights of a third party, the entrepreneur may have to stop using the software, defend against any infringement claims, and possibly pay damages for infringement. Due diligence becomes especially important if the open source software has no ready substitutes and will be important to the operation of the entrepreneur's product.

In addition, the entrepreneur must examine the license terms for the open source software carefully. Some open source licenses require that the licensee distribute as open source any software based on or incorporating the licensed open source code. If not part of the entrepreneur's business model, this result could have serious adverse effects. To comply with the license terms, the entrepreneur would have to make copies of his or her software freely distributable and make the source code available for examination and use by anyone, including competitors.

PUTTING IT INTO PRACTICE

As noted in Chapter 2, CCS had previously assigned to DataAccelleation all of its rights to the Saturn Data Booster (SDB) in exchange for equity. DataAccelleation now had to act promptly to protect these intellectual property rights.

DataAccelleation strengthened its copyright protection by filing a copyright registration for the SDB software and the documentation. Registering the copyrights was inexpensive but made it possible for DataAccelleation to recover statutory damages if its copyrights were infringed. This was particularly important because DataAccelleation's lack of an operating history would make it very difficult to prove actual damages.

DataAccelleation set up a basic trade secret protection program. Sanjay drafted a standard proprietary information and inventions agreement, which Kendra and all other employees were required to sign. To ensure that the agreements were supported by adequate consideration, all existing employees were paid a $100 bonus in exchange for signing the agreements. All future employees were required to sign the agreements as a condition of being hired.

Potential investors and others with whom any key technologies were to be shared were asked to sign nondisclosure agreements. When the venture capitalists refused to sign, Kendra took a different tack. She refrained from describing any key facets of the technology until discussions reached a serious stage with Centaur Partners; at that point, the technology experts who examined the SDB on behalf of Centaur were persuaded to sign.

Trademark protection for the names "DataAccelleation" and "Saturn Data Booster" and the availability of the DataAccelleation.com and SaturnBooster.com domain names were investigated early on as well.

Kendra met with Louise Johnson, a patent attorney in Michael's firm specializing in software patents, to consider whether the SDB technology contained any patentable inventions. Louise explained that Kendra's algorithm, taken alone, was not patentable, but that its use in a software program that significantly improved the performance of a database did appear to be a patentable invention. Louise used a well-known search firm to determine

continued...

continued...

whether there was any relevant prior art. Louise and Kendra carefully evaluated all of DataAccelleation's technology and the prior art and concluded that three separate inventions appeared to be patentable. Kendra also reviewed the findings of the patent search for helpful ideas about possible enhancements. Even if she had not pursued a patent, the novelty of the invention suggested that DataAccelleation should undertake a patent search to ensure that the SDB did not violate anyone else's patent rights.

The SDB had sales potential overseas, so Kendra and Louise discussed the advisability of filing patent applications in key foreign countries. Kendra decided to file applications in Japan and the European Union. In developing her funding requirements, Kendra budgeted for the considerable expense of obtaining the U.S. and foreign patents. Having a patent pending would help in fund-raising efforts.

Kendra and the other computer programmers had documented the timing of their progress in developing the SDB, which was critical because the U.S. patent rights go to the first to invent, not necessarily the first to file the patent application. Nevertheless, prompt filing would still be advantageous.

After Kendra had developed plans for a working prototype, she began the lengthy patent application process. Although Kendra prepared a draft of the description of the invention and the prior art, Louise drafted the claims, after explaining to Kendra that the claims section was the most legalistic and stylistic part of the application.

Once the patent application was filed, DataAccelleation released the SDB for public distribution. Sales were brisk. Two patents for key elements of the SDB were issued about eighteen months after the applications were filed. Louise was still working with the patent examiner to secure the third patent. With the two patents in hand, Kendra and the DataAccelleation board of directors turned to the matter of deciding whether to expand globally.

Notes

1. Kevin G. Rivette & David Kline, *Discovering New Value in Intellectual Property*, HARV. BUS. REV., Jan.–Feb. 2000, at 58.
2. *Id.*
3. Polaroid Corp. v. Eastman Kodak Co., 789 F.2d 1556 (Fed. Cir. 1986), *cert. denied*, 479 U.S. 850 (1986). *See* Lawrence Ingrassia & James S. Hirsch, *Polaroid's Patent-Case Award, Smaller than Anticipated, Is a Relief for Kodak*, WALL ST. J., Oct. 15, 1990, at A3.

4. Feist Publications, Inc. v. Rural Tel. Serv. Co., 499 U.S. 340 (1991).
5. Campbell v. Acuff-Rose Music, Inc., 510 U.S. 569 (1994).
6. Basic Books, Inc. v. Kinko's Graphics Corp., 758 F. Supp. 1522 (S.D.N.Y. 1991).
7. American Geophysical Union v. Texaco, Inc., 60 F.3d 913 (2d Cir. 1994).
8. A&M Records, Inc. v. Napster, Inc., 239 F.3d 1004 (9th Cir. 2001).
9. Sega Enters., Ltd. v. Accolade, Inc., 977 F.2d 1510 (9th Cir. 1992).
10. Sony Computer Enter., Inc. v. Connectix Corp., 203 F.3d 596 (9th Cir. 2000).
11. Fonovisa, Inc. v. Cherry Auction, Inc., 76 F.3d 259 (9th Cir. 1996).
12. Community for Creative Non-Violence v. Reid, 490 U.S. 730 (1989).
13. State Street Bank & Trust Co. v. Signature Fin. Group, Inc., 149 F.3d 1368 (Fed. Cir. 1998), *cert. denied,* 525 U.S. 1093 (1999).
14. *See* Constance E. Bagley & Michael J. Roberts, *Priceline.com v. Microsoft (A),* Harv. Bus. Sch. Case No. 9-802-074 (Oct. 10, 2001); Michael J. Roberts & Constance E. Bagley, *Priceline.com v. Microsoft (B),* Harv. Bus. Sch. Case No. 9-802-082 (Sept. 5, 2001).
15. Qualitex Co. v. Jacobson Prods. Co., 514 U.S. 159 (1995).
16. Wal-Mart Stores, Inc. v. Samara Bros., Inc., 529 U.S. 205 (2000).
17. TrafFix Devices, Inc. v. Marketing Displays, Inc., 532 U.S. 23 (2001).
18. Pro CD, Inc. v. Zeidenberg, 86 F.3d 1447 (7th Cir. 1996).
19. Specht v. Netscape Communications, Inc., 150 F. Supp. 2d 585 (S.D.N.Y. 2001).

Chapter 15

GOING GLOBAL

Traditionally, U.S. companies advanced their domestic business to a relatively mature stage before looking to overseas markets. In the last decade, this notion has been turned on its head. With the explosion of electronic commerce on the Internet, even start-up companies may seek an immediate outlet to customers worldwide.

Businesses can gain access to customers in foreign countries in several ways, ranging from sales or licenses to end-users (with no physical presence in the foreign country) to a merger with a foreign company, as occurred when Chrysler Corporation merged with Daimler Benz AG to form DaimlerChrysler AG. Each entrepreneur is driven by many factors and objectives when expanding internationally, but, by and large, the main choices and their respective benefits are outlined in Exhibit 15.1.

This chapter discusses key issues and decisions to consider when developing a global business. Although the chapter focuses primarily on the establishment of one or more overseas subsidiaries, many of the questions of control, intellectual property (IP) ownership, and financing apply equally to the establishment of a separate joint venture entity.

The chapter begins with a discussion of tax planning, then identifies the various forms available for conducting business overseas. It continues with a more detailed examination of corporate issues to consider when establishing an overseas subsidiary as well as hiring and employment concerns. Certain issues to consider when appointing a foreign distributor or sales agent are also identified. Protection of IP and funding and operational issues are then addressed. Product licensing and international IP protection are covered in detail in Chapter 14.

EXHIBIT 15.1

BENEFITS AND RISK LEVEL OF VARIOUS METHODS OF INTERNATIONAL EXPANSION

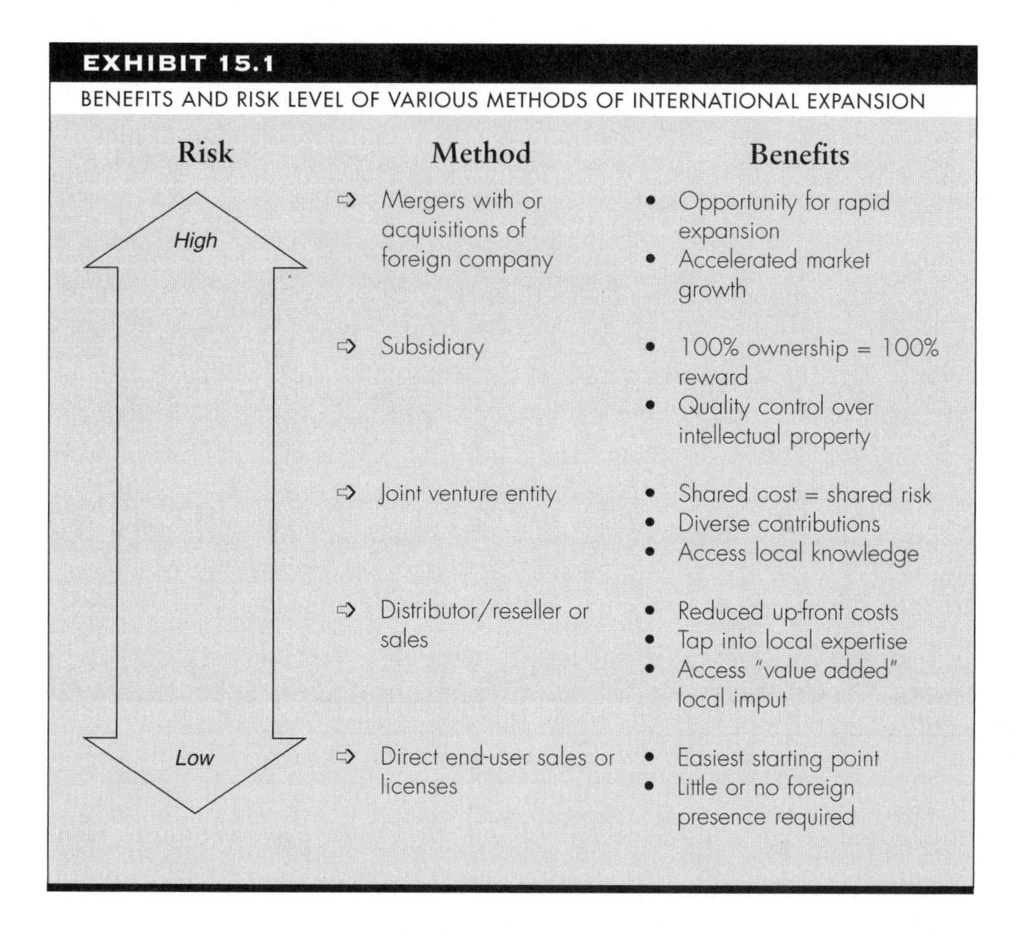

Risk	Method	Benefits
High	Mergers with or acquisitions of foreign company	• Opportunity for rapid expansion • Accelerated market growth
	Subsidiary	• 100% ownership = 100% reward • Quality control over intellectual property
	Joint venture entity	• Shared cost = shared risk • Diverse contributions • Access local knowledge
	Distributor/reseller or sales	• Reduced up-front costs • Tap into local expertise • Access "value added" local imput
Low	Direct end-user sales or licenses	• Easiest starting point • Little or no foreign presence required

Tax Planning

Although tax planning is not a popular topic, appreciating the tax consequences of international expansion is critical to deciding how to structure the growing business. Net operating losses (NOLs) in the United States will not help a subsidiary paying taxes in Europe. Corporate taxes vary enormously from country to country, as do employment taxes and social security contributions.

Permanent Establishment and Corporate Taxes

When considering the tax implications of selling goods or services overseas, entrepreneurs should always determine whether the overseas business constitutes a permanent establishment for tax purposes. If a business is deemed to have a *permanent establishment* (PE), then it will be liable to pay corporate taxes under the domestic tax regime of the relevant country on the business transacted there. Even one employee working from home or from a hotel room may be sufficient to trigger a PE or require registration as a branch in some countries.

Each country has different rules as to what level of activity triggers a PE. Tax authorities will often look behind the title of the operation to see what type of activity is actually taking place in the office and will base their assessment of whether a PE exists on their own analysis. The method of calculating "taxable profits" and the types of corporate deductions allowed also vary from country to country. With corporate tax rates ranging from (close to) 0 up to 50 percent or more, the magnitude of the corporate tax payable in a particular country may affect a company's decision whether to establish a presence there at all.

Fortunately, the negative impact of foreign corporate taxes is mitigated by several factors. First, under the system of bilateral tax treaties between the United States and many nations around the world, a credit for taxes paid overseas will often be available to offset liability for U.S. taxes. Second, corporate tax rates are often staggered, with relatively low rates applicable to smaller businesses. Third, a new subsidiary will almost always incur start-up costs as it works to build a new customer base, and it may generate significant NOLs (or their local equivalent) to offset any local corporate tax liabilities for many years. It is critical to obtain professional tax advice before setting up foreign subsidiaries or any other overseas structures.

Local Employment Taxes

Overseas foreign employees will be subject to the domestic tax regime in their own countries. Very often, and particularly in Europe, the employer is responsible for deducting employee income taxes and social security contributions, which must be paid to the government in the country concerned. Social security deductions can be significantly higher overseas, especially in countries where medical, disability, retirement, and other benefits are provided by the state. A small company may want to subcontract payroll and tax administration to a local agency or accounting firm.

Registration and VAT

Once a foreign subsidiary is established, it must register for corporate tax purposes. It must also register as an employer at the national, regional, and/or local level. In addition, European subsidiaries must register for *Value Added Tax (VAT)*, once certain minimum thresholds for suppliers of goods and services are met. Even if these thresholds are not met in the first few months of operation, early registration may be desirable to permit the new business to account for "input" taxes paid on purchases during the start-up phase. Generally, if the input taxes exceed the VAT charged by the business on sales to customers, the business may be entitled to claim a VAT refund. Many jurisdictions have similar sales or use taxes, such as the *goods and services tax* in Australia. Failure to register with the local tax authority there can have serious adverse consequences for the business.

Advantages of Creating an International IP-Holding Company

Companies that generate significant revenues from licensing technology developed by the U.S. company or from sales of products based on that technology should consider establishing an IP-holding company as part of their international corporate structure. The U.S. parent then makes all sales in the United States, and the offshore subsidiary makes all sales outside the United States. The goal of an international IP-holding company structure is to shift profits from sales outside the United States from a relatively high tax jurisdiction (such as the United States) to a company in a low-tax jurisdiction, such as the Cayman Islands or Switzerland. By transferring or assigning the right to develop and commercially exploit the U.S. company's IP outside the United States to a newly incorporated company in a low-tax jurisdiction, the U.S. parent and its group companies may be able to reduce their overall effective tax rate. The profits from the overseas sales remain offshore (perhaps for further expansion or development in Europe or Asia) and are normally taxable in the United States only if repatriated there.

These structures are fairly complex and involve significant professional costs for accounting and tax planning. For example, ownership of all IP needs to be verified, documented, and valued, and a transfer-pricing study should be completed to help determine the appropriate pricing structure and future IP development cost-sharing arrangements. Nevertheless, if a significant portion of the group's revenue will ultimately be derived from non-U.S. customers, the structure is worth considering at an early stage.

Selecting Among a Representative Office, a Branch, and a Subsidiary

Just as with the initial start-up of the U.S. business, several alternative forms are available for conducting business overseas, and some may be more appropriate than others. The three main choices of entity for an overseas operation are a representative office, a branch, or a subsidiary. The structure of the U.S. business will often influence the international structure. For example, because a U.S. S corporation generally cannot own more than 80 percent of another corporation, an S corporation could not establish a wholly owned subsidiary overseas.

Regulatory Issues

The first question to consider when choosing a form of business entity overseas is whether the country in question puts restrictions on foreign ownership of businesses. Some jurisdictions do not permit wholly owned foreign enterprises; in that case, a local partner who will own a substantial or even majority stake in the enterprise may be necessary. This raises additional issues, such as control over the day-to-day operations, strategic changes or acquisitions, financing of the local operation, and so on.

Representative Office

A *representative office* or *liaison office* is a minimal business presence. It may be the simplest to set up, but local laws usually limit what it can do. A representative office is usually permitted to generate sales leads, but these leads must be directed to the parent, which then decides whether to enter into a contract. The representative office will usually be required to register with the local governmental authority. Some countries, such as China, have a formal authorization process that must be followed before the office is permitted to conduct business.

Branch

A *branch* is a local office of the U.S. parent. It is part of the U.S. parent and not a separate legal entity. As a result, any assets or liabilities associated with the local branch are recorded in the financial statements of the U.S. parent. Formalities for a branch registration vary but usually include an application form, together with copies of the U.S. parent company's latest financial statements, which are filed with the relevant companies' authority and are often available in a public registry. Financial statements for subsequent financial years will also be publicly filed.

For this reason alone, it may be preferable to incorporate a separate subsidiary. That way, only the financial statements of the local subsidiary are publicly disclosed, rather than the U.S. parent's. The ability to limit disclosure may be particularly relevant for private U.S. companies that would otherwise restrict financial information to a very limited audience of investors, bankers, and shareholders. In addition, a branch will normally need to produce financial statements separate from the U.S. parent for the purpose of calculating local corporate taxes; consequently, complicated accounting systems may be required.

Subsidiary

By incorporating a *subsidiary* in a different country, a separate legal entity is established. The overseas subsidiary has its own assets, liabilities, business, and employees. Customers deal directly with the local business entity, although the U.S. parent is likely to be the owner of the IP and may provide certain central services (discussed later) at least initially.

Establishing a subsidiary will often enhance the credibility of the U.S. parent in the local market. By creating a local company, the U.S. parent indicates that it has made a long-term commitment to that market. This may be particularly important in jurisdictions, such as Japan, where business relationships are usually expected to last for many years.

For any operation that is likely to grow and develop into a significant business that will handle functions such as sales and marketing, technical or customer support, or localization of products, a subsidiary is invariably the way to go. At the very least, a subsidiary benefits from

FROM THE TRENCHES

A California software designer decided to open several offices in Europe to establish direct sales forces in various countries. Falsely believing that branch offices would be simpler, cheaper, and quicker to set up, the designer opened branches and recruited employees to staff them.

Twelve months later, when sales in Europe were picking up and the offices there were becoming self-supporting, the company decided that wholly owned subsidiaries were appropriate. In some cases, it sought local partners for specific country operations to help provide access to major public company customers. The company planned to issue equity in the local subsidiaries to the partners.

Much to its surprise, the company was advised that its branches were legally part of the U.S. parent. As a result, it not only had to incorporate its wholly owned subsidiaries in each country but also had to individually transfer all assets from each branch to each new subsidiary. This entailed drafting asset transfer agreements to assign and transfer to the subsidiaries all of the branches' customer contracts, IP, leases, employee contracts, and other assets. In addition, as a result of transferring some of the assets, the company had to pay unforeseen taxes, along with filing fees and notary fees in civil law countries. All in all, the transfers were a costly, involved, and management-intensive exercise.

limited liability. If the business fails or suffers unexpected liabilities (such as a lawsuit), the assets and liabilities of the subsidiary are segregated from those of the rest of the group, including the U.S. parent.

ESTABLISHING A LEGAL PRESENCE

Entrepreneurs may find the formalities for establishing an overseas presence to be detailed and costly, particularly in civil law countries, which generally require extensive filings and registrations. Adequate time for the registration or incorporation process needs to be scheduled into the expansion plans.

Setting up the Foreign Entity

Usually, setting up a representative office, branch, or subsidiary entails mandatory filings and authorizations. A local lawyer will be needed to draft the documents and complete the forms in the local language. The obligation to register the local entity is usually triggered as soon as business is conducted (or within thirty days of commencing business in some countries). Even the establishment of a small sales and marketing office overseas is likely to trigger requirements for registration, filing, or other formalities. Again, planning ahead is key.

Registration of a branch will normally require that the U.S. company's charter documents be translated into the local language. A subsidiary will require the local equivalent of a certificate of incorporation and bylaws. The time needed to register a branch or incorporate a subsidiary varies considerably from country to country, as does the cost. Initial costs include the registration fees, notary fees (in civil law countries), professional fees to prepare the documents, and, for subsidiaries, the initial equity (discussed below).

A fast and cost-effective way to incorporate in many common-law countries (such as the United Kingdom, Australia, and Ireland) is to purchase a shelf company, that is, a private company set up by lawyers, accountants, or company formation agents but left "on the shelf," neither transacting business nor incurring any liabilities. Shelf companies are not available in all countries and can cost more than simply incorporating a new company in others, so it is wise to check their suitability in the country concerned. Ownership of shelf companies can be transferred to the U.S. parent in a matter of hours or a day, with a minimum of formalities, because the company is already in existence. The U.S. parent receives the initial shares (usually just one or two shares) and appoints its own directors. The company name is changed at the same time, and the subsidiary is immediately ready for business.

Corporate Issues When Establishing an Overseas Subsidiary

Running an overseas subsidiary subjects the U.S. company to a different set of legal, tax, and accounting rules. The managers of the U.S. parent should endeavor to understand the workings and quirks of a foreign entity rather than leave too much to the local management.

The U.S. parent needs to find the right balance between controlling and delegating to the foreign office, which will often be staffed by personnel with a greater understanding of the local market. When the cat's away, the

FROM THE TRENCHES

In light of tremendous overseas demand for its accounting software, a privately held software company decided to set up subsidiaries in Europe and Asia. The U.S. vice president for sales persuaded his old friend, Claude, who lived in France to become the vice president for European sales. "Don't worry," said Claude. "I'll set up the company and deal with hiring and premises. It'll be my baby." Because all the incorporation documents, filings, leases, and the like were in French, Claude did not bother to send them back to the United States. He did, however, give monthly e-mail updates of how things were going.

Soon the business blossomed and a significant sales force was hired. Fifteen months later, when U.S. auditors reviewed the books in Paris, they discovered that Claude and several of his senior managers were all shareholders in the French company. The U.S. parent owned a bare majority of the shares and could not make key corporate decisions without the French shareholders' support. When questioned, Claude replied, "I have always taken equity in operations I run in France—you never said we could not hold shares." Protracted negotiations between the U.S. parent and French management ensued, resulting in significantly higher compensation and severance packages for the entire team.

Comment: Had the U.S. parent been more involved in the initial steps and worked closely with local counsel and French management, it would have avoided this scenario.

mice will play, however. Some of the most difficult problems to unwind are those created by unsupervised overseas subsidiaries that have run amok without adequate parental control.

Corporate Name and Business Name

The U.S. parent will usually want to use its own name abroad. Often it is possible to search company name registers in other countries in advance to check whether the name is available. In some cases, the name can be reserved pending incorporation.

If the parent's name is already registered and used by a local company as its corporate name in the foreign country, it may still be possible to register and use the parent's name as a business name there, providing the companies are in different lines of business and its use does not infringe a local trademark. Using the same or a similar business name where both companies are in the same line of business may expose the new subsidiary and its U.S. parent to trademark infringement as well as the local equivalent of misrepresentation claims or similar business torts.

Once the subsidiary is established, additional registrations may be required in other regions or territories within the country where business will be conducted. This is the same or similar to a "qualification to do business" that is required in various states in the United States for corporations doing business outside their state of incorporation. For example, a business name registration in Australia relates only to the state in which the registration is made; the other five states and territories must be considered separately.

Even if registration of the local business is not mandatory, it may well be worth doing to prevent anyone else from registering or using the company name in that region. Indeed, even if the U.S. parent is not quite ready to establish a business in a particular country, it should consider setting up a company there to protect the corporate name and prevent others from using it.

Shareholder Structure and Capitalization of an Overseas Subsidiary

Just as the entrepreneur and his or her team negotiate heavily the balance of ownership and control, various questions need to be addressed when setting up other entities, either in the United States or abroad. First, will nominee shareholders be required? Many countries require private companies to have two, five, or even seven shareholders. Since the subsidiary will usually be wholly owned, at least from an economic perspective, any additional shareholders required by local law must be carefully selected. These nominee shareholders will simply be the record owners, holding the shares on behalf of the U.S. parent. The best nominee may be a professional adviser, who will be under a contractual or fiduciary duty to act in accordance with the U.S. parent's instructions. If employees act as nominee shareholders, there is always the danger that they will leave the company, perhaps under unhappy circumstances such as a layoff; in that case, tracking them down and getting the nominee shares transferred could prove difficult.

The minimum capitalization for an overseas subsidiary can be significant. For example, the Netherlands, Switzerland, and Germany all require significant minimum share capital, up to $27,000 for private companies; it must be deposited in a blocked bank account before the local notary can incorporate the business. Although not usually significant, capital tax on the issuance of stock in the new subsidiary is often payable to the local government. Common-law countries usually have minimal share capital requirements (just £1 in the United Kingdom). A more significant equity stake may nonetheless be required to give the local subsidiary credibility with local customers, vendors, or suppliers.

Corporate Governance

Corporate governance and decision making overseas can vary significantly from the procedures used in the United States. For example, the structure and role of the decision-making bodies of a foreign subsidiary may vary substantially from those of the U.S. parent. Because most U.S. parents will expect to be involved in key decisions, it is essential to understand the corporate environment in which the subsidiary will operate even if its day-to-day operations are left to local management.

BOARD OF DIRECTORS In structuring the board of directors, or other decision-making body, it is important to understand what, if any, authority the various positions and titles bestow on local management. Several countries require local directors (nationals or permanent residents of the country concerned) or at least require a majority of the board to be local directors. Thus, selecting the board is important, as is the granting of titles to local personnel (discussed below).

Board meetings may be mandatory and must sometimes be held within the country concerned. Countries with a less advanced corporate law than the United States may not allow telephonic board meetings or written consents; thus, U.S. directors may be required to physically attend board meetings. A registered office in the country and a local company secretary will usually be required. In the early days of the subsidiary, it may well make sense to outsource the bookkeeping and company secretarial function to a local bookkeeper or accountant.

WORKS COUNCILS Several countries in continental Europe require or allow works councils or other employee representation, even in moderately small enterprises. Generally, employers must permit the establishment of works councils or other forms of employee representation once the business employs a certain number of people (fifty or more in France and five or more in Germany).

A works council will include one or more employee representatives, who will be involved in significant decisions or strategic changes to the subsidiary's business. Companies must usually provide information to the worker representatives before decisions are made and, in some instances, must consult with the works council or other representative body before implementing changes, particularly those affecting employees.

PERIODIC FILINGS AND PAYMENT OF FEES Most countries will require some form of annual or periodic filings and/or the payment of franchise fees, as do states in the United States. Many countries will also require the annual filing of financial statements, which may need to be audited by public accountants regardless of whether the U.S. parent conducts an audit. Financial statements are often available through searches of public registries and, in Europe, will disclose the identity (but not the financial information) of the U.S. parent.

Because local subsidiaries may be staffed with only sales and marketing personnel, at least in the early years, it is important to ensure that key local documents are directed to a competent adviser so that timely action can be taken. The penalty for noncompliance with local filings can range from a fine or to mandatory dissolution of the company for continued delinquency.

Flexibility for Various Exit Strategies

In setting up an overseas corporate structure, it is important to ensure that it is flexible enough for future transactions. For example, if businesses are set up on a country-by-country basis, with a separate subsidiary for each country, the U.S. parent has the flexibility to sell off some of the operations, or possibly bring in a major corporate partner in one or more countries, without affecting the ownership or control of the remaining members of the group. Alternatively, a very successful operation may be a suitable candidate for a local initial public offering in a particular country. The tax consequences of different exit strategies will vary enormously, so it is always wise to revisit the structure in light of changing tax laws and tax rates, both in the United States and overseas, to ensure that a flexible and tax-efficient structure is in place throughout the life of the company.

Hiring and Employment Overseas

Expansion overseas is often spearheaded by an experienced sales or marketing professional. Sometimes local agents or consultants will help establish the business, particularly where there are language barriers. Nevertheless, it is still essential for the U.S. parent to understand the employment environment in the foreign country. Failure to do so can lead to problems on many fronts.

No Employment At-Will

The first principle for the U.S. company to appreciate is that the doctrine of employment at-will does not exist outside the United States. This is especially true in Europe, where some countries have legislation that is *extremely* favorable to employees. In these nations, firing or removing a foreign employee can be an expensive and time-consuming process that will distract attention from other aspects of the business.

Documentation

When hiring overseas, proper documentation is essential. Care should be taken in communicating with candidates and potential employees in foreign countries, because even e-mails or faxes may include sufficient information to establish a legally binding employment contract between the U.S. parent and the overseas individual.

All employees in Europe and in most other parts of the world have written employment terms, either in the form of an employment agreement or a detailed offer letter. In addition, employment relationships in civil law countries are governed by labor codes and, in some countries, by collective-bargaining agreements covering specific industries or business sectors. Legislation enacted in the European Union (EU) usually requires the employer to give each employee certain written information, generally including the start date, job title and description, place of work, salary and benefits, details of the grievance/disciplinary procedure (if any), and so forth. For most countries in Europe, it will be sufficient to use a standard form or template, which can be amended as needed for new hires. More senior personnel will expect to negotiate individual employment agreements, with tailor-made employment terms, severance, and termination provisions.

Employees Versus Independent Contractors

As in the United States, simply calling a worker an "independent contractor" is often insufficient to avoid characterization as an employee. Many countries have their own test for deciding who is an independent contractor. If a person devotes all or substantially all of his or her time to projects for a single company, local law may infer an employer/employee relationship, irrespective of what the worker is called in an agreement.

Identifying the Employer

A U.S. company may need to quickly set up a local entity as a sales office to take advantage of a great business opportunity. Before the new sales team is on the ground, the U.S. parent may initiate the hiring process. If so, the parent should make certain that the local subsidiary is set up before offer letters or employment agreements are signed so that the subsidiary—and not the U.S. parent—is deemed the employer. The goal is to avoid *dual employment,* whereby overseas employees have the benefit of the mandatory employee protection laws in their home country and, at the same time, may have a cause of action against the U.S. parent if they are dismissed, because the parent signed their offer letter or employment agreement and is therefore technically the employer.

When Does Hiring Abroad Create a Business Presence?

As noted earlier, it is necessary to consider whether hiring one or more workers in a particular country will (1) trigger the need for either registration or incorporation (as either a branch or a subsidiary) under local corporate laws or (2) constitute a permanent establishment for tax purposes, requiring the local business to complete and file local tax returns and pay corporate taxes in the country on sales or business generated there. These two tests are often similar, but both need to be considered.

Recruiting Foreign Nationals

Recruiting foreign nationals can be a minefield if it is not handled properly. Local advisers should be consulted as part of the process. Recruiting methods used in the United States may be inappropriate, legally or culturally, elsewhere. More importantly, the U.S. parent needs guidance on the market rates of compensation, customary employee benefits, and other employer responsibilities in the country concerned. Otherwise, the first few employees may well get excessive compensation packages, including both the employee benefits that the U.S. employer makes available to U.S. personnel and various benefits that purportedly are standard or customary in the overseas country (e.g., "a sales representative here always gets a new Porsche!").

The relative cost of cars, mobile phones, and even housing can mean that employees overseas are much more interested in these benefits than in, for example, medical insurance, if most medical costs are paid by the state. Certain benefits may be heavily taxed, especially in Europe, so it is important to understand the employment and tax environment in which these negotiations take place. Another complication is the restriction on the transfer of personal data out of the EU (including personal information about employees, such as salary and tax information).

Data Protection and Employee Privacy

As mentioned in Chapter 9, the EU has issued a directive on data protection and privacy, which has been implemented through legislation enacted by its member nations. The directive restricts the use of consumer data by data collectors, which include technology companies and other businesses dealing with consumers and storing personal data about them. As noted earlier, these rules apply even to personal data regarding employees.

Further restrictions prevent the transfer of such data outside the EU to countries that do not have comparable restrictions on the use of personal data. The United States is such a country, which means that personal employee data (such as salary, tax payments, medical information, and the like) cannot be transferred to the United States unless a data protection policy is in place *and* each employee has agreed to the transfer and use of the personal data by the U.S. company and its personnel.

The data registration requirements and privacy protections afforded personal data vary from country to country and are complicated. As a first step, the U.S. parent will need to (1) put a data protection policy in place for overseas operations; (2) register with the local data protection registrar, commissioner, or the equivalent; and (3) comply with local laws when dealing with personal data, especially if the information is passed back to the United States. Failure to do so exposes the company to fines and may give employees additional claims against the company if they are terminated.

Mandatory Employee Benefits

Most countries will require that an employer provide certain mandatory employee benefits or make them available. Some European countries require a *minimum* of six weeks of vacation. This is just a starting point, so more senior or experienced personnel may expect more. Other state benefits, such as medical, disability, pension, and maternity benefits, are often compulsory and are paid for by social security taxes, which can exceed 20 percent or more of salary. Other countries allow a range of benefits to be provided either by the state or through private companies. Again, an understanding of the local employment rules and environment is key to negotiating a sensible employment arrangement that is fair to both parties.

Stock Options

Stock options of the type granted in the United States are rare or even unavailable in some jurisdictions due to their labor, securities, or tax laws. Even in countries where stock options are popular among senior management or other categories of employees, they are not as common as in the United States and may not afford the tax benefits available to U.S. employees receiving incentive stock options (ISOs). Because employee stock option plans have historically been designed and implemented under the auspices of the U.S. tax laws, these plans are unlikely to meet other countries' requirements for beneficial tax treatment.

Before granting options to overseas employees, the U.S. parent must carefully examine the requirements imposed by local laws and evaluate the benefits to the employer and employees of granting options in light of the regulatory and compliance burdens imposed. In addition to considering local tax and labor laws, it is important to determine whether registration of the options or the underlying stock is required under local securities laws or an exemption from registration is available. An exemption is often available when the company grants options to a small number of employees, generally not more than fifty but sometimes limited to as few as twenty to thirty-five individuals.

A U.S. parent wishing to grant options to employees overseas has several choices. Almost certainly, the U.S. parent will want to grant options at the parent company level, rather than at the subsidiary level. Options to acquire stock in the subsidiary are unlikely to be attractive to U.S. investors because ownership of the foreign subsidiary would be diluted once the options were exercised. They would also create valuation difficulties because the subsidiary would have to be valued on a stand-alone basis.

If a company anticipates eventually having a significant number of employees (say, more than twenty) in a foreign country, it may consider "qualifying" the stock option plan under local tax laws. This will give local employees in the foreign country the best available tax benefits upon grant and exercise of the options and again upon sale of the underlying stock. This process is not be available in all countries, however, and it may not be cost-effective if the company has only a small number of employees.

Another alternative is to issue options under the U.S. plan without qualifying the plan under local laws. This will usually have the effect of creating nonstatutory options (or their local equivalent) even when the category of employee and number of options would ordinarily qualify for ISO treatment in the United States.

Several fundamental consequences, some of which affect both the employer (the subsidiary) and the employee, should be considered before granting options to overseas employees. First, as the option will probably not be in the most tax-efficient form, taxes and/or social security payments may be triggered, either on grant, exercise, or even sale. It is important to find out when such payments are triggered under local laws; otherwise, employees could find themselves liable for significant tax or social security bills in the year benefits are given, even if the options have not vested and will not provide liquidity for tax bills if the U.S. parent is a private corporation. In addition, the grant of options will usually be treated as an employee benefit that is subject to income tax. As a result, the employer is required to deduct and pay the relevant amount of tax. Social security payments on the benefit can also be significant for both the employee and the subsidiary.

Taxes and social security payments are usually calculated based on the difference between the exercise price and the fair market value of the stock at exercise, but they may also be payable upon grant, based on the value of the benefit to the employee. For example, an employer's social security deductions on the U.K. equivalent of a nonstatutory option are roughly 11.9 percent in the United Kingdom. In some countries, it may be possible to pass that liability on to the employee if the proper documentation is in place.

Employee Inventions and IP Assignments

As noted in Chapter 14, it is common and good practice, particularly for technology companies, to obtain assignments of inventions and other IP rights from employees in the United States. Is such a mechanism needed or valid overseas? Many countries have legislation providing that inventions and IP produced by employees are automatically the property of the employer. However, each country is different. As a result, the type of proprietary information and assignment-of-inventions agreement used in the United States may be inadequate or, worse, ineffective in some countries. Accordingly, appropriate mechanisms to secure and protect IP ownership should always be discussed with local professional advisers.

Termination

Several consequences flow from the fact that employees overseas are not terminable at-will. Principally, this means that both the employer and the employee must give notice of termination of employment in accordance with the relevant minimum notice requirements. These requirements may be embodied in an employment contract or possibly a collective-bargaining agreement, or they may be determined by statute or local custom in the industry. If times are tough and the subsidiary needs to significantly reduce its workforce, notice periods can be weeks, if not months. Although some countries permit payment in lieu of notice, that is not always the case. More importantly, the termination process itself will be fundamentally different from that used in the United States.

Many countries require that the employer consult with the employees who potentially will be affected before giving any notice of termination. Indeed, on no account may employees be selected by the employer for termination ahead of the formal consultation and termination process in certain countries. Failure to follow local due process requirements can result in hefty liabilities for the employer.

Civil law countries often permit terminations only in very narrowly defined circumstances, and the consent of a local court or employment authority may have to be obtained before a termination becomes effective. Again, failure to follow set procedures can result in the employee receiving greater termination compensation and/or becoming entitled to reinstatement. In certain European countries, the termination is null and void unless the appropriate procedures have been followed.

If more than a few employees are being terminated, a more elaborate and formal process will often be required. For example, an employer in France may have to submit a formal social plan setting forth the basis of the terminations to the local court or tribunal before notice of termination can be sent to employees. In most European countries, the termination process is likely to take several months if a significant number of layoffs is involved.

When employees are laid off, severance pay will usually be required by contract and/or statute or local laws and customs. The amounts can be significant, based on length of service, local laws, and other factors. The effect of collective-bargaining agreements or works councils will also need to be taken into account in any consultation or termination process.

U.S. Expatriate Personnel

A U.S. parent company will often want one of its own senior managers to head up the newly created overseas subsidiary, and there are many benefits in doing so. The U.S. expatriate can keep the U.S. parent apprised of factors affecting the local market, including new opportunities, threats, and competitor actions. The U.S. expatriate can also educate the local team in the ways and culture of the U.S. business.

The U.S. expatriate will likely need a work permit or visa, both for the employee and for dependents residing with the expatriate overseas. The time required to obtain a visa varies enormously from country to country and should be built into the timeline for the establishment and operation of the new subsidiary.

Usually the expatriate's employment terms will need to be modified to produce an expatriate package. In addition to a hardship or overseas allowance, the expatriate may need housing and travel allowances and a mechanism for tax equalization; the latter is needed because the expatriate will usually be paying taxes in the foreign country on income earned there while remaining liable for U.S. taxes on worldwide income. As with corporations, the bilateral tax treaties between the United States

FROM THE TRENCHES

XYZ Corp., a public company, relied on a long-standing distributor in Asia when setting up a subsidiary in that region. Because XYZ knew the distributor and intended to hire him as its vice president for sales (Asia Pacific), it relied on him for information about market rates for salaries and benefits. XYZ did not obtain independent verification of the distributor's numbers and largely accepted the information he provided. XYZ signed a three-year fixed-term employment contract, which provided the distributor with mandatory severance payments of salary and benefits for the balance of the agreement or one year, whichever was greater. XYZ later discovered that the terms were not just overly generous but quite excessive compared to industry norms. This realization greatly soured the relationship.

and most other countries will often allow credit to be given in one jurisdiction for taxes paid in another.

All U.S. citizens employed by a U.S. employer or by an entity controlled by a U.S. employer are protected by the U.S. antidiscrimination and other civil rights laws described in Chapter 10 even if they are posted overseas. It is, therefore, important to ensure that both the U.S. parent and its subsidiaries have adequate policies and procedures in place dealing with employment discrimination and sexual harassment.

Distributors, Value-Added Resellers, and Sales Agents

To expand sales geographically or to develop additional channels of distribution, a U.S. company operating overseas may take on one or more distributors, value-added resellers, or sales agents as an alternative to, or in addition to, its direct sales and marketing team. The licenses allowing distributors, resellers, and sales agents to use or distribute products on behalf of the U.S. company or the subsidiary should be carefully crafted. Each party's rights over IP, whether copyrights in software or the U.S. parent's trademarks, should be narrowly and precisely spelled out.

It is important to distinguish between a *distributor* or *reseller* (who purchases goods from the U.S. parent or its overseas subsidiary and then sells them to end-users) and a *sales agent* (who locates potential customers and passes on sales leads to be accepted and fulfilled by the U.S. parent or subsidiary). Many countries have legislation protecting sales agents and, to a lesser extent, distributors.

For example, the European Commercial Agents Directive, now enacted throughout the EU, provides that certain terms and protections automatically apply to commercial sales agents, irrespective of what the agreement with the manufacturer provides. The legislation is designed to protect independent commercial agents, who are often individuals rather than companies, because their livelihoods can be severely jeopardized if a manufacturer takes away their ability to generate sales once they have built up a book of business. In furtherance of this objective,

FROM THE TRENCHES

An agent in the EU was appointed under a contract governed by California law. When the contract was terminated, the agent commenced proceedings pursuant to legislation enacted under the European Commercial Agents Directive seeking payment of commissions and compensation for damages suffered as a result of the termination of the contract. The issue before the European Court of Justice was whether the Directive applies when a commercial agent is appointed to carry out activities in a member state by a principal domiciled outside the EU pursuant to a contract that stipulates that the contract is governed by the law of the principal's country.

The Court ruled that the purpose of the Directive is to protect commercial agents after termination of the agency contract and to promote, for all agents, undistorted competition in the EU internal market. The Court concluded that it was essential that a principal based in a nonmember country, whose commercial agent carried on its activity within the EU, not be able to evade the provisions of the Directive by employing a choice-of-law clause. When a commercial agent carries out activity in the territory of a member state, the Directive applies irrespective of the law by which the parties intended their relationship to be governed.

Source: Ingmar GB Ltd. v. Eaton Tech., 2000 E.C.R. I-9305 (2000).

the legislation provides for mandatory compensation or indemnities upon termination of the sales agency. This rule can have a significant financial impact on the U.S. manufacturer or software producer.

INTELLECTUAL PROPERTY

Entrepreneurs' key assets are often their employees and their intellectual property. It is, therefore, essential that entrepreneurs understand how to protect their IP and put a strategy in place to manage and control those assets in the international arena. Even if the company plans to start in Europe, for example, and is unlikely to have a physical presence in Asia for some time, protection of IP assets on a global basis should be considered early on, as discussed in Chapter 14.

Before commencing any business overseas (whether using distributors or by establishing a more formal entity such as a subsidiary), the U.S. company should consider the adequacy of IP protection there. This is particularly critical if computer source code or other underlying IP assets are likely to be transferred or made available to the subsidiary or third parties in that country. For countries where IP protection is inadequate or timely redress through the courts for infringement is not available, the U.S. company may want to think long and hard about the appropriate business model for that country and make adaptations from the U.S. model as needed.

In addition, it may be appropriate to commence trademark applications overseas for key product and business names being registered as trademarks in the United States and, at the same time, apply for company names (or business name registrations) for the local subsidiary. In Europe, the Community Trade Mark (CTM) may be appropriate and has the advantage of requiring just one application to cover all member states of the EU.

FUNDING

Although the establishment of the euro-zone has reduced some of the previous foreign exchange headaches, several issues must still be considered when funding an overseas business. As noted earlier, some countries have significant capital requirements for the incorporation of a subsidiary. In addition, if the company is tackling a new market and building its overseas network, cash may be flowing out of the United States until the subsidiary is self-sufficient and revenue generating. Consideration should be given to the following items when preparing the initial budget for incorporating the subsidiary and funding its operations in the first six to twelve months of business.

- ***Capital Structure.*** What will be the initial capital contribution? (Cash? Does the country permit other tangible property, IP, or services to form part of the initial capital contribution?)
- ***Minimum Capital Requirements.*** Will the legal minimum capital be sufficient initially, or will customers, suppliers, or potential partners expect or require a higher amount?

- *"Thin Capitalization."* If working capital comes from bank borrowing, many countries require a balance of debt to equity in order for the interest on the debt to be deductible. A ratio of 1:1 may be required, so debt levels may need to be backed by equity from the U.S. parent.
- *Working Capital.* The new subsidiary may need substantial economic support in the first few months or even years, depending on the time to market for the local product and other factors, such as competition or other barriers to entry in the local market. Will the U.S. parent fund the initial start-up and growth, or will some or all of the funding come from bank borrowing, either in the United States or through a local facility? If the latter, and if the local subsidiary does not have adequate assets to secure the facility, parent company guaranties may well be required.

Local Bank Accounts

The new operation will need a working capital facility and a local bank account to pay local creditors and to handle payroll and related employee expenses. As with most aspects of operating overseas, formalities for setting up an account vary from country to country, but a few guiding principles apply in any jurisdiction.

When financing the local subsidiary, the U.S. parent needs to balance the need for flexibility with control over local expenditures. It is often appropriate to have signatories from the United States (particularly for board members) as well as local signatories, although the parent may want to ensure that checks or transfers above a certain monetary amount require dual signatures. The bylaws (or their equivalent) of the local subsidiary might also establish a mechanism for board approval of significant expenditures above a certain preset limit.

Bank signatories should be checked and updated at least once a year. The process of appointing or removing bank account signatories can be fairly formal, requiring board authorization or the production of various documents. If key people have left the operation, the subsidiary may not appreciate the inadequacy of its bank instructions until an urgent business need requires immediate action.

Financing International Sales

Both the U.S. parent and the local subsidiary need to consider how sales to customers in diverse parts of the globe will be financed. Although checking the creditworthiness of potential customers may be relatively easy in the United States or Western Europe, in many countries such information is simply not available, is unreliable, or is prohibitively expensive to obtain.

LETTERS OF CREDIT Even if a customer's credit standing can be checked prior to a sale, it may still be necessary to establish a reliable method of payment to ensure that the U.S. parent or its subsidiary receives payment promptly for goods shipped to the customer. In the absence of a reliable track record with the customer or prior dealings with businesses in a particular region, the best way to ensure reliable and prompt payment is to use letters of credit (*L/Cs*). There are two types of letters of credit: one type is usually referred to as a "documentary letter of credit" or just plain "letter of credit," and the other is a "standby letter of credit." Letters of credit are generally governed by Article 5 of the Uniform Commercial Code, although the parties may elect to be governed by a set of rules published by the International Chamber of Commerce.[1]

Documentary letters of credit are frequently used to secure payment for goods in international transactions. The overseas purchaser of the goods (known as the *applicant*) enters into a contract with the issuing bank (usually in its own country). The bank issues an L/C in favor of the seller (either the U.S. parent or its local subsidiary) as *beneficiary.* The L/C provides for payment of the purchase price by the issuing bank to the beneficiary upon delivery to the bank of specified documents (often the bill of lading issued by the carrier of the goods to the seller). A typical L/C requires the beneficiary to present a *clean bill of lading* to the bank, meaning one with no notations indicating defects or damage to the goods when they were received for transportation to the purchaser. Upon presentation of the relevant documents, the bank makes payment to the seller/beneficiary.

The key purpose of an L/C is to allow the issuing bank to pay based solely on the presentation of specified documents without requiring (or permitting) the bank to examine any underlying facts, including compliance by the purchaser and the seller with the terms of their sales contract. The sale of goods pursuant to an L/C therefore involves two contracts: one between the seller and the purchaser, and a second between the issuing bank and the seller. Absent proof of outright fraud, the issuing bank must pay the beneficiary even if, for example, the buyer asserts that the goods are defective. The buyer must then sue the seller for breach of contract to recover the purchase price paid to the seller by the bank.

It is customary for sellers to require irrevocable L/Cs when dealing with unfamiliar parties. An *irrevocable L/C* can be amended or canceled only with the consent of the beneficiary (the seller) and the issuing bank.

A *standby letter of credit* requires payment only if the purchaser of the goods has failed to perform its obligations under the sales contract, that is, to pay for the goods purchased. Payment by the issuing bank under a standby letter of credit is usually conditional upon a brief statement (in the precise language provided in the standby letter of credit) that the purchaser is in default and that the seller/beneficiary is therefore entitled to payment from the issuing bank. As with regular L/Cs, the issuing bank cannot inquire into the underlying transaction or assert defenses against payment the purchaser might have vis-à-vis the seller (other than blatant fraud). The bank must generally pay within seven business days following presentation of the specified documents.

Both types of L/Cs cost money. In an ongoing relationship, the purchasing customer usually presses for more favorable payment terms, including the possibility of substituting a guaranty for the L/C.

Property and Operations

Signing a lease overseas may trigger the creation of a permanent establishment in some situations, so the timing of the signing should be coordinated with the overseas expansion plans. In some parts of the world, property can be enormously expensive. For example, in many parts of Europe, leases tend to be much longer than is customary in the United

States. Doing some homework and investigation up front will avoid unpleasant surprises later.

Several different types of property may be available. Many major cities have serviced offices, where a U.S. start-up can rent the space it needs initially and also receive administrative support such as reception, switchboard, and security services. This type of service might be helpful for the first few months, until the sales and marketing operation has the critical mass to take on its own office space and associated personnel. Rents in the local market also dictate what is feasible. For example, Japan and Hong Kong are extremely expensive compared to other parts of the world, so property arrangements can be very important.

Because a subsidiary will usually have minimal assets to begin with, overseas' landlords may require the parent company to guarantee the subsidiary's obligations under the lease, particularly for longer leases where the total rental obligation may exceed the financial resources of the subsidiary for the foreseeable future. The financial obligations under these guaranties are often worded broadly and can cover all conceivable costs and expenses associated with the property, not just the rent and service charges. The rent guaranty could itself become a significant contingent liability for the U.S. parent.

FROM THE TRENCHES

A rapidly expanding business in the United Kingdom needed larger premises. Management there obtained authorization from the U.S. parent to find a lease for the appropriate space, up to an agreed cap on annual rent. The U.K. management found space and entered into a binding agreement to take up the lease. The formal closing required the parent company to deliver a guaranty in favor of the landlord.

On closer inspection, the U.S. parent realized that the guaranty obligation covered the entire life of the lease—twenty years. This possibility had never been anticipated or discussed before the binding agreement was signed and could not be negotiated away before the closing.

The new business overseas will also need equipment, which is often sourced locally in the country. Supply times may not be as short as in the United States, so entrepreneurs need to plan accordingly. This is also true of technology and communications links. Although the EU and many parts of Asia have services comparable to those available in the United States, this is not necessarily the case in other parts of the world. If the subsidiary needs fast Internet connections and a state-of-the-art communication system properly integrated with the head office in the United States, additional planning is necessary as well as extra time to obtain the telecom links and services from the local suppliers (many of which may be state-run enterprises or monopolies).

Another element to consider when establishing an overseas office is the adequate supply of products and associated components, manuals, and literature. Additional distribution channels may also be necessary to ensure reliable and timely distribution of products. This may involve the appointment of independent distributors or resellers to supplement the capabilities of the subsidiary or to assist it in achieving broader sales coverage in certain territories or regions. All agreements with distributors, resellers, or sales agents should be negotiated with the full knowledge of and input from the U.S. parent so that any new arrangements, especially if made on an exclusive basis, dovetail with existing agreements covering sales or supply.

If the overseas subsidiary is a manufacturing center as well as a sales and marketing site, it may be possible to obtain investment incentives, tax breaks, or other forms of financial assistance from the regional or national government. These incentives are often offered to attract new business into rural or depressed areas—locations that may not be the most suitable for technology businesses. Incentives are often not available if the company has already started building a facility or setting up an operation, so entrepreneurs should look into this possibility early on if incentives or grants are a key part of financing the new operation. Also, it is important to clearly understand the terms of the grant or incentive, which are often linked to the number of jobs created by the project. If economic conditions require a reduction in the workforce, some or all of the grant may become immediately repayable to the government or regional agency.

U.S. Support for Overseas Operations

A U.S. parent company will invariably supply some central services and support to its overseas offices, even when they are well established and relatively self-sufficient. The best practice is to formalize these arrangements at an early stage by putting them in writing. Intercompany agreements serve a variety of useful functions, from providing proper accounting and tax treatment for intragroup transactions to enabling both parties to budget for additional services to or from the other. These agreements typically spell out what sale, supply, and support arrangements will be provided for the overseas businesses and how the cost of these services will be calculated and adjusted from year to year. In addition, smaller subsidiaries can often piggyback on the U.S. parent's greater bargaining power with suppliers and vendors. Typical services supplied or procured by the head office include some or all of the following:

- Sales and marketing support and coordination.
- Advertising/public relations (launch and ongoing).
- Pricing policies.
- Technical support.
- Administration/human resources.
- Accounting/treasury.
- Other support services (strategic planning, legal services, supply chain management, and the like).

Regardless of whether the U.S. parent provides significant services directly to the overseas subsidiaries, it will have ongoing responsibilities with respect to their business. Continuing responsibilities will include overseeing their corporate governance and ensuring that all subsidiaries are current with their filings, registrations, and tax returns in the relevant jurisdictions. Periodic responsibilities will include involvement in acquisitions, joint ventures, or strategic partnering, which affect the group as a whole and not just the local subsidiary involved.

The U.S. business will also need to review other aspects of the overseas operations, such as risk management, where adequate local insurance coverage and suitable corporate policies should be an integral part of the business from day one. U.S. managers and senior personnel will often be sent to assist in running overseas operations, and those personnel will need to be rotated at appropriate intervals.

Last but by no means least, formal accounting and audit policies must be in place to ensure that the U.S. parent can properly supervise the financial and accounting activity of the subsidiary. This is especially important if the parent company is a public company or will shortly become one.

Finally, the U.S. parent should also be mindful of U.S. legal requirements regarding export control and the restriction of exports to certain countries. It should also comply with the antibribery and record-keeping requirements imposed by the Foreign Corrupt Practices Act (discussed in Chapter 11) and similar local legislation, which prohibit certain payments to foreign officials and impose criminal sanctions for violations.

Putting it into Practice

Within a few months of the first sales of the SDB, Kendra found that several of her U.S. customers were so pleased with its accelerated response time that they wanted to roll out the system in some of their larger overseas offices, particularly in Europe. Kendra realized that DataAccelleation did not have the personnel in California to spare sales staff and technicians to handle the sale and installation of products in Europe. At the same time, as most of DataAccelleation's customers were large financial and insurance institutions, Kendra was fully aware that if she could not scale her operations to meet their requirements, they would simply look for similar products from her overseas competitors.

After several discussions with Michael Cruz and the board of directors, Kendra formulated a preliminary plan to establish one or more subsidiaries in Europe to leverage the business links with her U.S. customers. While walking back to her office after the board meeting approving expansion into Europe, Kendra remembered Michael's parting words, "Establishing a subsidiary overseas is not nearly as daunting as it seems. What I suggest first, however, is an outline plan and timetable because international expansion will most certainly require input and assistance from every department in the company."

Kendra discussed the proposed overseas structure with her staff, beginning with a summary of what the board had approved. First, DataAccelleation would establish a European holding company in the Netherlands, a private limited liability company (known as a "BV"), because of the favorable tax treatment there for groups of companies. This process was expected to take four to six weeks, so Kendra planned to start immediately by committing the minimum capital required for a Dutch private company. The first operations center would be in the United Kingdom because London was a major business center for many of DataAccelleation's customers. The U.K. subsidiary would be a wholly owned subsidiary of the BV. As DataAccelleation rolled out in Germany, France, and other business centers in Europe, Kendra planned to establish local subsidiaries, each of which would be owned by the BV. This would give the company maximum flexibility. For example, if an opportunity to partner with a local company in any of those countries came along, a suitable vehicle would already be in place.

continued...

continued...

Michael recommended lawyers in his firm's offices in Amsterdam and London to deal with the incorporation process. They transferred a shelf company in the United Kingdom to DataAccelleation as sole shareholder and appointed Kendra and Philip to the board of directors. Kendra planned to add the U.K. country manager (once hired) to the board as well so that documents, checks, and the like could be signed in the United Kingdom. At the same time that she established the London subsidiary, Kendra started getting prices and delivery schedules for critical items of equipment and began thinking about the key technical and support services that would be supplied by DataAccelleation until the European operations were up and running.

Kendra spoke with an old friend involved in U.S. recruiting, who recommended a recruitment specialist in London who could assist with hiring the managing director for the United Kingdom, as well as the first two or three employees. Kendra and Philip traveled to London to interview suitable candidates. While there, they selected a small suite of offices that would be sufficient for the first twelve months. Kendra also visited the U.K. offices of her major customers to introduce the SDB product line and inform them of the opening of DataAccelleation's local office. Finally, Kendra and Philip opened a bank account in the name of the U.K. subsidiary and arranged a line of credit, supported by a guaranty from DataAccelleation, to ease cash flow in the first few months.

After hiring James Stout as the managing director for the U.K. subsidiary, Kendra brought him to California for a familiarization visit. This also gave the California staff a chance to meet the latest addition to the team. While in California, James and Kendra agreed on some ground rules regarding the sales and support of products in the United Kingdom, instituted weekly and monthly financial reporting policies, and prepared a preliminary budget for the U.K. operation.

Within a month, London had won its first contract from the European arm of one of DataAccelleation's key U.S. customers. They were all delighted with the progress, and the London attorneys quickly revised all of the company's customer contracts, licenses, and maintenance/support agreements to be used with U.K. customers to comply with local laws.

Six months later, business opportunities arose in Germany, France, Sweden, and Japan. Kendra and her board were pleased that they had a corporate structure and action plan in place to take advantage of the opportunities as they arose.

Having established a global presence, Kendra turned her attention back to expansion plans in the United States.

NOTE

1. *See* CHARLES DEL BUSTO, ICC GUIDE TO DOCUMENTARY CREDIT OPERATIONS FOR THE UNIFORM CUSTOMS AND PRACTICE FOR DOCUMENTARY CREDITS (UCP) 500: A STAGE-BY-STAGE PRESENTATION OF THE DOCUMENTARY CREDIT PROCESS (1994); INTERNATIONAL CHAMBER OF COMMERCE, INTERNATIONAL STANDBY PRACTICES—ISP 98 (1998). *See also* INTERNATIONAL CHAMBER OF COMMERCE, INCOTERMS 2000: ICC OFFICIAL RULES FOR THE INTERPRETATION OF TRADE TERMS (1999).

Chapter 16

BUYING AND SELLING A BUSINESS

For many early-stage companies, selling the company or buying another company (a *business combination*) may be the most effective method of accessing capital, establishing strategic relationships, and offering increased liquidity to the company's shareholders. Entering into a business combination can involve many complex issues, however, including those raised by tax and securities laws and those relating to the integration of the combined companies after the transaction is completed. Entrepreneurs should carefully consider the structure and potential implications of a proposed transaction before entering into any business combination.

This chapter introduces business combinations by discussing some of the issues that an entrepreneur should consider when deciding between a sale of the company and an initial public offering. The chapter then introduces the types of acquirers and typical forms of business combinations, including asset purchases, stock purchases, and mergers. Next, the chapter reviews the tax, securities law, accounting, and antitrust issues that frequently arise in connection with the purchase or sale of a business. It concludes by describing the process and terms of a typical merger, from the due diligence process and the memorialization of the basic terms of a transaction in a letter of intent or a term sheet, through the negotiation of the principal terms of a definitive merger agreement to the closing of the transaction. Common postclosing issues are also addressed.

Business Combination Versus Initial Public Offering

To obtain liquidity for shareholders, a company can either pursue a business combination or an initial public offering (IPO). Initial public offerings are discussed in detail in Chapter 17. Business combinations are a much more common method of obtaining liquidity for shareholders of private companies than IPOs, particularly if a company is experiencing slow but steady growth or operates in an industry not currently favored by the investment community.

Advantages of Business Combinations

The sale of a company for cash or for the stock of a public company can offer several advantages not available with an IPO. In a cash sale, the shareholders of the target company obtain immediate liquidity, and the value of the consideration paid for their shares is fixed. (For purposes of this discussion, *target company* refers to the entity whose assets are being sold, or whose stock is being sold, or which is being merged with the acquirer or a subsidiary of the acquirer in a transaction that will result in control being shifted from the target company's shareholders to the acquirer.) The target company's shareholders eliminate the risks associated with changing stock market conditions that may prevent completion of an IPO or adversely affect the price at which stock can be publicly offered by the company or sold by shareholders after the offering is completed. In addition, through an agreement referred to as a *lockup agreement,* underwriters of an IPO typically require most shareholders to agree not to sell or otherwise transfer their shares for at least six months after completion of an IPO, resulting in additional constraints on shareholder liquidity.

In a stock-for-stock combination with a public company, some market risk will remain. Usually, however, the market price of a more established public company is less volatile than that of a newly public company. In addition, shareholders can often reduce their risk by selling stock or engaging in other activities that would be precluded by a typical lockup agreement with the underwriters of an IPO. Perhaps most importantly, a business combination may enable a company to avoid the pressures of being a public company, including meeting or exceeding revenue and earnings estimates on a quarterly basis and communicating with and owing duties to a large number of shareholders.

Drawbacks of Business Combinations

A less positive feature of a business combination is a potential limitation on the return for the target company's shareholders. First, the price paid per share by an acquirer may be less than the target company could obtain in a public offering. Second, the target company's shareholders' *upside* (potential profit) is capped at the purchase price if the consideration is cash, or is determined by the performance of the acquirer's stock if the consideration is stock. Advantages and disadvantages of an IPO are discussed in Chapter 17.

FROM THE TRENCHES

A publicly held semiconductor manufacturer considered the possibility of acquiring a small privately held company whose principal asset was technology that could be applied in the public company's business but that also had applications in several other industries. One of the chief sticking points in negotiations between the two companies was the valuation of the privately held company. The public company acknowledged that it might be possible to develop the technology further for use in industries other than the semiconductor industry. Nonetheless, the public company was not willing to factor this potential into the calculation of the purchase price because it did not necessarily intend to develop this potential, which was far removed from its core competencies. The founders of the privately held company were faced with the choice of completing a transaction at a lower valuation than they thought their company was worth or continuing on their own while they sought to consummate a transaction with investors or another company that shared their vision for the development of their technology. Ultimately, the parties decided not to enter into a business combination.

TYPES OF ACQUIRERS

It is important for an entrepreneur to consider the different types of acquirers and the role that an acquirer will play in a target company after a business combination is completed. Of particular importance are the acquirer's long-term vision for the target company and the allocation of control of the combined entity. Often a financial acquirer's priority will be to fulfill the target company's potential for short-term financial return; as a consequence, the long-term vision of the target company may be sacrificed. This shift in priority may become manifest through a reduction of staff or research and development programs. In contrast, though strategic acquirers will often control the day-to-day operations of the target company, they will generally share its long-term vision. As a result, they may be less likely to take actions simply to increase the target's short-term financial value.

Potential acquirers often surface near the time that a company is ready to proceed with an IPO because acquirers are well aware that once a company is public, they will likely be required to pay a premium over the public market price to induce the target company's board of directors to approve the transaction. Information regarding different types of acquirers, including financial and strategic investors, and the advantages and disadvantages of each, is presented in detail in Chapter 7.

FORMS OF BUSINESS COMBINATIONS

Business combinations can take two basic forms: a purchase and sale of assets and a purchase and sale of equity interests. Equity transactions are further subdivided into stock purchase transactions and merger transactions.

Asset Purchase

In an *asset purchase,* the acquiring company purchases some or all of the target company's assets and assumes some or all of its liabilities. Exhibit 16.1 demonstrates the steps taken to accomplish an asset purchase and the result.

ADVANTAGES AND DISADVANTAGES TO THE ACQUIRER Acquirers often prefer to purchase assets instead of stock. By purchasing assets, the acquirer can purchase only those assets that it desires to acquire and agree to assume only specified liabilities of the target company. As a result, the acquirer can avoid the expense of purchasing unwanted assets and reduce the risk of assuming unknown liabilities.

An acquirer can never totally eliminate the risk of being saddled with some of the target company's liabilities, however. Even though the acquisition agreement will almost always limit the acquirer's assumption of liabilities to those expressly set forth in the agreement, certain federal and state laws may override the parties' contractual limitations. As a result, liabilities may be imposed on an acquirer that were unknown or unquantifiable by either the acquirer or the target company at the time of the transaction. For example, in some states, if the acquirer buys a business and continues selling the same products as the target company, the

EXHIBIT 16.1

ASSET PURCHASE

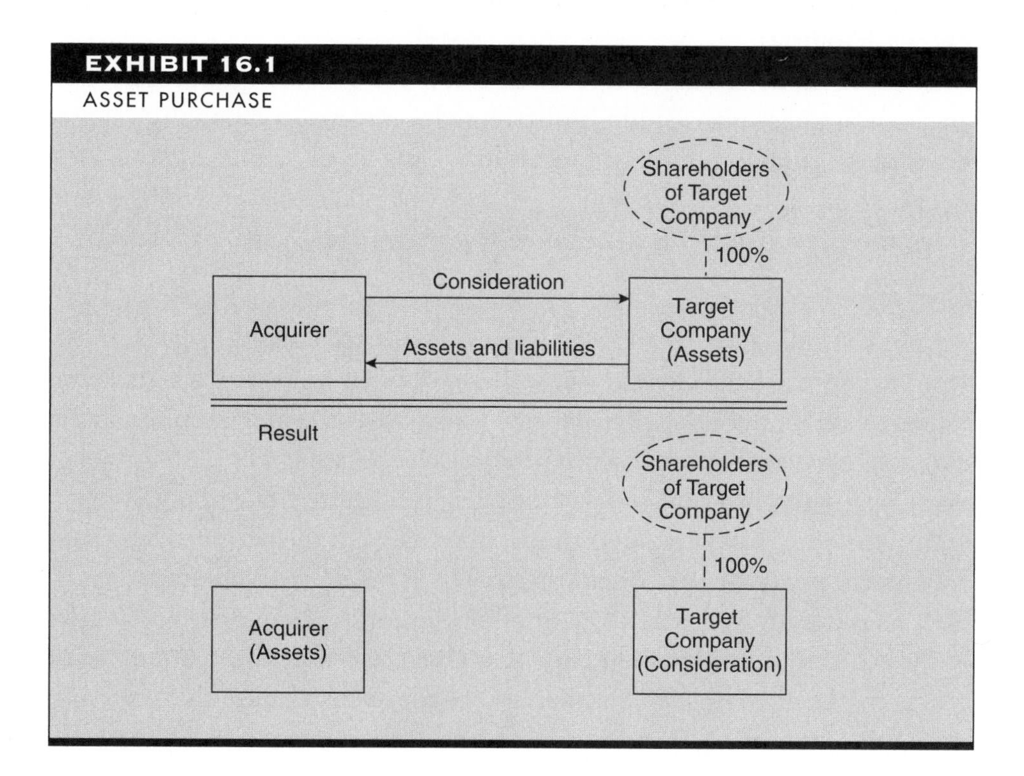

acquirer will be liable for defects in products sold by the target company *before* the acquisition. This is discussed further in Chapter 9.

Another potential advantage of a purchase of assets is that if the target company does not sell all, or substantially all, of its assets, then the completion of the asset purchase should not require shareholder approval or give rise to dissenters' rights (discussed below) for the target company's shareholders. As a result, an asset purchase transaction may be completed very quickly and without the possibility of additional payouts to the target company's shareholders.

An asset purchase may also entail potential disadvantages for an acquirer. For instance, the acquirer may not accurately identify all of the assets that it wishes to purchase and thus may acquire insufficient assets to develop the technology or operate the business line that it intended to purchase.

DISADVANTAGES TO THE TARGET COMPANY AND ITS SHAREHOLDERS From the perspective of the target company and its shareholders, an asset purchase is generally not as favorable as a stock acquisition. In particular, the target company may be forced to retain significant known or unknown liabilities.

In addition, as discussed further below, if the consideration received in an asset purchase transaction is distributed to the target company's shareholders, the asset purchase will result in double taxation of the gain on the sale: first, at the target company level, and, second, at the shareholder level when the consideration is distributed to the company's shareholders.

NEED FOR THIRD-PARTY CONSENTS When assets are purchased, contracts and permits (including real estate or equipment leases, technology licenses, or environmental or other governmental permits) often are either a part of, or fundamental to, the value of the assets. Many contracts and permits contain *anti-assignment* provisions, which prohibit the assignment of the contract or permit, or the transfer of the related rights, to third parties without the consent of the other party to the contract or the issuer of the permit. These anti-assignment provisions are often triggered when the target sells its assets.

If, as is usually the case, some or all of the contracts and permits critical to the acquired business limit assignment, then, as a practical matter, the acquirer will be unwilling to consummate the transaction unless the other parties approve their assignment to the acquirer. It is often not difficult to obtain a third-party consent, especially if the acquirer is economically sound and is not a competitor of the other party to the contract. However, this is not always the case. Sometimes the other party may refuse to grant its consent for business reasons that are unrelated to the proposed transaction. For example, if the target company had a below-market lease, then the lessor will usually elect to prohibit assignment so that it is free to lease the property to a new tenant at a market rate.

In addition, there may be disadvantages to seeking consent. The request for consent may force disclosure of the proposed asset sale to outside parties earlier than the acquirer and target company desire. Moreover, obtaining consent can take time and delay the completion of the transaction. The need to procure a third party's consent may give that party sufficient leverage to condition its consent on the acquirer's willingness to accept terms that are less favorable than those in the target company's original contract or permit.

Shareholder Approval and Dissenters' Rights in Sales of Substantially All of the Assets Under most states' laws, if the amount of assets being sold constitutes all, or substantially all, of the target company's assets, then the principal terms of the acquisition agreement must be approved by the target company's board of directors and its shareholders. The need to obtain shareholder approval can, at the very least, delay the closing of the transaction. It can also create uncertainty as to whether the target company will be able to obtain the necessary shareholder approval. In addition, some state corporate statutes provide that shareholders are entitled to dissenters' rights if the transaction constitutes a sale of all, or substantially all, of a company's assets. Shareholders who exercise dissenters' rights may be entitled to receive in cash the fair value of their shares of the target company. Shareholder approval and dissenters' rights are discussed in greater detail later in this chapter.

Bulk Sales Laws Some states have adopted *bulk sales laws,* which, among other things, require a target company that is selling a significant portion of its business or assets to give notice of the transaction (prior to its completion) to the target company's creditors. These laws, which typically apply only to certain types of assets and to transactions under a certain dollar amount, contain very specific requirements that can work to protect both an acquirer and creditors of the target company. On the other hand, if the target company fails to comply with the applicable bulk sales laws, then the acquirer may find itself liable to the target company's creditors.

Purchase of Equity

Two primary structures can be used to purchase the equity of a target company: a stock purchase and a merger. Depending on the structure, a target company may become a subsidiary of an acquirer, or it may be combined directly with an acquirer or a subsidiary of an acquirer. The two structures have some common features. These features and the specific characteristics of each form of equity purchase are set forth below.

ADVANTAGES TO THE TARGET COMPANY'S SHAREHOLDERS AND THE ACQUIRER The purchase of equity is generally more favorable to a target company's shareholders than a sale of assets. Although the target company's shareholders do not retain any assets of the target company after the equity is sold, they also typically rid themselves of the risks associated with its liabilities (unless the liabilities are otherwise allocated to the shareholders by contract). Moreover, this form of transaction will result in only a single level of taxation, at the shareholder level, rather than the double taxation, at both the target company and shareholder levels, commonly resulting from an asset purchase.

An acquirer may also favor an equity purchase because it is assured of obtaining all of the assets owned by the target company. An equity purchase may be preferable from a tax perspective as well because the acquirer may be able to take advantage of any net operating loss carryforwards that the target company has generated over time. Finally, as described in more detail below, the use of an equity purchase structure, as opposed to an asset purchase structure, may reduce the likelihood that the parties will need to obtain third-party consents prior to the completion of the transaction.

DISADVANTAGES TO THE ACQUIRER A primary disadvantage to the equity purchase structure for an acquirer is that the acquirer will, by virtue of its ownership of the target company following the completion of the transaction, assume all of the target company's liabilities, whether known or unknown, unless the liabilities are otherwise allocated to the target company's shareholders by contract. As a result, acquirers must perform extensive due diligence (a process described below) to attempt to confirm the extent of any possible exposure to such liabilities before the transaction is completed. The acquirer can also limit its exposure by having a separate subsidiary acquire the equity.

STOCK PURCHASE AND SALE

A stock purchase generally involves a contract between the acquirer and the target company's shareholders under which the acquirer agrees to purchase all outstanding shares of the target company's capital stock from the target's shareholders in exchange for cash, stock, or other consideration. Exhibit 16.2 outlines the steps involved and the result.

Technically, it is often not necessary for the target company to be a party to a stock purchase agreement. As a practical matter, however, the acquirer will often require the target company to be a party in order (1) to make representations and warranties regarding the target company and its business and operations and (2) to agree to certain covenants relating to the operation of the target company's business between the signing of the

EXHIBIT 16.2

STOCK PURCHASE

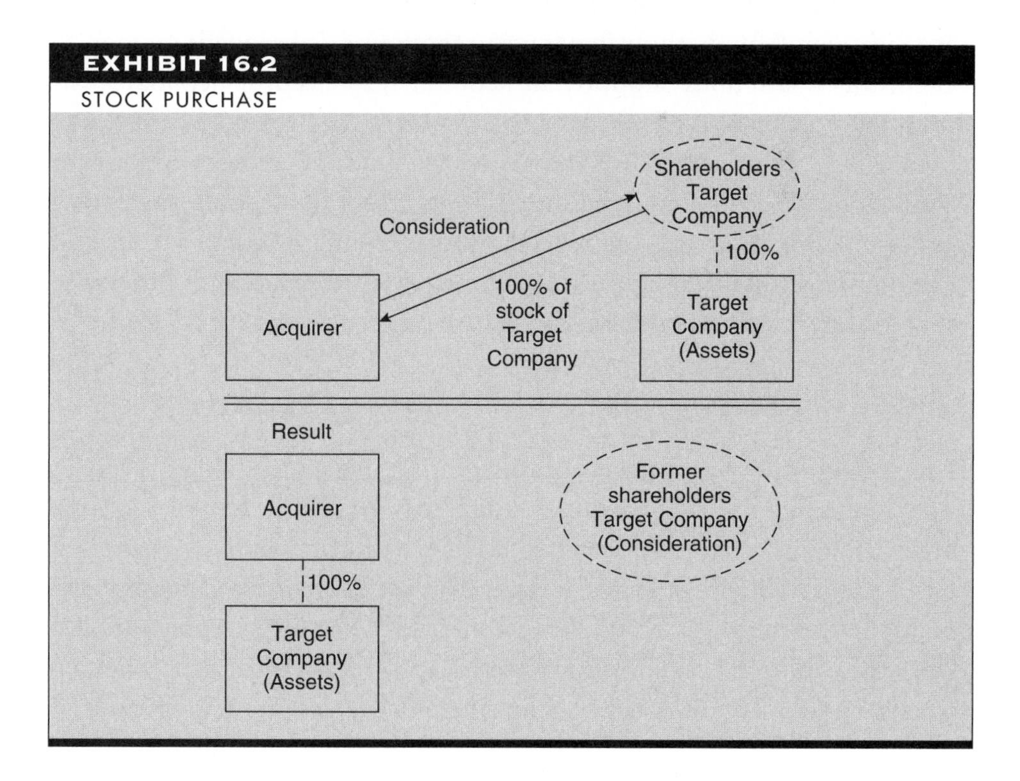

stock purchase agreement and the completion of the transaction. Stock purchase agreements in general are discussed in detail in Chapter 7.

Third-Party Consents

Upon the completion of a stock purchase transaction, the target company continues to exist; the only immediate change is in the ownership of its capital stock. Therefore, unlike in an asset purchase, there is no actual transfer of the target company's contracts or permits to the acquirer. Accordingly, under most states' laws, absent specific contractual provisions to the contrary, the parties will be required to obtain third-party consents for a sale of stock for only those contracts or permits that require consent to a change of control of the target company.

Shareholder Approval

In a stock purchase transaction, all shareholders must agree to sell their stock to an acquirer in order for the acquirer to gain complete control of the target company without having to carry out a subsequent merger. To obtain this unanimous support, an acquirer may need to negotiate with and make concessions to minority shareholders who would not necessarily have the same leverage in a merger transaction. These negotiations can significantly delay the completion of the transaction. Therefore, a stock purchase is typically used only when a target company's shareholder base is small and unified in support of the proposed transaction. Otherwise, most acquirers will use a merger structure rather than buy stock.

Acquiring the Balance of the Stock in a Second-Step Merger

If an acquirer that has elected not to structure the acquisition as a merger is unable to acquire all of a target company's securities directly from the target company's shareholders but holds a majority of the outstanding shares, then, under most states' laws, it may use its majority control to call a shareholder meeting and approve a merger of the target company with either the acquirer or a subsidiary of the acquirer. Majority shareholders may owe a fiduciary duty to the minority, however, so the acquirer should ensure that the terms of the "freeze-out" merger are procedurally and substantively fair to the minority.

For California corporations, if the acquirer owns more than 50 percent but less than 90 percent of the target company's shares, then, as a practical matter, the acquirer may not be able to eliminate the minority in a second-step merger if there is any substantial minority opposition. If the acquirer owns 90 percent or more of the target company's outstanding securities, many states (including California) permit the acquirer to complete the acquisition of the target company without a shareholder vote in a *short-form merger.*

MERGER

A *merger* is generally a transaction in which two corporations combine into one surviving corporation. The completion of a merger requires the approval of the board of directors of each of the combining companies. In certain circumstances as described below, approval of the shareholders of the combining companies may also be required. The surviving company will, by operation of the applicable state merger statute, assume all of the rights, assets, and liabilities of the disappearing company.

The principal advantage of a merger transaction over a stock purchase is that, unless a target company's articles of incorporation provide for a class or series vote, only the approval of shareholders holding a majority of the target company's outstanding shares, rather than unanimous approval of all shareholders, is typically required for a merger. This significantly reduces the ability of recalcitrant minority shareholders to block or delay the completion of the proposed transaction.

Types of Mergers

A merger will generally take one of three forms. In a *direct* or *forward merger,* the target company merges directly into the acquirer and does not survive the merger as a separate entity. The other two forms, a forward triangular merger and a reverse triangular merger, use a wholly owned subsidiary of the acquirer to effect the merger. In a *forward triangular merger,* the target company merges directly into a subsidiary of the acquirer and does not survive the merger. The subsidiary ends up with all of the assets and liabilities of the target company. In a *reverse triangular merger,* a subsidiary of the acquirer merges with and into a target company, and the target company survives the merger as a wholly owned subsidiary of the acquirer. Exhibits 16.3, 16.4, and 16.5 outline these three forms of merger.

The variety of available merger structures provides the parties with significant flexibility to structure a transaction that (1) shields the acquirer from direct exposure to the target company's liabilities, (2) optimizes the tax treatment for both the acquirer and the target company's shareholders, and (3) reduces the possibility of third-party interference in the transaction.

The use of a subsidiary corporation is often advantageous to an acquiring company for several reasons. It insulates the acquirer's assets (other than the value of its stock in the subsidiary) against liabilities of the target company, and it continues the target company's desirable tax attributes. In addition, unless the transaction requires a change in the acquirer's articles of incorporation or the acquirer is a publicly traded company and the transaction involves the issuance of a substantial amount of the acquirer's stock (generally 20 percent

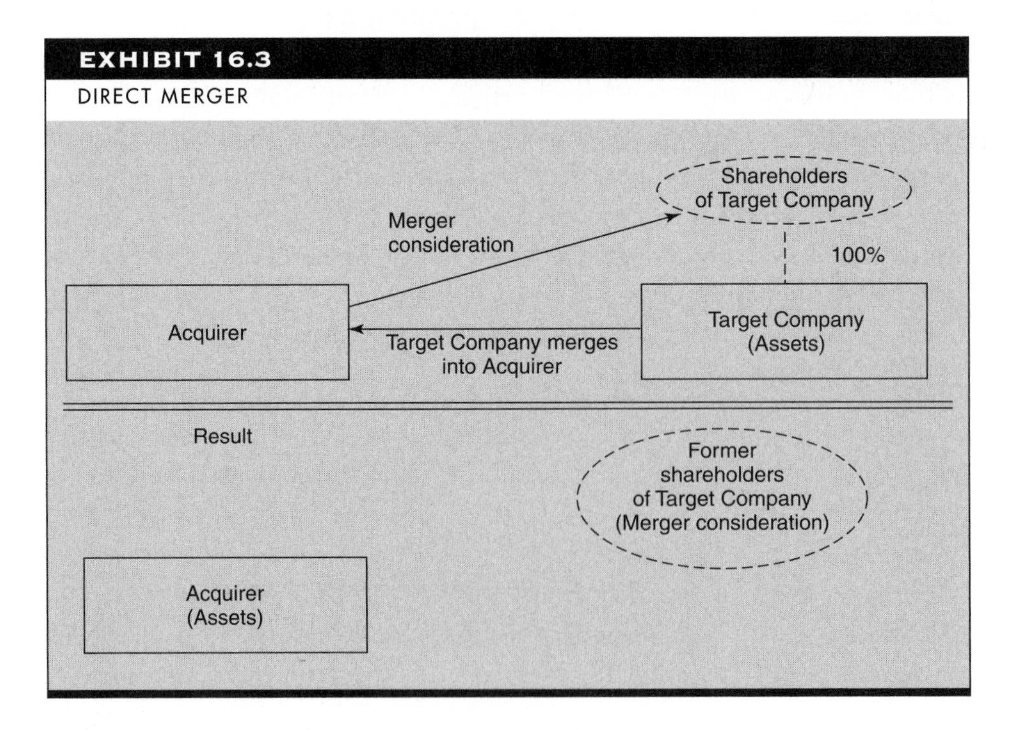

EXHIBIT 16.4

FORWARD TRIANGULAR MERGER

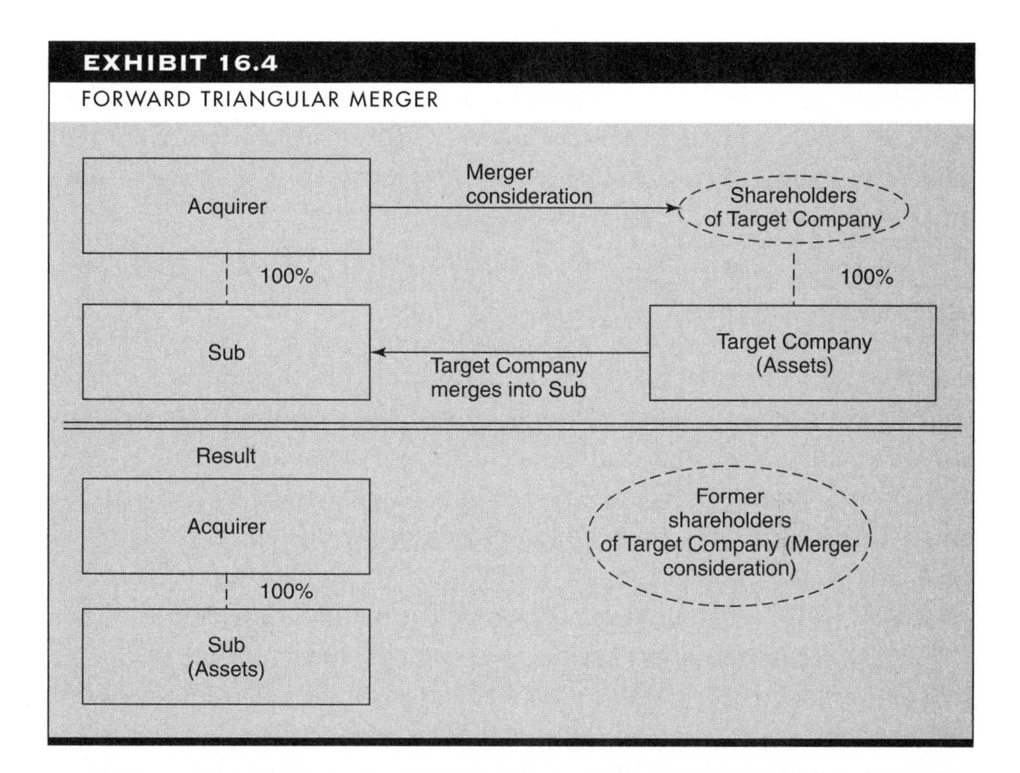

EXHIBIT 16.5

REVERSE TRIANGULAR MERGER

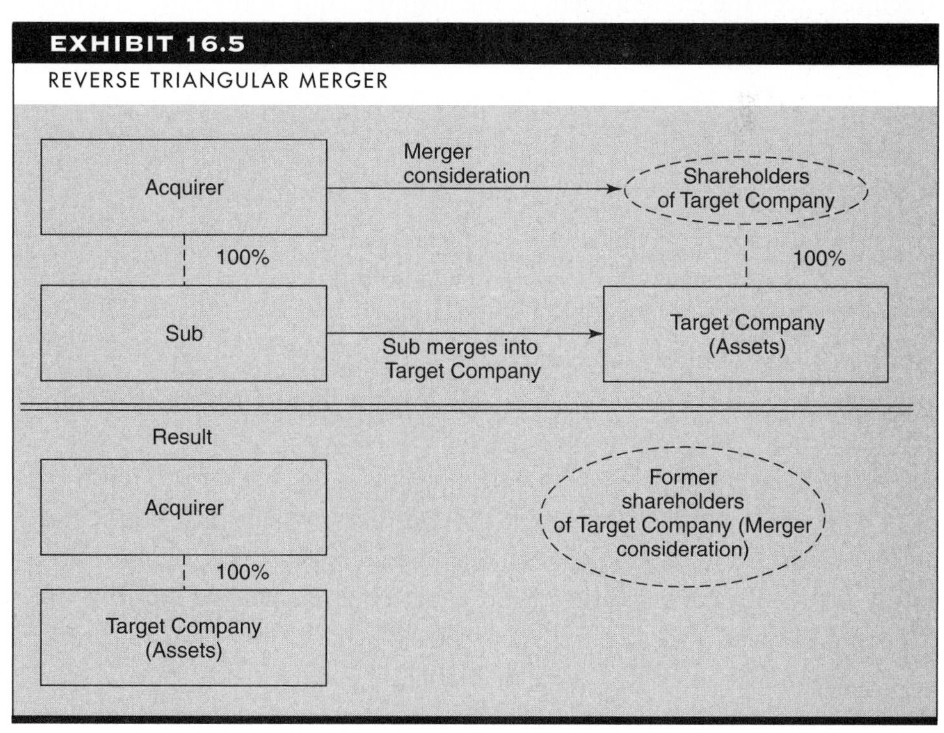

of an acquirer's outstanding shares at the time of the merger), the use of a subsidiary will generally obviate the need for the acquirer to obtain approval from its shareholders. Although the shareholders of the subsidiary must approve a triangular merger, this is a mere formality because the subsidiary's capital stock is all owned by the acquirer corporation.

Shareholder Approval and Dissenters' Rights

The completion of a merger requires the approval of shareholders holding at least a majority of the outstanding capital stock of the target company. If the target has more than one class of stock or more than one series of preferred stock, then the merger may have to be approved by each class or series voting separately. To mitigate the risk that this vote will not be attained, the acquirer may seek to obtain voting agreements from a portion of the target company's shareholders at the time the merger agreement is signed. In mergers requiring approval by the acquirer's shareholders, the target company may seek similar voting agreements from certain of the acquirer's shareholders. In addition to the shareholder vote requirement, in certain circumstances the shareholders of the acquirer and of the target company may be entitled to dissenters' rights in connection with the transaction.

Third-Party Consents

Whether the parties will need to obtain third-party consents in a merger depends on how the transaction is structured. In a direct or forward triangular merger (in which the target company will not survive the merger and all of its assets and liabilities will be assumed by the acquirer or a subsidiary of the acquirer), the contracts and permits of the target company often need to be assigned or transferred to the acquirer. Therefore, third-party consents will need to be obtained. In contrast, in a reverse triangular merger, the target company continues to exist. Therefore, there is no actual transfer of the target company's contracts or permits to the acquirer. In this circumstance, under most states' laws, absent specific contractual provisions to the contrary, the parties will be required to obtain third-party consents to the transaction for only those contracts or permits that require a consent to a change of control of the target company.

Pricing Issues and Forms of Consideration

In addition to determining how to structure the business combination, the parties must agree on the purchase price and the form of consideration to be used.

Purchase Price

Various formulations may be used to determine the purchase price. The simplest method is to set a *fixed dollar amount* that will be paid to the target company or its shareholders in cash at the closing of the transaction. Or the parties can agree on a *fixed number of shares* of the acquirer that will be distributed at closing.

Another method is to set a fixed dollar amount that is subject to a *postclosing adjustment.* An adjustment may be appropriate when there is a substantial period of time between the signing of the acquisition agreement and the closing of the acquisition or when the target company does not have audited financial statements. A postclosing adjustment may be based on an audit of the target company's financial statements on the closing date and may include, among other things, working capital adjustments and earnings tests.

Alternatively, the parties may agree that a portion of the purchase price will be paid through an *earn-out* in which a portion (or, rarely, all) of the purchase price is tied to events beyond the closing, including the ability of the target company to meet specified postclosing levels of earnings or to achieve certain milestones.

Earn-out arrangements can pose risks for both the target company and the acquirer. Because the acquirer will often control the management of the target company's business after the acquisition, the acquirer may be able, for example, to reduce the company's earnings by spending more during the earn-out period on research and development than the target company's management might have spent. Even if the acquirer is not deliberately manipulating earnings or taking similar actions, the target company's shareholders might still sue the acquirer, claiming that the acquirer breached an implied covenant of good faith and fair dealing or a fiduciary duty to the target company's shareholders by not maximizing the payouts due under the earn-out. To mitigate these risks, the parties should be as explicit and detailed as possible in the acquisition agreement about the duties owed by the acquirer and the consequences of certain transactions.

Form of Consideration

An acquirer can buy assets or stock of a target company, or effect a merger with the target company, by paying cash or delivering some combination of promissory notes, stock, and cash.

CASH PAYMENT AT CLOSING Cash will provide the target company and its shareholders with the least risk and the greatest liquidity. Except to the extent that the target company and its shareholders have agreed to indemnify the acquirer for breaches of the target company's representations and warranties (discussed below) or other matters, or have entered into other ongoing contractual obligations, once the consideration is delivered, there are no further obligations on the part of either party after the transaction is completed. A cash payment will result in an immediate taxable event for the target company or its shareholders, however.

DEFERRED CASH PAYMENTS OR PROMISSORY NOTES The acquirer may also offer deferred cash payments or promissory notes for all or a portion of the purchase price. These methods of payment are particularly advantageous for an acquirer that wants the ability to reduce future payments by deducting any indemnification payments or other amounts that may be owed to the acquirer by the target company or its shareholders. To ensure payment, the target company will often seek to have the amount of anticipated future payments placed into an *escrow account*, as discussed below. Under certain circumstances, the target's shareholders may be able to defer some of the tax on the gain by electing installment-sale treatment of the promissory notes.

PART CASH/PART STOCK OR ALL STOCK The acquirer may also offer the target company's shareholders a portion of the consideration in cash and a portion in stock. This structure helps reduce the shareholders' downside risk of accepting stock as consideration. It also provides the shareholders with some amount of immediate liquidity. Moreover, shareholders who receive stock may be entitled to receive tax-free treatment for the stock component of the consideration. The consideration to be used in a part cash/part stock transaction may be calculated using a formula specifying a fixed cash amount, a fixed or floating exchange ratio for the shares, or any other combination thereof.

SHARES OF THE ACQUIRER'S STOCK If the acquirer offers its securities as some or all of the consideration, additional issues and complexities are added to the transaction. In particular, if the acquirer's stock is publicly traded and the transaction will close some period of time after the acquisition agreement is signed, the parties will need to determine the effect, if any, of changes in the market value of the acquirer's stock between signing and closing.

Fixed Exchange Ratio The simplest pricing structure that the parties can use is a fixed exchange ratio. An *exchange ratio* is the number of an acquirer's shares that will be issued in exchange for each share of the target company's equity securities. A different exchange ratio may be designated for the target company's common stock and its preferred stock. In a *fixed exchange ratio* structure, the exchange ratio is fixed at the time the acquisition agreement is executed. A fixed exchange ratio provides each party with certainty as to the exact number of shares that will be issued in the transaction. It does not, however, permit an adjustment if an acquirer's stock price declines (or increases) between the time that the acquisition agreement is signed and the closing.

Though not a major issue in a transaction involving the issuance of stock of a private company, a substantial decrease in the market value of the acquirer's public securities may jeopardize the willingness of the target company's shareholders to approve the business combination. Similarly, market price increases may result in the issuance by the acquirer of shares with a greater value than was anticipated at the time that the acquisition agreement was signed. To at least partially mitigate these effects, the parties may negotiate a *collar* that provides that if the stock price moves outside specified upper and lower market price limits, then the exchange ratio will be adjusted. If the price fluctuates but does not move outside the specified range, no adjustment to the exchange ratio is made.

FROM THE TRENCHES

In the spring of 2000, when Bob Davis, the CEO of Lycos, was negotiating the sale of Lycos to Spanish media giant Telefonica in exchange for stock in Telefonica's publicly traded Terra subsidiary, Davis insisted on a collar, which protected Lycos shareholders if Terra's stock price dropped by as much as 20 percent. After the Nasdaq sharply declined in the summer of 2000, this clause ended up being worth more than $1 billion in the deal price.

Source: BOB DAVIS, SPEED IS LIFE 184 (2001).

Fixed Market Value Formula As an alternative to a fixed exchange ratio (with or without a collar), the parties may agree on a fixed market value formula, also referred to as a floating exchange ratio formula. With a *fixed market value formula,* the acquirer offers the target company's shareholders a fixed dollar amount of its shares in exchange for each target company share, with the exact number of the acquirer's shares to be determined based on the market price or value of the acquirer's stock during a specified period prior to closing. If the acquirer's stock price declines in value, the target company's shareholders receive the dollar consideration for their shares specified at the time of the signing of the acquisition agreement by receiving a higher number of the acquirer's shares than may have been anticipated at the time of the signing. On the other hand, if the acquirer's stock price increases in value, the target company's shareholders receive fewer of the acquirer's shares than may have been anticipated, although the dollar value, as of the closing, of the securities issued in exchange for the target's shares is the amount specified in the acquisition agreement.

To at least partially balance the potential fluctuations in the number of shares that may be issued, the parties may negotiate a maximum number of shares that will be issued in the transaction, referred to as a *cap,* or a minimum number of shares that will be issued, referred to as a *floor.* If the number of shares needed to equal the specified dollar amount falls below the floor or rises above the cap, then the acquisition agreement may permit one or both parties to terminate the agreement and not close.

Effect of a Business Combination on Preferred-Stock Rights and Stock Options

Preferred-Stock Rights Triggered by a Business Combination

The basic features of preferred stock and the rights that accompany it (including liquidation preferences) are set forth in detail in Chapter 13. The specific characteristics of preferred stock will vary greatly depending on the terms set forth in a company's certificate of incorporation and bylaws. Nevertheless, certain typical terms of preferred stock are of particular relevance to a business combination.

A business combination may trigger special rights for preferred shareholders, including a liquidation preference, dividend preference, antidilution protection, special voting rights, and redemption provisions. For example, the liquidation preference provides that, upon liquidation of the company, the preferred shareholders will receive the amount of their original investment and, possibly, a preferential return on their investment, including any accrued and declared but unpaid dividends, before the common shareholders receive anything from the transaction. In addition, the preferred shareholders may, after converting their shares into common stock, share the purchase proceeds with the common shareholders and enjoy any other rights given to common shareholders in connection with the transaction. An example of the activation of this liquidation preference appears in Chapter 13.

Treatment of Stock Options

Another factor to consider when planning a business combination is the treatment of stock options. Under many stock option plans, a business combination in which the target company's shareholders receive cash consideration will trigger acceleration of the vesting of the employee stock options. This acceleration may give the option holders the opportunity to exercise their options in full prior to the business combination and receive fully vested shares of stock. In a cash transaction, the target company's option holders will generally choose to exercise their stock options to the extent that their options are *in the money* (that is, to the extent that the consideration to be paid in the business combination exceeds the exercise price of the option).

The stock option plan may provide that any party who acquires the target company in a stock-for-stock transaction must assume the target company's stock option plans on the same terms and conditions as are in effect immediately prior to the business combination. In that case, the options may be exercised after the business combination only for shares of the acquirer's common stock, based on the merger exchange ratio. Under some option plans, the target company's board of directors has the discretion to determine whether the outstanding options will become vested or whether the acquirer will be given the alternative of assuming the stock option plan upon the closing of the transaction. As the treatment of stock options can change the number of shares of a target company's stock that are exchangeable in the transaction or the allocation of consideration between a target company's equity holders, the acquirer and the target company should carefully review the target company's stock option plans to determine how the transaction will affect them.

Tax Treatment

Tax considerations often dictate the form of acquisition in a business combination. An acquisition can be structured as a taxable purchase and sale of assets, a taxable purchase and sale of stock, a taxable merger, or a tax-free reorganization.

Taxable Purchase and Sale of Assets

In a *taxable sale of assets,* the target company must pay tax on the difference between the tax *basis* of the assets sold (which is generally equal to the cost of the assets less depreciation) and the consideration (e.g., cash) paid by the acquirer for the assets, including the amount of any assumed liabilities. Thus, for example, if a target company sells all of its assets, with a tax basis of $6 million, for $8 million in cash, plus the acquirer's assumption of $2 million of the target company's liabilities, then the target company will be required to pay tax on the $4 million gain ($8 million plus $2 million minus $6 million). On the positive side, the acquirer is often able to *step up* (increase) the tax basis of the assets acquired (the value attributable to the assets for tax purposes) to an amount equal to the cash and other consideration paid and the liabilities assumed. This permits the acquirer to depreciate the acquired assets going forward based on the higher, stepped-up value, thereby increasing the amount of depreciation deductions available and potentially decreasing the acquirer's tax liability. For example, if an acquirer pays $10 million for a target company whose assets had been depreciated to $6 million for tax purposes, the acquirer is eligible to take depreciation deductions of $10 million. On the other hand, the target company's net operating losses and other tax attributes are not transferred to the acquirer in a taxable asset purchase.

If the target company liquidates following a taxable asset sale, the target company's shareholders will face an additional level of tax, calculated based on the difference between each shareholder's basis in his or her shares (typically, the cost of those shares) and the amount of cash or other property distributed to the shareholder when the target company is liquidated. Gain or loss realized by the target company's shareholders in connection with a liquidating distribution will typically be a capital gain or loss.

Taxable Forward Merger

A *taxable forward merger* of the target company into the acquirer is taxed the same as an asset sale followed by liquidation of the target company. Tax is imposed at both the corporate level and the shareholder level.

Taxable Purchase and Sale of Stock

In a *taxable purchase and sale of stock*, the target company does not pay any tax, but its shareholders generally pay capital gains tax on the difference between the consideration paid by the acquirer for their stock and their basis for that stock. In a taxable stock purchase and sale, the tax attributes of the target company (such as net operating losses and tax credit carryovers) are generally preserved (in a limited sense), but the target company's basis in its assets remains the same as it was prior to the stock purchase. In other words, the acquirer does not receive a step-up (or step-down) in basis. In the example cited above, the acquirer would be eligible to depreciate only $6 million of asset value. In certain circumstances, a *Section 338 election* can be made to permit the acquirer in a taxable stock purchase to achieve a step-up in basis.

Taxable Reverse Triangular Merger

A *taxable reverse triangular merger* is taxed the same as a taxable stock purchase.

Choosing Among Taxable Alternatives

The interplay of the factors discussed above will determine the acquirer's choice of structure from a tax perspective. From the target company and its shareholders' viewpoint, whether a taxable asset sale or a taxable stock sale is preferable will turn on which alternative will produce the larger after-tax return. As noted above, gains on asset sales are generally taxed twice, first to the target company and subsequently to the target company's shareholders when the sale proceeds are distributed. This double level of taxation (in contrast to a sale of stock, which involves no entity-level tax) causes most taxable sales to be structured as stock sales, absent other factors.

Exceptions to this general rule include (1) sales by S corporations (which generally pay no corporate-level tax); (2) sales by corporations with operating losses, which can shelter the corporate-level tax; and (3) transactions in which nontax considerations are particularly important, as described below. The facts and circumstances of each situation and the objectives of each party must be examined to determine the optimal structure of a particular transaction from a tax perspective.

Tax-free Reorganizations

In addition to taxable purchases and sales of assets or stock and taxable mergers, an acquisition transaction can be structured as a tax-free reorganization. (The term is a bit of a misnomer: tax is not forgiven but merely postponed.) In a *tax-free reorganization,* stock of the acquiring company is exchanged for the stock or assets of the target company. Generally, the selling shareholders will not recognize the gain or loss until they sell the acquiring company stock received in the transaction. In certain types of tax-free reorganizations, the sellers may receive consideration in addition to stock; in that case, taxes are due immediately on the nonstock portion of the total consideration received. This taxable portion is called *boot.*

TYPES OF TAX-FREE REORGANIZATIONS The types of tax-free reorganizations include the following:

- A *statutory merger* under state law in which the target company disappears and, generally, at least 45 percent of the consideration paid by the acquirer to the target company's shareholders consists of the acquirer's stock (called an *A reorganization* because it is described in Section 368(a)(1)(A) of the Internal Revenue Code of 1986, as amended—the *Code*).
- A *stock-for-stock exchange* whereby the acquirer exchanges its voting stock for at least 80 percent of the stock of the target company (a *B reorganization,* described in Section 368(a)(1)(B) of the Code).
- An *exchange of stock of an acquirer for the assets* of a target company, followed by the liquidation of the target company and the distribution of the acquirer's stock to the target company's shareholders, in which at least 80 percent of the consideration paid by the acquirer consists of the acquirer's voting stock (a *C reorganization,* described in Section 368(a)(1)(C) of the Code).
- A *forward triangular merger* whereby the target company is merged into a subsidiary of the acquirer, and at least 45 percent of the total consideration paid by the acquirer to the target company's shareholders consists of the acquirer's stock (as described in Section 368(a)(2)(D) of the Code).
- A *reverse triangular merger* whereby a subsidiary of the acquirer is merged into the target company, and at least 80 percent of the consideration paid by the acquirer to the target company's shareholders consists of the acquirer's voting stock, and the acquirer obtains control of a target company in the transaction (as described in Section 368(a)(2)(E) of the Code).

Exhibits 16.6 to 16.10 outline the requirements for A, B, C, forward triangular merger, and reverse triangular merger reorganizations.

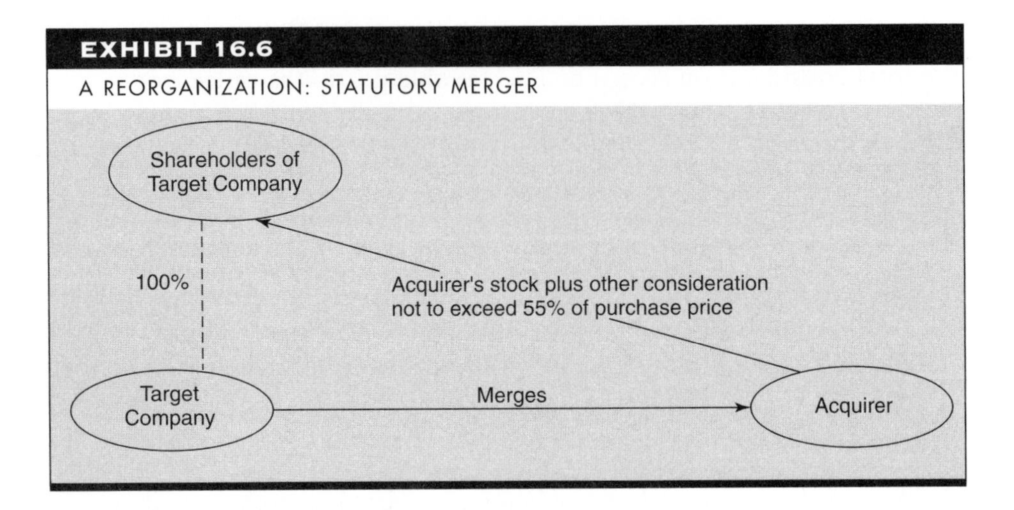

EXHIBIT 16.6

A REORGANIZATION: STATUTORY MERGER

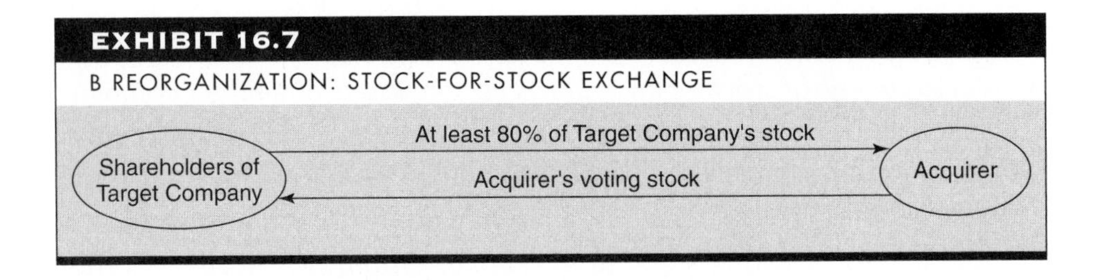

EXHIBIT 16.7

B REORGANIZATION: STOCK-FOR-STOCK EXCHANGE

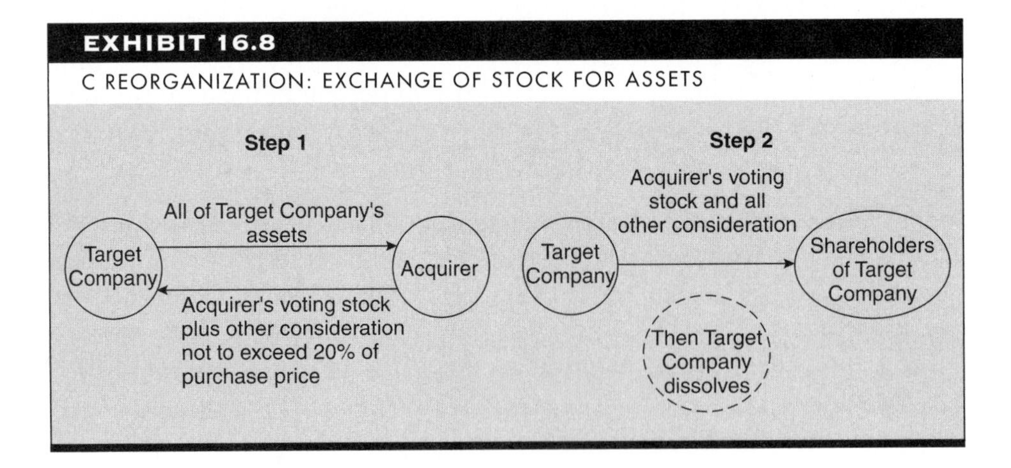

EXHIBIT 16.8

C REORGANIZATION: EXCHANGE OF STOCK FOR ASSETS

EXHIBIT 16.9

FORWARD TRIANGULAR MERGER

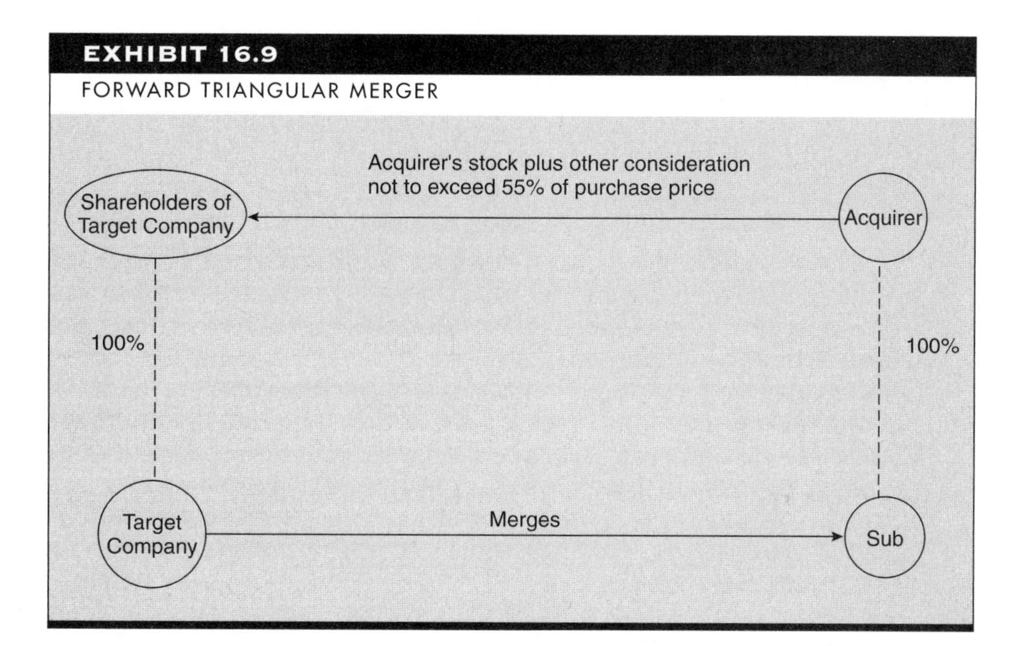

EXHIBIT 16.10

REVERSE TRIANGULAR MERGER

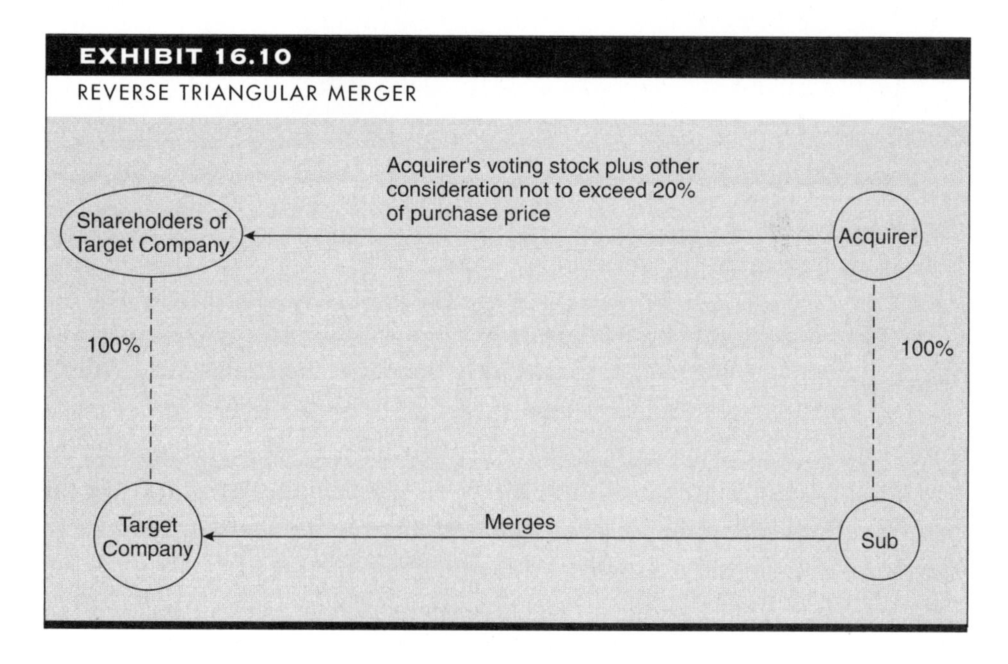

FROM THE TRENCHES

In early 2001, a well-funded, privately held software company entered into discussions with another private company regarding a possible business combination. The target company was quickly running out of cash. As a stopgap, the potential acquirer agreed to purchase shares of the target company's Series E preferred stock representing 25 percent of the target company's total voting stock outstanding. At some point following its initial investment, the acquirer proposed to purchase the rest of the target company's stock, in exchange for the acquirer's voting stock, by way of a reverse triangular merger intended to qualify as a tax-free reorganization.

Unfortunately, the companies faced the risk that the acquirer's Series E investment could cause a subsequent merger to be taxable. The Internal Revenue Service might argue that the transaction failed to meet the reorganization requirement that the acquirer obtain *control of the target company* (i.e., at least 80 percent of the voting power of the target company and at least 80 percent of the total number of shares of each class of the target company's nonvoting stock) *in the transaction* in exchange for the acquirer's voting stock. Fortunately, the parties recognized the issue in time and scaled back the Series E investment to less than 20 percent of the target company's outstanding voting shares. Ultimately, the target company was acquired in a tax-free reverse triangular merger.

NONTAX CONSIDERATIONS

Although tax consequences are critical in determining the structure of an acquisition (including, most importantly, whether the transaction will be tax-free to the shareholders of the target company), other factors come into play as well.[1] The acquirer may be unwilling to issue its stock in the transaction because of the dilutive effect on its earnings per share. On the other hand, the acquirer may be unable to borrow money or otherwise finance the transaction, so its stock may be its only currency.

Certain key contracts of the target company may not be assignable, thus preventing an asset sale. Alternatively, the acquirer may be unwilling to assume certain liabilities of the target company, thus precluding the acquisition of the target company's stock. The acquirer may be willing to take on these liabilities only in a subsidiary, however.

The acquirer may have significantly more favorable financial accounting reporting if it acquires the target company with the acquirer's stock. On the other hand, the target company may be unwilling to accept the risk in receiving the acquirer's stock and will insist on cash. All of these issues must enter the mix with tax considerations when the parties are negotiating the structure of the acquisition transaction.

Securities Law Requirements

If the consideration to be issued by the acquirer in a business combination includes stock or other securities, then the issuance of the securities must be in compliance with federal and state securities laws. As explained in Chapter 7, unless an exemption from registration or qualification is available, the offer and sale of any security must be registered with the Securities and Exchange Commission (SEC) under the Securities Act of 1933 (the 1933 Act) and qualified with the state securities commissions under any applicable Blue Sky laws. In a business combination entailing the issuance of stock that requires a shareholder vote, the decision by the target company's shareholders to approve the transaction is considered tantamount to the investment decision that investors make when deciding to buy securities. As a result, the securities law analysis is similar in both contexts.

A target company and an acquirer are also subject to federal and state laws concerning fraud and misrepresentation in connection with the offer and sale of securities. The antifraud rules apply even if the transaction is exempt from registration and qualification. These laws, along with the contractual provisions of the merger agreement, will offer each party limited protection from fraud by the other party.

Federal Securities Laws

The exemptions that are available for the issuance of securities in a business combination are generally the same as those available in any private placement financing pursuant to Sections 3(b) and 4(2) of the 1933 Act and Regulation D, which provides certain safe harbors under these sections. These include purely intrastate offerings under Section 3(b) and private placements under Section 4(2). Although an acquirer may consider proceeding directly under Section 4(2) of the 1933 Act if all of the target company's shareholders are able both to understand and to bear the risk of the investment, most acquirers will seek to qualify the transaction under the Regulation D safe harbors.

As explained in Chapter 7, offerings of securities of up to $1 million or up to $5 million may be exempted under Rules 504 and 505, respectively, of Regulation D. If the transaction involves the offering of more than $5 million of securities, then the acquirer will often seek to qualify for an exemption under Rule 506.

RULE 506 UNDER REGULATION D Meeting the requirements of Rule 506 can be more onerous in a business combination than when Rule 506 is used in a financing. In a financing, the issuer selects and agrees to each investor. In contrast, when attempting a business combination, the acquirer must work with a fixed group of the target company's shareholders, who may or may not meet the qualifications of Rule 506.

Under Rule 506, an acquirer (which is the issuer of the securities) may offer an unlimited value of securities to any number of *accredited investors* (as defined in Chapter 7) and to no more than thirty-five unaccredited shareholders who, either alone or with a purchaser representative, are deemed to be sophisticated. A *sophisticated* shareholder is one who has enough knowledge and experience in financial and business matters to be capable of evaluating the merits and risks of the prospective investment. The acquirer will generally require the target company's shareholders to complete an investor questionnaire to determine which of the shareholders are accredited and whether those who are not accredited are nonetheless sophisticated. If one or more shareholders oppose the transaction and are unwilling to complete the investor questionnaire, and the acquirer is not otherwise able to reasonably verify the shareholder's accreditation or sophistication, then Rule 506 may not be available as an exemption for the transaction.

If a shareholder is neither accredited nor sophisticated, then Rule 506 requires that a purchaser representative be appointed for that shareholder. A purchaser representative must meet specific requirements set forth in Regulation D and must be acknowledged by the shareholder as his or her

FROM THE TRENCHES

A privately held software company negotiated its sale to a successful public company for $50 million of the acquirer's common stock. One of the conditions for consummation of the transaction was that the acquirer have available an exemption from registration of the shares under Rule 506. The target company's option plan included an early exercise program, which enabled employees to exercise their options prior to the vesting of the options. Many employees had done so, which meant that the target company had approximately one hundred shareholders.

The parties confirmed that approximately seventy of the target company's shareholders could be considered accredited investors for purposes of Rule 506. Of the remaining thirty shareholders, twenty-two could be considered sophisticated because of their educational background and investment experience. The remaining eight shareholders, however, were not considered sophisticated for purposes of Rule 506 because they possessed neither the requisite educational background nor the investment experience.

The acquirer required these remaining eight shareholders to appoint the president of the target company as their purchaser representative. Seven of the eight shareholders were willing to do so; the remaining shareholder, who had been fired by the target company six months previously, refused to do so, thereby throwing the whole transaction into question. Fortunately, one of the other officers of the company was able to persuade the former employee that, whatever grievances he might have against management, his refusal to appoint a representative was only hurting his friends who remained employed by the company. Moreover, if the dissident preferred to appoint someone other than the president of the company as his own purchaser representative, he was free to do so. He also remained free to vote against the transaction if he believed it was not a good deal. Having had his fifteen minutes of fame, the former employee appointed one of the other shareholders who was an accredited investor as his purchaser representative, and the transaction was consummated.

representative. By agreeing to this representation, the shareholder becomes, in effect, sophisticated (albeit, not accredited).

REGULATION D INFORMATION REQUIREMENTS An acquirer can issue up to $1 million of its securities pursuant to the exemption set forth in Rule 504 of Regulation D without regard to the qualifications or number of the target company's shareholders. Acquirers offering securities pursuant to Rule 504 do not have to provide any particular information to the target's shareholders (although, as noted in Chapter 7, full disclosure is often prudent to avoid antifraud liability). If, however, (1) the transaction involves the issuance of more than $1 million of the acquirer's stock, and (2) any of the target's shareholders are not accredited investors, then Regulation D requires the acquirer to furnish the target company's shareholders with information regarding the securities and the business combination within a reasonable period of time prior to the closing of the transaction.

In particular, Rule 502 of Regulation D requires that the acquirer provide the target company's shareholders with information that is substantially similar to the information the acquirer would be required to provide if it were offering registered securities. The information required by Rule 502 is, however, limited to that which is "material to an understanding of the issuer [the acquirer], its business and the securities being offered." The disclosure document containing this information is often referred to as an *information statement* or a *private-placement memorandum*. This document is discussed in more detail in Chapter 7.

SECTION 3(A)(10) If the acquirer does not want to register the offering, but the offering does not qualify under Section 4(2) of the 1933 Act or any of the exemptions provided by Regulation D, an alternative to registration may be available under Section 3(a)(10) of the 1933 Act. Section 3(a)(10) provides an exemption from the federal registration requirements for securities issued in business combinations when a duly authorized state government agency has held a fairness hearing and approved of the terms and conditions of the transaction. A particular advantage of proceeding under Section 3(a)(10) is that stock issued in the transaction to shareholders who were not affiliates of the target is freely tradable and not subject to restrictions on resale.

The Section 3(a)(10) exemption is potentially quite useful, but unfortunately only a limited number of states (including California) provide a mechanism for fairness hearings. The states that do conduct fairness hearings generally require a nexus between the state and the parties to the business combination.

State Securities Laws

In addition to complying with federal securities laws, the acquirer must also comply with any applicable state securities laws. In general, the acquirer must comply with the Blue Sky laws of (1) the state where the acquirer has its principal place of business (and, if different, the state from which the offers will emanate), (2) the state where the target company has its principal place of business, and (3) the states where any of the target company's shareholders reside or have their principal place of business. Chapter 7 outlines exemptions available in certain states.

Protection from Fraud and Misrepresentation

The best way for a party to ensure that it is protected from fraud and misrepresentation in a business combination is to conduct a thorough due diligence investigation and to ensure that protective provisions are included in the merger agreement. The merger agreement will generally provide specific representations and warranties regarding the parties, and it may provide indemnification or other protection if the representations and warranties or covenants of a target company turn out to be false or misleading.

If, however, a party to the transaction believes that it has been misled by the other side, it may seek to go beyond the negotiated contractual protections in the acquisition agreement and bring an action for common-law fraud or, if the transaction involves securities, a claim under Rule 10b-5 of the Securities Exchange Act of 1934. In either case, the plaintiff faces an onerous task as the standard of proof to show fraud or misrepresentation is high. Parties to a privately negotiated sale of securities may find broader rights of recovery under the antifraud provisions of applicable state securities laws.

FROM THE TRENCHES

Randall Rissman owned two-thirds of the stock of Tiger Electronics, a toy and game company founded by his father. His brother Arnold owned the balance. After the brothers had a falling out, Arnold sold his shares to Randall for $17 million. Thirteen months later, Tiger sold its assets to toymaker Hasbro for $335 million. Arnold sued Randall, claiming that Randall had deceived him into thinking that Tiger would never be taken public or sold to a third party. Believing that his stock would remain illiquid and not pay further dividends, Arnold had sold his shares for whatever Randall was willing to pay. Arnold sought the extra $95 million he would have received had he retained his stock until the sale to Hasbro.

During the negotiation of the sale of his shares to Randall, Arnold asked Randall to represent in writing that Tiger would never be sold. Randall refused; instead, he warranted (accurately) that he was not aware of any offers to purchase Tiger and was not engaged in negotiations for its sale. Arnold and Randall also agreed that if Tiger were sold before Arnold had received all installments of the purchase price, then payment of the principal and interest would be accelerated. Arnold represented in the stock-sale agreement that "this Agreement is executed by [Arnold] freely and voluntarily, and without reliance upon any statement or representation by Purchaser, the Company, any of the Affiliates or O.R. Rissman or any of their attorneys or agents. . . ."

The court dismissed Arnold's securities law claims, reasoning that "[s]ecurities law does not permit a party to a stock transaction to disavow such representation—to say, in effect, 'I lied when I told you I wasn't relying on your prior statements' and then to seek damages for their contents." The court pointed out that Arnold could have avoided this result if he had negotiated an arrangement whereby he would accept less than what Randall was willing to pay unconditionally (say, $10 million) but receive a kicker if Tiger were sold or taken public.

Source: Rissman v. Rissman, 213 F.3d 381 (7th Cir. 2000).

Restrictions on Resale

In a business combination in which the target company's shareholders receive stock issued pursuant to an exemption under the 1933 Act, other than under Section 3(a)(10), the stock is deemed to be *restricted,* that is, subject to restrictions on resale. In addition, when affiliates of the target company receive stock in a business combination, that stock will also be deemed to be restricted. This is the case even when the stock has been registered under a registration statement filed with the SEC. Restricted securities may not be offered or sold by a target company's shareholders unless they are subsequently registered under the 1933 Act or exempted from registration.

RULES 144 AND 145 The most commonly relied upon exemption for the resale of restricted stock by the target company's shareholders is Rule 144 adopted by the SEC under the 1933 Act. As explained in Chapter 7, Rule 144 provides a safe harbor that often allows restricted securities issued by a publicly held company that provides current public information to be resold in the open market one year after the restricted stock is acquired, subject to certain volume and manner of sale requirements. Shares issued by a private company that have been held by a nonaffiliate seller for at least two years can be freely resold under Rule 144(k) without any restriction. Affiliates cannot sell under Rule 144(k). Registered securities and securities offered pursuant to Section 3(a)(10) that are issued to a target company's affiliates in a business combination are, pursuant to Rule 145 of the 1933 Act, deemed to be restricted; they can be sold in accordance with all of the resale limitations of Rule 144, except that there is no requirement that the seller own them for at least one year prior to resale.

In addition to restrictions on resale resulting from federal and state securities laws, the resale of acquirer stock may be restricted by contractual obligations agreed to by all, or some, of the target company's shareholders. Such restrictions will generally be in the form of a *lockup* agreement, which prohibits the shareholders from transferring or selling the securities for a certain period of time after the closing of the transaction or prior to a public offering or other specified event.

REGISTRATION RIGHTS If the target company's shareholders receive unregistered or restricted securities, the acquisition agreement may include provisions obligating the acquirer to register the shareholders' resale of the stock at some later date, typically on a short-form Form S-3 registration statement. Registration rights are discussed in more detail in Chapter 13.

Accounting Treatment

Pursuant to recent changes in U.S. generally accepted accounting principles, companies must account for all business combinations under the purchase method of accounting. Pooling treatment is no longer available. Under the *purchase method,* (1) all of the assets and liabilities acquired from the target company must be recorded on the acquirer's balance sheet at their fair value; (2) any excess of the purchase price over the fair value of the assets acquired must be recognized as goodwill; and (3) all intangible assets with finite lives must be amortized over their estimated useful lives. The goodwill will remain on the acquirer's books until the acquirer determines that the fair value of the goodwill is less than its carrying amount (that is, that it has become *impaired*). Any goodwill must be tested for *impairment* annually and upon the occurrence of certain significant events. Once the value of the goodwill has become impaired, the carrying amount of the goodwill on the acquirer's balance sheet must be reduced to its current fair value. Any reductions in goodwill must be taken as a charge against income; as a result, they will reduce earnings.

Antitrust Compliance

The U.S. Department of Justice and the Federal Trade Commission act as enforcement agents for the federal antitrust laws. They seek out information to determine whether any potential business combination or significant acquisition of assets (including those involving exclusive licenses) would lessen or stifle competition in any given market. Certain transactions, including most forms of business combinations, require companies to comply with federal notification and waiting period requirements, as set forth by the Hart-Scott-Rodino Antitrust Improvements Act of 1976, as amended (the HSR Act).

Transactions affecting competition in the European Union may require filing with the European Commission, which may impose its own requirements for approval. For example, General Electric's proposed acquisition of Honeywell was approved by the U.S. authorities but blocked by the European Commission.

Parties that engage in a transaction valued at more than $50 million generally trigger the HSR Act filing requirements and waiting periods. Transactions that do not exceed $50 million in value are not subject to the HSR Act notification and waiting period requirements. Parties to transactions that are valued at less than $50 million must pay particular attention to how their valuation is calculated. For private target companies, the value of a securities transaction will be the acquisition price. If the acquisition price has not been set, the value of the transaction will be the fair market value of the stock, as determined by the acquirer's board of directors.

The filing requirements call for disclosure of certain information and documents regarding the filing party and the proposed transaction. In addition, the acquiring party must pay a filing fee from the three-tiered filing fee structure of the HSR Act; fees range from $45,000 to $280,000, based on the size of the transaction. The parties to a business combination may negotiate to share or shift the obligation to pay the filing fee either initially or by reimbursing the other party later.

After making any required filings under the HSR Act, the parties will have to submit to a waiting period that lasts for a set number of days depending on the type of transaction (typically, thirty calendar days in a merger and fifteen days in a cash tender offer), unless the governing agency (1) approves a request for early termination or (2) launches a formal investigation by issuing a *second request*, demanding more information about the parties and the proposed transaction. If the agency requests more information, then the waiting period can extend for months, as happened in connection with the merger of America Online and Time Warner.

Shareholder Approval and Dissenters' Rights

In general, the shareholders of the constituent corporations in a business combination must approve the transaction. The *constituent corporations* generally include the target company, any subsidiary of the acquirer used in a triangular transaction, and, in certain cases, the acquirer. Although the acquirer may be deemed to be a constituent party to the transaction, under state law, most transactions that use a triangular structure do not require approval by the acquirer's shareholders unless the transaction requires a change in the acquirer's articles of incorporation. If, however, the acquirer is a publicly traded company and the transaction involves the issuance of a substantial amount of the acquirer's stock (generally, 20 percent of an acquirer's outstanding shares at the time of the merger), then stock exchange rules will generally require the acquirer to obtain the approval of its shareholders.

The target company will generally be required to obtain the affirmative vote of the holders of a majority of its outstanding shares to approve a

FROM THE TRENCHES

A privately held Internet company that could not secure a new round of venture financing agreed to be acquired by a large publicly held corporation for $20 million in cash in a reverse triangular merger. The holders of the Internet company's preferred stock, however, were entitled to receive a liquidation preference of $25 million upon the sale of the company before any proceeds from the sale would be distributable to the common shareholders. Accordingly, under the planned transaction, not only would the preferred shareholders not receive their full liquidation preference, but the common shareholders (mainly the founders and employees holding options) would not receive any consideration at all.

The target company was organized under California law. Therefore, the approval of the holders of a majority of its outstanding shares of common stock, voting as a class, was required, as well as the approval of the holders of a majority of its outstanding shares of preferred stock. The acquirer was concerned that as the common shareholders were to receive nothing for their shares, they would vote against the transaction. Moreover, the target company's employees, who were critical to the future success of the company's products, would probably be less motivated going forward if they received no reward for their past efforts.

Accordingly, the acquirer demanded that the preferred shareholders agree to reduce their liquidation preference so that $5 million of the purchase price could be allocated to the common shareholders. The acquirer also demanded that another $2 million of the purchase price be set aside in an employee retention pool, which would be payable over time to the employees if and when the target company met certain product development milestones. Faced with the prospect of not being able to secure the vote of the common shareholders and thus losing their last opportunity for a liquidity event, the preferred shareholders agreed to the acquirer's demands.

merger or consolidation, the sale of all or substantially all of the company's assets, or any other extraordinary transaction. However, some states and some companies' charter documents may require a higher percentage to approve a transaction. In addition, some states and the charter documents of some companies may provide that the company must obtain the affirmative vote of a majority of the holders of a certain class or series of the company's stock in order to approve the transaction. Finally, if the proposed transaction involves a stock purchase, asset purchase, or a merger with an interested shareholder, many jurisdictions will require a *supermajority* vote, typically 80 percent or higher, to approve the transaction.

As noted earlier, if the acquiring corporation holds 90 percent or more of the outstanding shares of a target company's stock, many states allow the completion of a merger without the approval of the target company's shareholders. In such a transaction, called a *short-form merger,* the acquiring corporation can effect the merger through a resolution of its board of directors and by filing the specified certificate with the target company's state of incorporation.

Dissenters' Rights

To protect the shareholders' ability to receive the fair value of their securities in a business combination, most states provide some form of *dissenters'* or *appraisal rights,* which entitle dissenting shareholders to receive cash equal to the fair market value of their target securities. Because fair market value is generally calculated without taking into account the effect of the merger or other transaction giving rise to the rights, the cash due the dissenting shareholders may be less than the acquisition consideration.

Dissenters' rights are generally available to shareholders of nonpublic companies who are required to vote on a business combination transaction. To exercise this right, shareholders must vote against the proposed transaction and give notice to the target company that they have so voted and that they are demanding an appraisal of the fair value of their securities. If the company and the shareholders are unable to agree on a satisfactory amount, the shareholders can file a claim for appraisal in court.

THE MERGER PROCESS

Although the following discussion speaks specifically to the completion of a merger, the process is generally similar in any form of business combination. Additional information regarding stock purchases and related issues can be found in Chapter 7.

Overview of Steps

As the first step in a business combination, small teams from both the target company and the potential acquirer will generally meet for preliminary discussions of the business and financial aspects of the proposed transaction. Some companies will engage an investment bank to provide financial advice at this stage. Once the parties decide to begin due diligence and engage in further discussions about the potential business combination, legal counsel will help prepare an agreement regarding the confidential treatment of nonpublic information and, potentially, an exclusivity agreement and other preliminary documents.

After the confidentiality agreement is in place, the parties will begin the due diligence review process, and management will begin strategic negotiations. The parties may prepare a letter of intent that outlines the principal terms of a transaction.

With guidance from management, legal counsel (generally, for the acquirer) will prepare a draft of the merger agreement, and the parties will negotiate the terms of the agreement. After the companies' respective boards of directors review the terms of the merger agreement and determine that the transaction is fair to the company and its shareholders, the agreement will be executed.

In cases where all necessary consents and approvals can be arranged in advance, the parties can close the transaction promptly. In this event, the merger agreement generally will not contain covenants or conditions of the parties and, as a result, is a much simpler document than an agreement that provides for a delayed closing. If the transaction will not close for some period of time after an acquisition agreement is signed, then the merger agreement will contain both covenants as to the behavior of the parties prior to the closing and conditions to both parties' obligations to complete the transaction.

Once the merger agreement is signed, the parties will make any necessary governmental or other filings, and the target company will set the date of its shareholders' meeting or commence the process of soliciting written consents from the shareholders. After the target company shareholders (and, if necessary, the acquirer's shareholders) have approved the merger, and all necessary third-party consents and other approvals have been received, the parties will close the transaction, file a certificate of merger in the target company's state of incorporation, begin integrating the companies, and deal with any postclosing purchase price adjustments. Exhibit 16.11 pre-sents an example of a merger timeline.

Confidentiality Agreements

In the preliminary stages of a business combination, each party will generally require access to confidential, nonpublic information regarding the other party. To protect the confidentiality of this information and to prevent it from being used unfairly if the merger negotiations break down, the parties will generally enter into a confidentiality agreement. Most confidentiality agreements set forth the parties' obligations regarding the use and disclosure of nonpublic information and various other related matters, including the return of confidential information if the merger is not completed. The parties should ensure that the confidentiality agreement is in place before they exchange any nonpublic information in the due diligence review or engage in discussions regarding their strategic plans and other nonpublic issues.

Exclusivity Agreements

Even in the early stages of a business combination, the negotiations and due diligence review can be very time-consuming and expensive. Accordingly, an acquirer may ask a target company to enter into an *exclusivity,* or *no-shop,* agreement, in which the target company agrees for a specified period of time not to solicit or encourage an acquisition proposal from

EXHIBIT 16.11

SAMPLE MERGER TIMELINE

Presigning Period	Signing	Period Between Signing and Closing	Closing	Post-closing Period
• Parties execute confidentiality agreement and, potentially, exclusivity agreement. • Acquirer conducts presigning due diligence review. • Parties determine transaction structure. • Parties may execute letter of intent or term sheet. • Parties negotiate definitive merger agreement.	• Parties execute definitive merger agreement.	• Parties make necessary governmental filings and obtain consents and approvals. • Target company's shareholders and, potentially, acquirer's shareholders, vote on transaction.	• Acquirer delivers consideration (stock, cash, or notes). • File agreement of merger with secretary of state.	• Make postclosing purchase price adjustments and assert potential indemnification claims. • Publicly announce merger. • Integrate companies.

any other company that may be interested in entering into merger negotiations and will not provide another company nonpublic information or participate in any potential merger-related discussions or negotiations. The duration and specific terms of a no-shop agreement will vary from deal to deal, but a typical no-shop agreement by a private company restricts the target company for approximately one month.

Because the directors of a corporation that has agreed to a transaction involving a change of control may, under certain circumstances, have a fiduciary duty to consider competing bids, the target company may request a *fiduciary out,* which permits the target board to take steps that might otherwise violate the exclusivity agreement if, in the good-faith judgment of the target directors, the steps are necessary to fulfill their fiduciary duties.

Letters of Intent

In the early stages of negotiating a business combination, the parties will generally want to settle the key terms of the transaction. These terms may include an agreement on the price or the pricing formula, the form of acquisition, tax treatment, closing conditions, and employee issues. To memorialize these details, the parties may decide to enter into a *letter of intent* or prepare a *term sheet.*

FROM THE TRENCHES

A target company entered into an exclusivity agreement barring it from considering any other offers unless, in the opinion of counsel for the target board of directors, such consideration was necessary to fulfill their fiduciary duties. Although the company's counsel opined that consideration of a competing offer was consistent with the directors' fiduciary obligation, counsel declined to opine that it was necessary. When the target directors decided that, in their minds, consideration of the competing bid was necessary to fulfill their fiduciary duties, the potential acquirer sued the target company for breach of contract. The Delaware Court of Chancery struck down the no-shop agreement, holding that the board could not delegate to its counsel the power to decide what was required to satisfy its fiduciary duties.

Source: Ace Ltd. v. Capital Re Corp., 747 A.2d 95 (Del. Ch. 1999).

A letter of intent or term sheet can help focus negotiations and make the process of finalizing terms for the merger agreement more efficient. A letter of intent or term sheet may also create a "moral" commitment that will influence a party's decision to propose a change in the terms of a transaction after a letter of intent is executed or the parties preliminarily agree on a term sheet. In addition, a letter of intent or term sheet will generally permit the parties to make any required filing under the HSR Act and to begin the HSR waiting period prior to the execution of the definitive merger agreement.

A letter of intent or term sheet can present a serious problem, however, if negotiations break down and one party tries to seek enforcement of the letter as a binding contract. If the document can be interpreted as binding, the terminating party may be liable to the other side if a merger agreement is not executed. To avoid this potential liability, it is generally not advisable for parties to enter into a binding letter of intent or term sheet. If the parties desire to enter into a letter of intent, it is important that the document specifically identify the terms that the parties intend to be binding, and those that are intended to be nonbinding. The execution of a letter of intent may also complicate the disclosure obligations of a public company.

Public Announcement of the Merger

Once the merger agreement has been executed, the companies will generally issue a joint press release announcing the terms of the transaction. If one or both of the parties are subject to the reporting requirements under the Securities Exchange Act of 1934, certain restrictions regarding disclosure will apply, and filings must be made with the SEC, depending on the type of transaction and its materiality to the parties.

DUE DILIGENCE

As in a venture financing, discussed in Chapter 13, or in preparation for a company's initial public offering, discussed in Chapter 17, due diligence is crucial in a business combination. Through this process, the acquirer examines the target company's business, financial condition, and legal affairs. Due diligence enables the acquirer to independently verify whether the target company's assets equal its expectations, to identify any required contractual or governmental consents, and to uncover any potential liabilities or issues that may make the merger unattractive. In addition, due diligence is often the best way of determining the true value of the target company to the acquirer.

In some acquisitions, generally those in which the acquirer's stock is offered as consideration, the target company may conduct a due diligence review of the acquirer. Usually, the target company's due diligence investigation will be less extensive than an acquirer's review.

Generally, the acquirer will provide the target company with a list of documents relating to the target company and each of its subsidiaries and predecessors that the acquirer wishes to examine. The acquirer will seek documents containing information concerning the following:

- General corporate matters such as minutes of the board of directors and charter documents.
- The target company's capital stock and other securities.
- Financial performance, including balance sheet and income statement.
- Any indebtedness.
- Taxes.
- Employment matters.
- Past, pending, or threatened litigation.
- Intellectual property, including schedules of patents, copyrights, and trademarks.
- Environmental issues and liabilities.

Gathering due diligence materials is time-consuming and difficult. Therefore, the requesting company should ensure that the due diligence request list is carefully tailored to reflect the specific terms of the transaction and the nature of the target company.

Generally, the acquiring company will lead the due diligence investigation and will allocate the review of certain information to its legal counsel and its accountants. In addition, if investment bankers have been retained to deliver an opinion as to the fairness of the transaction to the target company or the

FROM THE TRENCHES

In the summer of 2000, a software company sought to acquire a smaller start-up company that claimed to have rights to certain technology that was of significant value to the software company. The parties entered into negotiations and agreed on the basic terms for a proposed transaction prior to the commencement of a comprehensive due diligence investigation by the software company. Once the due diligence process began, it became clear to the software company that there was significant doubt as to whether the start-up company actually owned the desired technology. In particular, the founders of the start-up company appeared to have developed the technology while still employed by another company and prior to founding the start-up company. Although no single fact confirmed this doubt, the software company's due diligence team was able to determine that the start-up company was organized several weeks before the founders actually resigned their positions at their previous employer; furthermore, they had filed for a patent on the technology they claimed to have developed completely on their own within a week of their resignation. Although the founders might have conceived of the technology so quickly after resigning, it would have been almost impossible for them to have conceived of it, retained legal counsel, and prepared detailed patent applications in such a short period of time. Rather than risk facing a lawsuit from the founders' prior employer, the software company elected not to pursue the transaction further.

acquirer and its shareholders, the investment bankers may wish to review certain information. As the due diligence materials are being reviewed, and potential issues are uncovered, the reviewing teams should keep management fully informed. This information could be crucial to help management in the merger negotiations and may lead to the addition of representations and warranties or escrow, indemnification, or other protective provisions in the merger agreement to address potential liabilities. In addition, the due diligence review will be useful in analyzing the target company's disclosure schedule, discussed below. Finally, material issues uncovered during due diligence should be discussed with each party's board of directors to help the board fulfill its fiduciary obligations to make an informed decision regarding the transaction.

The Merger Agreement

The merger agreement sets forth the terms and conditions of the business combination and will govern the behavior of the parties prior to the closing of the merger and their rights and obligations to each other after the closing. Although details vary, most merger agreements have a similar overall structure.

General Provisions

Most merger agreements contain provisions that set forth the parties, the securities being acquired, the purchase price or exchange ratio (including any earn-out or escrow provisions), a description of the structure of the merger, the treatment of outstanding stock options, and the terms of any purchase price adjustment.

Representations and Warranties

Representations and warranties serve three main purposes in a merger agreement. First, they are a method for obtaining disclosure about the contracting parties before the execution of the merger agreement. Second, they serve as a foundation for a party's right to indemnification (and, potentially, a common-law claim for fraud) if a party discovers after the closing that the other party has breached one or more of its representations or warranties. Finally, they provide a basis for conditions to the parties' obligations to close the transaction. Indemnification provisions and closing conditions are discussed later in this chapter.

Each party to the merger agreement will make representations and warranties to the other party regarding its business and financial condition. Representations and warranties about the business of a target company generally include information regarding the target company's organization, the accuracy of its financial statements, title to its assets, the absence of liabilities and legal proceedings, compliance with laws, tax and environmental matters, contractual obligations, and full disclosure of all facts necessary to ensure that the representations and warranties are not misleading. The representations and warranties of an acquirer are typically much less extensive than those of a target company.

Representations and warranties can be absolute, such as "there is no pending legal proceeding and no person has threatened to commence any legal proceeding against the target company," or they can be modified by a *knowledge qualifier,* such as "to the best of the target company's knowledge, there is no pending legal proceeding and no person has threatened to commence any legal proceeding against the target company." Because knowledge qualifiers shift the risk that a representation or warranty may be untrue even though the target company believes it to be true, a target company will seek to include as many knowledge qualifiers as possible. An acquirer naturally will resist knowledge qualifiers because the damages resulting from an inaccurate representation are the same regardless of whether or not the target company knew of the problem.

An important part of the representations and warranties in most merger agreements is the information set forth in the accompanying disclosure schedule. Disclosure schedules are discussed in detail later in this chapter.

Covenants

Covenants include the obligations of the parties to take, or refrain from taking, certain actions between the execution of a merger agreement and the closing of the merger. The performance of all covenants is often a condition to each party's obligation to complete the transaction.

Indemnification Provisions

In a merger, the acquirer, or its subsidiary if a triangular structure is used, will assume all of the liabilities of the target company by operation of law. To avoid this liability, an acquirer may require a target company to provide indemnification with respect to any breach of the target company's representations and warranties in the merger agreement and potentially other identified liabilities. The provisions regarding indemnification raise many issues that are often among the most intensively negotiated in the merger agreement.

One indemnification issue is the extent to which a target company's shareholders should be liable for any potential indemnification. If the target company is owned by more than one shareholder, the acquirer will generally request that the shareholders who are selling their shares of the target company's stock be held jointly and severally liable for any potential indemnification claims. However, a shareholder's exposure to this potential liability will usually be limited to his or her percentage ownership in the target company. Moreover, in certain situations, it may be more appropriate to impose different liability on different shareholders, depending on the representations made. For example, the shareholders may be held jointly and severally liable for representations regarding the target company but be held individually liable for any representations regarding their individual shares.

Another issue is the duration of the indemnification. In general, a target company will seek to limit the time during which a claim for indemnification can be made (often one year), while an acquirer may require that a target company's shareholders be responsible for certain matters, such as environmental liabilities or liability under previously filed tax returns, for an indefinite period of time.

To secure payment of any indemnification claim, an acquirer may require that a portion of the purchase price (whether in cash or shares of the acquirer's stock) be placed in *escrow.* If an escrow is used, the release of the consideration from escrow will usually be tied to the expiration of the indemnification claim period set forth in the merger agreement, though the target company will often seek to provide for the release of the escrowed amount at an earlier time.

A target company will often seek limits on the indemnification obligations of its shareholders. One such limitation, called a *deductible,* sets a minimum amount of damages that must be exceeded before the target company's shareholders are liable to the acquirer. An acquirer will often agree to the deductible but may insist on characterizing it as a *threshold* that will entitle the acquirer to recover all damages that are incurred once the threshold is crossed, not merely the amount over the deductible. For example, in a recent contract for the sale of a distribution company for $50 million, the contract provided for a $500,000 threshold. Once the claims exceeded $500,000, the acquirer was permitted to recover every dollar of claims, not just claims above the initial $500,000. In the alternative, if the contract provided for a $500,000 deductible rather than a threshold, once the claims exceeded $500,000, the acquirer would be permitted to recover only claims above the initial $500,000 and would forgo recovery of the first $500,000 in damages.

In addition to a deductible or threshold, a target company will generally seek to limit the maximum exposure of its shareholders to all or a portion of the purchase price. If the acquirer seeks an escrow of a portion of the purchase price, the target company's shareholders will likely try to limit their total exposure to the amount of the escrow.

Conditions to the Closing

If the merger will not be closed shortly after the merger agreement is signed by the parties, the agreement will contain conditions that must be satisfied in order for the parties to be obligated to close the merger. These provisions are often of particular importance to the target company because tightly drawn closing conditions will reduce the likelihood that the acquirer will be able to withdraw from the merger. An acquirer may seek a closing condition that provides that the acquirer will not be obligated to close the transaction if it is not satisfied with the results of its due diligence investigation. In most circumstances, due diligence should be completed before a merger agreement is signed, and this closing condition should be resisted by the target company. An acquirer can almost always identify some problem uncovered during the due diligence process that can serve as a justification for not closing the transaction. As a result, a diligence-based closing condition effectively converts a merger agreement into an option to acquire the target company.

Common closing conditions include the following:

- The representations and warranties made by the other party are true and correct as of the date of the merger agreement and the closing date.
- The covenants or obligations of the parties have been performed or waived.
- The transaction is in compliance with federal and state securities laws.
- Shareholder approval and third-party consents have been received.

- Any necessary governmental approval has been obtained.
- Key employees have entered into new employment agreements.
- There has not been any material adverse effect on the other party.

In the negotiation of a merger agreement, parties generally focus particular attention on two closing conditions. The first is the accuracy of the representations and warranties made by the parties as of the date of the merger agreement and the closing date. The second is the effect of events between signing and closing that have had, or could have, a material adverse effect on the target company.

ACCURACY OF REPRESENTATIONS AND WARRANTIES If a party's representations and warranties are incorrect as of the date of the merger agreement or the closing date of the merger, the other party is often provided a right not to close the transaction. To enable a target company to avoid a situation in which an acquirer uses trivial breaches of the target company's representations to walk away from the transaction, closing conditions related to the accuracy of representations and warranties often include materiality qualifications. Such qualifications provide that the acquirer will be required to close the merger unless the representations and warranties are not true and correct *in all material respects* as of the date of the merger agreement or the closing date or unless any inaccuracies in the representations and warranties as of the date of the merger agreement or the closing date result in a *material adverse effect* on the target company.

ABSENCE OF MATERIAL ADVERSE EVENTS Typically, an acquirer will assume the ordinary course of business risks of a target company during the time between signing and closing. However, the assignment of risk for an event outside the ordinary course of business that has had, or could have, a material adverse effect on the business or financial condition of the target company is often heavily negotiated. From the target company's perspective, the events causing a material adverse effect could have occurred as a result of the announcement of the merger, so the risk is more properly borne by the acquirer. In addition, a target company may take the position that the risk should be borne by the acquirer because, once the merger agreement has been announced, the business community may view the target company as *damaged goods* that would have a lower value if it were to attempt a business combination with another party. From the acquirer's perspective, the allocation of this risk to the target company is more appropriate as, at the closing of the merger, the acquirer wants to obtain the company it agreed to acquire, not a potentially damaged company. A possible compromise is for the parties to agree that certain events, such as those caused by the announcement of the transaction or by a turn in the target company's industry or general economic conditions, will not alone, or collectively, constitute a material adverse effect. These exceptions must be carefully drafted, however, to ensure that the risks of a material adverse effect are properly allocated.

Termination

Typically, a merger agreement may be terminated by a party if there is a material breach by the other party. In addition, a merger agreement will generally provide that the agreement may be terminated by either party if the merger has not been completed by a specified date, if a court order has prohibited the merger, or if the required shareholder approval has been sought but not obtained.

If the merger agreement is terminated without fault from either party, there will generally not be any further obligations under the agreement, although each party will usually have a continuing obligation to pay its own expenses and maintain the confidentiality of the other party's information. However, if the terminating party shows that a breach by the other party caused the termination, certain rights and liabilities of the parties may remain in effect.

The Disclosure Schedule

A critical element of the representations and warranties of a target company is the *disclosure schedule,* also known as the *schedule of exceptions.* The disclosure schedule is a mechanism for the target company to provide information with respect to, or to disclose any exceptions to, the representations and warranties made in the merger agreement. For example, the merger agreement is likely to contain a representation that all material contracts of the target company are listed on the disclosure schedule.

When properly completed, the disclosure schedule will provide a complete picture of the representations and warranties made in the merger agreement and can provide an acquirer with a valuable reference to help it complete a thorough due diligence review. The acquirer should review the disclosure schedule very carefully, however, because it may include both material and immaterial information. The acquirer will be deemed to have been given notice of all information included in the disclosure schedule and will generally lose its right to terminate the transaction or to postclosing indemnification for matters identified in the disclosure schedule.

A target company will typically deliver the final disclosure schedule when the merger agreement is executed. If the transaction will close some period of time after an acquisition agreement is signed, the target company may need to add information to the disclosure schedule between signing and closing to include developments that occur prior to the closing. The parties will need to determine the effect of this additional disclosure on both the closing condition related to the continued accuracy of the representations and warranties and the indemnification obligations.

Board Approval and Fiduciary Duties

Generally, each party to the merger agreement must obtain approval to enter into the agreement from the respective party's board of directors. As explained in Chapter 6, under state and common law, directors have specific fiduciary duties to their constituent shareholders.

The duty of care requires that the board be fully informed prior to making the business decision to enter into the transaction. Therefore, prior to executing the merger agreement, the respective boards will meet and discuss the terms of the proposed transaction. The meeting may include a presentation from the company's investment advisers regarding the fairness of the transaction and the delivery of a fairness opinion. In addition, the company's legal advisers may explain the material legal terms of the transaction.

The duty of loyalty requires that the directors from the respective boards refrain from any conduct that could injure their company or its shareholders or deprive the target company or its shareholders of any profit or advantage. In other words, the directors must act in good faith and avoid transactions in which they have any personal or financial interest that is adverse to the interests of the company. If a director does have such an interest, certain procedures should be followed to ensure that the board, as a whole, is able to fulfill its obligations to the shareholders. The director may be required to abstain from voting on the transaction, to disclose his or her interests to the shareholders, or, in extreme circumstances, to delegate the consideration of the transaction to a special committee of directors who do not have such a personal or financial interest.

Although the board of directors must fulfill its fiduciary duties and carefully review the terms and conditions of the merger agreement, most, if not all, states provide that the board has satisfied its duties to the shareholders if the board acted on an informed basis, in good faith, and with the honest belief that the actions it was taking were in the best interests of the company. This presumption is called the *business judgment rule*. In circumstances involving a *sale of control* of a company, however, courts will review the actions of directors with *enhanced scrutiny* and will impose an obligation to obtain the highest price reasonably available to the company's shareholders. This duty is often referred to as the *Revlon duty*. "Revlon duties" do not apply in most stock-for-stock transactions, but it is not always clear whether a board is subject to "Revlon duties" with respect to a particular transaction. Finally, the business judgment rule may not apply if one or more of the directors has a financial or personal interest in the transaction. It is important to consult with counsel to ensure that the board is acting appropriately with respect to any business combination transaction.

Other Documents Related to the Merger

A business combination may also require various other documents including a general release, employment contracts, and noncompetition agreements.

General Release

In some transactions, an acquirer may be concerned that a target company has undisclosed liabilities to certain of its shareholders or other third parties. One way to limit the risk of this liability is to have the shareholders or other third parties enter into a general release, in which they agree to release the acquirer from any claims for known or potential liabilities that arise after the closing of the business combination. A general discussion of contracts can be found in Chapter 8.

Employment Agreements

An acquirer may decide that retaining key employees and members of a target company's management team, at least during the integration period following the closing of the transaction, is essential. To secure their retention, an acquirer may require that employment agreements by key personnel be secured prior to the signing of the merger agreement or that the execution of such agreements be made a condition to the obligation of the acquirer to complete the transaction. Although no contract can guarantee that personnel will remain with the target company after the merger is completed, employment agreements may give the acquirer more comfort. If an acquirer requires employment contracts as a condition to its obligation to close, the target company should seek to ensure that the employment arrangements are finalized before the acquisition agreement is executed and announced to reduce the possibility that negotiations with one or more employees could prevent the closing of the transaction. General information regarding employment agreements is found in Chapter 10.

Noncompetition Agreements

In addition to employment agreements, an acquirer may want to secure noncompetition agreements from key personnel who may leave the target company and compete directly with the surviving corporation. These agreements may be in the form of covenants not to compete in preexisting employment contracts or may be the subject of agreements entered into in contemplation of the business combination. Postemployment restrictions and covenants not to compete are discussed in detail in Chapter 2.

The Closing

At the closing, the parties will generally file a certificate of merger, articles of merger, or other form of notification with the relevant states in which the constituent companies are incorporated. Once such documentation has been filed, the merger will be complete, and the shares of the target company will generally be automatically exchanged for the right to receive the consideration offered by the acquirer. Prior to making the state filings, the parties will typically exchange other documentation, including officers' certificates attesting that certain conditions to the closing have been satisfied and opinions of counsel.

Postclosing: Integration

One of the most crucial and often underemphasized components of a successful merger is the integration of resources after the merger has been completed. Most often, the high-level merger negotiations will name executives and board members, but only rarely will the discussions deal with integrating accounting practices, management teams, or employee or facility redundancy. As a result, management and employees—and often clients and distributors—receive little information about how the merger will affect their relationships with the company. This lack of communication, and the resulting rumors, can lead to lower employee morale, higher employee turnover, and other adverse results for the newly merged company. For these reasons, among others, it is crucial that merging companies understand that postmerger integration is as important to the success of the merger as any other key issues.

From the perspective of employee compensation and benefits, a business combination presents many challenges and offers potential improvements for the merged company. The merged company will need to determine the optimal way to bring together the various compensation and benefits programs of the combining entities. If acquisitions have been a regular occurrence, this process may have become standardized for the acquirer, and with few exceptions it will know how to deal with the addition of a new group of employees. For less experienced acquirers—particularly when the combining entities are of nearly equal size—the integration process will require careful analysis of each compensation and benefit program with an eye to what is optimal for the merged entity. This may require the maintenance of parallel programs, at least for the short term, because regional differences and geographic distance dictate this result. One of the biggest challenges is to find the time, in the midst of frantic premerger activity, for the necessary analysis.

Putting it into Practice

About six months before DataAccelleation successfully launched its initial public offering, Kendra attended a trade show in San Jose, California. At the trade show, she met Jason Hubbel and Chris Cooder, the founders of Interseek, a two-year-old company based in Missoula, Montana, that was developing a product very similar to the SDB technology that DataAccelleation had developed. Jason and Chris explained to Kendra that Interseek's product was not yet production ready but that a trial version was undergoing beta testing with several companies based in the Midwest. Over the course of an hour, Jason and Chris explained their product to Kendra, who immediately recognized that Interseek's prototype contained certain features that, if developed properly, would enhance the SDB product that DataAccelleation currently offered. Kendra then invited Jason and Chris to meet with her and the DataAccelleation technical team for further discussions. Jason and Chris enthusiastically accepted the invitation, and plans were made to meet at DataAccelleation's offices the following Monday.

The next Monday, Jason, Chris, and Interseek's chief technologist, Sarah Gibson, came to DataAccelleation and gave a successful demonstration of Interseek's prototype product, SearchSmart. The features that initially interested Kendra appeared capable of incorporation into DataAccelleation's SDB product with a minimum of modification. Toward the end of the day-long meeting, Kendra asked Jason how much it would cost to license the technology from Interseek on an exclusive basis. Jason responded that with a licensing arrangement Interseek would not be able to market the product itself and thus would be totally dependent on the fortunes of DataAccelleation. "What would you think about possibly acquiring Interseek outright, Kendra?" asked Chris.

Kendra responded that her management team had considered that possibility but thought that integrating a Montana-based company into DataAccelleation's existing operations would be too costly and would divert scarce management resources from DataAccelleation's main efforts at a critical time in the company's development. "Anyway," Kendra declared, "why would you be interested in selling your company before your product has even been fully developed? Don't you expect a higher return if you have a market-ready product?"

continued...

continued...

Jason then explained that Interseek had encountered difficulties in obtaining a further round of venture financing to cover the company's expenses until SearchSmart began to generate revenue. With very little money left in the bank from their last round of financing and little or no hope of raising additional money through a venture round or a commercial debt facility, Jason and Chris were faced with the reality that Interseek might go out of business before SearchSmart made it to market. Accordingly, they were willing to sell provided that they had the opportunity to continue working on the product with a company that shared their vision of SearchSmart's potential. Although they understood that their dreams of a quick liquidity event would not be realized, they hoped that by combining with a better funded company with bright prospects, they might realize a higher return on their investment in the long term.

Kendra thanked Jason, Chris, and Sarah for their presentation and told them that her team would caucus further on the possibility of acquiring Interseek. She mentioned that she was concerned that even if the price was right, the integration issues still complicated the picture. "That should not be a problem," said Sarah. She, Jason, and Chris represented the brains behind SearchSmart, and they had already agreed that they would be willing to move to California if necessary. Kendra now realized that the day's meetings had essentially constituted a job interview for the three and that if what Sarah said was true, then Kendra now had the opportunity to dramatically enhance the SDB's capabilities for what she hoped would be a minimal cost to DataAccelleation! Trying to hide her excitement, Kendra agreed to get back to Jason within a week or two.

Kendra went back to her team and discussed the opportunity further. All agreed that the SearchSmart prototype contained several clever features that would greatly enhance the SDB technology without significant development time or cost. Moreover, as several people noted, the meeting had gone very well in part because of the meshing of personalities of the two technical teams. Sarah clearly was extremely experienced and talented, and Jason and Chris showed that they shared a common vision that they could see becoming reality as part of DataAccelleation.

Kendra next called a special meeting of her board of directors to discuss the prospect of acquiring Interseek. At the board meeting, the initial response was less than enthusiastic. Although the directors did not dispute the

continued...

continued...

benefits of the SearchSmart technology, a majority of the members expressed concern with the integration issues that Kendra's own management team had previously identified. After convincing the board that the technology was worth exploring regardless of how difficult the integration issues might be, Kendra received the board's approval to explore the acquisition further.

Kendra scheduled a further meeting at Interseek's offices in Missoula between her technical team and the Interseek team. Kendra made sure to block off some of her own time to sit down with Jason and Chris and discuss the integration issues that concerned the board. Jason and Chris sent Kendra a confidentiality agreement, which she signed after asking DataAccelleation's attorney, Michael Cruz, to review it.

DataAccelleation's team came away from the Missoula meetings more enthusiastic than ever. The full technical teams established an excellent working relationship, and Kendra made great progress resolving the potential integration issues. Her chief concern going into the Missoula meetings was that the development of the SearchSmart technology could not be completed without the assistance of Interseek personnel who would refuse to leave Missoula. Concerned that the acquisition might divert management's attention from other issues, DataAccelleation's directors had been very clear at the board meeting that they would not approve a transaction that resulted in an additional office in Montana. Chris was able to demonstrate to Kendra, however, that of the three engineers developing SearchSmart, two (Sarah and Jason) had already expressed their willingness to relocate, and the third was strongly considering that option. The other seven people then employed by Interseek would not leave Missoula, but their responsibilities would be assumed by those willing to relocate as well as by current DataAccelleation employees.

Kendra went back to her board and received approval to make an offer to acquire Interseek. The offer contemplated an acquisition of all of the outstanding equity interests of Interseek for approximately $5 million worth of DataAccelleation common stock pursuant to a reverse triangular merger. In addition, Jason, Chris, and Sarah would be hired to work with the DataAccelleation technical team. An offer would also be made to the other key technologist, Sam Kern. All four would be asked to sign noncompetition agreements in connection with the transaction and would receive benefitsand option packages comparable to those offered to similarly situated

continued...

continued...

DataAccelleation employees. Kendra asked Michael Cruz to prepare a term sheet reflecting these terms as well as the standard terms typically included in a term sheet, such as the structure of the transaction and the need for a definitive agreement before the offer would become binding.

Kendra e-mailed the term sheet to Jason and Chris and asked them to get back to her as soon as possible, which they did. Their chief concerns were the purchase price (the parties finally agreed on a $6 million purchase price) and the indemnification provisions. Jason and Chris explained that the business had been funded to date by their relatives and friends, as well as some of the local business leaders of Missoula. The term sheet provided that the representations and warranties that Interseek and its shareholders would be required to make in the definitive agreement would survive the closing of the transaction for a period of two years and that the sellers' indemnification obligations would be limited only by the amount of the purchase price each seller would receive in the transaction. In addition, 50 percent of the aggregate purchase price would be placed in escrow for the same period. This was not acceptable to Interseek's shareholders; they argued that it meant that no seller would know what he or she would actually receive in the transaction for two years.

Kendra countered that given the nature of Interseek, a small start-up without much operating history, she was concerned that possible infringement claims arising from the creation and development of the SearchSmart technology might not surface until after DataAccelleation had expended substantial sums of money and time and effort on incorporating SearchSmart into DataAccelleation's product offerings. After some further back and forth, the parties agreed that all representations and warranties made by Interseek would terminate a year after the closing of the transaction except for the representations dealing with intellectual property infringement, which would survive for eighteen months. Moreover, the amount held in escrow would be the sole and exclusive remedy of DataAccelleation for breaches of these representations and warranties. Forty percent of the purchase price would be held in escrow for the first year after the closing; after that time, the escrow fund would be reduced to 20 percent of the purchase price. After reaching agreement on these issues, the parties established a schedule for conducting due diligence and negotiating definitive agreements.

continued...

continued...

During the due diligence process, DataAccelleation's attorneys discovered that Interseek had approximately fifty-five shareholders. Further inquiry revealed that at least twenty-five were accredited investors, but it was unclear whether each of the remaining thirty investors possessed the requisite sophistication to satisfy the requirements of Rule 506 promulgated by the SEC pursuant to its authority under the Securities Act of 1933. Accordingly, Kendra explained to Jason and Chris that those investors not possessing the requisite sophistication would have to appoint someone to act as their purchaser representative. Chris offered to act as purchaser representative on behalf of the unsophisticated investors, each of whom readily agreed to his appointment.

Not everything, however, proceeded so smoothly. Sam Kern, whose role in the continuing development of the SearchSmart product was more instrumental than even Interseek had initially realized, decided that he did not wish to leave Missoula and relocate to Silicon Valley. A retired Intel engineer, Sam had moved to Missoula to escape the congestion of the Valley. He liked the slower pace of life in Missoula and had developed an almost spiritual attachment to the mountains and streams of his adopted region. Clearly then, some accommodations would have to be made with Sam if the transaction were to proceed.

After much internal discussion and further negotiation with Sam, it was agreed that he would be hired by DataAccelleation as a consultant and would work one week a month in the Bay Area and telecommute the rest of each month. Although this arrangement was not ideal for DataAccelleation, Kendra was hopeful that Sam could remain productive and be a valuable contributor to the product development efforts of the combined team from a distance. Sam assured her that he could and explained that he often worked separately from the main technology team at Interseek to keep himself free to think of new directions for the product rather than having to troubleshoot the existing technology.

The final sticking point in negotiations was the type of DataAccelleation capital stock that would be issued in exchange for the outstanding equity of Interseek. Although the parties had quickly reached agreement on a $6 million purchase price, if DataAccelleation were to issue $6 million worth of its common stock, the percentage interests of DataAccelleation's existing investors would be substantially diluted because of the extremely low price of DataAccelleation's common stock. On the other hand, DataAccelleation did

continued...

continued...

not wish to create an additional series of preferred stock issuable to Interseek's existing stockholders and optionholders; if it did, the employees of Interseek who would be employed by DataAccelleation would have the right to receive a better return on their options than similarly situated current DataAccelleation employees. Kendra observed to Chris and Jason that if they received stock, they would have better rights than she had as a founder in the event that DataAccelleation was sold for a price below the aggregate liquidation preferences of DataAccelleation's preferred stock.

Jason saw the bind that Kendra was in, but he noted that, with the exception of a small number of outstanding shares held by the company's founders, Jason and Chris, none of Interseek's employees held shares; rather, they all held options that had not yet been exercised. Jason said that issuing preferred stock to these optionholders would not create any compensation issues because none of these employees would be working for DataAccelleation. Moreover, Jason declared, he, Chris, Sarah, and Sam were willing to agree to terminate their existing Interseek options in exchange for receiving DataAccelleation options for common stock, provided that they were given credit in their vesting schedule for the time they worked at Interseek as well as some additional options to partly make up for the value they were ostensibly leaving on the table. Kendra readily accepted the offer, and the parties made plans to proceed with the closing of the transaction.

After obtaining the approval of the boards of both companies, the parties signed the definitive merger agreement. Within days of the execution of the definitive agreement, Interseek mailed an information statement to its existing stockholders that explained the transaction, provided information on DataAccelleation and Interseek, and solicited the approval of the transaction by the stockholders. Ten days later, Interseek had received sufficient written stockholder consents to satisfy the last condition to closing. The parties scheduled a closing date two days later at Michael Cruz's offices. At the closing, the attorneys exchanged signature pages for all the relevant documents while the business people discussed the press release that DataAccelleation would issue in the morning. When the attorneys were finally satisfied that everything was in order and that the transaction was closed, Kendra handed glasses of champagne to the newest members of the DataAccelleation team and toasted them with a heartfelt "Welcome aboard!"

Getting It In Writing

SAMPLE TERM SHEET FOR ACQUISITION OF A PRIVATELY HELD CORPORATION BY A PUBLIC COMPANY

TERM SHEET FOR PROPOSED ACQUISITION OF

PRIVATE CORP.

BY

PUBLICCO, INC.

This preliminary nonbinding term sheet sets forth certain key terms of a possible transaction involving Publicco, Inc. and Private Corp. Neither this term sheet nor any action taken in connection with the matters referred to in this term sheet will give rise to any obligation on the part of Publicco or Private Corp. to continue any discussions or negotiations or to pursue or enter into any transaction or relationship of any nature.

Parties:	Publicco, Inc. ("Acquirer") Private Corp. ("Target") _____, _____, _____, _____ and _____, who collectively hold approximately _____% of the outstanding common stock of Target on a fully diluted basis (the "Major Shareholders")
Acquisition of Outstanding Equity Target Securities:	Acquirer would acquire 100% of the outstanding equity securities of Target by means of a reverse triangular merger in which a newly formed subsidiary of Acquirer would be merged into Target (the "Transaction"). As a result of the Transaction, Target would become a wholly owned subsidiary of Acquirer.
Treatment of Outstanding Target Common Stock:	All outstanding shares of Target common stock would be exchanged for newly issued shares of Acquirer common stock in the Transaction. Any repurchase rights applicable to shares of Target common stock would remain in effect after the closing of the Transaction (the "Closing") and would become rights to repurchase the shares of Acquirer common stock issued in exchange for such shares of Target common stock.

continued...

continued...

Treatment of Outstanding Target Stock Options:	All outstanding Target stock options would be assumed by Acquirer in connection with the Transaction and would become options to purchase Acquirer common stock. The terms of the assumed stock options (including terms relating to vesting) would not change; there would be no acceleration of the vesting of unvested stock options.
Purchase Price:	The aggregate value of the consideration (including all shares of Acquirer common stock and all options to purchase Acquirer common stock) to be provided by Acquirer to the holders of Target's outstanding equity securities in the Transaction would be $_____. For purposes of the Transaction, Acquirer common stock would be valued at the average of the closing prices of Acquirer common stock for the 20 consecutive trading days immediately preceding the Closing.
Voting Undertakings:	The Major Shareholders would agree to vote their shares of Target stock in favor of the Transaction.
Tax Treatment:	It is expected that the Transaction would constitute a tax-free reorganization for U.S. federal income tax purposes.
Securities Law Matters:	Acquirer common stock to be issued in the Transaction would be issued in reliance upon the "Regulation D" exemption from the registration requirements of the federal securities laws.
Employment and Noncompetition Agreements:	Contemporaneously with the execution of the definitive agreement and plan of merger and reorganization relating to the Transaction (the "Merger Agreement"), certain key executives of Target would enter into employment agreements and one-year noncompetition agreements that would become effective as of the Closing.
Representation, Warranties, Indemnities, and Other Provisions:	In the Merger Agreement, Target and the Major Shareholders would make customary representations and warranties (which would survive the Closing) relating to the business, financial condition, contracts, liabilities, employees, and prospects of Target and would provide customary indemnities. A portion of the consideration to be provided by Acquirer in the Transaction would be held in escrow to secure Acquirer's rights of indemnity. The Merger Agreement would also contain customary covenants, closing conditions, and other provisions.

continued...

continued...

Transaction Expenses:	All legal fees and other expenses incurred on behalf of either party would be borne by that party, except that expenses of Target in connection with the Transaction would be borne by Target up to a maximum of $_____, after which all expenses of Target would be borne solely by the Major Shareholders.
"No-Shop" Agreement:	Target would execute a 45-day exclusivity ("no-shop") agreement on or before _____, 2002.

CAVEAT: *This form is intended only to serve as an example of a hypothetical term sheet. Every term sheet must be carefully tailored to reflect the specific terms of the transaction to which it relates; accordingly, it may be necessary to make substantial modifications to this form before it can be used in the context of any proposed transaction.*

NOTE

1. *See generally* MYRON SCHOLES ET AL., TAX PLANNING AND BUSINESS STRATEGY (2d ed. 2001).

Chapter 17

GOING PUBLIC

For many entrepreneurs, the company's *initial public offering* (*IPO*) is the realization of a dream. This first offering of the company's securities to the public represents recognition of the entrepreneur's vision as well as access to the capital required for the company to achieve its potential. It can also create substantial wealth for the entrepreneur, at least on paper.

The ease with which a company can go public fluctuates, and those who follow the IPO market know that the only thing predictable is the unpredictability. At times hundreds of companies are in the IPO pipeline, but at other times, there may be a slow month or series of months when only one or two companies go public. Recent history provides a stark example.

During the "dot-com" craze that began around 1998 and continued through the spring of 2000, hundreds of Internet and other technology companies went public in a great IPO market. Many of these companies had more limited operating histories and more substantial losses than any previous viable IPO candidates. This favorable momentum came to an abrupt halt shortly after the Nasdaq Composite Index reached its height in March 2000. By May, the IPO window had shut, and a number of companies had to terminate IPOs in progress. The dismal IPO market continued through the stock market slide of 2001, which was marked by economic uncertainty as well as external events, such as the tragic terrorist attack of September 11, 2001, that destroyed the World Trade Center and damaged the Pentagon. Yet, if history is a guide, the IPO window is likely to reopen.

This chapter first explores the reasons to consider going public, identifies certain disadvantages of being a public company, discusses matters to consider in deciding whether to sell the company, and outlines several factors to consider in determining whether a company is a good candidate for an IPO. The chapter then presents an overview of the public offering process, summarizes the contents of the prospectus, and describes what is usually done to prepare for an IPO. It continues with a discussion of contractual and securities law restrictions on the sale of shares not being sold in the IPO. The chapter concludes with a brief summary of the ongoing responsibilities of a public company and its board of directors.

WHY GO PUBLIC?

Initially, an entrepreneur finances the company's operations through private financing transactions, often involving the sale of preferred stock to venture funds and sophisticated individual investors, or through alliances with corporate partners. Although the timing varies by industry, most companies decide to go public when (1) the company has reached the point at which initial investors have invested the total amount of capital that they are willing to provide and are focused on *liquidity* (a return on their investment), and (2) the company has made sufficient progress to make a public offering viable. The company may need significant additional capital for research and development, product launches, or working capital to expand operations. As the company's value increases, however, the company may encounter difficulty in attracting new investors, who would rather target earlier-stage companies with a lower valuation but greater upside potential.

A public offering of securities provides a company access to broader financial markets to fund capital requirements. Once the company goes public, it can use its stock instead of cash to acquire strategic pieces of technology or other businesses. The company will also have the benefit of public visibility, and, as long as the company is performing well and the market is receptive, the company can return to the public market to raise additional capital. Finally, the IPO will value the company's shares at many (if not hundreds of) times the price paid by the founders and will afford them access to the public market for sale of their shares.

Going public can also entail a significant number of disadvantages, however. As explained in more detail below, a public company must meet a host of legal obligations that are inapplicable to private companies, including disclosure obligations and fiduciary duties owed to hundreds of shareholders whom the entrepreneur and the board have never met—and will never meet. The company will forever be in the fishbowl of public scrutiny. Disclosure requirements will apply not only to the company but also to officers and directors, who must inform the marketplace of the amount of the company's stock they and their family own and of any sales, gifts, purchases, or other changes in ownership of that stock, including stock option grants and exercises.

In addition, the going-public process is expensive, often costing more than $1 million in filing fees to the Securities and Exchange Commission, state securities filing fees, stock exchange or over-the-counter registration fees, legal fees, accounting fees, printing costs, and increased premiums for director and officer liability insurance. Also, the process consumes an enormous amount of management time during what is usually also a crucial period for business success. Once public, the company will spend significantly more in legal, accounting, and printing fees than in the past.

In addition, an entrepreneur contemplating a public offering because of the desire for liquidity for his or her stock should be aware of the restrictions on the sale of that stock, even if it is fully vested. As discussed below, the first impediment to sale is that the investment banks that manage the public offering will require the entrepreneur and all other significant shareholders to agree not to sell their stock, typically for six months after the offering. Second, after the lockup period has expired, rules against insider trading will severely limit when the stock can be sold without risk. Third, because the entrepreneur likely is an *affiliate* (an officer, director, or owner of more than 5 to 10 percent of the outstanding shares), the amount of stock that can be sold during any three-month period is limited by Rule 144 under the federal securities laws to, in most circumstances, 1 percent of the company's outstanding stock.

IPO Versus Sale of the Company

Because of the disadvantages of going public, an entrepreneur considering a public offering may wish to think about selling the company instead. Indeed, the sale alternative is a far more common path to liquidity, particularly for entrepreneurs with a company experiencing slow but steady growth or in an industry not currently favored by investment bankers. (Business combinations and contracts for the sale of an enterprise are discussed in Chapter 16.)

Often a larger corporation in the same general line of business will be interested in the purchase. For example, Boston Scientific, an integrated manufacturer of medical products, purchased or offered to purchase several companies (including Cardiovascular Imaging Systems, EP Technologies, and Vesica), either as the companies were contemplating public offerings or soon after their IPOs. The purpose was to expand Boston Scientific's product line. A buyout by an acquisition firm such as McCown De Leeuw & Co. or Genstar Capital is often an option for companies with assets against which the purchaser can borrow. Finally, direct competitors of the company may have an interest. In any event, many professionals, including business brokers and corporate finance personnel at investment banks, are available to help the interested entrepreneur find an appropriate buyer.

Potential buyers often surface about the time a company is ready to go public because they are well aware that once a company is public, they will have to pay a 15 to 30 percent premium over the public market price to induce the target company's board to approve the sale. A hot IPO market can also stimulate a hot acquisition market because buyers may fear they

FROM THE TRENCHES

A well-known maker of athletic equipment began the IPO process. The investment banks had advised the company that the public marketplace would value the outstanding shares at $125 million. Because of the disadvantages of being a public company, including the many restrictions on selling their own stock in the public marketplace after the offering, the founders seriously considered a third-party offer to buy the company for $95 million in cash, which was made after the offeror learned the public offering process had begun. The founders ultimately decided to go forward with the public offering, and after three years the public market valuation of the company was more than $800 million.

will lose the chance to get a company while it is still private. (Interestingly, after the stock market drops in 2000 and 2001, some private companies could still garner a relatively high acquisition price, while public companies were forced to sell at valuations lower than anticipated. This "public company discount" seemingly was attributable to the added complexity of acquiring a public company with a broad stockholder base.)

As discussed in Chapter 16, the sale of the company can offer several advantages compared to a public offering. In a cash sale, the shareholders of the target corporation can lock in their gains and have immediate liquidity, although they will have to pay taxes on their gain. The target shareholders will not be subject to the risk that stock market conditions will change and the IPO will be called off, or to market risk on their shares if the IPO does proceed.

If the sale is to be for stock of the acquiring company, the sellers will face certain restrictions on disposition of the stock, particularly if the transaction is to be tax-free. If the shares issued to shareholders of the target are registered, Rule 145 (the analog to Rule 144, discussed below, for stock acquired in a merger or acquisition transaction) will prohibit affiliates of the target from selling in any three-month period more than the greater of 1 percent of the acquirer's outstanding shares and its average weekly trading volume in the past four weeks. If the shares issued to the target shareholders are not registered, then all shareholders of the target must hold the shares for at least one year before they can sell their shares in the public markets.

Although market risk remains in a stock-for-stock deal because the entrepreneur now holds stock of another company, the market price of a more established company is usually less volatile than that of a newly public company, whose price can be depressed for years if early quarterly earnings do not meet the expectations of the market. In addition, the entrepreneur acquiring publicly traded stock in a merger or acquisition can engage in certain hedging activities against market risk that would be precluded by a lockup agreement with investment banks doing an IPO. But perhaps most important, the sale of the business enables the entrepreneur to avoid having to deal with the myriad pressures of being a public company, including meeting or exceeding revenue and earnings estimates quarter after quarter, dealing with stock analysts who are constantly seeking information and assurances, and communicating with and owing duties to shareholders the entrepreneur has never met.

Arguing against the sale of the business is the limitation on return. First, the price paid per share by a buyer will usually be less than the company could obtain in a public offering. Second, the entrepreneur's *upside* (potential profit) is capped at the purchase price if the consideration is cash or is determined by the stock market performance of the acquiring company if the consideration is stock. Many entrepreneurs do not want to let control of their upside slip from their own hands.

Is the Company an IPO Candidate?

The entrepreneur and the board must determine whether the company should pursue an immediate IPO or an alternative strategy, such as waiting until the company has made additional progress so that it can command a higher valuation in an IPO or pursuing a merger with a private or public company. Factors to consider include the nature of the company's existing products and product pipeline; the strength and depth of the company's research, development, and management teams; the competitive landscape; and the company's anticipated capital requirements.

The timing of an IPO is often dependent on conditions beyond the company's control, such as general market receptivity to IPOs at the time, whether the relevant industry is "hot," whether major institutional investors have exceeded the proportion of their portfolios reserved for investment in the relevant industry, and whether a competitor in the industry has announced disappointing financial or regulatory results that have caused the market to be wary of the industry as a whole. When faced with less than ideal conditions, some companies elect to seek bridge financing from existing investors or mezzanine (later-stage) financing from new investors to raise enough capital to permit the company to wait until market conditions improve or product milestones are achieved. If bridge financing is not available on acceptable terms and the IPO window closes, making it very difficult to get deals done (as happened in mid-2000 after a very active IPO market in 1999 and the first few months of 2000), the company may want to reevaluate its decision to go public and instead try to find a buyer for the company.

THE IPO PROCESS

Overview

The first four weeks of the IPO process are typically spent in a series of intensive drafting sessions to prepare the registration statement for filing with the Securities and Exchange Commission (SEC). The registration statement includes a detailed selling document called a *prospectus,* which describes the company and its business and management. *Due diligence,* which is a review of the company's business and legal affairs that is done to ensure the accuracy of the prospectus, is also conducted during this period. After the filing of the registration statement and typically one amendment to reflect SEC staff comments, 20,000 or more copies of the *preliminary prospectus* are printed and then distributed by members of the underwriting syndicate to potential buyers. The preliminary prospectus, which is preliminary because certain terms of the offering (such as price) are yet to be determined and some or all of the SEC staff's comments may not yet have been incorporated, is also known as the *red herring* because it contains a red legend mandated by the SEC on its front cover, warning of its preliminary and incomplete nature.

Once the registration statement has been filed, the company will work with the underwriters to prepare a presentation about the company for the road show. The *road show* is arranged by the underwriters and consists of a series of meetings, large and small, with potential investors in a number of major cities during a two- to three-week period. Increasingly, text or Webcast presentations are also made available to institutional investors over the Internet. Approximately thirty days (depending, among other things, on the workload of the SEC) after the registration statement has been filed, the SEC staff will send a letter with its comments on the registration statement to the company. The road show may commence prior to receipt of these comments, but issuers often wait until they receive the comments to ensure that no complex SEC hurdles are looming. An issuer may also wait until it has developed its responses and revised the prospectus to make "the story" substantially as it will be when the SEC completes its review and the prospectus is finalized. The goal is to complete the road show at about the same time as the company's and underwriters' counsel have satisfied the SEC by filing a series of *pre-effective amendments* to the registration statement. These amendments are called pre-effective because the registration statement has not yet been *declared effective* by the SEC; at the point when it is, the SEC gives permission for trading in the company's stock to commence. These pre-effective amendments typically revise the registration statement and the prospectus.

Once the SEC has declared the registration statement effective, the underwriters and the company, having completed the road show, agree on a final price and the final number of shares for the offering. Trading in the stock generally commences the next day.

The closing of the purchase and sale of the shares occurs three business days after trading commences. Following effectiveness, between 10,000 and 12,000 copies of the *final prospectus* will be printed and, as required by law, distributed to purchasers of the stock in the offering. The final prospectus includes the final price and number of shares offered and reflects changes to the preliminary prospectus suggested by the SEC or necessitated by events occurring subsequent to the date of the preliminary prospectus.

Selecting the Managing Underwriters

If the company is a suitable public offering candidate and the market is generally receptive, the first step is to establish a relationship with a financial institution that will assist the company with the offering. Virtually all public offerings are managed by investment banks that arrange for the purchase of the company's stock by institutions and individual investors in exchange for a commission. (In contrast, commercial or merchant banks lend their capital in exchange for interest.) An investment bank will also provide analysts who will publish ongoing research reports on the company's progress, which can foster investor interest after the offering.

Typically, the company will select two, three, or even four investment banks to act as managing underwriters. One bank is usually designated the *lead underwriter,* and sometimes there are co-leads. Other managing underwriters are known as *co-managers*. The company should seek underwriters that are willing to underwrite the offering on a firm commitment (as opposed to a best-efforts) basis. In a *firm commitment offering,* the underwriters actually purchase the shares from the company for resale to investors, thereby assuming some (albeit minimal) market risk in the transaction. In contrast, investment banks conducting a *best-efforts offering* are required only to use their best efforts to sell the securities.

The role of the managing underwriters is to position the company in the public market and to form a *syndicate* (a group of investment banks) to participate in the offering. The primary reasons for syndicating an offering are risk sharing and marketing. The syndicate will be composed of multiple underwriters that share liability under the securities laws and share in the underwriting component of the gross spread. In an IPO, the underwriters buy stock from the company at a discount (usually, 6 to 7 percent of the public offering price) and then sell it to the public at the full price. The *gross spread* is the difference between the offering price to the public and the proceeds to the company. The syndicate may also include selling group members or dealers who do not share liability with the underwriters. Selling group members or dealers agree only to purchase a specific number of shares at the public offering price less a selling commission (typically, 55 to 60 percent of the gross spread). Unless otherwise indicated, references in this chapter to underwriters mean the managing underwriters.

To be effective, a managing underwriter must be familiar with the company's industry and be able to differentiate the company and its products or services from others in its industry. The company should consider the reputation and experience of the underwriter in the relevant industry, its level of commitment to the deal, its ability to staff the offering appropriately with experienced and knowledgeable personnel, company management's impressions of the individual bankers who will shoulder the responsibility for the deal, the bank's marketing strength, and the quality of its support after the public offering (e.g., research analysts, market-making capabilities, and experience in mergers and acquisitions). The managing underwriters should have complementary strengths. For example, one might be stronger in making sales to institutional buyers, and another might have stronger retail distribution or a better-known analyst.

A company will often hold what has come to be called a *beauty contest* or *bake-off* among four or five investment banks before selecting the managing underwriters. In this process, each investment bank brings a team of three to five people to make a presentation to the board of directors. The investment bankers prepare and distribute elaborate bound materials (referred to as *books*). The books detail the strengths of the investment banking firm, its recent relevant IPOs, the post-IPO price performance of the companies it has taken public, and, perhaps most importantly, its preliminary views on how the market will value the company. These valuations are typically based on past and projected future earnings (initially supplied by the company but massaged by the bankers before the presentation); the *price/earnings ratio* (market price per share divided by earnings per share), or perhaps a different relevant ratio (for instance, a ratio of market price to revenues for companies not yet profitable), of comparable public companies; and the strengths and weaknesses of the company compared with its competitors. Despite the similarity of approach, the valuations among investment banks can vary tremendously. Given the various criteria that are important to the company and the process, the bank with the highest estimated valuation of the company is not

FROM THE TRENCHES

A Silicon Valley company invited six prestigious investment banks to engage in a beauty contest for the IPO. Although all the firms made impressive presentations, the company was attracted to the winner for two principal reasons. First, the bank had the industry's best analyst, which the company felt was important both for completing the IPO successfully and for providing ongoing research reports about the company. Second, the bank had completed many deals as a co-manager but only recently had begun to be selected as a lead underwriter in the particular industry. The company felt that the bank, intent on building its reputation, would provide excellent service during the offering and make certain the deal attracted significant attention in an overcrowded market. The offering was wildly successful as the preliminary orders exceeded the shares available in the offering by ten times.

necessarily the best choice. Following the presentations, the company will select the lead underwriter (or the co-leads) and one or more co-managers.

Timing

An IPO typically takes ten to fourteen weeks from start to finish, although it is sometimes possible to accelerate the schedule, and the schedule is sometimes extended in the event of company transactions, such as an acquisition, during the process. The underwriters typically prepare a time and responsibilities schedule setting out who does what and when those tasks must be completed. This schedule is handed out at the first *all-hands* or *organizational meeting,* which is attended by all of the key participants. Companies well prepared to move quickly will be in the best position to control the IPO timing and minimize market risk. For example, well-organized company counsel frequently will distribute a first draft of the registration statement before the organizational meeting. Exhibit 17.1 sets forth a sample timetable. Exhibit 17.2 is a sample agenda for the organizational meeting.

Registration Statement

Under the SEC's rules and regulations, an offering of securities to the public must be made pursuant to a form of registration statement filed with and reviewed by the SEC. In the case of an IPO by a company of its stock, the prescribed form is Form S-1, which is filed with the SEC in Washington, D.C. Smaller companies may qualify for filing on Form SB-2, which requires somewhat less disclosure. The SEC staff reviews the registration statement for compliance with SEC rules and reviews the substance of the disclosure in the prospectus, which is the part of the registration statement that will be printed and distributed to the public.

Participants in the IPO Process

The company's management plays a central role in the offering, guided by the underwriters, counsel, and the auditors. As discussed above, the major task of this *working group* is the preparation of the prospectus.

EXHIBIT 17.1

SAMPLE TIMETABLE

April

S	M	T	W	T	F	S
	1	2	3	4	5	6
7	8	9	10	11	12	13
14	15	16	17	18	19	20
21	22	23	24	25	26	27
28	29	30				

May

S	M	T	W	T	F	S
			1	2	3	4
5	6	7	8	9	10	11
12	13	14	15	16	17	18
19	20	21	22	23	24	25
26	27	28	29	30	31	

June

S	M	T	W	T	F	S
						1
2	3	4	5	6	7	8
9	10	11	12	13	14	15
16	17	18	19	20	21	22
23	24	25	26	27	28	29
30						

July

S	M	T	W	T	F	S
	1	2	3	4	5	6
7	8	9	10	11	12	13
14	15	16	17	18	19	20
21	22	23	24	25	26	27
28	29	30	31			

DataAccelleation, Inc.	Company
Representatives of the underwriters	UW
Company counsel	CC
Underwriter's counsel	UC
Auditors	AU

Summary

April 18 and 19	Organizational meeting and due diligence sessions
April 26	First draft of registration statement distributed
April 29	All-hands drafting sessions at CC at 8:00 A.M.
May 2 and 3	All-hands drafting sessions at CC at 8:00 A.M.
May 6 and 7	All-hands drafting sessions at CC at 8:00 A.M.
Week of May 13	All-hands drafting sessions at the printer
May 16	File registration statement with SEC
Week of May 27	Preparation of road show
Week of June 3	Road show presentation finalized
Weeks of June 10 and 17	Domestic and international road shows
June 20	Registration statement effective; pricing
June 21	Commence trading
June 26	Closing

EXHIBIT 17.2

SAMPLE AGENDA

SAMPLE AGENDA FOR ORGANIZATIONAL MEETING

I. Review and Complete Working Group List

II. Review Time Schedule

A. SEC review period
B. Drafting sessions and due diligence
C. Shareholder communications
   1. Piggyback rights
   2. Proposed lockup
D. Board of directors meetings
E. Filing/offering timing
F. Road show
G. Other lead-time items

III. Discuss Proposed Offering

A. Size of offering
B. Primary and secondary components
C. General discussion of use of proceeds
D. Green shoe option
E. Review existing shareholder list
   1. Registration rights
   2. Rule 144 stock
F. Number of shares authorized
G. Lockup agreement with principal shareholders
H. Distribution objectives
I. Directed shares
J. Possibility of confidential treatment being requested

IV. Review Legal Issues

A. Outstanding claims
B. Loan agreement restrictions or other consents needed to offer the shares
C. Blue Sky issues
D. Shareholder notes
E. Cheap stock
F. Stock options
G. Employment agreements
H. Board meetings
   1. Preparation of resolutions and appropriate board authorizations
I. Filing registration statement
J. Officers' and directors' questionnaires
K. Pricing committee

continued...

EXHIBIT 17.2 (CONTINUED)

SAMPLE AGENDA

L. Disclosure of confidential agreements
M. Related-party and certain transactions disclosures
N. Required shareholder approvals
O. Expert opinions

V. Discuss Financial and Accounting Matters

A. Audited financials
B. Availability of quarterly financials
C. Comfort letter
D. Management letters
E. Any special accounting issues

VI. Discuss Publicity Policy

A. Prefiling, postfiling/pre-effective, postoffering periods
B. Pending newspaper/magazine articles to be published
C. Other corporate announcements
D. Filing press release(s)

VII. Discuss Printing of Documents

A. Selection of printer and bank note company
B. Use of color, pictures
C. Volume requirements

VIII. Due Diligence Review

A. Management interviews
B. References for customer/supplier due diligence
C. Detailed competitive analysis
D. Projected financials (revenues, earnings, backlog)
E. Methodology and models for financial planning
F. Product brochures, trade press, other public relations materials

IX. Discuss Form and Contents of Registration Statement

X. Discuss Road Show Presentation

XI. Legal Due Diligence/Review of Corporate Records

The managing underwriters actively participate in the drafting of the prospectus and are responsible for the selling effort. They put together the syndicate of investment banks that will participate in the offering, organize the road show and marketing meetings, and coordinate other matters relating to the marketing and sale of the securities.

Company counsel, in addition to advising the company on compliance issues, coordinates the drafting of the registration statement and shepherds it through the SEC review process. He or she also helps the company select and coordinate with other participants in the process, such as stock exchange representatives, the printer, the transfer agent, and the bank note company. Company counsel participates in the negotiation of the *underwriting agreement* between the company and the managing underwriters, which covers all aspects of the offering, including the amount of the gross spread; the agreement is not actually entered into until the registration statement is declared effective, however.

Typically, company counsel will review the company's charter documents and legal records to determine what actions the company should take prior to becoming a public company. Company counsel also conducts a detailed review of the business, addressing any legal problems that may emerge and identifying items that require disclosure in the prospectus. If the company has separate patent counsel or regulatory counsel, they may be asked to participate in discussions with the working group and to review sections of the prospectus in their area of legal expertise and, in many cases, to render an opinion to the underwriters regarding those sections.

Underwriters' counsel participates on behalf of the underwriters in the drafting process and the due diligence effort, advises the underwriters on legal issues that arise, and prepares the underwriting agreement. In part to shield their clients from potential liability for misstatements or omissions in the prospectus, underwriters' counsel sometimes plays a devil's advocate role at drafting sessions, encouraging the inclusion of additional risk factors, toning down superfluous positive language, and challenging management to substantiate every statement in the prospectus. Given that an accurate prospectus is in the best interests of all participants, experienced company counsel will work closely with both management and underwriters' counsel to ensure that the language in the prospectus is satisfactory to both. Underwriters' counsel also coordinates the review of the underwriting arrangements by the National Association of Securities Dealers (NASD) and any filings required by state securities authorities.

The company's auditors provide accounting advice in connection with the offering and work closely with the company's chief financial officer in the preparation of the prospectus as it relates to accounting issues and financial disclosure. The auditors also address SEC comments related to accounting issues and prepare comfort letters. A *comfort letter* summarizes the procedures the auditors used to verify certain financial information in the prospectus and describes the scope of their review of the prospectus. It is delivered to the underwriters when the offering becomes effective and again at the closing.

Generally, the prospectus is printed by a financial printer. The printer must be experienced; able to produce a high-quality, timely, and accurate product; and able to respond quickly and cost-effectively to revisions prepared by the working group. A company should expect to spend more than $200,000 to print approximately 20,000 preliminary prospectuses and 10,000 final prospectuses and should obtain quotes from two or three reputable financial printers with extensive IPO experience.

In addition, the company will need a transfer agent, which is typically a specialized stock transfer company or a commercial bank, to issue and effect transfers of the company's shares and to coordinate mailings to shareholders. The company will also need to select a bank note company to help design and then print the new stock certificates that will be issued to the shareholders after the public offering.

Due Diligence

The company, the underwriters, and their respective counsel assemble and review the information about the company in the registration statement, thereby conducting a legal audit of the company and its business. This time-consuming process, along with the data and backup materials used by the company, its underwriters, and their counsel to verify the accuracy of this information, is called due diligence. Due diligence is also used to determine what additional information should be disclosed and to uncover any problems or risks that need to be addressed or disclosed in connection with the public offering. The company must make sure that all participants are aware of the importance of complete candor in the due diligence process to ensure that the information in the prospectus is complete and accurate.

The underwriters, their counsel, and company counsel ask numerous questions of the company's officers and key employees in order to understand thoroughly the company's business, its products and markets or potential markets, and their inherent risks. The due diligence review often includes discussions with key customers and suppliers; a review of environmental issues; analysis of projections, business plans, and product strategy; a review of industry publications; and consultations with patent counsel, technology advisers, and regulatory counsel. It also includes a legal audit of company records, including minutes of board and shareholder meetings, charter documents, qualifications to do business, and all material contracts.

The company must be prepared to back up the claims it makes in the prospectus. Even if a statement is cast as opinion, such as the company's belief that it is becoming the industry leader, the company must be able to demonstrate the reasonableness of this belief. Industry publications, market surveys, and company Web sites are common forms of support for statements regarding market size and the company's position in the market. The information collected in the due diligence process is useful in responding to the SEC if, as often happens, it asks for support for the company's assertions.

Due diligence also often reveals existing agreements or relationships that must or should be amended or terminated. These include agreements that grant certain shareholders rights to information, rights to participate in future financings, or other rights not appropriate for a public company. There might also be contractual or other provisions with third parties that could result in giving the parties inappropriate leverage or claims.

A company should expect the unexpected during the due diligence process. Matters of personal and professional character (such as any prior arrests) can become significant issues. The entrepreneur should discuss with counsel any and all issues, both real or perceived, that could affect the offering.

Determination of Stock Price and Offering Size

Although underwriters generally prefer the company's offering price to be more than $10 and less than $20 per share, the offering price and the size

FROM THE TRENCHES

For one company's officers, the prospect of personal liability for misstatements prompted the disclosure of unorthodox accounting practices by the chief financial officer and patterns of sexual harassment on the part of the chief executive officer. The revelations slowed the offering process and proved highly embarrassing when they were disclosed. The issues should have been discussed with company counsel before the offering process commenced so that counsel could have framed them for the bankers at the outset.

of the offering will be determined by negotiations between the company and its underwriters. The company often will need to effect a stock split of the outstanding stock prior to the offering to bring the expected price per share into this range.

The valuation of the company takes into account market conditions, comparable companies in the industry, past and projected financial performance, product and technology position, the management team, the potential for growth, and new products in development. As noted above, the managing underwriter will have proposed a preliminary valuation of the company at the outset of the IPO process. Additional due diligence by the underwriters' financial analysts and revisions to the company's financial models will take place before the registration statement is filed and before the red herring is printed. This may result in a valuation in the red herring different from that initially proposed. This valuation is still preliminary and is reflected in a *price range* set forth on the cover of the red herring, such as $14–$16 per share.

The final offering price is usually set after the SEC review process is completed and just before the commencement of the offering. The final price is based on the market and the reaction to the offering, as reflected in potential investors' nonbinding indications to the underwriters of intent to purchase shares (commonly referred to as the *underwriters' book*). Typically, underwriters like a book to be at least seven times the offering size. The underwriters generally try to price the shares slightly below the price at which they predict the stock will trade in secondary trading after the initial sale by the underwriters (the *target price*) to give the stock room to move up in the aftermarket. This *IPO discount* is typically 15 percent of the target price, although with the increased volatility of the stock market in recent years the discount has sometimes resulted in an offering price far below the value the underwriters expect the aftermarket to put on the stock.

The size of the offering is based on the company's capital needs, dilution to existing shareholders, the level of *public float* (shares held by investors other than officers, directors, and 10 percent shareholders) desirable to achieve an active trading market and to provide liquidity for existing shareholders, market receptivity, and the proposed price per share. The underwriters are typically granted an overallotment option, called the *green shoe*, to purchase additional shares at the IPO price. The option typically gives the underwriters the right to purchase an amount of additional shares equal to 15 percent of the amount originally offered, within a set period after the offering commences, usually thirty days. The option may be exercised only to cover overallotments, that is, to cover the underwriters' short positions when the offering has been oversold.

FROM THE TRENCHES

The relationship between the IPO price and subsequent trading prices is anything but predictable. Amgen, perhaps the most successful biotechnology company in history, remained at (and even below) its IPO price for several years before going on to give investors extraordinary returns. By contrast, Netscape Communications, originally expected to price at $13 per share, was raised to $28 on the eve of the IPO as demand continued to grow. On the first day of trading, the stock soared to $75 before coming to rest at $52 a few days later. Similarly, VA Linux Systems, Inc., a maker of computer products based on the Linux operating system, broke an IPO record in December 1999 when its IPO shares, which were priced at $30 per share, climbed as high as $320 on its first day and closed the day at $239.25. In September 2001, the VA Linux shares traded at less than $1 per share.

If the underwriters want to sell more shares than the company is willing to sell, the underwriters may invite certain shareholders to offer shares they own for resale as part of the initial offering. Moreover, some shareholders may have registration rights entitling them to sell shares in the offering pursuant to agreements entered into with the company at the time of their initial investment. These registration rights can usually be limited if the underwriters do not want to include selling shareholders because they believe that an offering limited to company shares is optimal or that management or significant investors may be perceived as bailing out if they make substantial sales. (Registration rights are discussed in more detail in Chapter 13.)

Confidential Treatment of Material Agreements

Generally, all of the company's material contracts must be filed as exhibits to the registration statement. These filings are public documents, and copies can be obtained by anyone, usually over the Internet. However, when documents contain information that could harm the company's legitimate business interests if disclosed, the company can seek to protect the information from public disclosure. In response to a narrowly framed request, the SEC may grant confidential treatment, for a limited number of years, of select portions of the agreements, such as royalty rates, payment amounts, volume discount rates, proprietary technical data or chemical compounds, and fields of research. A copy of the exhibit with the confidential portions carefully excised will then be available to the public. Requests for confidential treatment must be cleared with the SEC prior to effectiveness of the IPO. Prolonged negotiation with the SEC, or a third party who might be affected by such disclosure, may delay this clearance and thus delay the offering.

Exchanges, Nasdaq, and Blue Sky Laws

Each exchange has its own listing requirements, which must be satisfied for a company to be listed on that exchange. Underwriters typically recommend that companies apply to list their shares for trading on the Nasdaq Stock Market National Market System (*Nasdaq/NMS*) concurrently with the public offering. When stock is traded on the Nasdaq/NMS, brokers and traders are able to obtain real-time trading information. Listing on the Nasdaq/NMS is generally viewed as preferable to listing on the Nasdaq Small Cap Market because more information is available for Nasdaq/NMS companies, they are followed by more analysts and shareholders, and broad state securities law exemptions and corporate governance benefits are available. Alternatively, if the company satisfies the more stringent listing requirements of the New York Stock Exchange or the different requirements of the American Stock Exchange, the company may apply and be approved for listing there.

To list its stock on the Nasdaq/NMS, the company must file an application and satisfy specified criteria. It is important to begin the application process as early as possible; typically, the application is filed on the day the registration statement is filed or shortly afterward. The requirements for being listed on the Nasdaq/NMS are generally more stringent than those for the Nasdaq Small Cap Market and include financial as well as corporate governance requirements. As part of its Nasdaq/NMS listing application, the company must select a unique four-letter trading symbol.

Early-stage companies may have difficulty meeting the Nasdaq/NMS listing requirements. A special appeal process is available to permit the company to present additional facts to support its application.

Trading on the Nasdaq/NMS or an exchange requires the company to register under the Securities Exchange Act of 1934 (the 1934 Act), which subjects the company and its officers and directors to certain additional securities law requirements. Company counsel usually files to register the company under the 1934 Act at the time of the initial filing of the IPO registration statement with the SEC. Registration under the 1934 Act takes effect simultaneously with the commencement of trading on the Nasdaq/NMS or an exchange. Such registration would typically not otherwise be required for a number of months after a company's IPO.

The company must also comply with the securities or Blue Sky laws of each state in which shares are offered or sold except to the extent that such state laws are preempted by federal law. Underwriters typically ask a company to qualify in each state where the underwriters may offer the shares, as well as in Guam and Puerto Rico. Blue Sky qualification is usually handled by underwriters' counsel. The fees and expenses incurred in this process are typically paid by the company, subject to a cap on attorneys' fees. However, federal preemption enables a company that is listed for trading on the Nasdaq/NMS or certain exchanges to avoid time-consuming merit review by state regulators (whereby regulators evaluate the fairness of the terms of the offering) and eliminates the need for any pre-offering state filings.

The Road Show

After the registration statement is filed, the underwriters organize the road show. During this series of informational meetings, company management makes presentations to institutional investors and other prospective investors about the company, its business, and its strategy. Increasingly, the road show includes an Internet component as well. The underwriters typically time the road show to take place in the last weeks of the SEC review period. The meetings are set up for large audiences at select cities throughout the United States, and sometimes Europe and Asia, and are often followed by one-on-one meetings with certain potential investors. The road show can take two or three weeks and generally ends just prior to the expected effective date of the offering. The material presented in the road show must be consistent with, and cannot go

FROM THE TRENCHES

One of the most eagerly anticipated Internet IPOs was supposed to price in early October 1999 but was delayed for a one-month "cooling-off" period due to improprieties surrounding its road show. During a conference call for prospective investors, a representative of the company's underwriter shared its financial projections. The projections were not in the red herring, but they were subsequently published in an Internet periodical. The SEC not only ordered the cooling-off period but also required the company to describe what had happened in embarrassing detail in the final prospectus and to include the projections in the final prospectus, together with unusually detailed cautionary language concerning related risks and assumptions.

beyond, the information contained in the prospectus, and no written materials other than the preliminary prospectus should be distributed to the potential investors.

SEC Comments

The SEC's internal policies provide that comments to the prospectus will be delivered within thirty days after filing; during extremely busy periods, however, the comments may be delayed. The company responds to the SEC's staff comments by filing a pre-effective amendment to the registration statement, usually within a week after receiving the comments. The amendment is typically reviewed by the SEC examiner within a few days after receipt. If there are no additional comments, the examiner will indicate that the SEC will accept an acceleration request from the company and the managing underwriters to declare the registration statement immediately effective. Often more than one pre-effective amendment is filed, particularly when the initial comments are numerous or broad in nature. As the company is filing its amendments, the underwriters are finishing the road show and finalizing their book of nonbinding commitments.

Delayed or Terminated Offerings

Frequently, the IPO process is delayed or terminated. An IPO may be delayed for various reasons including a temporary downturn in the stock markets or the IPO climate; the need to incorporate another quarter's financial results into the prospectus; material developments, such as an acquisition, that must be completed and incorporated into the prospectus to permit adequate disclosure; regulatory problems in the case of highly regulated industries, such as medical devices and biotechnology; a change in company management; or the inability of the bankers to generate sufficient interest in the company's stock during the road show to fill the book and ensure that the offering will be fully sold. In many cases, a company will leave its registration statement on file, wait or take action as required to be in a position to continue the offering, and then go forward. Offerings are most frequently delayed (1) before responding to SEC comments and filing an amendment to the registration statement; (2) before printing the preliminary prospectus; and (3) in the case of an undersubscribed offering, at or near the completion of the road show. If the company and its bankers decide not to complete the IPO, then the company asks the SEC to withdraw its registration statement and continues corporate life as a private company. In the event of a terminated offering, securities laws severely limit the ability of a company to complete a private financing within six months of the termination. In early 2001 however, the SEC adopted a rule (Rule 155 under the Securities Act of 1933) that permits a company to complete such a financing by following certain requirements.

Pricing, Commencement of Trading, and Directed Shares

After the SEC review process is completed, the company and its underwriters will each request that the SEC declare the registration statement effective by submitting a request for acceleration. The underwriters and

FROM THE TRENCHES

The delicate timing of effectiveness can be unsettled by external events. In one case, a company was threatened with litigation a week prior to the proposed effective date. The working group was warned by company counsel that if they disclosed the threat in a pre-effective amendment to the registration statement, the SEC might delay the offering and require the company to recirculate a new preliminary prospectus with the additional disclosure. (Recirculation involves circulating the revised version of the preliminary prospectus to all persons who received a copy of the old version; it is often called for if material changes are made to the preliminary prospectus.) This risk could be avoided if no SEC filing were made and the lawsuit never materialized. On the other hand, if the lawsuit were filed on the eve of effectiveness, the offering most certainly would have to be delayed and the preliminary prospectus recirculated. The working group decided to fully disclose the risk in a pre-effective amendment to the registration statement; they reasoned that if the lawsuit were filed thereafter, the risk would have been fully disclosed. To the company's delight, no recirculation was required as a result of the amendment. The lawsuit was never filed, and the offering came to market as planned.

a subcommittee appointed by the company's board of directors to act as a pricing committee then negotiate the final price, usually after the stock market has closed on the day before the offering is to commence. This actual price is usually, but not necessarily, within the price range set out on the cover page of the preliminary prospectus. The company may reject the price proposed by the underwriters and elect not to proceed with the offering, although this rarely happens. Once the registration statement has been declared effective, the deal priced, and the underwriting agreement between the company and the underwriters signed, trading in the stock will commence, usually on the Nasdaq/NMS or an exchange, depending on where the stock is listed. Trading typically commences the morning after the pricing.

Often a portion of the shares to be sold is set aside by the underwriters and sold to purchasers specifically identified by the company. These transactions occur at the same time as the sales through the underwriting syndicate. These shares are called *"friends and family" shares,* or *directed shares.* Making directed shares available can be an effective way to permit persons and entities with which the company or its management has a relationship to participate in the offering and be part of the excitement. In the late 1990s, with the sharp increases in stock prices during first-day trading, many directed share programs proved very profitable for purchasers who might not otherwise have had the opportunity to purchase shares in an IPO. Consequently, directed shares became a hot topic during the IPO process. As one investment banker put it, the line of persons demanding directed shares was often "long and unruly."

If a company promises directed shares to customers or sells stock or issues warrants to customers shortly before an IPO at a price substantially below the IPO price, the SEC staff may become concerned that the company's reported revenues from those customers are overstated. The staff may require explicit disclosure of the sales to customers and, in extreme cases, may require the company to write down its revenues to reflect the portion of the amount paid that is attributable to the cheap stock.

The Closing

The offering is not *closed* (consummated) until the stock certificates are delivered and the funds are received. The closing usually takes place on the third business day after trading has commenced.

Restrictions on Sales of Shares

Lockup Agreements

The possibility of having additional shares of the company's stock come onto the market creates a very significant risk for the underwriters, the company, and the investors. Referred to as the *overhang*, an excess supply of shares in the marketplace can substantially depress stock prices. As a condition to the offering, underwriters typically require most shareholders, including all employees of the company, to sign *lockup agreements*, restricting their ability to sell any shares for a specified period of time, generally 180 days from the ef-

FROM THE TRENCHES

An experienced securities lawyer jumped from his prominent law firm to join a client, an Internet company, during the dot-com heyday. As part of his compensation package, he negotiated an option grant, with a portion to vest immediately and another sizable chunk to vest 120 days after the company's IPO. Both while at his law firm and after he joined the company, he worked to convince the underwriters to have a 120-day lockup rather than the usual 180 days. The underwriters agreed, perhaps because they expected the issue to be a high-volume stock that would be less affected if insiders began trading early. Following the IPO, the stock soared in value. One hundred and twenty days later, the lawyer was able to sell some of his stock for a multimillion-dollar profit. The company completed another public offering of its stock shortly thereafter, in which the lawyer and some of the company's executives sold additional shares, again for significant profits. The company's stock price subsequently dropped sharply with the market declines of 2000.

fective date of the IPO. As explained in Chapter 13, in many cases investors agree in advance to such a lockup at the time of their initial investment.

Most underwriters believe that unless the company secures lockups for at least 90 percent of the shares, an IPO could be jeopardized. Because of the risk, the underwriters may be reluctant to file the registration statement until sufficient lockup agreements have been obtained.

Trading of Stock Not Issued in Public Offering and the Impact of Rule 144

In addition to the lockup agreement provisions, trading of company stock acquired prior to the IPO is restricted under the federal securities laws. Common stock previously issued to employees and common stock issued when preferred stock is converted to common stock may not be sold in the open market unless certain conditions are satisfied. Employee shares issued prior to the IPO under written compensatory plans may generally be sold, pursuant to Rule 701 of the 1933 Act, ninety days after the IPO by employees who are not affiliates of the company and are not otherwise locked up. Employee shares held by affiliates (such as directors, executive officers, and significant shareholders of the company) may also be sold ninety days after the IPO pursuant to Rule 701, subject to the volume limitations described below. After the IPO, stock issued pursuant to employee plans is often registered with the SEC on Form S-8.

Restricted stock (i.e., stock not sold in a public offering) that was not issued under employee plans or for compensatory purposes must generally be resold in compliance with Rule 144 under the 1933 Act. Rule 144 generally requires that the securities be held for at least one year after purchase and be sold in limited quantities (*dribbled out*) through brokers or market makers. Rule 144 limits the amount that may be sold in a three-month period to the greater of 1 percent of the outstanding shares and the average weekly trading volume in the preceding four weeks. A Form 144 notice must be filed with the SEC when the order to sell is placed, and these filings are publicly available. However, nonaffiliates who have held their restricted stock for more than two years may sell their shares pursuant to Rule 144(k) without complying with any of these requirements.

Sales by affiliates must generally be made pursuant to Rule 144 even if they are selling stock acquired on the open market that was previously registered. However, sales by affiliates of such shares, or of stock acquired pursuant to employee plans under an S-8 registration statement or pursuant to Rule 701, are not subject to the usual one-year holding period requirement.

Contents of the Prospectus

Drafting the prospectus is a collaborative effort by company management, investment bankers, and attorneys. Company management can provide the most in-depth knowledge of the company itself, but the investment bankers and attorneys have the experience needed to shape the prospectus into a form that will win the approval of the SEC and can also be used as a marketing document to sell stock. In September 1998, the SEC's "plain English" rules went into effect to combat the complexity, repetition, and verboseness of the then-typical prospectus. The plain English rules encourage, and for many sections require, simple, straightforward language. Thanks to these rules, prospectuses look and read much differently now. Nevertheless, most prospectuses still follow a fairly standard format.

The prospectus begins with a short (one to three pages) summary of the offering, referred to as the *Box Summary,* which summarizes the key elements of the company's business and financial statements. Following the Box Summary is an extremely important section entitled *Risk Factors,* which alerts investors to the key risks and challenges faced by the company. It is important that risks specific to the company be identified and clearly explained. Additionally, an IPO prospectus usually addresses other risks that make the stock particularly speculative. These include the absence of an extended operating history or profitable operations, the fact that the nature of the business is inherently risky, the dependence on a sole supplier or particular customers, the uncertainties regarding technology or regulatory approvals, the uncertainty of proprietary rights, intense competition from more mature companies, and the lack of manufacturing or marketing experience. The Risk Factors section is intended to be cautionary, not optimistic; it highlights potential risks and serves as important protection in the event of shareholder litigation.

FROM THE TRENCHES

The underwriter and its counsel often must exert great effort to convince the company's chief executive officer to make the Risk Factors section in a prospectus as strong as possible. The CEO may believe that identifying all possible risks will have a negative effect on the offering and feel that it amounts to trashing the company's business in a public document. The underwriter, of course, wants to make certain that all conceivable risks are disclosed. In a recent offering, the CEO initially refused to permit certain risks to be included. Only after the managing underwriter offered to write him a letter to the effect that the inclusion of the risks would not have a negative impact on the IPO did the CEO relent.

The *Use of Proceeds* section describes how the company intends to use the proceeds of the offering in its business. The company should be able to support, by projections or otherwise, the proposed uses. The SEC staff has recently been insisting on fairly detailed discussions of the proposed uses of the funds, despite resistance from companies that want to avoid specific commitments of specific amounts to the extent possible or that do not have specific uses planned.

The *Management's Discussion and Analysis of Financial Condition and Results of Operations (MD&A)* section contains an analysis of the financial statements for at least the three most recent fiscal years and any applicable interim periods (unless the company has been in business for a shorter period of time). The analysis provides a year-to-year and period-to-period comparison, focusing on material changes and the reasons for those changes, as well as unusual or nonrecurring events that could cause the historical results to be a misleading indicator of future performance. The main point is to enable a reader to better understand the financial statements and financial condition of the company and known trends or uncertainties. This section has been the subject of heightened SEC scrutiny. Although projections *per se* are not required, the MD&A section does require a forward-looking analysis of the effect of known trends, events, or uncertainties, including information that may not be evident on the face of the financial statements. As part of the MD&A, the company's historical and projected sources of funds for the business must be discussed. In 2001-2002, in the wake of financial and accounting scandals involving Enron Corp. and other companies, there were multiple SEC pronouncements instructing companies to discuss more fully in their MD&A off-balance-sheet and related-party transactions and critical accounting policies, among other things. The SEC also instructed companies to provide extensive detail concerning financial prospects and sources and uses of capital.

The *Business* section provides a narrative description of the company, its strategies and goals, products or products in development, technology, manufacturing, and marketing. Within certain limits, this section can be customized in terms of both presentation and substance. It often has easy-to-read diagrams, graphs, or charts. Potential risks, such as technological uncertainties, shortages of raw materials, timing of new product introductions, or reliance on sole suppliers, are highlighted throughout. This section will reflect the tension between the need to provide complete disclosure of the risks of the investment and the desire to describe the company in a manner that will make it attractive to investors without revealing sensitive or competitive information.

The *Management* section provides biographical information about officers, directors, and key employees and describes executive compensation, employee benefit plans, and insider transactions. Disclosure of executive compensation is quite comprehensive and must follow certain prescribed tabular formats designed to facilitate comparisons among companies.

Audited Financial Statements are also required, including balance sheets as of the end of the last two fiscal years and income statements for the three most recent fiscal years. Unaudited interim financial statements are required for offerings that become effective 135 or more days after the end of the most recent fiscal year. All financial statements must conform to generally accepted accounting principles (GAAP) and to SEC accounting requirements.

If the company has recently (i.e., within twelve to eighteen months prior to effectiveness) granted stock options or otherwise issued stock at a price significantly below the IPO price, a charge to earnings to reflect the issuance of this so-called *cheap stock* may be required. The theory is that cheap stock issued to employees is actually additional compensation to the employees and should be accounted for as such, and that cheap stock sold to nonemployees represents a "deemed dividend" (in effect, a built-in gain) to the purchaser. Cheap stock is often the subject of SEC comment on the prospectus, and, if the proposed charge is significant, it can jeopardize the offering because of its impact on the company's financial statements. It is important to discuss this issue with the company's auditors prior to the organizational meeting.

The company need not but often does include photographs, illustrations, and graphs in the prospectus. Although color photographs or illustrations add to the cost of printing and require additional lead time, many companies and underwriters believe that they help readers who lack a technical background to understand the company's business and products. The SEC staff has commented negatively on the use of professional models rather than employees in product photographs. Photos of prototype products, fully disclosed as such, may be used in the prospectus.

FROM THE TRENCHES

One way to persuade the SEC that a cheap stock charge is inappropriate (or to reduce the amount of such a charge) is to obtain a valuation report from an independent expert concluding that the stock was issued at fair market value. In a recent deal, a company issued several hundred thousand shares of stock at a price of $1 per share seven months before the IPO. The proposed public offering price was $15 per share. Knowing that the SEC might argue that the company should recognize $11 per share of compensation expense (based on 80 percent of $15), amounting to several million dollars of charges over time, the company hired a valuation expert after the IPO process commenced to value the company's stock as of the issuance seven months before. The expert concluded, based on the company's precarious financial condition at that time, that a value of $3 per share was appropriate. The company took a charge based on this amount and filed the report with the SEC. No additional earning charges were required.

Liability for Misstatements in the Prospectus

Securities laws regulating IPOs and other registered public offerings of securities are geared, in large part, toward ensuring that sufficient disclosure of relevant facts is made to permit potential investors to make informed investment decisions. To further this goal, Section 11 of the 1933 Act makes certain persons associated with a registered offering of securities (including the company; the officers required to sign the registration statement, i.e., the chief executive officer, the chief financial officer, and the chief accounting officer; the directors; the named nominees for director; and the underwriters) civilly liable to the purchasers of the shares for any untrue statement of a material fact contained in a registration statement and for any failure to state a material fact necessary to make the other statements not misleading. The auditors are liable for any material misrepresentation or omission in the financial statements.

The company is absolutely liable for any material misrepresentation or omission, regardless of the degree of care that was used in preparing the prospectus. A director or an underwriter may avoid liability by establishing that he, she, or it exercised due diligence; that is, that, after undertaking a reasonable investigation, such person reasonably believed the statement at issue to be accurate. This *due diligence defense* is technically available to officers as well, but it is much more difficult for officers to demonstrate that they would not have been aware of the inaccuracy or omission if they had exercised due diligence. Underwriters, directors, and officers are often named as defendants in Section 11 lawsuits, and even a successful defense is expensive, time-consuming, and unpleasant.

Preparing for an IPO

Prefiling Publicity

Any publication of information or publicity effort made in advance of a proposed public offering that has the effect of conditioning the public mind or arousing public interest in the issuer or its securities may constitute an impermissible offer to sell securities under federal securities laws. This type of impermissible activity during the *prefiling period* (the period before the registration statement is filed) is referred to as *gun jumping*. Disclosures that may run afoul of the securities laws include marketing letters, press releases, speeches, presentations at seminars or conferences, articles in the financial press, and other forms of advertising. Gun-jumping violations, in addition to embarrassing the issuer and its underwriters, may delay the marketing of the securities because the SEC may refuse to declare a public offering registration statement effective until the effect of the violations has dissipated. Such violations may also result in criminal and civil actions against the issuer and the underwriters.

Companies in the midst of the registration process must be careful to avoid inappropriate publicity. During the prefiling period, it is illegal for

FROM THE TRENCHES

After years of unsuccessful attempts to attract press coverage, Amgen and its founder and then CEO, George Rathman, were unexpectedly featured in a prominent article published by *Business Week*. The article appeared on the day that the SEC received the company's registration statement. Counsel for the company spent a long weekend drafting a letter of explanation to the SEC, emphasizing that the interview was granted well before the offering process began, explaining that the company had no notice of publication, and requesting that the offering not be delayed. Fortunately, the request was granted.

In contrast, during the dot-com frenzy, huge publicity often surrounded upstart Internet companies. In October 1999, the IPO of online grocer Webvan was delayed for a month because of publicity during the waiting period. A *Forbes* article published during this period quoted the company's CEO, the former CEO of Andersen Consulting, as saying that "Webvan is all about leveraging technology and reinventing the grocery business, just as Andersen had reinvented consulting," and that Webvan will "set the rules for the largest consumer sector in the country. The creation of 26 distribution centers—each one bigger than 18 conventional supermarkets—will take the costs out of the equation." When Webvan was finally permitted to complete its offering, it had to include these statements in its final prospectus along with language disclaiming media reports and highlighting the risks of the enterprise. Notwithstanding the CEO's enthusiasm, Webvan shut down its business and filed for bankruptcy protection in mid-2001.

the company to offer to sell any securities pending registration. Therefore, during this period, the company's communications are most significantly restricted. For example, the company may not issue forecasts, projections, or predictions about its expected future performance. The only communication about the offering permitted during this period is a notice of proposed offering, the contents of which are narrowly prescribed by regulation. These notices are rarely used in connection with IPOs.

Nevertheless, the company need not completely discontinue its normal public relations activities. It is permitted to continue advertising that is consistent with past practices, to send out its customary reports to shareholders, and to make routine press announcements with regard to factual business developments, as long as such activities can be conducted without having an impact on the offering. The company should remember that newspaper and magazine articles often have a long lead time. Thus, an article currently being researched and written may not be published until many months later, when the public offering process is in full swing.

The company should consider setting up an internal control procedure to ensure that all public disclosures are properly reviewed and coordinated in advance. Counsel for the company and the underwriters should review all press releases and publicity, including product announcements, to be released for publication, broadcast, or distribution during the registration period. In addition, the company should establish a policy prohibiting employees, officers, and directors from recommending the company's securities, offering their opinions or forecasts regarding the company, or, without the advice of counsel, providing any information regarding the IPO.

Postfiling Publicity

After the registration statement is filed but before it is declared effective by the SEC, the company is in the *registration period* or *waiting period,* during which the company can offer its securities for sale but cannot actually sell them. The offer of securities must be made by means of the preliminary prospectus or through oral communications. During this time, the company and the underwriters will conduct the road show. Antifraud provisions of the securities laws still apply, and selective disclosure of material not included in the prospectus is problematic. Members of the press are typically excluded from the meetings with potential investors during the road show.

Industry conferences are extremely important opportunities for the company to meet the investment community. These conferences are planned long in advance, and invitations to present at them are intensely coveted. After discussion with counsel and the underwriters, a company may go forward with previously arranged conference presentations provided that the red-herring prospectus is available at the conference (and no other written materials are given out because they would be considered offering materials not included in the prospectus). The presentation should be the same as the road show presentation; the company will typically not participate in one-on-one or breakout sessions.

Posteffective Quiet Period

The twenty-five-day period after effectiveness of the registration statement and commencement of the IPO is called the *quiet period.* During this period, sales of the securities can begin, and the final prospectus is delivered. Distribution of other written literature is permitted, provided that it is accompanied or preceded by a prospectus. It is also traditional for the underwriters to run a tombstone advertisement in the financial press to announce the commencement of the sale of the securities. This tombstone advertisement is governed by both regulation and custom.

Even though the offering may be complete from the company's perspective once the closing has occurred, the SEC may consider an effort to publicize the offering to be an inappropriate attempt by the company to encourage the public to purchase shares from dealers who are still required to deliver a prospectus during this quiet period. As a result, issuers are generally careful to remain quiet, releasing information only as necessary in bare factual form. If material developments do occur during this period, it may be necessary to supplement, or sticker, the prospectus to reflect the new developments or, in some cases, to file a posteffective amendment with the SEC.

Board Composition

The company should review the composition of its board of directors prior to the offering. Public investors occasionally will be concerned if the

FROM THE TRENCHES

In a recent proposed IPO involving a Salt Lake City company, a significant shareholder (who owned 25 percent of the stock) had the contractual right to elect a majority of the company's board of directors. The shareholder wanted to maintain this right even after the IPO to protect its investment. The underwriters felt that board control by a single investor would adversely affect the marketability of the IPO. After extensive discussions, the investor agreed that it would retain only the right to elect one-third of the board. The offering proceeded.

board does not include enough *outside* or *independent directors*, that is, persons who are not officers or employees of the company or its subsidiaries and who do not otherwise have a relationship with the company that could interfere with their exercise of independent judgment in carrying out their responsibilities. (Independent directors and board composition are discussed in Chapter 6.)

Board committees, such as audit and compensation committees, become much more important once a company goes public. A company listed on the Nasdaq/NMS or the New York Stock Exchange must have an audit committee composed solely of at least three independent directors. The audit committee, which reviews the company's independent auditors and evaluates the company's accounting system and internal controls, is perceived as having a critical oversight role in preventing and detecting fraudulent financial reporting, especially after the demise of Enron Corp. and financial and accounting problems with numerous other companies. The audit committee is required to submit a report with the company's annual proxy statement detailing its independence and activities. The SEC's proxy rules also require a report from the compensation committee (or the full board if there is no such committee) on how the compensation of the company's executive officers was set. Additionally, a committee composed of at least two nonemployee directors generally must administer most of the company's employee stock plans if the company intends to take advantage of the favorable treatment afforded those plans by certain exemptions from liability for short-swing trading under Section 16 of the 1934 Act, discussed later in this chapter.

Reincorporation in Delaware

As explained in Chapter 5, companies choose to incorporate in Delaware for a number of reasons. Accordingly, companies not already incorporated in Delaware frequently reincorporate there as part of the IPO process. Shareholder protection measures available in Delaware to reduce a corporation's vulnerability to hostile takeover attempts are often adopted at the same time.

Responsibilities of a Public Company and its Board of Directors

The realities of being a public company include heightened public scrutiny and disclosure obligations that a private company does not face. Once public, a company must file a number of periodic reports and other documents with the SEC disclosing information about its business, management, and financial results and condition. The company's officers, directors, and principal shareholders must file documents with the SEC that disclose their ownership of and transactions in the company's securities. The company and its directors and officers also face increased potential liability as a result of their fiduciary responsibilities to public shareholders and their disclosure obligations.

The periodic reporting requirements, together with the need to issue press releases and deal with securities analysts and public shareholders, add significant pressure to achieve short-term results at the expense of long-term goals and may limit the flexibility of management and the board of directors in making strategic corporate decisions. Finally, the periodic reporting requirements bring additional costs to a public company in the form of increased legal, accounting, and printing expenses. The company may also need to hire additional management personnel to handle its expanded reporting and other obligations.

Periodic Reports

Public company status increases a company's responsibilities to its shareholders and to the trading market. The company will be required to file certain periodic reports with the SEC (e.g., annual reports on Form 10-K, quarterly reports on Form 10-Q, and current reports on Form 8-K) and will have to comply with the notification and filing requirements of the exchange that lists its shares. A newly public company will also have to make disclosures in its periodic reports concerning how the proceeds from its IPO have been used and how much remains. Additionally, public companies must comply with the SEC's proxy regulations when soliciting a vote or consent of shareholders.

FORM 10-K The report on Form 10-K, which is filed annually with the SEC, provides a continuing update of information about the company and its management substantially similar to that contained in the company's prospectus. It will include a description of the company's business for the preceding fiscal year, audited financial statements, and an MD&A section relating to the periods covered by those financial statements.

FORM 10-Q The report on Form 10-Q is filed quarterly with the SEC and includes summary unaudited quarterly financial statements, an MD&A section covering those results, and certain other specified disclosures, such as information concerning new developments in legal proceedings or shareholders' actions taken within the quarter.

FORM 8-K A report on Form 8-K is intended to supplement the normal recurring filing requirements (e.g., Form 10-K and Form 10-Q) when material events occur that should be brought to the prompt attention of the investing public, such as a merger, a change in control, a sale of significant assets, bankruptcy, or a change in accountants.

Effect of Proxy Rules

A company registered under the 1934 Act must comply with the SEC proxy rules when soliciting a shareholder vote or consent. Generally, these rules require that a proxy statement be mailed to each shareholder of record in advance of every shareholders' meeting. The proxy statement must set forth detailed information regarding the company's management and the matters to be voted on. For example, a proxy statement relating to the election of directors must include a report of the compensation committee (or the full board, if there is no such committee) explaining how executive compensation was determined and the relationship between pay and performance; it must also include a graph comparing performance of the company's stock against a broad-based index and an industry-group index. In some cases, such as a shareholder vote on a merger, the proxy statement and the form of proxy must first be submitted to the SEC for review and comment. Because of the filing and other procedural requirements applicable to proxy solicitations, the company should plan all meetings of shareholders well in advance.

Directors' Responsibilities in a Public Company

Because directors have a fiduciary relationship to both the company and its shareholders, they are bound by the duties of loyalty and care imposed by the law of the state where the company is incorporated. These duties are applicable to directors of all companies, whether public or private, and are discussed in Chapter 6.

DIRECTORS' LIABILITY FOR SECURITIES CLAIMS Companies and their officers and directors are subject to damage claims for securities fraud under the antifraud rules if their regular quarterly and annual disclosures to the SEC and the public are inaccurate in any material way. Similarly, the securities laws make it unlawful for any person to solicit proxies in contravention of the rules and regulations of the SEC. In this context, directors may be held liable if they knew, or through the exercise of due diligence should have known, that a proxy solicitation issued on their behalf contained material false or misleading statements or omissions. Beyond required disclosures, it is possible to incur liability for securities fraud in connection with the issuance of misleading press releases, reports to shareholders, or other communications that could be expected to reach investors and trading markets.

INDEMNIFICATION AND LIABILITY INSURANCE FOR DIRECTORS Under the laws of most states, companies have broad and flexible powers to indemnify directors who are made parties to proceedings and incur liability by reason of their status as directors. Delaware law generally provides broader powers and flexibility to companies to indemnify their directors, officers, employees, and agents than does the law in other states, and the case law regarding the interpretation of indemnification provisions is also more extensive in Delaware than in other states. For example, Delaware permits companies to eliminate monetary liability even for gross negligence, whereas California law requires directors to remain liable under certain circumstances for acts or omissions that constitute an unexcused pattern of inattention or reckless disregard of their duties. In addition, companies can acquire directors' and officers' (D&O) liability insurance. Most companies secure D&O liability insurance prior to completion of an IPO or consider increasing the company's current coverage while still a private company.

Insider Trading

Insider trading is the purchase or sale of any security on the basis of material nonpublic information about that security or the issuer in breach of a duty of trust or confidence owed the issuer of that security or its shareholders or the source of the information. Directors, officers, employees, accountants, attorneys, and consultants are considered insiders with a fiduciary duty to the company and its shareholders. An insider in possession of material nonpublic information must either disclose it before trading (which is often impossible for a variety of reasons) or refrain from trading. Failure to observe these restrictions may subject the individual (and perhaps the company) to both civil and criminal liability, including penalties of three times the profit or avoided loss on a transaction, fines of up to $1 million (up to $42.5 million for entities), and prison sentences.

Insiders are also prohibited from disclosing material inside information to others who might use the information to their advantage in trading in the company's securities. Both the person who discloses the information (the *tipper*) and the person who receives it (the *tippee*) may be liable under

FROM THE TRENCHES

It does not take a huge windfall to catch the attention of the SEC. An attorney was indicted for trading in the securities of his client at a time when he had knowledge of a pending merger. The resulting $14,000 profit could not have been worth the subsequent pain. He resigned from his firm and reportedly pled guilty to one count of insider trading, a felony charge with a maximum ten-year prison term.

the insider trading laws. In fact, the tipper can be held liable for the profits or losses avoided by the tippee even if the tipper does not share in the profits or losses avoided.

In past court cases involving insider trading, what the insiders or tippees thought or knew, or later claimed they thought or knew, has not necessarily provided a successful defense if, in hindsight, their personal securities transactions created the impression that they were in fact taking advantage of undisclosed information about the issuer. Thus, it is important that insiders and tippees avoid even the appearance of impropriety.

For example, assume that a director, who is also a partner in a venture capital firm, knows of a significant unannounced contract that the company has won. The director-partner does not communicate this information to anyone, but another partner in the venture capital firm, based entirely on public information, purchases securities of that company. Shortly thereafter, the company's securities increase substantially in value. Because it would be possible for an objective fact finder to find, based on appearances, that the director-partner had tipped the nondirector-partner, the partners and the firm could have significant exposure to litigation and potential liability for insider trading, even though they had not actually violated the law. Accordingly, persons with special relationships with insiders of a company are well advised to check with the insider before trading in the company's stock to make certain that the insider is not in possession of material nonpublic information about the company.

FROM THE TRENCHES

The son of the president of MCA Corp. overheard his father discussing the pending sale of MCA to Matsushita. The son heeded his father's warning not to trade on the information but passed it on to his ex-wife and her boyfriend. They traded for their own account and passed the information on to others who also traded. Following public announcement of the sale, MCA's stock rose sharply, and the SEC launched an investigation. Those who traded as a result of the son's tip settled with the SEC by disgorging their profits, plus penalties; the son settled by paying the SEC $418,000 in penalties, even though he had not traded and had not made a dime on the information he passed on.

New Safe Harbor for Preexisting Arrangements or Blind Trusts

In October 2000, new SEC regulations designed to permit trading in a company's stock by an insider under certain circumstances when the insider is in possession of material nonpublic information but does not trade on the basis of that information went into effect. Rule 10b5-1, promulgated by the SEC under the 1934 Act, provides that a trade will be deemed to be made on the basis of material nonpublic information if the person making the trade was aware of the information at the time of the trade unless the insider has taken specific measures to come within a new safe harbor set forth in Rule 10b5-1(c).

There are two ways to make trades under the safe harbor. First, an individual can, at a time when he or she has no material nonpublic information, expressly authorize trades in the future by (1) entering into a binding contract to make the trades, (2) instructing another to make the trades on his or her behalf, or (3) adopting a written plan for making trades. (Though the first two methods can be oral, written documentation would help validate when and under what terms the contract was entered into or the instructions given.) The contract, instruction, or plan must be specific as to the amount of shares and the price and trading date, or a formula or other specific manner of determining the amount, price, and date must be included. An insider using this method must not engage in hedging or any other activity designed to mitigate the risk of the trades; the insider must also be acting in good faith and not pursuant to a plan or scheme to evade the insider trading restrictions.

Alternatively, an insider can permit another person to make trades at his or her discretion; because the insider does not make the "investment decision," it will not be made on the basis of any material nonpublic information the insider might have. This empowerment of another to make trades is often referred to as a "blind trust." The person actually making the trades on behalf of the insider may not be in possession of any material nonpublic information at the time of the trades. The insider is also required to implement reasonable policies and procedures to prevent the trader from obtaining such information and to ensure that the trader will not trade if he or she does obtain such information.

The safe harbor provided by Rule 10b5-1(c) was not widely used during its first year, probably due to uncertainty as to its effectiveness upon challenge. Nonetheless, it does provide a useful mechanism to enable insiders to diversify their company holdings. Consequently, 10b5-1(c) plans, via either written plans or blind trust arrangements, are expected to become more common.

Company Liability

Legislation adopted in 1988 extends potential liability for insider trading violations to employers under certain circumstances. The Insider Trading and Securities Fraud Enforcement Act of 1988 (ITSFEA) provides that any controlling person who knew or recklessly disregarded the fact that a controlled person was likely to engage in acts constituting an insider trading violation and failed to take appropriate steps to prevent such acts before they occurred may independently be liable for a civil penalty of up to the greater of $1 million or treble the controlled person's profits or avoided losses resulting from the violation. This penalty provision theoretically would permit a court to assess a company a penalty of $1 million even if the insider trading by the employee involved only a few thousand dollars.

Adopting a written policy prohibiting insider trading can reduce the company's exposure for controlling-person liability. A well-drafted policy educates employees on the law of insider trading and establishes internal procedures to safeguard against both intentional and unintentional illegal trading. In the event that an employee does violate the law, the policy and related procedures reduce the risk that the company itself will be liable under the ITSFEA.

Some companies go beyond a simple insider trading policy applicable to all employees and adopt an additional policy limiting the times when directors, officers, and principal shareholders can sell or purchase stock. These so-called *window-period policies* typically prohibit the person from trading in the company's stock during a specific period, such as a period commencing four weeks before the end of a quarter and extending until seventy-two hours after the company has released its earnings report for that quarter (typically three weeks after the quarter has ended). The company usually retains the right to close the trading window early or not open it at all if there is undisclosed information that would make trades by insiders inappropriate. The company could provide for an exception to this policy, as well as to its insider trading policy, for trades properly conducted under Rule 10b5-1(c) discussed above.

The purpose of these policies is to protect the company from being sued because an officer or director traded stock at a time when the insider might have known how the quarter was going to turn out and the market did not. Defending such lawsuits takes management time and company resources, and the suits can bring ill repute to the company. In addition, the fact that insiders are trading can require the company to disclose pending developments (such as sensitive merger negotiations or major mineral finds) that the company might otherwise legally be entitled to keep quiet. Furthermore, if insiders sell substantial amounts of stock shortly before the company announces disappointing earnings, unhappy shareholders, who acquired stock prior to the announcement of the bad news and the ensuing drop in the stock price, will often sue the company for securities fraud and cite the insiders' sales as evidence that the insiders intentionally misled the market so they could sell their stock at an artificially high price. A window-period policy lessens the possibility of such lawsuits and makes it easier to get them dismissed.

Liability for Short-Swing Profits

Section 16 of the 1934 Act provides for the automatic recovery by the company of any profits made by executive officers, directors, and greater-than-10-percent shareholders on securities purchased and sold, or sold and purchased, within a six-month period (i.e., on *short-swing trading*). Section 16(b) is mechanically applied and liability is imposed regardless of the trader's intent to use, or actual use of, inside information. Furthermore, the reports filed by executive officers, directors, and greater-than-10-percent shareholders pursuant to Section 16(a) are monitored by professional plaintiffs' attorneys for indications of short-swing trading violations. Thus, even if a company might choose to ignore the short-swing trading of its insiders, insiders who have violated the strictures of Section 16(b) will still be pursued in shareholder derivative suits. Complex rules exist for the attribution to insiders of purchases and sales by persons and entities related to insiders for the purposes of Section 16(b).

Insider Reports

Executive officers and directors of public companies are subject to a number of reporting requirements designed, among other things, to provide the investing public with information regarding their holdings and trading activity in the securities of the companies by which they are employed or on whose boards they serve. Section 16(a), for instance, requires that each executive officer and director of a company involved in an IPO file a Form 3 detailing his or her beneficial ownership of the securities of that company. The Form 3 is typically filed at the same time as the public offering becomes effective. (A public company must also file a form within ten days of the election of any new director or officer of the company.) A Form 4 must be filed within ten days after the end of any month in which a change in beneficial ownership occurs, including gifts and transfers to trusts. A Form 5 must be filed annually to report certain transactions that were not otherwise reportable or reported. Finally, the company must disclose in its annual report on Form 10-K whether any officer or director has failed to file the required reports in a timely manner. It should be noted that, for purposes of these reporting requirements, complex rules exist regarding what constitutes beneficial ownership of securities.

The SEC has the power to seek monetary fines from individuals for violation of these laws up to the following limits: (1) up to $5,000 ($50,000 for entities) per violation for plain vanilla violations, such as a late filing or a nonfiling of a required form under Section 16; (2) up to $50,000 ($250,000 for entities) per violation for violations involving fraud, deceit, manipulation, or deliberate or reckless disregard of the law; and (3) up to $100,000 ($500,000 for entities) per violation for violations that not only involve fraud or reckless disregard of the law but also result in, or create a substantial risk of, substantial losses to others or a substantial gain to the individual involved. In the past, the SEC has taken the position that a new violation may occur for each day a filing is late or is not corrected.

Post-IPO Disclosure, Communications with Analysts, and Regulation FD

A public company should establish and follow a policy of prompt and complete disclosure through the press of all material developments, both favorable and unfavorable, that, if known, might reasonably be expected to influence the market price of the company's shares. In the absence of certain events or circumstances that trigger a duty to disclose, however, disclosure of even material information may sometimes be delayed for valid business reasons or if it is otherwise premature.

Disclosure Obligations

The securities laws impose a duty to disclose material information in a variety of circumstances. For example, a company must publicly disclose material information (1) when necessary to satisfy the SEC's periodic reporting requirements (including the inclusion of known trends and uncertainties in the MD&A section) or the company's obligations under listing agreements with Nasdaq or an exchange; (2) when the company or its insiders are trading in the company's own securities; (3) when necessary to correct a prior statement that the company learns was materially untrue or misleading at the time it was made; (4) when the company is otherwise making a public disclosure and the omission of material information could be misleading; (5) when material nonpublic information has been disclosed, intentionally or unintentionally, to one or a group of shareholders or to investment professionals, such as analysts, and not to the general public; or (6) when necessary to correct rumors in the marketplace that are attributable to the company.

Under the antifraud rules adopted by the SEC pursuant to the 1934 Act, a company may incur liability to any person who purchases or sells the company's securities in the market after the issuance of a misleading proxy statement, report, press release, or other communication reasonably expected to reach the investing public even if the company itself did not trade. For example, A.H. Robins was held liable for securities fraud when it failed to disclose new tests questioning the safety of its interuterine device (IUD) after publicly touting its safety record.

Information is considered *material* if its dissemination would be likely to affect the market price of the company's stock or would likely be considered important by a reasonable investor who is considering trading in the company's securities. In the event of nondisclosure for any reason, officers, directors, and other insiders should be advised against trading in the company's securities until the information has been adequately disseminated (subject, perhaps, to trades made in compliance with the safe harbor provided by Rule 10b5-1(c)). Otherwise, as noted earlier, a plaintiffs' attorney will use the fact that insiders were trading as evidence of intent to deceive the market.

Safe Harbor for Forward-Looking Statements

Federal legislation adopted in December 1995 made it easier for companies to protect themselves from litigation concerning certain disclosures made after an IPO. Congress established a safe harbor for certain oral and written forward-looking statements, such as projections, forecasts, and other statements about future operations, plans, or possible results. For a company to be protected, a statement must disclose that it is forward-looking and that the company's actual results may differ materially. In addition, the company must, in the case of a written statement, provide a detailed discussion of the factors that could result in a discrepancy and, in the case of an oral statement, refer the audience to a readily available written statement that contains such a discussion. Courts have repeatedly found this safe harbor and companies' properly worded cautions regarding forward-looking statements to be an effective defense to claims of inaccurate or misleading disclosures. Nevertheless, disclosure issues continue to be sensitive and should be discussed thoroughly with counsel.

Communications with Analysts, Selective Disclosure, and Regulation FD

Discussions with market analysts, who write reports following the progress of the company and generally keep the public informed of business developments, are inherently risky. No information given to an analyst is ever off the record. Casual or ill-considered disclosure to an analyst of material inside information can lead to shareholder lawsuits and SEC investigations for securities fraud and insider trading, as well as a violation of Regulation FD discussed below. Although it is important to maintain good relations with the press and analysts, it is also critical to avoid selective disclosure of material information. *Selective disclosure* is the release of material information on an individual basis without its simultaneous release to the public generally.

The SEC enacted Regulation FD (Fair Disclosure), effective in October 2000, as a mechanism to prevent and regulate selective disclosure and to reinforce a company's obligations to keep the public informed in a fair and evenhanded manner. Regulation FD has dramatically changed the way public companies disclose material information and the types of information they publicly disclose, particularly with respect to projections of future financial performance.

Regulation FD restricts a company's senior officers, and others who regularly communicate with analysts or investors, from selectively disclosing material nonpublic information to securities market professionals (such as investment advisers or analysts), as well as to shareholders when it is reasonably foreseeable that the shareholders will trade on the basis of such information. If a selective disclosure of material nonpublic information is intentional, the information must simultaneously be broadly disseminated to the general public. If a selective disclosure is unintentional, the company must broadly disseminate the information no later than twenty-four hours after the commencement of the next day's trading. As a result, with few exceptions, such as when the recipient agrees to "embargo" and not use the information, the senior officials of companies are required to broadly disseminate any material information they discuss with a small group of investors or investment professionals. This broad dissemination can take the form of a press release, a Form 8-K filing, or properly noticed conference calls or Internet broadcasts, but a company has flexibility in determining what is reasonable. A company can be liable in a suit by the SEC if (1) it knows, or is reckless in not knowing, that information selectively disclosed is both material and nonpublic; (2) it fails to promptly disseminate the information to the public; or (3) its methods of communication are not reasonably designed to prevent illegal selective disclosure. Individuals responsible for selective disclosure in violation of Regulation FD can also be liable, either as the direct violators or as aiders and abettors. Although only the SEC is empowered to sue for violations of Regulation FD, any affected shareholder can sue if the selective disclosure amounted to illegal tipping by an insider under Rule 10b-5.

The SEC has cautioned that an official who engages in a private discussion with an analyst seeking guidance about earnings estimates "takes on a high degree of risk under Regulation FD."[1] In most cases, however, it is permissible in dealing with analysts and the press to provide general background information or to fill in incremental details regarding a matter that has been disclosed in all material respects. The theory behind this is that a company may be able to selectively disclose bits of information that would

FROM THE TRENCHES

Not long ago, a company facing a disappointing earnings announcement decided that it might be able to soften the impact on the market by disclosing the news, several days before the public announcement, to two analysts who followed the company. One of the analysts decided to tell his firm's favored clients the news, and the company's stock began to fall rapidly. Not only did the company have to issue a press release quickly to respond to calls from panicky investors, but it also had to defend itself in an SEC insider trading investigation. Today, such communication would also constitute a clear violation of Regulation FD.

in themselves be immaterial to a "reasonable investor" (e.g., information about competitors, suppliers, or customers) but from which an analyst could create a "mosaic" of information that in its whole is material. In an attempt to avoid selective or premature disclosure problems, many companies observe a consistent no-comment policy with respect to certain material undisclosed corporate developments, such as acquisitions. Whenever material developments occur or the company becomes aware of rumors circulating in the marketplace, the company should always consult with counsel to determine whether a press release is appropriate.

When meeting informally with members of the business community, company representatives should also be careful not to inadvertently disclose nonpublic information that might be considered material. The antifraud provisions of the federal securities laws apply to all company statements that can be expected to reach investors and trading markets, not just to SEC filings or press releases.

LIABILITY FOR AN ANALYST'S REPORT If an analyst provides an inaccurate projection regarding a company, it is generally considered to be the analyst's assessment and not the company's unless the company confirms the information or otherwise becomes entangled in the analyst's report. Companies should always consult carefully with counsel whenever they are tempted to comment on an analyst's report. Disclaimers, warnings, and generalities can reduce the risk if the company decides to comment.

However, any spokesperson talking to analysts must understand that, if he or she comments on projections and forecasts, the company may be held liable if the projections prove incorrect or if the analyst uses the information to engage in trading before the information is released to the public. The comments or any other communication could also be a violation of Regulation FD. Generally, the safest course is for the company not to comment.

Putting it into Practice

Soon after the successful product launch of the SDB, Kendra met with the other DataAccelleation directors to decide whether to proceed with an IPO or to sell the company. They knew that DataAccelleation would need additional funds to enable it to accelerate its growth and continue to leapfrog over its competitors. Kendra and her board felt that it would be relatively easy to find a buyer for the company, given the enormous interest in the database management and navigation tools. In fact, two customers had already made unofficial overtures. But the directors also felt that DataAccelleation had a huge potential for growth that would not be reflected even in the IPO price, much less the price they would be able to command as a prepublic company. They also concluded that the current IPO environment was favorable: companies in their industry were completing IPOs, and the IPO window that had closed the year before appeared to have reopened. In the end, they were unwilling to cap the potential upside of an IPO by selling for cash or by taking stock in a larger company whose stock price would be determined in large part by the performances of businesses other than DataAccelleation. They were also excited by the challenge of taking DataAccelleation to the next level of growth as an independent company. After due consideration, the board unanimously decided to proceed with an IPO.

Once Kendra and her board reached this decision, Kendra assembled a team of investment bankers, lawyers, and accountants. The first step in picking an investment banking firm was to update and assemble a corporate profile to present to potential underwriters. This consisted of a business plan, marketing literature, and audited yearly and unaudited quarterly financial statements for the three years DataAccelleation had been in existence. Next, Kendra compiled a list of suitable and likely candidates for underwriters. She wanted to consider firms with (1) expertise in and commitment to companies in DataAccelleation's industry, (2) a track record of successful IPOs that were also successful in the aftermarket, (3) respected analysts who were likely to support the company by providing research reports to the investment community in the future, and (4) no conflicts of interest. The list of potential underwriters included firms that had expressed interest in the company in the past as well as others that were likely to be receptive to the company. Michael Cruz and other experienced securities counsel at his firm were helpful in providing leads and introductions.

continued...

continued...

Prior to the first organizational meeting, Kendra met with Michael and the company's auditors to determine whether there were any corporate or financial cleanup items that could affect the timing or success of the offering. At the organizational meeting, attended by Kendra, Philip, and Kristine on behalf of DataAccelleation, Michael and an associate from his firm as company counsel, the underwriters, underwriters' counsel, and the auditors, all such issues were fully aired and thoroughly discussed. By discussing these issues up front, the group was able to develop a realistic time line.

In addition to disclosure and timing issues, the DataAccelleation working group also discussed a number of other important issues at the organizational meeting, including the size of the offering, the price range, a required stock split, the length of lockup agreements and who would be required to execute them, reincorporation in Delaware, and other corporate matters. Then, and for the bulk of the day, the various executive officers and key employees of DataAccelleation introduced themselves, and each gave a short (thirty-minute) presentation on his or her respective area of responsibility. Kendra had reviewed the content of the presentations with the officers in advance. At a minimum, she wanted them to include an overview of the business, a review of the intellectual property portfolio, a description of significant corporate partners and strategic relationships, and a review of the company's current financial condition and projections.

After the organizational meeting, company counsel produced the first draft of the registration statement with significant input from Kendra and her partners. Kendra had prepared the first draft of the Business section, making it specific to her business but also including language based on several sample prospectuses Michael had provided her. Because all prospectuses have a particular style and tone with which Kendra and her partners were unfamiliar, Michael substantially revised the Business section to address certain standard points and to put the disclosure into "plain English." Once the first draft was completed and distributed, the working group met for a series of all-hands meetings. The dates for these meetings had been confirmed at the organizational meeting and took place at the offices of Michael's firm.

Once the draft had progressed sufficiently, a smaller group met at the financial printer's offices to finalize the document and file it with the SEC.

continued...

continued...

Kendra had chosen a printer early in the process based on competitive bids and the recommendations of the underwriters and counsel. Given the SEC requirement that all documents be transmitted to the SEC electronically (through a system referred to as EDGAR), it was important that Kendra retain an experienced financial printer that could meet the company's proposed schedule.

After the registration statement was filed with the SEC, Kendra and her partners turned their attention to corporate matters that had to be completed prior to the closing of the offering. For example, the company needed to undertake a shareholder mailing to obtain written shareholder consents to amend charter documents, reincorporate in Delaware, and effect a stock split.

The underwriters worked with Kendra and her team to develop the road show presentation and also recommended a consultant to assist in that process. They expected that the road show would commence following the filing of the first amendment to the registration statement. If all went well, the parties would be in a position to complete the road show about the time the registration statement became effective, with the offering to be priced very soon thereafter. At the direction of the bankers, Kendra planned to spend at least two or three weeks on the road show, making her presentation twenty to thirty times in as many as fifteen different U.S. cities. (The road show would have been even longer if Europe or Asia had been included.)

After approximately thirty days, the SEC staff provided comments on the registration statement. At this point, the working group reassembled at the printer to prepare the first amendment to the registration statement to respond to the comments. The group believed that certain of the SEC's comments were not clear or reflected a misunderstanding on the part of the SEC staff. In those cases, the company explained supplementally in a letter to the SEC why the company believed that the registration statement should not be revised in response to those comments. A number of the comments related to accounting matters, and Kendra obtained from the auditors a realistic estimate of the time they needed to revise any numbers, draft additional disclosures, and prepare any required supplemental response. In addition, the group assembled certain supplemental information that the SEC had requested so that it could determine whether other comments were appropriate.

continued...

continued...

After filing the amended registration statement, which also included financial statements and relevant information regarding the company's just-completed quarter, Kendra expected one or more additional sets of oral or written comments from the SEC, each of which would probably require another amendment to the registration statement. The company received the next "round" of comments one week after filing the first amendment, and subsequent comments were delivered within a few days after the filing of subsequent amendments. Each amendment was signed on behalf of the company and included an executed consent of the auditors. Once the SEC had no further comment, the company requested that the SEC declare the registration statement effective. This was done by means of a letter filed electronically with the SEC. By SEC rules, the underwriters were required to join in the request with their own letter.

On the day the offering was declared effective, the underwriters set up a telephonic conference call after the close of the market. The underwriters first congratulated Kendra on a successful road show and then proposed the final size of the offering, the offering price, and the underwriters' gross spread (commission). Kendra wanted to try to negotiate the gross spread and the price with the underwriters, so she came to the meeting armed with the latest information about DataAccelleation's competitors, particularly recent trends in their stock prices and price/earnings ratios. One or two underwriters had given her some indication of their preliminary numbers, and she had done her best prior to the call to justify increasing these numbers to a level where she still believed there would be a jump in the price in the aftermarket. Because DataAccelleation was considered "hot," she was able to negotiate a slightly higher price than first proposed, although (not surprisingly) the underwriters would not budge from a 7 percent gross spread. Once the deal was struck, the underwriting agreement was executed that same day. Trading commenced the following morning. The final prospectus was then prepared based on the final pricing information, and the offering closed three business days following the commencement of trading.

After the offering closed, Kendra invited Michael to visit the company to meet with her and the other executive officers to set up procedures to implement the company's insider trading and window-period policies, the SEC and

continued...

continued...

Nasdaq/NMS compliance procedures, and the investor relations strategy. Michael then spoke to the employees about the implications for them of owning stock in a public company and the applicable restrictions on trading.

After Michael finished, Kendra addressed the employees. She thanked them for their long nights and weekends of toil to get the SDB ready for the product launch. She also reminded the longtimers of the dark days before venture financing, when DataAccelleation's creditors were hounding the company and it almost failed. Finally, she spoke of the future. DataAccelleation had made remarkable progress from the time when it was merely a dream of its founders, but now it was time for the next stage. The challenges of entrepreneurship had been met, and the challenges of becoming a successful public company lay ahead. "But first," she declared, "let's break out the champagne and cookies—it's time to party!"

NOTE

1. Selective Disclosures and Insider Trading, SEC Release Nos. 33-7881, 34-43154, IC-24599, 17 C.F.R. pts. 240, 243, 249 (Aug. 15, 2000).

Internet Sources

General Information

The Small Business Association's site provides valuable information about starting and financing small businesses, a searchable online library, and links to other sites of interest (including the home pages for each state's department of corporations).
http://www.sbaonline.sba.gov/

The Harvard Business School Publishing site provides the Entrepreneurs Resource Center with searchable bibliographies and materials and very useful links to sites of interest to persons starting a business.
http://www.hbsp.harvard.edu/ideasatwork/entrep/

This page offers new students of the law a variety of materials, including guides to case citations and research materials.
http://www.lawlib.uh.edu/guides

Court Cases

The Web site for the U.S. Supreme Court offers a searchable full-text database of Supreme Court opinions. New opinions are usually posted the same day they are issued.
http://www.supremecourtus.gov/

Courts.net provides directory listings for courts throughout the nation on a state-by-state basis.
http://www.courts.net

Under the direction of the U.S. Department of Commerce, this page offers access to more than 7,000 U.S. Supreme Court opinions from 1937 to 1975, as well as to a wide range of information related to the federal government.
http://www.fedworld.gov/

Federal Legislation

"Thomas:" The U.S. Congress's Official Legislative Information Page, is an extremely well-organized page describing pending bills, committee information, and Internet sources.
http://thomas.loc.gov

Uniform State Laws

The National Conference of Commissioners on Uniform State Laws, in association with the University of Pennsylvania Law School, makes available drafts and revisions to finalized versions of the Uniform Commercial Code, the Uniform Partnership Act, the Uniform Limited Partnership Act, and the Uniform Limited Liability Company Act.
http://www.law.upenn.edu/bll/ulc/ulcframe.htm

The site for the National Conference of Commissioners on Uniform State Laws provides an updated list of which states have adopted various uniform acts.
http://www.nccusl.org

This site provides an updated list of states that have adopted UCITA.
http://www.ucitaonline.com

Employment

Equal Employment Opportunity Commission
http://www.eeoc.gov

Occupational Safety and Health Administration
http://www.osha.gov

The Department of Labor site includes information about Bureau of Labor statistics; OSHA data on occupational injuries; and laws and regulations administered and enforced by DOL agencies.
http://www.dol.gov

This site provides an index of laws and articles on employment law and the Labor and Employment Law Web Guide.
http://www.findlaw.com/01topics/27labor

The University of Chicago offers a guide for users of independent contractors that addresses many of the distinctions between independent contractors and employees.
http://admin-www.uchicago.edu/admincompt/icug/ic-contents.html

The Independent Contractor Report provides frequent updates on rulings and other issues relevant to users of independent contractors.
http://www.workerstatus.com/

Intellectual Property, Cyberlaw, and E-Commerce

U.S. Patent and Trademark Office
http://www.uspto.gov/

U.S. Copyright Office
http://lcweb.loc.gov/copyright/

Department of Commerce, Electronic Commerce Site
http://www.ecommerce.gov

This site, maintained by the U.S. Department of Justice Criminal Division's Computer Crime and Intellectual Property Section, provides information about cyber-crime.
http://www.cybercrime.gov

The Organization for Economic Cooperation and Development's Web site has guidelines on consumer protection in the context of electronic commerce and information regarding a forum on electronic commerce.
http://www.oecd.org/dsti/sti/it/consumer/prod/guidelines.htm

The World Intellectual Property Organization Electronic Commerce and Intellectual Property site provides information regarding WIPO's activities concerning intellectual property and electronic commerce, including the WIPO Arbitration and Mediation Center for the resolution of domain name disputes.
http://ecommerce.wipo.int/index-eng.html

The GigaLaw.com site provides legal information for Internet professionals, including a free daily e-mail update on breaking developments and articles of interest.
http://www.gigalaw.com

BNA's Internet Law News provides free daily e-mail updates.
http://ecommercecenter.bna.com/

The law firm of Baker & McKenzie provides a free weekly e-mail on developments in electronic commerce and cyberlaw throughout the world.
http://www.bakerinfo.com/elaw/

Consumer Protection and Privacy

The Federal Trade Commission's Web site provides information about its enforcement actions, consumer protection, and regional offices.
http://www.ftc.gov

This site, maintained by the FTC's Bureau of Consumer Protection, provides consumer news on product recalls, tips for avoiding scams, smart shopping suggestions, and contacts for lodging consumer complaints, as well as links to other Web sites containing consumer information.
http://www.consumer.gov

The Privacy Information page on the FTC's Web site contains information on how to protect personal information from public access, including sample "opt-out" letters for consumers to send to credit bureaus and the Direct Marketing Association requesting that their personal information not be sold, shared with third parties, or used for marketing purposes.
http://www.ftc.gov/privacy

The U.S. Consumer Product Safety Commission's Web site provides information about recent recalls and other agency activity.
http://www.cpsc.gov

Environmental Protection Agency
htp://www.epa.gov

Food and Drug Administration
http://www.fda.gov

The Privacy Forum site provides an online compendium of privacy-related topics.
http://www.vortex.com/privacy

The Better Business Bureau's Web site provides consumers with information about its private regulation of business, including recent warnings and local offices.
http://www.bbb.org/

The American Tort Reform Association hosts a page addressing various issues about tort reform, including information about states that have enacted tort reform measures and facts about the impact of tort liability on the economy.
http://www.atra.org

The Association of Trial Lawyers of America, a group of attorneys who represent plaintiffs in tort and consumer protection lawsuits, maintains a site with articles and news clippings regarding recent developments in tort litigation and reform.
http://www.atla.org

Securities Regulation

Securities and Exchange Commission
http://www.sec.gov

This site provides free access to electronic filings with the SEC.
http://www.freeedgar.com

Bankruptcy

This site provides links to bankruptcy journals and publications and to law firm Web sites providing bankruptcy information.
http://findlaw.com/01topics/03bankruptcy

This site, maintained by the American Bankruptcy Institute, includes legislative updates.
http://www.abiworld.org/legis

Arbitration and Mediation

The American Arbitration Association's home page offers avenues into its many services.
http://www.adr.org

The Mediation Information Research Center offers articles and other information about mediation as well as resources concerning professional mediators.
http://www.mediate.com

International Business

The European Union On-Line site is a searchable collection of official documents (such as Directives), news releases, the Official Journal of the European Communities, and case law of the European Court of Justice, with links.
http://www.europa.eu.int

The International Chamber of Commerce site provides information about doing business internationally and news alerts.
http://www.iccwbo.org/

Table of Cases

TABLE OF CASES

INDEX

U